The Study of Economics

Economics

Principles, Concepts & Applications

5th Edition   **Turley Mings**

■ This book is dedicated to the friends who enrich my life and make me laugh (except Steve, who isn't really all that funny).

■ About the Author: Dr. Turley Mings received his undergraduate degree in economics from Occidental College and his Ph.D. in economics from the University of California at Berkeley. He is Professor Emeritus of economics at San Jose State University where he taught the introductory course for 30 years. He served as director of the Center for Economic Education for 20 years, developing strategies for teaching economics and conducting in-service workshops at all levels.

The Study of Economics

Principles, Concepts & Applications

5th Edition **Turley Mings**

DPG

The Dushkin Publishing Group, Inc.

Credits and Acknowledgments

The illustrations in this book reflect the work of many professional artists and photographers. We, however, would particularly like to thank and acknowledge the following American and international corporations, institutions, and government agencies that have provided us with complimentary material: Apple Computer, American Egg Board, American Iron and Steel Institute, American Red Cross, Ben & Jerry's, Banque National de Paris, Busch Gardens, Chase Manhattan Bank, Chrysler Corporation, Congressional News Photos, Connecticut Department of Economic Development, Crafted with Pride in America, Environmental Protection Agency, EPA Documerica, Federal Aviation Association, Eastman Chemical Company, Equitable Agri-Business, Federal Reserve Bank, Ford New Holland, General Electric, General Motors, Greenpeace, Geo, Hind, Houston Industries, Inc., IBM, Krause Publications, Library of Congress, Matsushita Electric, Morrison Knudsen Corporation, National Cattlemen's Association, National Gallery of Art, National Institute of Standards and Technology, New York Convention and Visitors' Bureau, Old Dominion University, Philips, Pratt & Whitney, Port Authority of New York and New Jersey, StarKist Seafood Company, TRW, TVA Washington Office, Union Electric, University of Texas/Austin, World Health Organization, Yellow Freight.

Chapter 1   4 Steve Delaney/EPA; 8 Mike Eagle; 11 Pamela Carley; 13 ©Plowden 1989/Greenpeace; 14 Arthur Morris; 15 UN photo by Antoinette Jongen; 17 Connecticut Department of Economic Development; 18 Larry Murphy/University of Texas, Austin; 20 Steve Delaney/EPA; 25 Steve Delaney/EPA; 26 courtesy Paul Samuelson

Chapter 2   36 Rafal Olbinski; 39 Mike Eagle; 40 courtesy American Egg Board; 41 UPI/Bettmann, UPI/Bettmann; 46 courtesy Stuart L. Shalat; 47 Reuters/Bettmann; 51 Terry Husebye; 52 courtesy

(Continued on page 525)

Printed in the United States of America

Library of Congress Catalog Card Number 94-60668

International Standard Book Number (ISBN) 1-56134-303-X

Fifth Edition, First Printing

10 9 8 7 6 5 4 3 2 1

This book is printed on recycled paper.

The Dushkin Publishing Group, Inc.
Sluice Dock, Guilford, Connecticut 06437

Preface

This fifth edition of *The Study of Economics* draws upon a number of recent real-world events and problems to introduce and apply economic concepts—the abandonment of communism and the economic restructuring in Eastern Europe, the information superhighway, the North American Free Trade Agreement, the loss of rain forests, health care reform, and economic decline in Africa. In the 19 years since the first edition appeared, much has changed in economics. The world economy has become more integrated, and its impact on the domestic economy of the United States has become much greater. This change is reflected in an increase in the number of applications dealing with foreign economies and international issues.

Treatment of environmental issues has been further strengthened in this edition, running through the book from the introductory article for chapter 1 to the final section of the last chapter. In the article introducing chapter 1, the emphasis has shifted somewhat from global warming, the reality of which is challenged by some scientists, to destruction of the ozone layer, which is scientifically verified.

The article on the cigarette market, introducing the chapter on consumers, is even more relevant than when it first appeared because of increased controversy over cigarette marketing aimed at young people and the effects of raising taxes on cigarettes. To the coverage has been added a case application on the tobacco companies' increased marketing efforts in less developed countries.

The chapter 7 introductory article has undergone a metamorphosis from dealing with the loss of competitiveness of American industry in the last edition to industry's recent productivity rebound.

But the most extensive changes have been made in the last third of the book—changes in domestic macroeconomics and in the international economy. The question of health care reform in chapter 13 had not been settled at

the time of this writing, but it appeared that, whatever the near-term resolution, the health care issue would be revisited during the life of this edition. Therefore, the article deals with the problems in health care that need to be addressed rather than with the resolution.

The "death of the isms" is having great economic as well as political effects on the world. The changes are coming so rapidly that even monthly revision could not keep up with them. Chapter 17 describes these challenges and how they are being met in a variety of economies. It provides a framework for comparing economies and their performance.

In addition to the new topics for applying economic concepts, some new concepts have been added that have become part of economics debates since the last edition. These include the concepts of business process reengineering in chapter 7 and total factor productivity and catch-up in chapter 17.

The book retains the basic features that have characterized it since the first edition. One of these features is the presentation of economic concepts in the context of a real-world application that introduces each chapter. This is done to give the beginning student, for whom economics all too frequently seems abstract, a concrete setting to which new concepts can be related. A principle of learning theory is that the learner needs familiar intellectual pegs on which to hang unfamiliar ideas. For example, the concepts of alternative uses for resources, opportunity costs, and our economic goals are introduced in the second chapter within a discussion of the question of demilitarization and the "peace dividend."

The concepts in each chapter are grouped into three or four sections, and there is a different case application at the conclusion of each section. The intention throughout all of the applications is to integrate the explanations of economic concepts very closely with their applications. In this new fifth edition, 14 case applications have been labeled "comparative" and consider foreign economies and international issues, in whole or in part, in the text discussion. Each of the case applications is followed by questions that encourage the student to practice economic analysis and to apply the newly learned concepts. An important objective of this structure is to teach students to approach problems as an economist would. The numerous applications included in the text and the additional applications in the student workbook should help students to master basic concepts and increase their ability to transfer economic skills and knowledge to new problems as they arise in the real world.

Although the text makes extensive use of case applications, *The Study of Economics* is not a casebook. It presents economic theory in as systematic a framework of organization as more traditional texts. Each of the major areas of economics is discussed thoroughly, starting with economic methods and the fundamental choices about the use of resources and proceeding to deal in turn with markets, consumers, business and industrial organization and performance, government, labor and income distribution, money, economic instability, national income, public finance, policies for stabilization and growth, international trade and finance, alternative economic systems, and world economic development. Thus the text provides an evenly balanced presentation of the full range of economics. It is organized into four main units: Foundations (chapters 1–4), Microeconomics (chapters 5–9), Macroeconomics (chapters 10–14), and World Economics (chapters 15–18). While microeconomics is treated first in the text's organization, macroeconomics can just as easily be covered before microeconomics without any loss in student understanding.

It has been alleged that economics is the only discipline in which we have tried to teach everything we know about the subject in the beginning course. The rule in this text has been to include only those tools of economic analysis which will be useful to a student in understanding the real economic world. The book avoids purely technical devices that are relevant to advanced economic theory but have no immediate value to the beginning student. The close integration of concepts and models with real world applications has helped to exclude theory that does not have concrete applicability. When a simple model serves as well to explain a set of relationships, it has been used in place of a more complicated model. An example is the use of the GDP tank model in chapter 12 rather than the more abstract Keynesian cross diagram.

The questions following each case application and the study questions at the end of each chapter are designed to be useful for class discussion, either as a whole class with the teacher leading the discussion or in small discussion groups. There is a consistent pattern for the three questions that follow each case application. The first question of the three is one that a student who has read the material should not have too much difficulty in answering. Taxonomically, the first question is a concept recognition/simple application question. The second question is generally more difficult, requiring analytical thinking. It is a complex application/analysis type question. The third question is an open-ended question involving the student's own personal belief system and attitudes as well as the concepts in the text. These questions are of the integrative/valuation type.

Suggested answers to all of the application questions and to the study questions at the end of the chapter are given in the instructor's guide, *Teaching and Testing from The Study of Economics*. The instructor's guide also includes additional discussion of the text presentation and teaching strategies. It provides schematic outlines for each chapter that can be used as transparency masters for every section of the chapters. Also included are transparency masters for all of the charts and graphs in the text.

Supplementary materials include a testing program and a microcomputer test generator, a set of instructional color transparencies with overlays for overhead projection, and a student workbook, *Working with The Study of Economics*. The workbook contains review exercises, additional case applications with questions for each section of the chapters, self-test multiple-choice questions, and schematic outlines of every chapter section.

The schematic outlines serve a variety of purposes: as a preview of the material in the chapter, as an aid to the student in understanding the relationships between the economic concepts and models discussed, as a review, and, when displayed on an overhead projector, as a means for the teacher to orient the students to the material being covered in class.

Turley Mings

Contents Summary

Contents

Unit III. MACROECONOMICS 248

Chapter 10. Money 251

Chapter 11. Economic Instability 277

Chapter 12. The Economy's Output 307

To the Student

Welcome to the study of economics. I hope that you will find it interesting and worthwhile; I have done my best to make it so. Interest in economics is higher today than it has ever been, at least since the Depression era of the 1930s. Today's daily newspapers, weekly newsmagazines, and nightly newscasts are full of reporting on the latest economic developments and expert analysis of what those developments mean for us.

In order to help you gain an economic understanding of current events and problems, I have incorporated many applications of the economic concepts in the text. The applications are continuously interwoven with the explanations of economics to make it easier for you to see the relevance of the economic ideas and to make it more interesting. Economics sometimes has the reputation of being a difficult, dull, and abstract subject. I hope that this book will convince you that this doesn't have to be the case. Certainly economics is complicated, but by taking it one step at a time and being clear on just what each idea means and how it is used, you can enjoy it, master it, and find it useful.

What is economics? One definition is given in the cartoon panel below. "Economics is the social science concerned with how resources are used to satisfy people's wants." The subject matter of economics is divided into two major fields. One deals with the individual units in an economy, the individual businesses, workers, consumers, and so forth. This is called **microeconomics** because it takes a detailed look at the economic decisions made by individuals and businesses and the effect government policies have on them. The other major area is **macroeconomics**, which deals with the broad measurements of economic activity such as the average price level, employment, and total output. *The Study of Economics* is divided into 4 parts. The first part consists of 4 chapters on the fundamentals of economics. This is followed by 5 chapters on microeconomics, 5 chapters on macroeconomics, and 4 chapters on the world economy.

The organization of each chapter of the text follows a consistent pattern, and each part of the chapter has a specific function. The chapters begin with an introductory article on some event or problem related to the economic topics covered in the chapter. Chapter 4, for example, which deals with how markets work and how prices are set, begins with an article on what happened to the price and availability of peanut butter when there was a failure of the peanut crop. The economic concepts that explain how markets behave are then introduced in the context of what actually occurred in the peanut butter market. The introductory articles conclude with a preview of the content

of the chapter and a set of learning objectives that give you an idea of what the main things are that you should look for in the chapter. The next feature of the chapters is one that I hope you will enjoy. These pointed (and, I hope, amusing) cartoons relate the topic of the introductory article to the economic content of the body of the chapter.

The economic topics of the chapters are broken down into 3 or 4 *analysis sections*, each headed by an organizing question, such as *"What forces determine prices in the marketplace?"* Each of these sections is further subdivided into discussions of the individual concepts that are relevant to answering the organizing question. The contents explained under the above question are *demand, supply, and equilibrium*. When new concepts and unfamiliar terms are introduced, they are put in **bold face** type in the text, as microeconomics and macroeconomics are above, and defined in the *in-text glossary*. There is also an *end-of-the-book glossary,* keyed to the text pages and arranged alphabetically, incorporating all of these terms.

Each analysis section concludes with a short case that illustrates the application of the concepts covered in the section. The *case application* for the section on "What forces determine prices in the marketplace?" deals with the market for student academic talent. Recognizing the increased importance of the world economy to our own, 14 of the case applications in this edition are *comparative cases* that compare the United States to foreign countries or an international issue.

Following each case application are 3 questions that ask you to apply the economic concepts in the preceding section to the case application. The first of the 3 questions should be fairly easy for you to answer if you have read the section carefully. The second question will usually be somewhat more difficult, requiring you to employ your reasoning powers in applying economic concepts. Question number three calls for your opinion based on your own attitudes and judgments, as well as what you have learned about the topic.

There is a *Putting It Together* summary of the chapter's principal economic ideas at the end of each chapter. There is also an essay on some *perspective* of the topic covered in the chapter from the viewpoint of an influential economist or from a relevant historical event that has shaped our view. The chapters then conclude with the *For Further Study and Analysis* section that includes study questions, analytical exercises, and references to books for pursuing the material in more depth. The study questions are not review questions as such, but are intended to expand and reinforce your understanding of the material and, where appropriate, to give you a chance to apply it in your own locality.

There is available a study guide, *Working with The Study of Economics*, that contains review exercises, additional applications, practice questions, and a schematic outline of each section of the chapters. To get the most out of reading the text, it is recommended that you look over the schematic outline of a chapter section before you read it and then review the outline when you have finished reading the section.

The introductory articles and case applications in the chapters are similar to those reported on in the news media. They have been selected with two things in mind: their interest and relevance and their suitability for applying the economic concepts in the chapter. In some cases, the names of people and their experiences are composites of the experiences of different individuals and do not refer to an actual person.

I hope that you will look for opportunities to apply the economic understandings you gain from this book to stories currently in the news. There is a valuable collection of analytical tools in the intellectual toolbox of economics that, once you have learned how to use them, can be applied to the understanding and solution of new problems as they arise. The trick is to recognize which tools of analysis are useful for a particular problem. The knowledge and practice you get from this book should enable you to do that.

Turley Mings

Unit *I.* FOUNDATIONS

The foundations of economics are the ideas that form the basis of the discipline. They are fundamental to the different areas of economic applications.

Chapter 1. Economic Methods

Economics is a social science that is concerned with how resources are used to satisfy people's wants. By use of the scientific method and economic reasoning, economics enables us to understand and deal with problems that arise. The economics discipline has a set of factual and theoretical tools to apply to the solution of those problems. Descriptive charts and analytical diagrams are particularly useful tools in economics.

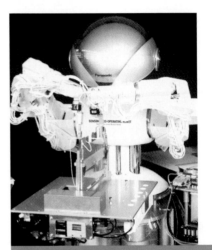

Chapter 2. Economic Choices

Scarcity of resources relative to our needs and wants requires that we make choices about the alternative uses of those resources. In allocating resources, an economy must resolve the basic economic questions of what, how, and for whom to produce. Societies make choices in accordance with certain economic and socioeconomic goals.

Chapter 3. The Economic System

Societies need a system to organize and co-ordinate economic activities in an efficient way. This makes the different elements in an economy interdependent. There are three principal types of economic systems, but modern economies are a mixture. The United States economy is predominantly market-directed.

Chapter 4. Market Pricing

In a market system, prices are determined by the demand for and the supply of goods and services. At the equilibrium price there is no shortage or surplus. If the conditions that determine demand or supply change, the equilibrium price and the quantity bought and sold will change.

Chapter 1. Economic Methods

■ **The study** of economics entails a special way of looking at the world around us and the way things work. This approach has been described as "the economic way of thinking." Once you learn it, it will come in handy in dealing with many types of situations, even some that are not necessarily thought of as being "economics." On the face of it, the subject of the introductory article for this first chapter might appear to be in the area of such natural sciences as meteorology or climatology rather than economics. But, as we shall see, its underlying causes and its ultimate effects are very much in the economics field.

Is the Sky Falling?

Are those scientists and politicians who worry about ecological disaster in the atmosphere just a bunch of Chicken Littles running around raising false alarms? Or are they prophets alerting the world to real devastation in the making?

There is certainly something in the air to worry about. In fact, there is a great deal too much in the air. There is too much carbon dioxide, too much methane, too much nitrous oxide, too many chlorine gases. In short, there is too much pollution.

Air pollution is nothing new. In the first half of this century, the air in many of the industrial cities of the East and Midwest was gritty with soot particles from the coal-burning furnaces of factories and homes. This type of air pollution was replaced in the years after World War II by smog from auto exhaust and manufacturing operations. According to the Environmental Protection Agency, some 150 million people in this country live in areas where the air is unfit to breathe.

While still wrestling with the problem of what to do about the growing smog problem, we have become aware that acid rain is killing our lakes and forests. The effects of air pollution are felt in rural wilderness areas as well as in the big cities.

Now we are faced with the potentially most destructive forms of air pollution yet. There is a depletion of the ozone layer, which protects us from harmful rays of the sun, and a threat of global warming that could bring catastrophic changes, both environmental and economic.

The old saying that "Everybody talks about the weather, but nobody does anything about it" is, unfortunately, no longer true. We have attained the capacity to cause worldwide changes in the weather. Accumulation of gases released into the atmosphere can produce a "greenhouse effect" by trapping heat near the surface of the earth. This may be likened to the way glass in a greenhouse traps heat from the sun. There is continuing controversy and ongoing research concerning the expected timing and severity of the greenhouse effect. Various climate experts predict that average temperatures will rise by anywhere from 3 to

9 degrees Fahrenheit by the middle of the next century, compared to "only" a 1 degree increase in the past 100 years. That would be an unprecedented change in such a short period. An increase of 3 degrees would be the largest change in recorded history. An increase of 9 degrees would make the world's climate hotter than it has been since the time of the dinosaurs, over 65 million years ago.

The consequences of such a global warming would be enormous. It would bring extreme conditions of heat, drought, and floods. There would be increased rainfall on coastal regions, with more violent storms and hurricanes. The most devastating effects could result from a melting of ice caps, snow cover, and the Antarctic, Greenland, and Alpine glaciers. With such melting, a thermal expansion of ocean waters could raise the level of the oceans and cover low-lying coastal territories around the world. This would flood large areas, including rich agricultural land in Bangladesh, the Nile Delta, China, Japan, and the Netherlands. It would displace an estimated 25 to 40 million people. Masses of environmental refugees would be forced to migrate.

In the United States, such cities as New York, New Orleans, and San Francisco would be flooded. Even whole states such as Delaware and Florida would be covered by water. Meanwhile, continental interiors would experience drought conditions. The corn and wheat belts would become deserts. The northern forests would be destroyed by insects and diseases. As rainfall declined by 40% in the central part of the country, the evaporation of Lake Michigan would leave acres of reeking mud flats around Chicago.

This is a worst-case scenario, projected by computer models. But even smaller climate changes would have great effects on our way of life and on economic conditions. And we may not have to wait 50 years to see those changes. We may already be experiencing them. Storms, floods, and droughts were 94% more frequent in the 1980s than in the 1970s. The six hottest years ever recorded occurred in the last decade.

These events could be merely normal climate variations. But there have been climatic indicators that fulfill the predictions for global warming. For example, ocean water warming above 80 degrees is conducive to hurricanes. The surface area of ocean waters warmer than 80 degrees has expanded one-sixth during the past 20 years. Another prediction fulfilled is the rising sea level. The sea level has risen 1 foot along the Atlantic coast of the United States in the last 100 years. As a result, beaches have receded an average of 200–300 feet. The sea level is the highest it has been in 5,000 years and is rising 10 times faster than before.

Whether or not it has actually started, there is no question that we are creating the conditions for a greenhouse effect. The primary cause is the increased amount of carbon dioxide released into the air. It accounts for about half of the greenhouse gas buildup. Carbon dioxide is a natural component of air, but the amount of atmospheric carbon dioxide has increased 25% since the 1850s. In the time since the beginning of the Industrial Revolution, we have dumped some 185 billion tons of carbon dioxide into the atmosphere by burning fossil fuels—coal and petroleum in particular—in factories, power plants, homes, and vehicles. Other gases that have contributed to the greenhouse problem are methane, nitrous oxides, and chlorofluorocarbons (CFCs).

The CFCs are doubly dangerous because not only do they add to the greenhouse effect, but their chlorine content eats away the ozone in the outer atmosphere, which serves to shield us and other life forms from the sun's damaging ultraviolet (UV) rays. For humans, the result is a rise in the frequency of skin cancer, an increasingly common cancer problem. There is evidence that excess UV radiation may also affect the body's immune system, reducing its ability to fight off disease. As for the effect on other life forms, research studies show that an increase in the size of the hole in the ozone over the Antarctic, letting in more ultraviolet rays, causes significant reductions in the growth of plankton, the tiny creatures that are the beginning of the ocean's food chain. Scientists from the University of California at Santa Barbara estimate that radiation from the ozone hole is decreasing the

Figure 1.

Sources of CFCs Worldwide

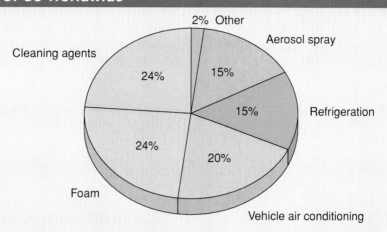

The chlorofluorocarbons that destroy the ozone layer come from a variety of sources.

productivity of phytoplankton by at least 10–12%. High doses of UV light can also reduce the yields of basic crops such as soybeans.

While heated controversy continues over the actual danger posed by the greenhouse effect, there is no doubt about the ozone depletion. Satellite measurements reveal that by 1993 the protective ozone had dropped to record low levels in the stratosphere above much of the planet. One molecule of CFCs will destroy 2,500 molecules of ozone; and with each percentage point drop in the amount of ozone, the strength of ultraviolet radiation increases as much as twice the percentage decrease in ozone.

The CFCs that eat away the ozone layer come from refrigeration gases used in refrigerators and air conditioners, from foam used in insulation and packaging materials, from cleaning fluids, and from aerosol sprays in those countries where such sprays have not been banned as they have in the United States. Figure 1 shows the relative sources of CFCs worldwide.

A start on solving the ozone depletion problem was made at a meeting in 1987 when three dozen nations signed the Montreal Protocol. They promised to cut the production of

CFCs by 50% by 1998. Then, in 1990, increasing recognition of the seriousness of the ozone layer destruction led to a treaty signed by 93 nations to ban CFCs altogether by the year 2000. Now most countries expect to beat that deadline because substitutes for CFCs are being introduced more rapidly than expected.

The end of CFC production can come none too soon because the gases continue to circulate for decades after they are emitted. Even if CFC production stopped today, researchers have concluded that the level of chlorine in the stratosphere would continue to rise until the first decade of the twenty-first century from the CFCs already dispersed. Stratospheric chlorine would not return to natural levels for at least a century.

Official attitudes toward the greenhouse effect have mirrored the treatment of the ozone problem. From 1974, when scientists first sounded the alarm, until 1985, when the existence of an ozone hole over the South Pole was positively confirmed, government authorities minimized the danger. Because cleaning up the atmosphere would be costly, governments have continued to be reluctant to admit that there is a problem. There is resistance to adopting policies that require a reduction in carbon dioxide, methane, and other greenhouse gases until evidence of an actual threat has been proven. But what concerns environmental scientists is that by the time there is a conclusive demonstration of the greenhouse effect, a great deal of damage may be done.

A start was made toward reducing the amount of carbon dioxide and other greenhouse gases through a voluntary "Climate Change Action Program" announced by President Bill Clinton in October 1993. The plan envisions a government/industry partnership program to invest in nonpolluting production methods, with industries investing $61 billion and the government contributing $1.9 billion. No one thinks that such a voluntary program will remedy the greenhouse effect, but until there is unmistakable evidence that it is a serious problem, more drastic (and costly) measures are unlikely.

■ Chapter Preview

Examining the problem of air pollution and its consequences provides a good illustration of economic methods. It is not an easy problem to resolve because it involves conflicting interests of different groups and public as well as private decisions. We will use it as a reference case for the questions: What is economics? What are the tools of economics? What are the uses of graphs? *The chapter is followed by an appendix on how to construct and interpret line graphs.*

■ Learning Objectives

After completing this chapter, you should be able to:

1. Explain scarcity as an economic term.

2. List the factors of production.

3. Describe the steps in the scientific method.

4. Describe three types of factual tools used in economics.

5. Describe the theoretical tools used in economics.

6. Give four examples of different types of charts.

7. Explain what an analytical diagram is used for.

8. Draw and label an analytical diagram showing the relationship between two variables.

What Is Economics?

A standard definition of economics is that "economics is the social science concerned with how **resources** are used to satisfy people's wants." This section discusses the basis of economics as a science and the methods it uses.

Scarcity : 정믹, 부족

Global warming and the destruction of the ozone layer are problems that naturally lend themselves to the study of economics for a number of reasons. Their underlying causes are economic. They have enormous economic consequences. Most importantly, they involve dealing with **scarcity**. The need for a science of economics comes from scarcity. We have only a limited amount of resources to satisfy our unlimited wants for goods and services. As a result, we need to economize on the use of those resources, to get the greatest benefit out of the resources available.

Resources used to produce goods and services, called the **factors of production**, consist of **land**, **labor**, and **capital**. Land includes all natural resources—the minerals under the

resources: the inputs that are used in production. Includes natural resources (minerals, timber, rivers), labor (blue collar, white collar), and capital (machinery, buildings).

scarcity: the limited resources for production relative to the demand for goods and services.

factors of production: another name for the production resources of land (natural resources), labor, and capital (machinery and buildings).

land: all natural resources, including fields, forests, mineral deposits, the sea, and other gifts of nature.

labor: all human resources, including manual, clerical, technical, professional, and managerial labor.

capital: the means of production, including factories, office buildings, machinery, tools, and equipment; alternatively, it can mean financial capital, the money to acquire the foregoing and employ land and labor resources.

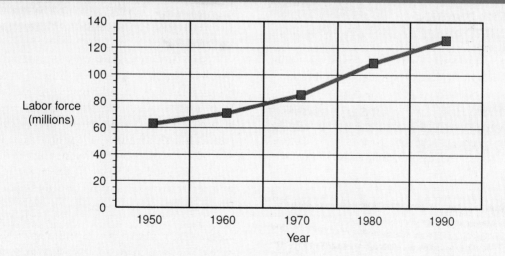

Figure 2.
Size of the U.S. Labor Force, 1950–1990

Labor force (millions)

Year

Source: U.S. Department of Commerce, Bureau of Labor Statistics, *Employment and Earnings*.

■ Labor is the most important factor of production. The United States added over twice as many workers to the labor force in the last 2 decades as it did in the previous 2 decades.

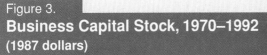

Figure 3.
Business Capital Stock, 1970–1992
(1987 dollars)

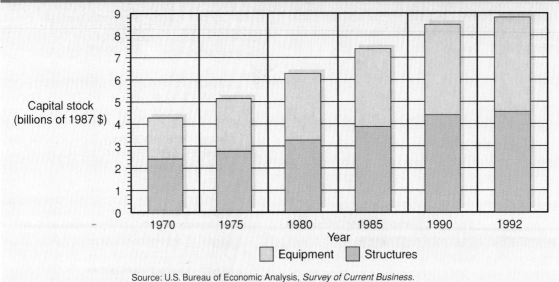

Capital stock (billions of 1987 $)

Year

☐ Equipment ◼ Structures

Source: U.S. Bureau of Economic Analysis, *Survey of Current Business.*

■ Capital is another important factor of production. The amount of real capital has more than doubled since 1970. The stock of equipment has increased faster than structures.

surface, the forests on it, and even the air above it. Labor refers to all types of human resources, managers and professionals as well as manual and clerical workers. **Entrepreneurs** are a particular type of human resource. They are individuals who see the possibility of profitable production and organize resources to produce a good or service.

Capital refers to the machinery, factories, and office buildings used in production. **Technology** and information, both of which have increasing importance in today's economy, are

entrepreneur: a business innovator who sees the opportunity to make a profit from a new product, new process, or unexploited raw material and then brings together the land, labor, and capital to exploit the opportunity, risking failure.

technology: the body of skills and knowledge that comprises the processes used in production.

financial capital: the money to acquire the factors of production.

also classified as capital resources. **Financial capital** is not a real resource like the factors of production, but it enables entrepreneurs and managers to purchase any of the factors of production.

Even in such a wealthy country as the United States, we do not have enough of these resources to satisfy all of our wants. How does resource scarcity apply to the case of air pollution? If there is one thing that you would think there is enough of, it is air. And there would be sufficient air—if only it were not used as a garbage dump for the by-products of our production and consumption activities.

This example underlines the fact that, in economics, scarcity is not the same thing as rarity. We have more air than anything else on the planet. But because of competing uses for it, air, at least pure air, has become very scarce. On the other hand, a thing that no one wants may be rare without being scarce. For example, radioactive waste is rare but not scarce.

■ There must be a demand for an item in order for it to be scarce in the economic sense. These one-clawed lobsters are rarer than lobsters with two claws, but because there is no great demand for them they are not considered scarce.

The Scientific Method

Economics, like other sciences, makes use of the **scientific method**. This consists of (1) observing an event, (2) devising an explanation (**hypothesis**) that accounts for that event, (3) testing the hypothesis by gathering additional information and observing whether a repeat of the conditions assumed by the hypothesis leads to the same result, and (4) tentatively accepting, revising, or rejecting the hypothesis, depending on whether it correctly predicts a repetition of the event.

For the study of ozone depletion, the scientific method involved observing the holes in the ozone layer of the upper atmosphere and its effects on earth. It required forming a hypothesis to explain the ozone depletion that was observed. The hypothesis was that ozone was being destroyed by chlorine gas, which came from CFCs. The scientific method then called for testing this hypothesis.

The testing itself entailed gathering information from satellite measurements on the decline in ozone levels. It required estimating the amount of chlorine gas produced as the sun broke down CFC molecules. It involved performing laboratory experiments on the destruction of ozone by chlorine.

The investigators then used computer models to predict future declines in the ozone levels as a result of increasing production of CFCs. Their predictions were realized, although the actual amounts of ozone depletion were greater than forecast. With the evidence supporting the hypothesis, it was tentatively accepted. A hypothesis is accepted pending any new information that might lead to a different conclusion.

Economics makes use of the scientific method, but it differs from some of the other sciences—laboratory sciences such as chemistry—because it is a social science. Economists

> **scientific method:** a procedure used by scientists to develop explanations for events and test the validity of those explanations.
>
> **hypothesis:** a tentative explanation of an event; used as a basis for further research.

Table 1.

The Scientific Method

Procedure	Example
1. Observe event.	1. Observe hole in the ozone layer.
2. Make an hypothesis to explain the event.	2. Chlorine gas from CFCs dispersed into the atmosphere is destroying the ozone.
3. Test the hypothesis by performing experiments (if that is possible), gathering additional evidence on the relationship between the effects and the assumed cause, predicting future events on the basis of the hypothesis, and observing whether or not the predictions are accurate.	3. Take measurements via satellite of changes in stratosphere ozone levels. In laboratory experiments, determine the effect of chlorine gas on ozone. Estimate the amount of CFCs in the air and the resulting amount of chlorine gas. Predict future changes in the ozone layer expected as a result of the chlorine gas. Observe whether the predictions are accurate.
4. Tentatively accept, revise, or reject the hypothesis, depending on whether it explains the event.	4. The hypothesis explaining ozone depletion is tentatively accepted because the predictions were fulfilled.

■ The scientific method of investigation can be applied to the specific case of global ozone depletion.

are not usually able to conduct controlled experiments in order to test hypotheses. They must depend on the observation of real-world events, which seldom occur under exactly the same conditions from one time to the next. Economics is not, therefore, an exact science.

Economic Reasoning

An alternative definition of economics is that economics is the way an economist thinks. The science of economics is characterized by a particular way of analyzing problems. It is called the economic way of thinking or **economic reasoning**. Whatever their personal and political views, economists have a similar approach to examining the way the world works. They make use of a common set of tools of economic analysis. (We will discuss what these tools are in the next section.)

economic reasoning: the application of theoretical and factual tools of economic analysis to explaining economic developments or solving economic problems.

free good: a production or consumption good that does not have a direct cost.

economic good: any good or service that sells for a price; that is, a good that is not free.

The case of air pollution provides an illustration of what is unique about the economic way of thinking. Air pollution has reached serious levels because individuals, businesses, and frequently even governments treat air as a **free good**. Since it does not have a direct cost, as do **economic goods**, air is freely used to dispose of exhaust gases, without regard to its scarcity. According to the economic way of thinking, on the other hand, all costs should be included as costs of production, whether they are paid by the producer or not.

The economic way of thinking would generally favor an antipollution policy that forces producers to bear all of the social costs of production. This includes the pollution costs. To most economists, that would be a better policy than one that imposes an outright ban on pollution. (Antipollution policies are discussed in chapter 8, "Government and Business.")

Since economics is not an exact science, economists depend to a great extent on logical analysis, making use of the principles of economics. These principles include assumptions about how people, businesses, and governments behave. On the basis of these assumptions, economists predict the results of particular

(Continued on page 15) ▥➧

Who Needs Rain Forests?

Who needs rain forests? In the United States, the remaining rain forests have, for the most part, become mere tourist attractions. But in other parts of the world—Central and South America, Southeast Asia, West Africa—the rain forests are a vital part of the environment and of the economy.

At the subsistence level, people who live in the tropical rain forests use the wood from felled trees as fuel for heating and cooking. Rain forest inhabitants are generally too poor to afford other types of fuel such as kerosene or liquefied petroleum gas.

Other, wealthier local and outside people often clear rain forest land of trees in order to plant crops. Governments sometimes encourage and subsidize this activity as a way promoting economic development of the region. These endeavors have frequently been unsuccessful and costly because rain forest soil has low nutrient quality—the nutrients are bound up in the foliage, not in the soil—and therefore agriculture is unproductive. There are also problems from countless varieties of insects inhabiting the jungles that attack the plants and from diseases that attack the workers.

Other people who need the rain forests are medical and scientific researchers. Rain forests are the only source of a variety of rare plants that have medicinal properties. Pharmacy shelves in the United States already contain 20 drugs that have been developed from rain forest plants. They include treatments for heart disease, inflammation, and malaria.

Recently, researchers have produced three anti-AIDS compounds from rare jungle plants. Finding plants that have medicinal properties is the first step in developing these new drugs. Isolating the active chemical compound is the

second step. Testing it, first on animals and then on humans, for effectiveness and safety is the third. Finally, the compound must be produced in sufficient quantity in the laboratory or, if that is not possible, by growing the plants under controlled conditions. (The plants are usually too rare and hard to find in the jungle to make that a dependable source.)

Rain forests are also an essential habitat for the preservation of animal and bird species. Many varieties of birds found in North America—warblers, thrushes, swifts, tana-

■ The Blackburnian warbler, which forages primarily in treetops, is finding survival harder because of deforestation in South America and fragmentation of the forests in the eastern United States to which it migrates each spring. Birds may sometimes signal to us danger in our environment: Miners would in the past take a caged canary down into the coal pits with them. If the canary died, they knew that there was not enough oxygen and their own lives were endangered.

gers, and flycatchers, to name some—migrate each year to rain forests in Central and South America and return. Loss of habitat due to deforestation is the principal cause of a precipitous decline in the populations of these birds and of a variety of animal species.

Indigenous people, agriculture and mining producers, researchers, and patients with certain illnesses, not to mention birds and other animals, need the rain forests, often for con-

flicting and incompatible purposes. But we now realize that we all need rain forests for a very important purpose. That purpose is to stabilize and cleanse the global environment. The rain forests absorb large quantities of carbon dioxide gas from the atmosphere and thereby counter the greenhouse effect.

However, according to Stanford University's Center for Conservation Biology, 74,000 acres of rain forest are destroyed every day. The Food and Agriculture Organization of the United Nations reports that deforestation has accelerated 50% in the last decade. The total acreage of tropical forests destroyed each year is equal in size to the whole state of Washington. And, to make matters worse, when the trees are burned for fuel or to clear the land, they release their stored carbon dioxide into the air.

Economic Reasoning

1. Rain forests are considered which factor of production?

2. Present a hypothesis that explains the relationship between a decline in rain forest area and the greenhouse effect. Can your hypothesis be tested? How?

3. Do you think that the industrialized countries should contribute money to save the remaining rain forests in the underdeveloped parts of the world? Why or why not?

⟫ *(Continued from page 12)*

events or policies; for example, what the results would be of taxing pollution. Economic reasoning consists of applying economic principles to explain events, predict outcomes, and recommend policies.

Because of differences in individual preferences and belief systems, economics must also take value judgments into account. A policy that makes sense economically may not be acceptable if it violates people's sense of what is right or just. For example, a number of the poorer developing countries have resisted international agreements to reduce air pollution. They argue that the developed countries are responsible for most of the world's air pollution, and that the developing countries should have the right to use the atmosphere as an inexpensive dump for disposing of industrial gases just as the now developed countries did in the past. International policies to reduce air pollution must take this value judgment into account.

Economic reasoning is similar to the process of critical thinking. You will have a chance to practice critical thinking skills frequently as you go through this book. For example, the Economic Reasoning questions following the Case Applications at the end of each chapter section call for critical thinking. The first question in each set of three is a comprehension question. The second question

■ In poor countries, the need to use forests for firewood often outweighs the economic—and environmental—consequences. Economic policies must take such value judgments into consideration.

involves economic analysis and critical thinking skills. The third question calls for you to apply your own value judgments, along with economic reasoning, in arriving at an answer.

What Are the Tools of Economics?

Important in the economic way of thinking are the factual and theoretical tools of economics. Many of them are useful in analyzing the problem of air pollution.

Factual Tools

The factual tools used by economists are **statistics**, history, and how **institutions** operate.

The term "statistics" has a couple of meanings. First, statistics are the data, the figures that economists use in various economic measurements such as production, prices, or unemployment. Second, statistics

can refer to the methods employed in studying the data, such as finding an average.

Statistics are often essential to understanding a problem and determining what to do about it. For example, data collected on ozone depletion were important in rallying in-

statistics: the data on economic variables; also the techniques of analyzing, interpreting, and presenting data.

institutions: decision-making units, established practices, or laws.

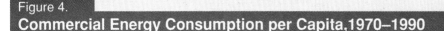

Figure 4.

Commercial Energy Consumption per Capita,1970–1990

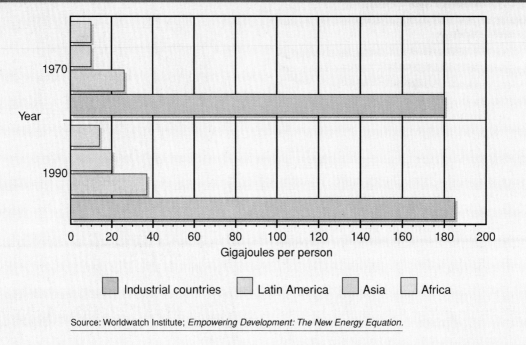

Source: Worldwatch Institute; *Empowering Development: The New Energy Equation.*

■ Per capita energy consumption in the industrial countries is many times greater than in the developing countries. But current growth rates of energy consumption in the developing countries are much higher.

---

ternational agreement on measures to protect the ozone layer. But obtaining accurate statistical information can be difficult.

History, especially economic history, is another useful tool in helping economists understand what is going on and how to deal with current problems. The experience of the industrial countries of North America and Western Europe has been that their economic growth was accompanied by greatly increased use of fossil fuels to power their economic expansion. If the developing countries of Asia, Africa, and Latin America follow the same path to economic growth, global warming will speed up. Figure 4 shows that, while commercial energy consumption per person is many times greater in the industrial countries than it is in the developing countries, the rate of growth of energy consumption is increasing much more rapidly on the developing continents.

Such high growth rates of energy production in the developing countries will bring about the worst-case scenario sooner.

Institutions are important organizations, customs, or patterns of behavior in a society. In economics, institutions can be a wide variety of things. They may vary from the banking system to labor unions, from the legal principle of private property ownership to the federal bureaucracy. They include the military, the media, accounting practices, and the zero population movement.

The institution of private property has permitted the owners of automobiles and factories to use their property in such a way that public welfare is injured by air pollution. To reduce the pollution problem, the institution of private property is now being modified. Owners are being restricted from using their property without regard to how the environment is affected.

■ State capitol buildings, like this one in Connecticut, symbolize an important legislative institution in the United States.

Theoretical Tools

The principal theoretical tools that are used in economics are concepts and models. **Economic concepts** are ideas. They are words or phrases that convey a specific meaning in economics. The subsections in the chapters of this book are organized by major concepts that are preceded by the color bar ▓▓▓▓ .

Other concepts are shown in **bold type** and defined in the marginal glossary, especially if their meaning in economics is different or more precise than the meaning of the word in general. Usually a concept means the same in economics as it does in ordinary usage. But sometimes it has a particular meaning. For instance, in economics the concept of scarcity does not indicate that there is necessarily only a small amount of something. Instead, it takes into account the amount available relative to the amount desired.

The most important theoretical tools of economists are **economic models**, which are simplified representations of the real world. Models are abstractions, reflecting only the most important aspects of a situation. A model of the greenhouse effect would show the relationship between the accumulation of gases in the atmosphere and global warming. It would not include other factors that might cause temperatures to vary from one year to the next, such as upper-atmosphere winds, particles from volcanic activity, and so forth. Random events are excluded from models in order to reveal the systematic relationships between the important **variables**.

economic concept: a word or phrase that conveys an economic idea.

economic model: a simplified representation of the cause-and-effect relationships in a particular situation. Models may be in verbal, graphic, or equation form.

variable: a quantity—such as number of workers, amount of carbon dioxide, or interest rate—whose value changes in relationship to changes in the values of other associated items.

Does It Pay to Go to College?

A question that faces students and their families in a time of sharply rising costs for higher education is whether or not it pays to go to college. A study by Frank S. Levy, an economist at the University of Maryland, showed that during the 1980s there was a rapidly widening gap between the value of a high school and college degree. In 1980 male college graduates over the age of 25 earned, on the average, 33% more than high school graduates of the same age. By 1990 the "college premium" had jumped to 60%. There was a similar increase in the earnings advantage of female college graduates, though not as large.

Not only did college graduates earn more, they were more likely to have a job. Richard B. Freeman of Harvard University found that male workers aged 25 to 34 with less than a high school education had a 12.1% unemployment rate in 1988. The unemployment rate for those with a high school degree was 6.7% and for college graduates a low 2.1%.

In the tough economic times of the early 1990s, however, the value of a college education was being questioned, especially in view of the large increase in college costs. For those graduates just getting their degrees, the job outlook was bleak. Among the 1.1 million stu-

■ More is involved in judging the value of a college education than a simple comparison of incomes with costs.

dents in the 1993 graduating class, less than 20% had lined up full-time employment by commencement day. And when they did find work, it was frequently not in a job that customarily called for a college degree. Labor Department economist Daniel Hecker has found that one-fifth of college graduates enter occupations that are not usually considered to require a college education (for example, sales, clerical, or manufacturing).

Does a college education still pay? Something that would help answer this question is an economic model called a *cost-benefit analysis*. A cost-benefit model compares the costs of a project (in this case, a college education) with the value of the benefits of the project. If the value of the benefits exceeds the costs, the project is worthwhile.

What would be included in a simple form of cost-benefit model of a college education? The most obvious benefit is the increased earning power of a college degree projected over a person's lifetime. The average expected lifetime earnings of a high school graduate is $1,667,000. By comparison, college graduates can expect to earn $4,142,000, on the average.

On the other side of the cost-benefit calculation, the largest costs are the direct costs of attending college and the sacrificed income that would have been earned by the student if he or she had not attended college.

Taking the college premium of increased earnings accumulated over a lifetime and dividing it into the sum of the direct and sacrificed earnings costs of attending college, the investment in college still appears to have a higher return than that of other long-term personal financial investments.

But for the individual student, whether or not it pays to get a college degree may depend on considerations other than purely financial ones. Does a degree provide a greater choice of occupations? Do college graduates express more job satisfaction than high school graduates? Is there more job security? More is involved in judging the value of a college education than a simple comparison of incomes with costs. A model is only as good as the assumptions on which it is built and the data that are fed into it, but in economics the model is an essential analytical tool.

Economic Reasoning

1. What factual tools of economic reasoning do you find in this application?

2. What theoretical tools of economic analysis do you find in this application?

3. What additional nonmonetary benefits of attending college might be included in a complete model of the advantages of a college education? Are there nonmonetary costs as well? What are they? In your view, would a complete cost-benefit model of a college education justify it or not? Why?

■ Owners of private property are being restricted from using it without regard to how the environment is affected. This North Carolina farmer is not free to spray his corn with whatever pesticide he chooses.

What Are the Uses of Graphs?

It is increasingly important to be able to read and use graphs. Besides being important in studying economics, it helps you understand a great deal of what appears in the news media. It is also becoming more necessary for today's occupations.

chart: a graphical representation of statistical data or other information.

Descriptive Charts

Charts are widely used to present information, such as statistical data, visually. One type of chart commonly seen is the *pie chart*. Pie charts are used to show the relative size of the components of a whole. An example is the chart on page 21 showing the amounts contributed by different sources to the greenhouse buildup. That chart is reproduced in its basic form as Figure 5.

The graph showing the size of the U.S. labor force, reproduced as Figure 6, represents

Figure 5.
Pie Chart

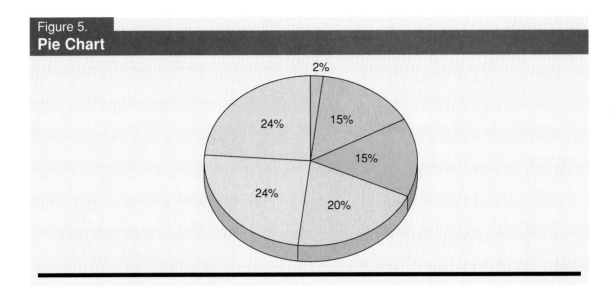

another type of chart. It is a *line graph* that shows how the number of workers in the labor force has changed over the years. The number of workers is a variable with the quantity measured by the scale on the left vertical axis of the graph. The years are shown on the bottom horizontal axis. This type of graph, with the values of the variable measured on the vertical axis and the years shown on the horizontal axis, is called a **time series**.

Another commonly seen graph is the *column chart*. It is useful in comparing the value of one variable with another or comparing the values of a variable over a period of time. An example of the column chart is Figure 3 on page 10. This is a stacked column chart which shows how the quantity of capital used by industries has increased over time. It also shows how much of the capital

> **time series:** the changes in the values of a variable over time; a chart in which time—generally years—is one of the variables.

Figure 6.
Line Graph

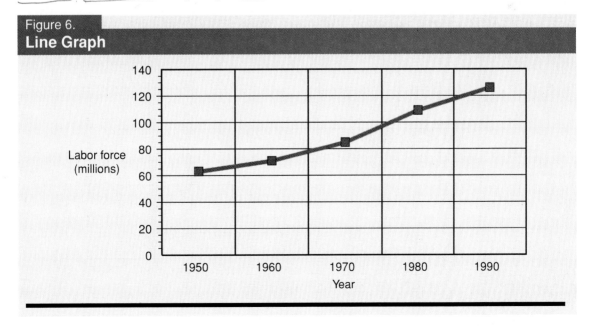

Figure 7.
Column Chart

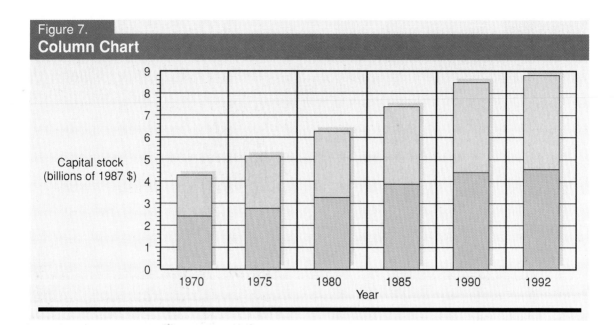

Capital stock (billions of 1987 $)

stock consists of machinery and equipment relative to factory buildings and other commercial structures. The basic form of the chart is shown as Figure 7.

Bar charts are like column charts turned on their side. Figure 4 on page 16, reproduced in Figure 8, shows how rates of growth in energy consumption per capita since 1970 differ between industrialized and developing countries.

An *area chart* is particularly well suited to demonstrating how the relative importance of different components of a variable change over time. The chart on page 283 is an area chart showing how the composition of total unemployment has changed. There are additional types of charts—scatter charts, range charts, three-dimensional charts—but the ones described above are those most commonly encountered.

Figure 8.
Bar Chart

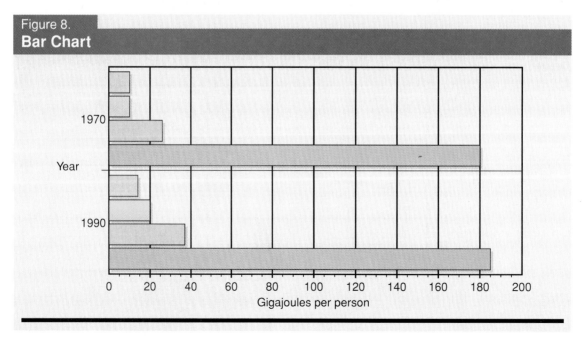

Analytical Diagrams

Economic **diagrams** are visual models. They resemble line charts, but instead of showing how a variable changes over time or with respect to a country or industry or other category, a diagram shows how two or more variables relate to each other. They are graphic models based on observation and economic reasoning.

As an example of such a model, let us take the relationship between energy production and air purity. In Figure 9, we measure the amount of energy production on the horizontal axis and the amount of pure air on the vertical axis. The measurements of the amounts of energy production and pure air both begin at 0 in the lower left corner of the diagram. The amount of energy production increases to the right on the horizontal axis and the amount of pure air increases as we move up the vertical axis. The purpose of the diagram is to show the interaction between energy production and air purity.

Figure 9 shows that the more energy that is produced, the less pure air there is. The relationship between the two variables is an **inverse relationship**; as the amount of one increases, the amount of the other decreases. (If two variables were to increase together and decrease together, they would have a **direct relationship**.) We will make more use of this type of model in the next chapter.

Diagrams are used a great deal in studying economics to illustrate economic principles. If you are not experienced with diagrams, you should read the appendix to this chapter and practice drawing diagrams to become familiar with them.

diagram: a graph that shows the relationship between two or more variables that may or may not have values that can actually be measured; a graphical model.

inverse relationship: a relationship between two variables in which the value of one decreases as the value of the other increases.

direct relationship: a relationship between two variables in which their values increase and decrease together.

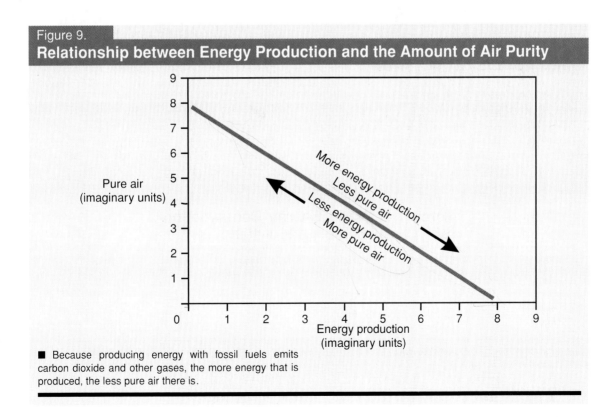

Figure 9.

Relationship between Energy Production and the Amount of Air Purity

Pure air (imaginary units)

More energy production
Less pure air

Less energy production
More pure air

Energy production (imaginary units)

■ Because producing energy with fossil fuels emits carbon dioxide and other gases, the more energy that is produced, the less pure air there is.

The Energy Gluttons

When we looked to see who the enemy was, it was us. In our concern over the greenhouse effect, we must recognize that the United States is the major contributor to the problem. We emit the most carbon dioxide and other greenhouse gases into the atmosphere. This country is responsible for over 20% of the carbon dioxide build-up in the atmosphere, although we have only 5% of the world's population. The explanation lies in our high energy consumption, energy that is produced mainly by burning fossil fuels. The United States consumes almost one-quarter of world energy production.

The U.S. share of world energy consumption is down, however, from earlier years. In 1960 it was 37% (see Table 2). Our high energy consumption correlates with our high level of production of goods and services. This country is responsible for nearly one-quarter of the world's output of goods and services.

Nevertheless, on an individual basis, we consume an excessive amount of energy. On the average, each American consumes twice the amount of energy consumed by someone in Japan. The largest portion of our energy consumption goes for transportation. Cars and trucks account for some 67% of the oil burned in this country. By contrast, only 44% of the oil used in Western Europe and 35% in Japan is linked to transportation.

To conserve oil and reduce carbon dioxide emissions, it has been proposed that we sharply increase the gasoline tax, to as much as $1.00 a gallon. It is hoped that such an increase would cause us to go on an energy diet and give up our gluttonous ways.

Economic Reasoning

1. Which type of graph would be appropriate to show the information in Table 2? Why?

2. Draw the graph and label it. Explain what the graph shows.

3. Are you in favor of raising the federal gas tax from 18¢ a gallon to $1.00 a gallon? Why or why not?

Table 2.   **Percent of World Energy Consumption by Region, 1960–1991**

Year	United States	Europe	Soviet Union*	Asia	Other
1960	37	27	15	13	8
1970	34	27	16	14	9
1980	28	25	17	19	11
1991	24	21	16	26	13

*In 1991, the Soviet Union dissolved; 11 of the 15 former Soviet republics joined to form the Commonwealth of Independent States.

Source: Statistical Office of the United Nations, *Energy Statistics Yearbook,* annual.

■ The U.S. share of world energy consumption is down from earlier years.

Putting It Together

Economics is the social science concerned with how resources are used to satisfy people's wants. The science of economics arises from the need to overcome *scarcity*. The *resources* available for production are not sufficient to satisfy all our wants. We therefore need to use them in such a way as to maximize output. These *factors of production* are *land* (all natural resources), *labor* (including managerial and professional), and *capital* (machinery, buildings, technology, and information). *Financial capital* is used by *entrepreneurs* and managers to purchase the factors of production.

The *scientific method* is a process of observing events, forming *hypotheses* concerning their causes, testing the hypotheses, and rejecting, revising, or tentatively accepting them. Economics makes use of the scientific method; but it is a social science, not a laboratory science, and cannot do controlled experiments. It applies logical analysis based on economic principles to explain events, predict outcomes, and recommend policies. Economic policies must take into account an individual's and a society's value judgments as well.

Economic reasoning is based on the application of economic principles and the use of a common set of tools of economic analysis. *Free goods* do not have a direct cost, while *economic goods* do.

Economics makes use of factual and theoretical tools. The factual tools are *statistics*, history, and the functioning of *institutions*. The theoretical tools are *economic concepts*, words that may have a more specialized meaning in economics than they do in general use, and *economic models*, simplified representations of the real world. Models may be in verbal, mathematical, or visual form.

Graphs may be charts that visually present statistical information, or they may be diagrams that show the relationship of vari-

■ Pollution from factories and other sources may cause average temperatures to rise 3 to 9 degrees Fahrenheit by the year 2050.

ables to each other in an economic model. It depends on the nature of the information to be shown. Charts may take the form of pie charts, line charts, columnar charts, bar charts, or others. Charts that show the values of a variable over a succession of years are called *time series*.

Diagrams are visual models based on observation and economic reasoning. In the case of energy production and air purity, the two variables have an *inverse* rather than a *direct* relationship.

The Master Model Builder

Paul Anthony Samuelson (born 1915)
Born in Gary, Indiana, Samuelson attended the University of Chicago, the temple of conservative economics. He studied under a number of the leading economists of the time, some with well-deserved reputations as tyrants in their classes. The young Samuelson had the guts and the knowledge to challenge them when he thought they had made a mistake—and get away with it.

He graduated in 1935 and would have been happy to pursue a doctoral degree at Chicago. But the scholarship that he received required him to change schools, so he went to Harvard, where he received his Ph.D. in 1941. Since 1940 he has been on the faculty of the Massachusetts Institute of Technology.

In 1947, at the age of 32, he published *Foundations of Modern Economics*. Milton Friedman, himself a University of Chicago product and quite conservative (see Perspective, p. 383), wrote that *Foundations* "immediately established his [Samuelson's] reputation as a brilliant and original mathematical economist" (*Newsweek,* November 9, 1970, p. 80).

Samuelson's introductory economics text was published a year later. It was subsequently translated into other languages and published in a number of countries. In 1958, in collaboration with two coauthors, he published *Linear Programming and Economic Analysis.*

In 1970, the second year that the Nobel Prize in economics was awarded, it went to an American, Paul Samuelson. It was in recognition of his outstanding work in constructing economic models. According to the Nobel Prize citation: "By his many contributions, Samuelson has done more than any other contemporary economist to raise the level of scientific analysis in economic theory."

Samuelson got off to a fast start in becoming the first American to win a Nobel Prize in economics. As an undergraduate student at the University of Chicago, he was allowed to attend graduate economics classes. Some leading economists today, who were then graduate students in those classes, report that they were intimidated by his intellectual ability. Remembering the "shock" of encountering Samuelson as a competitor in class, one of those graduate students, Martin Bronfenbrenner, now a renowned economist himself, has said of the course instructor, "I shall always be grateful for [the professor's] kindly assurances that one need not really be another Samuelson to pass muster as an economist" (Feiwel, p. 349. See Further Reading). Before he finished graduate school, Samuelson had published two papers that set forth models that were major contributions to economic theory. His subsequent articles fill the four large volumes of *The Collected Scientific Papers of Paul Samuelson*.

The mathematical models in those papers are not easy reading, even for other economists. But Samuelson proved his versatility by writing an introductory textbook that was the most successful economics text of all time. *Economics: An Introductory Analysis* (1948) was the leading introductory economics text for 2 decades, selling over 3 million copies.

In addition to his activities as a researcher and textbook writer, Samuelson has been a columnist for *Newsweek* magazine and was an adviser to the government during the Kennedy administration. He has been a teacher most of his life and an occasional speculator in the commodities market. The success of his textbook and commodities speculation made Samuelson a millionaire. By excelling in the world of finance as well as scholarship, he joins another great economist of the past, John Maynard Keynes, who is the subject of the Perspective in chapter 12.

Samuelson the scientist and capitalist is also Samuelson the social critic who believes that government economic activities have been too much "suppressed—so that we have public squalor along with private, really decadent, opulence" (*Science News*, Oct. 31, 1970, p. 348).

FOR FURTHER STUDY AND ANALYSIS

Study Questions

1. Give all of the examples of scarcity that you can find in the introductory article on air pollution.

2. Name something besides radioactive waste that is rare but not scarce.

3. What productive resources are used in your school? Do any of them appear to be more scarce than others? Which ones?

4. On the basis of your observation of which factors of production are especially scarce in your school, devise a hypothesis to explain their scarcity. How could that hypothesis be tested?

5. Why is information listed as a factor of production?

6. Name another "free good" besides air. Does excessive use of that good lead to problems in the way that unrestricted use of air has led to global warming and depletion of the ozone layer?

7. What example of each of the three factual tools used in economics do you find in the case application entitled "The Energy Gluttons" (p. 24)?

8. Do you find any economic concepts or models in that application? What are they?

9. What type of chart would be most appropriate for showing how your time is allocated during a weekday between attending school, traveling, eating, studying, engaging in leisure activities, sleeping, and other activities? Draw such a graph in its basic form and label it.

10. What variables are involved in the case application entitled "Who Needs Rain Forests?" on pages 13–14? Pick two of those variables that have an inverse relationship and draw a diagram that shows that inverse relationship.

Exercises in Analysis

1. Visit a local business and gather information on the factors of production used in that business. Ask the manager if there have been any recent technological improvements in the operations of the business. Write a short paper describing what resources are used in the business.

2. Prepare a short paper describing the school that you attend, using the factual tools of economic analysis.

3. Prepare a cost-benefit analysis model of your own education.

4. Find examples in newspapers or magazines of the following types of graphs: pie charts, line charts, column charts, and bar charts. For each type, identify the variable that is being measured and what it is being measured with respect to (time, industries, states, and so forth).

Further Reading

Bear, John, and Mariah P. Bear. *Guide to Finding Money for College.* Berkeley, CA: Ten Speed Press, 1993. Helpful information on various means of financing a college education.

Benedick, Richard Elliot. *Ozone Diplomacy: New Directions in Safeguarding the Planet.* Cambridge, MA: Harvard University Press, 1991. Covers the Vienna Convention for the Protection of the Ozone Layer in 1985 and the Protocols of 1987—laws on air pollution and legislation regarding ozone depletion.

Brown, E. Cary, and Robert M. Solow, eds. *Paul Samuelson and Modern Economic Theory.* New York: McGraw-Hill, 1983. This book is a *Festschrift*, a collection of articles published to honor a scholar; by contrast, the Feiwel collection listed at right is not intended to be a *Festschrift*. The lead monograph is by Samuelson himself and provides an insight into his personality.

Cagin, Seth, and Philip Dray. *Between Earth and Sky: How CFCs Changed Our World and Endangered the Ozone Layer.* New York: Pantheon Books, 1993. Describes the environmental effects of CFCs and the depletion of the ozone layer.

Cline, William R. *The Economics of Global Warming.* Washington, DC: The Institute for International Economics, 1992. Examines the economic aspects of air pollution and the economic implications of global warming.

Collins, Mark, ed. *The Last Rainforests: A World Conservation Atlas.* New York: Oxford University Press, 1990. Discusses what rain forests are, how they work, the pressures on them, and why we need them. Describes the people of the rain forests and the challenge of conservation.

The Encyclopedic Dictionary of Economics. 4th ed. Guilford, CT: The Dushkin Publishing Group, 1991. Explanations of economic terms, theories, and institutions, organized alphabetically.

Feiwel, George R., ed. *Samuelson and Neoclassical Economics.* Boston: Kluwer-Nijhoff Publishing, 1982. A varied selection of monographs by representative scholars of widely divergent perceptions discussing, sometimes critically, Samuelson's "history-making contributions to and impact on the economics of our age."

Flavin, Christopher. "Slowing Global Warming." In *Worldwatch Institute Report: State of the World—1990.* New York: W. W. Norton, 1990. The Worldwatch Institute publishes an annual report on "progress toward a sustainable society" which surveys the status of environmental and food conditions in the world. This article describes the causes of the greenhouse effect and alternative strategies for lessening its impact.

Gore, Albert. *Earth in the Balance: Ecology and the Human Spirit.* Boston: Houghton Mifflin, 1992. The vice president, who was a senator when this book was published, covers the concerns about environmental degradation in the context of human ecology. He discusses the environmental policies needed to ensure protection for the environment.

Grants for Scholarships, Student Aid and Loans: 1991–92. New York: Foundation Center, 1991. Provides directories for sources of scholarships, student aid, and student loans. Covers grants to colleges and universities on both undergraduate and graduate levels.

McKibben, William. *The End of Nature.* New York: Random House, 1989. A popular and personalized treatment of the greenhouse effect problem. The author suggests that we can follow one of two paths in dealing with environmental problems: we can defy nature and continue with our customary practices or we can humble ourselves to nature's requirements.

Park, Chris C. *Tropical Rainforests.* New York: Routledge, 1992. Examines the human ecology of the rain forests. Describes the deforestation of the rain forests that has taken place and conservation measures that could be taken in managing the remaining rain forests.

Peltz, Liz. *Take the Heat Off the Planet: How You Can Really Stop the Climate Change.* London: Friends of the Earth, 1993. A program of energy conservation to reduce emission of the gasses that can cause global warming.

Wyman, Richard, ed. *Global Climate Change and Life on Earth.* New York: Routledge, 1991. Covers the environmental aspects of global warming. Examines the conservation of biological diversity, the role of forests in affecting greenhouse gas composition of the atmosphere, and the impact of climate-induced sea level rise on coastal areas.

Constructing and Reading Diagrams

Here is how the points on a diagram are constructed. Let us take a noneconomic example that is familiar—an automobile trip. Our destination is 200 miles away. We are interested in how long it will take us to get there and where we will be at different times along the way.

In order to show this information graphically, let us draw a diagram that measures the driving time in hours on the horizontal axis and the distance covered in miles on the vertical axis. The axes with their appropriate scales are shown in Figure A.

How far we travel in a given amount of time depends, of course, on our driving speed. If we drive at a constant 40 miles per hour, at the end of the first hour we will have covered 40 miles, at the end of the second hour 80 miles, and so forth. The relationship between time and distance traveled is plotted in Figure B. At the 1-hour mark on the horizontal axis, a vertical line is drawn—referred to as a perpendicular. At the 40-mile mark on the vertical axis, an intersecting line is drawn—also called a perpendicular because it

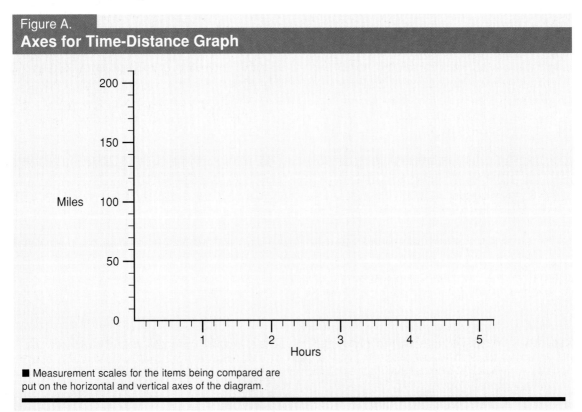

Figure A.
Axes for Time-Distance Graph

■ Measurement scales for the items being compared are put on the horizontal and vertical axes of the diagram.

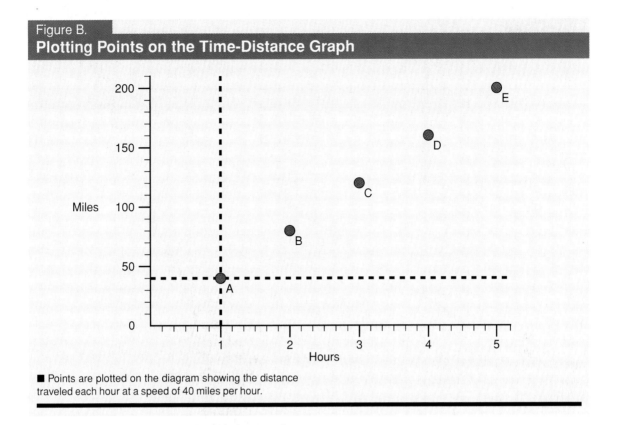

■ Points are plotted on the diagram showing the distance traveled each hour at a speed of 40 miles per hour.

is perpendicular to that axis. Where the two lines cross at point A is the first point plotted on the time-distance diagram.

If we plot the additional distances traveled at the end of each subsequent hour of driving time in the same fashion, we find points B, C, D, and E. At the end of 5 hours, we will reach our destination 200 miles away.

The dots in Figure B show how far we have gone at the end of each hour. Since we are traveling at a constant rate of speed, a line connecting the dots would show the distance traveled at any point in time. Such a line showing the relationship between two variables—here time and distance—is generally referred to as a curve, even when it is a straight line, as it would be in this case. The line in Figure C we can label the 40-mph Travel Curve.

To find how far we have traveled at any particular time, we draw a perpendicular from the horizontal axis to the travel curve and locate the corresponding point on the vertical axis. If we want to know how far we will have traveled in 3½ hours, we draw a perpendicular from the 3½-hour point on the horizontal

axis to the travel curve in Figure D. This gives point X on the curve. From point X we draw a perpendicular across to the vertical axis. The perpendicular intersects the vertical axis at 140 miles.

From the graph we could similarly find how long it would take to reach any particular place along the way. If we wished to know when we would pass through a town 100 miles from home, we draw a perpendicular in Figure D from the vertical axis at 100 miles to the travel curve. It intersects the travel curve at point Y. From that point we drop a perpendicular to the horizontal axis. It shows that we would pass through the town 2½ hours after we leave home.

If we wish to make the trip in less time, we can increase our speed. Figure E shows the travel curve for a speed of 50 miles an hour. Because more distance is covered each hour, the new travel curve rises more steeply than the previous one. It shows that we would reach our destination in 4 hours instead of 5. It also shows that we would pass through the town 100 miles from home in 2 hours.

Figure C.
40-mph Travel Curve

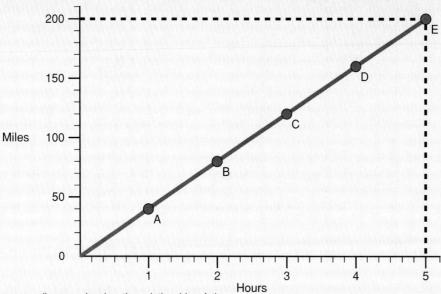

■ A line on a diagram showing the relationship of the variables is referred to as a curve, even when it is a straight line.

Using Travel-Curve Diagram

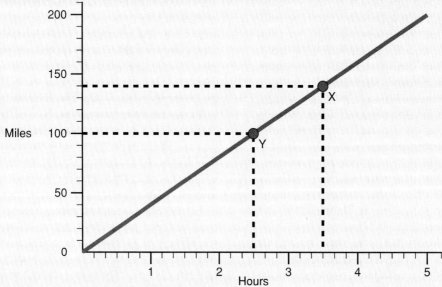

■ Information is obtained from a diagram by finding corresponding points on the axes with the use of perpendiculars.

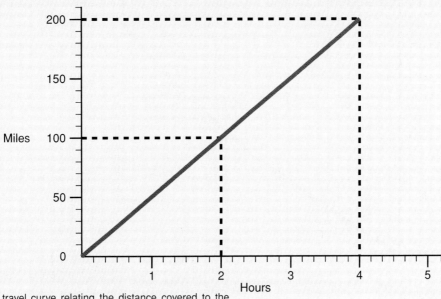

■ The travel curve relating the distance covered to the driving time is steeper for a speed of 50 miles per hour than for a speed of 40 miles per hour.

In these diagrams we have assumed a constant rate of speed during the whole trip, so the travel curve rises at a constant slope. What will happen if the rate of speed changes during the trip? Let us say that the first two hours we can drive only 40 miles per hour because of congested traffic, but the third hour we can drive 50 and after that 65 miles an hour. The travel curve based on those speeds is shown in Figure F. As speed increases, the slope of the curve becomes steeper. To find the time required to reach the destination, we draw a perpendicular from the 200-mile mark on the vertical axis to the travel curve. From that point we draw a perpendicular down to the horizontal axis where it intersects the time scale at 4 hours and 5 minutes.

The relationship of time to distance in the travel curve is positive (or direct). As one increases, so does the other. Therefore, the curve slopes upward to the right. The relationship of other variables may be negative (or inverse). As one increases, the other decreases. For example, the distance driven and the amount of gas remaining in the tank are in-versely related. In Figure G the miles driven are shown on the horizontal axis and the amount of gasoline in the tank on the vertical axis. Assuming that the car has a 15-gallon tank and gets 25 miles to a gallon, the amount of gas remaining at any point on the trip can be determined from the curve. If we wish to find the amount of gasoline remaining in the tank after 300 miles, we draw a perpendicular from the 300-mile mark on the horizontal axis up to the intersection with the curve and from that point draw a perpendicular across to the vertical axis. It shows that we have 3 gallons left and had better start looking for a filling station.

Because the relationship between miles driven and the amount of gas left in the tank is negative—as one increases the other de-creases—the curve slopes downward to the right. The curve ends at the horizontal axis because you cannot have less than zero gas in the tank.

However, there are some variables that can have negative values—become less than zero. Let us suppose that this trip we have been discussing is to visit some friends and

Travel Curve with Increasing Speeds

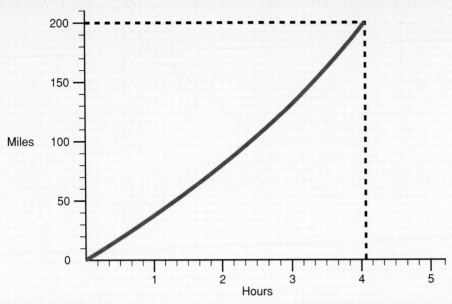

■ As the driving speed increases over time, the travel curve becomes steeper.

Gasoline-Distance Graph

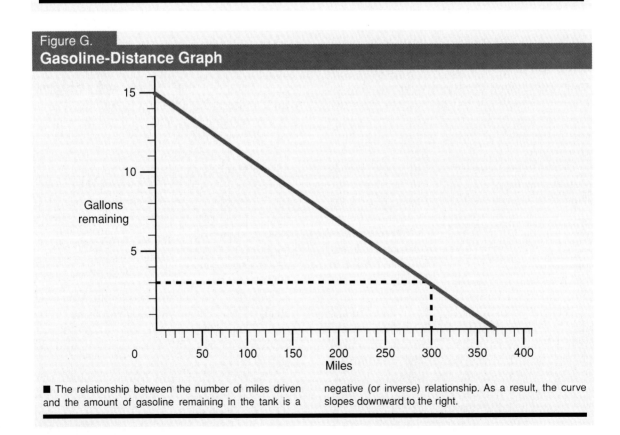

■ The relationship between the number of miles driven and the amount of gasoline remaining in the tank is a negative (or inverse) relationship. As a result, the curve slopes downward to the right.

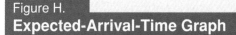

Expected-Arrival-Time Graph

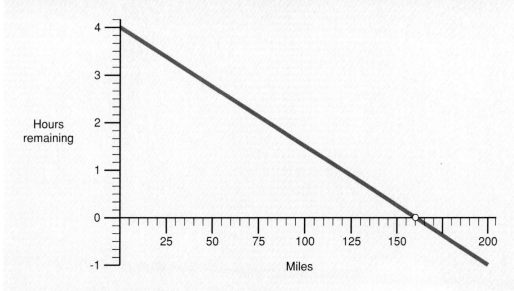

■ The part of a curve that falls below the horizontal axis indicates negative values of the variable measured on the vertical axis.

we have notified them that we expect to arrive at 4 P.M. We plan on leaving at noon and driving at a speed of 50 miles per hour. However, we encounter bad weather and are able to average only 40 miles an hour. The vertical axis in Figure H shows the amount of time remaining before our anticipated arrival. The distance driven is shown on the horizontal axis. We expected to cover the 200 miles in 4 hours, but due to the weather delay we cover only 160 miles at the end of 4 hours. The amount of time by which we are late in arriving is shown below the horizontal axis where the values are negative. We arrive at our destination an hour later than expected.

In becoming better acquainted with graphs and how to use them, it is helpful to draw diagrams yourself. You will be given the opportunity to do this in some of the Economic Reasoning questions following the Case Applications.

Here is a suggestion for a diagram that you could practice on now. Draw a graph showing the relationship of the number of weeks in your

economics course and the number of chapters that you are going to cover in the text. Put the number of weeks on the horizontal axis scale and the number of chapters on the vertical axis scale. Draw a curve showing the relationship between the number of weeks and the number of chapters if you were to cover the chapters at a constant rate. Draw another curve on the same diagram showing the relationship between the number of weeks and the number of chapters covered if you instead spend more time on the early chapters and less time on later chapters. (For the second curve don't bother to plot specific points; just make a freehand drawing of the curve showing its general shape and location in relation to the first curve.)

Practice using the diagram by locating, with the use of perpendiculars, in which weeks you will complete the first third of the chapters under each of the two assumptions—a constant rate of covering the material and an increasing rate.

■ **Making economic** choices is something we all do as consumers, as producers, and as members of society. Many personal and business choices are important—whether to buy a house, what product to produce—but among the most important are the choices citizens make about the use of the nation's resources. This chapter's introductory article deals with choices we face about the best uses for the "peace dividend."

Swords into Plowshares

Do you ever ask yourself "What couldn't I do with an extra $100 billion?" Well, you may get a chance to find out. Not the whole hundred billion for you personally, of course, but you may share in it if proposals for scaling back military spending are carried through. The collapse of the Soviet Union, ending the cold war, has created the promise of a "peace dividend," extra resources available to the civilian economy that were previously allocated to the military. Savings on the military budget in the 1990s could reach $100 billion per year. The projected spending in 1995 is $235.7 billion, down from $287.5 billion in 1991 (both figures in 1991 dollars).

If such a reduction in defense spending occurs, it will result in a massive redirection of resources away from preparation for war to civilian uses. There will be controversy over how to allocate the savings. The alternatives are (1) reducing the government deficit, (2) lowering taxes, and (3) increasing government spending on civilian programs. However the defense savings are allocated, there will be as much as $100 billion of resources available for civilian production each year that were not available before. Your per capita share of that $100 billion of resources would be about $400.

If you were allowed to decide how the resources were to be used, what would you choose? You might consider that if the defense budget savings were applied to reducing the deficit or cutting taxes, the resources could be used by the private sector—individuals and businesses—to purchase consumption or investment goods. If, instead, the savings in military spending were shifted to nonmilitary government programs, the resources could be used for such purposes as retraining displaced workers, construction of mass transit systems and "smart" highways using electronic traffic controls, cleaning up toxic waste sites, and so forth. An advantage of using the military savings for government civilian programs is that the programs would directly employ workers laid off from defense industries. Private spending would not be as certain to reemploy the displaced workers in the near future.

On the other hand, applying the peace dividend to reducing the government deficit would help to keep interest rates low. Low interest rates encourage investment. This increases our production capacity and improves the competitiveness of U.S. firms in world markets. Equally important, reducing defense spending will free research and development (R & D) resources for use in the civilian sector. There is a limited amount of skilled scientific and technical labor available, and a sizable amount of the most highly trained labor has been engaged in R & D work for military projects. Making those scarce resources available for consumer product development and increased production efficiency can help American industry to compete with foreign producers.

Allocating resources to repairing and improving our transportation, water, and energy systems would also make the nation more productive. It is estimated that the country is about $15 billion short of the amount that needs to be spent each year on public works for the economy to produce at its potential.

Others advocate using the peace dividend to reduce taxes. There is no scarcity of ideas about what to use the money and resources

for. But the shift of that much spending from defense to civilian purposes will not be without stresses and dangers. Those industries heavily dependent on defense contracts and the states in which they are located will be faced with a loss of jobs and income. Areas such as Los Angeles, St. Louis, and Dallas–Fort Worth, with their large concentrations of defense contractors, are especially affected.

In addition to the jobs lost in defense industries, the reduction in military spending will result in the discharge of a million, more or less, servicemen and -women and civilian employees of the military. If we were to cut the defense budget by the full $100 billion in one year, there would not be an opportunity for the reallocation of those service personnel and defense workers and other resources from military to nonmilitary production. Mass unemployment would occur.

Figure 1.

Actual Job Losses to 1993 and Anticipated Job Losses by 1997 as a Result of Cutbacks in States with the Most Defense Industry Spending

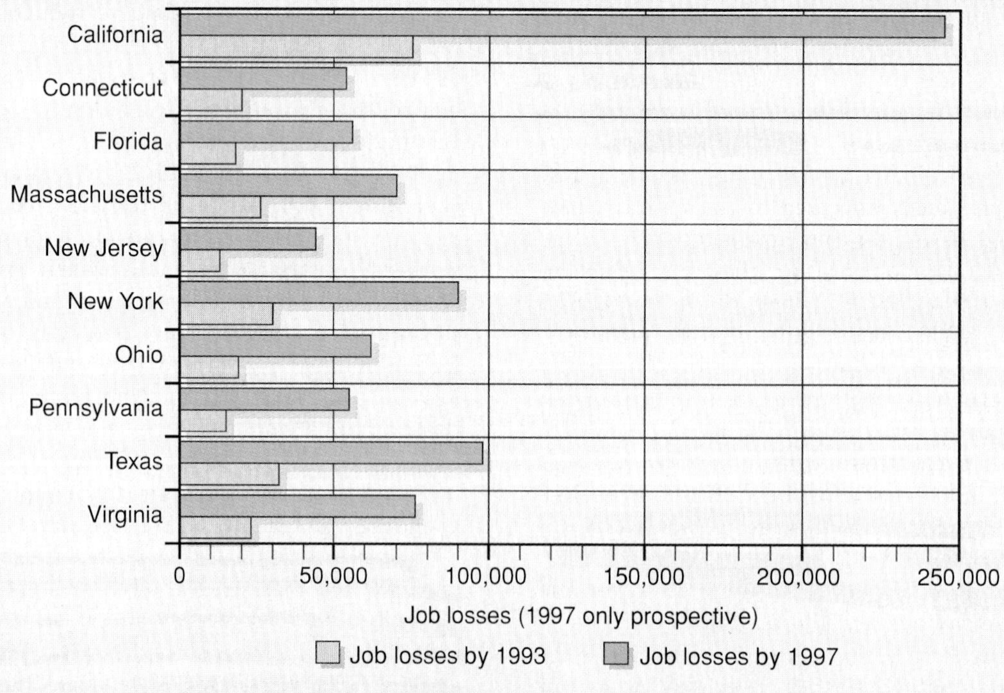

Job losses (1997 only prospective)

☐ Job losses by 1993   ☐ Job losses by 1997

Source: Federal Reserve Defense Budget Project.

For this reason, as well as due to caution in moving toward disarmament for strategic reasons, the cutback in military spending will continue to be gradual, involving reductions of around $10 billion each year. Getting even this amount of cuts in defense spending through the Congress is a difficult process, since every program reduction means a loss of jobs in some legislator's district.

The Gulf War and unsettled conditions in Eastern Europe and other parts of the world served to dampen expectations for the peace dividend. They provided ammunition for defense industry lobbyists and others opposed to sharp reductions in military spending. On the other hand, they have increased public and congressional interest in greater defense burden sharing by our allies.

Countries such as Japan and Germany have shown that a large defense budget is not necessary for a prospering economy. Part of the reason for their economic success in the last 20 years was that they allocated a much smaller part of their resources to the military than did the United States. The peace dividend offers us an opportunity to convert some of our resources to more productive uses.

■ Chapter Preview

Decisions about what to do with the peace dividend are examples of the kinds of choices that an economy must continually make regarding the use of resources. How successful we are at choosing the best allocation of our available resources determines how well we can achieve our economic goals. This chapter examines the questions: How do we make economic choices? What are the basic economic questions? What are society's economic goals?

■ Learning Objectives

After completing this chapter, you should be able to:

1. Define and give examples of economic trade-offs.

2. Explain opportunity cost.

3. Explain the production possibility frontier and increasing costs.

4. Give examples of the three basic economic questions.

5. List the four primarily economic goals of society.

6. Show the effect on output of increasing employment to full employment.

7. Show the effect on economic growth of producing more capital goods.

8. Give examples of trade-offs between economic and socioeconomic goals.

How Do We Make Economic Choices?

An abundant supply of everything relative to the demand for it would mean that individuals and society could be as wasteful as they pleased and not have to consider making choices. But because of scarcity, our choices involve **trade-offs**.

Trade-offs

Because resources are scarce in relation to the demand for them, using resources for one purpose means that other things will not be produced. The allocation of 6% of the nation's production to the military meant that resources were drawn away from production for civilian use. Being strong militarily involved a trade-off economically. Making our defense capability stronger made our economy weaker and our standard of living lower. This is sometimes referred to as the guns-for-butter trade-off.

Most trade-off decisions are made by individual consumers and producers, rather than by government. Every time you go to the store to shop, you affect the decisions about how resources are allocated. If consumers buy fewer eggs because of concern over their cholesterol content, resources flow out of the poultry businesses and into some other occupation. True, laying hens are not much good for anything but egg production, but the labor, feed, and capital in the industry can be transferred to other industries that better meet our needs.

When we turn from war production to peace, we do not literally beat our swords into plowshares, as may have been done in biblical times, or directly transform an armaments factory into a dairy in trading off guns for butter. But the trade-off consists of reallocating the land, labor, and capital—the factors of production—used to produce mili-

■ Egg production represents a trade-off in the allocation of resources. The resources (land, labor, and capital) that go into egg production are unavailable for other uses. If customers buy fewer eggs, resources flow out of the poultry businesses and into some other occupation.

tary goods, and reassigning those employed in the military services themselves, to increase output for civilian purposes.

Opportunity Costs

To make the best possible use of our limited resources, we need to compare the trade-off possibilities to find out what is gained and what is lost. If resources are used for armaments, they cannot be used for consumption or investment. The value of the sacrificed alternative is called the **opportunity cost** of whatever is produced. To give an idea of what the opportunity costs of our military spending

---

trade-off: the choice between alternative uses for a given quantity of a resource.

opportunity cost: real economic cost of a good or service produced measured by the value of the sacrificed alternative.

are, the $70 billion B-2 Stealth bomber program was the approximate cost of what the Ford Foundation estimated was needed to repair the "safety net" of social programs over 5 years—the school food programs, low-income housing, worker retraining, and other assistance.

The guns-to-butter trade-off is shown by the diagram in Figure 2 (p. 42). In this type of diagram, called a **production possibility frontier**, we can compare the opportunity costs of our alternative choices by showing the varying amounts of the two types of outputs that can be produced by the same fixed amount of resources. Figure 2 shows the amounts of armaments that could be produced in relation to the amounts of civilian goods that could be produced with a given amount of a hypothetical country's resources. The units of civilian goods are measured from left to right along the horizontal axis and the units of armaments are measured from bottom to top on the vertical axis.

If all of the available resources were put into military production, the country could produce 5 million units of armaments. If, instead, all of those same resources were put into increasing civilian goods, 10 million more units could be produced. (These units and quantities are imaginary; they are simply used to illustrate the principle of opportunity cost.) If we allocate part of the resources to produce armaments and the other part for civilian output, and if we assume that the trade-off between the two outputs is constant, the line marked PPF shows the different combinations of armaments and civilian goods that could be produced. PPF stands for production possibility frontier. It represents the maximum combinations of the two outputs that could be produced with the available resources.

If the nation chose to allocate its resources to produce the combination shown at point A, it could produce 4 million units of armaments and 2 million units of civilian goods. If it allocated its resources to produce at point B, it could produce 3 million units of armaments and 4 million units of civilian goods. The opportunity cost of changing the composition of output from A to B, of in-

■The opportunity cost of a program is the value of the sacrificed alternative. Military spending for such programs as the B-2 Stealth bomber (top) has an opportunity cost affecting spending on social programs, such as for the homeless (bottom).

creasing civilian production by 2 million units, is reducing armaments production by 1 million units. Similarly, if you go from B to A, the opportunity cost of increasing armaments production by 1 million units is decreasing civilian production by 2 million units. The opportunity costs would be the same wherever we moved the composition on the PPF because we assumed that the trade-off ratio was constant at 2:1.

> **production possibility frontier (PPF):** the line on a graph showing the different maximum output combinations of goods or services that can be obtained from a fixed amount of resources.

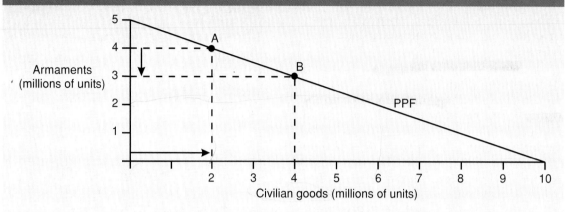

Increasing Costs

In the real world, however, trade-off ratios are seldom constant. The opportunity costs depend on what combination of outputs the country is producing, where it is on the production possibility frontier. If government spending goes largely for armaments and little for civilian output, it is likely that a large in-

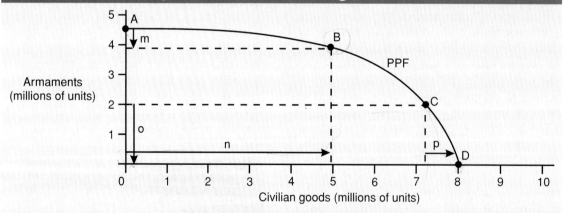

Dieting—The National Pastime

Even in America, a land of relative plenty, there are people who have insufficient food. And there would be millions more hungry if it were not for government and private food programs for the needy.

But in this country there is an even larger number of people who are overfed. According to the National Center for Health Statistics, there are in excess of 34 million Americans between the ages of 20 and 74 who are more than 20% above desirable body weight. It has been demonstrated that such overweight constitutes a health hazard for these individuals.

Although only a little over one-quarter of the population is clinically obese, about 100 million adult Americans are overweight and an even larger number think that they are. Overweight has been an increasing problem among adolescents. According to statistics, there are 50% more obese young people in the United States than there were 10 years ago.

In response to social and self-image pressures, as well as health considerations, dieting has become a national pastime. There are more than 8,000 commercial diet centers in the nation. Weight-loss firms have been known to advertise their rates by the pound. Along with the waste disposal industry, the "waist disposal" industry is one of the few businesses that charges you for what you give up rather than what you receive.

Although the recession of the early 1990s affected the weight loss businesses, as it did others, it caused them to fight more aggressively for market share. Their advertising claims became so extreme that the Federal Trade Commission had to crack down on some that could not be supported by evidence.

Despite the money and the physical and psychological energy expended, few dieters have had lasting success in weight reduction.

Studies of university programs show that only 5–10% of participants in weight loss programs haven kept the weight off a year or two after completing the diet.

There are many theories about why it proves so difficult for most people to lose weight and keep it off. Is it due to heredity, to childhood eating habits, to hormonal balance, to psychological tensions that are released by eating, to an automatic "starvation metabolism" reaction of the body to dieting, or to a combination of factors?

Most people find it difficult to stay on a diet. Many succumb to their craving for food, especially carbohydrates and fats, in response to anxiety, depression, or loneliness. Eating gives them a temporary feeling of well-being. A doughnut or a bag of potato chips is psychologically irresistible, even though the person may be well fed.

It has been shown that the most successful long-term weight loss programs are those that combine diet, exercise, and behavior therapy. Despite all of the advertised new diet drugs and systems, the outcome of the weight battle is resolved, as it always has been, by hard choices—the chocolate chip cookie versus the waistline.

Economic Reasoning

1. What is an example of a trade-off in this case application?

2. Where a dieter is concerned, are there different types of opportunity costs of a chocolate chip cookie? What are they?

3. Is the large amount of money spent each year on losing weight justified? Why or why not?

crease in civilian production can be had for a relatively small opportunity cost in military preparedness. At the other extreme, if resources were all being used for civilian production, with none for armaments, the opportunity cost of increased military purchases would be a relatively small decline in civilian production.

This situation is pictured in Figure 3 on page 42. Here the trade-offs are not constant. Still employing a given amount of resources, the opportunity costs of armaments and civilian goods vary, depending on where you are on the production possibility frontier. The closer you are to one axis or the other, the greater the opportunity cost of obtaining more of the output measured on that axis, and the smaller the opportunity cost of obtaining the other output. If the country were spending its whole budget on armaments and nothing on

civilian output (point A), it could obtain a large increase in units of civilian production with only a small sacrifice in arms (point B). It might, for example, give up a small amount of bomber production (m) to expand transportation facilities by a large amount (n). On the other hand, if it were at point C and changed output composition to point D, there would be a large opportunity cost in military preparedness (o) to obtain a small increase in civilian output (p).

The situation of increasing opportunity costs as resources are allocated exclusively to one output is the usual case. The more resources are devoted to the production of one good, the higher becomes its opportunity cost in the sacrifice of an alternative good, because some resources are better suited for the production of that other good. The typical production possibility frontier is more like Figure 3 than Figure 2.

What Are the Basic Economic Questions?

In allocating resources, there are three basic economic questions that must be resolved. How we resolve these questions determines to a large extent what kind of economic system we have.

What to Produce?
Because of the scarcity of resources, a society cannot produce everything it wants. Therefore, the economy must continually decide what mix of goods and services it is going to produce with the available resources. It must find the most efficient resolution of the **"what" question**.

How we allocate the peace dividend among deficit reduction, tax cuts, public works, and social programs will determine

> **"what" question:** the question concerning the decisions made by an economy about how much of the different alternative goods and services will be produced with the available resources.
>
> **"how" question:** the question concerning the decisions made by an economy about the technology used to produce goods and services.

what is produced. If the savings are directed toward deficit reduction, there will be a reduction of interest rates, which will encourage investment. This will mean more resources used in producing equipment, factories, and office buildings. There will also be more home construction and automobile production because there will be more money for lending to finance these purchases.

Using the savings to finance a tax cut will redirect resources into the production of consumer goods and services. Consumers will be able to purchase more electronic items, restaurant meals, and vacations. If the dividend is instead directed into public works, the construction industry will greatly expand. If it goes into social programs, there will be an increase in government services. What will the peace dividend be used to produce?

How to Produce?
Once an economy determines what mix of goods and services it is going to allocate its resources to produce, it must determine what production methods are going to be used. The resolution of the **"how" question** depends on

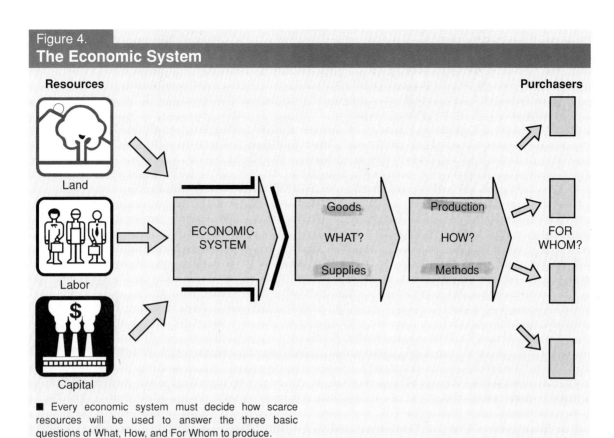

Figure 4.
The Economic System

Resources

Land

Labor

Capital

ECONOMIC SYSTEM

Goods

WHAT?

Supplies

Production

HOW?

Methods

FOR WHOM?

Purchasers

■ Every economic system must decide how scarce resources will be used to answer the three basic questions of What, How, and For Whom to produce.

the technology of production and on the particular combination of resources that will be used to produce each good or service.

How the peace dividend is allocated will affect production methods in the economy. If the resources go into investment, nonmilitary production will become more capital-intensive. In the civilian sectors of the economy, there will be more capital used in production relative to the amount of labor. There will also be more real capital, in this case public rather than private capital, if the savings go toward better highways, bridges, airports, and public transportation facilities—the **infrastructure** of the economy. This will similarly make the economy more productive.

An increase in capital investment, either private or public, would increase the competitiveness of the U.S. economy relative to those of Asia and Western Europe. An economic system needs to use the most efficient production

methods that are available to it, given its particular combination of resources, in resolving the "how" question.

▨ For Whom to Produce?

The third basic economic decision every economic system must make is how to allocate finished goods and services among its population. The resolution of the **"for whom" question** determines who gets how much of what is produced. Because the economy can't produce as much of everything as we would

(Continued on page 48) ⇒

infrastructure: an economy's stock of capital—much of it publicly owned—that provides basic services to producers and consumers. Includes such facilities as highways, electric power, water supplies, educational institutions, and health services.

"for whom" question: the question concerning the decisions made by an economy about income distribution—who gets how much of the goods and services produced.

Comparative Case Application

How Many Lives for Nuclear Power?

Electricity is a vital input for a modern industrial economy. Factories, businesses, and homes could hardly function without it, as anyone well knows who has experienced a power blackout. As growing demands for electric power tax the capacity of the generating plants fired by fossil fuels and those fuel resources become exhausted, how are we going to meet our future electricity needs?

In the 1960s the obvious answer was nuclear power. The energy contained in atoms had been vividly demonstrated by the atomic and hydrogen bombs. Having learned how to harness that energy to produce electricity, we expected to satisfy a limitless appetite for electricity at costs so low that it would be unnecessary even to meter the amounts used. Two decades later, after spending $112 billion constructing 100 nuclear power plants, and some $25 billion more on 111 nuclear power projects that were canceled or mothballed, we hit a wall of cost overruns and hazardous installations that stopped nuclear power dead in its tracks. There has not been an order placed for a new nuclear plant in the United States since 1978. What happened on the way to our bright future of cheap, clean, plentiful nuclear power?

The problems began showing up in the mid-1970s, when there was a serious accident at the Brown's Ferry nuclear reactor in Alabama and an escalation of construction expenses for new nuclear plants. The cost per kilowatt of electric capacity for nuclear plants rose from an approximate parity with the cost of coal-burning plants in the early 1970s to twice the cost of coal-fired plants by 1985.

But the real turning point was the 1979 accident at the Three Mile Island nuclear plant near Harrisburg, Pennsylvania, which very closely approached the ultimate disaster—a meltdown of the radioactive core. This incident focused attention on widespread weaknesses in construction methods and operations in the industry. A number of plants under construction could not be licensed without expensive redesign or extensive repairs on shoddy work. Many became uneconomical. The Marble Hill nuclear power station in Indiana, for example, had been projected to cost

■ Pilgrim Station nuclear power plant, Plymouth, Massachusetts.

$1.4 billion when construction began in 1978. By the time work was abandoned on the half-finished plant at the end of 1983, some $2.5 billion had already been spent; the estimated final cost would have been $7.7 billion or more. As a result of its losses on Marble Hill, the utility company increased the rates charged to the customers of its other electric generating facilities and reduced the dividend payments to its stockholders by 67 percent.

The future of nuclear power was dealt a further blow by an accident at Chernobyl, Ukraine, in the Soviet Union. On April 26, 1986, there was an explosion and fire in one of the Chernobyl nuclear reactors. The short-term consequences were the deaths from radiation of 30 people in the weeks immediately following the accident. But no one can say what the number of casualties will be in future years from the lingering effects. Some 100,000 people in the vicinity of the plant had to be evacuated, and the area became uninhabitable for miles around for an indefinite period due to high levels of radiation. Nuclear fallout carried in the atmosphere forced the destruction of crops in a number of European countries because of poisonous contamination.

The fear that these accidents aroused in the American people— fear that similar accidents could happen in their own backyard— along with the high construction costs and the losses sustained by electric utilities on abandoned nuclear plants, appeared to drive a stake into the heart of the atomic power industry. Similar fears and high costs abroad have slowed the development of nuclear power in other countries as well. Only Japan, because of its lack of fossil fuels, expects nuclear power to provide a much higher proportion of its electricity needs in the year 2005 than it does now.

But nuclear power refuses to stay dead. There are misgivings over our high dependence on imported oil. And with mounting concern over greenhouse warming—oil and coal-fired electric plants spew great amounts of carbon dioxide into the atmosphere—even many environmentalists have reconsidered their opposition to nuclear plants as possibly the lesser of two evils, providing, of course, that the

■ A youngster swallows an antiradiation solution in a Warsaw clinic in March 1986 as part of a precaution against fallout from the Chernobyl nuclear power plant accident in the neighboring Soviet Union.

questions over safety and disposal of radioactive waste can be satisfactorily resolved.

After conducting a 15-month federally funded study, the independent National Academy of Sciences has recommended the rapid development of a new generation of nuclear power plants. It would appear that, like strontium 90, plutonium, and other toxic by-products of the industry, atomic power has a long half-life.

Economic Reasoning

1. Which of the basic economic questions are involved in this case? In what way?

2. In what way does resource availability affect the resolution of the "how" question with respect to electric power generation in Japan as compared to the United States?

3. Who should pay the costs of failed nuclear projects? The customers of the utility company? The stockholders or bondholders of the company? The government (taxpayers)? What are the advantages and disadvantages of putting the burden on each group?

▨▶ *(Continued from page 45)*

like it to produce, the output must be rationed in some fashion.

The "for whom" question does not imply that a particular item is produced for a particular consumer, but rather that different groups will benefit from the peace dividend depending on how it is allocated. If it is used for deficit reduction, borrowers will benefit from lower interest rates to buy real estate or invest in capital goods. If it is allocated to social programs, the benefits will go more to the lowest income groups in society.

What Are Society's Economic Goals?

We make economic choices in the light of certain goals. There are four goals that societies aim to achieve that are principally economic in nature. In addition to these economic goals, there are other social goals with important economic dimensions. This section examines the goals that often underlie decisions as to what trade-offs a society will make and what opportunity costs it will bear in resolving the three basic economic questions.

efficiency: maximizing the amount of output obtained from a given amount of resources or minimizing the amount of resources used for a given amount of output.

Efficiency

Military production is notoriously inefficient. There are horror stories of $435 hammers, $7,622 coffee pots, and $449 pairs of pliers produced for the military. One way to achieve efficiency is to avoid waste. A part of the peace dividend would be the reallocation of resources to industries that are less wasteful than the defense industries. Given the scarcity of resources, it is important to use them with maximum efficiency to obtain the greatest output possible from the resources consumed.

Another way to achieve efficiency is to use the limited resources for their most important purposes. We need to resolve the "what" question in allocating peace dividend resources in the way that will best serve our needs. How

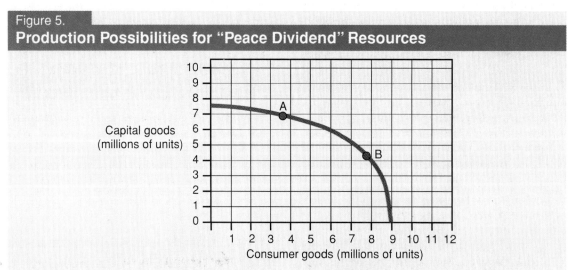

Figure 5.
Production Possibilities for "Peace Dividend" Resources

Capital goods (millions of units) — vertical axis 0 to 10
Consumer goods (millions of units) — horizontal axis 1 to 12

Points: A (at approximately 3, 7), B (at approximately 8, 4)

■ The resources that are made available by a decrease in military spending can be used to produce consumer goods and capital goods. Selecting the best combination of consumer and capital goods to produce with the available resources will result in efficiency in resource allocation.

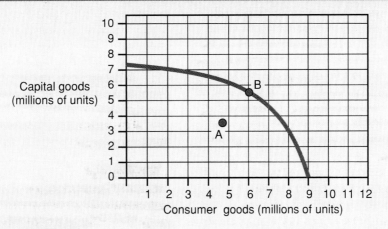

Figure 6.
Production with Unemployed Resources Compared to Full Employment Production

Capital goods (millions of units)

Consumer goods (millions of units)

■ Production at less than full employment is represented by point A, which lies inside the production possibilities curve. Point B on the PPF is full employment, with more output of consumer goods and capital goods. Maintaining full employment while demilitarizing the economy will be easier if the economy is healthy to begin with.

much should be directed toward investment in capital goods versus how much into consumer goods? The production possibility frontier in Figure 5 presents us with these choices. Which is the better combination of outputs for the peace dividend, combination A with more capital goods or combination B with more consumer goods? Combination B would provide a higher current standard of living, but combination A would increase the economy's production capacity (see discussion under **Growth** on page 50).

Finally, one of the most important ways we achieve increased efficiency is by improving the technology of production. Since much highly skilled labor is employed in the defense sector of the economy—scientists, engineers, technical personnel—and much capital is tied up in those industries, technology has been held back in the civilian sectors. This is one of the reasons why the United States, the world technology leader in the first half of the century, has fallen behind other countries that do not allocate as large a percentage of output to their military, such as Japan and Germany, in the technology of production.

Price Stability

Another economic goal is to maintain **price stability**. Price stability is the avoidance of rapid changes in the general price level of goods and services. Prices of individual goods and services go up and down in response to changes in the costs of producing them and the demand for them. When there is **inflation**, however, with the prices of most things rising rapidly at the same time, it can disrupt the economy.

The stop-and-go nature of military production—rapid increases in our defense output whenever the cold war heated up—tended to create price instability. The smaller the defense sector is in the future, the easier it will be to maintain stable prices.

price stability: a constant average level of prices for all goods and services.

inflation: a continuously rising general price level, resulting in a reduction in the purchasing power of money.

Full Employment

A stable price level is only one aspect of economic stability. The other is job stability at **full employment.** This means that nearly everyone who wants to work can find a job. Full employment is an important economic goal for two reasons. It is important because jobs are the main source of most people's incomes, and it is important because full employment is necessary for an economy to utilize fully its limited resources. Labor is a resource, and unemployed labor means loss of production from a resource that can never be recovered.

Unemployment is shown on the PPF diagram by operating at a point inside the production possibility frontier. In Figure 6 on page 49, point A is less than full employment

full employment: employment of nearly everyone who desires to work. In practice, an unemployment level of not more than 4–5% is considered full employment.

economic growth: an increase in the production capacity of the economy.

output. Moving to point B on the curve gives us full employment and increased production of both capital goods and consumer goods.

The trick in shifting resources from military to civilian production will be to minimize unemployment as labor moves from defense industries to industries producing for the civilian sector, to stay as close as possible to the PPF. This will be easier if the economy is healthy to begin with. It will also be easier if the shift is spread out over a number of years; however, this will delay the benefits of the peace dividend.

Growth

Efficiency, price stability and full employment contribute to achieving the fourth economic goal—growth. **Economic growth** means a continuing increase in the capacity of an economy to produce goods and services.

Channeling capital resources from defense industries into research and development for the civilian sector will speed up economic growth through new products and the use of advanced production methods. Growth will

---

Figure 7.

Growth of the Economy with Different Current Allocations of Resources Between Capital Goods and Consumption Goods

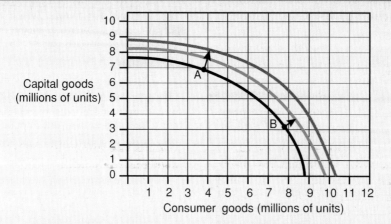

Capital goods (millions of units)

Consumer goods (millions of units)

■ If most of the peace dividend resources went into the production of consumer goods, as shown by point B, we would have a higher current standard of living; but economic growth during the next few years would only expand to the green line. If the resources were allocated as shown by point A, however, the economy would expand to the brown line, making even higher future living standards possible.

■ The peace dividend could help us achieve socioeconomic goals by reallocating resources from defense industries to the civilian sector. For example, the radar shown above, which was originally developed by Westinghouse for the military, now finds new uses: when attached to a dirigible, it can detect drug smugglers' aircraft crossing the border between the United States and Mexico.

also be promoted by a lowering of the deficit and the resulting reduction in interest rates, which encourages investment in new capital equipment. (The relationship between capital investment and output is covered in more depth in chapter 7.) Improvement in the economy's infrastructure will also facilitate growth by making investment more profitable.

Figure 7 illustrates that how we allocate the peace dividend will affect the rate of growth. If all of it were used for a tax cut, most of the increased output would be consumer goods (point B in Figure 7). This would give us a lower rate of growth, shown by the outward shift of the PPF curve only as far as the green line. On the other hand, if we used the peace dividend to reduce the deficit, a larger amount of investment would occur (point A). This larger investment would give us a higher growth rate, as shown by the outward shift of the PPF curve to the brown line.

■ One socioeconomic goal is just and unbiased treatment for all individuals in economic matters. Banks such as Chase Manhattan, for example, extend to anyone the opportunity to apply for credit.

Socioeconomic Goals

There is not much disagreement over the desirability of the four primarily economic goals discussed above (although there is a great deal of debate over how best to achieve them). There are some additional goals of society that are to a large degree economic in nature—what we might term **socioeconomic goals**—about which there is less universal agreement. An examination of public policies indicates that the following might be included among socioeconomic goals: protection of the environment from pollution, financial security for individuals, economic equity, just treatment for all individuals in economic matters, and freedom to carry out economic choices. The peace dividend should help us to achieve some of these socioeconomic goals. For example, conversion of government spending from defense against foreign attack to defense of the environment will help to solve some of the problems discussed in chapter 1. Conversion of spending to repair the safety net of social programs will help to meet some of the other socioeconomic goals.

socioeconomic goal: the type of social goal that has important economic dimensions.

The Robots Are Coming

The current generation of robots, relatively dumb brutes that perform repetitious tasks, may replace up to 1.3 million American workers by the year 2000. The industrial robot market was born in the United States some 30 years ago, but little happened in the industry until the late 1970s and early 1980s, when there was a surge of growth in the use of robots to meet competition from overseas, particularly in the automobile industry. Robots were assigned such jobs as welding, painting, and drilling motor blocks.

But sales flattened after the mid-1980s, and in 1993 there were still less than 50,000 robots at work in this country, compared to seven times that number in Japan. Now, however, a new generation of robots with senses of vision, touch, and hearing is coming on the scene and could have an impact on as many as 3.8 million jobs. Robots are performing a remarkable variety of tasks, everything from sorting parts (a worker can teach the robot's "eyes" to recognize a new part in less than 10 minutes) to acting as night watchmen at factories, assisting the blind and other disabled people, and handling radioactive waste.

The automobile industry is still the major employer of robots, and General Motors even has its own company to produce them. One of the things that delayed the spread of the use of robots was their high cost, but the price for the cruder type of robots has fallen. A welding robot that originally cost $150,000 now costs half that.

More sophisticated robots, such as the night watchmen, cost $100,000 and up. But robots can frequently save money in the long run compared to the cost of human workers. Not only can they do some jobs with more precision and less fatigue, but they don't have to

be paid wages, don't get fringe benefits, don't take coffee breaks, and have very low absenteeism rates.

Economic Reasoning

1. Which primarily economic goals are served by the use of production robots?

2. Does the use of robots involve a trade-off among different economic or socioeconomic goals? Which goals?

3. Do you favor or oppose a rapid increase in the use of robots to replace human workers? Why?

Putting It Together

Because resources are insufficient to produce all the things we want, we have to choose how best to use those resources. In deciding how to use our limited resources, certain *trade-offs* are necessary.

The value of what we give up when resources are used to produce one thing rather than another is the *opportunity cost* of what is produced. In order to get the greatest benefits from our limited resources, we should use them for the outputs that best serve our needs. If we don't, then the opportunity costs of what we produce will be too high.

A *production possibility frontier* (PPF) shows the trade-off between two alternative uses of a resource. (See Figures 2 and 3 on page 42.) The PPF shows the opportunity cost of producing more of one good by showing the amount of the alternative good that is sacrificed. Production possibility frontiers generally curve outward because of *increasing opportunity costs* incurred as more of one good is produced. Production possibility frontiers are economic tools helpful in analyzing the opportunity costs of trade-offs.

All economic systems must resolve three basic economic questions: *what to produce; how to produce;* and *for whom to produce.* Scarcity cannot efficiently be dealt with unless the economy allocates its resources to producing the goods and services most needed and desired. An economic system also needs to utilize the most efficient production methods with the resources available. Finally, an eco-

■ Decisions about what to do with the peace dividend are examples of the kinds of choices that an economy must continually make regarding the use of resources. How successful we are at choosing the best allocation of our available resources determines how well we can achieve our economic goals.

nomic system must determine who gets how much of what is produced.

There are four principally economic goals by which the effectiveness of an economy can be judged: *efficiency, price stability, full employment,* and *growth.* Some socioeconomic goals of our society are: *protection of the environment, financial security,* and *equity, justice, and freedom* in economic matters.

The Affluent Society

John Kenneth Galbraith (born 1908)
Galbraith is a lofty economist in more than one sense. at 6′ 8″, he towers over colleagues and debate opponents. Born on a farm in Ontario, Canada, he graduated from an agricultural college in the depths of the Depression in the 1930s. He came to the United States for graduate study and remained to teach at the University of California–Berkeley, at Princeton, and, most notably, at Harvard, retiring in 1973. He gave up the Harvard classroom to embark on a 3½-year project which took him to many locations around the world narrating a television series called "The Age of Uncertainty," which he wrote. "The Age of Uncertainty" was a broad, sweeping overview of the history of economic ideas. Of the 20-some books he has written, *The Affluent Society* and two others form an important triad on the functioning of our capitalist economy. The second book in the triad is *The New Industrial State* (1967), which examines the way decisions are made in modern corporations, their relationship to government, and the consequences for society. The third book is *Economics and the Public Purpose* (1973), in which Galbraith argues the necessity for government to act as a "countervailing power" against the economic and political power of big business and labor.

John Kenneth Galbraith, one of the most provocative modern economists, wrote a book in 1958 entitled *The Affluent Society*. In it he argued that the problem that had traditionally been of primary concern to economists, how to increase production, was no longer the most important problem in industrially advanced countries like the United States. He maintained that the problem of production had been so well solved that all citizens could have enough to satisfy their needs if output were distributed more equally. Furthermore, he said, a lot of what we produced was intentional waste, such as oversized cars. He noted that most of us eat too much, not too little.

Other social scientists have made the same point. Vance Packard maintained in *The Waste Makers* that the American economy has come to depend on consumption for the sake of consumption, planned obsolescence, and "progress through the throwaway spirit."

In the 1970s, the energy crunch, the decline in productivity and income growth, the shift to smaller cars, and the increased emphasis on conservation led to talk about "an age of limits" and cast doubt on the affluent society thesis. But these developments did not convince Galbraith to change his view that total output is not the main concern. Of more importance is the uses to which output is allocated. Poverty and hunger continue to persist in an economy of abundance. Public squalor in the streets of our cities contrasts with the opulence of the offices in the skyscrapers above. Many types of jobs are unnecessarily arduous, boring, or dangerous for the sake of maximizing total output.

Galbraith's thesis is contrary to the current movement in economic policy—the emphasis on increasing productivity and total output, the reduction of government spending in favor of private spending, the cutbacks in Occupational Safety and Health Agency activities, and the truce in the war on poverty, both at home and abroad. Being out of step with the popular parade is not unusual for Galbraith. He notes in his introduction to *The Affluent Society,* "I have read on occasion that I find perverse pleasure in attacking the conventional myth. I do not, and on the contrary, it is very hard work. Some day for recreation I intend to write a book affirming fully all the unquestioned economic truths."

FOR FURTHER STUDY AND ANALYSIS

Study Questions

1. Why are trade-offs necessary in our modern economic system?

2. Give an example of a personal economic choice you have made recently. What was the opportunity cost?

3. Give an example of an economic choice made by society as a whole. How was the choice made?

4. What are three examples of differences in the resolution of the "what" question in the United States today compared to 5 years ago?

5. How has the increased use of production robots affected the resolution of the "how" question?

6. What determines how much of the nation's output of goods and services is allocated to you?

7. Points on a production possibility frontier, such as points "A" and "B" in Figure 2, show the different combinations of two goods that could be produced with the available resources. Would it be possible to produce at a point outside the PPF curve? What would such a point mean?

8. Some economic and socioeconomic goals are complementary; achieving one goal helps to achieve another goal. What is one example where economic and socioeconomic goals are complementary?

9. In other cases, there are conflicts between different goals: efforts to achieve one make it more difficult to achieve another. What is an example of a conflict between economic goals?

10. What goals does Galbraith consider the most important in the United States today?

Exercises in Analysis

1. Prepare an analysis of the alternative uses of any selected natural resource (pine trees, for example) by considering the following questions: (a) What are three alternative uses of this resource? (b) What are the trade-offs for any one of the three uses you have selected? (c) What is the opportunity cost of using the natural resource for any one of the three uses you chose?

2. Select a local business and discuss how it resolves the "what," "how," and "for whom" questions.

3. Find out where the nearest nuclear power plant is located and what utility company owns it. Write to the utility company and request a copy of its latest annual report, a prospectus on any recent bond or stock issues, and a summary of any recent rate increase proposals submitted to the public utilities commission. On the basis of those reports, write a short paper on the economic effects of the nuclear power plant.

4. Prepare a list of government policy measures that promote goals of our society such as full employment, economic growth, protection of the environment, or financial security.

Further Reading

Ayres, Robert U., and Steven M. Miller. *Robotics: Applications and Social Implications*. Cambridge, MA: Ballinger, 1983. Discusses the technology and the costs and benefits of robots. Also examines the impact of robotization on employment and productivity and its policy implications.

Campbell, John E. *Collapse of an Industry: Nuclear Power and the Contradictions of U.S. Policy*. Ithaca, NY: Cornell University Press, 1988. Discusses the problems of the nuclear power industry, including its financial crisis.

Cohen, Bernard Leonard. *The Nuclear Energy Option: An Alternative for the 90s*. New York: Plenum Press, 1990. An analysis of energy needs and comparison of nuclear energy with other energy sources in satisfying the needs.

Gold, David. *The Impact of Defense Spending on Investment, Productivity and Economic Growth*. Washington, DC: Center for Budget and Policy Priorities, 1990. A study of how much defense expenditures affect the civilian sectors of the economy.

Logue, A. W. *The Psychology of Eating and Drinking*. New York: W. H. Freeman, 1986. Describes scientific inquiries into food consumption, both normal behaviors and abnormal behaviors such as overeating and obesity.

Lall, Betty G., and John Tepper Marlin. *Building a Peace Economy: Opportunities and Problems of Post–Cold War Defense Cuts*. Boulder, CO: Westview Press, 1992. Discusses the impact of defense cuts on contractors and labor, on bases, and on the national laboratories. Examines state and local strategies for conversion.

Lynch, John E., ed. *Economic Adjustment and Conversion of Defense Industries*. Boulder, CO: Westview Press, 1987. Chapters on such topics as community adjustments to defense plant closings, conversion of plants to nonmilitary production, civilian product market opportunities for defense plants, and worker assistance and placement.

Medvedev, Grigorii. *No Breathing Room: The Aftermath of Chernobyl*. New York: Basic Books, 1993. A first-person account of the Chernobyl accident and what followed by a department chief in the Directorate for Nuclear Energy in the former Soviet Union.

Pligt, J. van der. *Nuclear Energy and the Public*. Cambridge, MA: Blackwell, 1992. Examines public opinion concerning the nuclear industry and the effects of accidents at nuclear plants.

Read, Piers Paul. *Ablaze: The Story of Chernobyl*. London: Secker & Warburg, 1993. Covers the environmental impact of the nuclear accident and the radiation injuries.

Ross, Alastair. *Dynamic Factory Automation: Creating Flexible Work Systems for Competitive Manufacturing*. New York: McGraw-Hill, 1992. An examination of modern robots in industry and the use of automation to be competitive in the world marketplace.

Wolfson, Richard. *Nuclear Choices: A Citizen's Guide to Nuclear Technology*. Cambridge, MA: MIT Press, 1991. A cost/benefit examination of the peaceful uses of nuclear power.

Chapter 3. The Economic System

■ **Every society,** even the most primitive, has an economic system that organizes the production and distribution of goods and services. Although these systems have basic identifiable charac-teristics that remain consistent over long periods of time, change in the systems inevitably takes place.

Ranch to Table: A Different Story Now

In 1856 a Texan named Bill Hayden went on a cattle-buying trip to Oklahoma. Hayden bought a few dozen head of longhorn cattle from different ranchers until he had a herd of about 600 head of cattle. Hayden's plan was to drive the cattle east and sell them in New York City, where the price of beef was high.

It was spring when Hayden's cowhands started the longhorns on their trek. The rains were heavy and the steers often had to be pulled out of thick mud holes. When the summer sun baked the mud, the cattle stirred up huge dust clouds, and the cow-hands had to cover their faces with necker-chiefs in order to breathe. Many of the longhorns died along the way from hunger, thirst, and exhaustion. When winter came, the drive halted and the cattle had to be penned up and fed corn.

The following spring, Hayden and his trailhands pushed the longhorns on until they reached a railroad in Illinois. The steers were loaded onto cattle cars and shipped the rest of the way to New York. The drive had taken Hayden a year and a half, but the price he got for his cattle in New York was high enough to make the trip worthwhile.

Today, cross-country cattle drives are a thing of the past, and modern beef cattle are not much like Bill Hayden's longhorns. José and María Ruiz have a cattle ranch in the high plateau country of northwest Texas. They raise short, heavy cattle that yield large amounts of high-quality beef. A century ago, the longhorn was a tough, rangy animal that could survive bad weather, scarce water, and long drives. The Ruizes' cattle require protec-tion from bad weather, plentiful water and feed, and a relatively calm existence.

The Ruizes' cattle rarely walk more than a few hundred yards at a time. They are kept on the ranch until they reach 450 to 500 pounds, then they are trucked to feedlots. In the feedlots, the cattle may eat up to 24 pounds of specially prepared feed and gain 3 pounds a day—about a pound of beef for each 8 pounds of feed. The feed is a rich mixture of wheat, barley, corn, chopped alfalfa, corn silage, cottonseed hulls, molasses, tallow, and other ingredients. The ideal mixture of ingre-dients for each stage of the steer's develop-ment is determined by nutritionists. In 5 months each steer doubles in weight to a total of 1,000 pounds or more.

■ Cattle are sent from the ranch to feedlots, where they double in weight to 1,000 pounds or more. This specialization in modern beef production increases the supply and lowers prices to consumers.

In the 1850s it took Bill Hayden over a year to move his longhorns to market. Today, cattle are trucked from feedlots to slaughterhouses in a matter of hours. Within a few more hours they are slaughtered, loaded into refrigerated trucks, and shipped to butcher shops or supermarkets.

Although beef is relatively expensive to produce when compared to many other foods, specialization of various tasks in beef production has made it possible to keep beef prices low enough so that most of us can afford to eat at least some beef. From the birth of the calf on the ranch to the sale of packages of meat in a supermarket, each stage of production is handled by specialists. The result is a better product at a lower price.

The way cattle are produced and brought to market has changed over the past 100 years in an effort to better satisfy the economic goal of efficiency. The manner in which society organizes production to deal with the problem of scarcity is continually evolving. In some countries it has evolved in different directions than in others. But every society has to resolve the same basic economic questions. This chapter will examine the way societies are organized to deal with scarcity by asking the following questions: Why are economic systems needed? What are the principal types of economic systems? How does a market system resolve the three basic economic questions?

After completing this chapter, you should be able to:

1. Distinguish between absolute and comparative advantage.

2. Explain why specialization based on absolute or comparative advantage results in greater economic efficiency and interdependence.

3. Identify the three major types of economic systems, and explain how they differ.

4. Explain how a market system resolves the three basic economic questions.

5. Distinguish between goods and services sold in product markets and those that are sold in factor markets.

6. Diagram the circular flow of a market economy.

Why Are Economic Systems Needed?

Back in 1856, Bill Hayden and his cowhands were largely on their own when they drove their cattle from Oklahoma to Illinois. Today, José and María Ruiz depend on many different people to help them raise cattle. They depend on feed suppliers, veterinarians, gasoline distributors, and government cattle inspectors, among others. In many ways the Ruizes' cattle ranch is much like the economy as a whole. In achieving greater efficiency in production, we have become more dependent on others, thereby increasing the need for an economic system to organize and coordinate diverse economic activities of our society.

Specialization

A century ago many Americans raised their own beef cattle. In rural areas there was a high degree of self-sufficiency in food production. But people in large cities did not raise their own cattle. Thus, cattlemen like Bill Hayden found a profitable opportunity in that particular **specialization**—raising cattle in

an area well suited for it and supplying the beef to city dwellers.

Today, the modern cattle business is very highly specialized. Ranchers such as the Ruizes concentrate on raising cattle. Truckers ship the cattle to feedlots. Nutritionists use computers to create diets for the cattle. At slaughterhouses, people with specialized skills dispatch the cattle with efficiency, and butchers at supermarkets trim various cuts for the consumer. In the production of beef and most other products there is a division of labor into specialized tasks that results in greater efficiency and a lower-cost product.

One reason why this division of labor results in greater efficiency and lower costs is

specialization: concentrating the activity of a unit of a production resource—especially labor—on a single task or production operation. Also applies to the specialization of nations in producing those goods and services that their resources are best suited to produce.

■ New York City obviously lacks the grazing space necessary to cattle production that is found in the western plains states. Thus, our western states have an absolute advantage over New York City in cattle raising. However, New York City has an absolute advantage over some cattle-producing areas in banking and finance due to its location.

that specialization enables the producer to concentrate on only one job. A veterinarian, for example, is much better at keeping cattle healthy than are the Ruizes because the veterinarian has specialized knowledge and experience.

Absolute and Comparative Advantage

In addition to the advantages of specialization as such, specialization is most efficient when it is based on natural advantages. The residents of New York City cannot very well produce beef there. Grazing cattle in Manhattan

> **absolute advantage:** when each of two producers can produce a different good or service more efficiently than can the other producer, each of the producers has an absolute advantage in the good or service that he produces most efficiently.

would be difficult, to say the least. City dwellers must get their beef from a place where the conditions are more suitable for producing it, such as on the plains of the western states. That area has an **absolute advantage** over New York City in beef production because the resources are more suitable for the production of cattle, and the production costs are therefore much less. New York, for its part, has an absolute advantage over the western plains states in such things as banking and finance because New York is a hub of commerce. Its advantages were originally due to its strategic geographical location on a natural harbor and then to the historical development of its institutions.

Oklahoma obviously has an absolute advantage over New York City in raising cattle, but absolute advantage does not account for all, or even most, specialization. It is apparent why you wouldn't raise cattle in New York City. But why not produce the beef for New Yorkers someplace closer than Oklahoma or Texas? It is possible, for example, to raise cattle just across the Hudson River in New Jersey, and, in fact, some cattle are raised there. But most of the limited agricultural land in New Jersey is better allocated to farming and dairying because cattle grazing takes too much room in a state where land is scarce. New Jersey can make better use of its scarce land resources in farming and dairying, which take less space. It has a greater advantage in these economic activities than it does in raising beef cattle. Although New Jersey with its fertile land has the resources to produce either vegetables and dairy products or beef, it has a **comparative advantage** relative to the plains states in farming and dairying because those activities take less space than raising beef cattle. The plains states, on the other hand, have a comparative advantage in cattle raising because their vast land resources are better suited to that activity.

The distinction between specialization based on comparative advantage and that based on absolute advantage is important. Assume that the best surgeon in town is also the best auto mechanic. Such a person would have an absolute advantage in both surgery and auto repair, but that person's time would be spent more valuably in healing sick people than sick automobiles because the economic value of a surgeon's time is greater than the economic value of an auto mechanic's time. Although the surgeon has an absolute advantage in both endeavors, the comparative advantage lies in surgery. Individuals, regions within a country, and nations all tend to produce those things in which they have a comparative advantage.

Interdependence

Specialization results in **interdependence**—the reliance of different individuals and businesses on each other. José and María Ruiz could not specialize in raising cattle without the help and cooperation of others. They depend on the veterinarian to keep the cattle healthy; on various manufacturers to supply trucks, gasoline, and equipment; and on the feedlot operator to fatten the cattle for market. They depend on the government to protect their herd from epidemics of hoof-and-mouth disease. And they depend on consumers in cities to buy the beef produced.

This interdependence requires an economic system to coordinate the various activities. As the degree of specialization and interdependence has increased over the years, so has the complexity of the economic system. When Bill Hayden drove his long-horns across the country, our economic system was much simpler than it is today. People were not as dependent on each other or on government services. Now, because of interdependence, it is more important than ever that the economic system function effectively.

---

comparative advantage: when one producer has an efficiency advantage over another producer in two separate products, but has a greater advantage in one product than in the other, the efficient producer has a comparative advantage in the product in which he has the greater relative efficiency; and the inefficient producer, on the other hand, has a comparative advantage in the product in which his efficiency disadvantage is not as large.

interdependence: the relationship between individuals and institutions in a country or between countries that arises because of specialization of production.

The Efficiencyburger

In 1948, the McDonald brothers opened a small restaurant in San Bernardino, California, specializing in the production of hamburgers. They developed a method of producing hamburgers so easily and inexpensively that they could be sold profitably at 15 cents each.

Today, the McDonald's chain of restaurants (the original McDonald brothers are no longer associated with it) sells more hamburgers than any comparable operation. The key to the McDonald's method of hamburger production is specialization. The menu at a McDonald's restaurant is limited to a select number of items. This cuts food waste to a minimum and eliminates much of the expense of a full-line restaurant. The company tried expanding its offerings to include pizzas in order to increase nighttime patronage. The attempt was a failure, and McDonald's had to abandon the effort to diversify.

For the sake of efficiency, each job in the McDonald's operation has been refined and simplified. Workers have one speciality, although they can also perform other jobs. A typical restaurant has a fry specialist, a grill specialist, and a shakes specialist, all coordinated by a production control specialist. To learn the system of operation, owners and operators of individual restaurants attend McDonald's "Hamburger University" in Elk Grove, Illinois, where they take a 19-day course that leads to a "Bachelor of Hamburgerology, with a minor in French Fries."

The McDonald's operation is dedicated to speed. A hamburger, french fries, and a shake can be turned out in 50 seconds. Production is tightly controlled in an effort to maintain freshness. Unsold burgers are to be destroyed if not sold within 10 minutes, french fries after 7 minutes.

Everything is done the same way at each of the McDonald's restaurants—the way hamburgers are made, the napkins used, even the greetings used by the salespeople are the same.

Everything is even done the same way at the Moscow McDonald's, opened in 1990. The first fast-food restaurant in Russia, it is the biggest McDonald's in the world, serving nearly 50,000 customers a day. Every hour an enormous machine spits out 10,000 perfectly formed hamburger patties, each containing between 15.8% and 16.5% fat. Technicians in the upstairs laboratories test the stickiness of the hot fudge and the acidity of the ketchup. They make sure that every batch of apple pie filling has exactly 40% apples.

However, the elements of the operation not directly under control of McDonald's do not function with the same precision. Initially, nearly all of the basic ingredients were supplied by collective and state farms. These food supplies proved undependable. The suppliers "don't care much about the schedule," according to the branch distribution manager. "It's a big headache to make all these suppliers produce their goods at the proper time."

As a result, McDonald's took over supervision of much of the production, processing, and distribution of its inputs. It increased its original 2 trucks to a fleet of 15. It expanded the capacity of its supply center—Foodtown—to provide such items as lettuce, hamburger buns, and pasteurized milk not only to the McDonald's outlet but also to foreign embassies in Moscow.

Economic Reasoning

1. What economic principle did McDonald's adopt that was so successful that it was copied by others?

2. How does the Moscow McDonald's operation reflect the relationship between specialization and interdependence?

3. One objective of economics is to avoid waste, but McDonald's policy is to destroy hamburgers if not sold within 10 minutes. Is this a good idea? Why or why not?

What Are the Principal Types of Economic Systems?

The greater the specialization and interdependence in economic activities, the more important is the development of an economic system to organize and coordinate production and distribution. Different types of economic systems have evolved. All of them must resolve the questions of what to produce, how to produce it, and how to allocate what is produced. But different economic systems make these determinations in different ways.

Market Economies

The key to allocating resources and finished products in a **market economy** is the function of the price system in the **marketplace.** In 1856 beef sold for such a high price in New York that it made it worthwhile for Bill Hayden to spend a year and a half bringing cattle all the way from Oklahoma to market them there. Today, the Ruizes decide how many head of cattle to breed on the basis of beef prices in the marketplace, and they decide how to raise their cattle on the basis of feed prices and other production costs. Prices also determine who will consume the beef; namely, those who can afford it and are willing to pay the price.

Market economies are often called capitalist or free enterprise economies. We will examine in more detail how such an economic system resolves the "what," "how," and "for whom" questions in the next section of this chapter.

Centrally Directed Economies

In **centrally directed** or **command economies**, most production is controlled by the government. The major decisions concerning what to produce, how to produce, and for whom to produce are made by centralized authoritarian agencies. Typically, a central planning commission draws up a master plan, which is then put into effect by regional and local government agencies. The natural resources and capital goods are owned by the government. Workers are generally employed in

■ Resources and finished products in a market economy are allocated by the functioning of the price system in the marketplace.

> **market economy:** an economic system in which the basic questions of what, how, and for whom to produce are resolved primarily by buyers and sellers interacting in markets.
>
> **marketplace (market):** a network of dealings between buyers and sellers of a resource or product (good or service); the dealings may take place at a particular location, or they may take place by communication at a distance with no face-to-face contact between buyers and sellers.
>
> **centrally directed (command) economy:** an economic system in which the basic questions of what, how, and for whom to produce are resolved primarily by governmental authority.

■ Tradition can often determine what goods and services are available. In India, strong cultural and religious norms limit beef consumption.

government enterprises or in the government agencies that plan and administer the system.

Resources are allocated in a much different way in a centrally directed economy than they are in a market economy. In a market economy, ranchers like the Ruizes, responding to signals from the market for beef, decide how much beef will be produced. In a command economy, the central planning authority decides how much beef will be produced. The ranchers are given production goals and permission to buy the supplies necessary to produce the amount of beef decided upon. They may also be given directions about most of the details involved in cattle production from the selection of feed to the number of steers to be slaughtered.

Once the beef is produced, it is placed on sale in government-owned stores. The price, rather than being determined by the interplay between sellers and buyers in the market-place, is determined by the government. When there is an insufficient quantity available to satisfy all who would like to purchase it, meat may be allocated to buyers by a formal rationing system, with each customer limited to buying a certain amount of meat each week or month. Or it may be allocated on a first come, first served basis, resulting in lines of customers at stores when there are supplies available. The operation of centrally directed economies is also covered in chapter 17 (see p. 442), which includes a more detailed examination of the differences in contemporary economic systems.

Traditional Economies

In earlier ages, and, to some extent in non-industrialized countries today, basic economic decisions depended on tradition and not on the function of markets or the commands of a centralized authority. In **traditional economies** goods are produced and distributed in

> **traditional economy:** an economic system in which the basic questions of what, how, and for whom to produce are resolved primarily by custom and tradition.

certain ways because that is the way it has always been done.

We have seen how the raising of beef cattle can be controlled by decisions based on market considerations or by the decisions of a centrally directed planning authority. In India, which in many ways has a traditional economy, the business of raising beef cattle is very limited because the majority of people are Hindu and it is against Hindu tradition and religion to eat beef. Cattle are numerous in India, but most of them are not slaughtered and marketed because by tradition beef is not considered a food source. Another example of tradition at work in India is the way jobs are allocated. For centuries, India's population was divided by a caste system, a way of classifying people according to the social class, or caste, into which they were born. People born into certain castes could do only the kinds of jobs those castes traditionally did. Although now prohibited by Indian law, the tradition of the caste system may prevail in rural areas where education and mobility are restricted. Here it may still determine to an extent what kinds of occupations are open to which people, how much they earn, and, therefore, how much income they will have to purchase goods and services.

Experience has shown that tradition is still very strong in many nonindustrial nations that are trying to industrialize. Even the lure of profits, an almost irresistible force in most places, is frequently unable to overcome the force of custom in traditional societies. The nonindustrialized countries are the subject of chapter 18.

Mixed Economies

The actual systems in existence throughout the world are not pure market, pure centrally directed, or pure traditional economies. They are mixtures of the three, and

(Continued on page 70) ⇒

mixed economy: an economic system in which the basic questions of what, how, and for whom to produce are resolved by a mixture of market forces with governmental direction and/or custom and tradition.

■ A hydroelectric dam is an example of the type of good produced by government in mixed economies such as the United States.

A Mixed (Up) Economy

The problem of changing an almost totally centrally controlled economy into a market-directed economy is illustrated by the difficulties of Avedis Seferyan, a Moscow bakery owner. Seferyan was a director of the Bread and Confectionery Factory No. 19 under the old communist system in Russia. When it became possible, he opened his own bakery in 1992. But he immediately ran afoul of MosKhlebTorg (Moscow Bread Sales), MosKhleb-

■ Lines and rationing are typical features of a centrally directed economy and may persist during a transition to a market economy. These customers were lined up at a Moscow bakery in October 1993 just before the government was to free bread prices.

Trans (Moscow Bread Deliveries), and other state monopolies still operating under government ownership.

For 8 months, MosKhlebTorg blocked his efforts to open a bread shop that would compete with its government retail outlets. And delivery trucks from MosKhlebTrans might or might not show up at his bakery in the mornings as promised. If not, the fresh bread just sat on the delivery docks.

The Russian economy is part state-run, according to the old authoritarian model, and part private enterprise, modeled on a market system unfamiliar in Russian experience. Seferyan had to learn the hard way some things that businesspeople in market economies take for granted. When the costs of making one of his specialty items—a rich chocolate-covered wafer cake called "Valentina"—rose to 62 rubles, he raised the selling price from 40 rubles to 100. As a consequence, his sales dropped from 30 cakes a day to 12. He reduced the price to 75 rubles, and he concentrated on producing less costly pastries that didn't run into so much consumer price resistance.

In addition to the small private businesses started by individuals like Seferyan, some state-owned firms have been privatized. At the end of 1992, in order to facilitate the transition to a market economy, every Russian citizen was given a privatization voucher by the government. Each voucher had a nominal value of 10,000 rubles, then worth about $25. The vouchers were to be used to acquire shares of state-owned businesses when they were privatized. At that time, many Russians had no faith that privatization would occur or that the enterprises would succeed. As a consequence, so many vouchers were offered for sale that the going price soon fell to 4,500 rubles. However, as privatization was gradually put into effect, the value of the vouchers recovered; and by the end of 1993 their price went above 30,000 rubles.

The fraction of the Russian economy that is market-directed is hard to gauge because of inadequate statistics. But it was estimated that by mid-decade as much as half or more of Russia's output would be produced in the market sector, either from small businesses started by individuals, from joint ventures and investments by foreign firms, or from enterprises privatized by the government. With experiences such as those of Seferyan and McDonald's (see the preceding case application on p. 64), the question arises how well the market sector and the remaining centrally directed sector of the economy can coexist.

Economic Reasoning

1. What type of economic system did Seferyan's new bakery represent? How can you tell?

2. Why did Seferyan not have to be concerned about making the prices of the bakery products cover the costs of producing them or about unsold merchandise when he was a director of the Bread and Confectionery Factory No. 19?

3. Do you think that former communist administrators like Seferyan should be able to take advantage of their experience and contacts to make profits in the new Russian economic system? Why or why not?

▪▶ (Continued from page 67)

these **mixed economies** take many different forms. Some, such as that of the United States, are basically market economies with a mixture of government regulation and government ownership. For example, in the cattle industry the government encourages beef production through favorable tax benefits for investment in the industry. The government inspects cattle for disease and regulates sanitary conditions in meat processing. There have been times when it even imposed price controls on meat. The U.S. government does not produce the beef, but it does own many dams that supply water and electricity to the ranches. The government also owns land that it leases to ranchers for cattle grazing.

Other economies, such as that of China, are primarily centrally directed, but with some private ownership and sales. The countries that were formerly part of the Soviet Union and the countries of Eastern Europe are in transition from centrally directed economies to market economies. As for India, its economy combines all three forms—market, command, and traditional—in a very mixed system.

Most of this book, with the exception of the final two chapters, describes the operation of the type of economic system found in the United States and other western industrialized countries. They are basically market economies in which the government plays a significant but secondary role.

How Does a Market System Resolve the Three Basic Economic Questions?

As we have seen, there are three basic types of economic systems. The one we are most familiar with is that of the United States—the market economy. A market economy determines what to produce, how production will take place, and how output will be allocated to individuals largely on the basis of market forces. What these forces are and how they form the answers to the basic questions are surveyed here and examined more closely in the following chapters.

Markets

The word "market" can have a variety of meanings. Markets differ in the way they are structured and the way they operate. Some are highly organized and are found in particular locations to which the buyers and sellers come. José and María Ruiz sell their cattle at a cattle auction—a market where the buyers and sellers of beef cattle come together. The buyers bid against each other for the animals

offered for sale by the sellers. The highest bidder gets the cattle. Both buyers and sellers get what they want at the best prices they are able to obtain, and the market is usually cleared of all merchandise as every seller finds a willing buyer.

Other markets are more dispersed and unorganized. The hamburger meat that is made from the Ruizes' cattle is sold in many different supermarkets at various prices. Sometimes a supermarket does not sell all of its hamburger, while at other times it may sell out its stock, which means its customers have to look elsewhere or do without.

Product and Factor Markets

Hamburger meat sold by a supermarket to its customers is sold in what economists call a **product market**—a market in which a finished product is sold to the consumer. However, if the hamburger meat is sold to McDonald's or to other commercial buyers, it is then part of a **factor market**—a market in which goods and services are purchased and then used to make final products. The land, labor, and capital resources used in production are sold in factor markets.

> **product market:** a market in which finished goods and services are exchanged.
>
> **factor market:** a market in which resources and semifinished products are exchanged.

■ Retail stores are primary examples of product markets that sell finished products such as the packaged meats found in supermarkets.

The Ruizes buy their cattle feed, hire their ranch hands, and acquire stud bulls for breeding purposes in factor markets. They also sell their fattened cattle in a factor market, because the cattle are part of the production input for a slaughterhouse. The butchered beef is sold in the factor market to supermarket chains, and it is not until the hamburger, roasts, or steaks are sold to the consumer that the beef is finally sold in a product market.

Incentives

Why do markets function in the first place? What is it that makes them work? Bill Hayden's story provides some of the answers to these questions. In 1856, Hayden felt that New Yorkers would pay enough for beef to make his cross-country cattle drive profitable for him. The high prices New Yorkers were willing to pay for beef provided Hayden with an **incentive**. In a market system, the opportunity to make a profit is the usual incentive for providing a good or service.

The profit incentive also motivates the Ruizes. Today, just as 140 years ago, if there are people who are able and willing to pay a price high enough to cover production costs and yield some profit, an incentive exists for someone to produce the good or service wanted. A rise in price is generally an incentive to produce more. A decrease in price generally brings a decrease in production.

A rise in beef prices would probably provide the incentive needed for ranchers to increase their cattle stocks and encourage more ranchers to raise cattle. It might also induce feedlot operators to fatten their beef for a

incentive: a motivation to undertake an action or to refrain from undertaking an action; in a market economy profits are the incentive to produce.

longer time in order to get heavier animals to sell at the higher prices. A decline in beef prices would be a signal to ranchers to produce fewer cattle and perhaps cause some ranchers to stop raising cattle altogether. Ranch hands would be laid off, and there would be less investment in breeding stock because of poorer profit prospects. In the market system, prices and the profit motive determine

> **production inputs (inputs):** the factors of production used in producing a good or service.
>
> **household:** an economic unit consisting of an individual or a family.
>
> **rent:** a factor payment for the use of land.
>
> **wage or salary:** a factor payment for labor service.
>
> **interest:** a factor payment for the use of capital.
>
> **factor incomes:** the return to factors of production as a reward for productive activity.

what will be produced, how it will be produced, and for whom.

Circular Flow of the Economy

In a market economy, the factor and product markets support each other and keep the system going. Owners of resources provide the **production inputs**—the land, labor, and capital—that business firms need to function, and business firms provide the finished goods and services consumers want. The owners of resources are also the consumers, who are sometimes referred to as **households**. Firms pay money to the households for the use of the factors of production. These payments are **rent** for land, **wages and salaries** for labor, and **interest** for the use of capital. Households, for their part, use the **factor incomes** that they receive to purchase the

(Continued on page 75) ⬛➡

Figure 1.
Circular Flow Diagram

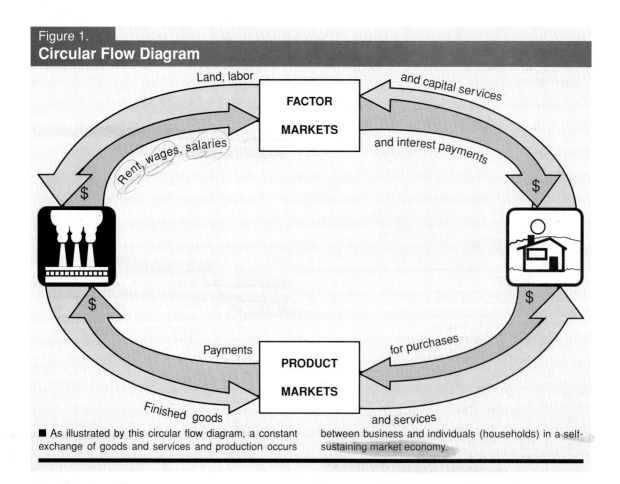

■ As illustrated by this circular flow diagram, a constant exchange of goods and services and production occurs between business and individuals (households) in a self-sustaining market economy.

What Will Keep the Lights Burning?

The United States has an ever increasing demand for energy (see "The Energy Gluttons," chapter 1, p. 24). With the problems inherent in increasing our energy supplies from petroleum or nuclear power (see "How Many Lives for Nuclear Power?" chapter 2, p. 46), the electric utility companies are being forced to consider other energy sources to meet future needs.

Coal is one possible answer because the United States has so much of it. It is estimated that we have a 200-year supply of coal reserves in the ground. Will coal again become, as it was earlier in our history, the "king" of energy?

The main problem with coal is that it is an even "dirtier" source of energy than petroleum. To begin with, coal mining operations despoil the landscape, especially through strip mining, in which scoops gouge out the coal from enormous pits. But the most serious drawback of coal is that when it is burned in utility generating plants or factory furnaces, it pollutes the air with particles and with gases that cause acid rain and contribute to the greenhouse effect.

Another possible candidate to take over from petroleum is natural gas. It is much cleaner and neater to obtain, to transport, and to burn than coal. One problem with a big increase in the use of natural gas is that of getting it from the sources, mainly in the south-central states and the Rocky Mountains, to the utility companies where it is needed on the eastern and western seaboards and in the Midwest. The existing cross-country pipelines are already at capacity, and laying new lines would be very costly and have a negative environmental impact.

There is an alternative energy resource that is "clean," without environmental harm,

■ This solar-powered car represents one potential use of solar energy, a clean, renewable alternative to fossil fuels.

and limitless in supply. That resource is solar power.

Until recently, solar power was considered a long shot as an energy replacement for petroleum because of the high costs it entailed per unit of energy produced. Technological developments in solar power equipment, however, have continued to bring down those costs until it is now being taken seriously by the electric utility companies. The price of the photovoltaic cells that convert sunlight to electricity has fallen from $500 per watt in 1960 to under $4, and it is expected to reach $2 in the near future.

Electricity produced from the cells is still quite a bit more expensive than electricity produced from petroleum (if the environmental costs are disregarded), but the gap is expected to continue to close. Electric utility companies are sufficiently optimistic about solar power that 68 of them have formed a consortium to purchase $500 million worth of solar panels between 1994 and 2000.

Economic Reasoning

1. Natural gas piped to a homeowner for heating a house is sold in what kind of market? Natural gas piped to a factory for heating its boilers is sold in what kind of market? Why can the same good be sold by the same supplier in two different types of markets?

2. What will determine which of the alternative resources replaces petroleum in meeting future energy needs?

3. In the late 1970s, President Jimmy Carter undertook government encouragement of the development of solar power. President Ronald Reagan, when he took office in 1981, stopped all government promotion of solar power and took a hands-off approach to the energy question. Should the government intervene in the energy market by aiding in the development of a particular energy source, or should it leave the determination entirely to the marketplace? Indicate what forms government intervention might take and give the reasons for your answer.

■ These "Sun-Spot" solar collector modules are heating the Environmental Science building and supplying all the hot water for that building on the campus of Rutgers University, New Brunswick, New Jersey.

➠ *(Continued from page 72)*

goods and services that they want from the business firms. Everyone's receipts are someone else's expenditures.

The basic functioning of a market economy can be shown as a **circular flow diagram** with two complementary circles flowing in opposite directions. The outer circle shows the flow of inputs and outputs from firms and households—the production inputs provided by the households to the firms and the finished outputs provided by the firms to the households. The inner circle shows the corresponding money payments made for the inputs—the rents, wages, and interest—and the money payments for the finished goods and services purchased.

The model of the market system shown here is overly simplified. The transactions between firms in the business sector are not shown in our diagram, nor are the effects of government, foreign trade, or the banking system. The diagram shows a closed, static system without growth. It is a useful model, however, for illustrating the interdependence of economic sectors and the self-sustaining operation of a market economy. We will make use of a more elaborate model for studying how the economy works in later chapters.

Market System Resolution vs. Alternatives

During most of this century (from the 1920s to the late 1980s) there were two rather well-defined competing systems: free-market and centrally directed. Each had elements of the other—the government postal service and public transportation in market economies, and farmers' markets for fruits and vegetables in command economies—but the basic foundations of how the systems worked were quite different. Today, the contrast of economies is less distinct.

Putting It Together

In the course of attempting to overcome the problem of scarcity, *specialization* in production has developed in order to increase efficiency and enlarge output. Workers, regions, and nations get the largest returns for their efforts by concentrating on the economic activity that they perform most efficiently.

A producer who can produce a good or service with a smaller amount of factor inputs of land, labor, and capital than another producer has an *absolute advantage* in the production of that good or service.

If one producer has an absolute advantage in the production of two or more goods or services, it would pay for that producer to specialize in that good or service produced with the greatest efficiency relative to another producer of the same goods or services. The second producer, who is less efficient in producing both outputs, should specialize in producing that good or service which is produced with the least relative inefficiency. This is a case of *comparative advantage*.

Specialization results in *interdependence*. Workers and firms are dependent on each other and on the buyers of the finished products. They are often dependent on government services as well. The more specialized and interdependent economic activities become, the greater is the importance of a smoothly functioning economic system to coordinate production and distribution.

There are three basic types of economic systems and each resolves the "what," "how," and "for whom" questions in a different way. In a *market economy*, the interplay of buyers and sellers in many various markets determines what will be produced, how it will be produced, and for whom it will be produced. Markets are places or arrangements for the exchange of goods and services. In a *command economy*, a centrally directed, authoritarian

circular flow diagram: a schematic drawing showing the economic relationships between the major sectors of an economic system.

agency decides what to produce, how to produce it, and for whom to produce it. *Traditional economies* use custom to resolve these basic questions. Most economic systems today are actually *mixed economies* with elements of traditional, command, and market economies.

The United States basically has a market economy. Producers in this economic system react to price signals from markets and the desire to make a profit when deciding what to produce and how to produce it. The prices of goods and services and individuals' ability to pay for them determine who will get these products.

There are basically two types of markets in our market economy—*product markets* and *factor markets*. A factor is anything that is used to produce goods and services. Factor markets deal in goods and services that will be used in production. Product markets provide goods and services used directly by the consumer. It is *households* that provide the production inputs to the business firms that supply semifinished and finished products.

In our market economy, each person's spending is another person's income. The *rent, wages,* and *interest* paid out by business firms to households are spent by households in exchange for the goods and services produced by business firms. The flows of finished goods and services and factor inputs are paid for by the counterflows of *factor incomes* and sales revenues. Together they form a *circular flow* in our economy that is self-perpetuating.

■ The manner in which society organizes production to deal with the problem of scarcity is continually evolving to better satisfy the economic goal of efficiency.

The Industrial Revolution

James Watt and his improved steam engine, which was perhaps the most important invention of the Industrial Revolution.

Additional information on the Industrial Revolution can be found in *The Industrial Revolution* by T. S. Ashton (New York: Oxford University Press, 1961); *The Industrial Revolution and Economic Growth* by R. M. Hartwell (Oxford: Blackwell, 1970); and *Workers in the Industrial Revolution* by P. N. Stearns (New Brunswick, NJ: Transaction Books, 1974).

The Industrial Revolution was a period of great change during which basically agricultural countries with small, home-based "cottage industries" were transformed into industrial societies characterized by machine-dominated factory production centered in heavily populated cities.

The Industrial Revolution first took place in Great Britain between 1750 and 1850. It did not become widely diffused in the rest of Europe and in North America until the second half of the nineteenth century, and it is only now spreading to some parts of the world, as the nonindustrialized nations strive to change from agricultural economies to industrial economies.

During the century between the mid-1700s and the mid-1800s drastic changes in production methods and in the products themselves occurred. The changes were initiated by the invention of spinning and weaving equipment in the textile industry, which took textile production out of homes and put it into factories. Perhaps the most important invention was the improved steam engine developed by James Watt in 1769, because it provided an efficient motive source to power the other new inventions. It also advanced the art of machine toolmaking.

The production of textiles, metal products, and other goods with the use of power equipment instead of hand tools gave the United Kingdom (which encompassed Great Britain) such a large competitive edge over other countries that it became the wealthiest and most powerful country of the nineteenth century.

The wealth created by the Industrial Revolution at first did not benefit the workers. In fact, many workers viewed the new machinery as a competitive threat to their livelihood. They feared machines would put them out of work. There were riots, and factories and machinery were destroyed. As a result, laws were passed that made the willful destruction of any building containing machinery an offense punishable by death. Working conditions were very bad; and labor, especially child labor, was grossly exploited in the early factory system of the Industrial Revolution.

In our time, we have reaped the benefits of the Industrial Revolution—high consumption levels and increased leisure time—along with its costs, such as pollution of the environment and depletion of our energy and other resources. The slowing of productivity growth in recent decades has led to calls for a "new Industrial Revolution," which might again transform not only production methods but society itself.

FOR FURTHER STUDY AND ANALYSIS

Study Questions

1. Does the operation of the Ruizes' cattle ranch represent specialization according to absolute advantage or comparative advantage or both? Why?

2. What is an example of a specialized job with which you are personally familiar? How is that job performed efficiently as a result of specialization?

3. Specialization and interdependence increase efficiency, but what disadvantage might result from interdependence? Give an example.

4. What instances of interdependence can you identify in the cattle industry?

5. Was the 1856 cattle drive of Bill Hayden representative of a traditional economy or a market economy? Why?

6. How does tradition in the United States affect the resolution of any one of the three basic economic questions?

7. What is an example of a relatively well organized market in your area? What is an example of a relatively unorganized market in your area?

8. What changes in Russia are making use of incentives?

9. Give an example of a factor market in which you have participated. What factor did you provide and what was the factor income called?

10. How did the Industrial Revolution affect the outcome of the three basic economic questions?

Exercises in Analysis

1. Visit a local fast-food restaurant and observe the job specialization in production there. Write a short paper on what you observe.

2. The case application "A Mixed (Up) Economy" showed how some parts of the Russian economy are command segments and some are market directed. Prepare a short paper showing how elements of command and traditional economies can be found in the United States.

3. On the basis of what you know about different countries and using any available resource materials, make a list of countries that would be classified as basically market economies, centrally directed economies, or traditional economies.

4. Write a short essay on what will determine the type of energy production that market economies will use in the future.

Further Reading

Cartledge, Bryan, ed. *Energy and the Environment*. New York: Oxford University Press, 1993. Examines the environmental aspects of energy development and what is required for sustainable development.

Fishwick, Marshall, ed. *Ronald Revisited: The World of Ronald McDonald*. Bowling Green, OH: Bowling Green University Popular Press, 1983. A collection of essays on McDonald's and the fast-food industry.

Goldman, Minton F., ed. *Global Studies: Russia, Eurasia, and Central/Eastern Europe*. Fifth edition. Guilford, CT: The Dushkin Publishing Group, 1994. A comprehensive volume including regional essays, country reports, current statistics, and articles from world sources on the states of Eastern Europe and the former Soviet Union.

Jarrige, R., and C. Beranger, eds. *Beef Cattle Production*. New York: Elsevier, 1992. Covers reproduction of the beef herd and genetic improvement of beef cows; hormonal control of growth in beef cattle; and feeding, nutrition, and feedlot fattening.

Lachmann, Ludwig M. *The Market as an Economic Process*. Oxford: Blackwell Scientific Publications, 1986. An examination of how markets function and what they accomplish, looked at from an economic doctrines approach.

Nellis, John. *Improving the Performance of Soviet Enterprises*. Washington, DC: World Bank Publications, 1991. Examines the history of state enterprises and compares their productivity with that of the newer forms of business organization emerging in the former Soviet states.

Oppenheimer, Harold L. *Cowboy Arithmetic: Cattle as an Investment*. Danville, IL: The Interstate Printers and Publishers, 1961. Explains the operations and economics of cattle ranching.

Schipper, Lee, and Stephen Meyers. *Energy Efficiency and Human Activity: Past Trends, Future Prospects*. New York: Cambridge University Press, 1992. Examines energy consumption and the possibilities for "obtaining" energy by conservation.

■ **The American** economy is basically run by the marketplace, with each individual helping to direct the economy by the market choices he or she makes. The marketplace, however, sets its own terms; and both consumers and producers are forced to adjust their decisions to market changes. This chapter's introductory article illustrates how an act of nature can alter the market and our behavior.

The Peanut Butter Crunch

Peanut butter sandwiches are almost as much a part of American food culture as apple pie. Generations of children have been raised on them. Not even the fear of peanut butter sticking to the roof of our mouth (called Arachibutyrophobia) deters us from consuming great quantities of it. In the camps set up for homeless refugees of the 1994 Los Angeles earthquake, peanut butter was the food most in demand, suggesting that it has a comforting effect. Americans consume over 800 million pounds of the gooey stuff every year at a cost of more than $1 billion.

It was therefore a blow to American families and their budgets when the great peanut butter shortage hit in 1981, emptying grocery shelves and causing prices to double in a single year. Who was responsible for this rapid rise in peanut butter prices? Was there a sinister international peanut conspiracy manipulating the market to drive prices up? No, not really. Actually, it was just nature playing tricks with agricultural production again. A summer drought in Georgia, Texas, and other peanut-growing states reduced the peanut crop by 42%. This shortage raised peanut prices from the government-supported price level of $445 a ton to as high as $2,000 a ton.

Faced with such high peanut butter prices, some buyers turned to a substitute made with cotton nut kernels flavored with peanut oil. While this substitute had fewer calories and was considered more nutritious than peanut butter, the substitute's best attribute was its price, which was about one-third less than peanut butter.

However, those with a real passion for peanut butter stuck to the high-priced original in such numbers that the shelves in many stores were cleared of it. Although there was a good deal of consumer resistance to the high price, not everyone was willing to settle for a substitute. Actually, the decline in peanut butter sales was proportionally smaller than the decline in the peanut harvest. This was probably because peanut butter manufacturers purchased more of the available peanuts than the customary 50% of the crop they normally used.

When peanut supplies are normal, the crop amounts to 1.6 million tons annually. As the crop was reduced by the drought, peanut butter producers were willing to pay higher

■ Droughts are not the only reason for higher peanut butter prices. Federal government restrictions on the amount of acreage allowed for commercial peanut growing squeeze the supply and push prices higher.

prices for peanuts in order to acquire a larger share of the smaller supply available. They were induced to do this in part because many consumers would not give up peanut butter even in the face of rising prices and in part because the cost of the peanuts is only a frac-

tion of the total costs of producing and selling peanut butter. The demand behavior of consumers and the behavior of production costs combined to determine what quantity peanut butter companies would produce and at what price they could sell their output.

Market prices are the result of many influences, including consumer preferences, available supplies, and government price supports. The prices of agricultural products are especially sensitive to these influences. They are affected by weather conditions, damage from insects or disease, changes in foreign demand for agricultural products from the United States, changes in the prices of products that can be used as close substitutes, and, of course, government regulations. This chapter will explore how market influences interact to establish prices. We shall investigate the following questions: What forces determine prices in the marketplace? What determines demand? What determines supply? Why do prices change?

■ **Learning Objectives**

After completing this chapter, you should be able to:

1. Explain the laws of demand and supply.

2. List the determinants of demand.

3. List the determinants of supply.

4. Distinguish between short-run and long-run supply.

5. Identify the causes of shifts in demand and how they affect market equilibrium.

6. Identify the causes of shifts in supply and how they affect market equilibrium.

7. Explain why prices move toward an equilibrium price.

8. Distinguish between a change in demand and a change in quantity demanded.

What Forces Determine Prices in the Marketplace?

The key element in the functioning of a market economy is the allocation of resources through the voluntary exchange of goods and services. These goods and services are not directly traded for each other in our modern economy, as they would be in a primitive barter economy. Instead they are bought and sold in markets where each good and service has its price. This analysis section examines how prices are determined.

Demand

Households in the United States consume over 800 million pounds of peanut butter every year. It is a staple of the American diet. When the price of peanut butter nearly doubled, some people cut back their purchases. The **quantity demanded** decreased because of the higher price. For virtually every product or service, an increase in price results in a smaller amount demanded. This is the **law of**

demand: a rise in price causes a fall in the quantity demanded, whereas a decline in price causes an increase in the quantity demanded.

There are two reasons why people behave according to the law of demand. One reason is that when the price of a product goes down, people can afford to buy more of it, and when the price goes up, they can't afford to buy as much. This is the **income effect**.

> **quantity demanded:** the amount of a good or service that consumers would purchase at a particular price.
>
> **law of demand:** the quantity demanded of a good or service varies inversely with its price; the lower the price the larger the quantity demanded, and the higher the price the smaller the quantity demanded.
>
> **income effect:** the effect of a change in the price of a good or service on the amount purchased that results from a change in purchasing power of the consumer's income due to the price change.

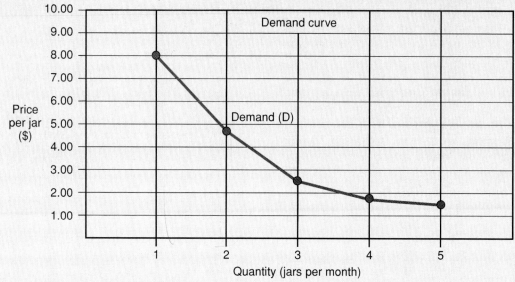

Figure 1.
Yang Demand for Peanut Butter

Demand curve

Demand (D)

Price per jar ($)

Quantity (jars per month)

■ The number of jars of peanut butter that the Yang family would buy in a month depends on the price.

The second reason why people behave according to the law of demand is that when the price of a product rises, people tend to buy less of that product and buy a cheaper substitute instead. This is the **substitution effect**, replacing a more costly item with a less costly one.

Let's take a look at a hypothetical family—the Yangs—buying peanut butter at alternative prices. At $2.50 a jar, the Yangs buy three jars of peanut butter a month. If the price rises to $4.70 a jar, they cut back their purchases to two jars a month. If another year's drought causes the price to go up to $8.00 a jar, the Yangs cut down to one jar a month. At prices higher than $8.00 a jar, the

Table 1.   Yang Demand Schedule

Price per jar	Number of jars per month
$1.50	5
1.80	4
2.50	3
4.70	2
8.00	1

Yangs give up peanut butter altogether as a luxury they can't afford.

On the other hand, if the government eliminates price supports, and the price of a jar of peanut butter falls to $1.80 a jar, the Yangs increase their consumption to four jars a month. With a further drop to $1.50 a jar, the Yangs would increase consumption to five jars a month.

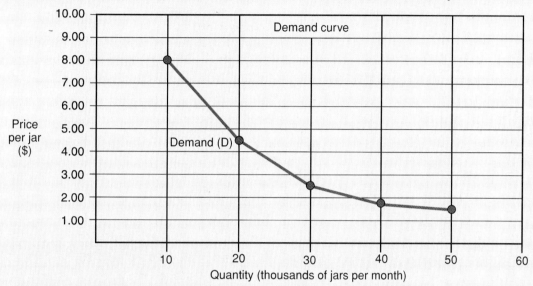

Figure 2.
Community Demand for Peanut Butter

■ The number of jars that 10,000 families similar to the Yangs would buy in a month depends on the price.

Table 2. Community Demand Schedule

Price per jar	Number of jars per month
$1.50	50,000
1.80	40,000
2.50	30,000
4.70	20,000
8.00	10,000

The Yangs' **demand** for peanut butter is given in Table 1, which shows the number of jars they would buy each month at different possible prices. This is the Yangs' **demand schedule** for peanut butter.

A demand schedule also can be shown in the form of a diagram as in Figure 1. In this diagram of the Yangs' demand schedule for peanut butter, the alternative prices for pea-

nut butter are shown on the vertical axis and the corresponding quantities of peanut butter that they would buy on the horizontal axis. This is the customary way to diagram a market situation. Prices are always on the vertical axis, and quantities are always on the horizontal axis.

If we locate for each price on the vertical axis the corresponding quantity demanded at that price on the horizontal axis, given in Table 1, and then draw a line connecting these points, we have a **demand curve**. (We locate

demand: the relationship between the quantities of a good or service that consumers desire to purchase at any particular time and the various prices that can exist for the good or service.

demand schedule: a table recording the number of units of a good or service demanded at various possible prices.

demand curve: a graphic representation of the relationship between price and quantity demanded.

Figure 3.

Bif Supply of Peanut Butter

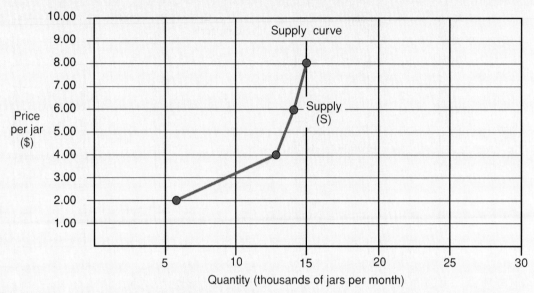

■ The number of jars of peanut butter that the Bif Company would like to sell in a month depends on the price.

points on the demand curve by drawing perpendiculars from corresponding prices and quantities, as shown in the appendix to chapter 1, p. 30.) Just as the law of demand dictates, the quantity demanded increases when the price decreases. The demand curve on our chart slopes downward from upper left to lower right. The lower the price, the more the Yangs would buy; the higher the price, the less the Yangs would buy.

That is the individual household demand for peanut butter. How about the whole market demand for peanut butter? Let us assume that in the town where the Yangs live there are 9,999 other families who have the same demand for peanut butter that the Yangs

community demand schedule: the sum of all the individual demand schedules in a particular market showing the total quantities demanded by the buyers in the market at each of the various possible prices.

Table 3.   Bif Supply Schedule

Price per jar	Number of jars per month
$2.00	5,625
4.00	13,125
6.00	14,500
8.00	15,000

have. If we multiply the number of jars that the Yang family would buy at different prices by 10,000, we get a hypothetical **community demand schedule** for peanut butter. This is shown in Table 2. To assume that all the families have the same demand for peanut butter is, of course, a simplification. In real life, different families have different demands for peanut butter as well as for other products

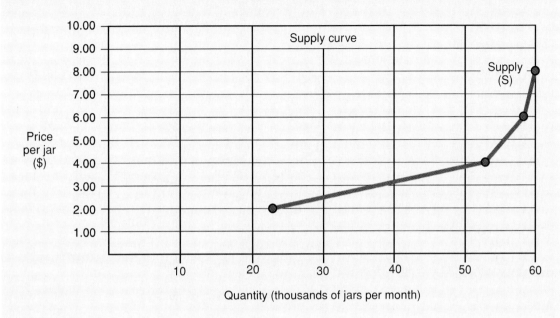

Figure 4.
Market Supply of Peanut Butter

Price per jar ($) vs **Quantity (thousands of jars per month)**

Supply curve

Supply (S)

■ The number of jars that the four peanut butter producers would like to sell in a month depends on the price.

Table 4. Market Supply Schedule

Price per jar	Number of jars per month
$2.00	22,500
4.00	52,500
6.00	58,000
8.00	60,000

and services. (We will see in the next analysis section what determines each individual's demand.)

The data in Table 2 are plotted on the diagram in Figure 2. This shows how much peanut butter would be demanded at different prices ranging from $1.50 to $8.00 per jar in a community composed of 10,000 families, each with the same demand for peanut butter as the Yangs.

Supply

Demand schedules are economic models that help us understand consumer reaction to various prices of a product. To see the behavior of **supply** on the sellers' side of the market, we make use of a **supply schedule**. Sellers have just the opposite attitude toward prices that consumers have. The higher the price of a product, the more of the product sellers are

supply: the relationship between the quantities of a good or service that sellers wish to market at any particular time and the various prices that can exist for the good or service.

supply schedule: a table recording the number of units of a good or service supplied at various possible prices.

Figure 5.
Market Price

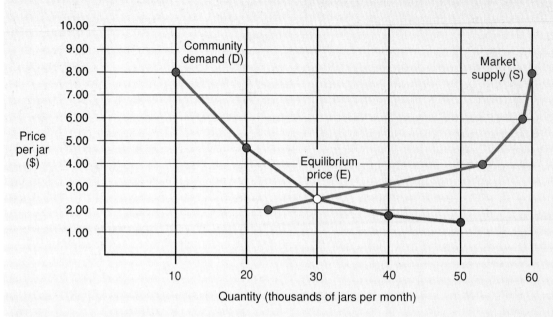

- The equilibrium price in the market is the price at which the quantity that consumers would like to buy is identical to the quantity that suppliers would like to sell.

willing to offer for sale. Table 3 on page 86 shows the amounts of peanut butter one hypothetical seller, Bif Peanut Butter, would have offered at different prices before the drought. At low prices, Bif is not willing to supply much peanut butter. At higher prices, the company offers more for sale. Table 3 is the supply schedule for one producer of peanut butter. (In the third section of this chapter we will examine what determines the quantities sellers are willing to offer at different prices.)

If we plot the points indicating how much peanut butter Bif will supply at different

supply curve: a graphic representation of the relationship between price and quantity supplied.

law of supply: the quantity supplied of a good or service varies directly with its price; the lower the price the smaller the quantity supplied, and the higher the price the larger the quantity supplied.

prices and then connect these points, we get the **supply curve** shown in Figure 3 on page 86. Note that the supply curve slopes upward to the right, indicating that higher prices are associated with larger quantities supplied. In providing more peanut butter at higher prices, Bif is complying with the **law of supply:** the higher the price of a good or service, the more will be offered for sale.

If we assume that there are three other peanut butter suppliers similar to Bif in the market, we create the market supply schedule shown in Table 4 and the market supply curve shown in Figure 4. Note that the supply curves indicate only what quantities sellers would like to sell at various prices, not how much they *can* sell. How much they can sell depends on the demand schedule. Supply and demand schedules are determined independently by different considerations, but they jointly determine price as shown in the following section.

Equilibrium

The Yang family, along with all of the other potential peanut butter customers in their community, determines the demand by their willingness to buy a certain number of jars at any particular price. It may not be until they see what the price is on the supermarket shelf that they decide how many jars they are going to buy. But the community demand schedule accurately describes their behavior on the average. If the Yang family doesn't buy any peanut butter one month because they are on vacation, another family is just as likely to buy twice as much because they are having a picnic. With demand curves, as with many economic variables, individual variations from the norm tend to cancel each other out when you are dealing with large numbers.

Bif and the other peanut butter suppliers determine what the supply will be at different prices by their willingness to produce and market a certain number of jars. The sellers are likely to plan in advance how much they will offer for sale depending upon the price they can get. The market supply schedule gives the total amounts they will offer to sell at different prices.

The actual market price is determined when the two sides of the market, the buyers and the sellers, come together. Out of all the possible prices, only one price can exist in a market at a given time when all of the selling conditions are identical. Normally, that is the price that "clears" that market—the price at which the amount the buyers are willing to purchase just equals the amount the sellers are willing to supply. That price is called the **equilibrium price**.

Market equilibrium is shown when we put the demand curve and the supply curve on the same diagram. The point at which they cross shows the price that clears the market. The equilibrium price for peanut butter in our example is $2.50, as shown in Figure 5.

At a price of $2.50 per jar, the families in the community wanted to buy 30,000 jars of peanut butter a month, which the suppliers were willing to sell. If the market price had been less than $2.50, the buyers would have

■ Bologna is one of the more popular ingredients found in sandwiches. Consumer preference for meat and an affordable price keep demand high.

wanted more, but the suppliers would not have been willing to sell as much. As a result, a shortage would have developed. Whenever there is a shortage, the price goes up. Buyers, in effect, would have been bidding against one another for the short supply. This would have raised the price to the equilibrium level.

If the market price had been higher than $2.50, there would have been a surplus of peanut butter and the higher price would not have been maintained. Competition among sellers to get rid of their overstock would have driven the price down to $2.50. Whenever there is a surplus, the price goes down. Freely competitive markets are self-equilibrating, with the price always adjusting to the level that clears the market over a period of time. In our economy, however, we sometimes find markets that are not freely competitive, as in the case of government-regulated prices. In such noncompetitive markets, surpluses or shortages can persist for a long time.

---

equilibrium price: the price at which the quantity of a good or service offered by suppliers is exactly equal to the quantity that is demanded by purchasers in a particular period of time.

How Much Is a Good Student Worth?

Colleges have long recognized the value to the school in having outstanding athletes. This recognition takes the form of scholarships, part-time jobs, and other inducements. Vigorous competition among colleges for star high school athletes has created a market in which the athlete, in a sense, "sells" his or her services to the highest bidder, although there are many restrictions on what the school can offer.

In recent years a similar market has developed for top academic students. For prestige purposes, to strengthen their academic programs, and to diversify their student body, colleges are trying to attract high academic achievers by offering monetary inducements. It is not new for colleges to give academic scholarships, but the competition and the size of the offerings have greatly increased as the result of two developments in the past decade. One of these developments is the leveling-off of college enrollments. The other is the decline in the supply of top students, as evidenced by SAT scores and other tests.

As a result of the competition, some colleges now engage in recruiting practices for top students that formerly were reserved for star quarterbacks. College officials visit students' homes and bid against rival schools for the students. Scholarship offers can reach $40,000 or more.

The amount spent on financial aid by colleges and universities has increased over 600% in the past 20 years. In order to avoid an all-out bidding war for top students, a group of financial aid officers from some prestigious northeastern colleges began to meet annually to discuss the amounts of aid they would offer to students who applied to various schools. Differences in the aid amounts that the schools intended to offer to a particular student were resolved before the offers were mailed out.

The U.S. Justice Department objected to this practice, maintaining that the schools were illegally conspiring to fix student aid "prices." The eight "Ivy League" schools gave in to the Justice Department ruling and agreed to stop the practice. The Massachusetts Institute of Technology, however, chose to fight the ruling in court, maintaining that scholarships are charity and as such are exempt from antitrust regulations.

Economic Reasoning

1. In the market for academic talent, what are the two sides of the market? Who is represented on the two sides of the market?

2. What has happened to the equilibrium price for top high school students? Why?

3. Should the Justice Department intervene in the cooperation among colleges regarding the awarding of scholarships? Why or why not?

What Determines Demand?

We have seen that there is a predictable relationship between the price of a good or service and the quantity demanded—the lower the price, the larger the quantity. But what determines how much demand there will be for a good or service at any particular price? Or, for that matter, whether there will be any demand at all? This analysis section examines the determinants of demand.

Tastes and Preferences

Consumer tastes and preferences are particularly important determinants of demand. Eating peanut butter is a taste that many people acquire when they are young and retain to a greater or lesser extent throughout their lives. The fact that people like or dislike peanut butter is the first thing that determines their demand for the product. As they grow older, their tastes may change, and they may not want as much peanut butter as before.

Income

In order for demand to exist for a product, the desire for the product must be backed up by the ability to pay for it. This is sometimes called **effective demand**. Without the ability to pay for a product, demand for that product does not exist. Our income determines how much money we have to spend; therefore, a person's income plays an important role in determining that person's demand for a product. Increases in income enable people to purchase more goods and services, including more peanut butter, if that is what they choose to spend part of their increased income for.

Substitutes and Complements

A third determinant of demand for a particular product is the availability and price of **substitutes** and **complements**. There are some close substitutes for peanut butter that are made from nuts such as almonds, or from cotton nut kernels or sunflower seeds. More general substitutes—not in looks or taste, but in function—are cheese, salami, and tuna fish. With these substitutes available, many families might not

■ The demand for one product is influenced by the availability of others. These meats and sausages offer many substitute choices.

be willing to pay higher prices for peanut butter, at least not for as many jars of peanut butter as they had been purchasing.

Among the products that complement peanut butter, a favorite one is jelly. A rise in the price of jelly would result in less peanut butter being demanded, since peanut butter and jelly are used together so often. While a rise in the price of a substitute, cheese for example, generally results in an increase in the demand for a product like peanut butter, a rise in the price of a complement such as jelly results in a decrease in the demand for the product. Conversely, a drop in the price of cheese would cause the de-

---

consumer tastes and preferences: individual liking or partiality for specific goods or services.

effective demand: the desire and the ability to purchase a certain number of units of a good or service at a given price.

substitute: a product that is interchangeable in use with another product.

complement: a product that is employed jointly in conjunction with another product.

Pedal Power

Bicycling was already the third most popular sports activity in the United States (after swimming and fishing), but the televising of the sport during the 1984 Olympic Games in Los Angeles gave it a further boost. A 1985 Gallup poll found that 33% of all Americans bicycled at least once during the year. And when American Greg LeMond won the Tour de France, the "Super Bowl" of world cycling competition, in 1986, 1989, and 1990, U.S. interest in the sport reached an even higher pitch.

There has been a generally increased interest in sports activities and in the sales of sports equipment as people become more aware of the relationship between exercise and good health. As a result, bicycles and bicycle accessories have become big business. The number of bicycle shops in the United States grew to 6,500, and some of the more fancy bicycles are priced in four figures.

The most rapidly growing part of the market was not the bikes themselves but the accessories, especially cycle clothing. Sales of eye-catching uniforms, shoes, and headgear for cycling enthusiasts grew at a rate of 25% each year. The popularity of the hip-hugging shorts and flashy jerseys is such that stores sprang up which sold only cycling-style clothing but not bicycles. As with participants in such other sports as jogging, skiing, and health spa training, cyclists not only want to get in shape, but they want to look good while doing it.

The recession of the early 1990s hurt sales of high-end recreational goods, as it did other discretionary purchases. When white-collar and professional employees either lost their jobs or feared that they might do so, high-cost bicycles and cycle clothing became luxuries that were dispensable. Nevertheless, in addition to the 89 bicycle companies producing 1,043 stock models in 1993, there were 73 custom builders making high-priced specialty bikes.

At the low-cost end of the market, increasing numbers of workers elect to use bicycles as a means of commuting to work. Cycling not only

saves on the costs of gas, automobile maintenance, and parking, but it is easier on the environment.

Economic Reasoning

1. Which of the determinants of demand were responsible for expanding the market in bicycles and accessories? Which caused a slowdown in sales of high-end bikes and expensive accessories?

2. If lower import taxes were to reduce the prices of bicycles, how would this affect the demand for cycle clothing? Why?

3. Are changes in the bicycle market a good thing or a bad thing? What changes and why?

mand for peanut butter to go down, while a fall in jelly prices would cause it to go up.

Population

Finally, the demand for a product depends on the number of people in the market area. Since peanut butter is eaten in every part of the United States and is an easily transported, non-perishable item, the potential domestic market population is over 250 million. Increases in population result in greater demand for virtually everything that is produced. Selling in other countries also results in larger demand for the domestically produced product.

What Determines Supply?

The determinants of supply are totally different from the determinants of demand. It should be noted from the outset that demand does not determine supply. Of course if there is no demand for a product, it will not be produced. But the amounts that producers are willing to offer for sale at different prices are not the same as the amounts that are demanded at those prices. The supply schedule, as we have seen, is independent of the demand schedule.

The most important determinant of supply is the cost of production. In the peanut butter industry, the price of peanuts, the wages of factory workers, and the price of jars, as well as how efficiently these factors are used in production, are among the things that determine production cost.

Short Run

How costs behave also depends on the time period under consideration. At any given time, peanut butter producers can adjust their output only over a limited range. They have only so many ovens for roasting peanuts, just so much factory space for processing them, and only so many canning machines for filling jars. In the **short run** they can vary their output only within the limits of their existing plant and equipment. They can increase production by purchasing more peanuts and jars and hiring more workers. They can put on a night shift of workers to increase output. But in the short run, they cannot add to their existing plant and equipment to increase the amount of output.

■ The expansion of a plant can increase product output in the long run.

Increasing the output in the short run generally increases the cost of producing each unit. More workers in the plant means that each one has a smaller amount of capital equipment to work with, so average labor output falls. Consequently, producers will have to get higher prices to induce them to expand production.

short run: a period of time so short that the amount of some factor inputs cannot be varied.

Jojoba: A Desert Weed That Smells Like Money

Before sperm whales came under the protection of international whaling agreements, millions of pounds a year of sperm whale oil were used in the production of leather, textiles, carbon paper, drugs, and polishes. Much whale oil also was used as a lubricant. It prevented corrosion in tractor and automobile transmissions, gears, and machine parts. There was no close substitute. Sperm oil was so vital that it was stockpiled against emergencies. However, in the early 1970s, the United States and Canada banned the import of all whale products because sperm whales were in danger of extinction, and a search for substitutes for whale oil began.

A desert bush called the jojoba ("ho ho ba"), native to the southwestern United States and to Mexico, provides one of the best of these substitutes. Peanut-sized seeds from the jojoba contain a colorless liquid wax with properties that are very similar to whale oil. Jojoba oil is significantly purer than whale oil and is nearly odorless. It never gets rancid and does not deteriorate even after long periods of high-pressure, high-temperature use. The jojoba is a workable substitute for animal oils and waxes, which are difficult to synthesize commercially. Ancestors of Native Americans in this region used jojoba wax as a hair conditioner, and modern cosmetics manufacturers have been the biggest customers for seeds of the wild plants.

The jojoba is a renewable resource. Each bush lives for 100 to 200 years and apparently is not subject to serious insect damage or disease. It responds well to cultivation. But it takes five years for the plant to produce harvestable numbers of seeds. The supply of wild seeds was so limited that, when its uses as a substitute for sperm whale oil were first recognized, the price of jojoba oil nearly tripled in one year to over $7,000 per barrel.

Now, however, commercial growing of jojoba, which got under way with the first commercial

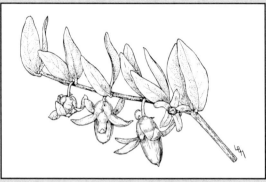

■ Seeds of the jojoba bush produce a wax used in commercial lubricants, cosmetics, and hair products.

farm planted in 1978, has brought down the cost substantially. A jojoba harvesting machine shakes beans off of the rows of bushes onto a conveyor belt where a blower removes the chaff, and the beans are bagged for transport to the processing plant. Rising supply is matching demand as more uses are found for the versatile jojoba.

Economic Reasoning

1. What period of time is the long run for increasing jojoba oil production?

2. How much did jojoba oil cost in the short run? Why was it so expensive? Why did it become cheaper in the long run?

3. Investment in commercial jojoba farms was encouraged by especially favorable tax credits. Should jojoba farm investors be given special tax benefits? Why or why not?

Long Run

Production costs in the **long run** differ from short-run costs in that the size of the plant and the amounts and types of equipment can be altered. If market conditions justify it, a producer can expand output in the long run by building larger production facilities. Additional outputs can then be produced more efficiently in the long run than they can in the short run.

The exact time period that divides the short run from the long run varies from industry to industry. A copy firm that duplicates printed materials for customers may have a long run of a few weeks—only as long as it takes to rent additional floor space and install some more copying machines. For an electric power company, however, the long run is a matter of years. Building additional electric power production capacity takes a long time.

Why Do Prices Change?

Prices generally do not remain constant for very long in our economy. They are always changing because the factors determining demand change, or the factors determining supply change, or both do. Changes in demand and supply cause prices to change, and not the other way around. In this section of the chapter we will examine why prices change.

> **long run:** a period of time sufficiently long that the amount of all factor inputs can be varied.

Figure 6.
Shift in Demand

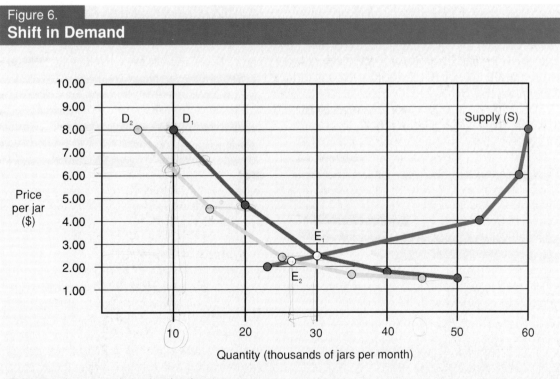

■ A report that peanut butter is related to acne causes the demand to shift from D_1 to D_2 and the equilibrium price to fall from $2.50 to $2.32.

Shifts in Demand

If there is a change in any of the four determinants of demand for a good or service—tastes, incomes, the prices and availability of substitutes and complements, or population size—there will be a **shift in the demand** schedule. More or less of the item will be demanded at each and every price.

Assume, for example, that research were to show peanut butter was a major cause of acne. Publication of this news would probably result in a significant decline in the quantity of peanut butter demanded at every price. Such a demand shift is shown in Figure 6. The original equilibrium price of a jar of peanut butter, as reflected in Figure 5, was $2.50. Let us assume the news story causes the demand to fall by 5,000 jars per month. This is reflected by a shift of the demand schedule from D_1 to D_2. As a result of this shift, the price of a jar of peanut butter drops to $2.32 and the number of jars purchased falls to 27,500.

Notice that the decrease in quantity purchased is less than the decrease in demand. The news story caused demand to decrease by 5,000 jars. At any given price, the consumers wanted 5,000 fewer jars than before. However, the quantity purchased fell from 30,000 to 27,500, a decline of only 2,500 jars. The reason that the decrease in the quantity purchased was not as great as the decrease in demand is because of the price reduction. Decreasing demand causes suppliers to cut their prices. This is shown in Figure 6 by the movement down the supply curve (which has not changed) from E_1 to E_2. Suppliers cut their price because with smaller output their short-run production costs are lower.

In summary, the news story about the alleged relationship between peanut butter and acne caused a downward shift in demand from

D_1 to D_2, a reduction of 5,000 jars. This fall in demand caused a reduction of the price of a jar of peanut butter from $2.50 to $2.32. At this new equilibrium price the quantity demanded and supplied is 27,500 jars. The demand shift caused a reduction in the quantity demand and the quantity supplied of 2,500 jars. Note that there has been no change in the supply schedule. At any given price, suppliers would be willing to sell as much as before the demand shift.

Shifts in Supply

The rise in the cost of peanuts because of the drought caused a **shift in the supply** schedule for peanut butter. In Figure 7, the original hypothetical supply of peanut butter is represented by S_1. The rise in production costs because of higher peanut prices in the drought resulted in a fall in the peanut butter supply to S_2. At each price, sellers were offering a smaller quantity for sale than the year before.

As a result, the market equilibrium as shown in Figure 7 moved from E_1 to E_2. The

shift in demand: a change in the quantity of a good or service that would be purchased at each possible price.

shift in supply: a change in the quantity of a good or service that would be offered for sale at each possible price.

Figure 7.

Shift in Supply

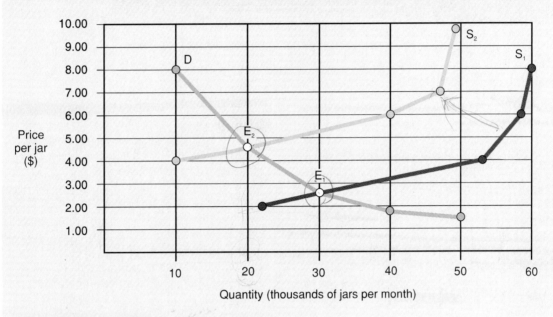

■ The higher cost of peanuts during the shortage causes the supply of peanut butter to shift from S₁ to S₂ and the equilibrium price to increase from $2.50 to $4.70.

jump in prices from $2.50 to $4.70 a jar caused families to cut back on their peanut butter consumption. This did not represent a shift in demand, but rather a movement back along the existing demand curve to a smaller quantity at the higher price. The quantity demanded decreased because of the change in supply, not because of any change in demand (shift in the demand schedule).

It is easy to confuse the causes of market changes between those changes that are the result of changed demand and those that are the result of changed supply. If peanut prices were to decline because of reform of the government agricultural price support program and as a result families began consuming more peanut butter, people might refer to this increased consumption as an increase in de-

mand. The real reason for the changed consumption, however, would be the increase in supply. An increase in supply, by reducing the market price, causes an increase in the *quantity demanded*—represented by a movement downward to the right on the existing demand curve. This is different from an increase in *demand*—represented by a shift upward to the right of the whole demand curve.

To determine whether a market change is the result of a change in demand or a change in supply, look at the cause of the change. If it is due to a change in tastes, incomes, the availability or prices of substitutes and complements, or population size, the cause is a change in demand. If the market change is due to a change in production costs, the cause is a change in supply.

(Continued on page 100) ⟹

Case Application

Prices at the Pump

Since 1973 the price of gasoline has been on a roller coaster. It was in that year that OPEC (the Organization of Petroleum Exporting Countries, a combine of largely Arab oil producers) imposed an embargo on crude oil shipments to the United States in retaliation for U.S. support of Israel. Prior to that, gas prices had been quite stable, rising a few cents in the summer months of heavy demand and settling back to their previous level in the fall.

This price pattern was violently disrupted by the embargo of 1973–1974 and by the oil shortage resulting from the Iranian revolution in 1979. The power over world oil prices obtained by OPEC as a result of these events has since been the dominant factor in the market.

The resulting fluctuation in prices at the pump is shown in Figure 8. When OPEC was putting the squeeze on petroleum supplies, gas prices went up. When OPEC was unable to get agreement among all its members on production quotas or when members cheated on their quotas, which was often the case, pump prices fell.

Figure 8.
Gasoline Prices at the Pump—Unleaded Regular
1977–1993

Source: Energy Information Administration, *Monthly Energy Review.*

■ Gasoline prices rose rapidly in the 1970s as a result of OPEC petroleum supply restrictions. Since then they have been on a roller coaster.

That is not to say that demand has not had an effect on prices as well. The shift to smaller, more fuel-efficient cars has slowed the rise in demand for petroleum. This has made it more difficult for OPEC to raise prices and maintain sales volume. But the principal force in the market has been OPEC supply policies.

This situation may now have come to an end. According to Philip Verleger, author of *Adjusting to Volatile Energy Prices,* "OPEC has lost its market power," and petroleum has become a "true commodity" with prices determined by normal market forces of demand and supply.

Economic Reasoning

1. What determinant of supply affected gasoline prices in 1973? How?

2. Which way did the supply curve shift as a result of OPEC policy? Diagram the shift in the supply curve and show the effect on the equilibrium price.

3. In 1994 federal taxes on gasoline were raised. How did this increase affect our dependence on OPEC? Are higher gas taxes justified? Why or why not?

■ This 1994 Geo Metro, an excellent example of the trend toward smaller, more fuel-efficient automobiles, is considered the Number One enemy of OPEC by a consumer car magazine!

Putting It Together

In our economic system resources are allocated through the exchange of goods and services between producers and consumers. Each good or service commands a price. These prices are determined by the interplay between the *demand* for a product and its *supply*. A *demand schedule* and its graphic representation, the *demand curve,* show the amounts of a good or service buyers would purchase at different prices. For almost any item, the higher the price, the smaller the *quantity demanded*. This is referred to as the *law of demand.* People buy less of an item at higher prices because of the *income effect—* they can't afford to buy as much—and because of the *substitution effect—*they buy relatively less costly substitutes instead.

A *supply schedule* and its graphic representation, the *supply curve,* show the amounts of a good or service sellers would offer for sale at different prices. For virtually any good or service, the higher the price, the larger the quantity that will be offered for sale. This is referred to as the *law of supply.*

When buyers and sellers come together in the market, an *equilibrium price* is established where the quantity demanded equals the quantity supplied. This is the market-clearing price at which there are no shortages and no surpluses. In competitive markets, prices cannot stay above or below the equilibrium point for very long. Competitive pressures push prices back down or up to the equilibrium point.

The determinants of demand are *consumer tastes and preferences,* income levels, the availability and prices of substitutes and *complements,* and the population size of the market.

Supply is determined by production costs. The *short-run* situation assumes that plant size, equipment, and technology do not change; the *long-run* situation assumes that

■ Agricultural products like peanut butter are particularly sensitive to the influences that cause shifts in demand and supply.

production capacity and technology can change.

A change in demand or supply is reflected by changes along the entire demand or supply schedule. This causes the schedule to shift left or right. *Shifts in demand* and *shifts in supply* cause equilibrium prices to change in the marketplace. In contrast to shifts in the whole schedule, changes in the quantity demanded or the quantity supplied reflect movements by sellers or buyers along existing demand or supply curves. These changes in quantity demanded or supplied are the result of price changes.

An increase in demand will raise prices and cause suppliers to offer more for sale in the short run. If they expect the increased demand to be permanent, they will invest in new plant and equipment and thereby increase production capacity and long-run supply.

Adam Smith's Marketplace

Adam Smith (1723–1790)
Smith was born in Scotland. At the age of 3, he was kidnapped by gypsies. He was, however, soon rescued. He was sickly as a child and was in the habit of talking to himself when alone. Absent-minded throughout his life, he nevertheless had an extraordinary memory. At the age of 28, he became professor of moral philosophy at the University of Glasgow in Scotland. He was a popular lecturer, and his classes were very well attended. When he was 40, after the publication of his first book, *The Theory of Moral Sentiments,* he accepted an appointment as traveling tutor to the young duke of Buccleuch. He accompanied the duke to France, where he became acquainted with the intellectual leaders of the country, including a number of Physiocrats. When he returned to England, Smith worked on his masterpiece, *The Wealth of Nations,* for a decade before its publication in 1776. Two years later he was appointed commissioner of customs in Scotland. Not long before his death in 1790, he expressed the regret that he had "done so little" in his lifetime.

Adam Smith is considered the father of economics. Before him, economics was studied either as a branch of politics called political economy or as an area of philosophy. Economics was born as a distinct discipline with the publication of Smith's *The Wealth of Nations* in 1776. It was a remarkable book setting forth expositions of basic economic ideas, which hold up very well today, along with a mind-boggling amount of factual data.

Among the most important and enduring contributions to economic thought was Smith's explanation of the beneficial workings of the free marketplace. He explained market equilibrium as follows:

> The quantity of every commodity brought to market naturally suits itself to the effectual demand. It is the interest of all those who employ their land, labour, or stock [capital] in bringing any commodity to market, that the quantity never should exceed the effectual demand; and it is the interest of all other people that it never should fall short of that demand.

A major thrust of *The Wealth of Nations* was that market prices and quantities should be permitted to adjust to their equilibrium levels without any interference from the government. Smith was arguing in opposition to the system of mercantilism under which the government exercised a great deal of control over economic life. The government regulated production and trade with the objective of bringing gold and silver into the coffers of the state.

Smith contended that a nation's real wealth would be maximized by allowing individuals to make economic decisions based on the forces of the marketplace, unhindered by government regulations. He maintained that in pursuing their own self-interest, people would be guided by an *invisible hand* to maximize their personal contribution to the economy. Smith's views had been greatly influenced by the 3 years he spent in France associating with the French Physiocrats. The Physiocrats promoted a policy of *laissez-faire,* which called for the government to keep its hands off trade and allow prices to seek their natural levels.

Because of his *laissez-faire* doctrine, Adam Smith is greatly admired by economic conservatives today. But Smith was anything but a conservative in his day. He was, in fact, someone that we might today call a consumer advocate, protesting the special interests backed by governments that profited at the expense of the general public.

FOR FURTHER STUDY AND ANALYSIS

Study Questions

1. "Retail Chain Stores Increase Sales of Tennis Balls." Does this headline reflect a change in demand for tennis balls? Explain.

2. "Lobsters Found to Contain Harmful Levels of Mercury." How would this discovery affect your demand for lobster meat? Explain how some consumers might actually buy more lobster after the market adjusted to the news.

3. "Cane Sugar Prices Rise Dramatically." How would this price rise affect the demand for beet sugar?

4. "Record Number of Hockey Fans Paid Higher Prices." Explain how this situation could have occurred, and then use supply and demand curves to illustrate your answer.

5. "Pollution Curbs on Steel Mill Urged." What effect would this proposal to curb pollution have on the supply of steel? How would such a law affect the long-run planning for steel production?

6. "New Auto Sales Off by 25%." What changes in demand and/or supply might have accounted for this headline?

7. If a friend said to you, "I really need a new car, but I can't afford one for at least 6 months," does your friend have an automobile demand in economic terms? What is the meaning of demand in economics?

8. Is the time period that divides the short run from the long run in a particular industry different depending on whether firms in the industry are increasing production capacity or decreasing production capacity? In the case study on jojoba oil production, does it take the same number of years to increase the quantity of jojoba beans grown as to decrease the quantity of jojoba beans grown?

9. What is the difference between a "change in demand" and a "change in the quantity demanded"? What is the cause of each? How is each represented on a diagram of the market?

10. Adam Smith strongly believed that governments should not interfere in the marketplace. What examples of government interference in the marketplace do you find in this chapter?

Exercises in Analysis

1. Make a table of the number of times you would attend the movies at different possible admission prices from $1 to $10 in steps of $1. Then draw a diagram of your demand for theater movies. Total the demand schedules for a group of seven students to obtain a community demand schedule; then draw the demand curve. Save the results for use in an exercise at the end of chapter 5.

2. Take a disc or tape of a popular singer or group to campus and ask a sample of 10 students how much they would pay for the disc or tape at a store. Assuming each student in the sample represents one-tenth of the total number of students at your school, use the data to draw a demand schedule of the campus demand for that disc or tape. (Keep in mind that the students who name a particular price are also willing to buy the disc or tape at any price less than that.)

3. From a financial publication, such as the *Wall Street Journal,* find the current world market price of a barrel of petroleum. What has caused the change in the price from what it was in 1980? Diagram the change in market conditions that has resulted in the price change.

4. Look up "Physiocrats" in the encyclopedia. Write an explanation of their beliefs in your own words.

Further Reading

Deutschman, Alan. *Winning Money for College*. 3rd ed. Princeton, NJ: Peterson's Guides, 1992. This is a "how-to" book on the strategies for winning college scholarships. For each scholarship program, it gives the rules and procedures, helpful hints, program deadlines, and where to obtain more information.

Haase, Edward F., and William G. McGinnies, eds. *Jojoba and Its Uses*. Tucson: University of Arizona Press, 1972. An examination of the various types of applications that jojoba can substitute for other products and in what ways it is superior.

Horsnell, Paul, and Robert Mobra. *Oil Markets and Prices*. Oxford: Oxford University Press, 1993. A more technical treatise on the setting of prices in the petroleum market.

Leider, Robert, and Anna Leider. *Leider's Lecture: A Complete Course in Understanding Financial Aid*. Alexandria, VA: Octameron Press, 1992. A handbook of sources of student aid and how to go about applying for scholarships.

Linam, Del. *Jojoba Fever: A Survey of a New Agricultural Industry*. Burbank, CA: Burbank Books, 1981. A look at the emergence of jojoba growing as an industry.

Seymour, Adam. *The Oil Price and Non-OPEC Supplies.* Oxford: Oxford Institute for Energy Studies, 1990. Examines how new petroleum supplies coming on line from other areas have weakened the power of OPEC to control world oil prices.

Tempest, Paul, ed. *The Politics of Middle East Oil.* London: Graham & Trotman, 1993. A study of the political aspects of the petroleum industry and trade in oil.

Verleger, Philip K., Jr. *Adjusting to Volatile Energy Prices.* Washington, DC: Institute for International Economics, 1994. Covers the pricing of petroleum products, the industry's structure, and the market behavior.

Unit *II.* MICROECONOMICS

The field of economics is divided into two major areas, microeconomics and macroeconomics. Microeconomics includes the topics that have to do with the individual units of the economy, the households and the firms, and with the way markets for products and resources behave.

Chapter 5. The Consumer

In a market economy, consumers dictate what is produced by their spending decisions. They make their spending and saving decisions in the way that obtains the most satisfaction from their incomes, based on the information available.

Chapter 6. The Business Firm and Market Structure

Business firms are of three different types of organization, each with its particular advantages and disadvantages. Firms decide what prices to charge and how much to produce in order to obtain the largest profit possible. The market outcome depends on the structure of the industry they are in.

Chapter 7. Industry Performance

The performance of industries is measured by their efficiency, the quality of their product, their responsiveness to the market, and their responsiveness to social concerns. There are various ways that American industries can improve their performance. The amount of industry concentration affects performance.

Chapter 9. Labor and Income Distribution

The price of labor is wages or salaries, which are determined by forces in the labor market. One of these forces is labor unions. Other income shares come from rents, interest, and profits. Incomes are unequally distributed because of differences in productivity, opportunity, and the ownership of assets. Public policy is particularly concerned with household income levels below the poverty line.

Chapter 8. Government and Business

The government intervenes in business in various ways, regulating industries and sometimes producing goods and services. There are a variety of government agencies that enforce laws and regulations to protect consumers, workers, and the environment.

Chapter 5. The Consumer

■ **The end result** of nearly all economic activity is consumption. The consumer is said to be king or queen in our economy. Consumer demand in the market is presumed to dictate what will be produced. But sometimes, it seems, there is a Madison Avenue Merlin behind the scenes manipulating royalty's decisions.

Blowing Smoke Rings

In 1964 the surgeon general of the United States published a report on medical findings indicating that cigarette smoking is linked to lung cancer. Additional research since then has implicated cigarettes in heart disease, emphysema, and other health problems. A RAND Corporation study estimates that for each pack of cigarettes smoked, a person's life expectancy is reduced by more than 2 hours.

According to the U.S. Centers for Disease Control and Prevention, tobacco use causes the deaths of about 418,000 people a year. Nonsmokers subjected to long-term exposure to secondhand smoke, especially children, are also at significant risk for smoking-related diseases. Secondhand smoke kills an estimated 9,000 nonsmokers a year and aggravates asthma and other health problems for others.

As the public has become aware of the dangers of cigarette smoking, per capita consumption has declined. The proportion of the U.S. population that smokes, which amounted to 40% at the time of the surgeon general's report, is only just over one out of four today. But about 1 million teenagers take up smoking each year; and the total number of smokers, 46.3 million, is almost the same as it was in 1964, when 50 million smoked. (The percentage of smokers has declined as total population has increased.)

The wholesale value of cigarette sales is more than $20 billion a year; and, despite the industry's recent setbacks, cigarette makers are still among the most profitable companies in the nation. The profit margin of Philip Morris, the industry leader, is 27%, an even larger profit rate than exists among the pharmaceutical makers, criticized for excessive profits. If another product had experienced the bad press that cigarettes have had in the last 3 decades, we would expect the producers to be in big trouble financially. How is it, then, that the cigarette companies are doing so well?

One important reason is that their customers have a particular type of loyalty not found in most products: namely, addiction. This has helped make tobacco a very profitable industry in the face of a shrinking market. Even with a decline in the number of packs sold due to a 10-fold increase in cigarette prices since the surgeon general's report, the operating profits of the tobacco companies have nevertheless remained high. Whether measured as a percentage of sales or as a percentage of the amount invested in the companies, the profits of cigarette manufacturers have always been, and still continue to be, among the highest for any industry.

One way the tobacco companies have ensured that profits continue to roll in is by spending large sums on promoting their product, $339.8 million in 1993. Philip Morris got to the top of the heap with successful advertising campaigns that created images of the macho, tattooed Marlboro man and the liberated Virginia Slims woman. Ironically, the original model for the Marlboro man died in 1987 of emphysema, a lung disease caused by smoking.

A more recent advertising campaign that has drawn heated criticism from health officials and antismoking groups is the Old Joe Camel character promoted by R. J. Reynolds Tobacco Company, the number two producer. Old Joe is a cartoon character that has served as a mascot for Camel cigarettes, helping to boost sales from 2.7% to 3.1% of the market. According to critics, backed by studies showing the popularity of the character among children as young as 6, Old Joe has contributed to the increase in smoking by children. Children, young women, and African Americans are the only groups that have shown a rise in the rate of smoking since the surgeon general's report.

The combination of physical and psychological addiction to smoking plus heavy advertising promotion enables the tobacco companies to raise prices, even in the face of the negative health reports. The average price of a pack of cigarettes increased 65% between 1987 and 1992. The cigarette makers believe that because their customers are hooked on the product anyhow, price is not as important as image in purchasing decisions.

However, a study by the National Bureau of Economic Research shows that those assumptions are not true for all groups of smokers and potential smokers. It determined that for those in whom the cigarette habit is well established, smokers over 25, a rise in the price of cigarettes causes them to reduce their consumption by only 10% as much as the price increase. But for younger people between 20 and 25, for whom the habit is not as ingrained, the effect of higher prices is much greater. Their consumption of cigarettes decreases by nearly 90% of the amount of the price increase. Another study shows that for beginning smokers in the 12–17 age range, consumption decreases by 140% of the price rise. In other words, a 10% increase in price results in a 14% decrease in cigarette smoking among the youngest smokers.

Possibly with that group of future hardcore customers in mind, and because of increased competition among the producers for customers in a shrinking market, some companies began marketing less expensive brands, offering discounts, and selling "generic" cigarettes. This price cutting had only a tempo-

rary effect on prices in the market. Philip Morris responded by cutting the price of Marlboros by 40¢ a pack, but within a year began raising prices again. The attitude among major cigarette producers is that image is more important than price. They are convinced that blowing advertising smoke rings will distract smokers both from the unpleasant medical reports and from concerns about how much their habit costs.

■ Chapter Preview

When consumers spend a part of their income on cigarettes, they must give up some other use for the money—a trade-off. Just as the economy doesn't have enough resources to produce everything desired, people do not have enough income to purchase everything they want. Their spending reflects their priorities. Those priorities are conditioned by the information made available to them, notably by advertising. In this chapter we will examine the decisions consumers make and how they make them. The questions to be discussed are: What choices do consumers make? How do consumers make choices? How can consumers make better choices?

■ Learning Objectives

After completing this chapter, you should be able to:

1. Define elasticity of demand.

2. Define the terms perfectly elastic, relatively elastic, unitary elasticity, relatively inelastic, and perfectly inelastic.

3. Compute elasticity ratios.

4. Define consumer sovereignty and show how it is related to the allocation of resources.

5. Define average propensity to consume and average propensity to save.

6. Show the relationship of marginal utility to total utility.

7. Explain the principle of diminishing marginal utility.

8. State the conditions necessary for consumer equilibrium.

9. Explain the effects of product information and advertising on consumer choices.

What Choices Do Consumers Make?

The interplay between demand and supply in a market economy determines the prices of goods and services. Prices, in turn, influence consumer choices between different goods and services. They also affect consumer decisions about how much to save rather than spend.

Spending Choices

People are faced with spending choices every day. They make these spending decisions to satisfy their consumption needs and desires.

Spending decisions depend on personal preferences and the prices of different goods and services in the marketplace. Consumption purchases can be classified as **necessities**—items people must have, including food, clothing, shelter, and medical care—or **luxuries**—items they would like to have but don't necessarily need. For the average household, about $7 of every $10 spent is used for ne-

> **necessity:** a good or service which is considered essential to a person's well-being.
>
> **luxury:** a good or service which increases satisfaction but is not considered essential to well-being.

■ Americans require more income each year to buy the necessities of life. The growth of home entertainment, such as these stereo systems, however, demonstrates that the demand for recreational products remains high.

cessities. The other $3 goes for nonessential luxuries such as camcorders, video games, movies, and holiday trips.

In their spending decisions, consumers react differently to price changes depending on whether a good or service is a necessity or a luxury. When the price of a luxury rises, consumers are likely to cut back their purchases of the item much more than they would if it were a necessity. An item such as cigarettes would normally be considered a luxury purchase. But because of the addictiveness of cigarettes, smokers react to changes in the price of cigarettes as if the cigarettes were necessities rather than luxuries.

The extent to which the quantity demanded of a good or service varies with small changes in its price is its **price elasticity of demand**, a term usually shortened to elasticity of demand. If demand for an item is very **elastic**, the quantity demanded will decrease a great deal with a small increase in its price. The demand for cigarettes, however, is **inelastic**, especially among established smokers. Younger smokers, who are not as hooked on smoking, have a more elastic demand for cigarettes. If the price increases, their purchases of cigarettes will decrease by anywhere from 90% to 140% as much as the increase in price. For example, take a 20-year-old smoking 10 packs a week with cigarettes costing $2 a pack. If the price rose to $2.20 a pack, the 20-year-old would cut back approximately 1 pack to purchase about 9 packs a week. In other words, a 10% increase in price leads to a 10% decrease in purchases. Established smokers, by contrast, would on the average

price elasticity of demand: the relative size of the change in the quantity demanded of a good or service as a result of a small change in its price.

elastic: a demand condition in which the relative size of the change in quantity demanded is greater than the size of the price change.

inelastic: a demand condition in which the relative size of the change in the quantity demanded is less than the size of the price change.

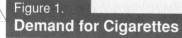

Figure 1.
Demand for Cigarettes

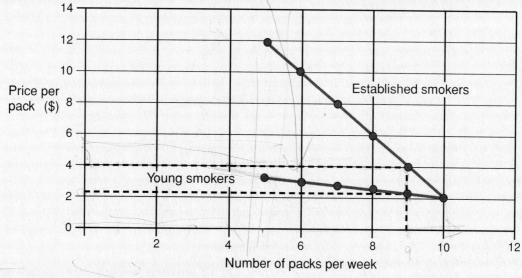

■ The demand for cigarettes by young smokers is more elastic than the demand by established smokers.

reduce their purchases by only one-tenth of a pack per week. To get established smokers (using 10 packs a week) to reduce their smoking by one pack a week, the price of a pack of cigarettes would have to go to over $4.00.

The cigarette demand by established smokers is thus much more inelastic than the demand by younger smokers. The amount of cigarettes they purchase is less responsive to changes in the price. The difference in the behavior of demand for the two groups is shown in Figure 1. The more vertical demand curve represents the demand by established smokers. Changes in price, shown on the vertical axis, result in only very small changes in the amounts purchased, shown on the horizontal axis. The curve showing the demand by younger smokers indicates that a change in price results in a larger change in the quantity purchased.

A very elastic demand curve is more horizontal. It shows that small changes in price result in large changes in the amounts purchased. At the extreme, an absolutely flat demand curve indicates that a rise in the price would reduce purchases to zero. This is **perfectly elastic** demand. At the other extreme, if changes in price resulted in no change whatsoever in the amounts purchased, the demand is **perfectly inelastic,** shown by a curve that is straight up and down. The various degrees of elasticity are represented in Figure 2.

Price elasticity of demand is an important characteristic of consumer behavior. It is vital to understanding spending decisions by consumers and pricing decisions by producers. Elasticity is also important to such governmental decisions as what fares to charge on

perfectly elastic: a demand condition in which the quantity demanded varies from zero to infinity when there is a change in the price.

perfectly inelastic: a demand condition in which there is no change in the quantity demanded when price changes.

Figure 2.

Types of Demand Elasticity

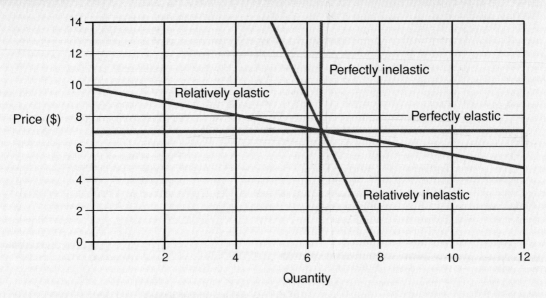

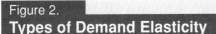

■ The degree of elasticity of demand for a good or service can range from perfectly elastic (horizontal demand curve) to perfectly inelastic (vertical demand curve). The elasticity of demand is usually somewhere in between these extremes.

public transit systems and what taxes to levy on goods such as gasoline, cigarettes, and liquor. It is important to understand what the effects are of governmental regulations on prices and thus on demand. It is useful, therefore, to have a measurement of elasticity. If we know how much change there is in the amount of an item people will buy when its price changes, we can calculate its demand elasticity by dividing the percentage change in the quantity demanded by the percentage change in price. This is the **elasticity ratio**.

$$\text{Elasticity Ratio} = \frac{\% \text{ change in Q (quantity)}}{\% \text{ change in P (price)}}$$

elasticity ratio: a measurement of the degree of the response of a change in quantity to a change in price.

unitary elasticity: a demand condition in which the relative change in the quantity demanded is the same as the size of the price change.

From this equation it can be seen that if the percentage change in quantity demanded is greater than the percentage change in price, the elasticity ratio will be greater than one. If the elasticity ratio is greater than one, demand is elastic. If it is less than one, demand is inelastic. If the ratio is exactly one, the demand elasticity is unitary. **Unitary elasticity** exists when the relative change in quantity is identical to the relative change in price, when demand is neither elastic nor inelastic but right in between. If the demand for cigarettes were unitary, doubling the price would cut consumption in half.

But the study by the National Bureau of Economic Research on the reactions of smokers to higher cigarette prices showed that elasticity was much less than unitary. Established smokers cut back on purchases of cigarettes only one-tenth as much as prices increased. If prices increased 100% from $2 a pack to $4, a 10-pack-a-week confirmed smoker would cut down to 9 packs, a 10% decrease.

■ Since 1964, the surgeon general of the United States has required all advertising and packaging of cigarettes to carry a warning of the health hazards of smoking, like the one on this billboard.

$$\text{Elasticity Ratio} = \frac{\%\text{ change in Q}}{\%\text{ change in P}} = \frac{10\%}{100\%} = 0.1$$

The established smoker's elasticity of demand for cigarettes is 0.1 or one-tenth. The average 20- to 25-year-old smoker's elasticity of demand is much greater; it is 0.9 or nine-tenths. Nevertheless, it is still inelastic, at that price, because the elasticity ratio is less than one.

For the 12–17 age group, however, the percentage change in quantity is greater than the percentage change in price. A rise in the price of 10% causes a 14% decrease in purchases. The elasticity ratio is thus 14/10 or 1.4. Since the ratio is greater than one, those very young smokers have an elastic demand for cigarettes. This has implications for the types of public policies which might discourage teenagers from taking up smoking.

In general, goods and services for which demand tends to be inelastic are those which are necessities, those for which there are either no or few close substitutes, and those which take an insignificant part of our total spending. Salt is a very good example of an item with highly inelastic demand. It has few close substitutes, and the amount we pay for salt is an insignificant part of our total spending. Those goods and services that tend to have an elastic demand are luxuries, those that have many close substitutes, and those that cost us a significant amount of money. Satin sheets are a good for which there is an elastic demand. Real satin sheets are expensive, and there are a variety of other materials for sheets that are close substitutes.

Consumer Sovereignty

Consumer spending decisions are crucial in the functioning of a market economy because they are the most important determinant of the allocation of resources. These decisions are the basis of resolving the "what to produce" question. Producers generally provide goods and services for which there is sufficient consumer demand and stop producing goods and services for which demand is insufficient. In this way producers reflect the will of the consumer. **Consumer sovereignty** exists when the choices of consumers in the market determine what producers make.

When the news first appeared about the effects of cigarette smoking on health, many concerned smokers switched to cigarettes with less tar and nicotine, the suspected causes of damage. Encouraged by cigarette company advertisements, they thought that by switching to reduced-tar brands they could have their cigarettes and their health too. As a result, the manufacturers increased production of reduced-tar cigarettes until they constituted 53% of the total amount produced. As it turned out, a lot of those who switched found that they were smoking more of the less flavorful brands, thus defeating the purpose, and went back to the stronger cigarettes. Even though consumers sometimes aren't sure *what* they want, consumer sovereignty, influenced by advertising, determines what is produced.

Savings Choices

Consumers have two alternatives for their after-tax income: they can spend it, or they can save it. On the average, we in the United States currently spend about 95% of our disposable income on goods and services. This is the **average propensity to consume.** Propensity means inclination. In this case, we are inclined to spend 95 cents of every after-tax dollar we receive. We put the remaining 5 cents of each dollar of after-tax income

■ Savings accounts are one of a wide range of alternative ways to save offered by banks, with differing rates of return and different degrees of risk.

into savings. Our **average propensity to save** is 5%.

Savers try to find the best way to save in order to get the largest returns (interest, dividends, or growth) from their savings for the amount of risk they are willing to take. At one time some people kept their savings in old shoes or under floorboards, and maybe there are some who still do. But this is an expensive way to save, because the savings earn no returns. There is a wide choice of alternative ways to save with differing rates of return and different degrees of risk, ranging from passbook savings accounts to stocks and bonds. For most people, the largest amount of savings they have is the **equity** in their house. Equity is the money value of a property less the value of outstanding mortgages.

Deciding how to save is important to the individual and to the economy as a whole because savings provide the funds other individuals and business firms borrow to begin or expand production. Savings are channeled by banks, brokerage firms, pension funds, and insurance companies into productive investments. Therefore, individual consumer decisions on saving can have a significant impact on the entire economy.

consumer sovereignty: the condition in a market economy by which consumer decisions about which goods and services to purchase determine resource allocation.

average propensity to consume: the percentage of after-tax income which, on the average, consumers spend on goods and services.

average propensity to save: the percentage of after-tax income which, on the average, consumers save.

equity: the owner's share of the value of property or other assets, net of mortgages or other liabilities.

Comparative Case Application

Exporting the Habit

As cigarette sales in the United States decline, being expected to fall some 15% by the end of the decade, American tobacco producers are turning to overseas markets. Philip Morris increased its international revenues from cigarette sales from $8.4 billion in 1989 to $15.7 billion in 1993. Sixty percent of its sales now come from outside the United States. Overall, American cigarette exports are growing at a rate of 6% to 8% a year.

The markets that U.S. tobacco companies are looking to for expansion are especially those of Eastern Europe and Asia. The manufacturers have acquired tobacco-production plants in Hungary, the Czech Republic, Russia, Lithuania, and Kazakhstan. Expanding aggressively into Asia, American brands now account for 17.5% of the Japanese cigarette market. But the big Asian prize they are eyeing is China, with its 298 million smokers, more than the entire population of the United States.

The overseas markets are considered ripe for increased tobacco sales because of rising consumer disposable incomes combined with low social awareness of the health risks. Weak or nonexistent government antismoking campaigns, illiteracy, and cultural attitudes leave the cigarette markets in nonindustrial countries wide open for penetration by the sophisticated marketing techniques of American tobacco companies. Furthermore, their paid advertising is supplemented by "free advertising" in the old Hollywood films shown in those countries, projecting the image of smoking as glamorous and upscale.

But not everything about the overseas market is pleasing to U.S. tobacco companies. High distribution costs and competition from cheap local brands hold down profit margins. Philip Morris averages a profit of only 11.5¢ on each pack it sells overseas, compared to 30¢ a pack on domestic sales. Domestic sales account for less than half its total tobacco sales, but 75% of the tobacco profits. However, American producers expect profit margins on foreign sales to improve as incomes and prices rise abroad.

The American government previously promoted cigarette exports by a policy of challenging health-related restrictions on cigarette imports by foreign countries as a violation of U.S. trade laws. In 1993, the U.S. trade representative announced that this policy would no longer be pursued.

Economic Reasoning

1. If tobacco company advertising in foreign countries succeeds in increasing consumer spending on cigarettes, will this have an effect on the savings rate in those countries? Under what assumptions?

2. How does the elasticity of demand for cigarettes in the nonindustrialized countries compare with that in the United States? Why? What are the indications?

3. Considering the effects on health of cigarette smoking, should American tobacco companies be free to compensate for declining domestic sales by boosting sales in other countries? Should they be encouraged to do so by U.S. government policies, or should their overseas sales be discouraged? Why?

How Do Consumers Make Choices?

There are two types of choices facing consumers. First they must decide how to allocate their income between spending and saving. Second, they must determine exactly what specific spending and saving choices they want to make. People are not necessarily conscious of why they make the choices they do. There are psychological and economic factors involved in all spending and saving decisions. This section explores how consumers make these choices.

Utility

In deciding what to spend their incomes on, consumers may purchase a particular item for a wide variety of reasons: because it adds to their comfort or convenience; because they get pleasure from it; or because it satisfies their egos. Whatever the individual reasons, people buy something because they derive satisfaction from it. The amount of satisfaction that they obtain from a purchase is its **utility**. Utility is the ability of a good or service to provide satisfaction to its consumer. People purchase the necessities and luxuries that they think will provide them with the greatest utility.

Smokers buy cigarettes because they expect the cigarettes to provide them with a certain amount of satisfaction. The amount of satisfaction they derive from smoking a certain number of packs is the **total utility** they receive from their cigarette purchases.

But since they have limited income and other needs and desires, how do smokers de-

■ Former surgeon general Joycelyn Elders launched a campaign warning of the dangers for children of exposure to secondhand smoke. Knowledge of the effects of smoking may decrease the utility of cigarettes for consumers.

cide how many packs of cigarettes to buy in a certain time period? The answer to this question lies in how smokers perceive the **marginal utility** of each additional pack they buy. Marginal utility is the value or satisfaction received by a consumer from one more unit of consumption—in this case, an additional pack of cigarettes. Up to a point, each pack purchased adds to the total utility of cigarettes for a smoker. But each pack will add less utility than the one before.

For a smoker, the first cigarette of the day has a very high utility. If he or she only smoked one cigarette a day, the marginal utility of that one cigarette would be very large. Additional cigarettes would add to total utility, but the second would have less satisfaction than the first, the third less than the second and so on. This characteristic of **diminishing marginal utility** is true not only for cigarettes but for virtually everything else.

> **utility:** the amount of satisfaction a consumer derives from consumption of a good or service.
>
> **total utility:** the amount of satisfaction a consumer derives from all of the units of a particular good or service consumed in a given time period.
>
> **marginal utility:** the amount of satisfaction a consumer derives from consuming one additional unit (or the last unit consumed) of a particular good or service.
>
> **diminishing marginal utility:** the common condition in which the marginal utility obtained from consuming an additional unit of a good or service is smaller than the marginal utility obtained from consuming the preceding unit of the good or service.

Figure 3.
Consumer Utility

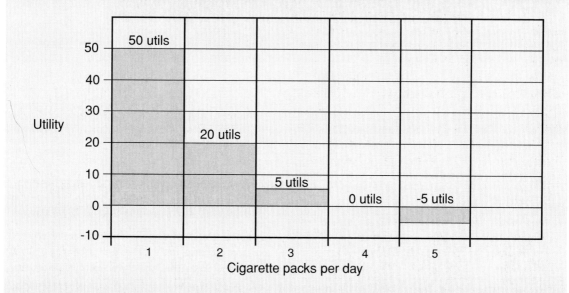

■ Marginal utility diminishes with each additional pack purchased. Generally, the more we have of a good or service, the less we will be willing to pay for an additional amount.

Figure 3 shows the utility a smoker might derive from packs of cigarettes in a day. There are no actual measurements of utility, but we can use a hypothetical unit and call it a "util." Each additional pack purchased adds so many utils to the total utility the smoker obtains from smoking cigarettes during the day.

We will assign the first pack 50 utils of utility. We will assume a second pack adds 20 utils. The third pack adds 5 utils more, and the fourth 0 utils, since even confirmed cigarette addicts seldom enjoy smoking that many cigarettes a day, not to mention the devastating health effects of such heavy smoking. We can suppose that, even for this hypothetical heavy smoker, a fifth pack of cigarettes in a day would have negative marginal utility. The smoker would not only not enjoy the fifth pack, but would have to be paid to smoke it.

As Figure 3 shows, the marginal utility is less for each additional pack purchased than for the preceding pack. The principle of diminishing marginal utility means that, all other things being equal, the more we have of a good or service, the less we will be willing to pay for an additional amount of the same good or service.

The total utility a consumer gets from a good or service is the sum of the marginal utilities. If the smoker in the above example bought 3 packs of cigarettes a day, the total utility would be 50 plus 20 plus 5, a total of 75 units of utility.

Consumer Equilibrium
How many packs of cigarettes, or anything else, a consumer buys depends on comparing the marginal utility of the good or service to its price. The objective is to obtain the largest amount of utility possible with our limited incomes. This is accomplished when the last dollar spent on any item provides the consumer with the same marginal utility as the last dollar spent on any other good or service. That spend-

The Channel Race

A lot of competitors have plunged into the channel race on cable television. Subscribers now have their choice of all-news, all-sports, all-children's, all-music-video, all-comedy, all-religious, and all-cultural channels, among others. In some cities, you can add a channel that allows you to push a button to respond electronically to questions asked in the broadcast studio.

In addition to paying a basic service fee, many cable subscribers are subscribing to additional "premium" channels at extra cost. Some are paying for more than one movie channel, although the channels often show the same films. Even with the increase in cable subscribers, many of the companies that supply programs to the cable stations operate at a loss, and some have gone broke. But these losses have not deterred new companies from entering the field.

New technologies, such as fiber-optic cables and super satellites, now promise to increase the number of potential channels available to over 500. The question is, how many channels will the viewing public support?

Economic Reasoning

1. How would adding a second movie channel to a cable subscription affect the subscriber's total and marginal utility from pay television?

2. What criterion would you use, in economic terms, in deciding how many premium cable channels to subscribe to?

3. Do you think that there is a danger that people might spend too much of their income on cable/satellite television? Why or why not?

ing allocation results in **consumer equilibrium** because the consumers obtain more satisfaction from whatever they spend their money on than from any other pattern of spending.

Consumer equilibrium is reached for smokers when the last dollar they spend on additional packs of cigarettes provides as much added satisfaction as the last dollar spent on gasoline, hamburgers, movie tickets, rent, or anything else. The marginal utility per dollar spent on the various goods and services our hypothetical smoker buys should also be equal to the marginal utility received from an additional dollar saved. When consumers have allocated their incomes so that the marginal utility of every item purchased divided by its price is equal to the marginal utility of every other item divided by its price, the consumers are doing as well as they can with their incomes. If they can't do any better, they are at consumer equilibrium. They have maximized the satisfaction they can get from their income because any other allocation of their income would result in lower total utility.

$$\frac{MU}{P}$$

How Can Consumers Make Better Choices?

Consumers try to get the most they can out of the dollars they spend or save. However, obtaining the maximum utility from our income is not always easy. This analysis section examines under what conditions consumers can make proper consumption or savings decisions.

Information

An essential requirement for making wise consumer spending and saving decisions is to have sufficient and accurate information about your choices. For product information, the consumer should know what goods and services are available, where they can be obtained, what prices they are selling for, their quality and serviceability, and their distinctive characteristics.

With respect to cigarettes, an important piece of information consumers did not have prior to the surgeon general's report was the effects of smoking on health. Smokers who died of lung cancer or other smoking-related diseases were not able to make informed decisions about the allocation of their spending in the absence of information concerning the relationship between cigarette consumption and health. With that information, they might decide to continue smoking, to cut down on the amount, to switch to lower-tar cigarettes, or to quit smoking. Whatever their choice, it would be a more efficient allocation of income if based on full knowledge about the product.

> SURGEON GENERAL'S WARNING: Smoking By Pregnant Women May Result in Fetal Injury, Premature Birth, And Low Birth Weight.

Similarly, in making savings decisions, consumers need to know how secure the savings are against being reduced in value, how easily they can be turned into cash (their liquidity), and how much the earnings on the savings will be. In the case of borrowing, it is important to know what the **real interest rate** is as well as all the loan repayment conditions.

Ideally, consumers can achieve the greatest total utility from their incomes by having complete information about all goods and services. But there is a cost to obtaining information—the opportunity cost of the time involved in seeking the information. If you were in the market for an automobile, it would

consumer equilibrium: the condition in which consumers allocate their income in such a way that the last dollar spent on each good or service and the last dollar saved provide equal amounts of utility.

real interest rate: the quoted interest rate calculated on an annual basis and adjusted for changes in the purchasing power of money during the duration of the loan.

■ Information, such as an automobile's gas mileage, is an essential requirement for making wise consumer spending decisions.

be wise to visit a number of dealers, get comparative prices, read brochures and test reports on the characteristics and quality of the different makes, and talk to car owners. On the other hand, if you are buying a can of tomatoes, it doesn't pay to put that much time into deciding which brand to buy and where to buy it.

Even with such an insignificant purchase as a can of tomatoes, however, we would like to know that the quality of the product is good. For this information we often depend on the reputation of the brand name and the producer's desire to maintain a good reputation. For some products, especially foods and drugs, we also depend on government-imposed standards and testing. The government requires firms in certain industries to make information available about their products, such as the contents of mattresses, pillows, and sleeping bags, the energy efficiency of home appliances, and the ingredients in packaged foods.

Cigarette manufacturers must print warnings about the health dangers of their products on the packages and in their advertisements. The government also requires lending institutions to inform borrowers in writing of the actual rates of interest they will be paying and other conditions of a loan. A major purpose of these government requirements is to reduce information costs for consumers and enable them to obtain greater utility from their income.

Advertising

The most prevalent source of information about products and services is advertising. There is a good deal of dispute over the merits of advertising. Some of advertising's benefits are that it informs consumers of what is available, where, and at what price. Advertisements also often present the distinguishing characteristics of different products and services. This is essential information in making consumer choices. In some cases, advertising may lower production costs per unit by expanding a producer's market. By identifying producers, it may encourage them to maintain the quality of and service for the product.

On the negative side, advertising generally adds to the cost of products and thus reduces consumers' purchasing power. (It is calculated that in 1993 "free" television cost every American household $30 in higher prices for the products it bought.) Advertising may help eliminate all but the biggest firms from production—the ones that can afford the high advertising costs in certain industries. It also helps create wants and fads and thereby affects consumer sovereignty. If the advertising is false or misleading, it will reduce consumer satisfaction.

The heavy advertising by cigarette companies is credited for maintaining a large market for their product in the face of information about its detrimental effects on health. The image created by advertising that smoking is sophisticated, sexy, macho, or whatever the advertising firms think people might identify with has been effective in offsetting the health warnings, especially in inducing those who have not yet developed the habit to begin smoking.

Counterfeit Commodities

When you buy a shirt with an American manufacturer's insignia on the front, it may not have been made by that firm. Counterfeit copies of clothes with well-known trademark symbols have been produced by foreign producers and sold in regular retail outlets as the legitimate article.

What is worse, you could be driving your car after having the brakes relined and have an accident because the brake linings that were installed were inferior imitations of a name brand. Automobile parts have long been a favorite target of counterfeit manufacturers. A car company executive collected over 225 different parts that were sold with Ford company markings but were not legitimate Ford products.

Other favorites of the counterfeiters have been Rolex watches, Gucci leather goods, Levi's jeans, Spalding sporting goods, Apple computers, and pirated music and videotapes and computer software. More recently, the product forgers have moved on to new industry targets such as over-the-counter pharmaceuticals, industrial parts, and electronic components. Since the fake products generally do not meet the quality standards of the originals, there are potential health and safety problems. Counterfeit birth control pills labeled as G. D. Searle brand were delivered to pharmacists, forcing the company to recall more than 1 million pills to find the bogus ones. The cause of a helicopter crash and the death of its pilot have been traced to a defective counterfeit part in the rotor assembly.

Most of these imitation goods are produced by countries in the Far East. Pressured by U.S. officials, who are in turn being pressured by the legitimate American manufacturers, those countries have begun to crack down on the counterfeit manufacturers. Taiwan, once the capital of counterfeit goods production, has led this fight by passing tough new anticounterfeiting laws.

The laws in this country have also been strengthened. In 1984 Congress passed legislation bolstering the trademark laws and giving customs agents more powers to search out and confiscate imitation products coming into the country. However, with the Customs Service concentrating on narcotics smuggling, only a small fraction of the counterfeit imports are caught.

The merchandise counterfeiters are taking advantage of the reputation and market success of name brand producers. The public's familiarity with manufacturers' trademarks was built up by a great amount of promotional advertising, as well as by the quality of the products themselves. The prices of the legitimate products include those advertising costs. Thus, even if the imitation products were of as high a quality as the originals, they could be sold at lower prices because they do not have to cover the promotional costs.

Economic Reasoning

1. What consumer information is conveyed by a trademark?

2. How does counterfeiting of trademarks affect consumer utility?

3. Would you knowingly buy an imitation Apple computer made in Hong Kong if you could get it at a greatly discounted price, say one-half the price of a legitimate Apple, and try it out before you bought it? Why or why not?

Putting It Together

WORLD HEALTH

Smoking or Health the choice is yours!

■ The decision to smoke or not to smoke is an economic as well as a health choice, involving such concepts as trade-offs and utility.

Consumers dictate what will be produced in a market economy. They express their wants through their purchases of the goods and services they desire at the prices they are willing to pay. This is *consumer sovereignty*.

Some goods such as food, housing, clothing, and medical care are *necessities* for all consumers. Other goods and services, on which we may choose to spend our incomes, are *luxuries*.

If we do not change the amount we buy of something by very much when its price changes, it has an *inelastic demand*. If the amount demanded varies a great deal with changes in the price, the item has an *elastic demand*. The *elasticity ratio* is measured by dividing the percentage change in the quantity demanded of a good or service by the percentage change in its price. If the elasticity ratio is less than one, demand is inelastic. If the elasticity ratio is greater than one, demand is elastic. If the elasticity ratio is exactly one, demand elasticity is *unitary*.

The percentage of our total disposable income that we spend on goods and services is our *average propensity to consume*. The percentage that we put into savings is our *average propensity to save*.

The amount of satisfaction that a good or service provides to its purchaser is called its *utility*. The total satisfaction provided by all units of the item consumed is its *total utility*. The extra satisfaction provided by one additional unit of the item is its *marginal utility*. The marginal utility diminishes as more units are purchased because our wants for the item are more fully satisfied.

The consumer is getting the maximum satisfaction possible when income is allocated so that the marginal utility from the last dollar of expenditure on a good or service is the same as the marginal utility from the last dollar of expenditure on every other item consumed and also the same as the marginal utility from the last dollar put into savings. This situation is called *consumer equilibrium*.

In order to obtain the maximum utility from our spending and saving, we need full and accurate information on which to base our decisions. Commercial advertising is one source of product information, and to the extent that it provides useful information, it is helpful in making consumer choices. However, it may add to the cost of products; and when it does not provide accurate, useful information, it is wasteful at best and sometimes misleading.

Conspicuous Consumption

Thorstein Veblen (1857–1929)
Of Norwegian parentage, Veblen was raised in a Wisconsin farm community. He was educated at some of the country's best universities (Johns Hopkins, Yale, and Cornell), but his agricultural background gave him an appreciation for the realities of life that shaped his thinking about economics. He mistrusted the theoretical formulations of the marginalist school of economists, who held that the economy worked according to certain economic "laws" and automatically made adjustments "at the margin" to give the optimum outcome. Instead, Veblen emphasized the importance of the way a society's culture and institutions dictate economic outcomes, and he is credited with being the founder of the institutionalist school of economics.

In addition to *The Theory of the Leisure Class* (1899), Veblen's books on economics include *The Theory of Business Enterprise* (1904), *The Engineers and the Price System* (1921), and *Absentee Ownership and Business Enterprise* (1923). He also wrote on other subjects such as the way universities are run, the subject of *The Higher Learning in America* (1918), as well as publishing articles on sociology and anthropology and a translation of ancient Nordic sagas, *The Laxdoela Saga* (1925).

Consumers are supposed to be calculating buyers, spending their limited income to get the most utility. But are they? Why do they spend $100 for a pair of designer jeans with a particular label on the back or $50 for a knit shirt with a trademark insignia on the pocket when for about half the price they could buy very similar items without the identifying trademarks? How can shops on exclusive Rodeo Drive in Beverly Hills charge so much more for merchandise than stores do only a few blocks away on Wilshire Boulevard in West Los Angeles?

These phenomena were explained as far back as 1899 by an American economist, Thorstein Veblen. In his best-known work, *The Theory of the Leisure Class,* Veblen pointed out that people at the high end of the income ladder, whom he referred to as the "leisure class," set the consumption standards that other income classes try to emulate. "Conspicuous consumption of valuable goods is a means of reputability to the gentleman of leisure," Veblen said, and "members of each [social] stratum accept as their ideal of decency the scheme of life in vogue in the next higher stratum, and bend their energies to live up to that ideal." In other words, people try to copy the lifestyle of those above them on the income ladder, and the ones at the top display their purchasing power by *conspicuous consumption* of expensive things. Purchasing things because they are expensively chic has been termed "the Veblen effect."

A similar but somewhat different consumption behavior is "the snob effect." The snob effect depends on the consumption of a good being confined to a very limited number of people. Buying a Mercedes automobile might be an example of the Veblen effect at work, while buying a gold-plated Mercedes would be an example of the snob effect.

We have another type of consumer motivation at work at the other extreme, "the bandwagon effect." The bandwagon effect arises when people purchase a good because "everyone else has one." An example of the bandwagon effect is the popularity of high-tech sneakers.

Do the various psychological motivations that drive people to buy certain goods undermine the idea of maximizing total utility? Not at all. Utility comes from psychological satisfaction as well as from satisfaction in use. In the words of Veblen, we derive satisfaction from "the utility of consumption as an evidence of wealth."

FOR FURTHER STUDY AND ANALYSIS

Study Questions

1. What goods and services do you consider to be necessities in your own consumption? How do you differentiate between a necessity and a luxury?

2. What luxuries do you think would have a higher price elasticity of demand than others? Give three examples and explain why you think they would have an exceptionally high elasticity.

3. Besides salt and drinking water, what other items that you use regularly have an inelastic demand? Pick one of those items and explain why if its price went up 10% you would reduce your consumption of the item by less than 10%.

4. If you were the owner of a business and trying to decide what price to charge for your product or service, why would the elasticity of demand be an important consideration?

5. A hamburger stand raised the price of its hamburgers from $2.00 to $2.50. As a result, its sales of hamburgers fell from 200 per day to 180 per day. Was the demand for its hamburgers elastic or inelastic? How can you tell?

6. Why would something that has many close substitutes tend to have an elastic demand?

7. If the average propensity to consume was 90% of after-tax income, what would the average propensity to save be?

8. How does tobacco company advertising affect the cigarette market? Does it influence the elasticity of demand for cigarettes? How?

9. Chemically, all aspirin is the same, but some aspirin sells for much more than other aspirin. Why do consumers often purchase the higher-priced aspirin when all aspirin is chemically the same?

10. What are examples of purchases you have made because of the Veblen effect, the snob effect, and the bandwagon effect?

Exercises in Analysis

1. In the first exercise at the end of chapter 4, you constructed the demand schedule of a group of students for movie theater tickets. Using the data from that demand schedule, calculate the elasticity of demand for movie theater tickets when the price falls from $7 to $6. Then calculate the elasticity of demand when the price is reduced from $3 to $2. How do the two elasticity ratios compare? Compare the elasticity ratios for your group's demand with those calculated by the other groups for their demand schedules. Can you draw any generalizations from these comparisons about the behavior of elasticity of demand at high prices compared to low prices? Save the results of this exercise for use in an exercise at the end of chapter 6.

2. Sometimes things that are considered luxuries at one time come to be looked upon as necessities by later generations. Using the recent past, demonstrate how a good or service once considered a luxury might become a necessity.

3. The theory of consumer sovereignty holds that only those goods and services consumers want are produced. Prepare a report showing the principle of consumer sovereignty at work in the automobile industry in recent years.

4. Write a paper comparing the advertising in a section of the daily newspaper with the advertising in an hour of prime-time television. Which has the most useful information for the consumer? Which has the most uninformative, repetitive, and/or misleading advertising?

Further Reading

Bradbury, David E. *A Uses and Gratification Study of Three Audiences: Cable Decliners, Basic Cable Subscribers, and Pay Cable Subscribers.* Philadelphia: Temple University theses, 1990. Research into what motivates people to subscribe to multiple cable channels.

Chollat-Traquet, Claire. *Women and Tobacco.* Geneva: World Health Organization, 1992. An examination of the rising incidence of use of tobacco among the female population.

Earl, Peter. *Lifestyle Economics.* New York: St. Martin's Press, 1986. Analyzes the processes of consumer choice making.

Fritschler, A. Lee. *Smoking and Politics.* 4th ed. Englewood Cliffs, NJ: Prentice Hall, 1989. This book examines the response of the government bureaucracy to the health threat posed by smoking and the administrative politics of rule making.

Napier, Christine, ed. *Issues in Tobacco.* New York: American Council on Science and Health, 1992. A study of the toxological effects of tobacco and the health aspects of smoking.

O'Shaughnessy, John. *Why People Buy.* New York: Oxford University Press, 1987. Examines consumer behavior with respect to what motivates people to buy specific products and brands. It makes use of a social science survey approach, based on buyers' statements.

Otnes, Per, ed. *The Sociology of Consumption.* Atlantic Highlands, NJ: Humanities Press International, 1988. A study of consumer behavior from the standpoint of economic and sociological doctrines.

Penz, G. Peter. *Consumer Sovereignty and Human Interests.* Cambridge: Cambridge University Press, 1986. A view of the operation of consumer sovereignty with respect to private-want satisfaction, social wants, and human interests and deprivation.

_____. *Strategies to Control Tobacco Use in the United States: A Blueprint for Public Health Action in the 1990s.* Bethesda, MD: National Cancer Institute, 1991. Smoking prevention and control.

White, Larry C. *Merchants of Death: The American Tobacco Industry.* New York: William Morrow, 1988. This book attacks "the big lie" put forth by the cigarette companies that there is no proof that smoking kills. It investigates the role of advertising in promoting and romanticizing smoking.

Whitman, M. J. *Tobacco Through the Smokescreen.* New York: M. J. Whitman, 1993. Explores product liability in the tobacco industry.

6. The Business Firm and Market Structure

■ **In the American** economy, decisions about what, how, and for whom to produce are made primarily by private business firms. Their decisions are dictated by the marketplace; but for some the market is more dictatorial than for others. For farmers the market is often fickle, as the following article shows.

Corn Belt-Tightening

The farm crisis of the 1980s accelerated the departure of hundreds of thousands of small farmers from farming, a process that has been going on for decades (see Figure 1). Some 400,000 farmers either went into bankruptcy in 1985 or quit before the creditors took over. The farm population fell by 14% in the decade. As a result, many small farm communities in Iowa, Illinois, Minnesota, Missouri and other corn belt states have become near ghost towns. The community of Gravity, Iowa, at its peak counted a population of over 1,000. By 1993 it was down to 218.

Nearly every Iowa farm county and all the country towns, even the county seats, have experienced population losses since World War II. Between 1960 and 1990, some three-fourths of Iowa's counties lost 55% or more of their population. The same is true in other farming states. The loss of young people has been especially pronounced. According to the Census Bureau, most of the small towns have practically no teenagers; and in some, from 60% to 70% of the population consists of retired people.

The population losses have been accompanied by a loss in income. The farm support businesses have left town. The feed stores, farm equipment dealers, banks, even the groceries, shoe stores, and gas stations are gone. Along with the businesses have gone the paychecks. The small towns, once comprised of self-sufficient farmers and other proud entrepreneurs, now must depend on welfare checks from the government. In Gravity, 22% of the people live below the poverty line. In many other towns, the percentage is even higher.

As if things weren't bad enough, the Great Flood of 1993 added another crushing burden to the distress in the corn belt. It flooded 354 counties in 9 states. The billions of dollars in damage were to a large extent covered by federal assistance, but not completely.

But not all is gloom and doom down on the farm. Crop prices are up more than 40% since the late 1980s, and farmers' debt burdens have been cut in half. Innovations in farm machinery and bioengineered seeds have reduced the amount of labor needed to run some farms by as much as a third. As a result of the higher prices and improved efficiency, profits on the average farm have nearly tripled since their low point in 1984. Positive developments for the future are the new trade agreements negotiated with other nations in

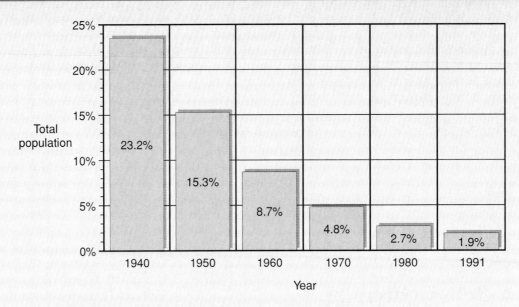

Figure 1.
Farm Population as a Percent of Total Population, 1940–1991

Total population

25%

20%

15%

10%

5%

0%

23.2%

15.3%

8.7%

4.8%

2.7%

1.9%

1940   1950   1960   1970   1980   1991

Year

Source: U.S. Bureau of the Census, *Current Population Reports*.

■ In the last half century the proportion of the population engaged in farming has decreased to less than one-tenth of what it was.

the General Agreement on Tariffs and Trade (GATT) and with our neighboring countries in the North American Free Trade Agreement (NAFTA). (For a discussion of these agreements, see the introductory article to chapter 15, p. 389.) Because U.S. farming is the world's most efficient, reductions in barriers to our exports will especially benefit the farmers.

It will be mainly the larger farmers, however, who benefit. This is in part because the agricultural sector is more and more dominated by big individual and corporate farms. The largest 67,000 farm operators (out of a total of more than 2 million) account for over half of agricultural production, while the million smallest farmers produce less than 5%.

In addition, it appears that large farms will have an increasing advantage over small farmers as a result of the high-tech tools becoming available to agriculture. For example, the application of new developments in com-

puter and genetic engineering technology to farm operations reduces production costs, but only for those who can afford them.

Up to now, computers have been used in farming in much the same ways they are used in other businesses: for record keeping and accessing information via modem, such as the latest market prices and weather. But now computers are going out into the fields to increase efficiency. One use of computers is the satellite mapping of farmland with the aid of the satellite global positioning system (GPS). Created by the Defense Department for military purposes, GPS is now being used to provide the farmer with a method to locate a position on his land to within 3 feet; and the position is automatically mapped on a portable computer for future reference. This enables the farmer to tailor the application rate of fertilizers and pesticides to the exact needs of the soil on every part of the farm, rather than simply applying a uniform supply, as was done in the past. This not

only saves fertilizer and pesticides, but is also beneficial for the environment.

This system of site-specific or prescription farming is affordable only by large farms because of the investment needed in equipment—up to $100,000. Smaller farmers may be able to access the technology, however, if it is made available by chemical application services in their area.

Other technological advances in the offing for farmers include genetically tailored crops. In 1994 the "Flavr Savr" tomato was the first genetically engineered crop to come on the market. More will follow. Other advances include optical soil sensors as a substitute for expensive, laborious chemical soil testing.

■ Chapter Preview

Farmers traditionally represent the epitome of free enterprise in action. In a market economy, the private business firm is the principal supplier of goods and services. Consumers express their will in the marketplace, and it is up to the individual enterprises to put together the labor, capital, and natural resources to satisfy these consumer demands.

This chapter will explain how the business sector of our economy works. The market structure of an industry determines the quantity of goods or services produced and the prices charged. These matters are explored under the questions: What are the forms and economic functions of business firms? What determines a firm's profits? How does industry market structure affect price and output decisions?

■ Learning Objectives

After completing this chapter, you should be able to:

1. List the three main forms of business organization and cite the advantages and disadvantages of each.

2. Describe the four economic functions of business firms.

3. Distinguish between fixed costs and variable costs.

4. Show the relationship of total cost and total revenue to output.

5. Locate the break-even point and point of maximum profit.

6. Distinguish between normal rate of return and economic profits.

7. List the characteristics of purely competitive industries.

8. Explain the principle of diminishing returns.

9. Explain the short-run and long-run adjustments to changes in demand in a purely competitive industry.

10. Differentiate between pure monopoly, shared monopoly, and differentiated competition.

What Are the Forms and Economic Functions of Business Firms?

The three basic allocation questions that an economic system must resolve were described in chapter 2 as the "what to produce," "how to produce," and "for whom to produce" questions. In a market economy, it is the interplay of demand and supply in the marketplace that resolves these three allocation questions by directing the decisions of business firms. In this section, we will first examine what the different forms of business organization are, and then discuss what economic functions businesses perform.

Forms of Business Organization

By far the overwhelming majority of farms are individual **proprietorships**, owned and operated by one individual or one family. This type of business organization accounts for some 87% of the total number of farms and 70% of farm real assets (value of land and buildings). About 10% of farms are **partnerships**, which own 16% of farm real assets. Only 3% are **corporations**, but they have over 11% of the real assets. These are the three main forms of business organization. In addition, there are some farm **cooperatives**.

There is a trend toward fewer and larger farms. This has led to concerns about the consequences if family farms are allowed to go under and be replaced by corporate farming. Since food is a necessity of life, what would be the results if all agriculture fell into the hands of a few giant corporations? Could this happen, and would these corporations then raise food prices to levels people couldn't afford? Will the agricultural industry end up like the automobile industry, with just a handful of giant producers?

The economic organization of agriculture differs from the economic organization of other types of industries. In nonfarm industries taken together, 73% of the firms are proprietorships, but those proprietorships account for only 6% of total industry sales, while corporations account for 90%. In agriculture, on the other hand, proprietorships receive 56% of the revenue from farm sales, compared with only 26% for farm corporations. At present the corporate form of business does not dominate in agriculture as it does in manufacturing. Whether it will in the future depends on the relative costs of the different types of business organization in agriculture.

Proprietorships, partnerships, and corporations each have their advantages and disadvantages, which are of varying importance in different industries. One of the advantages of a proprietorship is that, depending on the type of business, it can be relatively inexpensive to start. Over one-fourth of all farms are less than 50 acres in size. The average investment in land and buildings for a family farm is less than $300,000, not a big investment compared to a manufacturing plant. Another advantage of proprietorships is that the owner-operator makes all of the decisions and keeps all of the profits, on which only personal income taxes are paid.

On the other side, a major disadvantage of a proprietorship business is that the owner is personally responsible for the debts of the business if it goes bankrupt. Some of the other disadvantages are that the business is legally terminated when the owner dies, and a single owner often does not have access to enough capital to make the business succeed.

proprietorship: a business enterprise with a single private owner.

partnership: a nonincorporated business enterprise with two or more owners.

corporation: a business enterprise that is chartered by a state government or, occasionally, by the federal government to do business as a legal entity.

cooperatives: producer and worker cooperatives are associations in which the members join in production and marketing and share the profits. Consumer cooperatives are associations of consumers engaged in retail trade, sharing the profits as a dividend among the members.

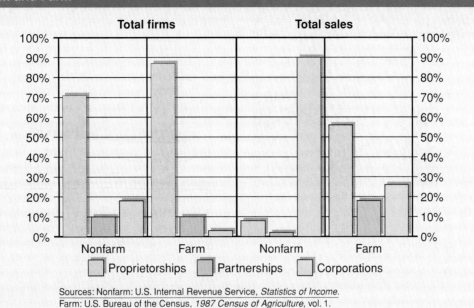

Figure 2.
Types of Business Organization
Nonfarm and Farm

Total firms

Total sales

Proprietorships   Partnerships   Corporations

Sources: Nonfarm: U.S. Internal Revenue Service, *Statistics of Income*.
Farm: U.S. Bureau of the Census, *1987 Census of Agriculture*, vol. 1.

■ Total sales by corporations in industries other than agriculture are many times the sales of proprietorships, even though the number of corporations is only about one-fourth the number of proprietorships. In farming, however, proprietorships dominate the industry in sales as well as in numbers.

For all businesses outside of farming, there are only 15% as many partnerships as there are individual proprietorships; but since partnerships tend to be larger in size than proprietorships, their total sales are over half of the total sales of proprietorships. The principal advantage partnerships have over proprietorships is that they enable two or more people to pool their capital and/or talents to make a business successful. A disadvantage is that each individual is personally liable for all decisions made and for all financial obligations of the company. Another drawback of the partnership form of business organization is that if one of the partners dies, the business is dissolved in the eyes of the law, just as a proprietorship is when the owner dies.

Proprietorships and partnerships allow individuals with ideas, talent, and a willingness to work the opportunity to take a risk on their abilities. If they succeed, they reap the financial and personal rewards of their efforts, and the economy benefits from the availability of a product or service at a price people are willing to pay. If they fail, they suffer the brunt of the failure. It is a ruthless process because the overwhelming majority of new businesses do fail, but it serves an economizing function. Businesses normally do not continue in operation when they do not satisfy a demand efficiently.

The corporate form of business is one in which ownership is represented by stock purchases. A corporation is a legal "person" in the eyes of the law. As such, the corporation has the advantage of **limited liability** for the stockholders. Unlike proprietorships and part-

limited liability: a legal provision that protects individual stockholders of a corporation from being sued by creditors of the corporation to collect unpaid debts of the firm.

■ Ben Cohen and Jerry Greenfield were the founders of the ice cream maker Ben & Jerry's Homemade. Although many people might assume that Ben & Jerry's is a partnership, it is in fact a corporation; most partnerships are small businesses or professional firms.

nerships, the owners of a corporation are normally not personally liable for debts of the company. The corporation is legally treated as an individual and is responsible for its financial obligations. If it fails, its stockholders can only lose the amount they have invested in their stock. Furthermore, when ownership of a corporation changes through the sale of shares in the company, the corporate firm is not legally dissolved.

The corporate form of business organization has some specific disadvantages: corporations are more regulated by the government than other businesses; they must pay corporation taxes on their earnings; there are state and legal fees charged for incorporation. Corporations must be chartered by the state in which they are legally headquartered or, in some cases, by the federal government. The costs of incorporation tend to discourage small firms from incorporating. There are some small corporations, including professionals such as doctors who incorporate, but the typical corporation is quite large. Although only 20% of the nation's businesses are corporations, they account for 90% of total business receipts.

When a large corporation fails, the economy tends to suffer more than when a small proprietorship fails. More jobs are lost by corporate failure, more suppliers are hurt, more buildings and equipment are wasted, and the government loses more potential tax revenue. If the company is sufficiently important, the government may step in to save it, as it did with Lockheed in 1971, Chrysler in 1980, and Continental Illinois in 1984, by guaranteeing new loans extended by creditors to keep the firm functioning.

Identifying Consumer Wants

The first function of any type of business firm is to determine what will be produced by identifying what consumers want and will pay for. Farmers have a particularly difficult time predicting this because they must make their production decisions at planting time on the basis of what they think the market will be the following year at harvesttime. And because American farmers are so dependent on foreign markets to dispose of a large part of their output, their decision about what to produce is complicated by the need to know what world demand will be as well as what domestic demand will be.

But producers in other industries have different problems in identifying consumer wants. At least farmers are producing necessities that are always in demand—food and fibers. Producers of luxury goods are at the mercy of changing fads. Identifying what new products consumers will buy is the first task of the entrepreneur.

Organizing Production

The second function of businesses is to organize production—to resolve the "how" question. It is the most complex function of business firms. How effectively they perform it usually determines whether they succeed or fail. Business firms must decide what mix of the factors of production—land, labor, and capital—will best achieve the desired output.

Many farmers invested too heavily in farm equipment in the 1970s and too heavily in land in the 1980s and found themselves capital-poor because they spent so much on equipment as well as land-poor because of land investment when markets weakened and

■ The sprawling Chrysler headquarters and plant illustrate the large amount of capital and labor involved in a major corporate enterprise. Government loan guarantees saved Chrysler from a possible permanent shutdown.

land prices fell. They had so much invested in expensive equipment and land that they couldn't meet their current bills. Farmers who had invested less in land and capital equipment, hiring the large machinery when it was needed, and depending more on their labor for cultivating and harvesting, fared better. Corporate farms, on the other hand, were able to make efficient use of capital equipment because with their large size they could employ it more continuously; the machinery was not idle as much of the time as on a small farm.

Allocating Revenues

As part of the circular flow of economic activity, businesses allocate the revenue they receive from sales to pay their employees, suppliers, and investors. When farmers are in an economic squeeze, it spreads to their suppliers—the farm equipment dealers, the fertilizer companies, the banks that lend them money—and to whole farm communities.

Businesses decide not only what will be produced and how, but they also decide how purchasing power is allocated. This is their third function. In resolving the "for whom" question, they do not decide who will purchase their products. Consumers decide for themselves what they will purchase under the principle of consumer sovereignty. But businesses do determine how much will be paid to the suppliers of inputs and therefore how much purchasing power each supplier has. The income received by the firm's employees and other factor inputs is spent, in turn, on other goods and services, or it is saved. In a freely functioning market economy, it is purchasing power that determines the answer to the "for whom" question.

Real Capital Investment

The fourth function of business firms is to increase the economy's stock of **real capital**—the barns, factories, office buildings, machinery, tools, and equipment used to produce goods and services. This investment in real capital is an important economic function because it makes possible the expansion and modernization of production. One thing that has led to such an increase in agricultural production

(Continued on page 137) ⟹

real capital: the buildings, machinery, tools, and equipment used in production.

Running with the Bulls

In the decade of the 1980s and on into the early 1990s, the stock market bulls were unstoppable, setting new records for daily and weekly advances in stock prices and numbers of shares traded. The bulls—speculators who expect rising stock prices—were buying on every price increase and contracting for future deliveries of stock, expecting to turn around and sell the stock for more than they paid. They were reinforced from 1991 to early 1994 by hoards of money pouring out of bank certificates of deposit into mutual funds, seeking higher returns in a low interest rate environment.

Against this tidal wave of speculation and income refuge, the bears were helpless. Bears expect prices to fall and sell short, contracting to make future delivery of stock they don't own in hopes the price will drop before they have to cover the transaction. The market was pushed to ever-higher levels as the bulls routed the bears and drove them into hibernation.

But the bears had their days, notably October 19, 1987, when the Dow Jones index of prices of a group of major industrial corporation stocks fell by a record 508 points. The fall was another instance of the stock market adage that what goes up must come down. The only questions are when and how far. Anyone having the answers to those questions would hold the keys to the capitalist kingdom. There is no shortage of "experts" who profess to know the answers—and sell them for a price. However, examinations of the predictions of stock market analysts suggest that one can do just as well by consulting the stars, or the length of women's skirts, or which professional football conference wins the Super Bowl. All of these have been better indicators of the direction stock prices would take in the following year, presumably by pure coincidence, than the predictions of security analysts.

Furthermore, stock market analysts' predictions of the performance of individual stocks have been no better than their predictions of market trends. As Burton Malkiel has shown in his book *A Random Walk Down Wall Street* (see Further Reading at the end of the chapter), one could do just as well at picking stocks by throwing darts at a page of stock listings as by following the advice of the market experts.

Why are the security analysts no better at predicting the direction of stock prices than simply taking the recent trend and no better at picking individual stocks than pure chance? The explanation is not analysts' incompetence, but the nature of the stock market. Analysts are unable to predict accurately the direction of stock prices because what the market does depends less on the real factors affecting the market—profits, interest rates, inflation, employment—than it does on the psychological factors—how investors think other investors will react to economic and market developments. The "Great Bull Market" was propelled less by actual economic conditions than it was by the desire of investors, particularly institutional investors, not to be left behind when stock prices rose.

In their ability to pick individual stocks, market analysts can do no better than random chance because securities are traded in a "perfect" market. A perfect market is one in which all relevant information is available to everyone. As a result, the price of a stock reflects any good or bad news that is likely to affect its future earnings, or what people think its value will be. Because stocks are traded in a perfect market, their prices correspond to their relative expected values. Except in retrospect, there are no bargains in the stock market. The current market price of a stock is the best estimate of what it is worth. If it turns out to be worth more, it was a bargain at that price. But it will just as often turn out to be worth less.

An experiment carried out in Sweden, reported on by the Stockholm newspaper *Expressen*, seems to verify Malkiel's hypothesis regarding stock prices. The experiment pitted five professional stock analysts and a chimpanzee against one another in picking stocks over a month-long period. While the stock experts made their stock picks on the basis of carefully evalu-

How to Read the Daily Stock Market Report

High Low Stock	Div.	Yld%	P-E Ratio	Sales 100s	High Low Close	Net Chg.
$49\frac{3}{8}$ $30\frac{1}{8}$ GAP	.48	1.4	17	8819	$33\frac{7}{8}$ 32 $33\frac{5}{8}$	+ $1\frac{3}{8}$
The price of GAP shares in current year.	Annual dividend per share in dollars to stock-holders.	Yield = Div. × 100 ÷ closing price	Price-earnings ratio: the number of times the current market value of the company exceeds its annual profits.	Number of shares that changed hands (881,900).	In day	Net price change from previous day's closing price (expressed as a fraction of a dollar).

ating the companies and industries, Ola the chimp made his selections by throwing darts at a printout of the companies listed on the Stockholm securities exchange. You guessed it, the stocks picked by the chimpanzee did better than those picked by the experts. To scientifically validate the outcome of this experiment, it would have to be repeated by others. But the results do tend to support the thesis that the stock market is a perfect market.

Stock market analysts are not useless, however. One function they serve is to help make it a perfect market. After surveying the performance of Wall Street security analysts and fund managers, Anne B. Fisher writes: "All in all, the record doesn't really refute the widespread suspicion that security analysts aren't very good at picking stocks. . . . [But] in gathering and disseminating huge gobs of information about companies and stocks that investors wouldn't otherwise have, the analysts over the long run help to insure that stocks are fairly valued. Maybe that's all we can ask of them" (*Fortune,* October 1, 1984, p. 136).

The only advantage anyone can have in the market—so-called expert or not—is to know something about a company that others do not know. For example, if someone knew that a company was about to be acquired by another firm at a price for its stock higher than the current market price, the person could buy a large block of the company's stock and sell it at a profit when the merger took place. But the use of such "insider" information is illegal. The Securities and Exchange Commission, the government watchdog agency over the securities business, investigates reports or indications of "insider trading" and prosecutes offenders.

Does all of this mean that you can't make a profit in the stock market or that it is just a gamble? Attempting to "play" the market by short-term trading in stocks is definitely a gamble, more likely to enrich the brokers with commissions than to enrich the investors. But long-term investment in stocks, the so-called "buy and hold" strategy, can be profitable. On the average, over a long period of time stock ownership has provided a real return to investors, after taking inflation into account, of 6%. This may not appear to be a high figure, but when you consider that it is in addition to increases in the consumer price level and that the earnings compound if you leave them invested, a real return of 6% can mount up significantly over a period of years. It doubles the purchasing power of your investment in 12 years and triples it in 19 years, minus any income taxes on the earnings.

In order to avoid the risk of selecting a stock or stocks that, for some unexpected reason, do worse than anticipated, it is considered good investment strategy to diversify investments into different companies in a variety of industries. A convenient way for investors to do this is by purchasing shares in mutual funds. Mutual stock funds are pools of stocks in a variety of companies, where the investment decisions are made by a professional fund manager. Some funds charge a sales fee, ranging up to 8% of the amount invested; others are "no-load" funds, meaning that they charge the buyer no sales fee. For both load and no-load funds, the fund managers collect administrative fees from the fund assets at regular intervals, and frequently also collect "performance" fees based on increases in the value of the fund shares.

Different funds have varying investment objectives. The aggressive growth funds invest in stocks with greater risk but with the potential to return higher profits. More conservative funds frequently have at least a part of their portfolio invested in bonds, which have a fixed return and

are considered safer than stocks. Some journals, such as *Forbes* magazine, annually publish reports on the performance of mutual funds by type of fund, showing their returns over the past year, 5-year, and 10-year periods. The funds themselves publish prospectuses that give their investment objectives, the fees they charge, and the names of fund administrators. A fund must provide its prospectus to anyone interested in investing in the fund before selling them any shares.

The rapid growth of mutual funds in recent years has contributed to the volatility of the stock market. Institutional investors—mutual funds, pension funds, insurance companies—have increasingly dominated the market. Their enormous buy and sell orders cause wild swings in the prices of stocks. The small investor who engages in short-term trading can be tripped up by the rapid price movements.

Most institutional investment takes place in stocks traded on the two major exchanges: the New York Stock Exchange, where stocks of the nation's largest companies are traded, and the smaller American Stock Exchange, also located in New York. In addition, there are half a dozen regional exchanges around the country that trade many of the same stocks listed on the major exchanges. But the stocks of the overwhelming number of compa-

nies, the tens of thousands of small corporations that have publicly traded stocks, are not sold on any stock exchange floor. They are sold by individual brokers "over the counter."

The stock exchanges do not handle new issues of stock. When a company wishes to issue new shares of stock, it negotiates a sale of the stock to an investment bank, or if it is a major corporation raising a very large amount of money, to a group of investment banks referred to as a consortium. Investment banks then sell the stocks through brokers to the public.

Small "start-up" companies are frequently financed by venture capitalists, financiers who provide funds for promising new ventures in return for part ownership in the company. If the company succeeds well enough to "go public," that is, make a stock offering to the general public, the venture capitalist can reap rewards many times the amount of the capital invested in the company.

Although the stock exchanges do not trade new issues of stock, they are important to the ability of companies to raise investment capital. Investors would be reluctant to buy stock in a company if there were no ready way to dispose of it when they wanted to get their money out. The efficiency of the U.S. stock market is important to the dynamism of our economy. However, excessive speculation in the stock market can create big problems, as it did in the financial collapse of 1929. Running with the bulls is exciting, but a bull can cause havoc in a china-shop economy.

Economic Reasoning

1. Are shares of ownership of most business organizations traded in the stock market? What types of businesses are traded there?

2. Which of the functions of business firms are most affected by the stock market? How?

3. Should the Securities and Exchange Commission reduce the amount of speculation in the stock market by prohibiting investors from buying stock on credit, paying only a fraction in cash, and pledging the stock as collateral on the balance owed? Why should such "buying on the margin" be allowed, or why should it be prohibited?

⟫ *(Continued from page 133)*

in this country that it can supply its food needs with fewer and fewer farmers is the investment in real capital. American agriculture is the most productive in the world. Although this has not always benefited the farmers, it has been very good for consumers.

Investment is an aspect of the resolution of the "what" question because if all resources were allocated to the production of consumption goods and none used for capital goods, the economy would not grow. By investing in real capital, business firms shift some resources from production for present consumption to production for increasing future consumption. This is sometimes referred to as the "when to produce" question.

Real capital investment is also important in resolving the "how" question. It may be possible to change production methods to increase efficiency without new capital investment, perhaps by organizing workers into production teams and giving the teams broad decision-making authority. But most changes in production methods are associated with the installation of new, more technologically advanced machinery and equipment, which is expensive and calls for new investment capital.

What Determines a Firm's Profits?

The objective of producers in all types of business organizations is to make the largest possible profit. Profit is the difference between the revenue a firm takes in and the costs it incurs. A survey of 1,920 Kansas farms showed the 480 most profitable farms averaging $104,000 in profits. The 480 least profitable farms lost an average of $3,000 each—negative profits where costs were greater than revenues. Like other producers, farmers try to maximize profits or minimize losses. This is accomplished by producing the most profitable quantity of output with the resources available. We will use a farm operation to illustrate how costs and revenue are determined and how they determine profits.

▒ Costs

To illustrate how a firm's costs affect production decisions, we will use the example of a chicken farm. A chicken farm with 300,000 laying hens might have three employees and an owner-manager. A large percentage of the hens will have to be replaced each year because hens have a limited time of productivity. During its productive span, a hen will lay, on the average, about 250 eggs a year. Modern chicken farms keep the hens in environmentally controlled cages, with feeding equipment and egg collection both automated. In contrast to farms that grow crops, chicken farms do not need much land, just a few acres.

Like other businesses, chicken farms have two categories of costs: fixed and variable. **Fixed costs** are those that do not change with changes in the quantity of goods or services produced. The principal fixed costs of a business are the costs of its buildings, equipment, and land—the real capital invested. When a building is constructed and machinery and equipment purchased, they are expected to have specified lifetimes before needing replacement. If a building is expected to have a useful lifetime of 40 years, one-fortieth of the cost of the building is charged as a fixed cost of the business each year. This is called **depreciation**. If a piece of equipment is expected to have a productive life of 10 years, one-tenth of the cost of the equipment is charged as a fixed cost for depreciation for each year of its expected productive life. The productive life of machinery and equipment usually depends more on the rate of technological advances in an industry than it does on actual physical wear and tear. If an industry is undergoing rapid technological change, the capital goods used in the industry usually

> **fixed costs:** production costs that do not change with changes in the quantity of output.
>
> **depreciation:** the costs of buildings, machinery, tools, and equipment that are allocated to output during a given production period.

■ A major cost of chicken farming is hen depreciation.

become obsolete and inefficient and have to be replaced long before they wear out.

The fixed costs of a chicken farm include depreciation of the buildings and equipment and replacement of the hen flock. Unlike machinery, laying hens do not become obsolete, but they do wear out and have to be replaced—hen depreciation.

The monthly fixed costs of a representative chicken farm with 300,000 laying hens are:

Depreciation on buildings and equipment:	$18,800
Hen depreciation:	$59,100
Total fixed costs/month:	$77,900

Variable costs of a business are those costs that increase with each additional unit of a product that is provided. Variable costs include the labor, raw materials, and other costs that depend upon the quantity of goods produced and sold. Variable costs are calculated on a per unit basis.

> **variable costs:** production costs that change with changes in the quantity of output.
>
> **total costs:** the sum of fixed costs and variable costs.
>
> **average costs:** total costs divided by the number of units produced.

The largest cost item in producing eggs is feed, which amounts to about two-thirds of the total cost. Other variable costs include labor, energy for lighting and temperature control of the henhouses, medication, litter, and other supplies.

The variable costs per dozen eggs are:

Feed:	$0.28
Labor:	$0.03
Energy and miscellaneous:	$0.02
Variable costs/dozen eggs:	$0.33

Total costs are the fixed costs plus the variable costs for a particular level of output. At zero output, total costs equal fixed costs. Total costs rise with output by the amount of additional variable costs. An equation measuring total costs would be:

Total Costs (TC) = Fixed Costs (FC) + Variable Costs (VC)

The total monthly costs of the chicken farm when it is producing 520,000 dozen eggs per month are:

TC = FC + (VC/doz. eggs × # of doz.)
TC = $77,900 + ($0.33 × 520,000) = $77,900 + $171,600 = $249,500

The total costs of the chicken farm are $249,500. Its **average cost** (AC) per dozen is the total costs divided by the output (Q).

AC = TC/Q = $249,500/520,000 doz. = $0.48/doz.

The farm could produce less or more than 520,000 dozen eggs per month by culling (that is, disposing of) more or fewer hens at a time, changing the amount or mixture of feed, or altering the length of time the henhouses are lit each day (light makes the hens lay more eggs). However, the most efficient output for this size of farm with the existing buildings and equipment is 520,000 dozen eggs, and increasing or decreasing the output would raise the production costs per dozen because that is its most efficient output level. Operating at any other output level would make it difficult for the farm to sell its eggs in competition with other egg producers.

Revenue

The money that a firm receives from the sale of its products or services is the company's **revenue**. **Total revenue** is the price of the product times the number of units sold.

Total Revenue (TR) = Price (P) × Quantity (Q)

For an egg farm, the monthly revenue is the price it receives for a dozen eggs times the number of dozen sold in the month. Because there are a number of farms trying to sell their eggs to the same buyers and eggs are a standardized commodity, the egg producer (the farm owner, that is, not the hen) has little control over the price. The producer must sell eggs of a given size and type from that farm at the going market price, whatever the price is and however small or large the farm's egg production.

If the average wholesale market price for eggs is $0.53 a dozen and the farm produces 520,000 dozen eggs per month, the farm's total revenue per month is:

TR = P × Q
TR = $0.53 × 520,000 doz. = $275,600

Profits

Profits are determined by subtracting total costs from total revenue.

Profit (P) = Total Revenue (TR) – Total Cost (TC)

The egg farm we have been looking at would appear to have profits of $26,100 a month.

P = TR – TC
P = $275,600 – $249,500 = $26,100

However, this profit figure does not take into account some economic costs to the owner of operating the farm. It does not, for instance, take into account the managerial costs of running the farm. Since the owner is the manager, unless he or she pays himself or herself a salary, the accounting profit figure overstates

the actual profitability of the business. Part of that $26,100 is really compensation to the owner for performing the managerial functions of running the farm. If we assume that the value of the management service provided by the owner—the salary and benefits that would have to be paid to someone else to manage the operation or the amount the owner could earn managing some other egg farm—is $5,200 a month, the profit figure is reduced to $20,900.

Another cost not included in computing the farm's profits is a fair return on the money the owner has invested in the business. If the investment in land, buildings, equipment, and hens were financed with borrowed money, the interest on the loan would appear as a fixed cost along with depreciation. But if the investment is the owner's own capital, which is the case here, there is no actual interest payment. Nevertheless, there is a cost to the owner of the capital tied up in the business—an opportunity cost of the money, which could otherwise be earning a return on loan to another business or in some other investment.

The return calculated on the owner's invested capital should be what the capital would earn on the average if put into some other investment having the same degree of risk. This expected return on the capital invested in the business is the **normal rate of return** and is included as a cost when determining the firm's **economic profits**.

The chicken farm has a capital investment of $1,800,000. If the normal rate of return on investments with a similar amount of risk is 15%, the monthly cost to the owner of having his or her capital tied up in the chicken

---

revenue: the receipts from sales of goods and services.

total revenue: the sum of receipts from all of the units sold; price × quantity.

profits: the net returns after subtracting total costs from total revenue. If costs are greater than revenue, profits are negative.

normal rate of return: the rate of earnings on invested capital that is normal for a given degree of risk.

economic profits: earnings on invested capital that are in excess of the normal rate of return.

Aging Rockers Hit the Road One More Time

Over two decades after they rode the wave of rock and roll popularity to the top of the charts, aging rock stars such as the Who, the Rolling Stones, Starship, the Grateful Dead, Tina Turner, and Paul McCartney are cashing in on the nostalgia of the 1960s generation and the curiosity of that generation's children. The sixties-era parents and their children sometimes attend the concerts together as a sharing experience (although some parents use protective earplugs). Other families prefer to share the experience separately.

Whether it's together or separately, the two generations have been buying enough tickets to support the concerts of the superstars of the past. They and a few, but not most, of the more transient current rock-and-roll groups can still sell out performances. But many concert promoters have discovered that lesser-known groups don't draw well enough to cover expenses. Costs have greatly increased. The cost of liability insurance, for example, has multiplied many times over. If promoters have to guarantee the performers $80,000, lay out another $20,000 for rental of the arena, purchase liability insurance, rent sound and lighting systems, and pay for radio and newspaper advertisements, they face at least a $150,000 outlay before they even start to sell tickets. Performance costs such as hiring ushers, security guards, and the many ticket checkers needed to counter widespread counterfeiting of concert tickets add to promoters' expenses. They also have to pay the ticket agencies a percentage of each ticket sold and pay state taxes on the tickets.

The costs for a medium-size rock concert are shown in Table 1.

With these high costs for a less established group that may or may not draw a ca-

Table 1.	Costs of a Rock Concert	
Expense		**Cost**
Performers		$80,000
Arena rental		20,000
Insurance		9,500
Sound system		5,700
Lighting system		3,250
Radio advertising		9,800
Newspaper advertising		6,700
Personnel (ushers, etc.)		3.40 per ticket sold
Ticket agency		1.50 per ticket sold
State taxes		1.80 per ticket sold

pacity crowd, it is not surprising that promoters turn to the '60s rock stars who can draw on two generations of fans to fill the arenas.

Economic Reasoning

1. What are the fixed costs shown for a rock concert? What are the variable costs?

2. About how many tickets would the promoter have to sell at $30 each to cover the above costs of a concert?

3. If the promoter could count on selling only enough tickets to cover those costs, do you think it would be a good idea to go ahead and put on the concert? Why or why not?

how can it be?

farm is $22,500. When this is added to the other costs of the business, total costs are greater than the revenue. The economic profits are a minus—a loss of $1,200 a month. In effect, the owner is subsidizing the business with his labor and the use of his capital. This is not unusual where proprietorships are concerned. Small business owners frequently pay a price for being their own boss.

As with other branches of farming, the egg business is undergoing consolidation. Since 1980 about half of the egg growers with more than 10,000 laying hens have left the business. The industry is becoming dominated by corporate firms such as Cargill, the nation's largest egg company, with a flock under contract of about 9 million birds, as well as Rose Acre Farms and Michael Foods. Cargill achieved its dominant position in part because it is an integrated company, producing the chicken feed purchased by its own and other growers and marketing its eggs under the Sunny Fresh label.

How Does Industry Market Structure Affect Price and Output Decisions?

Although the egg industry discussed in the previous section is becoming more dominated by giant corporate firms, there are still well over a thousand large-scale egg farmers. In other types of farming, there are even more producers in the market. Other industries, however, have different market characteristics from those of farming. There are four types of industry market structure and, although firms in each of the four types attempt to maximize their profits, the results are different in the four different types of industries.

Pure Competition

Agriculture represents an industry that is as close to **pure competition** as one can find. Purely competitive industries are those in which there are a large number of producers supplying a standardized product. Firms in such industries don't have any choice about what price they charge. It is relatively easy for new producers to get into the purely competitive industries or for existing producers to drop out. If a wheat farmer tries to charge more for wheat than the going price in the wheat market, he won't find any buyers. Nor would it pay wheat farmers to set their price below the market price because they can sell all of their wheat at that price. Wheat farmers, therefore, because they sell a standardized product in competition with many other suppliers, have no control over price. The only

■ This combine can harvest enough wheat in 9 seconds to provide flour to make 70 loaves of bread. Wheat farming is a purely competitive business, and wheat farmers cannot raise prices to increase revenues.

pure competition: a condition prevailing in an industry in which there are such a large number of firms producing a standardized product that no single firm can noticeably affect the market price by changing its output; also an industry in which firms can easily enter or leave.

Figure 3.

Firm in Pure Competition
Total Revenue

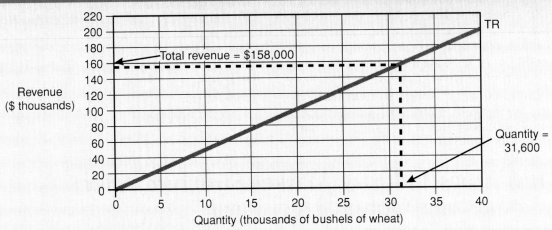

■ If the market price of wheat is $5 a bushel, the farmer's total revenue rises $5 for each additional bushel produced and sold. In pure competition, the total revenue of the individual firm increases at a constant rate with increasing output.

choice they have is how much wheat to sell at the going price. If wheat is selling for $5 a bushel, their total revenue will be $5 multiplied by the number of bushels they sell, as shown by the total revenue curve in Figure 3.

The yearly quantity of wheat produced on the farm is shown along the bottom axis. The revenue from sale of the wheat is shown on the vertical axis. The total revenue is the price per bushel times the number of bushels sold $(TR = P \times Q)$. This is shown by the TR curve on the diagram. The farmer's revenue, beginning at zero with zero output, would rise at a constant rate with each additional bushel of wheat produced and sold. At an output of 31,600 bushels, the total revenue is $158,000 ($5 × 31,600 bushels).

The wheat farmer's costs are shown in Figure 4. The fixed costs are $62,000, whatever the level of output. This fixed cost in-

cludes not only depreciation on the buildings and equipment and interest on the borrowed capital, but also an allowance for the normal rate of return on the farmer's own capital invested in the farm and his management input. The variable costs are added to the fixed costs, depending on how much wheat is produced. They include seed, fertilizer, irrigation water, and hired labor costs. The total costs are the sum of the fixed and variable costs. Total costs are $140,000 at an output of 31,600 bushels of wheat.

Notice that costs go up at an increasing rate, especially after about 25,000 bushels, as shown by the TC curve rising more and more steeply. Wheat farmers can increase wheat production by using more seed, fertilizer, and irrigation and by cultivating land more intensively. But if the amount of land on which they are growing wheat is fixed, costs per bushel of wheat grown increase as they cultivate the land more intensively. This is due to the principle of **diminishing returns.** When one factor input is fixed, in this case, land, it requires successively larger amounts of the other in-

diminishing returns: the common condition in which additional inputs produce successively smaller increments of output.

Figure 4.

Firm in Pure Competition
Total Cost

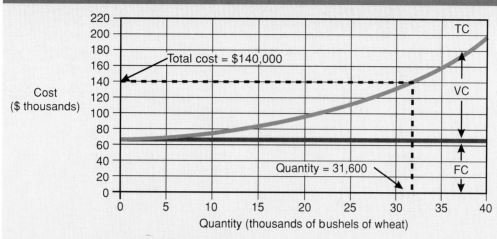

Cost ($ thousands)

Quantity (thousands of bushels of wheat)

■ The total costs for each level of output are the fixed costs plus the variable costs. Variable costs go up at an increasing rate because of diminishing returns.

puts to obtain an additional unit of output. As a result of diminishing returns, a farmer's costs go up faster than his or her output.

Total cost and total revenue together determine profits (P = TR – TC). This is shown in Figure 5. The levels of output where total revenue equals total cost are the **break-even points**. The lower break-even point is just under 20,000 bushels of wheat and the upper break-even point is around 40,000 bushels. Producing any output between the lower and upper break-even points will give the farm a profit. But the **maximum profit level** will be at an output of 31,600 bushels, where total revenue exceeds total cost by the greatest amount. At that output, the total cost is $140,000 and the total revenue is $158,000, providing a profit of $18,000.

Since the costs were calculated to include a normal rate of return on the capital invested by the farmer and a salary for the farmer's labor input, the $18,000 is pure profit—economic profit. However, in pure competition, where entry into the industry is easy, any profit earnings in the industry greater than

the normal rate of return on capital attract additional producers into the industry. The resulting increase in supply causes the price to fall. This is what happens in the wheat industry when there are economic profits, as shown in Figure 6 on page 145.

With the supply of wheat S_1 and the demand D, the equilibrium price was $5 a bushel. At this price, wheat farmers were making above-normal profits. This short-run situation does not last in purely competitive industries. It results in an increase in the production of wheat, shifting the supply to S_2. The new market equilibrium, E_2, lowers the price for wheat to $4.30 a bushel. At this price, wheat farmers are just covering their costs, as shown in Figure 7 on page 146.

break-even point: the output level of a firm at which total revenue equals total costs (TR = TC).

maximum profit level: the output level of a firm at which the revenue from one additional unit of production (marginal revenue) is equal to the cost of producing that unit (marginal cost).

Figure 5.
Firm in Pure Competition
Short-Run Profit

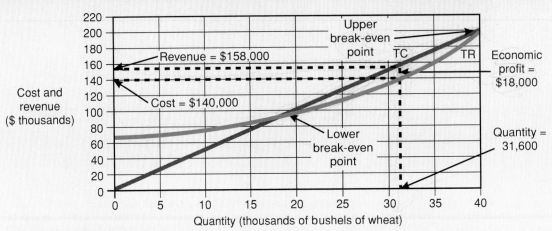

■ A firm can maximize profits by producing the output at which total revenue exceeds total cost by the largest amount. For a firm in pure competition, economic profits are only possible in the short run because they attract new entry into the industry.

pure monopoly: an industry in which there is only one firm.

public utility: an industry that produces an essential public service such as electricity, gas, water, and telephone service; normally, a single firm is granted a local monopoly to provide the service.

The new total revenue curve, TR₂, reflects the lower wheat price of $4.30. At this price, total revenue equals total cost, including a normal rate of return on the farmer's capital. With no economic profits to attract more farmers into wheat production, the supply is stabilized. This is the long-run equilibrium in pure competition, where the producers are just covering their costs, including a normal return on their investment. They must produce at the level of output that minimizes their costs per unit. If their average costs are higher than for other producers in the industry, they cannot stay in business.

Pure Monopoly

At the opposite end of the spectrum from pure competition is the industry with only one firm, **pure monopoly.** Except for **public utilities**—industries such as electricity, gas, water, and local telephone service—there are not many examples of pure monopolies. One industry that is a virtual monopoly is the diamond industry. De Beers Consolidated Mines, a South African company, controls over 80%

Figure 6.

Purely Competitive Market Adjustment

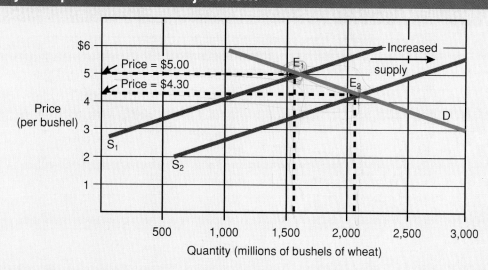

- Above-normal profit returns in a purely competitive industry result in an increase in the market supply. The increased supply causes the price to fall to the level at which producers no longer make economic profits.

of the world's wholesale diamond business. As a result, it has been able to manipulate prices by controlling the supply ever since 1934.

In the early 1980s, there was a break in the diamond market because of a sharp drop in the demand for diamonds by investors. In just one year, diamond prices fell by one-third. The price of a flawless, one-carat diamond dropped from $63,000 to $40,000. To stop the slide in prices, De Beers cut back sales of diamonds to dealers. The changes in the diamond market are shown in Figure 8 on page 147.

Because of the lessened demand for diamonds by investors and speculators, the market demand fell from D_1 to D_2. To stop the price decline, De Beers reduced the supply of uncut diamonds offered to dealers from S_1 to S_2. De Beers might have attempted to raise the price back to P_1 by reducing the supply even further. But they felt that the March 1980 price, inflated by speculation, was too high to maintain a healthy diamond market and maximize profits. To get the price of a flawless, one-carat diamond back up to $60,000, they would have to have cut production by more than 60%.

There are few pure monopolies—even the monopoly control De Beers has over diamond prices is threatened by the possibility of increased supplies from Russia and Angola—but most industries have some degree of monopolistic pricing. Unlike producers in a purely competitive industry, who have to sell their product at the prevailing market price, firms in monopolistic industries can raise or lower their prices to maximize their profits. If they lower prices, they will sell more because their product has a downward-sloping demand curve—the lower the price, the more of the product customers will buy. If they raise prices, they will sell less but receive more per unit sold. As a result, their total revenue does not rise at a constant rate with increasing output as it does under pure competition. The amount of revenue at different prices depends on the demand schedule.

Table 2 on page 147 shows the quantities that a hypothetical monopolist could sell at different prices and the resulting total revenue.

The data in Table 2 are shown as a diagram in Figure 9 on page 148 with the reve-

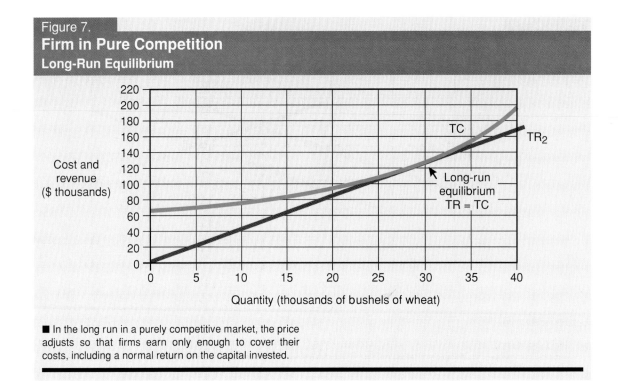

Figure 7.

Figure 7.
Firm in Pure Competition
Long-Run Equilibrium

Cost and revenue ($ thousands)

TC

TR₂

Long-run equilibrium
TR = TC

Quantity (thousands of bushels of wheat)

■ In the long run in a purely competitive market, the price adjusts so that firms earn only enough to cover their costs, including a normal return on the capital invested.

nue measured on the vertical axis and the number of units produced on the horizontal axis.

The firm could maximize its revenue by producing 375 units, which it could sell at $7.50 each for a total revenue of $2,812.50. However, the purpose is not to maximize revenue but to maximize profit, P = TR – TC. The maximum profit output is shown in Figure 10 on page 149.

Because diminishing returns cause costs to rise more rapidly for outputs greater than 300 units, it does not pay to produce more even though revenue would be greater. At an output of 375, which provides the highest revenue, the firm would be losing money because costs are even higher than revenue.

The rule for maximizing profits is to produce the quantity at which total revenue is rising at the same rate as total cost. For this

firm, as output is increased up to about 300 units, total revenue is rising more rapidly than total cost for each additional unit produced and profits are getting larger. Up to this point, costs increase at a diminishing rate—the TC curve rises less steeply—because of an increase in plant efficiency. But as output exceeds the most efficient production level of the plant and equipment, total costs rise more rapidly. Beyond an output level of 300 units, total revenue is not rising as fast as total cost and profits are shrinking, as shown by the narrowing difference between TR and TC in Figure 10. At more than 340 units of output (the upper break-even point), costs exceed revenue and profits become negative.

The increase in total revenue from producing one more unit is called **marginal revenue** (MR). The increase in total cost from producing that one additional unit is **marginal cost** (MC). The output level at which revenue and cost are increasing at the same rate (MR = MC) is the maximum profit level of output.

marginal revenue: the addition to total revenue from the sale of an additional unit of output.

marginal cost: the addition to total cost from the production of an additional unit of output.

Figure 8.
Diamond Monopoly

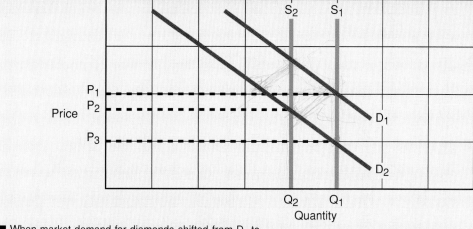

■ When market demand for diamonds shifted from D_1 to D_2, De Beers reduced the supply from S_1 to S_2 in order to keep the equilibrium price from falling to P_3.

Table 2. **Demand Schedule and Total Revenue for a Hypothetical Monopolistic Firm**

Price	× Quantity	= Total Revenue
$15	0	$0
14	50	700
13	100	1,300
12	150	1,800
11	200	2,200
10	250	2,500
9	300	2,700
8	350	2,800
7	400	2,800
6	450	2,700
5	500	2,500
4	550	2,200
3	600	1,800
2	650	1,300
1	700	700
0	750	0

Shared Monopoly

Single-firm monopolies like De Beers are rare, but there are many industries in which the market is controlled by only a few firms. According to the most common measurement, any industry in which four firms or fewer account for over 50% of industry sales is considered a **shared monopoly**. If there is a formal agreement among the firms regarding pricing and/or dividing up the market, the group of firms is called a **cartel**. OPEC is a prominent example of a cartel. If there is no formal agreement among the firms, the industry is called an **oligopoly**. Many industries in the United States are oligopolistic, including the steel, aluminum, cigarette, met-

shared monopoly: an industry in which there are only a few firms; more specifically, an industry in which four or fewer firms account for more than 50% of industry sales.

cartel: an industry in which the firms have an agreement to set prices and/or divide the market among members of the cartel.

oligopoly: a shared monopoly in which there is no explicit agreement among the firms.

Figure 9.

Monopolistic Firm
Total Revenue

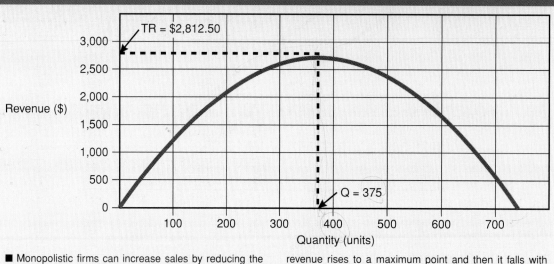

- Monopolistic firms can increase sales by reducing the price. As the price declines and sales increase, total revenue rises to a maximum point and then it falls with further price cuts.

al can, and automobile industries. The steel and aluminum industries produce **homogeneous products**, while the cigarette and automobile industries produce **differentiated products.**

As in pure monopolies, above-normal profit returns in shared monopoly industries can be maintained over the long run by restricting output. Because it is difficult or impossible for new competitors to enter the industry, there is no increase in supply to lower the price. The smaller the number of firms in the industry, the easier it is for them to maintain maximum monopoly profits.

It benefits the firms in a shared monopoly to cooperate and produce the quantity and charge the price that a pure monopolist would. But where there is no formal agreement among the firms in the industry, and sometimes even when there is, this cooperation is difficult to sustain because of the desire of each firm to get a larger share of the market.

The danger of a price war among the different firms is a threat to profits in a shared monopoly. As a result, we frequently see a practice of **price leadership** in this type of industry. One firm, usually the most powerful, takes the lead in setting the price. The other firms follow its price leadership and avoid price competition. Price leadership is most likely to be found in industries with a standardized product such as steel.

Differentiated Competition

An industry with **differentiated competition**, sometimes called monopolistic competition, is one in which there are many firms.

homogeneous products: identical products produced by different firms.

differentiated products: similar but not identical products produced by different firms.

price leadership: a common practice in shared monopoly industries by which one of the firms in the industry, normally one of the largest, changes its prices, and the other firms follow its lead.

differentiated competition: an industry in which there are a large number of firms producing similar but not identical products; sometimes called monopolistic competition.

■ McDonald's used to package their hamburgers in distinctive styrofoam containers. Now, bowing to concern about the environment, the company has changed its packaging to biodegradable paper.

But, unlike in pure competition, the product is not standardized. Each firm differentiates its product to make it unique and to appeal to customers. The fast-food industry is a good example of differentiated competition. The "Big Mac," the "Whopper," and Wendy's burger are all hamburgers that the producers attempt to differentiate from the competition.

As a result of the relative ease of entry into differentiated competition industries, monopolistic profits tend not to last in the long run. Firms in these industries spend a lot of money on advertising and packaging in order to differentiate their product and carve out a mini-monopoly position in the industry. But since other firms in the industry are doing the same thing, profits tend to fall to the normal rate of return on capital, and economic profits disappear over time.

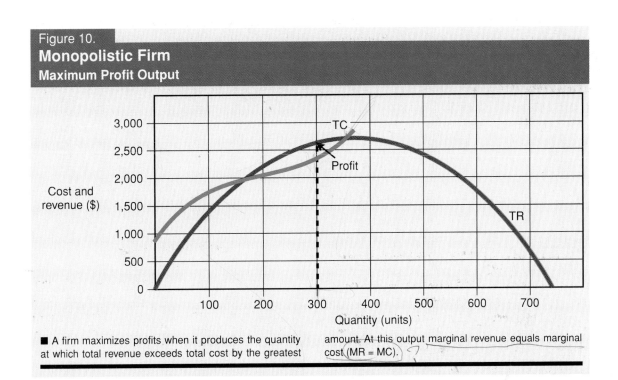

Figure 10.
Monopolistic Firm
Maximum Profit Output

■ A firm maximizes profits when it produces the quantity at which total revenue exceeds total cost by the greatest amount. At this output marginal revenue equals marginal cost (MR = MC).

Hard Decisions for the Software Industry

It is always a difficult problem knowing how best to price a product when it is first brought to market. When the product is one in a new and rapidly evolving industry, the decision is doubly difficult.

The microcomputer software industry did not exist until the 1980s. At first the owners of personal computers were so hungry for software to use on their new machines that nearly any useful software could be sold at whatever price, reasonable or not. Software industry sales doubled every year. Major software programs—word processing, spreadsheet, database—sold for hundreds of dollars, although the direct production costs were only a few dollars for each disk. The major costs of the programs were the developmental expenses—the labor hours (number of programmers times the hours they worked) required to write and debug the programs. Those fixed costs had to be recovered from sales of the disks, of course. But there was little relationship between the costs of producing the software and the price charged, and successful programs could be priced well above their total costs.

As more software developers entered the industry—totaling over 3,000 companies at one point—competition forced a reassessment of pricing policies. Was it best to charge a high price and sell a smaller number of disks or charge a lower price and aim for volume? One software producer decided to find out what price would give it the most profits by actually testing the market at different prices.

The firm, Noumenon Corporation, had initially priced its Intuit accounting program for the IBM PC at $395. In spite of extensive advertising, the program wasn't selling. In order to find the best price, the company first reduced the price to $50 and then each week raised it by an additional $20. After trying prices in increments of $20 all the way up to $210, at which point sales virtually dried up, they found that total revenue was maximized at a price of $90. As a result of this experiment, they decided to advertise and market Intuit at $89.95, much lower than the prices of competing software programs.

Other software producers also began to adopt competitive pricing policies. Dac Software set a price of $70 for an accounting package that was equivalent to programs for which some companies were charging $300 or more. Even the major software firms—Microsoft, Lotus, Ashton-Tate—have felt the heat of competition. Borland International has cut the price of its Quattro spreadsheet program from $495 to $50 since 1992. According to Phillipe Kahn, founder and president of Borland, "After technology, the most important decision to be made in software is pricing; and pricing decisions are always agonizing and difficult."

It is unusual for a company to actually experiment with a wide range of prices for their product as Noumenon did for Intuit. But computer software is not an ordinary industry. It is continually innovating and developing new types of programs, even programs to determine the best price to charge for new products.

Software is maturing as an industry. The recent era of vigorous price competition cut profit margins to the bone and left some producers in financial difficulty. As a result, the industry is going through a period of consolidation. Early in 1994 a number of acquisitions and mergers were announced, including a proposed merger of major desktop publishing software makers Adobe and Aldus. Novell, a producer of network systems, announced that it would spend $1.5 billion to acquire WordPerfect, a leading word processing program, and Borland's Quattro. The purchases nearly doubled Novell's annual sales.

Economic Reasoning

1. In what type of market structure have the software firms been operating? How can you tell?

2. Is a software company likely to price its programs near the price that maximizes total revenue? Why? Diagram the total cost and total revenue situation of a hypothetical software producer and show whether maximum profit output is close to maximum revenue output. (It is unnecessary to put in quantity and revenue figures. Only the relative positions of the TR and TC curves are important.)

3. Do you think that it is beneficial to have software companies merge or acquire other firms producing similar software products? Why or why not?

■ Because of the relative ease of entry into the microcomputer software industry, a factor that tends to drive down monopolistic profits, software makers must frequently introduce new versions of their products to differentiate them from the products of other software makers.

Putting It Together

Businesses may be organized as individual *proprietorships, partnerships,* or *corporations.* Proprietorships are the most numerous, but because they are typically small, they account for only a minor percentage of total business sales. Partnerships make possible the pooling of the capital and/or abilities of two or more people. The advantages of proprietorships and partnerships are that they are easily and inexpensively started and the owners have the responsibility for success or failure of the business and reap the rewards or suffer the losses. The disadvantages of proprietorships and partnerships include the following: owners are personally responsible for the debts of the business if it goes bankrupt; the business legally terminates if an owner dies or withdraws; and owners may not have sufficient capital to enable the business to succeed.

The corporate form of business organization is one in which the ownership is represented by stock. Corporations, although fewer in number than proprietorships, do most of the nation's business because of their large size. Stockholders are not personally responsible for actions of the firm or for its indebtedness. The selling of stock makes it possible for corporations to pool large amounts of capital. Change of ownership does not terminate the life of the firm, since a corporation is a legal entity (or "person"). The disadvantages of the corporate form are as follows: it costs money to get a corporate charter; corporations are more regulated than other businesses, especially in that they must publicly disclose information about themselves; and corporations must pay corporate taxes on their earnings.

The economic functions of business firms are to identify needs (what to produce), organize production (how to produce), allocate revenues (for whom to produce), and invest in real capital (plant and equipment).

The costs of production are divided into *fixed costs* and *variable costs.* Fixed costs are those that are paid regardless of the level of output. Even if the firm stops production al-

■ Whether they are owned by individuals or by corporations, farms represent the free enterprise system in action. The market structure of an industry will determine the quantity of goods or services produced and the prices charged.

together, fixed costs continue in the short run. In general, fixed costs are the costs of depreciation on plant and equipment and interest charges on borrowed funds. In economic analysis, fixed costs also include the opportunity cost of the owners' capital invested in the business. This is calculated as the *normal rate of return* on investments with similar risks. Variable costs are the costs that increase with each additional unit produced. They are generally the costs of labor and raw materials. *Total costs* are the fixed costs plus the variable costs for a particular level of output. At zero output, total costs are the amount of fixed costs. As output increases, total costs rise by the amount of additional variable costs.

In agriculture, and in fact in industries in general, firms encounter *diminishing returns* with expanding output. In the short run, with fixed size of plant and equipment, adding variable inputs results in smaller and smaller additions to output. These diminishing returns cause costs to rise at an increasing rate for a firm.

Total revenue is the price of the product multiplied by the number of units sold. If the firm can sell more without lowering its price, as is the case with a firm in a purely competitive industry, total revenue rises at a constant rate with increasing output.

Profits are total revenue minus total cost. The output level at which total revenue just equals total cost is the *break-even point*. Profits are maximized at the output level where total revenue exceeds total cost by the greatest amount.

Purely competitive industries are those in which there are a large number of firms producing a standardized product. Each firm in the industry produces such a small part of the total industry output that it cannot noticeably affect the market price. Purely competitive firms can earn *economic profits* in the short run. But the ease of entry of new firms into the industry will result in an increased supply. Prices drop, and profits will fall to the normal rate of return in the long run. Because of competition, purely competitive firms must operate at their most efficient level of output, which is also their break-even point.

A *pure monopoly* is an industry in which there is only one firm producing a product, and the product has no close substitutes. Monopolistic firms, unlike purely competitive firms, can adjust the price to obtain maximum profits. They produce the quantity of output that provides the greatest difference between total revenue and total cost. At this output, total revenue is rising at the same rate as total cost so that *marginal revenue* equals *marginal cost*.

A *shared monopoly* is an industry in which there are only a few firms that account for the majority of industry sales. They may produce a *homogeneous product* such as aluminum or a *differentiated product* such as automobiles. Firms in these industries tend to avoid price competition. They may establish a *cartel* with a formal agreement, like OPEC, or they may be an *oligopoly* and follow a practice of *price leadership*.

An industry with *differentiated competition* has many firms producing a similar but not identical product. Promotional costs tend to be high in these industries, while profits tend to be low in the long run because of competition.

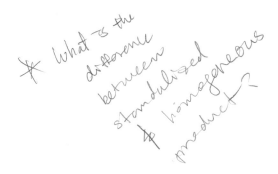

The Evolution of the Modern Corporation

A Dutch East India Company seashore market in Batavia (about 1682) represents the activities of one of the world's earliest corporations.

Additional information about the evolution of corporations can be found in *The Modern Corporation and Private Property* by Adolf A. Berle and Gardner Means (Buffalo, NY: W. S. Hein, 1982 [reprint of 1933 edition]); *Essays in the Earlier History of American Corporations* by Joseph S. Davis (Cambridge, MA: Harvard University Press, 1917); *Great Enterprise: Growth and Behavior of the Big Corporation* by Herrymon Maurer (New York: Macmillan, 1955); and *The Corporation in the Emergent American Society* by William L. Warner (New York: Harper & Row, 1962).

Technological changes in production techniques associated with the Industrial Revolution (see Perspective in chapter 3) are generally credited with establishing the nature of our present economy. But changes in business organization and management have also played a crucial role. If it were not for a parallel revolution in business organization, the mass production methods of the Industrial Revolution could not have been as extensively implemented as they were.

The most important aspect of this business revolution was the development of the modern corporation. The corporate form of business organization actually existed in Roman times, although it was not well evolved. It first achieved some importance as the form of organization for trading companies of the sixteenth and seventeenth centuries.

The Dutch East India Company, chartered in 1602, used the capital of its investors to finance voyages to procure spices and other exotic merchandise from Asia for sale in Europe. The British government chartered private trading companies, such as the Hudson's Bay Company (chartered in 1670), to develop trade and settlements in the New World in order to secure its colonization. Until well into the nineteenth century, corporate charters in Europe were granted by the king or parliament only for special purposes. In 1800, England and France together had only a few dozen such corporations.

It was in the United States that the corporate form of business first obtained widespread importance. By 1800 there were already some 300 private business corporations. At first, state legislatures, like the kings and parliaments of Europe, granted individual corporate charters. But in 1811 New York enacted a general incorporation law providing for corporate charters to be issued by New York's secretary of state. Today state governments grant most corporate charters, but the federal government also charters firms in some fields such as banking (federal savings and loan banks), transportation (railroads), and communications (Comsat).

Today there are over 2 million corporations in the United States. About 100 of them own one-half of the total corporate wealth, and the trend is continuing toward fewer and larger corporations.

FOR FURTHER STUDY AND ANALYSIS

Study Questions

1. Why isn't it a good idea to join in a partnership if you do not know the other partners very well? Does the same consideration apply to buying shares in a corporation?

2. Why would the capital equipment of a firm in a dynamic industry such as electronics depreciate more rapidly than in an industry such as textile manufacturing?

3. What is the difference between accounting profits and economic profits?

4. Why does the total revenue of an egg farmer rise at a constant rate with increasing sales while the total revenue of a monopolistic firm rises at a decreasing rate, reaches a maximum, and then declines with increasing sales?

5. If a firm increases its output beyond the level where MR = MC, what happens to its profits? Why?

6. Why is a firm more likely to encounter diminishing returns in the short run than in the long run?

7. Why do economic profits tend to disappear in pure competition in the long run?

8. Why do purely competitive firms in the long run have to operate at the level of output that minimizes their average cost while monopolists do not?

9. What are examples of firms in your area that represent each of the four types of industry structure? If there are not any firms that correspond exactly to one or more of the four types, what firm comes closest to the industry type?

10. What are three examples of industries in which advertising expenditures appear to be especially large? Are these industries purely competitive, monopolies, shared monopolies with standardized products or with differentiated products, or differentiated competition industries?

Exercises in Analysis

1. Select a corporation, preferably one in your community, and request a copy of its annual report. Using the report as a source, write a short paper on the operations of the company, including such information as the amount of capital investment, annual sales, fixed and variable costs, and profits.

2. Interview the owner of a business in your area. Find out what type of industry the business is in, whether it is purely competitive, monopolistic, shared monopoly, or differentiated competition. Find out how the business decides what price to charge. Ask the owner if he or she experiments with different prices to see the effect on total revenue and profits. Write a report on the interview.

3. From the demand schedule computed for your group's demand for movie theater tickets in the first exercise at the end of chapter 4, construct a total revenue curve for sales of movie tickets to the group.

4. In Exercise 1 at the end of chapter 5, you calculated the elasticity of demand of your group for movie theater tickets for price changes from $7 to $6 and from $3 to $2. Calculate the effect of these same price changes on total revenue. Compare the results for your group with the results found by other groups in the class. From this information, can you make any generalizations about the relationship between elasticity of demand and the effect of price changes on total revenue?

Further Reading

Caves, Richard. *American Industry: Structure, Conduct, Performance.* 6th ed. Englewood Cliffs, NJ: Prentice Hall, 1987. A short book on the economics of industrial organization.

Davidson, Osha Gray. *Broken Heartland: The Rise of America's Rural Ghetto.* New York: Free Press, 1990. Traces rural conditions and the situation of the rural poor in the United States. Describes the social conditions affecting farmers.

Dunnan, Nancy. *The Stock Market.* Englewood Cliffs, NJ: Silver Burdett Press, 1990. A simplified description of what stocks are, how they are bought and sold, and the functions and operations of stock exchanges.

Frank, Werner. *Critical Issues in Software: A Guide to Software Economics, Strategy, and Profitability.* New York: John Wiley, 1983. Covers the economics of the computer software industry, including the effects on profits of alternative pricing policies for microcomputer software.

Giles, A. K. *Getting Out of Farming?* Reading, U.K.: University of Reading, 1991. An examination of the management of agricultural resources.

Goering, Peter. *From the Ground Up: Rethinking Industrial Agriculture.* Berkeley, CA: International Society for Ecology and Agriculture, 1993. A study of the economic and ecological aspects of agriculture. It looks at what is necessary for sustainable agriculture and the effects of agricultural innovations.

Hamlin, Christopher, and Philip T. Shepard. *Deep Disagreement in U.S. Agriculture: Making Sense of Policy Conflict.* Boulder, CO: Westview Press, 1992. An inquiry into U.S. agricultural policies and their consequences.

Malkiel, Burton G. *A Random Walk Down Wall Street.* 4th ed. New York: W. W. Norton, 1985. "Taken to its logical extreme, [the random walk principle] means that a blindfolded monkey throwing darts at a newspaper's financial pages could select a portfolio that would do just as well as one carefully selected by the experts" (p. 16).

Mamis, Justine. *The Nature of Risk: Stock Market Survival and the Meaning of Life.* Reading, MA: Addison-Wesley, 1991. The nature of risk and the psychology of risk taking as applied to speculation in stocks.

Mayer, Martin. *Stealing the Market: How the Giant Brokerage Firms, with Help from the SEC, Stole the Stock Market from Investors.* New York: Basic Books, 1992. Examines the changes in the dynamics of the stock market and the role played by the Securities and Exchange Commission.

Rogers, Kenny, and Len Epand. *Making It with Music: Kenny Rogers' Guide to the Music Business.* New York: Harper & Row, 1978. An examination of the economic aspects of the music business from the standpoint of the performer.

Shover, John. *First Majority—Last Minority: The Transforming of Rural Life in America.* De Kalb, IL: Northern Illinois University Press, 1976. Traces the revolution in American agriculture that has transformed a one-time majority of the population into a vanishing minority—the parts played by technology, agribusiness, and the federal government.

Sokoloff, Kiril. *The Thinking Investor's Guide to the Stock Market.* New York: McGraw-Hill, 1984. A serious discussion of the principles of stock market investment. Less technical than many others.

Thompson, Paul B., Robert J. Mathews, and Eileen D. van Ravenswaay. *Ethics, Public Policy and Agriculture.* New York: Macmillan, 1994. An examination of the moral and ethical aspects of the treatment of the agricultural sector. The role of the federal government in agriculture.

Tweeten, Luther. *Causes and Consequences of Structural Change in the Farming Industry.* Washington, DC: National Planning Association, 1984. Discusses farm size and technology with respect to the causes and consequences of structural change in agriculture.

Chapter 7. Industry Performance

■ **As this** decade opened, U.S. industry was on the ropes, seemingly near death. Productivity was down; many industries were losing out to foreign competitors; some of the largest, most powerful corporations were in financial difficulty; and the economy was heading into recession. But a few short years later, it is making a comeback. U.S. industrial decline and recovery are the subject of this introductory article.

The Industrial Phoenix

Resembling the phoenix of Egyptian mythology, U.S. industry has been reborn from the ashes of its funeral pyre. Like that legendary bird, it has exhibited the power of self-regeneration.

Between 1978 and 1988, the U.S. share of world automobile production fell from 29% to 18%. Its share of world machine tools production declined by half, from 14% to 7%. In the new high-tech industries, mostly pioneered by U.S. firms, the losses were even more striking. U.S. production of DRAMs (dynamic random-access memory chips) fell from 73% of the world supply to 17%, and its output of floppy disks for computers dropped from 66% to just 4%.

For 2 decades, in fact, the world's most powerful economy lost ground to its foreign competitors. Most of the losses by American firms went to Japanese industries. From 1971 to 1991, the Japanese economy grew at nearly twice the rate of the American economy. Total real output growth in the United States during those years averaged 2.5%, while Japanese growth averaged 4.4%.

Ironically, the success of Japanese industry was due in no small way to the part played by American tutors. During the occupation of Japan by the U.S. Army following World War II, General Douglas MacArthur sent for a U.S. electronics engineer to restart the Japanese radio industry. The occupation authorities needed to be able to communicate with the Japanese people. The engineer, Homer Sarasohn, found that of the first batch of radio vacuum tubes produced by the Japanese factories, 99% were defective. "The idea of quality they did not understand," he said. Discovering that the Japanese lacked any knowledge of modern business practices, he and a colleague, with MacArthur's blessing, set up a course of instruction for Japanese managers. Among the principles taught in the course were that a company must have a concise and complete statement of the purpose of the company, providing direction for the efforts of management and labor; that quality is the first consideration and profits follow; and that every employee deserves the same respect accorded to managers, since democratic management is good management. Out of the course came the future leaders of some of Japan's most successful companies: Sony, Matsushita, and Mitsubishi, among others. The course was still being taught to Japanese executives 25 years after Sarasohn departed.

During the postwar period, the Japanese put to use the principles taught in the course and stayed with them. Meanwhile, American businesses were turning their attention from a focus on production to a focus on finance and marketing. Increasingly, top management in U.S. industry came from the accounting or sales departments of a company rather than from the production side.

Japanese managers were more alert than Americans in taking advantage of technological advances. In one case, an American firm invented a major consumer electronics product—the home videotape recorder—only to forfeit its production to Japan. The original patents for videotape recording machines were held by Ampex Corporation of Redwood City, California. In the 1960s Ampex produced videotape equipment for the broadcast industry and attempted to develop a model for the consumer market. Due to inadequate engineering know-how and managerial indecision, it failed to mass-produce its videotape recorder design successfully. Even though Ampex put $90 million into the VTR venture, the company failed to produce a machine that was small enough, reliable enough, and cheap enough to sell in the consumer market. Other U.S. companies, such as RCA and Cartrivision, also attempted to develop home VTRs. Cartrivision even got as far as marketing a model in 1972, but it was unsuccessful.

Meanwhile, Sony and other Japanese companies were working to improve the design and simplify the production process in order to make videotape recorders acceptable and affordable to consumers. In 1975, when Sony put its first Betamax on the market, Japan was on its way to adding the videotape recorder industry to its trophy case of consumer electronics industries, along with audio cassettes, television sets, calculators, and digital watches.

But because of the American automobile industry's great importance in the economy, Japanese market incursion had the greatest impact there. By itself, the auto industry accounts for 4.2% of total U.S. output, and more if you include related industries. By 1991 Japanese producers had captured 40% of the American market, counting Japanese cars sold by U.S. companies under their brand names.

As U.S. automakers lost market share to the Japanese, they saw their profits evaporate. General Motors suffered financial losses of $38 billion in its North American auto market between 1990 and 1993. It was forced to shut down dozens of plants and lay off some 200,000 workers. Further downsizing was expected to reduce the firm to one half its 1985 size by 1995. Chrysler nearly went bankrupt twice, once in the early 1980s, when it was saved by a government bailout, and again in the early 1990s.

The striking successes of the Japanese in one industry after another in taking market share away from American firms shook the U.S. business community, especially Detroit, out of its complacency. American firms began to study and adopt Japanese business practices. In some cases they formed joint ventures with Japanese companies to facilitate the transfer of management and operations know-how.

Belatedly getting themselves in competitive fighting trim, the U.S. automakers began to regain market share. First, in 1992 the Ford Taurus won the title of best-selling car away from the previous favorite, the Honda Accord. Then Chrysler's Stratus and Cirrus took more market share away from Honda. Even General Motors broke into the black in 1993, although it was its foreign car-making divisions and other subsidiaries that provided the profit margin; U.S. car sales were still in the red.

By the end of 1993, the U.S. auto industry had turned the corner on market share. Increased auto sales accounted for nearly half of the rise in the nation's output in the fourth quarter of the year. As of January 1994, the Japanese share was down to 28.7%. Other U.S. industries were also fighting back, some even more successfully. These included laptop computer makers, the semiconductor industry, and even the steel industry, which many observers had written off two decades ago. The

semiconductor industry, which had lost its leading position as world supplier of electronic chips to the Japanese in 1985, regained that distinction in 1992.

The successful turnaround of American industries has been accompanied by problems cropping up for the Japanese economy: rising interest rates, scandals in government and finance, wild movements on the stock market, and declines in asset values. There are also sectors of the Japanese economy that are quite unproductive. This is especially true of the agricultural and distribution systems. Japanese laws protect uneconomical small

■ Chapter Preview

The comeback of American industry was due to a number of transformations in such areas as the firm's utilization of its labor force, its quicker response to changes in consumer preferences, and its organizational structure. We will look at these changes under the sections on: What determines industry performance? How can industry performance be improved? What are the effects of industry concentration on performance?

■ Learning Objectives

After completing this chapter, you should be able to:

1. Describe four factors that determine industry performance.

2. Define productivity and state how it is usually measured.

3. Explain why product quality is important and how it can be improved.

4. Describe why and how businesses respond to social concerns, and give three examples.

5. Explain the importance of investment in capital equipment, why the investment rate is low in the United States, and how it can be increased.

6. Describe investment in human capital and show how it affects the learning curve.

7. Explain R & D spending and its importance.

8. Describe process innovations and explain how they improve productivity.

9. List and give an example of three types of EI teams.

10. Describe market concentration and define the degree of market concentration in terms of the concentration ratio.

11. Explain the difference between market concentration and aggregate concentration.

12. Describe four consequences of high concentration in industries.

farms and mom-and-pop retail stores to keep them in business. As a result, the Japanese pay up to 3 times as much as Americans for food and staples. Rice in Japan costs 10 times the world price because of government subsidies to the politically powerful farm bloc. A multilayered, high-cost distribution system adds as much as 60% to the price of Japanese products. As a result, a third of the country's export industry goods cost more in Japan than in the United States—a camera that cost $380 in New York City, for example, was priced at $539 in Tokyo.

As a consequence of such large markups and the inflated price of land in Japan, where it takes a family an average of 17 years before they can afford to buy their own home, the costs of living in Japan are very high. The desire for a better standard of living makes Japanese workers put in an average of 300 more hours on the job per year than workers in the United States. This includes a great deal of overtime. There are recent indications that the Japanese are beginning to rebel against the austerity of high living costs and long work hours.

As for the United States, Japanese competition actually did us a favor by forcing U.S. industries to refocus on quality and productivity. With the increasing interdependence of world markets, the competitive stimulus and lessons learned from Japanese producers in the 1980s are proving invaluable to American industries in the 1990s.

What Determines Industry Performance?

In chapter 2 we noted that one of the principal goals of an economic system is efficiency. How do we achieve efficiency in production? Why did the Japanese and other producers appear to be outdistancing the United States in efficiency? In this section we will examine those things that affect the efficiency of firms, and why American producers fell behind in some industries.

Productivity

Overall U.S. industrial **productivity** has been stagnating since 1973. During the 15 years up to 1973, output per labor hour grew at an average of 2.5% a year. Increases have averaged 2% a year from the very beginning of the century. But from 1974 to 1993, productivity rose on the average less than 1% per year.

While the difference between 1% and 2% per year may not sound like much, it has a great impact over a period of time. With annual increases in productivity of 2%, output per person doubles every 35 years due to compounding. At 1% productivity growth, it takes twice as long, 70 years, to get the same increase in output.

Overall, the United States still leads Japan and other countries in productivity, resulting from the advantages of a large integrated market, wealth of resources, and the encouragement of competition and prohibition of anticompetitive practices (see chapter 8, p. 192). But a study by McKinsey Global Institute covering the years 1987–1990 showed that in five of the nine industries covered in the study, the Japanese labor force was more productive than American workers. The industries in which Japanese productivity excelled were carmaking, car parts, consumer electronics, metalworking, and steel. Overall Japanese productivity is dragged down by low worker productivity in the food industry, where the United States is much more efficient.

In 1993 productivity in U.S. manufacturing accelerated—a customary occurrence during the recovery from a recession. Productivity growth reached 2.4%, accounting for about half of the growth in total output (Figure 1).

> **productivity:** a ratio of the amount of output per unit of input; denotes the efficiency with which resources (people, tools, knowledge, and energy) are used to produce goods and services; usually measured as output per hour of labor.

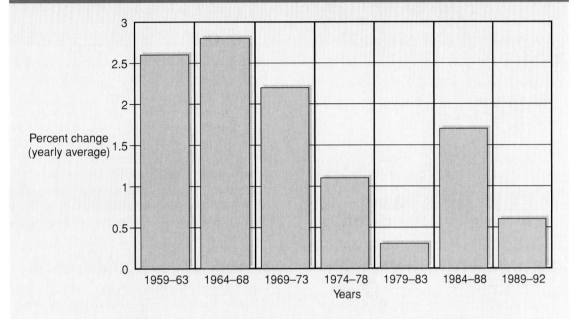

Figure 1.
Rates of Increase in Productivity per Hour of Labor in the U.S. Nonfarm Business Sector, 1959–1992

Percent change (yearly average)

Years

Source: U.S. Department of Labor, Bureau of Labor Statistics.

■ From 1959 to 1973, U.S. productivity per hour of labor rose an average of 2.5% a year. Since then, productivity gains have averaged less than 1% a year.

Quality

In addition to the problem of lagging productivity in the 1980s, American industry suffered in comparison with other producers in the area of quality. This was especially obvious in the case of U.S. automobiles compared to Japanese. The number of defects per vehicle built by U.S. automakers averaged 1.7 per vehicle in 1990, while the number of defects of Japanese cars sold in the United States averaged 1.2, a 30% lower level. By 1993 the differential had been reduced to 22%.

The concern with quality starts with the parts purchased from suppliers. The U.S. suppliers of parts for cars produced by Nissan in this country averaged 2 defects per 1,000 parts compared to only 1 defect per 1,000 parts from its Japanese suppliers. Japanese manufacturers are more demanding of quality from suppliers than their American counterparts. Honda examined over 250 potential suppliers of metal stampings before choosing 6. Mazda was in contact with 1,000 U.S. suppliers when setting up its manufacturing facilities in this country but found only 65 that satisfied its standards.

After Japanese firms choose a supplier, they work closely with the supplier to reduce the defect rate even further. The practice of American producers, on the other hand, has in the past been to maintain a distance from their suppliers, constantly bidding them against competing firms to get the lowest possible prices. Chrysler was the first U.S. automaker to switch to the Japanese system of "presourcing" parts. For its new Chrysler Cirrus and Dodge Stratus, 95% of the parts were from suppliers chosen be-

■ One way that industry performance and efficiency can be improved is by increasing the quality of the product. Eastman Chemical Company was the winner of the 1993 Malcolm Baldrige National Quality Award in the large-manufacturing category.

fore the parts were designed, eliminating competitive bidding.

In order to promote attention to quality by American firms, Congress established the Malcolm Baldrige National Quality Award, given annually. Of the tens of thousands of firms eligible to compete for the award, only 106 applied in the first 2 years. Those that entered, and even some who didn't yet feel ready, found that the standards for the competition brought an urgency to the firm's concern with quality improvements. Motorola, one of the first American firms to adopt Japanese management practices and a Baldrige award winner in the first year, insisted that

all of its eligible suppliers also prepare to compete. It dropped 200 who refused.

Responsiveness to the Market

Producing a quality product efficiently is not good enough unless it is a product that people want to buy. What features does a customer want in a product? When does the customer need delivery? What level of support, including maintenance, does the customer require after delivery? Firms that respond quickly to such questions are more likely to be successful. Japanese producers take pains to satisfy their clients, possibly because their Japanese customers in the domestic market are very particular. They demand not only high-quality products, but good service to back them up. If the car of a Japanese customer breaks down, the dealer will often pick it up, repair it promptly, and return it free of charge. A few American auto companies have adopted the Japanese service approach by offering prompt roadside assistance for mechanical problems on new cars.

Japanese manufacturers have responded to changes in market preferences more quickly than U.S. firms. The lead time for producing a new model automobile from design to production is only 3 to 4 years for Japanese car companies. By comparison, it took 5 years for American manufacturers to get a new model in production. This gave the Japanese greater flexibility in responding to changing consumer tastes and introducing advanced engineering and styling features.

This situation changed in the early 1990s. In the 20 years up to 1992, Chrysler introduced only three basic chassis designs. Between 1992 and 1994 alone, it introduced five new chassis designs. Ford and General Motors also began to introduce new models at record rates.

More and more products are being targeted at specific market niches. Producers in the United States have traditionally planned for long production runs in order to reduce the average cost of a product. Japanese firms, on the other hand, build flexible plants that can readily be shifted between the production of differentiated products according to market demand. This enables them to satisfy customer preferences quickly and at the same time hold down the costs of inventory storage.

Responsiveness to Social Concerns

Another measure of industry performance today is the responsibility shown by firms with respect to such social concerns as environmental protection, resource conservation, product safety, and equal opportunity for employees. To a large extent, these concerns are forced upon firms by government regulations, about which more will be said in the next chapter.

Public opinion and liability suits are also causing businesses to clean up their acts. Polls show that 83% of the American public is concerned about the environment and only 36% think that industry is doing an adequate job of protecting it. The rising voice of concern by the citizenry over air and water pollution, accumulation of garbage—especially nonbiodegradable plastics—and waste of natural resources has led to changes in corporate behavior.

In the past, businesses tended to ignore environmental problems and oppose environmental protection laws because of the costs involved. But in the face of aroused public opinion and legal pressures, corporations are showing more environmental awareness. Some are even taking a leading role. As stated by Elliot Hoffman, president of Just Desserts, Inc., "Once content to focus solely on the bottom line and leave other issues to government, business has become a proactive force on the front lines of social change. This phenomenon is called social responsibility, a term increasingly heard in boardrooms across America as companies—some gladly, some kicking and screaming—take a hard look at themselves and their practices."

One important example of a company responding to the pressure for environmental responsibility occurred in 1990. Under threat of a consumer **boycott** of all of its products, the H. J. Heinz Company announced that its StarKist cannery would no longer buy tuna from fishing boats using gill nets. Such gill nets killed thousands of dolphins each year. Other tuna canners immediately followed suit.

■ Responsiveness to social concerns is another measure of industry performance. Businesses such as StarKist often find that it makes economic sense to pay attention to public opinion on issues like environmental protection, rather than risk being boycotted.

Electronics firms have stopped using CFC chemicals that destroy the ozone layer and contribute to global warming (see chapter 1). The American Paper Institute, an industry association, says that 40% of all paper produced in 1995 will be recycled, thereby saving millions of trees.

Social responsibility is one area of industry performance in which the Japanese have lagged behind. The United Nations Environmental Program has ranked Japan last in overall environmental concern and awareness among 14 countries surveyed. It was one of the last countries to stop slaughtering whales and continues to be one of the worst offenders in the illicit marketing of endangered wildlife. It gives little attention to recycling, and the Japanese landscape is littered with

boycott: refusal by consumers to buy the products or services of a firm.

Comparative Case Application

A Tantalizing Market Feast

With the internationalization of markets and the lessening of market restrictions in emerging economies, auto producers are salivating over the vast number of potential customers in Asia, Latin America, and Eastern Europe. While the auto markets in the United States, Europe, and Japan are relatively saturated, with one car for every 1.7 people in the United States, one for every 2.5 people in Europe, and one for every 3 in Japan, there is only one car per 680 people in China, 70 people in Thailand, 14 in Brazil, 12.5 in Mexico, and 6 in Poland. With the economies in these countries growing at much faster rates than in the advanced industrialized countries, their markets have attracted a lot of new attention. In 1993 new car sales grew 12% in the developing countries while falling in Western Europe and Japan.

The Big Three U.S. auto producers are scrambling to establish or expand footholds in these markets, as are foreign producers such as VW, Fiat, Toyota, and Nissan. But they are finding that they cannot simply duplicate the same models produced the same way as in their home markets. They must customize the engineering of their cars for particular markets: heavier suspensions for the rough roads in Southeast Asia, gasohol (a mixture of grain alcohol with gasoline) engines for Brazil, and engines that take leaded fuel in China. Small pickups that have rugged suspensions, carry heavy loads, and are easy to maintain and repair are needed in countries with primitive road systems. Subcompacts that are relatively nonpolluting are needed in countries with densely populated metropolitan areas. The particular demands of foreign markets are now being taken into account early in the design of new models.

Besides producing cars for unfamiliar markets, the auto companies have to manufacture the cars under unfamiliar production conditions. Infrastructure facilities such as transportation, power, and water are often undependable. Governed by local-content rules which require them to acquire a certain percentage of their components from local suppliers, foreign producers encounter delivery and quality problems. A VW plant in Shanghai, for example, must test all of the dome light switches it receives because one-fifth of them don't work. Supply bottlenecks, traffic congestion, and cultural dictates regarding labor play havoc with production schedules.

In the past, Detroit has given lip service to adapting its products and production methods for foreign markets more than it has actually undertaken to do so. The Japanese have been more aggressive in adapting vehicles to other markets. For example, Nissan Motor Company designed a station wagon specifically for Thailand to take advantage of the rising Thai market for cars replacing pickups. Detroit may be forced by international competition to replace rhetoric with action in the markets in emerging countries as it was in the domestic market.

Economic Reasoning

1. In what respects do automobile producers have to respond to market needs in the emerging economies? Give examples.

2. How would you expect the productivity of U.S. auto plants in developing countries to compare with productivity in domestic plants? Why?

3. Is competition from Japanese and European car companies in the emerging markets of Asia, Latin America, and Eastern Europe beneficial for the Detroit Big Three, or is it detrimental? Why?

solid waste. Stung by world environmentalist accusations of irresponsibility, however, the Japanese government has embarked on an effort to turn the country around on environmental concerns.

As far as American firms are concerned, does their improved social behavior represent a basic attitude change by business or only a temporary accommodation to the pressures? A survey of top MBA candidates at the nation's business schools found 89% of them saying that corporations should become more directly involved in solving the country's major social problems. By comparison, only 69% of current business executives believe that. Many business schools have introduced ethics courses into the curriculum. They have been encouraged to do this by those in the corporate community who see an urgent need to prepare future business leaders to deal with complex ethical questions. The large accounting firm Arthur Andersen & Company is spending $5 million over 5 years to produce ethics case studies and other ethics teaching materials for business schools. A donor has pledged $20 million to Harvard to improve the teaching of ethics. There are those, however, including some teachers who have taught such courses, who are skeptical about whether ethics can be instilled by a course in school.

How Can Industry Performance Be Improved?

Faced with increasing threat of competition from Japanese and other foreign producers, American industries are being forced to get back into shape in order to ward off the challenges. In this section we will investigate the factors that increase productivity and improve other aspects of industry performance.

Investment in Capital Equipment

Although productivity is commonly measured as output per hour of labor, the quantity of output depends greatly on the amount of investment in **capital equipment**. This includes machine tools, robots, computers, and the like that labor works with. Net investment in producers' durable equipment (investment in new equipment minus depreciation of existing equipment), measured in constant dollars, reached a peak in 1979 that it has not since regained (Figure 2).

Real investment in equipment falls during periods of slow economic activity and rises when economic activity is expanding. In order to increase productivity, net new investment in producers' durable equipment must exceed the rate of increase in the size of the labor force. Although the U.S. labor force has been growing at a faster rate than that of Japan, fixed capital formation in this country as a percentage of total output has been only half the Japanese rate in recent years (Figure 3).

One of the reasons for the low investment rate in the United States in the 1980s was the high cost of financial capital—the high interest rate for borrowed money. A study by B. Douglas Bernheim of Northwestern University and John B. Shoven of Stanford University showed that U.S. firms incurred the highest after-tax costs of capital among all of the leading industrialized nations, over 5%. At the same time, capital cost Japanese firms less than 3%, while the cost to British and West German companies was in between.

Financial capital is cheaper in Japan in large part because of their high savings rate. Savings are the major source of funds for investment, and the savings rate in the United States, both private and public, reached his-

> **capital equipment:** the machinery and tools used to produce goods and services.
>
> **real investment:** the purchase of business structures and capital equipment; investment measured in dollars of constant value to adjust for inflation.

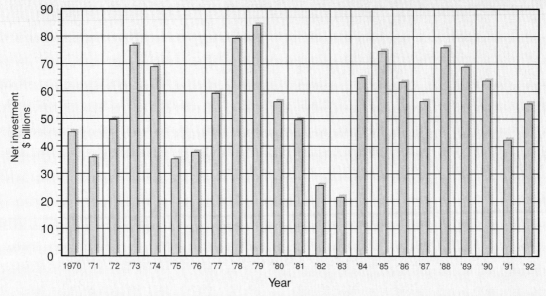

Figure 2.
Net Fixed Investment in Producers' Durable Equipment, 1970–1992
Measured in 1987 Dollars

Source: U.S. Department of Commerce, Bureau of Economic Analysis.

■ Net investment by U.S. industries in capital equipment declines during periods of slow business activity and low sales volume. A smaller capital stock results in lower productivity of labor.

toric lows in the decade of the eighties. (Public savings, the difference between government revenues and government spending, are covered in chapter 13.)

Another reason for the low rate of real capital investment in the 1980s was the diversion of financial capital from the purchase of new plant and equipment into the purchase of existing firms. These buyouts, financed in great measure by **junk bonds** (see "Corporate Raiders, LBOs, and the Feeding Frenzy," p. 181) drove interest rates higher and made real investment less attractive.

The investment rate by U.S. firms also tends to be lower than that of their Japanese counterparts because of the shorter time ho-

junk bonds: bonds that are issued paying higher than normal interest rates because they have a greater risk of default.

rizon of corporation objectives in this country. If American corporate executives do not see the likelihood that an investment in new plant and equipment will pay for itself and return a profit in a very few years, they will not undertake it. Japanese business leaders, on the other hand, are willing to invest for the long term. They believe that increasing their companies' market share by reducing production costs and improving the product will pay off in the future. The heads of American corporations are not in a position to be as patient. They are under pressure from stockholders and Wall Street analysts to show good earnings reports every quarter. If they do not, the value of the company's stock may fall and the president may be ousted, or at the least not given the customary year-end bonus.

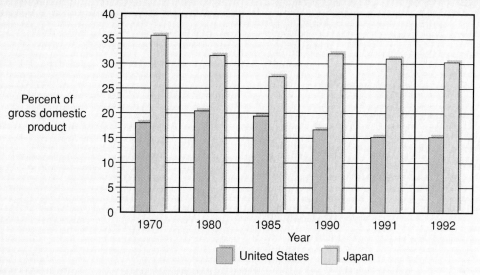

Figure 3.
Ratio of Gross Domestic Capital Formation to Total Output, 1970–1992

Percent of gross domestic product

1970   1980   1985   1990   1991   1992
Year

■ United States   □ Japan

Source: U.S. Department of Commerce, International Trade Administration.

■ Fixed capital formation as a percentage of total output is only half as large in the United States as in Japan, although the U.S. labor force is growing at a faster rate than the Japanese labor force. As a result, productivity in the United States has suffered by comparison.

Some of the ways that real capital investment can be increased, thus raising productivity and lowering production costs, are

1. to lower interest rates by increasing private and public savings,

2. to redirect capital from financial speculation to new investment, and

3. to shift the pressures on corporate executives from short-term to long-term performance objectives.

Investment in Human Capital

Another lesson that American industry needs to learn from the Japanese is the value of investing in its workers. The investment in productive equipment must be accompanied by the training of workers to use the equipment. Studies have shown that investment in **human capital** is actually more effective in raising productivity than investment in physical facilities. American firms, however, invest 10 times more in new plant and equipment than

they do in employee training. According to research conducted by Martin K. Starr of Columbia University, Japanese companies in the United States spend twice as much on training as U.S. companies. A report by the American Society for Training and Development for the U.S. Department of Labor says that industry needs to double the $30 billion a year it currently spends on employee training.

Studies of increasing labor productivity in specific firms have shown the existence of a **learning curve**. A plant with new equipment and new technology will achieve increasing labor productivity for a period of time as the total number of units produced increases. However, the successive increases of output per worker will be greater at first and then

human capital: labor that is literate, skilled, trained, healthy, and economically motivated.

learning curve: a diagram showing how labor productivity or labor costs change as the total number of units produced by a new plant or with new technology increases over time.

■ Investment in human capital is an important way of improving industry performance. At TRW's Rogersville, Tennessee, steering plant, training programs help workers learn critical, technical, and interpersonal skills.

gradually diminish as the learning curve flattens out. The steeper the initial slope of the learning curve, the faster costs of production will drop and the more profitable the investment will be. One reason that Japanese firms are able to be so competitive in world markets is that the learning curve in Japanese industries appears to be steeper than it is in American industries, as the hypothetical learning curves in Figure 4 illustrate. The steepness of the learning curve depends upon the amount and quality of the training given to workers, attitudes of workers toward their jobs and the employer, and the degree of flexibility of work rules.

One of the first companies to get the message on the importance of worker training was Motorola. In order to compete with global challengers to its electronics business, it invested heavily in computer-controlled robots in its factories. To operate the high-tech equipment, it needed workers with higher skill lev-

cross-training: giving workers training in performing more than one task.

els than those of its existing workforce. The company determined that employees should have at least fifth-grade math skills and seventh-grade reading skills to work in its plants. It discovered, however, that fully half of its workers needed remedial training to reach this level. To retrain its existing workforce and train new employees, it established a $10 million center for training and education where workers attended classes 5 hours a day for 4 months. To upgrade performance on a continuing basis, the company has set a goal that every employee from janitor up to the president of the company receive 40 hours of training each year.

Some companies have adopted the Japanese practice of **cross-training** workers for different jobs. This provides a more flexible workforce that can switch from one operation to another as production demands require, detect flaws in each other's work, and jointly solve production problems. It also has the side benefit of reducing worker boredom, a problem on traditional assembly lines where the worker does one repetitive job all day long, day after day.

Research and Development

A statistical analysis commissioned by *Business Week* "demonstrated beyond any doubt" that the companies that were most successful in their markets were those that spent the most on research and development per dollar of sales and per employee. But industry-funded R & D spending in the United States as a percentage of total output has lagged behind both Japan and the Federal Republic of Germany for two decades. In industries such as electrical equipment and ceramics, Japanese companies regularly spend 30% to 60% more on R & D than do their U.S. counterparts.

Investment in R & D may result in new products or in new production technologies. The importance of earlier R & D spending for new technology is demonstrated in a study by Edward F. Denison on the factors contributing to production growth in the United States from 1929 to 1982. It shows that technology made the second largest contribution to in-

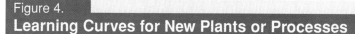

Figure 4.
Learning Curves for New Plants or Processes

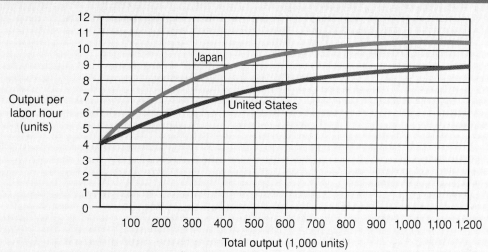

Output per labor hour (units)

Total output (1,000 units)

Japan

United States

■ As more units are produced in a new plant or with a new process, labor productivity increases at a diminishing rate.

creased output. It ranked just behind the amount of labor input and ahead of both the quantity of capital and the contribution of education (Table 1).

The importance of increased private R & D spending in this country is greater as a result of declining government spending on R & D for the military. Also, a higher level of cooperation between industry and universities is necessary, particularly to stimulate more applied research. Scientific discoveries in university research are too slowly implemented in industry production.

Organization of Production

Research and development results in product innovation, but the real secret of Japanese industry success seems to be their **process innovation**. This entails improvements in the methods of organizing production to reduce costs, improve quality, and satisfy the demands of customers. Process innovation can take different forms, such as the incorporation of manufacturing feasibility in product design decisions; the **automation** of production with the use of computer-controlled equipment; the integration

of ordering, scheduling, accounting, and production operations with the aid of a computer network; the use of **just-in-time** manufacturing methods; and, most importantly, the inclusion of workers in decision making, generally by forming one or more types of worker teams or worker-management teams.

Industry studies show that as much as 75% of all manufacturing costs are locked in by the product design. In Japanese firms, the product design engineers work closely with the manufacturing departments to avoid designs that will present manufacturing problems or be costly to make. In the United States, conversely, it has been traditional for

process innovation: introducing improved methods of organizing production.

automation: production techniques that adjust automatically to the needs of the processing operation by the use of control devices.

just-in-time: a system that provides for raw materials and subassemblies to be delivered by suppliers to the location where they will be processed at the time they are needed rather than being stored in inventories.

Table 1. Factors Responsible for Production Growth in the United States, 1929–1982

Factor	% Total Growth
Labor input	32
Technology	28
Capital input	19
Education	14
Economies of scale	9
Improved resource allocation	8
Negative growth factors costs of pollution abatement, protecting worker safety and health, dishonesty and crime, etc.	−10
	100

Source: Based on data from Edward F. Denison, *Trends in American Economic Growth, 1929–1982* (Washington, DC: The Brookings Institution, 1985).

the white-collar design people to have little contact with the blue-collar manufacturing people. Ford was the first American auto company to adopt a new approach to product development called **design for manufacturability and assembly (DFMA)**. It is estimated that in one year alone DFMA trimmed manufacturing costs by more than $1.2 billion at Ford. This helped Ford edge out General Motors as the nation's most profitable automaker, despite a lower sales volume.

design for manufacturability and assembly (DFMA): a system of designing products in which the design engineers consult with manufacturing personnel during the designing process to avoid designs that will be difficult or costly to manufacture.

flexible manufacturing systems (FMS): the use of computer-controlled capital equipment that can be readily shifted from the production of one part to a different part.

computer-integrated manufacturing (CIM): a system of integrating all the operations of different departments in a plant by means of a central computer and a network of workstation computers.

employee involvement (EI): various programs for incorporating hourly-wage workers in decision making; may involve decisions on production methods, work scheduling, and purchase of capital equipment.

Some companies—Lockheed, Caterpillar, Hughes, General Electric, and Borg-Warner, to name a few—have installed **flexible manufacturing systems (FMS)**. These systems, which use automated equipment controlled by computers, are costly—the average outlay for a FMS is $4 million—but efficient. A General Electric plant in Somersworth, New Hampshire, can be programmed to make up to 2,000 variations of 40 basic models of an electric meter. American companies were pioneers in FMS development in the 1970s. Nevertheless, it was competition from the Japanese, who custom-tailor their products for buyers, that stimulated heavy new investment by U.S. firms in FMS.

More expensive yet are totally **computer-integrated manufacturing (CIM)** plants. With CIM, all of the various production operations of the company are fed into a mainframe computer. This provides a common pool of data for the various departments—ordering, scheduling, accounting, and production—where factory versions of personal computers, communicating through local networks, control the operations. It is estimated that more than 30% of Japanese companies now have CIM installed and that the number will expand to 70% by the end of the century.

Even before CIM, Japanese producers made use of just-in-time manufacturing methods. Under this system, raw materials and subassemblies from suppliers are delivered to the plant at the time they are needed. This eliminates investment in inventories, and it reduces warehouse and distribution costs. Incoming supplies can often be delivered directly to their processing area. Many U.S. firms have implemented just-in-time methods in recent years. Some Japanese voices, however, have been raised in criticism of the just-in-time system because of all of the delivery trucks running around Tokyo and other major cities contributing to traffic congestion and smog.

Much less expensive than CIM—and possibly providing even larger productivity and quality returns—are **employee involvement (EI)** programs. These programs provide for worker participation in organizing production. This concept was first introduced in the United

States in the 1920s under the title of "industrial democracy." But it remained for the Japanese to make extensive use of the idea.

Employee involvement can take different forms, from self-contained teams of workers that operate without direct supervision to worker participation in such managerial decisions as what types of investment to undertake. There are three basic types of EI teams:

1. Self-managing teams. These are customarily made up of 5 to 15 employees, who produce an entire product rather than make subunits. Team members learn all jobs and rotate from job to job. They take on such managerial functions as work and vacation scheduling and materials ordering. The Volvo auto company in Sweden led in the use of this type of EI team. Example: Teams at a General Mills cereal plant in Lodi, California, operate production and maintain the machinery so effectively that the factory runs with no managers present during the night shift.

2. Problem-solving teams. These consist of hourly and salaried volunteers, generally 5 to 12, from different areas of a department. They meet one or two hours a week to discuss ways of improving quality, efficiency, and work environment. Known as "quality circles," this type of EI team was developed and used widely in Japan. Now the system is in use in thousands of American companies. Example: A team of Federal Express clerks, meeting weekly, spotted and solved a billing problem that was costing the company $2.1 million a year.

3. Special-purpose teams. These teams are made up of workers and managers who undertake such tasks as designing and introducing work reforms and new technology, meeting with suppliers and customers, or linking separate functions within the plant. This type of team is more common in the United States than in Japan. Example: A team of Chaparral Steel mill workers examined new production machinery in other countries before selecting and installing machines that helped make their mill one of the world's most efficient.

There has in the past been a basic difference in philosophy about the use of labor in

■ An employee involvement program, called "work cells," is in operation at Pratt & Whitney. Such a program encourages participation by labor in management decisions.

Japanese and U.S. companies. Japanese companies view their workers as valuable assets, the use of which should be maximized. Management in this country, on the other hand, has tended to view workers as expensive inputs, the cost of which should be minimized. The nature of relationships within a company is also different in the two countries. U.S. companies have vertical lines of authority like the military. Communications between different departments in a company go up a chain of command to a high level and back down another chain of command. In Japanese companies there are continual communications between members of different departments at the same level and levels above and below as well. This is a flatter system of organization than that of U.S. businesses.

Employee involvement programs have been very helpful to some U.S. companies in increasing productivity and improving quality. A study of 101 industrial companies found that the EI companies outscored those that had no participatory management programs on 13 of 14 financial measures.

Despite the benefits from employee involvement, EI programs have not had an easy time in this country. According to one study, about 75% of all EI programs introduced in the early 1980s failed. Another survey, conducted by the U.S. General Accounting Office, found that among 476 large companies some 27% were using work teams. But even in those companies, the programs usually involved less than a fifth of their employees.

Opposition to EI has come from labor unions and from middle management. Some labor leaders see EI as just a cover for management to get more work out of its employees for the same wages—a new version of the old work speed-up routine. The president of a paperworkers' union local was quoted as saying:

> What the company wants is for us to work like the Japanese. Everybody go out and do jumping jacks in the morning and kiss each other when they go home at night. You work as a team, rat on each other, and lose control of your destiny. That's not going to work in this country.*

Many unions, on the other hand, have gone along with EI in the hope that it would enable the company to compete more effectively with imports and save union jobs.

At another level of employee incentive are profit-sharing and employee stock ownership plans (ESOPs). About one in every six companies with more than 100 employees has a profit-sharing plan. Unions, historically cool toward profit-sharing in lieu of wages, have shown more interest in profit-sharing as a part of employee contracts since 1993, when Chrysler paid an average of $4,300 to its employees as a year-end bonus. This amounted to more than 10% of their annual salaries. And although still few, an increasing number of companies are totally or majority owned by their employees—United Airlines, Avis Car Rental, Health Trust hospital management, Amsted Manufacturing, Weirton Steel, and Dan River Textiles as examples.

More damaging to EI programs than unions has been the opposition of middle managers and foremen. They see worker participation as a threat not only to their authority but to their jobs, and not without reason. Changing from a vertical system of management to a flatter organizational system often means that half or more of the middle management positions are eliminated.

These changes require a total reorganization of the company. The term **business process reengineering (BPR)** was coined in 1993 to describe the bottom-up redesign of companies that incorporates just-in-time methods, DFMA and DMS, and multidisciplinary teams of workers. BPR has as a goal getting the product to the consumer in a short time and free of defects. Indicating the resurgence of American industry, BPR was first implemented in the United States, from where it spread to Europe. But because it entails diminished importance of the traditional bureaucratic power centers in the company—sales, marketing, accounts—unless there is inclusive agreement within the company to bring about radical change, BPR is not likely to succeed.

---

*John Brodie, president, United Paperworkers Local 448, Chester, Pennsylvania. Quoted in *Business Week*, July 10, 1989, p. 56.

business process reengineering (BPR): a reorganization of a company to make use of just-in-time methods, DFMA and DMS, and multidisciplinary teams of workers aimed at production in least time with no defects.

The New Industrial Revolution

The first Industrial Revolution (see Perspective, p. 184) was the second most important economic event in humankind's history, exceeded in significance only by the change from nomadic wandering to settled agriculture. We are now in the midst of a second Industrial Revolution, which also may have far-reaching effects. At the heart of this new revolution is a tiny piece of silicon, a "chip," less than the size of a fingernail. This chip is a microprocessor, which can do everything from controlling the shutter speed on a camera to weighing the cargo of a truck. When linked to input-output and programming units on separate chips, it forms the central processing unit (CPU) of a computer.

The public is most familiar with the uses of microprocessors in consumer goods such as pocket calculators, automobile controls, and personal computers, but it is their industrial applications that may ultimately have a greater impact on our lives. A Kansas City, Missouri, firm manufacturing air conditioning refrigeration systems for buildings formerly needed months of engineering work and production time to custom design and fabricate a system for a new building. Now it can do the job in a few weeks with only one-fourth the personnel formerly needed. It is able to do this through the use of CAD/CAM (computer-aided design/computer-aided manufacturing). CAD/CAM is to the second Industrial Revolution what the steam engine was to the first.

The biggest CAD project to date was the development of the Boeing 777, introduced in 1994. Previously, airplanes had been designed with the aid of physical mock-ups to ensure that the millions of parts fit together. With the 777, the fit was all done by means of an electronic mock-up on the computer.

■ The tiny silicon chip is at the heart of the second Industrial Revolution.

The maximum use of CAD/CAM is the factory totally automated by computer-integrated manufacturing (CIM). What effect will CIM have on workers' jobs? Is the U.S. labor force going to be thrown out of work en masse? Will we see workers riot as they did when machines were installed in factories at the beginning of the Industrial Revolution? The answer to these questions is probably not. Just as the first Industrial Revolution was responsible for creating more jobs than the total number of workers employed when it began, this second revolution will very likely create more than

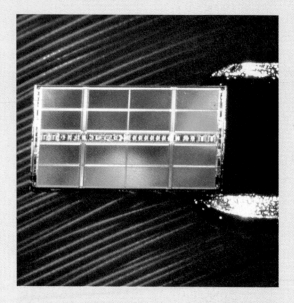

enough new opportunities to offset the jobs eliminated. However, this technological revolution will radically alter the types of jobs available and most likely cause temporary dislocations. There will be jobs in the industries that produce the new equipment, jobs in operating and maintaining the equipment, and, most of all, jobs in a variety of new industries created by the reduction in costs due to CIM.

The transition will not occur overnight. Only about one-quarter of all industrial plants in the United States—mainly auto and auto parts, aerospace, electronics, electrical and mechanical engineering, food, and paper companies—are currently making use of CAD/CAM.

The adoption of computerized automation is slow because of the high cost of the equipment. It can cost anywhere from $100,000 to $1,000,000 for one device. The vast sums of money needed to finance the second Industrial Revolution will be difficult to find. But firms that do not make the investments will not be able to compete. CIM enables companies to produce custom-made products of the highest quality to the customer's order at the least cost. Increasingly, as time goes on, companies that do not install CIM systems will not be able to match the quality and prices of those producers that do, both domestic and foreign.

Another cost of automation is the extensive retraining of workers and managers required. Since only 30% or 40% of the costs of production have anything to do with actually producing a part, the main impact of CIM will be on planning, scheduling, and controlling the use of equipment. This change will totally transform the functions of management. In the second Industrial Revolution, the managers may resist the introduction of the new production techniques more than the workers.

Economic Reasoning

1. What is an example of investment in real capital that is improving industry performance in this application?

2. Why does automation of production require investment in human capital?

3. Do you think EI teams of workers and managers should decide on investments in CAD/CAM, or should investment decisions be left to management and owners? Why? If such decisions do include workers, which of the three types of EI teams would be involved?

What Are the Effects of Industry Concentration on Performance?

In the last section of chapter 6, we examined the different types of industry structure, from pure competition to pure monopoly. Industry performance can be affected by how monopolistic the industry is—how close it is to pure monopoly.

Market Concentration

The degree of concentration in an industry is determined by the number of firms in the industry that are competing for customers. The degree of **market concentration** ranges from pure monopoly as the most concentrated to pure competition as the least concentrated. Reduction of the number of firms in an industry increases market concentration and enables the firms in the industry to exert more control over prices. When there are fewer firms, each firm faces a demand curve for its output that is more inelastic. As a result, it can raise prices without as much loss in sales. Also, the more concentrated an industry is, the more likely it is to follow the practice of price leadership and avoid price competition.

The degree of concentration in an industry is measured by the proportion of total sales accounted for by the largest firms in that industry. The percentage of industry sales accounted for by the four largest firms is the most commonly used **concentration ratio**. Industries in which the four largest firms account for over 50% of sales can be considered shared monopolies. In the United States, these include the motor vehicle, photographic equipment, tire, aircraft, and soap industries. When the concentration ratio is less than 25%, industries are assumed to be competitive. This is the case with such industries as printing, sawmills, fluid milk, meatpacking, plastics, and paper mills.

Approximately one-third of the sales of American industry fall into the shared monopoly category, and another third are competitive. The remaining third, those in industries with concentration ratios between 25% and 50%, are neither clearly monopolistic nor clearly competitive.

The extent of monopoly power in American business as defined by the concentration ratio, however, is perhaps understated. There can be local monopolies that have as much power in their area as national monopolies do in the nation as a whole. Furthermore, the way industries are defined frequently masks the actual amount of monopoly that exists in the economy. For example, the largest four producers of salt account for 80% of salt sales. But in the data on which concentration ratios are based, salt producers are lumped together with firms producing other chemical compounds. As a result of including salt producers with producers of other chemicals that do not compete with salt, the entire industry is classified as competitive.

Aggregate Concentration

If instead of market concentration we look at the **aggregate concentration** of all industries, we see that there has been a dramatic increase in the overall amount of concentration in American industry. Aggregate concentration is the percentage of total sales of all industries accounted for by the nation's largest corporations. Today, fewer than 200 corporations control the same proportion of business assets that the 1,000 largest corporations controlled in 1941.

The idealized concept of a market economy is one in which large numbers of small firms compete for customers by offering better

> **market concentration:** a measure of the number of firms in an industry.
>
> **concentration ratio:** the percentage of total sales of an industry accounted for by the largest four firms. An alternative measure is the percentage of sales accounted for by the largest eight firms.
>
> **aggregate concentration:** a measure of the proportion of the total sales of all industries accounted for by the largest firms in the country. There is no common standard for measuring the aggregate concentration ratio.

products and lower prices. This market model does not correspond to the real world of concentrated industries.

◼ Concentration and Industry Performance

Concentration in an industry may result from **mergers**, **barriers to entry**, or **predatory business practices**, including such illegal ones as **price discrimination**, sales below cost, and **kickbacks**.

In the 1980s a controversy arose among economists regarding the effects of industry concentration. Up until then there was general agreement, at least among economists in industrialized countries, that unregulated monopolies have undesirable effects on the economy and on consumer welfare. One of the most obvious effects is **monopolistic pricing**. With only a few firms in an industry, barriers to entry of new firms, and a lack of close substitutes for products sold under monopolistic conditions, firms can charge prices substantially above their costs of production and make monopoly profits. The Federal Trade Commission once estimated that eliminating concentration in industries would reduce prices by 25% or more.

Another unfortunate result of concentration is **misallocation of resources**. Monopolies keep prices high by limiting the supply of the product on the market. As a result, monopolistic industries have less need for labor, raw materials, and capital equipment than they would if they were more competitive. The resources squeezed out of monopolistic industries by restricting output are diverted to other industries where they are in surplus. The surplus of these factors in the other industries lowers the incomes of the households that provide them. Too few resources are used in a particular industry when that industry is monopolistic. Our resources would be used more efficiently if prices were more competitive. One estimate is that the misallocation of resources, resulting from monopoly pricing, costs the economy between $48 billion and $60 billion a year in lower total output.

Although large firms can have lower costs than small firms because of **economies of scale**, monopoly may instead result in higher costs. Firms in competitive industries are forced by market pressures to operate at or near their most efficient production levels. Monopolistic firms are not subject to this pressure and may therefore permit costs to rise above the lowest possible cost per unit.

One reason for higher costs in shared monopoly and differentiated competition industries is the amount of money they spend on advertising. If advertising provides useful information to buyers, it is not wasteful of resources. Advertising that describes real attributes of the product, where it can be purchased, and at what price is a productive service that improves the operation of markets. This is the case with most newspaper advertising. But much advertising is repetitive and is purchased only for the purpose of countering a rival's advertising claims, such as in many national television ad campaigns.

Competitive firms selling a standardized product do not have large advertising budgets. They do not need them because there are buyers at the market price for all that they can

merger: a contractual joining of the assets of one formerly independent company with those of another; may be a horizontal merger of companies producing the same product, a vertical merger of companies producing different stages of a product in the same industry, or a conglomerate merger of companies producing in different industries.

barrier to entry: an obstacle to the entry of new firms into an industry.

predatory business practice: any action on the part of a firm carried out solely to interfere with a competitor.

price discrimination: selling a product to two different buyers at different prices where all other conditions are the same.

kickback: the return of a portion of a payment or commission in accordance with a secret agreement.

monopolistic pricing: setting a price above the level necessary to bring a product to market by restricting the supply of the product.

misallocation of resources: not producing the mix of products and services that would maximize consumer satisfaction.

economies of scale: decreasing costs per unit as plant size increases.

■ Finding a new way to package a product will help differentiate it from its competitors, but can also add greatly to the cost of the product.

produce, and they cannot afford large advertising outlays because they must keep their costs down to be able to sell at the market price.

Other forms of non-price competition that drive up costs are **product differentiation** and packaging. In differentiated competition industries, a firm will often attempt to differentiate its product in the minds of consumers from that of its competitors in order to segment the market and make the demand for its product more inelastic. Product differentiation purely for the sake of promotion is found extensively in the detergent, soft drink, and cosmetics industries, among others. Differentiation may take the form of "additives," product appearance, or packaging. Distinctive packaging for the sake of product differentiation adds greatly to the cost of many products. A University of California study showed that $1 of every $11 spent on products goes for packaging, and in one-fourth of the industries studied, the packaging cost more than the contents.

Industry concentration may also result in greater economic instability, due to the pricing practices in monopolistic industries. During periods of good business with booming sales, all businesses are likely to raise prices. During times of depressed business conditions,

firms in competitive industries are forced by falling sales and the resulting price competition to reduce prices. This helps to maintain sales and cushion the amount of unemployment. But such is not the case in monopolistic industries. When sales decline, shared monopolies are likely to hold their prices stable or even raise them in order to increase their margin of profit on each unit sold to compensate for the reduction in sales volume.

Against this view of the drawbacks of concentration in industry, some economists now argue that the emergence of global competition has made national monopolies irrelevant. If domestic monopolies charge prices that are higher than costs of production, including a normal profit, foreign producers will enter the market and drive prices down.

Furthermore, they maintain, global competition calls for companies that are very large and also for cooperation among the firms in a country's industries. Small, independent firms do not have the financial resources to develop and market products in competition with aggressive manufacturing giants outside the United States.

According to these economists, cooperation among firms plays a large part in the Japanese national competitive advantage. In the semiconductor industry, for example, such companies as Hitachi, NEC, and Fujitsu are **vertically integrated**. Individual firms are associated with industrial groups in which they have close ties with each other, with large Tokyo banks, with their suppliers, and with the government. Industrial policies and export strategies are devised and promoted by the Ministry of International Trade and Industry (MITI). It encourages cooperation among firms to carry out the strategies.

But the idea that Japan's success in world markets is due to cartel practices in its indus-

> **product differentiation:** a device used by business firms to distinguish their product from the products of other firms in the same industry.
>
> **vertically integrated:** separate divisions of one company producing the different stages of a product and marketing their output to one another.

tries, aided and abetted by MITI, is challenged by Michael Porter of the Harvard Business School in *The Competitive Advantage of Nations* (see Further Reading at the end of the chapter). Porter maintains that the success of Japanese firms is due not to their cooperation or to assistance by the government, but rather to vigorous domestic rivalry among companies in their home market. The Japanese industries in which there is the fiercest competition among the firms in the domestic market— autos, consumer electronics, televisions, cam-

eras—are the very ones that have been the most successful abroad. On the other hand, in those Japanese industries in which there are strong cartels and government restrictions on competition—construction, agriculture, food, paper, commodity chemicals, and fibers—costs are so high that Japan cannot compete with other countries. According to Porter, this is no accident. It is competition at home that has made Japanese companies lean and mean for kung-fu assaults on foreign markets.

■ This recently unveiled wall-hanging "plasma display panel" (PDP) has a 40-inch television screen that is less than 3 inches deep. It is a good example of the innovation that results from the competitive spirit among Japanese firms.

Corporate Raiders, LBOs, and the Feeding Frenzy

Of the companies that were on the *Fortune* 500 list of the nation's largest industrial corporations in 1983, 143 had disappeared from the list by 1988. In 102 of those cases the reasons were acquisition or merger.

We are accustomed to thinking of acquisitions in terms of large, successful companies buying up small, less successful companies—big fish swallowing little fish. In the 1980s there was a lot of this going on, but more characteristic of the decade was the acquisition of one giant corporation by another—big fish swallowing other big fish. Gulf Oil, the 11th largest company in 1983, was acquired by Standard Oil of California (now Chevron), the 9th largest; General Foods, 38th on the list of the 500 largest in 1985, was purchased by Philip Morris, number 27, as was Kraft in 1987, when it was 31st and Philip Morris 12th; and number 54 in 1984, Nabisco, was acquired by R. J. Reynolds, number 23.

In the latter part of the decade, the feeding frenzy increased as a result of corporate raiders and leveraged buyouts (LBOs). Leading raiders such as T. Boone Pickens, Sir James Goldsmith, and Irv ("the Liquidator") Jacobs were constantly on the lookout for likely takeover targets with undervalued assets or complacent managements. Sometimes the raiders succeeded in getting control of the company's assets. Other times they arranged to be bought off by management with "greenmail," payments for the raiders' stockholdings at far above the market price for the stock.

Leveraged buyouts are a means of financing the takeover of a corporation by selling securities which are secured by the assets of the company. Since the price raiders pay for a company is often well above the previous market value of the company's stock, the LBO saddles the company with a large debt burden. By the end of the decade, U.S. corporations on the average were paying over half of their pre-tax earnings in interest on their debts.

In order to induce investors to buy the risky security issues that financed LBO transactions, interest rates on the securities were higher than normal. These securities acquired the name "junk bonds" because of their high risk. If the company did not earn enough to pay the large interest charges on its debt, it could be forced into bankruptcy, leaving the bond purchasers holding the bag.

As the decade of the 1980s came to a close, the acquisition feeding frenzy spent itself from its excesses. The "inventor" of junk bonds to finance LBOs, Michael Milken of the investment banking firm of Drexel Burnham Lambert, paid $600 million in fines and restitutions and went to prison for fraud. Drexel Burnham Lambert was forced to dissolve, and other aggressive acquisition financiers pulled back.

As the economy began to recover from recession, however, so did merger and acquisition fever. In 1993 there were $230 billion worth of deals initiated. The junk bond market was resurrected to finance many of the deals. But unlike the hostile takeovers of the 1980s, most acquisitions were friendly mergers. And with tighter regulations and once-burned-twice-shy investors, it is unlikely that the heedless experience of the 1980s will be repeated in the 1990s.

Economic Reasoning

1. What effect did Chevron's acquisition of Gulf Oil have on market concentration?

2. How could the acquisition of General Foods, Kraft, and other food companies by Philip Morris affect the price of food and the allocation of resources?

3. Was the creation of the junk bond market good for American business? Why or why not?

Putting It Together

A principal determinant of industry performance is *productivity*. Productivity is customarily measured by the amount of output per hour of labor. Productivity growth in the United States in the past two decades has been lower than in Japan and a number of other countries.

Another indication of performance is the quality of goods and services produced by industry. In order to encourage U.S. firms to devote more effort to improving quality, Congress established the Malcolm Baldrige National Quality Award in 1988.

The level of industry performance also depends on the responsiveness of companies to market preferences and changes. Production is increasingly targeted at specific market niches, which necessitates flexible plants.

Today industry performance is also measured by the extent to which businesses act responsibly in environmental protection, resource conservation, product safety, and equal opportunity for employees.

A means of raising productivity is increasing the amount of *real investment* in *capital equipment*. Financial capital is more costly in the United States than in Japan because the savings rate is lower here both for households and government, because financial capital has been diverted from real investment to financial speculation, and because of the short time horizon of U.S. corporation executives, who are under pressure to show good profit reports every quarter.

Another way of increasing productivity and also improving quality is investment in *human capital*. When new equipment and technology are introduced in a plant, there is a *learning curve* of rising productivity.

The learning curve for Japanese companies is steeper than for American companies, in part because the Japanese invest more in training their workers than do U.S. firms. Cross-training workers provides a more flexible labor force and reduces worker boredom.

Spending on research and development has in the past been the second most impor-

tant factor responsible for growth in the U.S. economy. Private R & D spending takes on increased importance today as the government cuts back on military-related R & D, and more cooperation between industry and universities is needed.

The most successful Japanese business innovations have not been their product innovations but their *process innovations*. These include the inclusion of manufacturing feasibility considerations in product design, installing flexible manufacturing systems, integrating the various operations in a plant by means of a computer network, using just-in-time manufacturing methods, and including workers in decision making.

Design for manufacturability and assembly (DFMA) is a system of product design that reduces production costs. *Flexible manufacturing systems (FMS)* enable workers and equipment to shift quickly from producing one item to producing a different one. *Computer-inte-*

grated manufacturing (CIM) plants tie together the different production operations by means of a computer network. *Just-in-time* manufacturing methods allow raw materials and subassemblies to be delivered by suppliers to the location where they are needed at the time they are needed.

A process innovation first introduced in the United States but extensively put to use in Japan is *employee involvement (EI)*. EI programs may be self-managing teams, problem-solving teams, or special-purpose teams.

Japanese firms view their workers as valuable assets to be maximized, while U.S. firms have been inclined to view their workers as expensive inputs to be minimized. In U.S. firms, the organization is vertical, while in Japanese firms, it is flatter, resulting in closer communications. Some labor leaders and middle managers in the United States have opposed EI programs.

Total reorganization of a company, incorporating just-in-time methods, DFMA and DMS, and multidisciplinary teams of workers, is termed *business process reengineering (BPR)*.

Market concentration is determined by the number of firms in an industry. The *concentration ratio* is customarily measured by the percentage of industry sales accounted for by the four largest firms. If it is over 50%, the industry is a shared monopoly. If it is less than 25%, the industry is competitive.

Aggregate concentration is the share of total output of all industries accounted for by the nation's largest firms.

Concentration may result from *mergers*, *barriers to entry*, or *predatory business practices* such as *price discrimination*, sales below cost, and *kickbacks*.

The consequences of high industry concentration include *monopolistic pricing*, *misallocation of resources* (despite *economies of scale*), uneconomical *product differentiation*, and greater economic instability.

Contrary to conventional wisdom in this country about the reasons for Japanese success in exporting, it is not so much the result of cartels and government help, but is due more to the vigorous competition between Japanese firms in their home markets.

An Imperfect World

Joan Violet Robinson (1903–1984)

The daughter of a British major-general, Joan Robinson received an "upper class" education in exclusive English schools. She taught at Cambridge University for 42 years until her retirement in 1973. She visited the United States to deliver lectures to various groups, including the American Economic Association, and she spent a few months at Stanford University in 1969 as a special professor.

Referred to at times by other economists as "the magnificent queen" and "the magnificent tigress," her small stature belied the force of her presence. In face-to-face debates, the rigor of her uncompromising intellectual honesty was a match for such leading American economists as Nobel Prize–winners Paul Samuelson and Robert Solow.

In addition to her work on the structure of industry and capital theory, she wrote on such subjects as Marxian economics (*Essay on Marxian Economics*, 1942) and China (*The Cultural Revolution in China*, 1969).

Classical economists, starting with Adam Smith (1723–1790) and culminating in the neoclassical writings of Alfred Marshall (1842–1924), formulated their economic ideas around the concept of pure competition and its antithesis, pure monopoly. But the world is not composed of purely competitive and purely monopolistic markets. In the real world, industries lie somewhere between these extremes.

One of the first economists to light the way through the murky regions of imperfect competition was Joan Robinson. In her classic work, *The Economics of Imperfect Competition* (1933), she developed a model of an economy consisting of shared monopolies. Reversing the approach of earlier economists, she treated pure competition as a special case, just as it is in the real world.

In her subsequent writings, Robinson explored the relationship of the market behavior of business enterprises and labor unions to the economic growth and stability of the capitalist system. In her view, the desire of capitalists to retain as much as they can of sales revenues for reinvestment and growth is in conflict with the desire of labor unions to obtain a larger share of the proceeds for the workers.

The struggle between these two monopolistic forces, big business and big labor, creates uncertainty in the business world and causes fluctuations in economic growth. Robinson believed the efforts of businesses and unionized workers to increase their respective shares of business income also contribute to inflation.

Robinson was one of the century's leading economic theorists and was considered a prime candidate for the Nobel Prize in economics. Nonetheless, she had disdain for the abstract mathematical manipulations that are so common in modern economic theory. She described the mathematical economists' models as being "such a thin story that they have to put it into algebra."

More than most of her contemporaries, Robinson's approach to economics was strongly tied to the realities of market practices. She made significant contributions to economics by wedding the theoretical models of the neoclassical and marginalist schools of economics to the pragmatism of Veblen and the institutionalists.

FOR FURTHER STUDY AND ANALYSIS

Study Questions

1. According to Figure 1, page 163, what was the period of highest productivity growth in the past 30 years? What was the period of lowest productivity growth? Approximately what was the difference in productivity growth rates during those two periods?

2. Why did Motorola insist that its suppliers compete for the Malcolm Baldrige Award?

3. What is a recent example of a product, domestic or imported, that was targeted at a specific market niche?

4. If the increase in new producers' durable equipment does not keep pace with the increase in the size of the labor force, what will happen to productivity? Why?

5. Table 1 lists some negative growth factors that have reduced the growth of output. Should businesses avoid these costs? How are they related to the socioeconomic goals discussed in chapter 2, page 52?

6. What sorts of worker skills are necessary in order for EI programs to work successfully?

7. In 1992, total sales of the aerospace industry in the United States amounted to $135 billion. The largest producers were Boeing with $30 billion in sales, United Technologies with $22 billion in sales, McDonnell Douglas with $18 billion in sales, and Allied/Signal with $12 billion in sales. What was the concentration ratio in the aerospace industry? Was the industry monopolistic, competitive, or in between?

8. How do monopolies manage to keep prices higher than they would be in a competitive market? Why do they not raise their prices even higher?

9. Do the companies that have the largest sales also have the largest profits? What might explain differences between the sales rank of a company and its profits rank?

10. What are examples of informative advertising? What are examples of noninformative advertising?

Exercises in Analysis

1. From the most recent Economic Report of the President or another source find the productivity increase for the previous year and compare it with the average for 1989–1992 shown in Figure 1.

2. Survey local industries or firms that you know about through personal contacts and write a paper on their worker training programs.

3. Select an industry that is important in your state or province and write a short paper on the extent to which that industry is concentrated.

4. Write a short paper defending or attacking the results of concentration of industry in the United States over the past 25 years.

Further Reading

Craypo, Charles, and Bruce Nissen, eds. *Grand Designs: The Impact of Corporate Strategies on Workers.* Ithaca, NY: ILR Press, 1993. Examines the effects of corporate conduct such as restructuring, plant shutdowns, and relocation on workers, communities, and unemployment.

Dertouzos, Michael L., Richard K. Lester, and Robert M. Solow. *Made in America: Regaining the Productive Edge.* Cambridge, MA: MIT Press, 1989. This is a thorough examination of the performance of American industry and how it can be improved, the results of a 2-year study by a Massachusetts Institute of Technology Commission on Industrial Productivity.

Emmott, Bill. *Japanophobia: The Myth of the Invincible Japanese.* New York: Times Books, 1993. Emmott does not subscribe to the common view of Japanese economic dominance. He points to many mistakes the Japanese government and industries have made.

Fallows, James. *Looking at the Sun.* New York: Pantheon, 1994. Fallows argues that, despite Japan's difficulties in the early 1990s, for us to write it off would be a big mistake.

Helfgott, Roy B. *Computerized Manufacturing and Human Resources: Innovation through Employee Involvement.* Lexington, MA: Lexington Books, 1988. The economic aspects of computer-integrated manufacturing systems and the necessary labor involvement in the technological innovations.

Hornbeck, David M., and Lester M. Salamon, eds. *Human Capital and America's Future: An Economic Strategy for the 90's.* Baltimore: Johns Hopkins University Press, 1991. How manpower policy can solve the productivity problem and again make the United States the competitive leader worldwide.

Ishinomori, Sho-taro. *Japan Inc.: An Introduction to Japanese Economics.* Berkeley, CA: University of California Press, 1988. This book explores the operation of the Japanese economy and its economic relations with other countries in an unusual format—as a comic book. It was written for the Japanese people, especially students, and subsequently translated for U.S. publication.

Karier, Thomas. *Beyond Competition: The Economics of Mergers and Monopoly Power.* Armonk, NY: M. E. Sharp, 1993. A new look at how the current movements in industry concentration affect competitive markets and economic performance.

Keller, Maryann. *Collision: GM, Toyota, Volkswagen, and the Race to Own the 21st Century.* New York: Currency Doubleday, 1993. An analyst of the automobile industry for the securities business looks at U.S., German, and Japanese car producers in their positioning to capture market share in world markets.

Kolberg, William H., and Foster C. Smith. *Rebuilding America's Workforce: Business Strategies to Close the Competitive Gap.* Homewood, IL: Business One Irwin, 1992. The authors examine the way to maximize human capital in the United States with manpower planning and occupational training.

Pine, B. Joseph. *Mass Customization: The New Frontier in Business Competition.* Boston:

Harvard Business School Press, 1993. Technological innovations in production and managerial methods permit flexible manufacturing and service to meet special customer needs.

Porter, Michael. *The Competitive Advantage of Nations*. New York: The Free Press, 1990. The results of a four-year study of the degree of success in global markets of ten countries shows that the ability to compete internationally depends on improvements in technology and productivity that result from vigorous competition in a nation's markets.

Robinson, Stanley L. *Harnessing Technology: The Management of Technology for the Nontechnologist*. New York: Van Nostrand Reinhold, 1991. Discusses the automation of manufacturing processes as viewed by managers who are not technically trained.

Ross, Alastair. *Dynamic Factory Automation: Creating Flexible Systems for Competitive Manufacturing*. New York: McGraw-Hill, 1992. Examines the use of industrial robots to increase plant productivity from a more technical standpoint than Robinson presents in his book listed above.

Rutledge, John, and Deborah Allen. *Rust to Riches: The Coming of the Second Industrial Revolution*. New York: Harper & Row, 1989. The authors begin this book with a futuristic look backwards from the year 2041 on the reasons for the demise of General Motors. Despite this dour introduction, the book's outlook is optimistic. Its authors believe that the baby boomers will rescue the U.S. economy as they mature and shift from consumption to savings, thus providing more capital for investment. At the same time, the Japanese economy is expected to slow because of increased consumer materialism and decreased savings there.

Sobel, Robert. *Car Wars*. New York: E. P. Dutton, 1984. The story of how the U.S. auto industry succumbed to foreign competition, then rebounded.

Stalk, George. *Competing against Time: How Time-Based Competition Is Reshaping Global Markets*. New York: Free Press, 1990. Examines the importance of time management in production and delivery in today's highly competitive international markets. Argues that comparative advantage is now often based on timeliness.

Chapter 8. Government and Business

■ **We have seen** major changes in the automobile industry, but they are as nothing compared to the coming changes in the communications industry. The communications industry has historically been regulated by the government. The pace of change in the industry is making it difficult for government regulation to keep up.

Where Is the Information Superhighway Taking Us?

In September 1993, the Clinton administration released a plan for development of a telecommunications highway that will electronically connect homes, schools, businesses, and government. This information superhighway promises to have an even greater impact on the U.S. economy and its citizens than the construction of the interstate highway system in the 1950s and 1960s. But it raises a lot more questions and concerns about where it will take our society—issues of equal access, control of information, privacy, and others.

Because of the importance to the public and businesses of accessible communications and because of the monopolistic nature of the industry, in the past, telecommunications were strictly regulated by government. From its beginning in the last century the telephone industry was dominated by the American Telephone and Telegraph Company (AT&T). AT&T's dominance was given official sanction by the Communications Act of 1934, which made it an "authorized monopoly" in providing local and long-distance telephone service.

Although the rates charged and services provided by AT&T were regulated by the government, Ma Bell, as it was not-so-affectionately known by its customers, was in continual hot water with the Justice Department for abusing its monopolistic position. Eventually, in 1984, the telephone industry was restructured by a compromise agreement, a so-called "consent decree" that settled a decade-long court suit. In the settlement AT&T was divorced from the local telephone service companies, which were reorganized into seven independent regional "Baby Bells." AT&T was left with its long-distance services, its manufacturing subsidiary, Western Electric, and the freedom to enter the newly emerging telecommunications markets.

It was apparent even then—before the term "information highway" was coined—that new technologies were going to make the traditional telephone business, if not obsolete, at least of diminishing importance. The marriage of computers with new transmission paths such as satellites and fiber optics promised to create entirely new markets. These included data processing and E-mail for business, lessons via satellite for schools, movies-on-demand and electronic games for couch potatoes, electronic forums for every interest group, and

universal access to information on Internet, an international computer network.

The struggle is now engaged to determine who will provide the path over which the information highway travels. AT&T is only one entrant in the fray, along with cable television companies, the regional Bells, which have the important local switching equipment, and others. Some companies have attempted to secure a place in the new industries through mega-mergers. AT&T acquired computer maker NCR in a hostile takeover; and in a no-holds-barred battle for possession of a major film library, Viacom merged with the Blockbuster video chain to outbid the QVC home shopping network for Paramount Communications.

Whoever succeeds in gaining control over the information superhighway, there are serious public policy questions that will need to be resolved. One of these is equal access. When information comes via printed materials, it is relatively accessible to everyone through such free or inexpensive sources as public libraries, schools, newspapers, and journals. But when it is delivered electronically, access to it requires hardware, software, and user expertise that is not available to everyone. Good employment opportunities in the future will be dependent on a close familiarity with the information highway. Inequality of access to it will widen the existing gap between the haves and the have-nots.

Another problem is ensuring that delivery of information and entertainment over the system is not controlled by those who provide the pathways for their own purposes. Could a QVC-type merchandiser own the fiber-optic cables over which interactive transactions take place and exclude competing sellers? Could the system owner charge monopolistic rates for use of the system? Could the owner discriminate in favor of or against any groups or any particular types of messages?

When communications are digitized (messages put into the numerical form used by computers), privacy becomes more of a problem because the messages can be easily captured, stored, and processed by third parties. One of the less ominous uses of information would be to gather a record of consumer purchases for use in targeted marketing, as is done on a limited scale now in the mail order business and at the supermarket checkout. Of greater concern would be the gathering of information on what forum groups a person participates in, what organizations one requests information from, or the political programs that one tunes into. Without adequate checks, all of this information and much more could be easily obtained by the provider of the highway and sold to anyone.

The information highway promises revolutionary changes in our way of life and our way of doing business. But in the absence of traffic controls, there could be some societal crashes along the way.

■ **Chapter Preview**

In the mixed economy of the United States, government plays a large role in the nation's business. In this chapter we shall examine the relationship between government and business by asking: What does the government do to regulate monopoly? Why, in a market economy, does the government produce goods and services? What is the role of government in protecting consumers, workers, and the environment?

■ **Learning Objectives**

After completing this chapter, you should be able to:

1. Explain the purposes of the Interstate Commerce Act and the Sherman, Clayton, and Celler-Kefauver Acts.

2. Explain the purpose of industry R & D consortiums and why they are exempt from the antitrust laws.

3. List the causes of natural monopoly and indicate what industries fall under that classification.

4. Explain how public policy deals with natural monopolies.

5. Discuss the positive and negative aspects of regulation.

6. Explain the reasons for and the consequences of deregulation.

7. Identify the kinds of goods and services that constitute collective goods, and explain why the government provides them.

8. Explain the concepts of external economies and external costs.

9. Explain how the government protects workers and consumers.

10. Describe three alternative ways by which the government can reduce pollution by getting firms to internalize the external costs of environmental pollution.

What Does the Government Do to Regulate Monopoly?

The last section in the preceding chapter discussed the economic consequences of monopolistic industries. The disadvantages for the economy of monopoly behavior were recognized at least as early as the eighteenth century, pointed out by Adam Smith in *The Wealth of Nations*. But it wasn't until the end of the nineteenth century that government undertook measures to curb monopolies.

Antitrust Legislation

Much as AT&T dominated the telephone industry in this century, the powerhouses of the previous century were the railroad **trusts**. They generated a great deal of public resentment because of their monopolistic behavior. Especially angry were the farmers, who were almost totally dependent on railroads to trans-

port their crops to market. Because farmers had little choice of transportation services, the railroads serving particular farming regions could charge extremely high rates. This enabled the railroads to give rebates (partial returns of payments) to large industrial shippers as a means of attracting their business. These and other abuses led to the passage of the Interstate Commerce Act by Congress in 1887. This law required that all rail rates for railroad traffic between states be fair and reasonable. The Interstate Commerce Act strictly forbade competing railroads from making arrangements for sharing traffic

> **trust:** a combination of producers in the same industry under joint direction for the purpose of exerting monopoly power.

Been Rolling a Little too High.

■ Policing the railroad monopoly was the first mandate of the ICC, as shown in this early cartoon.

and earnings. It required that all rates be published and adhered to, thus limiting **rate discrimination**. To oversee the application of the Interstate Commerce Act, Congress established the Interstate Commerce Commission (ICC).

The Interstate Commerce Act was the first **antitrust legislation**, but because the railroads were not the only businesses abusing monopoly powers, a more comprehensive law soon followed. The Sherman Antitrust Act was passed in 1890 declaring illegal all contracts, combinations of business firms, and conspiracies that were in restraint of interstate or foreign trade. Any person who monopolized, attempted to monopolize, or conspired with others to monopolize any part of commerce between the states or with foreign countries was guilty of a misdemeanor.

rate discrimination (price discrimination): charging different customers different rates for services of equal production cost.

antitrust legislation: laws that prohibit or limit monopolies or monopolistic practices.

The Sherman Act formed the basic national antitrust legislation. However, lack of enforcement funding, nonaggressive attorneys general, and conservative interpretation of the law by the courts made the Sherman Act relatively ineffective in the years following its passage. In fact, many monopoly practices became more apparent after its enactment. The Clayton Antitrust Act (1914) helped to remedy this situation by putting teeth in the Sherman Act. Among other things, it prevented firms from acquiring stock in competing companies and it prohibited price discrimination if the price discrimination injures competition. Later, price discrimination that injures buyers was also outlawed unless the difference in prices charged to two buyers could be justified by actual differences in the costs of supplying the buyers.

The Sherman and Clayton Acts were aimed at preventing collusion among firms to raise prices and at practices that reduced competition in the marketplace. But the merger of two competing firms into a single company was not prohibited, and there were many such mergers following the end of World War II. As a result, the Celler-Kefauver Antimerger Act was passed in 1950 to slow down the wave of mergers. Congress was concerned about the increasing amount of concentration in American industry. The Celler-Kefauver Act forbids mergers in which a company acquires the assets of another company when this lessens competition. It has greatly reduced horizontal mergers, but not vertical and conglomerate mergers, which do not directly increase the concentration ratio.

Industrial Consortiums

In order to meet the challenge of global competition described in the last chapter, there has been some modification of antitrust policy. The National Co-operative Research Act of 1984 exempts companies engaged in joint R & D projects from some antitrust provisions. Its purpose was to enable firms to pool resources and expertise in order to spread the costs and risks of developing new technologies. More than 300 research agreements are now registered with the Justice Department.

The government has taken even more direct action by initiating a program to encourage collaboration among the firms in certain industries in research and development. The most important instance was in 1987 when the Commerce Department organized the leading semiconductor companies into an **industry consortium** for development of advanced chip-making technology. The consortium, Semiconductor Manufacturing Technology (Sematech), was formed of 14 companies and funded 50% by the Pentagon. Sematech was important in helping the American semiconductor industry to recapture world leadership in chip making from the Japanese.

In other actions to facilitate cooperative research efforts, the government has created more than 30 research centers at universities with the goal of promoting rapid application of the most recent technological discoveries to production. Since 1985 the government-funded National Science Foundation has set up 18 Engineering Research Centers at universities to encourage academic research specifically related to the needs of industry. Legislation passed in 1986 permits the government's own laboratories to collaborate with industries in turning the results of their research into useful products.

There is pressure from business to relax the antitrust laws further in order to allow for joint manufacturing and marketing activities as well as research. Such a liberalization of antitrust policies, however, could be expected to result in less domestic competition, higher prices, a greater rate of inflation, rising interest rates, and ultimately lower investment. As indicated in the last chapter, vigorous domestic competition among firms in an industry is the best guarantee that the industry will be competitive in the international marketplace.

Public Utility Regulation

There are, however, some industries in which competitive conditions, having a number of firms competing in the same market, would be inefficient. These are industries where **natural monopolies** exist, industries where the market is best served when there is only one firm. Public utility companies fall in this category. Gas, water, and electricity service are examples of natural monopolies. It would be wasteful to duplicate the networks of pipes and wires that distribute these throughout a city.

Natural monopolies arise when there are economies of scale in production that encompass the market. One large utility company serving a city or region is considered more efficient than a number of smaller ones. Because of the lower costs that result when one firm supplies the whole market, the government treats public utilities differently from other industries. It either grants a franchise to a single firm and then closely regulates it or provides the service itself, as with community-owned utilities.

In order to prevent privately owned public utilities from charging monopolistic prices or providing inadequate service, **public utility commissions** are appointed to regulate the companies. When the utility wants to raise its rates or reduce the level of its service, the commission holds public hearings at which concerned parties, including consumers, give testimony. It then approves, disapproves, or modifies the proposed changes. If a commission finds that a utility company has been overcharging customers, it can order refunds to be made.

Government regulation of public utilities faces the problem of reconciling adequate service with a fair return to the investors. Up until 1989 AT&T was allowed a profit rate of 12.75% on its investment in interstate transmission facilities. This was considered a fair

---

industry consortium: a combination of firms in an industry to carry out a common purpose.

natural monopoly: an industry in which the economies of scale are so extensive that a single firm can supply the whole market more efficiently than two or more firms could; natural monopolies are generally public utilities.

public utility commission: a regulatory body whose members are appointed by government to set rates and services provided by public utility firms.

■ Due to economies of scale, electricity is often more efficiently provided by one utility. The utility is then considered a natural monopoly and is subject to regulation by a public utility commission.

return for a public utility, for which the investment risks are less than for other businesses. Such calculations, however, are beset with pitfalls. If the equipment that AT&T invested in was produced by its subsidiary Western Electric and was overpriced, AT&T would make more than a fair return. Also, there was no way to determine how much of AT&T's central administrative costs should be allocated to its long-distance telephone services. But the greatest drawback to the fair-return principle of regulation is that it discourages improvements in efficiency and innovation because any resulting increase in profits is eliminated by offsetting rate reductions.

deregulation: the process of eliminating government regulations and reducing the scope and power of regulatory bodies.

Deregulation

The difficulty of establishing rates that return no more or less than a fair profit on a regulated company's investment is only one of the problems faced by government regulation. With respect to regulated industries other than public utilities, the original purpose of government regulation was to prevent monopoly and foster competition. However, in many cases, regulation resulted in restricting competition rather than promoting it. The airline and trucking industries are examples of industries that were regulated in such a way as to prevent competition.

Growing dissatisfaction with the results of regulation has led to widespread **deregulation** in recent years. Railroad regulatory reform acts in 1976 and 1980 allowed railroads to set prices, start new services, abandon old services, and sign long-term contracts without Interstate Commerce Commission approval.

■ Deregulation of the airlines provided consumers with a wider selection of services at lower prices. But when an airline went bankrupt in the competitive market, passengers were sometimes left stranded with useless tickets.

Under the Airline Deregulation Act of 1978, the airlines were freed to select their routes and set their prices for the first time in 40 years. The Motor Carrier Act of 1980 did the same thing for the interstate trucking industry, despite opposition by the large trucking firms and the Teamsters Union. Both feared that increased competition would reduce hauling rates, profits, and wages in the industry. Partial deregulation has also been applied to banks, savings and loan associations, and other financial services firms.

In a 1993 study by Clifford Winston of the Brookings Institution published in the *Journal of Economic Literature,* it was shown that deregulation of seven industries in the 1970s and 1980s resulted in lower prices and better services for the consumers. Furthermore, the producers benefited as well in increased profits. The net gain to the economy is calculated at from $36 billion to $46 billion a year.

Deregulation has not been accomplished without pain. Some older firms could not meet the new competition and failed, putting their employees out of work. Some new firms expanded too aggressively and also failed. Labor unions in industries where regulation limited competition enjoyed high wages by forcing the firms to share their monopolistic revenues. After deregulation introduced competitive pricing into such industries, many union members were forced to take pay cuts. Others lost their jobs due to cost-cutting reorganizations by the firms. Even customers sometimes suffered. Airline passengers were left stranded with useless tickets when an airline could no longer pay its bills and had to shut down. Bank depositors were hit with large increases in service charges when banks had to pay competitive interest rates and made up the revenue losses by raising their service fees. Families, whose basic telephone service had been subsidized by revenue from business long-distance calls under AT&T, found bigger telephone bills after decentralization of the industry.

Despite these numerous problems, deregulation has in general achieved its aims. It has revitalized industries, providing consumers with a wider selection of services, usually at lower prices. Where prices have gone up—local telephone service charges, for example—the increases can be attributed to an end to artificial pricing structures that do not reflect actual costs.

It is a basic tenet of economics that prices should be in accord with costs in order to bring about the most efficient allocation of resources. If prices are higher than production costs, not enough can be sold to employ sufficient resources in the industry. Consumer wants will not be satisfied as fully as with a price system that reflects actual production costs. Achieving a more rational allocation of our resources is one of the main objectives of deregulation.

Air Warfare

Prior to the Airline Deregulation Act of 1978, the domestic airline industry was a government-controlled cartel. Routes between cities were allocated to specific carriers by the Civil Aeronautics Board (CAB), and competition from other airlines was not permitted. The CAB set fares according to the distance flown.

After deregulation came into effect in 1982–1983, a number of new airlines entered the industry, and existing airlines expanded their services to routes that had previously been closed to them. There were constant fare wars to attract passengers to these expanded services.

Not all areas of the country benefited from more air service. Under CAB regulation, airlines had been forced to provide unprofitable service to small cities in order to be granted routes to service major markets. After deregulation, some small cities lost all airline service.

There was concern that safety would also suffer under deregulation. With cutthroat price competition and rapid expansion of routes, it was feared that airlines would skimp on equipment maintenance and allow unsafe planes to take off. These fears have proved groundless. Although the CAB was phased out of existence, the Federal Aviation Administration (FAA) has responsibility for inspecting airline equipment maintenance and safety procedures.

The safety record for air travel has actually improved significantly since deregulation. In the decade following deregulation, the average number of commercial airline accidents decreased by more than one-third compared to the decade before deregulation. Considering the great increase in the number of people flying, the safety improvement was even more striking. There was a decrease of 57% in fatal accidents per million passenger miles traveled. These safety improvements are credited to advancing technology and better understanding of dangers like wind shear rather than to deregulation, but deregulation apparently has not been detrimental to safety.

Other aspects of air travel have not fared as well under deregulation. The increased number of flights, especially during the popular morning and evening departure and arrival hours, has resulted in frequent delays. There is flagrant overbooking, causing passengers to be bumped from flights. Complaints about lost and battered luggage have increased faster than passenger traffic. And complaints about inedible airline food are louder than ever. Critics of the industry observe that the airlines ignore such complaints until they get into financial difficulties. Only when they are about to go under, as a last desperate measure, do they attempt to improve passenger comfort. By then it may be too late to save themselves.

The airlines know that the prime consideration for most passengers is ticket prices. Deregulation clearly made flying more affordable and to a large extent was responsible for the great expansion of air travel. The Winston study cited on page 195 estimates that consumers have pocketed between $8.8 and $14.8 billion since deregulation compared to the amount they would have paid without it.

But more surprising is the finding that airline profits have increased as well. There were many airlines that could not adjust to the competitive environment and failed, with more than 50 mergers and 150 bankruptcies since deregulation. But new start-ups and expansion by small regional carriers have taken their place. Winston calculates that the airline industry has made nearly $5 billion more in profits with deregulation than it would have without.

However, not all is sweetness and equality in the industry. The nation's two largest airlines, American and United, have had a big advantage over competing carriers because of their ownership of the two computerized reservation systems over which travel agents book flights. Although government regulations prohibit bias in the use of those systems, it is estimated that the airlines owning the systems gain an advantage of $2–$3 billion in ticket sales over competing carriers.

And savings on fares have been unequal, depending on routes. Fares are higher for those cities where one carrier dominates the market. Following deregulation, airlines went to a route system based on hub cities. Major carriers have one or two hub cities for their fleet. They fly passengers from their point of origin to the airline's hub city, where they are consolidated into planes flying to a passenger's final destination. This is cost-effective for the airlines, though for passengers it is more time consuming than nonstop flights.

Another advantage the hub-and-spoke system gives the airlines is more control over prices. Since flights into and out of each hub city are dominated by the airline that uses that hub, it has a near monopoly on that market. At nine major airports, over 60% of all traffic is controlled by a single airline. The effect on prices of this lack of competition is clear. A study of airline pricing, conducted by Severin Borstein of the University of Michigan, revealed a strong link between prices and the amount of competition in a particular market. He found, for example, that USAir, whose hub is Pittsburgh, charges 20.5¢ per mile on flights to and from Pittsburgh where it has an 85% share of the market, while it charges only 15.8¢ per mile on flights to other destinations. Similar differences exist in pricing for TWA in St. Louis (83% market share), Northwest in Minneapolis (79%), American in Dallas (63%), Delta in Atlanta (59%), and United in Chicago (51%). The General Accounting Office found that fares were 27% higher at airports dominated by one carrier than at airports with competition.

Winston estimates that the airline industry is still short by $4.9 billion of providing customers with the value for their money that they could have in an industry operating under ideal competitive conditions. Continued vigorous contention for customers could lead the industry closer to the competitive ideal. Or, on the other hand, continuing airline fare wars could bankrupt smaller carriers, force additional mergers and consolidations, and leave the industry with just a few mega-carriers, resulting in a shared monopoly industry and a return of high fares.

Economic Reasoning

1. Is air transportation a natural monopoly? Explain.

2. What benefits resulted from deregulating the airline industry? What drawbacks?

3. Should the Celler-Kefauver Act be rigorously applied to the airline industry? Why or why not?

Why Does the Government Produce Goods and Services?

In a market economy, consumer sovereignty is supposed to dictate what is produced. Consumers voting with their dollars in the marketplace decide how resources will be allocated: this product or service will be supplied because it can be sold at a profit, and that product or service won't be supplied because it can't be sold at a profit. If that is the way the system is supposed to work, why does the government provide a variety of goods and services that do not produce profits? Why does it provide mail service, highways, bridges, dams, lighthouses, harbors, air traffic controls, national defense, and, at the local level, schools and police and fire departments? This next section examines these questions.

Collective Goods

Among major countries, a privately owned and operated telephone system serving the nation is unique to the United States. In other countries, the telephone system, like the postal system here, is a government agency. In many countries, in fact, the telephone and postal systems are operated by the same government agency. The railroad, electric power, and various other industries are also government owned in most countries, even those countries that are considered capitalist.

Goods and services produced by the government are **collective goods**. One reason for the existence of collective goods is that, for some types of production, it is not feasible or efficient to recover the full costs by charging the people who use the product or service directly. If the good or service is considered of sufficient importance to society to justify its production but it cannot be sold for a price that covers its production and distribution costs, it may be sup-

collective good (public good): an economic good (includes services) that is supplied by the government either with no direct payment by the recipient or at a price less than the cost of providing it.

■ Air traffic controllers are trained and paid by the Federal Aviation Administration.

plied by the government. Since the profit-making private sector is not motivated by profit to provide these goods or services, the government does. It pays for them both by fees for service and by tax money. Collective goods are also called public goods.

Some things must clearly be public goods. National defense is an obvious case. It is not feasible for individuals to purchase their own ICBMs to protect their homes against attack from foreign enemies. In the case of other collective goods, such as sidewalks, it might be possible to collect user fees to pay for the service, but the collection costs would be too great to make it workable. In earlier times, some towns had privately owned, for-profit fire departments. When the fire truck arrived at a fire, homeowners sometimes had to negotiate the fee for putting out the fire while watching their house burn.

National defense, sidewalks, and fire departments are obvious cases of collective goods. Other collective goods such as Amtrak, the postal service, libraries, museums, and

■ The Patriot missile is an example of a government-owned collective good. Shown above is a Patriot missile being fired to intercept a target Lance missile at White Sands Missile Range, New Mexico.

public schools are not so obvious. There have been proposals to turn each of these services over to the private sector of the economy, or in some cases, if they can't pay their way, abolish them altogether.

External Economies

Goods and services sometimes benefit people other than the purchasers. A telephone, for instance, not only benefits the subscriber but also provides benefits to everyone who places a call to that number. The subscriber pays for the telephone and pays the monthly service charges, but all of the callers receive benefits from that telephone as well, even though they do not pay for it. Of course, most of them have telephones of their own, which they do pay for. But the more people that have telephones, the more useful a telephone is to each person. A telephone is a good that has **external economies**; it benefits not only the purchaser but other people as well.

The existence of external economies is often a reason for governments to provide collective goods. If goods and services are supplied by private enterprises, the price must cover their costs. Buyers must pay for the total costs of production and distribution. If people are unwilling to pay the price, the goods and services are not produced. However, there are some products for which the external economies are so significant that their production is justified even if buyers are unwilling to pay the price.

External economies, for example, are a justification for the government to pay for education. If our country did not have a literate population, it could not operate its industries efficiently or provide the professional services needed by people. Also, the public could not effectively participate in the political process. As a result, the country would be less productive and probably less politically stable. Because of the external economies resulting from education, families are not required to pay the full costs of their children's schooling. The government pays most of the costs for public education. Public health services, medical research, postal services, and city transit systems are other instances where services benefit people other than those directly receiving the services.

Libraries and museums are a variation of this type of collective good. They are considered **merit goods**. They enrich our entire culture, not just individuals. Because the social value of such services is greater than the price buyers will pay, the government provides the services either for free or at less than full cost.

external economies: benefits that accrue to parties other than the producer and purchaser of the good or service; benefits for which payment is not collected.

merit goods: goods (including services) that have a social value over and above their utility for the individual consumer.

■ The National Gallery represents a greater value than what some consumers would be willing to pay for its services. Governments often support museums and other institutions that benefit all of society.

Collective Goods and Equity

Sometimes collective goods are provided in order to meet the goal of greater equity. Public transportation, for example, is most heavily used by lower-income groups, including young people and the elderly. This is one of the justifications for government subsidies to public transit systems. It helps to achieve the socioeconomic goal of greater economic equity.

An alternate way to achieve the goal of greater equity would be direct subsidies to low-income people. In some ways, this would satisfy the goal of equity more efficiently. Income supplements might help low-income people more than subsidized bus fares because such supplements permit them to choose the best transportation means for their particular

externalities: external economies or external diseconomies (external costs).

circumstances. The same reasoning has led to rent supplements for the poor as an alternative to public housing.

The argument over which is the best approach, income supplements or public services, continues. The answer may depend on whether providing a particular public service satisfies other objectives as well as equity. It is possible that direct income supplements to low-income families to help them pay for private transportation could be less expensive than maintaining public transit. But it would also result in more pollution, greater traffic and parking congestion, and more vehicle accidents.

It has been proposed that collective goods be subjected to cost-benefit analyses to balance total costs against total benefits. Such analyses are difficult, however, where **externalities** and equity considerations are involved.

Case Application

Private Participation in Public Education

Education is the most important collective good provided by state and local governments. It absorbs over one-third of all state and local government spending (see chapter 13).

There is widespread concern over the condition of education in this country today. Over one-fourth of students drop out of school before graduation. Some 13% of the nation's 17-year-olds are functionally illiterate. Achievement tests given to students in 13 industrialized countries show American students rank 11th in chemistry, 9th in physics (for students who have taken 2 years of physics), and last in biology. Average Japanese 12th graders have a better command of mathematics than the top 5% of their American counterparts generally do.

This situation disturbs parents, educators, and politicians. It also disturbs leaders of American industry, who wonder where they are going to get the workers they need in coming years for their high-tech factories and offices. As an example, Baldor Electric Company installed a new "flexible flow" manufacturing system at its Columbus, Mississippi, plant. Production was disrupted because, although computer-generated work orders clearly told employees *not* to weld motor shafts to rotors, they were welding them anyhow. Investigation turned up the fact that many of Baldor's employees simply couldn't read those orders. At a new Motorola factory that makes cellular phones in Schaumburg, Illinois, using highly automated equipment, just 25 out of 200 workers passed a basic skills test for jobs. Japanese automakers that have opened U.S. plants found that they have to hire college graduates to fill assembly jobs that would have been filled by high school graduates in Japan.

In coming years there will be a shortage of skilled labor at all levels. It was predicted that there would be a growth of 38% in job openings for technicians in the 1990s. The National Science Foundation estimates that the United States will experience a shortage of 700,000 scientists by the year 2010. Currently, more than half of the engineering Ph.D. degrees awarded in this country go to foreign nationals.

Concern over meeting the needs of American business for a competent labor force has led a number of companies and executives to get involved in the effort to improve education. In a 1990 *Fortune* magazine poll of its list of the 500 largest industrial corporations and the 500 largest service corporations, 98% of the companies responding contributed to public education. The principal form of assistance was contributing money (78% of the companies). Sizable percentages also provided students with summer jobs (76%), contributed materials or equipment to schools (64%), participated in school partnerships (48%), and encouraged employees to run for school boards (59%) or to tutor or teach (50%).

In the past, most corporate contributions have been at the college level, but businesses are increasingly getting involved in public education in the high schools and the lower grades. They have come to understand that worker competency in basic skills is as important to them as the contribution of the highly trained part of the labor force. Companies realize that they need to be part of the solution.

Economic Reasoning

1. Is all education a collective good? Explain.

2. Do corporations contribute to education because of the external benefits? Explain.

3. There are those who argue that education would have better results if it were not a collective good but instead turned over to private enterprise, with government subsidies for families with schoolchildren. Do you think that "privatizing" education would be a good idea? Why or why not?

What Is the Role of Government in Protecting Consumers, Workers, and the Environment?

Beginning in the 1960s, there has been a large increase in government involvement in the welfare of consumers, workers, and the environment. The activities of government in these respects are discussed in this analysis section.

Consumer Protection

As civilized society has developed, the dangers we face have become more of our own making than from nature—poisonous chemicals, polluted air, automobile accidents, defective products. And as the nature of the dangers has changed, so has the way we respond. We have increasingly looked to government to protect us from man-made dangers from which we feel incapable of protecting ourselves.

One dangerous place in modern society is the highway. Around 40,000 people are killed in automobile accidents in the United States each year. In order to reduce the death and injury rate, the Department of Transportation (DOT) has required automobile manufacturers to provide certain safety features such as seat belts, air bags, and secure fuel tanks. The DOT conducts crash tests on new car models to determine which ones give the passengers the most protection.

One of the most important government agencies dealing with product safety is the Food and Drug Administration (FDA). If foods or medicines are found to be unsafe, the FDA has the power to order them off the market. The agency conducts tests on prepared foods to find out if any of the ingredients are cancer-causing. No new drugs may be put on the market without the FDA's approval.

Another federal agency concerned with consumer safety is the Consumer Product Safety Commission. It has issued a recall of asbestos-insulated hair dryers, put an end to

■ The U.S. Department of Transportation conducts crash tests such as this to evaluate automobile safety, in response to increasing consumer concerns. This is one example of how consumer protection has become a function of government.

Table 1.   Selected Government Regulatory Agencies

Agency	Year Created	Regulates
Agencies that regulate specific industries:		
Interstate Commerce Commission (ICC)	1887	Railroads, trucking, pipelines, barges, express carriers
Food and Drug Administration (FDA)	1906	Food, drugs, cosmetics
Federal Reserve Board (FRB)	1913	Banks
Federal Power Commission (FPC)	1930	Public utilities
Federal Communications Commission (FCC)	1934	Radio, television, telephone, telegraph
Federal Aviation Administration (FAA)	1967	Airline safety
National Highway Traffic Safety Administration (NHTSA)	1970	Motor vehicles
Nuclear Regulatory Commission (NRC)	1975	Nuclear power plants
Agencies that regulate specific functions:		
Federal Trade Commission (FTC)	1914	Unfair business practices
Securities and Exchange Commission (SEC)	1934	Sales of securities
National Labor Relations Board (NLRB)	1935	Labor-management relations
Equal Employment Opportunity Commission (EEOC)	1964	Hiring practices
Environmental Protection Agency (EPA)	1970	Pollution of the environment
Occupational Safety and Health Administration (OSHA)	1971	Conditions in workplaces
Consumer Product Safety Commission (CPSC)	1972	Design and labeling of goods

the use of benzene in paint removers, banned the use of Tris—a cancer-causing flame retardant in children's clothing—and required that slats on baby cribs be set close together to prevent strangulation.

There are government agencies not only to protect our health, but to protect our pocketbooks. The Federal Trade Commission tries to prevent deceptive advertising. It has made producers of aspirin pills, diet breads, toothpastes, cigarettes, and numerous other products either prove their claims or change their advertisements.

To protect the interests of investors and provide more stability to the financial markets, the Securities and Exchange Commission was set up in 1934 to regulate the stock market. It requires full disclosure of a company's financial condition when new stock is issued, and this has helped eliminate stock swindles.

In recent years there has been legislation requiring financial institutions and companies extending credit to provide the borrower with complete information about the true interest charges and payment conditions. In some states, customers are allowed to cancel certain kinds of purchase contracts within a few days after signing them. Some of the types of contracts that can be canceled are land purchases

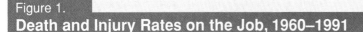

Figure 1.

Death and Injury Rates on the Job, 1960–1991

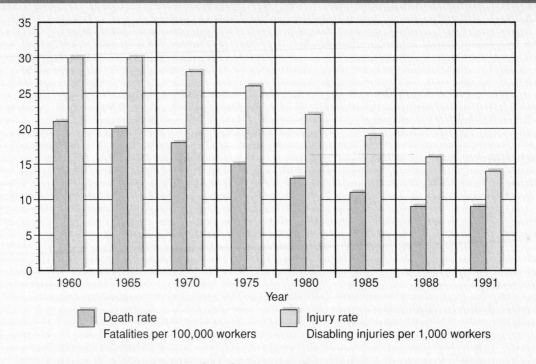

Year

☐ Death rate
Fatalities per 100,000 workers

☐ Injury rate
Disabling injuries per 1,000 workers

Source: Based on data from the National Safety Council, *Accident Facts,* annual.

■ The rates of worker fatalities and disabling injuries on the job have been steadily decreasing, especially since the establishment of the Occupational Safety and Health Administration in 1971. Improvement in the rates has slowed since 1988. The most hazardous industries are agriculture and mining and quarrying.

in undeveloped land promotions and contracts signed with door-to-door salespeople. These laws are designed to protect consumers from being manipulated into hasty, unwise decisions by high-pressure sales techniques.

Worker Protection

Some 10,000 workers are killed on the job each year and 1.7 million suffer disabling injuries. As high as these figures are, they are lower than they were in the 1960s, despite a near doubling of the size of the labor force.

Improved safety on the job is credited at least in part to the establishment of the Occupational Safety and Health Administration (OSHA) in 1971. The Occupational Safety and Health Act gave OSHA, in the Department of Labor, the power and responsibility to set standards for the workplace to protect workers from work-caused injury and illness. Since 1970, the year before OSHA was established, the rate of job fatalities has been cut in half, and disabling injuries have declined from 30 to 14 for every million workers during the year. The improvement in the rates of workplace casualties is even greater than the data indicates, due to more complete reporting of casualties now than earlier.

However, OSHA regulations and plant inspections have been vigorously opposed by some businesses. It has been claimed that OSHA regulations cost industry too much, that they drive some companies out of business, and that they make competition with imports difficult because the increased costs must be reflected in higher prices. The American Textile Manufacturers Institute and 12 textile companies filed suit to overturn OSHA standards requiring mills to reduce cotton dust levels. Cotton dust causes brown lung disease among the workers. The textile firms maintained that the air filtration systems needed to meet the standards would impose unreasonable costs on the firms. But the Supreme Court rejected the arguments of the textile industry. The Court held that the law required only that the needed safety measures be "feasible," not that they meet cost-benefit criteria; and therefore the textile plants were required to install the filtration equipment.

OSHA is prevented from regulating the greater part of the most dangerous industry of all—farming—where the annual death rate is 44 per 100,000 workers, higher than mining (43) and construction (31). By comparison, the death rate in manufacturing is only 4 per 100,000. More than 95% of all farms are off-limits to OSHA inspectors. Nor does the government do much to inform farmers of the dangers a farm family faces in operating machinery and using chemicals. It spends only 30¢ a year per farmer on safety education, while at the same time spending $4.48 per worker in industry and $244 per mine worker.

Environmental Protection

The ozone depletion and greenhouse effects discussed in chapter 1 are only two of the environmental problems with which the country has recently become concerned. Others are regional air and water pollution, toxic waste dumping, the accumulation of nonbiodegradable plastic and other garbage, and urban noise pollution.

As the U.S. public becomes more aware of the dangers of pollution, it is demanding that the sources of pollution be curbed. One of the principal reasons why pollution has become so bad is that producers and consumers in some circumstances do not pay the full costs of what they use, including the environmental costs. Consumers of electricity do not have to pay on their utility bills the costs of environmental damage done by smoke from the power plants. Motorists do not have to include in the cost of running their cars the health and environ-

■ The worker above covers toxic waste with plastic. Adding to the problem of pollution is the fact that producers and consumers often do not pay the full costs of what they use, including the environmental costs.

mental damage resulting from automobile exhaust emissions. Airlines, and their passengers, do not generally have to pay for the noise pollution that they create in the neighborhoods of airports when landing and taking off. These costs, which are not paid by the user, are called **external costs** because they are imposed on other people.

The existence of external costs means that too much of a good is being produced and used. External costs often arise because the environment is treated as a free good (see chapter 1, p. 12). From the standpoint of economic efficiency, prices should always reflect the full production costs of a good or service. When there are external costs that are not covered by the market price, the equilibrium price is too low and the quantity produced too large for the most efficient allocation of resources. Just as prices should not be higher than production costs, as we've seen in the

external costs: costs of the production process that are not carried by the producer unit or by the purchaser of the product and are therefore not taken into consideration in production and consumption decisions.

case of monopoly, neither should they be lower than the costs of the good, including the costs of any environmental damage resulting from its use.

The solution for this problem is to **internalize the external costs** by requiring producers and buyers to shoulder the full costs of production. In the case of electric power generation, this is accomplished by requiring the installation of smoke scrubbers on power plant stacks. For auto exhaust pollution, installation and proper maintenance of exhaust emission control devices are required. In the case of airport noise, the solutions are to require airlines to fly planes with quieter engines, limit their hours of takeoffs and landings, and restrict their flight patterns. The cost of these pollution abatement requirements raises prices to consumers. But without such regulations, society subsidizes the production of pollution. Somebody has to pay the costs, and it is more resource-efficient for the user to pay than to allow external costs to shift the burden to others.

The above examples of direct regulation are the most common means used by government to protect the environment. Alternatives to these **command-and-control regulations** have been proposed as more economically efficient, saving costs.

One way to force an internalization of external environmental costs is to impose an emission charge on firms for the environmental damage they do. These are sometimes referred to as **eco-taxes**. The electric utility industry, for example, might be taxed $2 billion a year or more for spewing pollutants into the air. This would provide a strong incentive for the utilities to internalize their external costs by reducing smokestack emissions. Eco-taxes would be a more flexible and market-directed and less bureaucratic means of reducing industry environmental damage than regulation. The emission charges could be set high enough to get the level of environmental compliance desired. There would be the additional benefit that whatever amount of pollution remained would provide a source of government revenue.

A similar and even more market-oriented approach, one that is favored by many economists, would be for the government to sell emission allowances—so much per ton of emissions. This method would encourage those firms that found emission control less costly than buying the permits to clean up. At the same time it would enable other companies, for whom emission control was more costly, to purchase the right to continue polluting. There would be a market for emission allowances, allowing firms to buy and sell them. As with eco-taxes, the price of the permits could be set to achieve any desired level of environmental cleanliness, given that a totally pure environment is not technically or economically feasible. The comprehensive clean air bill that was passed in 1990 permits, among other things, the sale of emission allowances, which are granted to plants faced with heavy pollution control costs. The receipts from sale of the allowances enable the firms to recover some of the costs imposed on them by the bill.

---

internalize external costs: the process of transforming external costs into internal costs so that the producer and consumer of a good pay the full cost of its production.

command-and-control regulations: a system of administrative or statutory rules that requires the use of specific control devices to reduce pollution.

eco-tax: a fee levied by the government on each unit of environmental pollutant emitted.

What Are You Worth?

How much are you really worth—in economic terms? Putting a money value on a human life may seem callous, but it must be done. The most common reason for establishing the value of a life is to determine the amount of liability in a wrongful death suit. If someone is killed through highway, industrial, medical, or other negligence, the person's family is entitled to collect damages. There must be some guidelines for the jury to determine the amount of damages to award.

Another need for establishing the value of a human life arises when governments allocate spending on safety measures. How to allocate available funds in making highway and public transit safer is a question that must continually be resolved. How much should be spent on center dividers? On improved lighting? On grading for curves? How much should be allocated by the government or required of private carriers to improve airline and airport safety? To upgrade railroad track beds and rolling stock? To increase municipal transit safety?

And how strict should the Occupational Safety and Health Administration regulations on business be? Safety costs money. Society cannot afford totally safe environments. (If we really did consider a human life priceless, we would have speed limits of no more than 10 miles an hour on our highways.) So there must be a way of objectively measuring the value of human life.

There are two methods of setting the economic value of an individual—the "human capital" and the "willingness to pay" approaches. The basis of valuing life according to the "human capital" approach is to calculate the lost earnings potential of a victim. If the family of a breadwinner killed in an accident is to be recompensed, it is important to know that person's expected lifetime income. If the victim is not gainfully employed—say a nonworking spouse or a child—an estimate is made. The expected lifetime earnings then are customarily discounted by a certain percentage because future income is worth less today than current payment.

The "human capital" method of calculating a victim's value, however, neglects other considerations. A victim's life is worth more to the family members left behind—not to mention to the victim him- or herself—than merely the sacrificed future income. Consequently, the alternative "willingness to pay" approach is used in some places. According to this method, an attempt is made to ascertain what people would be willing to pay for improved personal safety. One way to determine this is to ask them what they would be willing to pay to avoid particular types and degrees of danger. This gives, of course, very subjective results. More indirect approaches are sometimes used, such as examining the wage premium that must be paid to attract workers into dangerous occupations.

This method is flawed as well; but taking the different measurements into account, governments have established standards for valuing the lives of their citizens. Some countries use the "human capital" method and some the "willingness to pay" method. The United States, along with Great Britain and Sweden, uses "willingness to pay." Countries that use "human capital" include Germany, France, the Netherlands, and Portugal.

The countries that use the "willingness to pay" approach arrive at much higher values for a human life than those using "human capital." The values established by the former group range from a high of $2.6 million in the United States to $1.1 million in Great Britain. The highest value calculated in "human capital" countries is $928,000 in Germany, ranging down to $20,000 in Portugal.

1. Why do governments need to calculate the monetary value of a human life?

2. Would estimating the value of human life be relevant to determining environmental protection regulations? How? Give an example.

3. Do you think the value of a human life should be based on a calculation of "human capital," on "willingness to pay," or on neither one? Why?

Putting It Together

In the last quarter of the nineteenth century, the growth of industries in which there were a few large firms conspiring to fix prices inspired legislation to curb their monopolistic behavior. The Interstate Commerce Act of 1887 put an end to the railroad *trusts'* market-sharing agreements and *rate discrimination.* In 1890 the passage of the fundamental *antitrust legislation,* the Sherman Antitrust Act, made monopolies and attempts to monopolize illegal. The generality and vagueness of the Sherman Act made its enforcement difficult, so the Clayton Act (1914) spelled out specific anticompetitive practices which were prohibited. The wave of mergers after World War II led to the Celler-Kefauver Antimerger Act (1950), which prohibits one firm from acquiring the assets of another when this would substantially lessen competition.

To assist U.S. industry in meeting foreign competition, strict application of the antitrust laws has been modified by the National Cooperative Research Act. It permits companies to form an *industry consortium* for purposes of sharing the costs and results of R & D. Also, the government has established research centers at universities to promote a rapid application of new technology in production and permits government laboratories to collaborate with industries.

Certain types of monopolies are not illegal. These are *natural monopolies* such as *public utility* companies, which, for technological reasons, are more efficiently operated as single firms.

In the last decade, some regulated industries, such as railroads, trucking, airlines, petroleum, and banking, have been either partly or totally deregulated. One of the principal reasons for this *deregulation* was that the regulatory agencies were in some instances protecting and enforcing monopolization. De-

■ The breakup of the long-distance telephone service industry provides one example of the reasons for government intervention in a market economy and the problems that are involved.

regulation is aimed at increasing competition, lowering prices, and increasing service in these industries.

Some types of goods and services do not lend themselves to distribution through normal market channels. National defense, highways and bridges, police and fire protection, and public transportation systems are examples of *collective goods*. One reason for the government's supplying goods and services not provided by the private sector is the existence of *external economies*. Merit goods such as libraries and museums are provided by the government because they enrich the culture. Another justification for publicly provided goods and services is that such actions help achieve the goal of greater economic equity.

Among the numerous government agencies that establish and enforce regulations to protect consumers are the Food and Drug Administration, the Consumer Product Safety Commission, the Department of Transportation, the Interstate Commerce Commission, the Federal Trade Commission, and the Securities and Exchange Commission. Protection of workers on the job is provided under the Occupational Safety and Health Act, which is enforced by the Department of Labor.

One of the reasons for the extent of environmental pollution is that the environment is considered a free good by consumers and producers. They do not have to pay for dumping their wastes into it. Pollution can be reduced and resources, including the environment, more efficiently used if these *external costs* are *internalized*. Forcing industries to internalize the external costs of pollution can be accomplished by regulating the amount of pollution, imposing *eco-taxes*, or selling pollution permits.

■ The exhaust fumes from this bus are just one example of the pollution that has resulted because consumers and producers consider the environment to be a free good.

The Interstate Highway to Serfdom

Friedrich August von Hayek (1899–1992)
Friedrich Hayek, as he is known in the United States, was born in Vienna, Austria. He began his teaching career there but in 1931 went to teach at the University of London, where he stayed for nearly 2 decades. In 1950 he moved to the University of Chicago, where he was appointed Professor of Social and Moral Sciences. This impressive title reflected the expanse of Hayek's interests and writings, the scope of which includes economic theory and policy, political philosophy, legal theory, social and moral values, and experimental psychology. After 12 years at Chicago, Hayek taught for 7 years in Germany before returning to Austria to live. Some of his major publications include *Prices and Production* (1931), *The Pure Theory of Capital* (1941), *The Road to Serfdom* (1944), *Individualism and Economic Order* (1948), *The Constitution of Liberty* (1960), and *The Fatal Conceit: The Errors of Socialism* (1989).

According to an old saying, "The road to hell is paved with good intentions." According to Friedrich von Hayek, the Nobel Prize–winning economist, the road to totalitarian slavery is paved with government planning. His views have gained a wide following, and *Business Week* magazine has referred to him as "the intellectual godfather of today's conservative economics."

It was Hayek's work in theoretical economics dating back to the 1930s that earned him the Nobel Prize in 1974, but he is best known for his 1944 book on political philosophy, *The Road to Serfdom.* In that book he warns of the dangers of government intervention in the economy. He maintains that government planning and economic control are incompatible with competition and individualism. If the government attempts to manipulate the economy to achieve some objective such as greater equity, says Hayek, it will increasingly resort to totalitarian measures until all freedom is lost and democracy is extinguished.

In later writings, Hayek has labeled those who advocate collectivist ideas and urge government intervention in the economy as "constructivists." Constructivists are those who think that society can consciously devise policies and programs to change the way the economic system works and achieve certain goals. Constructivist programs do not work, according to Hayek, because they ignore fundamental rules of behavior that have evolved in society over a long period of time. Disregarding these rules, which have enabled existing societies to survive and prosper, will lead to social and economic decline. Hayek believes in an economic Darwinism by which the fittest have survived.

In his last book, *The Fatal Conceit: The Errors of Socialism,* published when he was 89, Hayek states that man's "fatal conceit" is his belief that he "is able to shape the world around him according to his wishes."

Hayek is not altogether dogmatic, however, in his opposition to government regulations and programs. In *The Road to Serfdom* he allows that some types of government intervention might be justified as long as they do not unduly diminish competition.

"The only question here," Hayek wrote, "is whether in the particular instance the advantages gained are greater than the social costs they impose."

In other words, Hayek would apply a type of cost-benefit analysis to any regulation.

FOR FURTHER STUDY AND ANALYSIS

Study Questions

1. How did the monopolistic practices of the railroads in the nineteenth century frustrate the functioning of a free market?

2. How did the various laws passed by the federal government deal with the monopolistic abuses of certain industries?

3. Would you agree or disagree with the statement, "Once a natural monopoly, always a natural monopoly"? Why?

4. How are natural monopolies, such as utility companies, prevented from indulging in monopolistic practices?

5. Why should investors in utility companies be guaranteed a fair return on their investments? How would a fair return be determined?

6. Have you used any public goods (services) in the past week? What are they? Could you have obtained them from the private sector?

7. Why does the government subsidize public transportation when most people do not use it?

8. What would happen if the government got out of the lighthouse business? Would lighthouses be provided by private industry?

9. What are some external economies derived from goods or services that you have benefited from but have not used or paid for yourself?

10. Prior to the 1970s, it was common practice for utility companies to give discounts on quantity consumption by large users of electrical power, thus promoting increased power consumption. Today, utility companies give their lowest rates to their smallest consumers—thereby promoting conservation of electrical power. Why do you think this reversal of policy has taken place?

Exercises in Analysis

1. Long-distance telephone companies may charge different rates for phone calls at different times of the day. Does this practice reflect price discrimination? Defend your answer with facts and logic.

2. Locate at least five business firms in your community that have had to internalize previously external costs. What effects did these newly internalized costs have on profits and on the prices charged for the companies' goods or services?

3. Use your library or media center to research the history of federal government regulations in the past year. List any new regulations that went into effect and any older regulations that were dropped.

4. Investigate the operations of the nearest mass transit system. How is it funded? What percentage of costs comes from fares? What percentage from subsidies? From what level of government do the subsidies come? What is the financial condition of the mass transit system you have investigated?

Further Reading

Asch, Peter. *Consumer Safety Regulation: Putting a Price on Life and Limb*. New York: Oxford University Press, 1988. A technical treatment of the need for public protection and policies to provide it.

Barrows, Paul. *The Economic Theory of Pollution Control*. Cambridge, MA: The MIT Press, 1980. Discusses external costs, market failure, and pollution control policies.

Harrison, Bennett, and Barry Bluestone. *The Great U-Turn: Corporate Restructuring and the Polarizing of America*. New York: Basic Books, 1988. Examines what has happened to American business and living standards in recent years, the reasons for U.S. economic reversals, and the role of government in turning the economy around.

Irwin, Manley Rutherford. *Telecommunications America: Markets without Boundaries*. Westport, CT: Quorum Books, 1984. Takes the position that technology and government regulation are not compatible, and that "the world of regulation and the world of technology stand in sharp contrast" (p. 125).

MacAvoy, Paul W. *Industry Regulation and the Performance of the American Economy*. New York: W. W. Norton, 1992. The effects of regulation and how deregulation in the 1970s and 1980s changed industry performance.

Marine, April. *Internet: Getting Started*. Englewood Cliffs, NJ: PTR Prentice Hall, 1993. An introduction to the ultimate information network. How to access the network to communicate and to search databases.

Murray, Denise E. *Conversation for Action: The Computer Terminal as Medium of Communication*. Philadelphia: J. Benjamins, 1991. Examines how interpersonal communications can be handled through computers to accomplish objectives.

Petulla, Joseph M. *Environmental Protection in the United States*. San Francisco: San Francisco Study Center, 1987. Reviews the history of environmental protection, the roles of industry and government in environmental protection, the problems associated with it, and what can be done.

Samuels, Sheldon W., ed. *The Environment of the Workplace and Human Values*. New York: Alan R. Liss, 1986. Various dimensions of the health conditions of workplaces are considered from labor, business, legal, moral, economic, and political viewpoints.

Sigler, Jay A., and Joseph E. Murphy, eds. *Corporate Lawbreaking and Interactive Compliance: Resolving the Regulation-Deregulation Dichotomy*. New York: Quorum Books, 1991. Examines the legal and criminal aspects of corporations violating statutes and regulations, and how society is affected by such corporate behavior.

■ **Measured by** its contributions to the output of business and to the income of households, labor is the most important factor of production. There-fore, labor problems are of great concern to the economy. The introductory article deals with a con-troversial aspect of the labor market.

Immigrants—Part of the Problem or Part of the Solution?

There are over 600,000 immigrants admitted to the United States each year. Most of them need jobs, and they also need public services such as health care, schools, transportation fa-cilities, and other collective goods. In addition to the legal immigrants, there are annually an-other half-million or so illegal immigrants for whom there is no accounting and little control.

An estimated 60% of the illegals enter by crossing the Mexican border, sometimes with the help of a "coyote" who is paid to sneak them across and transport them to a city where they can disappear into the Mexican barrio. Some of the remainder are illegally landed from boats, but most enter the country on temporary visitor visas and then simply disappear. When the Immigration and Natu-ralization Service (INS) computerized its rec-ords, it found that of the approximately 10 million visitors who arrive each year, there was no record of some 2 million of them hav-ing departed. How many of those that over-stay their visas become illegal residents no one knows.

Concern over illegal immigration led to the passage of the Immigration Reform and Control Act (IRCA) of 1986. The law was counted on to reduce illegal immigration by providing that employers could be fined for knowingly hiring an illegal alien. The penal-ties were stiff—from $250 to $10,000—and employers were required to keep accurate rec-ords of the citizenship documentation of every worker hired or face additional fines of up to $1,000 for each incomplete record.

At the same time, IRCA provided amnesty to 3 million illegal aliens already in the coun-try who could prove that they had been here for a period of time. This provision was im-portant to farm owners, fruit and vegetable growers in particular, who complained that they could not operate without the low-cost immigrant farm workers.

The first 2 years after the passage of IRCA there was a decline in the numbers of new illegal immigrants. But when it became apparent that there was not effective enforce-ment of the employment provisions of the law, illegal immigration climbed back to previous levels. It is estimated that there are again be-tween 2 million and 4 million illegals in the country.

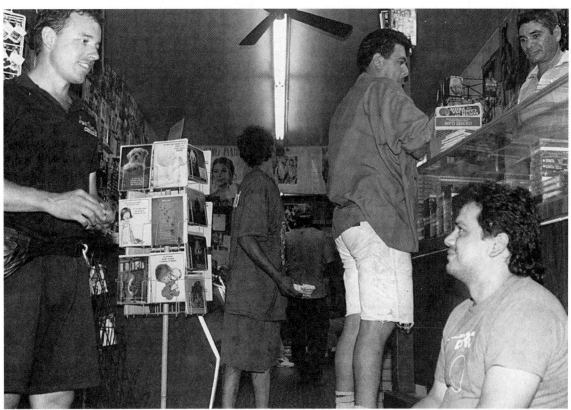

■ In the late seventeenth century, persecuted Huguenots came from France to the New World. Today, Mexican, Peruvian, and Cuban immigrants own many of the shops and restaurants on Huguenot Street in New Rochelle, New York. According to the U.S. Bureau of Labor Statistics, the number of job openings in this country will increase 19.2% by the end of the century, while the labor force will increase only 17.8%. The bureau predicts severe labor shortages in such sectors as health care, retailing, and business support services.

The current surge of immigrants, legal and illegal, is the largest in our history in total numbers. The nearest comparable period was 1901–1910, when there was an inflow averaging 879,500 per year. As a percentage of the population, however, immigration is much smaller now than it was then. During that first decade of the century, the number of immigrants each year averaged more than 1% of the population. Today it is less than half that.

The concerns about immigration are that the immigrants take jobs from native-born workers, put downward pressure on wages, and increase the cost of public services. It was such considerations that led to the passage of IRCA. The bill was backed by labor unions, fearful that immigrants willing to work for low wages deprive union members of jobs and make it more difficult to get pay raises.

What is the validity of these concerns? A number of studies have been done and are summarized by Julian Simon in *The Economic Consequences of Immigration*. (See Further Reading. Chapters 5 and 12 of Simon's book are particularly relevant.) The studies generally conclude that immigrants generate as many new jobs as the number of jobs that they occupy, that their effect on wages is small or nonexistent, and that they pay more in federal, Social Security, state, and local taxes than the amount they cost in social services.

Some recent studies, however, have come to different conclusions. Donald Huddle of Rice University has calculated that immigrants—legal and illegal together—receive over twice as much in government services as they pay in taxes. Another study by George Borjas of the

University of California, San Diego, finds that the earnings of immigrants compared to native-born workers have been declining. Whereas in 1970 the average earnings of immigrants were 3% higher than those of the native-born, by 1990 they were earning 16% less and paying correspondingly less in taxes. But with respect to the impact of immigration on native-born workers, Borjas finds not "a single shred of evidence" that American workers suffer as a result of immigration.

Rather than being part of the problem, immigrants may, on the other hand, be part of the solution to our production problems in coming years. According to the U.S. Bureau of Labor Statistics, the number of job openings in this country will increase 19.2% by the end of the century, while the labor force will increase only 17.8%. The bureau predicts severe labor shortages in such sectors as health care, retailing, and business support services.

Immigration can help to close the gap between the needs for labor and the supply of native-born workers available. But there is a call for changing the criteria by which immigrants are selected for admission. Since 1952, immigration laws have given preference to the relatives of current residents—the spouses, children, and siblings of earlier immigrants. Upon becoming citizens, they in turn bring in their families.

It is proposed that, to meet the nation's occupational needs and increase productivity, immigration policies be altered to favor those with skills that are in short supply, as Canada and Australia have done. Currently only about 140,000 out of the 810,000 visas granted annually by the United States are awarded on the basis of the applicant's education and abilities.

Although the studies cited above show that immigrants have little direct effect on wage rates, there may be a long-term effect on labor productivity and wages. An expanding labor supply means that there is less incentive for companies to invest in labor-saving equipment. As a result, labor productivity and wages do not increase as rapidly as if there were more investment. In Japan, with an aging population—the oldest industrial labor force in the world by the end of the century—and little immigration, there will be much worse labor shortages than in the United States. Japanese companies are expected to compensate by increasing their investment rate above its already high level.

Another aspect of immigration is the impact of a growing population on crowding and the environment. Although the population density of the United States is only about two-thirds of the world average, the Zero Population Growth organization and others concerned with protecting the environment are opposed to immigration because of negative effects on the quality of life.

■ Chapter Preview

The effect of immigrant labor on the economy is a subject of continuing debate. To help understand how immigration and various other forces affect income distribution, we will examine the following questions: What determines wages? What determines other incomes? What causes unequal distribution of income? Who is poor in the United States?

■ Learning Objectives

After completing this chapter, you should be able to:

1. Explain what determines the demand for and supply of labor and how demand and supply influence wages.

2. Discuss how capital availability affects labor demand and wages.

3. Describe the effects of minimum wage laws.

4. Explain what labor unions do.

5. Explain what "sticky" wages are and discuss their impacts in labor markets.

6. Describe the different income sources that make up the functional distribution of income.

7. Identify the unique characteristics of the determination of rent compared to the determination of other sources of income.

8. Describe how the personal distribution of income is measured, how it has changed over time, and how the distribution is shown on a Lorenz curve.

9. Describe the causes of unequal distribution of personal income.

10. Explain how poverty is defined and describe the programs for reducing poverty.

What Determines Wages?

Wages, the price of labor services, are determined in much the same way other prices are determined—by demand and supply. But many factors enter into this determination, including the amount of capital goods available, natural resources, the level of technology, the education and training of the labor force, and the number of workers in the labor force.

▨ Derived Demand

The demand for labor services is a **derived demand** because it is dependent upon consumer demand for goods and services. For example, as the consumer demand for electronic

products increases or decreases, the demand for parts-assembly labor shifts as well. The demand for labor to pick crops depends on the consumer demand for fruits and vegetables. The demand for restaurant workers depends on desires of consumers to go out to eat and how much income they have to satisfy those desires.

▨ Labor Supply

If there is a large supply of unskilled workers as a result of illegal immigration, wages tend to be lower in agriculture, restaurant and hotel service, parts-assembly work, and other unskilled and semiskilled occupations. The effect of immigrant labor on the agricultural labor supply and farm wages is illustrated in Figure 1, where the number of workers hired in agriculture is on the bottom axis and the farm workers' wage is on the vertical axis. The figures are hypothetical.

derived demand: the demand for a factor of production, not because it directly provides utility, but because it is needed to produce finished products that do provide utility.

Figure 1.

Effect on Wages of an Increase in the Labor Supply

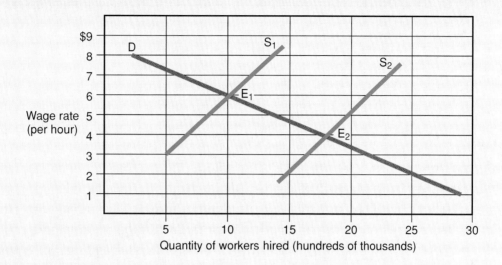

■ The equilibrium wage is determined by labor demand and supply. Other things remaining the same, the addition of immigrant workers to the labor supply shifts the supply curve from S_1 to S_2 and lowers the equilibrium wage rate from E_1 to E_2.

The demand for labor in agriculture is derived from the demand for farm produce and also depends on the productivity of the workers. The supply of native farm labor is shown by S_1. With this limited supply, the wage rate in agriculture would be $6 an hour. Immigrant labor inflow increases the supply to S_2. This results in an equilibrium wage rate of $4 an hour, other things remaining the same.

However, if the studies referred to in the introductory article are correct in finding that wages are not lowered by an increase in immigrant labor, other things do not remain the same. For one thing, there will be an increase in the demand for food as a result of the larger population. This explains part but not all of an upward shift in demand, since the new agricultural workers produce more food than they and their families eat. An additional cause of increasing demand for agricultural labor may be an increase in food exports as prices are reduced.

The demand for immigrant labor is also increased by the number of immigrants who start small businesses, including farms. The proportion of immigrants that start their own businesses is larger than that for the population as a whole.

But the main reason immigrant labor does not result in lower wages is that, by spending their income on a wide variety of goods and services, the immigrant workers increase the incomes of other workers, who in turn spend more on food and other products.

The increase in demand resulting from immigration is shown in Figure 2. Demand shifts from D_1 to D_2, offsetting most of the effect on wages from the increase in labor supply. There is a small net reduction in agricultural wages from $6 an hour to $5.50 an hour. (The figures, again, are hypothetical.) This outcome is in accord with some studies that show that the effect of additional new immigrants on wages is a small reduction in the income of the immigrants that preceded them.

Figure 2.

Net Effect on Wages of an Increase in Labor Supply and Demand

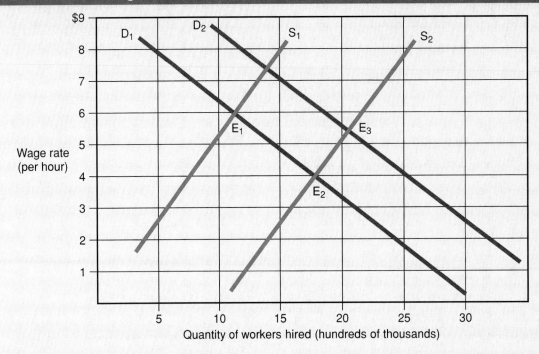

■ Immigration increases the demand for labor as well as the supply. As the result of a shift in demand from D_1 to D_2, the equilibrium wage rate in the labor market in which the immigrants are employed is E_3, a 50-cent reduction from the wage rate before immigration. Wages overall in the economy are not reduced as a result of immigration because of the increase in demand for other goods and services.

This does not result in an overall reduction in incomes because of the increased demand for goods and services generated by the immigrants.

Capital Available

The amount and quality of capital goods available in an industry affect the wages workers are paid. The tools, machines, and other capital goods labor has to work with are a major determinant of labor productivity and wages. In modern industrial plants this capital equipment is frequently controlled by computers (see chapter 7, p. 172). Such automation increases labor productivity and makes the workers more valu-

net value: the market value of a worker's output after subtracting the other production costs, such as raw materials.

able. As automation increases a worker's productivity, more workers will be demanded by industries. More workers will be hired so long as the **net value** of an additional worker's output exceeds the wage rate.

If there is a shortage of labor in an industry and wages increase, firms in the industry find it profitable to invest more in laborsaving equipment. In coming years the shortage of labor in Japan will likely bring about a change in the competitive relationship between U.S. and Japanese industries. In earlier times, Japanese producers depended on low-wage labor to be competitive. Now, and to an even greater extent in the future, increasing investment in automation by Japanese firms to compensate for the declining availability of new workers will raise the productivity of workers and their wages. Japan will depend more on

■ Children were a source of cheap labor shortly after the Industrial Revolution began. They often worked 72-hour weeks at low pay until passage of the Fair Labor Standards Act of 1938 prohibited such practices.

capital-intensive, high-wage, high-productivity industries to be competitive.

Minimum wage laws are also a stimulus for producers to substitute capital equipment for labor. If the minimum wage is higher than the net value of worker output in an industry, the number of workers employed in the industry will be reduced. When it is possible to offset the higher labor price by increased investment in capital equipment, labor productivity will rise. The current low level of minimum wages provides little incentive for employers to invest in capital equipment if there is a sufficient supply of unskilled labor available.

Unions

Labor unions affect wages, although perhaps not as much as people think. Through **collec-** **tive bargaining**, the unions negotiate better wages and working conditions. Collective bargaining was established as the basis of labor-management relations by the National Labor Relations Act in 1935, generally referred to as the Wagner Act. This law states that employers cannot "interfere with, restrain, or coerce employees," or "dominate or interfere with the formation or administration of any labor organization or contribute financial support to it." Employers are also forbidden to discriminate

minimum wage laws: federal or state laws that prohibit employers from paying less than a specified hourly wage to their employees.

collective bargaining: a process by which decisions regarding the wages, hours, and conditions of employment are determined by the interaction of workers acting through their unions and employers.

Table 1.   Legislation Concerning Labor

Legislation (Year enacted)	Provisions
Clayton Act (1914)	Exempts labor organizations from antitrust law prohibitions against concerted actions, thus making strikes legal.
Norris-La Guardia Act (1932)	Makes yellow-dog contracts (by which employers prevent their workers from joining unions) unenforceable. Limits court injunctions that restrict strikes and other union activities.
Wagner Act (1935)	Guarantees workers the right to join unions and bargain collectively. Prohibits management from engaging in unfair labor practices such as organizing company unions, discriminating against union members, or failing to bargain in good faith.
Fair Labor Standards Act (1938)	Established the minimum wage, originally 25 cents an hour. Also regulates child labor and the length of the workweek.
Taft-Harley Act (1947)	Prohibits unfair union practices such as secondary boycotts or strikes against firms doing business with a struck company, jurisdictional strikes, and closed shops (requiring that a person already be a member of the union in order to be hired). It permits states to pass right-to-work laws outlawing union shops (requiring employees to join the union after they are hired).
Landrum-Griffen Act (1959)	Regulates the administration of unions, such as governing the election of union officers, prohibiting felons from holding union office, and requiring the filing of union financial reports with the secretary of labor. Also requires employers to file reports on any payments they make to union officers.
Civil Rights Act (1964)	Prohibits discrimination in hiring, firing, or promotion on the basis of race, color, religion, sex, or national origin. Establishes the Equal Employment Opportunity Commission to enforce the act.
Age Discrimination Act (1967)	Provides protection against discrimination based on age to workers between 40 and 65.

against union employees in hiring or firing policies. Most important, the Wagner Act established the National Labor Relations Board (NLRB) to enforce and administer the law.

Collective bargaining allows workers to bargain as a group rather than as individuals. The result of collective bargaining is the signing of a contract between the union and the employer regarding pay and working condi-tions for a specified period of time, generally 1 to 3 years. When labor and management cannot reach agreement on a contract, the union may undertake **job actions** such as **strikes** and, occasionally, boycotts of the firm's products.

Union membership as a percentage of the labor force has been declining since the 1940s, when it reached a peak of 35%. By 1994, only 12% of the private-sector nonfarm workers belonged to unions. Unions represent an additional 2% of workers who are not union members in contract negotiations. Although unions do not have nearly the influence on wages they did formerly, they are still a major factor in the manufacturing sector.

According to the traditional theory of wage determination, with no unions and a

> **job action:** a concerted action by employees to disrupt production or distribution in order to put pressure on employers to grant concessions. Job actions may consist of lesser actions such as work slowdowns or work-to-rule (performing the minimum tasks stipulated in the job description) as an alternative to a strike.
>
> **strike:** a collective refusal by employees to work.

Figure 3.

Labor Market Adjustment with Flexible Wage Rates

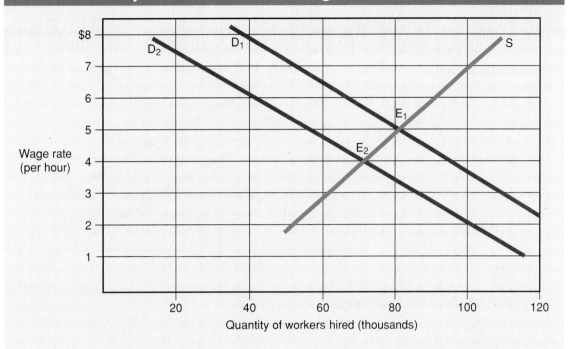

■ Under early-twentieth-century economic assumptions, a shift in the demand for hospital orderlies from D1 to D2 would lead to a fall in the equilibrium wage rate from E_1 to E_2 and voluntary exodus from the occupation.

perfectly competitive labor market, wage rates were determined by equilibrium between the demand for and supply of labor. It was assumed that if there were unemployed workers, wage rates would fall until all of the unemployed had jobs. Figure 3 shows a hypothetical demand and supply for hospital orderlies in a competitive labor market. The original point of equilibrium, E_1, represents a situation in which the wage rate is at a level where the number of workers that employers demand equals the amount of labor willingly supplied. Anybody willing to work for $5.00 an hour would be working.

Suppose a reduction in the demand for hospital services reduced the net value of hospital orderlies' labor. Hospitals would no longer find it profitable to hire as many orderlies as before, and the wage rate would fall until the last worker hired produced a net value equal to the new lower wage rate.

As shown in Figure 3, hospital administrators cut back their demand for orderlies from D_1 to D_2. As a result, the wage rate for orderlies would fall from $5.00 an hour to $4.00 an hour, equal to the net value of the work performed by the 70,000th orderly employed in the industry. At E_2, the new equilibrium, 10,000 orderlies would quit their jobs because they chose not to work at that job at the lower wage rate. Those workers would be rehired elsewhere at wages between $4.00 and $5.00. The costs of hospital care would fall.

Modern economic analysis interprets the labor market differently. When demand falls off, wages seldom drop rapidly. They tend to be rigid, or, in economists' terminology, "sticky." Workers, both union and nonunion, strongly resist any lowering of wages.

Figure 4 demonstrates the concept that if wages are rigid, a fall in the demand for a good or service brings an initial reduction in

Figure 4.

Labor Market Adjustment With Rigid Wage Rates

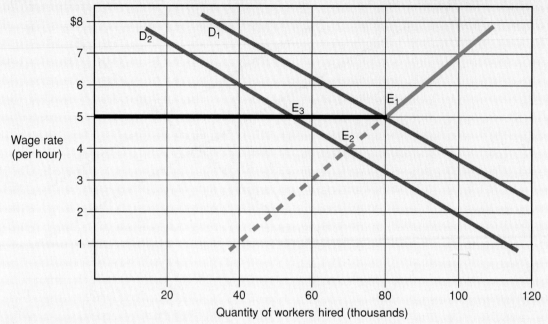

Wage rate (per hour)

Quantity of workers hired (thousands)

■ When the wage rate is fixed, the decrease in demand from D₁ to D₂ forces a new equilibrium at a point E₃, causing involuntary unemployment.

the quantity produced rather than in its price. If the demand for hospital orderlies declines from D_1 to D_2, wages do not fall to a new equilibrium at E_2. Instead, if the orderlies are unionized and the union refuses to let the wage rate fall below $5.00 per hour, 25,000 orderlies will be laid off. The new equilibrium will be at E_3, where hospitals would be willing to hire only 55,000 workers, since that is the employment level at which the net value of the last worker is $5.00 per hour. The costs of hospital care will not decline. If there is adequate demand in other fields, and labor is mobile between jobs, workers may find other jobs. In the meantime, there is involuntary unemployment.

In spite of being the subject of numerous studies, the actual effect of unions on wages remains unclear. Members of strong unions, those with a large amount of monopoly power in the labor market, generally do receive

higher wages than nonorganized or weakly represented workers, as shown in Figure 5. The "union effect" on wages may be in the neighborhood of 20% for blue-collar workers, and much less for white-collar workers. But it is uncertain how much of this effect is due strictly to wage bargaining and how much to other factors. In some ways, the effect of unions on wages is similar to that of minimum wage laws. By forcing wages up, they accelerate the introduction of laborsaving technology. This increases labor productivity and the value of an hour of labor. High wages also encourage employers to seek to hire the most productive workers and attract such workers to the job. But the ability of labor unions to increase the relative wage rates of their members in the long run has been questioned. Some observers suggest that unions only enable their membership to hold their own in relation to nonunion employees in the marketplace.

Comparative Case Application

Europe Copes with Immigration

■ A would-be immigrant rests beside her baggage on arrival at a railway station in Berlin in 1990. After accepting hundreds of thousands of refugees from Eastern European countries, Germany recently changed its immigration laws to limit new inflows.

The United States is not the only country that is wrestling with an immigration problem. Europe is facing the same set of contradictions in public policy toward immigrants as the United States, and with the same ambivalence.

During the boom years of the 1960s and 1970s, West Germany, France, and Great Brit-

ain accepted many immigrants to supplement their domestic labor forces, which had been reduced by low birthrates and World War II casualties. West Germany, especially, recruited "guest workers," mainly from countries bordering the Mediterranean.

But when serious unemployment problems developed in the European economies in the 1990s, the recent worker arrivals were no longer welcome. In Germany, following reunification of East and West, there were physical attacks on foreign worker settlements by bands of young toughs. Workers from Turkey were assaulted and even murdered. In France, also, there was violence against immigrants from her former North African colonies, perpetrated by supporters of far-right "national front" organizations.

But among the European countries, it is Italy that is coping with the most internal ambivalence toward immigrants. In the first years after the war, Italy was a supplier of "cheap labor" to its northern neighbors. But as the Italian economy flourished in the boom years, it became a net importer of labor. A public policy debate emerged in the 1990s regarding Italian immigration policy—whether it should continue to be liberal, accepting large numbers of legal immigrants and not cracking down on illegal immigration, or whether it should become restrictive. Supporting continued liberal, relatively unrestricted, immigration policy were Catholic organizations, the trade unions, and the far left. Pushing for a ban on immigration were the right wing political groups.

Italy is faced by two "Rio Grande" situations that will make it difficult for her to seal off her borders from an expected future influx of immigrants. On one side are the former communist countries of Eastern Europe, from which there is a rising exodus of economic refugees. An even greater potential immigrant problem lies to the south, across the Mediterranean. The African continent has the highest birthrate and poorest economic prospects of

any place on earth. (For a detailed look at the problems of Africa, see chapter 18.)

The free borders within the European Economic Union make Italy's immigration problems Europe-wide problems. By comparison, the future immigration problems faced by the United States may be relatively mild. Economic conditions in neighboring Mexico are improving and expected to get even better in the years ahead. Western Europe's African and Eastern European neighbors, on the other hand, are going through difficult economic and political times, which generate great numbers of would-be immigrants.

Economic Reasoning

1. How does immigration from the East and South affect the supply of labor in European countries? How does it affect the demand for labor?

2. Unemployment in Italy is highest in the undeveloped, largely agricultural, southern part of the country. Is that section affected differently by immigration than more industrialized parts of Italy? How? (Hint: You might draw an analogy with California farming and immigration from Mexico.)

3. Should Europe accept immigrants from the former communist countries to the east? Why or why not? Should it accept immigrants from the countries of Africa? Should it discriminate between immigrants from those two areas? Why or why not?

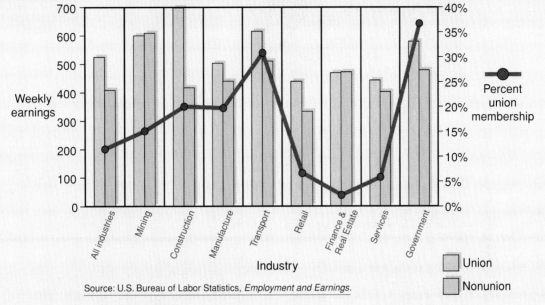

Figure 5.

Average Weekly Earnings of Union and Nonunion Workers, 1992

All and Selected Industries and Government

Source: U.S. Bureau of Labor Statistics, *Employment and Earnings*.

■ The wages of union workers are higher than those of nonunion workers, but the specific effects of unions on wages are unclear; and the percentage of union membership in an industry is not correlated with the wage differences between union and nonunion workers.

What Determines Other Incomes?

In the last analysis section we examined the factors that determine wage levels. Variations in labor income are only one, and not the major, explanation for differences in people's incomes. Income from sources other than wages and salaries results in greater inequalities in income distribution. In this section we shall look at the other types of income and what determines them.

Functional Income Distribution

Incomes are received from various sources. Most people earn the largest part of their income from wages and salaries. Other types of income are rent, interest, and profits. The **functional distribution of income** is the allocation of income according to type—wages and salaries, rent, interest, or profits. Figure 6 shows the relative proportions of different types of income that made up the nation's income in 1992. It shows that over three-fifths of total national income came from wages and salaries.

Looked at in economic rather than accounting terms, the proportion is somewhat greater. Part of the income of proprietors, generally the largest part, is **implicit wages**. Implicit wages measure the value of the owners'

> **functional income distribution:** the shares of total income distributed according to the type of factor service for which they are paid, that is, rent as a payment for land, wages for labor, and interest for capital.
>
> **implicit wages:** income that is the result of labor input but is not received in the form of wages or salaries, but in some other form such as net proprietor's income (profits).

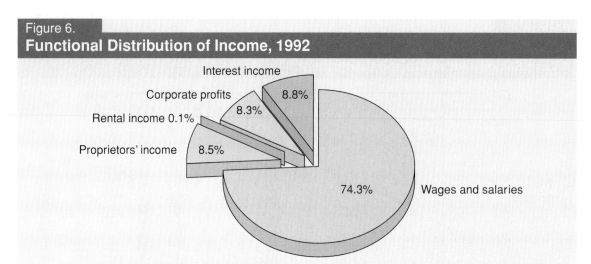

Figure 6.
Functional Distribution of Income, 1992

Interest income 8.8%

Corporate profits 8.3%

Rental income 0.1%

Proprietors' income 8.5%

74.3% Wages and salaries

Source: U.S. Department of Commerce, Bureau of Economic Analysis.

■ Amost three-fourths of the income in the United States is from wages and salaries. The remainder is in the form of proprietors' income, rent, corporate profits, and interest.

time that is spent in running their businesses. The balance of proprietors' income should be added to corporate profits, an 8.3% share, to give the total share of profits in the nation's income.

Rent

Rent received by persons, not including rent receipts of businesses, is the smallest of the income shares, accounting for only one-tenth of one percent of national income. The total amount of rent people receive is about 10 times as large, but the depreciation on their property is deducted in calculating net rental income.

In economic analysis, rent is the payment made for the use of land. Because land is pretty much fixed (unchanging) in supply, the level of rent depends almost entirely on the demand for the resource. A big demand results in a very high rent, and a small demand results in a low rent. This is so because the supply is fixed and can't expand or contract in response to price changes. The effect of an increase in demand on rent is compared with

the effect of an increase in demand on the prices of other types of factors in Figure 7.

The supply schedule for land is shown by S_1. It is perfectly inelastic because the quantity of land is fixed and does not change with changes in the price of using it (rent). If the demand for land increases from D_1 to D_2, the rent on land will increase from P_1 to P_2, but the quantity transacted stays at Q_1. With land, the whole adjustment to an increase in demand is accommodated by an increase in rent. With other types of factor inputs that do not have a perfectly inelastic supply, an increase in demand is partly accommodated by an increase in the quantity supplied. If the factor has a supply schedule such as S_2, an increase in demand from D_1 to D_2 results in a smaller price increase from P_1 to P_3 and some increase in the quantity transacted from Q_1 to Q_2. If the factor has a perfectly elastic supply such as S_3, the increase in demand results in no change in the price. The increased demand is accommodated by an increase in the quantity supplied, reflected in the move from Q_1 to Q_3.

Although rents compose the smallest share of income receipts, rent-type earnings are frequently found in other **factor shares**. This helps explain why such large differences

factor share: the part of national income received by a particular factor of production.

Figure 7.
Factor Market Adjustments to an Increase in Demand

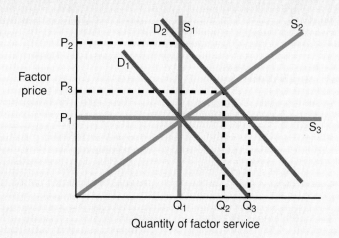

■ An increase in demand for a factor from D_1 to D_2 will have more of an effect on price or on quantity depending on whether the factor supply is perfectly inelastic, like S_1, which represents land, more elastic, like S_2, which might be skilled labor, or perfectly elastic, like S_3, which might be unskilled labor.

can exist in wages and salaries. The estimated $5 million in salary and bonuses paid to quarterback Joe Montana by the Kansas City Chiefs to play in 1993 was more like a rent than a salary. The same is true of the incomes of movie and pop music stars.

For most occupations, an increase in demand only raises wages by a small amount. The increase in the supply of workers attracted by higher wages accommodates the balance of the increased demand. But when there is a unique talent involved and the supply cannot be increased, the wage may go very high as demand increases. The market adjustment to an increase in the demand for a scarce or unusual talent such as hitting well in baseball is shown by the S_1 outcome in Figure 7. By comparison, the adjustment to an increase in the demand for unskilled labor would be more like that for S_3, while an increase in the demand for a skilled occupation would lie in between, as in the S_2 case.

Interest

Interest income accounts for nearly 9% of total income. Interest is the factor payment for the use of financial capital. Financial capital comes mainly from savings, and the interest rate depends on the amount of capital available relative to the demand for capital for investing or for financing personal or government debt.

Generally, a rise in the interest rate should make more capital available by making it more profitable for people to save a larger percentage of their income rather than to spend it. However, people who have a specific savings goal for retirement or for some other specified amount such as the down payment on a house will receive more interest income on their savings if interest rates go up. Consequently, they can achieve their goal with a smaller amount of savings each month. The net effect of a change in the interest rate on the amount of savings is not predictable.

Interest rates, like other prices, play an important rationing function. Higher interest rates discourage some uses of capital. When capital is scarce, only the most productive types of investment can justify using the expensive capital.

Profits

Profits are often the least understood type of income. It is clear what the other factor pay-

Four Strikes in Baseball?

Everybody knows that in baseball there are only three strikes. Not anymore. Now there are four. The first strike in baseball, of the labor-management type, that is, was at the beginning of the regular season in 1972. The second was during the exhibition season in 1980. Both were short-lived. Strike three came in the middle of the 1981 season and lasted 50 days. The fourth strike, in 1994, resulted in cancellation of the remainder of the regular season and the World Series as well.

Baseball strikes are not a big deal as far as the economy is concerned. The $2 billion dollars generated by baseball is not a large amount in comparison with other industries, but the strikes result in significant losses to those involved. Besides the players and owners, there are big losses to a number of third parties—cities lose tax revenues and rent on city-owned stadiums; park concessionaires and their employees lose income from food, drink, and parking; hotels, bars, restaurants, airlines, and city transportation suffer untold losses. But possibly the biggest losers, certainly the most numerous, do not count their losses in dollars, but in psychic deprivation. These are the baseball fans, especially the avid fans, who depend on the national pastime in the summer like bees depend on nectar.

The 1994 strike was particularly maddening to the fans in view of its cause. The issue over which the strike was called was a salary cap proposed by the owners. Here were two groups of millionaires fighting over the spoils: owners who, whether or not they are making annual profits, benefit from a steady rise in the market value of their franchises and "workers" earning millions of dollars for "part-time" work. Members of other unions, earning $20,000 a year or so, do not feel much brotherhood identification with the Major League Players Association. They fear higher player salaries mean higher ticket prices.

Economic Reasoning

1. According to functional income distribution, what types of income were affected by the baseball strikes?

2. Why do members of the Major League Players Association earn so much more than members of most unions?

3. Are the high salaries paid to professional athletes justified? Why or why not?

■ Quarterback Joe Montana's income can be considered to be more a rent than a salary. Whenever there is a unique talent involved and the supply cannot be increased, the wage may go very high to reflect demand.

ments are for: wages are the payment for labor services, rents for the use of land, and interest for the use of financial capital. But for what factor service are profits paid? Profits are sometimes said to be the payment to entrepreneurs for perceiving a need for a new or better good or service, organizing the factors of production to satisfy that need, and taking the necessary financial risks.

When proprietors use their own capital in their business, there is an **implicit interest** cost that should be charged against revenues in calculating economic profits. As we saw in chapter 6, accounting profits are the difference between the total revenue of a company and its total costs. But much of accounting profits is actually an implicit interest payment to owners for the use of their capital, which they have invested in their business. Only the profits in excess of the normal rate of return on capital are considered economic profits.

In markets where there is no monopoly control, economic profits tend to disappear in the long run because of the entry of new firms, which increases supply and reduces the profit rate (see Figure 6 in chapter 6, p. 145). Economic profits persist only in cases of monopoly.

What Causes Unequal Distribution of Income?

In the previous two sections of the chapter we examined the functional distribution of income according to its source. In this section we will take a look at the distribution of income according to those who receive it and what causes income differences.

Personal Income Distribution

Functional income distribution is one way of looking at how income is distributed. Another way of looking at income distribution is to look at the pattern of distribution according to the relative size of people's income—**personal income distribution**. Table 2 shows the distribution of personal income in the United States

implicit interest: income that derives from the use of capital but is not paid as interest but rather as a part of accounting profits.

personal income distribution: the pattern of income distribution according to the relative size of people's income.

Table 2.

Income Distribution, 1960–1991
Money Income of Families
(percentage distribution of total income)*

Year	Lowest fifth	Second fifth	Third fifth	Fourth fifth	Highest fifth
1960	4.8	12.2	17.8	24.0	41.3
1965	5.2	12.2	17.8	23.9	40.9
1970	5.4	12.2	17.6	23.8	40.9
1975	5.4	11.8	17.6	24.1	41.1
1980	5.1	11.6	17.5	24.3	41.6
1984	4.7	11.0	17.0	24.4	42.9
1987	4.6	10.8	16.9	24.1	43.7
1991	4.5	10.7	16.6	24.1	44.2
Income classes 1991	below $17,000	$17,001 to $29,111	$29,112 to $43,000	$43,001 to $62,991	above $62,992

*Row totals may not add to 100% because of rounding.

Source: U.S. Bureau of the Census, *Current Population Reports*.

During the 1960s income distribution became somewhat more equal. Since then it has become more unequal than it was in 1960. The highest fifth of income receivers have gained at the expense of the lower three-fifths.

according to five income classes for the years 1960–1991. Each class represents 20% of all income receivers, ranging from the 20% receiving the lowest incomes to the 20% receiving the highest incomes. The numbers in the table show the percentage of total income received by that group of income receivers. Comparing the percentage of total income received by the people in each fifth of the income scale, we can see the distribution of income in the United States between lower- and upper-income groups.

A good way to make this comparison is with a **Lorenz curve** diagram as shown in Figure 8. The bottom axis shows households divided into five equal groups according to amount of income received. The vertical axis shows the percentage of total income that is earned by each fifth of the population. Perfect

Lorenz curve: a diagram showing the distribution of income among groups of people; an indicator of the degree of inequality of income distribution.

equality of income distribution would be represented by a diagonal straight line from the lower-left corner to the upper-right corner, with 20% of the population earning 20% of total income, 40% of the population earning 40% of the income, and so forth.

The extent to which the actual income distribution shown by the Lorenz curve varies from a diagonal straight line indicates the extent of inequality in income distribution. The more the curve bows away from the straight line, the greater the inequality in income distribution.

Figure 8 shows the Lorenz curve for income distribution in 1991. The bottom 20% of income receivers earned 4.5% of total income, while the top 20% of income receivers earned 44.2% of total income. The lowest 40% of the population received 15.2% of the income, while the highest 40% received 68.2% of the income.

During the 1960s, as Table 2 shows, income distribution was becoming somewhat

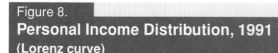

Figure 8.
Personal Income Distribution, 1991
(Lorenz curve)

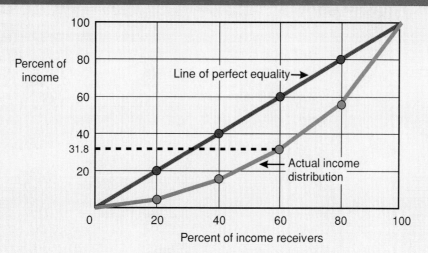

Source: U.S. Bureau of the Census, *Current Population Reports*.

■ The degree of inequality of income distribution is shown by the extent of deviation from the straight line. In 1991 the lower 60% of income receivers got 31.8% of the income, while the highest 40% got 68.2%.

more equal. The lowest 20% of income receivers increased their share of total income, while the shares received by the highest groups declined. During the 1970s the highest two-fifths regained their earlier relative shares at the expense of the second fifth, the lower-middle-income group.

Since 1980 income distribution has become more unequal than at any time since the data have been published. The highest fifth of income receivers have increased their share of income at the expense of the lower three-fifths of families. Between 1975 and 1991 the share of total income going to the upper fifth of income receivers increased 3.1%. It represented a shift of income of $112.5 billion from the lower 60% of income receivers to the top 20%. This amounted to an average of $2,791 less income per family in the lower 60% and $8,374 more income per family in the upper 20%.

Differences in Productivity
One of the causes of inequality in income distribution is differences in productivity. Labor

incomes in particular are closely related to productivity. As we saw in the last chapter, the wages of workers are determined by the net value of the output of the last worker it pays an employer to hire. The greater the value of the output of a particular type of worker, the more income such workers will receive. Workers in low-productivity jobs generally receive small incomes. Workers in high-productivity jobs generally earn relatively high incomes. The productivity of skilled workers is greater than that of unskilled workers, and their earnings are related to their productivity.

Some of the differences in productivity between occupations are due to differences in education, training, and ability. However, productivity also depends on the amount of capital equipment that a worker has to work with. Labor in automated firms is more productive than labor in firms that do not have much capital investment per worker. The high-wage industries generally have a great deal of capital equipment per worker, while the low-wage

■ The workers in New York's garment industry earn $8 an hour. Outside of New York, the rate is closer to $7.25. It is interesting to note that women account for 80% of this workforce.

industries generally have much smaller amounts of capital investment per worker.

As U.S. industry has become more competitive, in the way described in chapter 7, virtually all of the wealth created by the increased productivity has flowed to the upper 20% of income receivers. As shown by economist William Baumol of Princeton and New York Universities, the productivity growth in Japan and Europe has yielded more equitable income distributions.

Differences in Opportunity

While differences in productivity explain differences in income among different types of jobs, productivity does not explain differences in income among different population groups. Men are not inherently more productive than women, yet according to Bureau of Labor Statistics figures for full-time workers, women earn only 75¢ for every dollar paid to men. (This is an improvement from 10 years earlier, when women earned only 67% as much as men.) Nor are there any innate racial or eth-

nic productivity differences, but the median weekly earnings of white full-time workers in 1992 were $462, while black full-time workers earned only $357.

The income discrepancies between the sexes and among racial and ethnic groups result from differences in opportunities. Title VII of the Civil Rights Act of 1964 prohibits employers from discriminating in the hiring, firing, promotion, job assignment, compensation, training, and other "terms, conditions, or privileges of employment." It is the task of the Equal Employment Opportunity Commission (EEOC) to enforce these provisions of the law.

Discriminatory attitudes and practices, however, cannot be easily reversed. Racism, sexism, and ageism have not been eliminated from society and its institutions. This is one reason for income inequality and poverty.

Lack of educational opportunities and motivations in the past is another explanation of current differences in earnings between population groups. While 25.2% of all white males have completed college, only 19.1% of white

Case Application

Created Equal, But . . .

When the 1964 Civil Rights Act made it illegal for employers to discriminate on the basis of race, religion, or sex, the focus of public attention was on the discrimination against black and other minority workers. The better-paying jobs were frequently open to white workers only. The median weekly earnings of black workers were only 70% as large as the earnings of white workers. Since the passage of the Civil Rights Act, the income gap for black workers has been reduced from 30% less than white workers to 23% less. But the relative income of women was and still is the lowest of all, in 1992 only 75% as large as that of white males.

In terms of family income rather than weekly earnings, which is a better measure of economic welfare, women are at an even greater disadvantage. Families with women as heads of the household have an average income that is only 59% as much as households headed by men. This compares with interracial and interethnic differences in family income: black families average 57% and Hispanic families 63% of the median income of white families. But the situation of women heads of households with children is the most desperate of all. Such families have a median income that is only 31% that of married-couple families with children.

The main reason for the low earnings of women is that women workers are concentrated in low-wage occupations. A study by the National Academy of Sciences has shown that the more an occupation is dominated by women, the less it tends to pay. Women constitute over 80% of the workforce in six of eight low-paying jobs: practical nurses, stitchers and sewers, child-care workers, hairdressers, nurse's aides, and health care workers. The only two of the low-paying jobs in which they do not predominate are cooks (50% are women) and farm laborers (less than 15%).

The most important reason for the slow growth of productivity in the 1980s was the low rate of productivity growth in the service industries, less than 1% a year. This was in part due to the availability of female labor to fill the low-paying jobs in that sector of the economy. Large numbers of women entered the labor force during the decade, increasing the labor force participation rate of women by 6 percentage points and adding some 15 million workers. The great majority of these new female workers went into service occupations.

The availability of this pool of cheap labor meant that service industries did not have to invest in new capital equipment to meet rising demand. In Western Europe and Japan, which did not have such a pool of cheap labor available, service companies invested heavily in new technology that resulted in productivity gains of 2% to 4% per year. The difference in productivity growth between other industrialized countries and the United States has left the United States at a disadvantage in global competition. Substandard pay for women is not only a hardship for them, but a drag on the economy as well.

Economic Reasoning

1. In which income classes of Table 2 (see p. 232) would you expect to find an unusually large proportion of women?

2. Considering the causes of income inequality, why do women predominate in six of the eight low-paying jobs?

3. Do you think that affirmative action in the hiring and promotion of women and minorities is a good idea? Why or why not?

females, 11.9% of black males, and 10.2% of Hispanic males have college degrees. The most educationally disadvantaged group is Hispanic females, of whom only 8.5% have 4-year college educations. The gap is closing between white males and females in educational attainment, but it is increasing between black and white males. There has been no increase in the percentage of black male college graduates in the 1990s, though there has been of black females. The educational attainment level of black females now exceeds that of black males.

Differences in Asset Ownership

While there are wide differences in income between different occupations, the greatest income variations result from differences in earnings from asset ownership. Of those people with incomes of more than $1 million a year, the largest source of income, by far, is the **capital gains** on their assets. The second largest source of their incomes is dividends on stock.

The third largest source of income among millionaires is salaries. They receive less than one-fifth as much in salaries, on the average, as the sum of their capital gains and dividend income. Most people who receive incomes at the top of the scale earn them from assets rather than from wages and salaries.

What Is the Answer to Poverty?

As we have seen, unequal distribution of income can be the result of a variety of causes. The result for those at the bottom of the income distribution ladder is poverty. This section of the chapter looks at what constitutes poverty and some of the methods used to combat it.

The Poverty Line

The dividing line between those officially considered poor and those not officially considered poor is called the **poverty line**. The initial poverty line was established in 1964 and was based on the cost of an economical food expenditure budget for a family. The poverty income threshold was calculated at 3 times a family's economical food budget. This income level has been adjusted each year for changes in the cost of living. In 1975 the poverty line was $5,500 for a non-farm family of four. In 1980 the poverty line for such a family was $8,414, and in 1991

it was $13,924. By adjusting the poverty line to reflect inflation, the government can keep the poverty threshold constant in real purchasing power.

The total number of people below the poverty threshold declined from almost 40 million in 1960 to a low of 23 million in 1973. Since then it has been increasing, and in 1991 it stood at 35.7 million. This comprised 14.2% of the population.

The poverty line measurement, however, may understate the increase in poverty for some groups and overstate it for others. Consumption patterns, living standards, and relative costs have changed since the measure was devised. Food's share of family budgets has shrunk from one-third of family income to one-fifth of income. Meanwhile, housing's share has risen from one-third of income to over two-fifths of income for the average family, two-thirds for poor families. As a consequence, the poverty threshold based on food expenditures does not reflect a family's actual living costs today. Using a housing-based poverty measure in place of the food-based poverty line would raise the poverty rate some 10 percentage points.

Another objection to the poverty line measurement is the different criteria used in

---

capital gain: net income realized from an increase in the market value of a real or financial asset when it is sold.

poverty line: the family income level below which people are officially classified as poor.

■ Over 100 million people around the world have no home at all. Here, in a tunnel under the West Side Highway in Manhattan, squatters called the Mole People are sharing a Thanksgiving turkey that has been roasted in a foil-lined rusty file drawer.

computing the needs of the elderly compared to those used for the rest of the population. Because the food needs of the elderly were about 10% below those of the nonelderly, the poverty threshold was set lower for those 65 and older. This adjustment, which is still made, ignores the higher health care costs for the elderly. They spend more than twice as much of their budgets on health care costs not covered by Medicare as other households spend on health care. If the same poverty criterion is used for the elderly as for others, the percentage of elderly living in poverty is higher than average, rather than lower, as shown by the existing poverty line.

On the side of overstatement, it appears on the surface that low-income groups have suffered an absolute, as well as a relative, reduction in their real incomes since 1980. Recent research, however, has brought into question whether they are actually worse off. Although the real incomes of poor families have declined in the past 2 decades, their consumption levels have gone up. A study by Christopher Jencks of Northwestern University and Susan Mayer of the University of Chicago found that for a quarter of a century America's poorest families have spent much

more each year than the total amount of income they reported receiving. The main reason for this apparent contradiction is that income earned at odd jobs or received from family and friends is frequently not reported in order to remain eligible for welfare benefits and to reduce tax liability. The poorest 10% of households with children reported a mean income of $5,588 in 1988–1989 but spent more than twice as much, an average of $13,558. The gap between reported income and actual spending has been growing.

This finding does not necessarily mean that the extent of poverty is substantially exaggerated. Jencks and Mayer did not include the poorest of the poor—the homeless—in their study, or single individuals, who typically do not have support networks. Jencks believes that although the poor have more income than previously thought, the poverty line is set too low to cover necessary expenses and should be raised.

However measured, poverty is unequally distributed among population groups. The majority of families below the poverty line are those in which women are the heads of household, although such families are only 10% of the total population. Racial and ethnic minorities are also disproportionately represented among the poor. The proportion of minority families falling below the poverty line is two to three times that of white families. Children constitute a disproportionately large share of those below the poverty line.

Increased Opportunity

A major objective of the Civil Rights Act of 1964, the Age Discrimination Act of 1967, and the Americans With Disabilities Act of 1990 was to remove obstacles to economic opportunity caused by racial, religious, sex, age, or disability discrimination. The actions of the Equal Employment Opportunity Commission have opened doors of increased opportunities that were previously closed to minorities, women, older people, and people with disabilities.

The antipoverty programs initiated by the Johnson administration in 1965 and expanded under following administrations reduced the percentage of people living below the poverty line from 22.2% of the population in 1960 to 11.1% in 1973. This was accomplished in part by equal employment opportunities and **affirmative action programs** in government and private employment, and by government-funded jobs for the hard-core unemployed.

Reductions in federal government funding for the antipoverty programs in the 1980s, decreases in work training opportunities, and elimination of day-care centers, which had given mothers of young children more opportunity to work, slowed progress on increasing opportunities for economically disadvantaged groups.

affirmative action program: a program devised by employers to increase their hiring of women and minorities; frequently mandated by government regulations.

transfer payments: expenditures for which no goods or services are exchanged. Welfare, Social Security, and unemployment compensation are government transfer payments.

entitlement program: government benefits that qualified recipients are entitled to by law, such as Social Security old-age benefits.

food stamps: certificates that can be used in place of money to purchase food items.

■ The Food Stamp Program, one of the government's largest transfer payment programs, enables low-income persons to buy more groceries.

Transfer Payments

Providing increased employment and educational opportunities is one way of raising people out of poverty. But this approach misses many of those currently in need. A more direct method of assisting those living in poverty is **transfer payments**. Government transfer payments to low-income households are subsidies paid out of tax receipts to supplement the income of impoverished families. These transfers include money payments such as welfare, Social Security benefits, and unemployment compensation.

One of the largest **entitlement programs** to supplement the cash income of the poor is federally financed **food stamps**. The Food Stamp Program was authorized by Congress in 1964 with the stated goal of helping low-income households obtain more balanced and nutritious diets. Stamps that can be used to purchase food vary in cost depending on the income of the recipient. The program is administered by the Department of Agriculture through state and local welfare offices. Many cities also have federally funded programs that provide hot meals to the elderly each day. In order to ensure nutrition for the young, schoolchildren of low-income families are provided free or discounted lunches and, in some cases, breakfasts.

Another major entitlement program is **Aid to Families with Dependent Children (AFDC)**. This program was begun to provide income maintenance and social services for that most needy of all groups, families below the poverty line with women heads of household. **Medicaid** is a federally financed program to provide adequate health care for low-income families. There are also subsidies that assist the poor in obtaining adequate housing.

Transfer payments substantially reduce the portion of the nation that is poverty stricken. Without antipoverty transfer payments and nonmonetary benefits, the poverty rate would be nearly twice as high—over one-fifth of the population. The poverty programs have sometimes been criticized for "throwing money at the problem." Long-term solutions to poverty such as increased opportunities are essential, but in the short run "throwing money at the problem" raises some 30 million people out of poverty.

The **earned income tax credit (EITC)** is a type of negative income tax for the working poor, who comprise 60% of all those in poverty. It was originally instituted in 1975 as a way to offset the federal tax liabilities of the poor. Succeeding tax bills have increased the maximum amount of the tax credit and provided an adjustment for inflation. As a result, many low-income families are entitled to credits that exceed their tax liabilities.

Workfare

Another alternative to the ordinary income transfer programs is **workfare**. Originally, workfare referred to programs that required public assistance recipients to "work off" the value of their welfare checks—perhaps $100 a month—by community service in government or nonprofit organizations. Several states adopted such programs under the AFDC program, though recipients who were unable to work or had preschool children were typically exempt from the requirements.

■ The term workfare covers a number of different programs that enable people to enter or reenter the job market. Above, one workfare recipient helps clean up a park in the East Bay Region Park District in Oakland, California.

More recently, workfare has been used to refer to a variety of education, training, work experience, and job placement programs designed to increase the self-sufficiency of public assistance recipients. Federal laws authorize such programs for AFDC recipients, and several states—most notably California and Massachusetts—have mounted major programs. Child-care and transportation expenses may be subsidized to enable public assistance recipients to participate in the programs. Some states have also experimented with "grant diversion," under which the assistance payments are diverted to serve as wage subsidies to support on-the-job training by employers who hire welfare recipients.

Aid to Families with Dependent Children (AFDC): a federally subsidized public assistance program to provide income maintenance and social services to needy families with dependent children.

Medicaid: a federally subsidized, state-administered program to pay for medical and hospital costs of low-income families.

earned income tax credit (EITC): a federal tax credit for poor families with earnings that offsets their tax liabilities and, for the poorest, provides a tax subsidy.

workfare: originally a program that required nonexempt welfare recipients to work at public service jobs for a given number of hours a month; now may also include job training and wage subsidies.

Case Application

The Rich Get Richer and the Poor Get Ketchup

Income distribution has become more unequal in the last decade, as shown in Table 2 on page 232. When we adjust for inflation, families in the lowest 20% of income receivers have less purchasing power now than they did in 1980. A typical family in the top 20%, by contrast, has seen its real earnings rise by more than 10%; and a family in the top 5% of income receivers has experienced a healthy 15% gain in inflation-adjusted income.

These average figures for income classes do not show the income changes that particu-

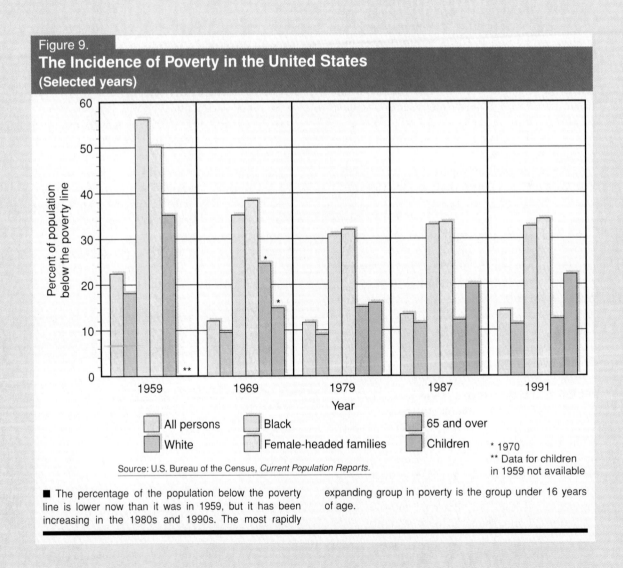

Figure 9.

The Incidence of Poverty in the United States

(Selected years)

Percent of population below the poverty line

Year

- All persons
- White
- Black
- Female-headed families
- 65 and over
- Children

* 1970
** Data for children in 1959 not available

Source: U.S. Bureau of the Census, *Current Population Reports*.

■ The percentage of the population below the poverty line is lower now than it was in 1959, but it has been increasing in the 1980s and 1990s. The most rapidly expanding group in poverty is the group under 16 years of age.

lar subgroups have experienced, which in many cases are even more inequitable. Racial and ethnic minorities are disproportionately represented among those people below the poverty threshold. One-third of the black population is classified as poor. The incidence of poverty among minorities in general is two to three times that of the white population. Families with black female householders have the highest incidence of poverty, with more than one-half such families below the poverty level.

Because of the low average earnings of women, families exclusively dependent on the income of a female householder constitute over half of the families below the poverty line, although such families are only 10% of the population. Looked at another way, over three-fourths of all the poor are women and children. Families below the poverty line are more likely to include children under 16 than families above the poverty line. More than one child in five lives in poverty. More than two out of every five black and Hispanic children live below the poverty level. The younger the children, the more likely they are to be poor: half of all black children under the age of 6 live in poverty. Children are now the poorest group in the country, having displaced the elderly from this unfavorable distinction as far back as 1974, when 15% of children were below the poverty level. Since then their economic position has deteriorated further, and now over 22% are living in poverty.

Families headed by people under 30 have been especially hard hit by the changes in income distribution. Their poverty rate has doubled in the last two decades. This high poverty rate among young families foreshadows a continuation of this problem well into the future. Poverty tends to reproduce itself, creating a self-perpetuating underclass. For example, 36% of girls from welfare families end up on welfare in later years themselves, compared to 9% from nonwelfare families.

A congressional analysis of the causes of the increase in poverty found that nearly one-half of the increase was attributable to cutbacks in state and federal aid. Decreased funding for antipoverty programs during the 1980s affected the range of antipoverty programs. Living stipends paid to welfare families with children fell 35% below the 1970 level, adjusted for inflation. A million people were eliminated from the food stamp program. Two million children were dropped from eligibility for school lunches. One cutback was reversed, however, by public reaction. There was an attempt to save money on the school lunch program by classifying ketchup as a vegetable in satisfying nutritional requirements, since ketchup was cheaper than a serving of a vegetable. The public outcry over this instance of government ecomomizing at the expense of children's health forced a cancellation of the change.

Economic Reasoning

1. What group experienced the largest increase between 1979 and 1991 in the percentage of the group living below the poverty line? Approximately how many percentage points was the increase?

2. How do government programs such as the school lunch program increase opportunities for rising out of poverty?

3. Do you think women receiving AFDC should be required to participate in workfare? Why or why not?

Putting It Together

Wages are determined basically the same way other prices are, by demand and supply. The demand for labor is a *derived demand,* because it depends upon consumer demand for goods and services. The value of what a worker produces, after subtracting the costs of the other inputs, determines the demand for that worker's services. An increase in the labor supply, say, by immigration, also increases the demand for labor as a result of greater spending on goods and services.

The amount and quality of capital equipment available per worker is a major determinant of productivity and wages. More workers will be hired in an industry as long as the *net value* of an additional worker's output exceeds the wage rate.

Minimum wage laws may increase wages by accelerating capital investment. When wages are thus pushed up, in the long run either the number of workers in the industry will decline or labor productivity will be increased so that the last worker hired brings in as much added revenue as the wage paid.

Under *collective bargaining,* established by the National Labor Relations (Wagner) Act in 1935, agreements are negotiated between a firm and a labor union to determine wages and working conditions. If agreement on a contract cannot be reached, the union may resort to *job actions* such as a *strike* or boycott.

According to the traditional theory of wage determination, in a free labor market wages fall to the level at which all workers are employed. But modern economics holds that wages are "sticky" in the downward direction. They do not readily fall when there is unemployment. This is one difference between the price of labor and the price of most things: a surplus of labor often does not cause a fall in its price to an equilibrium level, where the surplus would be eliminated. When unions hold wages above the free-market level, higher labor costs accelerate the introduction of laborsaving equipment, as in the case of minimum wages.

Functional income distribution reflects the way income is distributed according to its source: labor, land, capital, or entrepreneurship. Each of the resources has a function in production. Wages and salaries are paid for labor. Rent is payment for the use of land, which includes not only real estate but everything provided by nature. The payment for the use of financial capital is interest, and the income from entrepreneurship is profit. In addition to being the source of people's income, factor payments ration productive resources to their most valuable uses and serve as an incentive to produce.

Most income, about three-quarters of the total, is composed of wages and salaries. Although rent income, as such, is less than 1% of total income, some other incomes are similar to rent in that the supply of the factor is fixed. A unique human skill or ability that cannot be replicated by education, training, or practice earns an income that is more similar to rent than to wages. When the factor supply is perfectly inelastic, the factor price depends entirely on the level of demand. An increase in demand is accommodated exclusively by a rise in price, since the quantity supplied cannot increase.

From the standpoint of their economic function, proprietors' accounting profits consist to a large extent of *implicit interest* returns on the owners' capital, including a premium for risk taking, and *implicit wages* for the owners' labor. These are not economic profits. In competitive markets, economic profits tend to disappear. If economic profits persist, it is because of monopolistic power in the market.

Personal income distribution is the proportion of income going to different groups of income receivers. The most usual measure of income distribution is the percentage of total income received by each fifth of income receivers. A *Lorenz curve* plots these data on a diagram. The further the curve deviates from a straight diagonal line, the more unequally is income distributed.

Unequal income distribution results from differences in productivity, differences in economic opportunity, and differences in the amount of income-earning assets owned. Productivity differences are due to varying amounts of capital equipment per worker and variations in the training and skills of workers. Opportunity differences are often due to lack of access to education and lack of access to higher-paying jobs in industry and the professions. The Civil Rights Act of 1964 prohibits discrimination in job opportunities. The widest variations in income result from earnings on financial assets, of which capital gains are the most significant for the highest-income receivers.

The *poverty line* is the income level below which people are officially designated as poor. The poverty line is based on the amount of money that a family needs to spend on an economical food budget. That amount is multiplied by 3 to determine the total income needed for a family's basic living costs. Each year it is adjusted upward to reflect rising prices.

During the 1960s and early 1970s the number of people below the poverty line was decreasing. Since 1973 the number has been increasing. Women, children, and racial and ethnic minorities make up a disproportionate share of those living in poverty.

Government programs to increase the economic opportunities of poor people include job training programs, child-care facilities for working mothers, higher-education grants and student loans, early-childhood education programs, and *affirmative action program* requirements for employment and education. *Transfer payments* to increase the real income of poor people include *entitlement programs* such as *food stamps, Aid to Families with Dependent Children, Medicaid,* housing subsidies, and food programs for schoolchildren and the elderly.

Earned income tax credits are a type of negative income tax used to raise the income of the working poor. Many states have initiated *workfare* programs for those on welfare, requiring a given number of hours of work per month in public-service agency jobs. Some states incorporate job training in their programs to get welfare recipients into private-sector jobs or provide wage subsidies to employers hiring someone on welfare.

The Haymarket Affair

The Haymarket Square riot in Chicago, 1886. A dynamite bomb exploding among the police touched off large-scale bloodshed.

Additional information on the Haymarket Affair and labor union history can be found in *The Haymarket Tragedy* by Paul Avrich (Princeton, NJ: Princeton University Press, 1984); *Labor in America: A History* by Foster Dulles (New York: Crowell, 1966); *History of the Labor Movement in the United States* by Philip Foner (New York: International Publishers, 1947); and *Working Men: The Story of Labor* by Sidney Lenz (New York: G. P. Putnam's Sons, 1960).

On the evening of May 4, 1886, a rally was held in Chicago's Haymarket Square to protest the deaths of six striking workers, killed the previous day by police at the McCormick Harvester factory. The events were the outgrowth of a nationwide demonstration held on May 1 to reinforce labor demands for an 8-hour day to replace the average 10- or 11-hour workday existing at the time.

The Haymarket Square demonstration was attended by about 1,500 people, and as police were attempting to disperse them, a bomb was thrown, killing or wounding a number of policemen. The police then opened fire on the crowd, inflicting over 200 casualties. It was never determined who threw the bomb, but eight labor organizers were arrested, tried, and convicted of murder. Only one of the eight had been at the demonstration, and he was speaking on the platform at the time the bomb was thrown. Nevertheless, all were found guilty of contributing to the crime because of inflammatory speeches they had made on other occasions. One of the condemned men committed suicide in prison, four were hanged, and the other three were eventually pardoned after serving 7 years in prison. John Altgeld, the Illinois governor who pardoned them, stated that all eight were completely innocent and had been the victims of a biased judge and a packed jury.

The Haymarket Affair was a turning point in labor union history. Before then unions had been weak and transitory. If a union was defeated in a strike, it generally went out of existence. Economic depressions virtually wiped out the whole union movement. Union organizers were blacklisted by employers and could not get jobs. Job applicants were required to sign pledges that they would not join a union. The extensive use of children and immigrant labor in the factories undercut the unions. Immigrant workers were recruited from other countries, and many strikes were broken by pitting one nationality group against another.

Prior to the Haymarket Affair, no national union had ever lasted. But a few months after that episode, the American Federation of Labor was formed under the leadership of Samuel Gompers. It was the first federation of unions that proved able to survive depressions. In the 1930s a second national union was organized, the Congress of Industrial Organizations, and in 1955 the two merged to form the AFL-CIO.

FOR FURTHER STUDY AND ANALYSIS

Study Questions

1. How would an increase in the demand for a product affect the wages of workers in that industry? Why?

2. What effects does the use of more capital equipment have on the productivity of labor in a particular industry? How can increased investment in capital equipment sometimes result in less demand for labor and at other times result in more demand for labor?

3. For most things, a higher price results in a larger quantity being supplied, but higher wages for labor have led to shorter workweeks. How do you account for this?

4. How do minimum wage laws affect youth employment? What would be the effects of reducing or abolishing minimum wage laws for people under 20?

5. In what ways might labor unions affect the rate of technological development?

6. What differences between U.S. industries result in some being high-wage industries and others being low-wage industries?

7. If the proprietor of a dry-cleaning establishment has $200,000 in personal capital invested in the business, works an average of 60 hours a week running the firm, and averages $35,000 in proprietor's income a year, would you estimate the proprietor's economic profits to be positive or negative? Why?

8. Are the high prices paid for admission to professional games the result of high players' salaries or the cause of high players' salaries? Or are these high salaries not related at all to high ticket prices? Why?

9. Has the relative income of the middle fifth of income receivers improved or worsened compared with that of other income receivers since 1960? What explanations might be found for the change in the relative income of middle-income earners?

10. Why do workers who work with large amounts of capital equipment generally earn more than workers who do not use large amounts of capital equipment?

Exercises in Analysis

1. By researching the labor movement in your state or province, determine if "union shops" are legal. Then prepare a position paper supporting either the concept of the "union shop" or the reasoning behind "right-to-work" laws.

2. In what ways, if any, do government workers differ from workers in private industry in their right to organize unions and enforce their demands with strikes? Prepare a position paper defending or attacking the right of public employees to organize unions and to strike.

3. Draw a Lorenz curve based on the following data:

Percent of Population	Percent of Income
Lowest 20%	6%
Next 20%	12%
Next 20%	18%
Next 20%	24%
Highest 20%	40%

4. Using the latest census data available, create a line graph reflecting the income level of American women as compared to American men for the past 10 years.

Further Reading

Burton, C. Emory. *The Poverty Debate: Politics and the Poor in America*. New York: Greenwood Press, 1992. An examination of the social conditions of the poor in America. The situation of welfare recipients and the role of employment.

Borjas, George J. *Friends or Strangers: The Impact of Immigrants on the U.S. Economy*. New York: Basic Books, 1990. Examines the impact of immigrants on earnings and employment, immigrant poverty and government programs, immigrant entrepreneurship, and international competition for immigrants.

Bohning, W. R. *Studies in International Labour Migration*. New York: St. Martin's Press, 1984. "It would be ridiculous to attempt to show whether the effects of immigration are a 'good thing' or a 'bad thing.' . . . There can be no peremptory conclusion to a controversy in which there are so many factors and so many intermingled and conflicting interests" (p. 61, quoting M. Allefresde).

Collinson, Sarah. *Europe and International Migration*. New York: St. Martin's Press, 1993. A study of immigration problems in Europe that are similar to those in the United States.

Freeman, Richard B., and James S. Metdoff. *What Do Unions Do?* New York: Basic Books, 1984. Covers the effects of unions on wages, wage inequality, nonorganized labor, productivity, and profits.

Handler, Joel F., and Yeheskel Hasenfeld. *The Moral Construction of Poverty: Welfare Reform in America*. Newbury Park: Sage Publications, 1991. Examines the moral and ethical aspects of public welfare and critiques the welfare service policies of government.

Haveman, Robert. *Starting Even: An Equal Opportunity Program to Combat the Nation's New Poverty*. New York: Simon & Schuster, 1988. Discusses the relationship between inequality of income distribution and efficiency, the effect government has had on inequality, and a program for equality with efficiency.

Hollifield, James F. *Migrants, Markets, and States: The Political Economy of Postwar Europe*. Boston: Harvard University Press, 1992. A study of recent immigration in the United States and Europe and the political and economic factors that prompted them. Examines the conflict between maintaining the labor supply and protecting citizenship.

Levitt, Martin, and Terry Conrow. *Confessions of a Union Buster*. New York: Crown, 1993. Physical assaults on union members no longer take place as they did in the time of the Haymarket Affair; but unions are still under attack in more devious ways, as exposed by a former "labor relations management consultant" hired by companies to undermine unions attempting to organize workers in the firms' plants.

Mead, Lawrence M. *The New Politics of Poverty: The Nonworking Poor in America*. New York: Basic Books, 1992. How the "new poor" came into existence; the economic conditions that led to the present welfare dilemma.

Rivera-Batiz, Francisco L., Selig L. Sechzer, and Ira N. Gang, eds. *U.S. Immigration Reform in the 1980s: A Preliminary Assessment*.

New York: Praeger, 1991. Covers various aspects of the changes in immigration laws and policies and the effects of those changes.

Ropers, Richard H. *Persistent Poverty: The American Dream Turned Nightmare.* New York: Plenum Press, 1991. Examines the deterioration of the social and economic conditions that have resulted in a rise in poverty and homelessness.

Simon, Julian L. *The Economic Consequences of Immigration.* Cambridge, MA: Basil Blackwell, 1989. A technical treatment of the consequences of immigration for public finance, native workers' incomes, productivity, and the environment.

VanderStaay, Steven. *Street Lives: An Oral History of Homeless Americans.* Philadelphia: New Society Publishers, 1992. The author paints a verbal picture of life on the street and illustrates with photographs the runaway youth, veterans, mentally ill, and families living homeless.

Unit *III.* MACROECONOMICS

Macroeconomics covers the overall aspects of the economy. It deals with the total performance of the economy rather than with the behavior of individual units.

Chapter 10. Money

Money comes in different forms and serves various purposes. The ways in which it is created and controlled have a major effect on the economy.

Chapter II. Unemployment and Inflation

The two big problems that macroeconomics has to deal with are unemployment and inflation. There are three different types of unemployment and a similar number of causes of inflation. The trade-off between unemployment and inflation changes at different times.

Chapter 12. The Economy's Output

There are two different ways of measuring the total output of the economy, giving the same result. There are also two different explanations for what determines the level of total output—demand-side economics and supply-side economics—which do not come to the same conclusions.

Chapter 14. Policies for Economic Stability and Growth

The government attempts to solve the unemployment and inflation problems and simultaneously maximize total output through the use of monetary and fiscal policies. The goal of economic growth can be achieved by increasing capital investment and capital efficiency and by improvements in the quality of the labor force.

Chapter 13. Public Finance

Spending by the three levels of government—federal, state, and local—equals about one-third of total spending in the economy and accounts for 18% of total output. What this money is spent on and what its sources are depend on the level of government concerned. The way in which government spending is financed affects households and the economy.

■ **People often** associate economics with money. As we have seen in the first half of this book, economics deals with much more than just money, but now it is necessary to take a closer look at money. The introductory article examines its origins.

That Curious Commodity

Money is a curious commodity. Cattle were commonly used as money in pre-Christian times, and even recently by some primitive tribes. In fact, our word *pecuniary,* which means "related to money," comes from the Latin word *pecus,* meaning "cattle." Cloth, corn, slaves, knives, and even beer have been used as money in different places at various times. These were types of money that had a real value. But that was not true of all forms of money used in the past. Seashells, porpoise teeth, and woodpecker scalps have little practical use; but, at one time or other, in various places, all of these items have been used as money.

Metal coins were first used as money in the seventh century B.C. in ancient Lydia, which was located in what is now Turkey. Lydian coins were stamped with the head of a lion. Coins from other places sported turtles, owls, and horses with wings. These coins were usually made from an alloy of gold and silver. The designs on coins, especially those minted by the city-states of ancient Greece, became works of art, designed by some of the greatest artists of the day. The beautiful artwork helped the coins gain recognition and acceptance.

Paper money originated with goldsmiths during the seventeenth century in London. Because the goldsmiths had safes in which to keep the precious metals that they worked with, people would bring them coins and gold and silver for safekeeping. The goldsmith gave the "depositors" receipts for their coins and precious metals.

It developed that these receipts would then be transferred from person to person as a means of payment. And if a wily goldsmith made out a few extra receipts and used them as a means of payment, no one would know it as long as everyone with receipts did not come to claim his or her precious metals or coins at the same time.

In the United States, after the Revolutionary War and during the next century, paper money in the form of banknotes was issued by privately owned banks. These banks were chartered by the federal government and the state governments. The state-chartered banks tended to be reckless in creating money. If someone presented a banknote for redemption, it had to be redeemed in gold or silver. Since the banks, following the example of the goldsmiths, issued more paper money than they had reserves of gold and silver, they preferred that the notes not be redeemed. Some banks made it difficult for people to find them by locating in out-of-the-way places. These hard-to-find locations were out in the "wilds," and this gave rise to the term "wildcat banking."

When the Civil War broke out, the federal government put an end to the freewheeling

practices of state-chartered banks. The federal government printed paper money itself—"greenbacks"—to help finance the war. But it was not until 1913, when the Federal Reserve System was established, that the federal government monopolized the issuance of banknotes.

Today, the production of currency is a big operation. There is a factory in Washington, D.C., that prints tens of millions of dollars in paper money every day. Tight security measures are used to protect this operation. Closed-circuit television cameras monitor production and inventory, and each employee must have a security clearance. This factory, the Bureau of Printing and Engraving, operates 24 hours a day, 7 days a week, including holidays.

New currency leaves the Bureau of Printing and Engraving in armored trucks for distribution to the 12 Federal Reserve banks around the country. The Federal Reserve banks act as wholesalers in passing the currency to commercial banks and other financial institutions. It is from these that the public obtains currency.

If we used currency for all of our money transactions, the printing presses in the Washington printing factory couldn't possibly keep up with the demand. But we don't use currency for all our money transactions. In terms of the total amount paid, 90% of all our monetary transactions are paid by check rather than currency.

The way we pay for goods and services is undergoing another change. One indication of this change is the increasing use of credit cards. In 1980, 86.1 million holders of bank, store, gas, and other credit cards held 526 million cards, on which they charged $201.2 billion of purchases. By 1991 this had increased to 111.3 million cardholders with 1.027 billion cards charging $481 billion.

Another aspect of the changing payments mechanism is the emergent use of electronic transfers of funds to replace writing checks in making payments. Transactions by automated teller machines and point of sale (POS) transfers, using debit cards that draw directly on the customer's bank deposit, have doubled from 3.6 billion transactions in 1985 to 7.5 billion in 1992.

These changes are altering the nature of banking. Handling currency becomes unnecessary. Dallas's Lone Star National Bank became the nation's first cashless bank in 1984. It kept no currency on hand. Among other advantages, this eliminated any danger of robberies. On the sides of the bank were signs announcing "No cash on premises."

The newest innovation in payments is the "smart card." The first such smart card to be introduced was the Mondex system, field-tested by a British bank as an alternative to cash. An amount of purchasing power is programmed into electronic chips embedded in a plastic card. As the card is used to make purchases, machines at stores, restaurants, and other establishments with the necessary equipment deduct the amount of the purchase from the balance on the card until it is exhausted.

Chapter Preview

Although you can use a dollar bill to clean the lenses of your glasses or a coin as an emergency screwdriver, modern money is not a very useful commodity. Its only value is that other people have confidence in it and are willing to accept it in exchange for goods and services. This chapter explores the behavior of money by examining the following questions: What is money? What does money do? How is money created? How is the supply of money controlled?

Learning Objectives

After completing this chapter, you should be able to:

1. Discuss the history of money.

2. Define the M1 money supply and describe its components.

3. Explain how near money differs from money and discuss how near money relates to the broader money definitions of M2, M3, and L.

4. List the three functions of money and explain the characteristics money must have in order to be functional.

5. Discuss how currency is affected by public demand and explain money creation.

6. Describe the Federal Reserve System.

7. Explain how the Federal Reserve System controls the money supply.

The same equipment may then be used to replenish the amount of "money" in the card from the customer's bank account. The card can hold balances in up to five different currencies, making money changing at borders unnecessary. There is a "lock" programmed into the card to prevent others from using it.

The volume of electronic payments is likely to exceed the amount paid by checks in the future. Even the paper symbols of money payments are being replaced by invisible electrical impulses. Money, that curious commodity, has come a long way from seashells and woodpecker scalps.

What Is Money?

As we have seen, money has taken many forms throughout the centuries. It can be anything that society generally accepts as payment for goods and services. This section will discuss what serves as money in our contemporary economy.

Currency

In the United States today, only about one-fourth of our money supply is **currency**. The amount of currency in circulation increases each year by varying amounts. After regularly increasing 9–10% a year during the last half of the 1970s, the rate of growth slowed to an average of less than 8% during the 1980s, and then increased again to an average of 9.5% in the first 4 years of the 1990s. The amount of

currency in circulation depends on how much is desired by individuals and businesses. In February 1994 it totaled $329 billion. Individual and business withdrawal of currency from banks determines how much the banks will order from the **Federal Reserve System**. The government mints enough coins and prints sufficient paper money to satisfy this demand. Cur-

currency: that part of the money supply consisting of coins and paper bills.

Federal Reserve System (Fed): the central bank of the United States; a system established by the Federal Reserve Act of 1913 to issue paper currency, supervise the nation's banking system, and implement monetary policy.

Figure 1.
Money Supply Components (M1)
Percent of the Total Supply

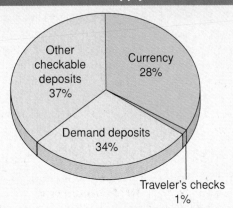

Source: Board of Governors of the Federal Reserve System.

■ Demand deposits and other checkable deposits make up 71% of the money supply.

rency held by the government or by banks is not considered part of the money supply.

At one time federal law required that the amount of currency in circulation be limited to a legally fixed ratio to the value of the banking system's gold reserves. In 1968 this requirement was eliminated. The value of currency today depends only on people's confidence in the stability of the U.S. economy.

The percentage of currency in the money supply increased gradually from 20% in 1960 to 28% in 1980 and has stayed at that level since. Monetary experts are not sure why there are variations in the demand for currency. One view is that the percentage of currency in the money supply always rises whenever there is a publicized failure of a business or a bank. In the year following the failure of Oklahoma's Penn Square Bank in 1982, the growth of currency in circulation

Figure 2.
The Supply of Money and Near Monies, 1975–1993

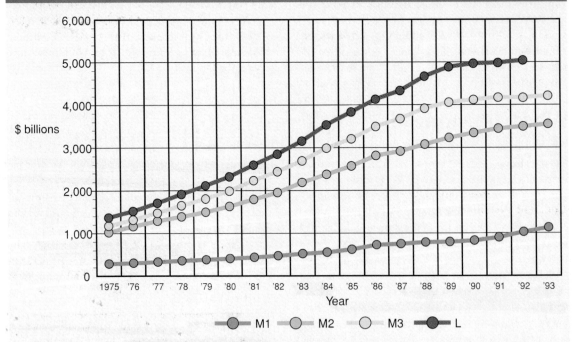

Source: Board of Governors of the Federal Reserve System.

■ The supplies of near monies have been increasing more rapidly than the money supply. This is due in large part to the growth of new money instruments, such as money market funds and money market accounts, that combine high liquidity with higher returns than savings accounts.

■ When people withdraw cash from their checking accounts to pay for purchases, the money supply is not changed.

temporarily increased, lending support to that idea. On the other hand, widespread failures of savings and loan institutions in the late 1980s had no appreciable effect on the currency component of the money supply.

There are also variations in the amount of currency in circulation during the year, especially around December, when it reaches a peak to accommodate the holiday buying rush. At any given time, a number of factors can affect how much of their wealth people desire to hold in the form of currency.

Demand Deposits

The largest part of the money supply is not currency but **demand deposits** and **other checkable deposits**—the obligations of a financial institution that are payable whenever the depositor writes a **check**. These deposits, which may be in either commercial banks, savings banks, savings and loan associations, or credit unions, do not consist of currency. A deposit is a liability, a sum that the bank must stand ready to pay immediately upon request. A check is a written order instructing the institution to do so, to transfer funds from one account to another. In this respect, it is similar to an IOU given to a friend in exchange for a cash loan. Checks written on demand deposits differ from personal IOUs in their widespread general

acceptability as money. Unlike a check written on a demand deposit, a personal IOU normally cannot be used for purchases.

Because checks drawn on deposit accounts are used to pay for goods and services, these deposits are considered money. When people make cash withdrawals from their checking accounts to pay for purchases, or when they deposit cash into their checking accounts, the money supply is not changed. One type of money is exchanged for another type, with the total remaining the same.

The most commonly used measurement of the money supply includes currency, traveler's checks, demand deposits, and other checkable deposits such as **NOW accounts**. This measurement of the money supply is known as **M1**. Demand and other checkable deposits constitute 71% of the money supply (see Figure 1).

Near Money

There are various types of financial assets that can be turned into money more or less easily. These assets are considered **near monies** (see Figure 2). They include **savings deposits, cer-**

(Continued on page 258) ⫸

demand deposits (checking accounts): liabilities of depository institutions to their customers that are payable on demand.

other checkable deposits: accounts, other than demand deposit accounts in commercial banks, on which checks can be drawn, principally negotiable order of withdrawal (NOW) accounts in savings and loan banks.

check: a written order to a depository institution to pay a person or institution named on it a specified sum of money.

negotiable order of withdrawal (NOW) accounts: savings and loan bank customer accounts on which checks can be drawn.

M1: a measure of the money supply that includes currency in circulation, demand deposit accounts, negotiable order of withdrawal (NOW) accounts, automatic transfer savings (ATS) accounts, traveler's checks, and checkable money market accounts.

near money (monies): assets with a specified monetary value that are readily redeemable as money; savings accounts, certificates of deposit, and shares in money market mutual funds.

savings deposits: liabilities of depository institutions to their customers that are not transferable by check and for which the institution may require advance notice before withdrawal.

Dealing the Cards

■ Walter Cavanagh, also known as "Mr. Plastic Fantastic," displays some of his 1,356 different credit cards. Even with his record-breaking collection, however, Mr. Cavanagh possesses only 12% of the different kinds of credit cards that are available.

The stakes in the plastic card game are high and everybody wants in on the action. There are some 80 million holders of bank credit cards, a figure projected to grow another 10 million before the end of the decade. In 1991 these bankcard holders charged $260 billion of purchases on their cards, up from only $53 billion in 1980. Bankcard charges are projected to grow to $494 billion in the year 2000. With these universal cards—Visa and Master-Card along with the American Express and Discover cards—you can buy anything from a toothbrush to an automobile. Besides the universal cards, there are also innumerable specialized credit cards issued by oil companies, department stores, airlines, hotels, and the telephone companies. By the beginning of the next century, total credit card purchases will be approaching $1 trillion per year.

From the standpoint of the customer, the explosion in the popularity of credit cards is due to a number of attractions: their convenience, the chance to spread out the payments over a period of time, the "float" (the delay between the date of the purchase and the date when the credit card payment is due), and the reduced risk of having cash lost or stolen. For some transactions—renting a car, ordering merchandise over the phone—a credit card is a virtual necessity. Most bankcards offer the cardholder the option of paying all bills in one lump sum or stretching out payments.

From the standpoint of the banks issuing the cards, the attraction is the high rate of interest they earn on outstanding balances. Interest charges on credit card balances are typically 18–20%, substantially higher than the 12–13% banks charge on other types of personal loans. The banks maintain that the costs of credit card fraud and defaults necessitate the high interest rates. Furthermore, they claim, cardholders are not concerned about what interest they pay, but only about the convenience of their charge cards.

The evidence suggests that banks may be right about the claim that cardholders generally are not concerned about the interest they pay. They are wrong, however, about the claim that it is economically necessary for them to charge such high rates. According to Federal Reserve data, since 1982 the profit margin on credit card business has been higher than for any other type of bank lending. Further evidence of the profitability of credit cards is the premium price paid when one bank buys the credit card business of another bank. In 10 such transactions for which the price was publicly disclosed, the accounts sold at an average premium of 17% above their value, reflecting the expected future profitability of the accounts.

Despite the high interest rates, some people are credit card junkies. Like compulsive gamblers, they are unable to control their use of the credit cards. They find themselves over their heads in debt and unable to meet their payments. This often means that the cards are canceled and the cardholder gets a bad credit rating. Other people choose to make minimum use of credit cards in order to keep their spending under control. If they can pay off the balance each month, as about one-third of all cardholders do, they benefit from the convenience of credit cards but avoid the high interest charges. The issuing banks don't like this much, but they still make a profit from the annual fees paid by the cardholder plus the amounts they collect from merchants for processing charge slips.

Some credit card users elect to carry only a few cards so that in case the cards get lost or stolen it won't be difficult to notify the companies. At the other extreme are the credit card collectors. According to the *Guinness Book of World Records,* the champion cardholder is Walter Cavanagh of Santa Clara, California, who has 1,356 valid credit cards. He has the nickname of Mr. Plastic Fantastic. He keeps his credit cards in a fold-out wallet that is 250 feet long and weighs 37½ pounds. The total amount of credit available to him with the cards is over $1.6 million. However, he makes a practice of paying off all of his bills each month.

Economic Reasoning

1. Is "plastic money" included in the money supply measured by M1? How can you tell whether it is?

2. If credit cards are not money, can their use lead to an increase in the money supply? How?

3. Should the government tighten restrictions on credit card companies? What kinds of restrictions might be imposed?

⟹ (Continued from page 255)

tificates of deposit (CDs), and shares in **money market mutual funds**. The ease with which near monies can be converted into money is called their **liquidity**. Depending upon how liquid these various financial assets are, they may be included in broader definitions of the money supply referred to as **M2, M3,** and **L**.

With the deregulation of the banking system and the evolution of new types of finan-

cial assets, the line between money and near money has become blurred. Banks now provide **automatic transfer services (ATS)** from savings deposits to demand deposits. Money market funds permit investors to write checks on their fund accounts. These new types of accounts cross over the line from near money to money.

What Does Money Do?

Not only does money take different forms, but it also serves various functions. In this section, we'll examine the different functions of money.

certificate of deposit (CD): a deposit of a specified sum of money for a specified period of time that cannot be redeemed prior to the date specified.

money market mutual fund: an investment fund that pools the assets of investors and puts the cash into debt securities that mature in less than 1 year: short-term bank CDs, commercial paper of corporations, and 6-month Treasury bills.

liquidity: the degree of ease with which an asset can be converted into cash without appreciable loss in value.

M2: a measure of the money supply that includes M1 plus savings deposits, small time deposits (CDs), and certain money market mutual funds.

M3: a measure of the money supply that includes M2 plus large time deposits (CDs).

L: a measure of the money supply that includes M3 plus commercial paper, savings bonds, and government securities with maturities of 18 months or less.

automatic transfer services (ATS): a type of account that provides for the depository institution to automatically transfer funds from the depositor's savings account to her or his checking account when it has been drawn down.

medium of exchange: a commodity accepted by common consent in payment for goods and services and as settlement of debts and contracts.

barter: direct exchange of goods and services without the use of money.

unit of measurement (standard of value or unit of account): a common denominator of value in which prices are stated and accounts recorded.

Medium of Exchange

One function of money is that it is used as a **medium of exchange**, something that people will accept in exchange for goods or services.

The use of money to pay for things evolved as an alternative to **barter**. Using money as a medium of exchange for goods and services of all kinds is much easier than attempting to trade those goods and services directly for each other. Money generally simplifies the exchange process. There is no need in a monetary economy to waste time looking for someone who has exactly that good or service you want and who wants exactly what you have to trade. The use of money greatly simplifies exchange.

In order to serve well as a medium of exchange, whatever is used as money should be universally recognized, have an adequate but limited supply, not be easily reproduced (forged), be easily portable, and be durable. The evolution of money from seashells to bank drafts has been one long attempt to satisfy these requirements.

Unit of Measurement

Some of the earlier forms of money did not serve very well as a medium of exchange. Cows, for example, are not exactly portable. However, they did serve another function of money, that of providing a **unit of measurement**. The money unit serves as a common denominator that can specify the value of something else. In societies where cattle were used for money, everyone knew pretty well the value of a cow. The value of other

POW Money

During World War II, captured servicemen in prisoner of war (POW) camps in Germany and Italy created a simple but complete economic system to serve their needs. The prisoners received Red Cross rations, which included canned milk, chocolate bars, jam, sugar, crackers, and cigarettes. Some also received gift packages from home through the mail. These rations and gifts comprised a flow of real income to the prisoners, although they had no money.

The Red Cross rations were fairly standardized, and a POW would likely find himself with a shortage of his favorite commodities and an excess of other commodities that he did not want.

The prisoners soon began to make exchanges. Out of these exchanges a market system was born. The essence of exchange is that both parties benefit. A nonsmoker gives up cigarettes he does not value for chocolate, which he does like. So the smoker gets the cigarettes and the candy lover gets the chocolate.

Exchanges at first were made through a simple barter procedure, whereby one item was swapped for another. But this process was awkward and time consuming. If one POW had some crackers and chocolate bars and wished to exchange the chocolate bars for jam to eat with the crackers, he would have to find someone else who had jam but preferred to have chocolate bars instead. Some prisoners in the camp became very good at making advantageous swaps and made a business venture of it—POW capitalists.

To get around the inconvenience of barter, a money economy gradually developed in the camps, complete with buyers, sellers, and even a merchant class. Cigarettes were used as money, and the prices of all other items were quoted in terms of how many cigarettes they were worth.

Economic Reasoning

1. Which functions of money did cigarettes perform in the POW camp?

2. Heavy air raids in the vicinity of the camp increased the consumption of cigarettes. What effect did this have on the prices of things?

3. Sometimes the successful POW capitalists who profited from buying and selling things were resented by other prisoners. Was the hostility directed toward them justified? Were they providing a useful service, or were they merely leeches on the POW society?

things could therefore be expressed in terms of how much of each was equivalent to the value of a cow.

Normally, the unit of measurement is the same as the medium of exchange, but not always. In international transactions where countries use different mediums of exchange (French francs, German marks, British pounds), the American dollar is frequently used as a unit of measurement. The price of OPEC oil, for example, is quoted in U.S. dollars per barrel all over the world.

A unit of measurement should itself be stable in value. Because of fluctuations in the value of the dollar, there have been suggestions that the world adopt a new unit of measurement. It would be based on the value of commodities rather than on the value of the dollar or any other currency.

Store of Value

The third function of money is to serve as a **store of value**, a form in which wealth can be held. Any form of wealth may be used as a store of value, but money has the advantage of being more liquid than other forms of wealth. Near monies are not perfectly liquid, because in order to use them for purchases you must normally convert them into currency or a demand deposit. You run the risk that converting them at a particular time may result in a loss. Holding money itself, however, results in a loss during times of rising prices. As prices rise, the real purchasing power of money declines.

How Is Money Created?

The manner in which money is created has evolved quite a bit since the Lydians stamped out their lion-headed coins 26 centuries ago. In this section we will look at how money is created in a modern economy.

Currency

As we have seen, this part of the money supply is produced by the federal government, which supplies coins and paper money in the amounts required by the public. Currency enters businesses and households through banks. An increase in the amount of currency in circulation, however, does not necessarily mean an increase in the money supply. People who need more currency buy it from their banks by writing checks on their deposits for the bills or coins desired. The increase in currency has been offset by a decrease in demand deposits, leaving the total money supply unchanged.

It would be possible for the federal government to increase the money supply by printing more currency if it used the currency directly to pay government bills rather than selling the currency to the public through the banking system. This is not the usual practice in this country, however, and the government

commodity: an economic good.

store of value: a means of conserving purchasing power for a future time.

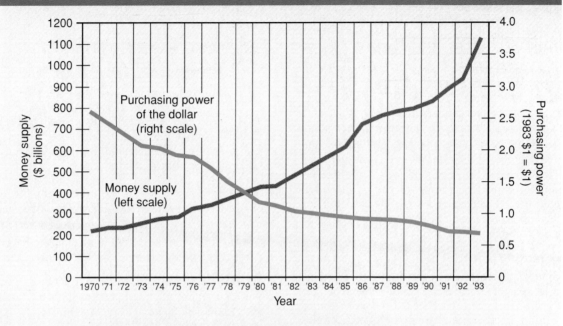

Figure 3.
Comparisons of the Money Supply (M1) and the Purchasing Power of the Dollar, 1970–1993
(purchasing power in 1983 dollars)

Sources: Money supply: Board of Governors of the Federal Reserve System.
Purchasing power of the dollar: U.S. Bureau of Labor Statistics.

■ As the money supply increased, the amount each dollar would buy decreased. As a result, money has not served very well as a store of value. Inflation diminishes this function of money.

normally produces currency only in response to the demands from businesses and the general public.

■ The Lydians of western Anatolia minted the first gold and silver coins and set up the first permanent retail stores in the seventh century B.C.

Private Borrowing

Borrowing from a bank increases the supply of money by increasing the amount of demand deposits. The borrower, in exchange for promising to repay a given sum (usually this promise is represented by a **promissory note**), receives the amount in his or her checking account. This added deposit does not reduce anyone else's deposit and, as such, represents a net increase in the supply of money. The individual is then able to use that money to purchase goods and services by writing a check on the account. The new money created by the loan is thereby transferred to someone else, who in turn may use it for other purchases.

promissory note (IOU): a written obligation to pay a specified amount at a specified time.

How to Create Money

One way you can create money is to print it on a printing press in your basement. But if you were to do that you could get into a lot of trouble. A perfectly legal way you can create money, however, is to take out a loan at a bank. Imagine that you have decided that you will buy a computer that costs $1,200. You go to the bank for a loan, and if the bank approves your loan for $1,200, you sign a promissory note. The banker makes out a deposit slip to be credited to your demand deposit account, and you can then write a check to pay for the computer.

When the purchase is made and the computer dealer deposits your check in the bank, it is presented to your bank for payment. Your demand deposit account is decreased by the amount of the check. What has happened to your personal wealth? You now own a computer worth $1,200. You have also increased your liability by the amount of the loan ($1,200), so your personal wealth has not changed. Your assets and liabilities from this transaction are equal. But you have succeeded in increasing the money supply in the economy. That money is now in the computer dealer's checking account. When the computer dealer spends it, it will move to someone else's account.

Economic Reasoning

1. If you borrowed the $1,200 in cash rather than having it credited to your checking account, would the effect on the money supply be the same? Why or why not?

2. When you pay off your bank loan, what happens to the money supply? Is the effect on the money supply any different depending on whether you pay the bank by check or with currency?

3. There is an old adage that bankers are only willing to loan money to people who don't need it. Those who have plenty of financial assets that can readily be turned into cash have little trouble getting a loan, whereas those who have no assets have a great deal of difficulty. Should bankers make loans only to those who have enough assets to guarantee repayment of the loan? What are the consequences of making loans to people who are not good credit risks?

■ In a throwback to earlier forms of money, these cumbersome stones, while not easily portable, serve as a unit of measurement on the islands of Yap.

If the borrower repays the loan from the bank when the note comes due, the money supply is reduced by that amount. Changes in the money supply depend on the amount of new loans relative to the amount of repayment of previous loans. When the volume of new lending by banks exceeds the repayment of previous loans, the money supply increases.

Government Borrowing

When the local, state, or federal government borrows from a bank, the initial effect upon the money supply is much the same as in the case of private borrowing. New deposits are created. A government borrows by promising future repayment in return for a current deposit. The government can then write checks on the deposit to cover its expenditures. **Treasury bills** and **bonds** are government promises to repay its loans.

Thus the federal government does not customarily increase the money supply by printing money. It increases the money supply in the same way businesses and individuals increase the money supply—by borrowing.

How Is the Supply of Money Controlled?

In order for our monetary system to function successfully, people must have confidence in the value of money. This confidence can be maintained only if the quantity of money in circulation does not fluctuate excessively. Here we will examine how the money supply is controlled to prevent excessive variations in the quantity and value of money.

The Federal Reserve System

Banks in the nineteenth century engaged in unrestrained issuance of currency and imprudent lending. This caused wild fluctuations in the money supply. Excessive creation of money alternated with bank failures and the collapse of the monetary system. Finally, after the panic of 1907, when a run on banks by people attempting to withdraw their deposits forced many banks to close, the government established a National Monetary Commission to formulate a plan for a new American banking system. The recommendations in its report led to the establishment of the Federal Reserve System in 1913. The Federal Reserve, commonly referred to as "the **Fed**," is the **central bank** of the United States. It is a government institution that acts as a "banker's bank," serves the monetary needs of the federal government, and controls the monetary system.

There are 12 regional Federal Reserve banks in the country. Each one services and regulates the banks in its district. The Federal Reserve Districts are shown in Figure 4 on

Treasury bill: a short-term, marketable federal government security with a maturity of 1 year or less.

bond: a long-term, interest-bearing certificate issued by a business firm or government that promises to pay the bondholder a specified sum of money on a specified date.

Fed: Federal Reserve System.

central bank: a government institution that controls the issuance of currency, provides banking services to the government and to the other banks, and implements the nation's monetary policy; in the United States the Federal Reserve is the central bank.

Table 1.

Organization of the Federal Reserve System

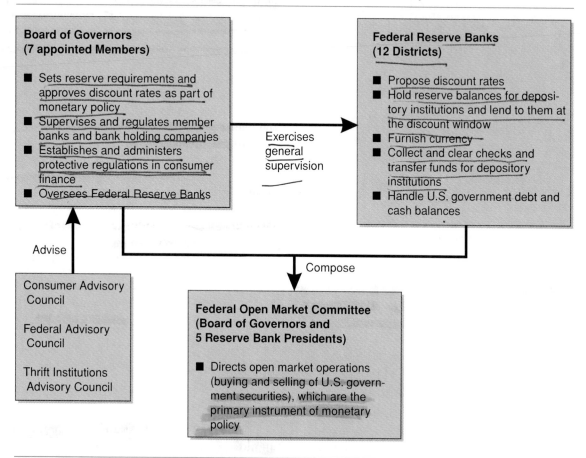

Board of Governors
(7 appointed Members)

- Sets reserve requirements and approves discount rates as part of monetary policy
- Supervises and regulates member banks and bank holding companies
- Establishes and administers protective regulations in consumer finance
- Oversees Federal Reserve Banks

Exercises general supervision

Federal Reserve Banks
(12 Districts)

- Propose discount rates
- Hold reserve balances for depository institutions and lend to them at the discount window
- Furnish currency
- Collect and clear checks and transfer funds for depository institutions
- Handle U.S. government debt and cash balances

Advise

Consumer Advisory Council

Federal Advisory Council

Thrift Institutions Advisory Council

Compose

Federal Open Market Committee
(Board of Governors and
5 Reserve Bank Presidents)

- Directs open market operations (buying and selling of U.S. government securities), which are the primary instrument of monetary policy

Source: Board of Governors of the Federal Reserve System, Division of Support Services, *Purposes and Functions*, 1984.

page 265. The system is under the overall authority of the **Board of Governors** in Washington, D.C. The seven members of the board are appointed by the president of the United States and confirmed by the Senate for staggered 14-year terms. The board's chairman and vice chairman are named by the president, and confirmed by the Senate, from among the members of the board. They are appointed to serve for 4-year terms, with the

possibility of reappointment so long as their board terms have not expired.

Only about half of the nation's commercial banks, some 7,000 banks with 39,000 branches, are members of the Federal Reserve System. These include the nation's larger, most influential banks. The state-chartered commercial banks that are not members of the Federal Reserve System, the savings and loan banks, and the federally insured credit unions are supervised at the federal level by three other agencies: the Federal Deposit Insurance Corporation, the Office of Thrift Supervision, and the National Credit Union Administration, respectively. There are a variety of proposals before Congress to revamp the present

Fed Board of Governors: the governing body of the Federal Reserve System, consisting of seven members appointed by the president for 14-year terms.

Figure 4.
The Federal Reserve System

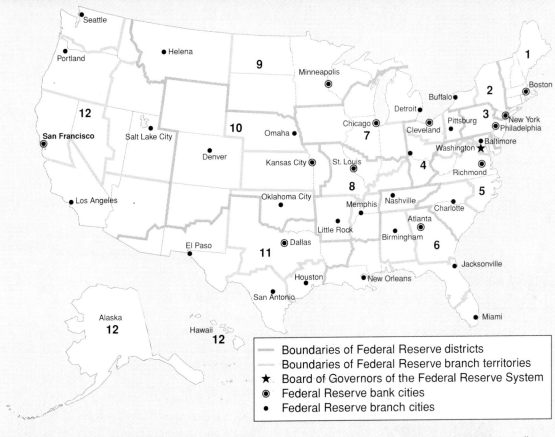

Boundaries of Federal Reserve districts
Boundaries of Federal Reserve branch territories
★ Board of Governors of the Federal Reserve System
◉ Federal Reserve bank cities
• Federal Reserve branch cities

■ This map shows the network of Federal Reserve bank districts in the United States. Before the Fed's establishment in 1913, bank failures and monetary collapse threatened the economic system.

structure of monetary supervision and control. The Fed has opposed the proposed changes because they would tend to lessen its authority and independence.

The most important function of the Federal Reserve System is to control the creation of money by **depository institutions.** There are three ways by which it accomplishes this: (1) by setting **legal reserve requirements**; (2) by varying the **discount rate**; (3) by **open market operations.**

Reserve Requirements

All banks are required to have a reserve on deposit with the Federal Reserve bank in their district. These deposits are the banks' **re-quired reserves.** A bank may have in its reserve account more than the legal minimum

> **depository institutions:** financial institutions that maintain deposit account obligations to their customers; includes commercial banks, savings banks, savings and loan associations, and credit unions.
>
> **legal reserve requirement (required reserves):** the minimum amount of reserves that a depository institution must have on deposit with the Federal Reserve bank, stated as a percentage of its deposit liabilities.
>
> **discount rate:** the interest rate charged by the Federal Reserve on loans to depository institutions.
>
> **open market operations:** the purchase or sale of government securities by the Federal Reserve to implement monetary policy.
>
> **required reserves:** see legal reserve requirement.

Table 2 Seventh Bank of Commerce Year-End Balance Sheet
(thousands of dollars)

Assets		Liabilities	
Reserves at Federal Reserve	$15,843	Demand deposits (private)	$91,145
Vault cash	3,721	Time deposits (private)	63,025
Deposits at other banks	12,210	Deposits of U.S. government	1,670
Checks in process of collection	5,776	Deposits of state & local governments	26,145
U.S. government securities	23,680	Liabilities to financial institutions	7,445
Securities of state & local governments	24,370	Other liabilities	6,760
Other securities	2,420	Total Liabilities	$196,190
Loans and discounts	114,155		
Bank premises	5,305	**Capital**	
Other assets	3,310	Common stock	$2,265
Total Assets	$210,790	Capital surplus	5,360
		Undivided profits	4,700
		Reserves	2,205
		Total Capital	$14,600
		Total Liabilities and Capital	$210,790

■ The balance sheet of a hypothetical bank. Required and excess reserves are an asset. Deposits are liabilities.

specified, but it is not allowed to operate with less. Reserves over the legal minimum are referred to as **excess reserves.**

Under the Monetary Control Act, the Federal Reserve Board specifies the legal reserve requirements of all banks as a percentage of each bank's customer deposits—whether checking, savings, or time deposits. These reserve requirements can be varied by the Fed within statutory limits. The highest reserve requirements are imposed on checking and "checkable" savings (NOW and ATS) accounts and can vary from 8% to 14%.

> **excess reserves:** reserves of depository institutions over and above the legally required minimum on deposit with the Federal Reserve.
>
> **reserve requirement ratio:** the percentage of a depository institution's deposit obligations to its depositors that must be maintained in reserves.
>
> **deposit liabilities:** the amount that a depository institution is obligated to pay out to its depositors.

Let us assume for illustration that the **reserve requirement ratio** is 10%. This means that the bank must have on deposit in its reserve account with the Fed at least $1 for every $10 in customer deposits on its books. If the balance sheet of the bank shows **deposit liabilities** of $100 million, the bank must have no less than $10 million in its reserve deposit. If by some chance the bank's reserves stand at less than $10 million, it must obtain additional reserves. It can do this by selling some of its financial assets, such as the government securities it owns, or by borrowing funds from the Fed or from other banks. If the bank wants to avoid doing one of these possibly costly things, it must reduce its deposit liabilities to a level that does not exceed 10 times its reserves.

How does the Fed control the supply of money by altering the legal reserve requirements? Let us assume that the bank we are discussing has not loaned all the money it was allowed to loan. Instead of having $10 million

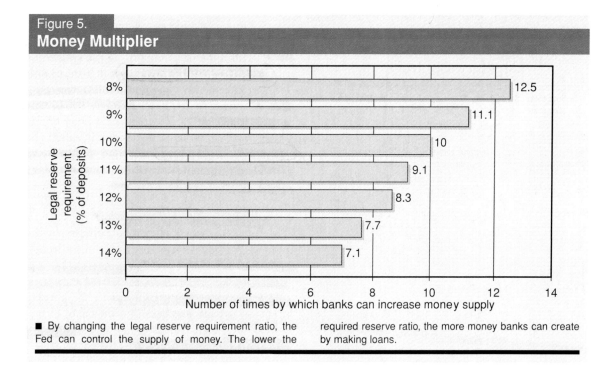

Figure 5.
Money Multiplier

Legal reserve requirement (% of deposits)

	Number of times
8%	12.5
9%	11.1
10%	10
11%	9.1
12%	8.3
13%	7.7
14%	7.1

Number of times by which banks can increase money supply

■ By changing the legal reserve requirement ratio, the Fed can control the supply of money. The lower the required reserve ratio, the more money banks can create by making loans.

in reserves, it has $12 million. In addition to its $10 million required reserves, it has $2 million in excess reserves. The bank could profit by expanding its credit business and making new loans. If the Fed Board of Governors does not want banks to expand their lending because the money supply is growing too rapidly, it can prevent the bank from making new loans by raising the reserve requirement to 12%. Since the bank's $12 million reserve is 12% of its demand deposit liabilities, the bank has made as many loans as it can. It cannot extend additional loans to borrowers without first increasing its reserves. Thus the money supply has been prevented from growing.

The reserve requirement ratio determines by how much the banking system can expand the money supply. If the reserve requirement is 10%, the maximum expansion of the money supply is 10 times the increase in bank reserves. If the reserve requirement is 12.5%, the maximum expansion of the money supply is only 8 times the amount of the increase in bank reserves. The ratio of maximum money supply creation to bank-required reserves is

the **money multiplier**. If the reserve requirement were 100%, commercial banks would be unable to expand the money supply at all. This would make it very difficult for businesses to borrow money and would seriously hamper economic activity.

Discounting

If a bank wishes to expand its lending activity but has no excess reserves, or if it finds itself below the legal reserve requirement, it may add to its reserves by borrowing from the Fed. Federal Reserve lending to commercial banks is called **discounting,** and the interest charged by the Fed for such loans is the discount rate. By increasing this rate, the Fed can discourage banks from coming to the "discount window" and asking for a loan. On the

> **money multiplier:** the ratio of the maximum increase in the money supply to an increase in bank reserves. Determined by the required reserve ratio.

> **discounting:** assigning a present value to future returns; making a loan with the interest subtracted in advance from the principal.

Table 3. **Major Tools of Federal Reserve Monetary Control**

Federal Reserve Tool	Action	Effect on Money Supply
Reserve Requirement	Raise required reserve ratio	Decreases
	Lower required reserve ratio	Increases
Discount Rate	Raise discount rate	Decreases
	Lower discount rate	Increases
Open Market Operations	Buy U.S. Treasury securities	Increases
	Sell U.S. Treasury securities	Decreases

other hand, if the Fed wishes to see an expansion of the money supply, it can lower the discount rate and thereby lessen the cost of the loan. This makes borrowing additional reserves a more attractive possibility for the bank.

Federal Funds market: the market among depository institutions for temporary transfer of excess reserves from one institution to another.

Federal Funds rate: the interest rate paid on Federal Funds borrowed.

Federal Open Market Committee: a committee consisting of the Federal Reserve Board and the presidents of five regional Federal Reserve banks that decides on the purchase or sale of government securities by the Federal Reserve to implement monetary policy.

A bank can also supplement its reserves by borrowing the excess reserves of another bank. This type of borrowing is referred to as the **Federal Funds market.** Such interbank lending is typically only overnight or for a few days at most to cover the bank's short-term reserve needs. The interest rate that banks charge each other for these loans is called the **Federal Funds rate.** It is one of the most closely watched interest rates because of its effect on other interest rates.

Open Market Operations

The third way in which the Fed influences the money-creating power of banks is through open market operations. This means that the Fed purchases or sells U.S. government securities (bonds or Treasury bills) in the government securities market. The decision to buy or sell such securities is made by the **Federal Open Market Committee.** This committee is made up of the seven members of the board of governors together with the presidents of five of the Federal Reserve banks.

When the Fed purchases government securities, the amount it pays for them ends up as new reserves for the banks. The new excess reserves in turn make it possible for these banks to create more demand deposits by making new loans. When the Fed sells securities, the opposite happens. Reserves flow out of the banks' Federal Reserve accounts, and bank deposit creation is curtailed.

In practice, open market operations are the tool most commonly used by the Fed to control the money supply. The reason that this is the most popular instrument of monetary policy is that it is the most flexible. It permits the banks the greatest amount of leeway in adjusting to their individual circumstances.

Case Application

Cheap Money

Figure 6.

Prime Interest Rate, Real Interest Rate, and Tax-Adjusted Real Interest Rate, 1970–1993

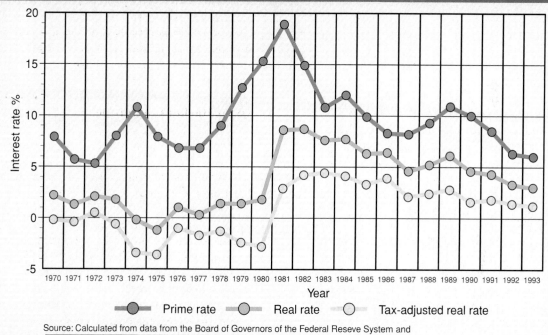

Source: Calculated from data from the Board of Governors of the Federal Reseve System and the Department of Labor, Bureau of Labor Statistics.

■ The real interest rate, the prime rate adjusted for inflation, was near or below zero in the 1970s. After rising in the 1980s, it has again been at less than 5% since 1990. The tax-adjusted real interest rate for those in the 30% bracket was negative in the 1970s and has fallen below 2% in the 1990s.

Money is a real bargain in the United States. The price of money is the interest rate. But the actual cost of money is less than the quoted interest rate, the so-called "nominal rate."

One reason interest costs are less than the nominal rate is inflation. As a result of inflation, when you pay back a loan, the dol-lars that you use to make the payment are not worth as much as the dollars that you bor-rowed. The real rate of interest is the nominal rate minus the rate of inflation. If the interest rate is 10% and the inflation rate is 10%, you get the use of the money free.

The real interest rate is the actual cost of money to the borrower in purchasing power.

Figure 6 shows the prime interest rates and the corresponding real interest rates, after subtracting the rate of inflation, for the years 1970 to 1993. As you see, the real interest rate was less than zero in 1974 and 1975. This means that lenders were subsidizing borrowers to use the lenders' money.

Of course, only the most successful, creditworthy businesses can borrow money at the prime rate. Individuals and other businesses must pay higher rates, reflecting the higher loan risks. Nonetheless, real interest rates were quite low during the 1970s.

This situation changed in the 1980s as a result of a variety of factors. One was the realization by lenders, after a succession of years of high inflation rates, that inflation was apparently going to persist and the rates they charged should take this into account. Reinforcing this movement to higher rates was the deregulation of the banking system, which eliminated interest ceilings on bank deposits. Competition for customers among banks and other financial institutions, such as money market funds, raised the cost of money to lenders, which the lenders passed on in higher interest rates charged to borrowers.

Nominal and real interest rates in some countries, Japan for example, are normally lower than in the United States. But, in this country, the real interest rate is not the "really real" interest rate. The real interest rate takes into account only inflation. It does not take into account the tax benefits to borrowers. Un-like the tax systems in other countries, our tax laws have allowed taxpayers to deduct certain interest payments from their incomes before computing their taxes.

This means that the government subsidizes borrowing. If the borrower's combined federal and state marginal income tax rate is 30%, government picks up 30% of the nominal interest cost on eligible loans. The tax-adjusted real prime interest rates for borrowers in the 30% tax bracket are shown in Figure 6. From 1973 to 1980 they were negative. From a cost standpoint, adjusting for inflation and taxes, borrowing was cheaper than saving. By allowing deductions for interest costs and taxing interest earnings, the government discourages savings.

Economic Reasoning

1. What effect would an increase in the Fed discount rate have on the money supply? Why?

2. What effect would it have on the interest rates shown in Figure 6? Why?

3. Should the tax laws stop subsidizing all borrowing by individuals? By businesses? Why or why not? Should interest earnings on savings be exempt from taxation? What effect would this have on income distribution between the wealthy and the poor?

Putting It Together

Money can be anything that society generally accepts as payment for goods and services. What we consider money today includes not only *currency,* but also travelers' checks, *demand deposits,* and other checkable deposits such as *negotiable orders of withdrawal.* Currency, which consists of coins and bills not held by the banking system, constitutes just over one-fourth of the country's money supply. The remainder is principally made up of bank deposits on which people can write *checks.* The measurement of the money supply, referred to as *M1,* includes *other checkable deposits* in depository institutions such as savings banks and credit unions, as well as those in commercial banks. Other types of financial assets that are not used directly to pay for goods and services but can be turned into money quickly and easily are called *near monies.* Near monies with a high degree of *liquidity* are *savings deposits, certificates of deposit,* and shares in *money market mutual funds.*

Money serves three distinct functions. First, it serves as a *medium of exchange* in conducting transactions. It is much more efficient in facilitating the transfer of goods and services than a *barter* system would be. The second function of money is that it serves as a *unit of measurement.* Whether or not any transactions take place, the value of goods and services is measured in units of money. The unit of measurement within each country is the currency of that country. The unit of measurement in international transactions is quite often the U.S. dollar. Finally, money can be used as a *store of value.* During periods of rapidly rising prices, however, it does not serve this function well.

Currency is produced by the government in response to the demand for it by businesses and the general public. The currency enters the economic system when people purchase it from banks, paying for it by check. Therefore, an increase in currency in circulation does not increase the money supply. It is merely exchanged for a different form of money—demand deposits. The money

■ Federal Reserve banks shred 7,000 tons of worn-out paper currency each year. The life expectancy of a $1 bill is 18 to 22 months (higher denominations have a greater expectancy); it may eventually be replaced with a $1 coin, which would have a much longer life span.

supply is increased when banks lend funds to businesses, individuals, or governments. The bank loans are in the form of demand deposits, which borrowers can then transfer to someone else by writing checks. The amount borrowed continues to circulate in the banking system as additional money until the loan is repaid.

The responsibility for controlling the money supply is in the hands of the *Federal Reserve System*. The Fed has three tools of monetary control. First, it can limit or expand the ability of banks to make loans by raising or lowering banks' reserve requirements. The *required reserves* are equal to a specified percentage of the bank's total *deposit liabilities* that must be deposited with the regional Federal Reserve bank. Any reserves that a bank has deposited over and above the required minimum are *excess reserves* and can form the basis for an increase in loans extended by the bank to borrowers. The ratio of the maximum increase in the money supply to an increase in bank reserves is the *money multiplier*. Its size is determined by the required reserve ratio. The second instrument of the Federal Reserve monetary control is the *discount rate*.

This is the interest rate that banks must pay on funds borrowed from the Fed. Lowering the discount rate encourages banks to borrow from the Federal Reserve to acquire excess reserves in order to expand loan business. Raising the discount rate discourages them from making new loans. The third and most often employed monetary tool of the Federal Reserve is *open market operations*. This is the purchase and sale of U.S. government securities by the Fed in order to increase or decrease bank reserves. When the Fed purchases a bond in the government securities market, the amount of the check that it issues to pay for the bond becomes an addition to the reserves of the banking system. If the Fed sells a bond, the amount that it receives from the sale diminishes bank reserves.

The Big Bank Controversy

An engraving of the Bank of the United States in Philadelphia about 1799. Further information on the evolution of the nation's banking system can be found in *The Second Bank of the United States* by R. C. H. Caterall (Chicago: University of Chicago Press, 1960); *The Theory and History of Banking* by Charles Dunbar (New York: G. P. Putnam's Sons, 1917); and *Money: Whence It Came, Where It Went* by John Kenneth Galbraith (Boston: Houghton Mifflin, 1975).

From the earliest days of the American republic, there has been conflict over states' rights versus the power of the federal government. One of the first important battles in this conflict was over the control of the nation's banking system. The Federalists, led by Alexander Hamilton, wanted a strong national banking system to finance the expansion of industry. The Anti-Federalists, under the leadership of Thomas Jefferson, wanted to minimize the power of the banking system, which they did not trust to protect the predominantly agricultural interests of the country.

The initial victory went to Hamilton and the Federalists when Congress chartered the first Bank of the United States in 1791 for a period of 20 years. One-fifth of the capital needed to finance the bank was provided by the federal government and the remaining four-fifths by private investors. The national bank established branches in major cities and engaged in commercial banking activities and central bank functions. It accepted deposits from and made loans to private borrowers. It also lent money to the federal government and acted as the depository for government funds. It issued banknotes of its own and acted to curb the issuance of banknotes by state-chartered or private banks.

This latter activity generated a great deal of hostility on the part of the state banks. When the charter of the first Bank of the United States expired, it was not renewed by Congress. Freed from the restraints imposed by the national bank, state banks went on a note-issuing spree. They more than doubled their note issues in 5 years. Most of them stopped redeeming their notes for gold and silver. As a result, the notes of many banks became practically worthless. There was chaos in the banking system and numerous bank failures and alternating periods of excessive money expansion and contraction.

As a result, the second Bank of the United States was chartered in 1816. It was similar in its financing and operations to the first bank. It also had a similar fate, its charter being allowed to lapse in 1836. The state banks again had the banking field to themselves until the National Banking Act of 1864. The act provided for a system of federally chartered banks to take over the note-issuing function of the state banks. Congress also intended these national banks to help finance government spending for the Civil War. It was not, however, until the establishment of the Federal Reserve System in 1913 that a true central bank was created.

FOR FURTHER STUDY AND ANALYSIS

Study Questions

1. Have you ever transformed near money into money? How?

2. Are there any barter transactions that take place in today's economy? Why would anyone prefer barter to money transactions?

3. Using the criteria by which money is judged, how well would each of the following serve as a medium of exchange? (1) empty beer cans, (2) four-leaf clovers, (3) IOUs written on cards with the name and address of the writer, (4) fresh fish.

4. Which of the above items could serve one or both of the other two functions of money, even if it isn't a good medium of exchange?

5. Because many people take vacations in the summer, there is an increased demand for currency. How is this additional demand satisfied? Does it increase the money supply? Why or why not?

6. Suppose that in one week the First National Bank made loans of $217,000. During that same week repayment on earlier loans amounted to $220,000. What happened to the money supply as a result?

7. Which would have a more expansionary effect on the money supply, the Treasury's sale of securities to the banks or to the general public? Why?

8. If banks have no excess reserves, what happens when the Fed raises the required reserve ratio?

9. Since bank interest rates are always higher than the Fed discount rate, why does a rise in the discount rate discourage banks from making new loans?

10. Why does appointing members of the Federal Reserve Board of Governors for terms of 14 years make the board independent? Why was this provision put in when the Federal Reserve System was established?

Exercises in Analysis

1. Determine what Federal Reserve district you live in and write a short paper on the Federal Reserve bank that serves the district. Include such information as what states are served by the bank and the bank's capitalization, assets, and liabilities. This information can be obtained from the bank or from the *Federal Reserve Bulletin.*

2. Assume the banking system is fully loaned up and the required reserve ratio is 12.5%. If the Fed then purchases $10 billion worth of U.S. Treasury securities from the banks, what is the effect on bank reserves? What is the total potential effect on the money supply?

3. Make a table showing current interest rates for different types of borrowing. Include interest rates on the following types of bank accounts, loans, and investments: deposit accounts; automobile loans; mortgage loans; 90-day certificates of deposit; money market funds; prime rate; Fed discount rate; Federal Funds rate; 26-week Treasury bills. (The first three rates can be obtained at local banking institutions and may vary from one to another; the remainder can be found in the *Wall Street Journal* or other financial publications.)

4. From issues of the *Wall Street Journal,* or another source, plot the money supply for each month for the past year. Write a brief description of changes.

Further Reading

De Rosa, Paul, and Gary H. Stern. *In the Name of Money*. New York: McGraw-Hill, 1981. How the Fed implements monetary policy.

Garcia, Gillian, and Elizabeth Plautz. *The Federal Reserve: Lender of Last Resort*. Cambridge, MA: Ballinger, 1988. Discusses the need for the Fed as a lender of last resort and its effectiveness in handling crises.

Graziano, Loretta. *Interpreting the Money Supply*. New York: Quorum Books, 1987. The author takes the position that "the money supply is in the eye of the beholder." She discusses the pitfalls in interpreting data on the money supply. She draws conclusions regarding the relationships between the money supply and interest rates and the money supply and inflation.

Kurtzman, Joel. *The Death of Money: How the Electronic Economy Has Destabilized the World's Markets and Created Financial Chaos*. New York: Simon & Schuster, 1993. In the context of the twentieth-century history of money and of the financial services industry, examines how electronic funds transfers have changed the rules of the game. The resulting consequences for the economy have been negative, according to the author. Also looks at the effects on the securities market of program trading.

Mayer, Martin. *The Money Bazaars*. New York: E. P. Dutton, 1984. Banks are being replaced by "financial services institutions." How the new system works and how it is changing the country's financial operations are examined.

Melton, William C. *Inside the Fed: Making Monetary Policy*. Homewood, IL: Dow Jones–Irwin, 1985. Examines how the Fed operates, how to interpret its behavior, and the results of its actions.

Yablonsky, Lewis. *The Emotional Meaning of Money*. New York: Gardner Press, 1991. Money is more than just a means of exchange, a standard of value, and a store of wealth. According to the author, it has social and psychological aspects in addition to its traditional three functions.

Chapter 11. Economic Instability

■ **Money is** necessary to get along in our economic system. The access to money is generally gained by means of having a job. Without a job, the ability to acquire the necessities of life, not to mention the luxuries that enhance life, is limited or nonexistent. The introductory article examines the changing outlook for employment among the new generation.

Jobs for Generation X?

When an economy pulls out of an economic slump, you expect the number of job openings to expand. As overall production picks up, you expect the demand for all types of labor to increase. The recovery in the early 1990s did not meet these expectations.

The recovery itself was weak and hesitant, not as vigorous as we have seen in previous recoveries. But more than that, many jobs continued to disappear. The first year of recovery, 1991–1992, saw rising unemployment. Subsequent employment gains in the next 2 years were far below the levels experienced in earlier recovery periods. Three years into a recovery, there is normally an increase in jobs of over 60% of the rate of increase in output. At that point in the 1991–94 recovery period, however, employment had grown less than half that much. Also, while the total number of unemployed fell, the number of long-term unemployed (those out of work for more than 6 months) rose to over one-fifth of the total unemployed. The average amount of time an unemployed worker was out of a job before finding another increased from 3 months in 1989 to 4½ months in 1993.

A number of large businesses were downsizing as part of a company restructuring program. Even large and profitable companies such as Proctor & Gamble and General Electric continued to shrink their labor forces as the economy expanded. A survey by the American Management Association showed that nearly half of its members reduced their staffs in the first 2 years of the recovery—by an average of 9.3% in 1991–92 and an additional 10.4% in 1992–93.

But stubborn unemployment in the face of economic expansion may not be the biggest employment problem that the country faces. A greater problem in the long term lies in the fact that the new jobs created differ from the old jobs lost in a variety of ways. For one thing, the newly created jobs to a large extent consist of part-time or temporary jobs, replacing full-time jobs. Restructuring companies are using more "contingent" workers because they want a flexible labor force and wish to avoid the costs of benefits for full-time permanent employees. Some 22.5 million workers—nearly one in every five—now work part time. Nine of every ten workers with jobs of less than 35 hours per week do not have employer-

paid health insurance, compared with only one in four workers with jobs of 35 hours per week or more.

Many of the new job openings are in low-wage industries. In the first 2 years of the recovery, the company that created more new job openings than any other was Wal-Mart, the giant chain of discount stores. The wages for those jobs were generally $5 to $9 an hour. A study of workers laid off by RJR Nabisco found that the pay of those hired elsewhere averaged only 47% of the amount they had previously earned.

These difficulties, however, do not constitute the crux of our employment problem. It is not true, for example, that all or even most of the new jobs are in low-paying occupations. In 1993, in fact, 48% of all new jobs were in relatively well-paying managerial and professional occupations. Others were in skilled technical positions that commanded high salaries.

The real problem of future employment in this country is a lack of correspondence between the types of jobs being created and the skills of the labor force available to fill those jobs. Innovations, advances in production technology, and expanding foreign trade have created and will in the coming decades create even more high-productivity jobs.

There has been a rapid increase in the demand for educated labor. The differential between income with a college degree and income with a high school degree has been in-creasing, especially for new workers (see "Does It Pay to Go to College?" chapter 1, p. 18). The college premium for workers aged 25–34 has increased 100% in the last 2 decades. Although the fraction of college graduates in the population has continued to grow, the demand for educated workers has grown faster.

As we saw in chapter 9, the wage rate depends on the relationship between the demand for labor in a particular occupation and the supply of labor available to fill jobs in that occupation (pp. 222–223). There is a growing gap between the wages for workers in jobs that require a high level of training and skill and the wages of workers in unskilled jobs. The low pay for jobs at Wal-Mart and Taco Bell is attributable to the large numbers of workers who are available to fill those jobs, while the premium pay for jobs at high-tech companies is due to the limited number of workers with the training to fill those positions.

The employment problem faced by Generation X—those born between 1965 and 1979*—is not that there will be no jobs available. The economy will continue to create jobs, normally enough jobs to employ 94% to 95% of those in the labor force. The problem is that

*"Generation X" is the name applied to that age cohort by Douglas Coupland in his book of the same name (*Generation X: Tales for an Accelerated Culture.* New York: St. Martin's Press, 1991).

■ **Chapter Preview**
The experience of slow job growth and persistent unemployment even during an economic recovery illustrates that unemployment has a variety of causes. On the other hand, the slowness of price increases during this period was attributable to some extent to the lack of vigorous job growth. This leads us into an investigation of the following questions on economic instability: What causes unemployment? What causes inflation? Is there a trade-off between unemployment and inflation? What are the consequences of unemployment and inflation?

■ **Learning Objectives**
After completing this chapter, you should be able to:

1. Describe the three major causes of unemployment.

2. Explain why some unemployment is hidden.

3. State the meaning of inflation and the CPI.

4. Describe three causes of inflation and explain the usage of the quantity equation.

5. Explain the relationship between unemployment and inflation and use the Phillips curve to show this relationship.

6. Define stagflation and relate the price level to output and employment levels by use of the aggregate supply and aggregate demand curves.

7. Explain how the natural rate of unemployment affects inflation.

8. Explain the consequences of unemployment and inflation.

unless the members of Generation X and succeeding generations acquire the skills for highly productive occupations, their wages may be so low that they cannot maintain a satisfactory standard of living. We have already seen a substantial increase in the numbers of the "working poor." If we do not find a way to bring the skill level of the workforce into line with the demands of the evolving new production system, the pessimistic expectations of Generation X—75% of whom do not think they will have as high a standard of living as their parents—may be fulfilled. (Measures that can be taken to improve the fit between the requirements of jobs and the capabilities of the labor force are discussed in chapter 14, p. 379).

What Causes Unemployment?

A market system operates on the assumption that people who want to work can obtain employment to earn the income necessary for consumption. This chapter analysis section looks at the reasons why this assumption isn't always fulfilled.

Frictional Unemployment

It is expected that in a market economy a certain number of people will be changing jobs at any given time. They may have quit their jobs to find better ones, or they may have lost their jobs because they were laid off, or their firms may have relocated. In a dynamic economy there will always be some workers between jobs. This type of unemployment is called **frictional unemployment**. However, in a healthy economy, workers who are experiencing frictional unemployment should be able to find other jobs within a few weeks.

frictional unemployment: the lack of work that occurs from time lost changing jobs.

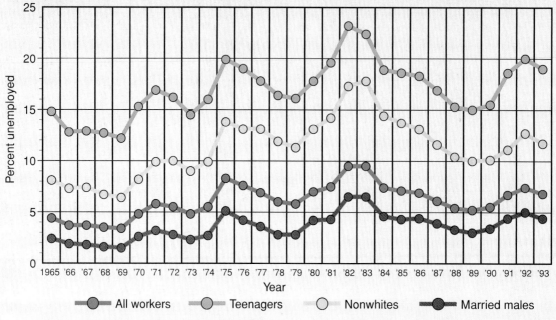

Figure 1.
Unemployment Rates for All Workers and for Selected Groups, 1965–1993

Source: U.S. Department of Labor, Bureau of Labor Statistics.

■ Married males experience the lowest unemployment rates and teenagers the highest. Unemployment has increased for all groups since the 1960s.

From the end of World War II until the 1970s, 3% to 4% frictional unemployment was considered normal. If no more than 4% of the labor force was without a job, the economy was considered to be at full employment. As can be seen from Figure 1, the unemployment rate for all workers has not been this low since the 1960s.

Structural Unemployment

It is not certain why the "full employment" unemployment rate—that level of unemployment that exists at times of greatest output—has increased in recent decades. There is no reason why frictional unemployment should

structural unemployment: the lack of work that occurs because of changes in the basic characteristics of a market, such as a new substitute product, a change in consumer tastes, or new technology in production.

have gone up. The availability of job placement facilities, labor mobility, and, presumably, the efficiency of market clearing in labor markets should be better than in the past. The reason cited most often for the apparent rise in the "natural" rate of unemployment is an increase in **structural unemployment**. Structural unemployment may arise from changes in the market conditions of a particular industry or geographic region. Labor in the U.S. auto industry was hard hit by structural unemployment. First, the industry became uncompetitive in the 1980s (see the introductory article for chapter 7, p. 159). Then, to lower costs and regain its share of the market, it automated production to save on labor costs. Production and sales are back up, but employment in the industry may never be as great as before. Detroit and other traditional auto producing centers are suffering from structural unemployment.

Structural unemployment occurs when the quantity demanded of particular kinds of labor falls short of the quantity offered in the job market at the going wage rate. When a large number of workers in an industry lose their jobs, it may be difficult or impossible to absorb them into other industries, even in the best of times. Skills and work experience in one line of work are not always easily transferred to another line of work. The skilled auto worker who is laid off is not automatically employable in the field of medical technology, even though there are numerous jobs in that field. Even if workers have transferable skills, they may not know about available jobs or may not be able to take them. Unemployed workers in Detroit may not be aware that they have the qualifications for job openings in Atlanta, Georgia. Even if they knew about a job in Atlanta, they might not be in a position to pull up stakes and move there.

There has always been a certain amount of structural unemployment. It goes with a dynamic market economy, as some industries decline while others expand. But the amount of structural unemployment may have taken an upward shift, resulting in a permanently higher rate of unemployment, due to the mismatch between new job requirements and available labor skills. The rate of technological change has speeded up. With labor education and training lagging behind, the full employment unemployment rate increased from the 4% level to 5% in the 1970s; and some economists think it has taken another jump to 6%. The President's Council of Economic Advisers, however, does not believe that the equilibrium rate of unemployment has increased since the 1970s.

Inadequate Aggregate (Total) Demand

Frictional and structural unemployment are distressing for the particular individuals and communities affected. But they are necessary in a market economy for flexibility in the allocation of resources. Changing consumer tastes and the development of new products and production technologies require a continual reallocation of resources, including labor.

A more disturbing type of unemployment for the economy, one that can affect much

■ An unemployed worker, during a recession, is about to file an unemployment claim. There are different types of unemployment and many reasons why those who want work cannot always find it.

larger numbers of workers, is **cyclical unemployment** associated with inadequate total demand. When demand is down in the whole economy, there are simply not enough jobs to employ the labor force fully.

The total spending for all types of goods and services is called **aggregate demand**. When aggregate demand is below the full employment level, people will be out of work, some of them for long periods of time. **Full employment aggregate demand** is the amount of goods and services that the economy can produce when it is using all of its capacity. During a **recession**, such as the one in 1990–1991, the economy is operating far below its capacity.

cyclical unemployment: the lack of work that occurs because the total effective demand for goods and services is insufficient to employ all workers in the labor force.

aggregate demand: the total effective demand for the nation's output of goods and services.

full employment aggregate demand: the level of total effective demand that is just sufficient to employ all workers in the labor force.

recession: a decline for at least 2 successive quarters in the nation's total output of goods and services.

Figure 2.

Production Capacity and Unemployment

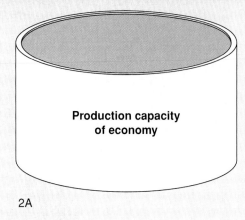

**Unused capacity
(unemployment)**

**Production capacity
of economy**

**Actual production
of
goods and services**

2A

2B

■ When aggregate demand is at the full employment level, the production capacity is fully utilized (2A). However, when aggregate demand falls below the full employment level, it causes unused production capacity, creating unemployment (2B).

Figure 2 illustrates the relationship between unemployment and aggregate demand. It shows a tank much like a water tank. The size of the tank represents the capacity of the economy to produce goods and services, and the purple represents the aggregate demand for those goods and services. When aggregate demand reaches the top of the tank, as shown on the left, full employment results. When aggregate demand is not sufficient to employ all of the labor, capital, and other resources of the economy, a recession occurs; or, if the excess capacity is very large, a **depression**. This situation is illustrated on the right in Figure 2. The white space between the purple and the top of the tank is unemployment.

In a recession there is too little buying to keep the economic wheels turning at a rate that will provide full use of the available resources. A recession tends to spread throughout the system and affect all parts of the nation's economy. It may be aggravated by structural problems, such as those in the auto industry, but the main problem is inadequate total spending. When workers are unemployed, they have less to spend and therefore reduce their purchases. This results in more workers being laid off and spending less, and aggregate demand falls even further. A downward spiral is created that, if it isn't stopped, leads to a depression.

The total number of unemployed for frictional and structural reasons consists of those who have lost their jobs, those who have quit, those reentering the labor force, and new entrants (see Figure 3 on p. 283).

Hidden Unemployment

The labor force is made up of persons who are either working or unemployed but actively looking for work. Someone who would like to have a job but is not actively looking for work is not counted among the unemployed. Such individuals are part of the **hidden unemployment** in the United States.

Some of those who have looked for a job for a long time without finding one become

---

depression: a severe and prolonged period of decline in the level of business activity.

hidden unemployment: that part of the unemployed population not reflected in official unemployment figures.

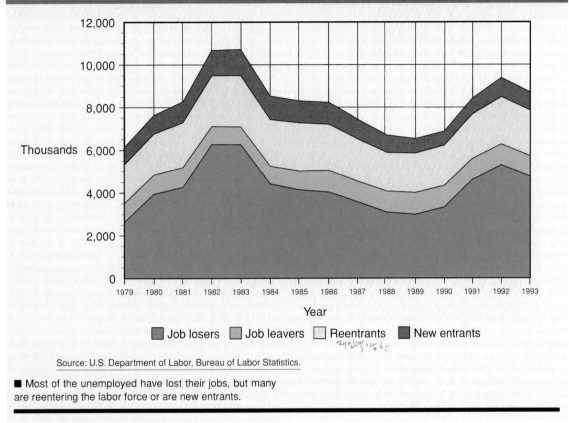

Figure 3.
Unemployment by Origination, 1979–1993
Cumulative Numbers of Unemployed 16 Years of Age and Older

Legend: ■ Job losers ■ Job leavers □ Reentrants ■ New entrants

Source: U.S. Department of Labor, Bureau of Labor Statistics.

■ Most of the unemployed have lost their jobs, but many are reentering the labor force or are new entrants.

discouraged. They decide that it is useless to look for work and stop trying to find employment. In the employment statistics, they are then no longer counted as unemployed. The Bureau of Labor Statistics has put the number of discouraged workers at about 1 million. Others, outside of government, have estimated the number to be almost 3 million.

Another form of hidden unemployment is represented by the workers who have had their work hours reduced involuntarily. If a factory cuts back from a 40-hour workweek to a 30-hour week as a result of slow sales, the official measure of unemployment is not af-

fected. For the workers involved, however, this situation is the same as a 25% drop in their employment level, and a change from a full-time job to a part-time one. The term **underemployed** has been used to describe those workers who can find only part-time work or jobs that are beneath those for which they are qualified. Between August 1990 and December 1993, part-time employment increased by 6.4% as full-time employment was rising only 1.7%.

underemployed: workers who cannot obtain full-time employment or who are working at jobs for which they are overqualified.

Comparative Case Application

El desempleo

El desempleo, le chômage involontaire, die Arbeitslosigkeit—whether you say it in Spanish, French, German, or English, unemployment is a bad word in Europe these days. The major European countries have not been accustomed to such mass unemployment since the Great Depression of the 1930s. For 3 decades following recovery from World War II, unemployment rates in the dominant economies of Europe were lower—generally much lower—than in the United States (Figure 4).

This is no longer the case. In the mid-1980s unemployment rates in Europe caught up with and surpassed the unemployment rate in the United States. In 1994 unemployment in the European Union reached an average of over 11%, almost double the U.S. rate. Even worse, nearly half of those unemployed in Europe were without work for over a year. The percentage of long-term unemployed in the United States was small by comparison.

Those figures for Europe are the official rates. The real rates of joblessness, including discouraged workers and the underemployed, are much worse. Also, in some European countries the numbers of individuals subtracted from the labor rolls because of being on disability are exceedingly large, forming another group of hidden unemployed. According to a 1992 study, fully one-quarter of the Dutch labor force over the age of 45 was on disability payments. A large fraction of those were actually able-bodied workers given disability pensions only as a means of removing them from the labor rolls. If they were counted among

the unemployed, it is estimated that the official unemployment rate would have been double that reported.

European workers who lose their jobs can expect to be out of work for a long time. Only 5% find another job within a month. In the United States, on the other hand, about half of those out of work find employment within a month. The U.S. economy has proven much more prolific in creating new jobs than European economies.

The other side of the picture, however, is not so rosy for American workers. For one thing, it is also much easier to lose your job in America than in Europe. Labor turnover rates are much higher. In the late 1980s, 2% of U.S. workers became unemployed each month, while in Europe the figure was only 0.4%.

Another difference is that in the United States many of the jobs available are so low paying that they leave the worker in or just above poverty. In Europe, low-income workers in comparable deciles earn 44% more, based on the purchasing power of their wages, than in America. A European worker in the lowest 10% of wage earners earns 68% of the average European pay. The U.S. worker in the lowest decile earns only 38% of the average.

And for the unemployed, European countries are much more generous than the United States. Unemployment benefits last longer and are a larger percentage of the unemployed worker's previous earnings in Europe. And a major problem for the unemployed U.S.

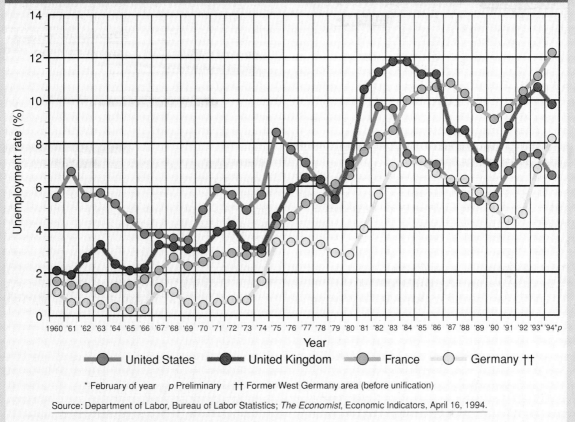

Figure 4.
Unemployment Rates in the United States and Major European Countries, 1960–1994

Year

United States   United Kingdom   France   Germany ††

* February of year   p Preliminary   †† Former West Germany area (before unification)

Source: Department of Labor, Bureau of Labor Statistics; *The Economist*, Economic Indicators, April 16, 1994.

■ Unemployment rates were lower in major European countries than in the United States until the 1980s. Since then, unemployment in Europe has climbed well above that in the United States.

---

worker, at least prior to health care reform (chapter 13, p. 333), has been the loss of health insurance along with the job. In all of the major European countries, every citizen is covered for health care, regardless of work status.

Economic Reasoning

1. What are some examples of hidden unemployment in Europe?

2. Which European country had the lowest unemployment rate in the period covered by Figure 4? In what year? What type of unemployment do you think was represented in that country at the time? Why? (Refer to "Europe Copes with Immigration," p. 225.)

3. Which workers do you think are better off with respect to unemployment problems, American or European? Why?

What Causes Inflation?

Unemployment is one of the twin devils of economic instability; the other is inflation. This section sheds some light on the forces that give rise to inflation, forces that can arise on the demand side of the economy or on the supply side. First we will examine what inflation is and how it is measured.

Measuring Inflation

Inflation is a period of generally rising prices in the economy as a whole. In a market econ-

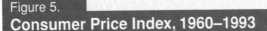
consumer price index (CPI): a statistical measure of changes in the prices of a representative sample of urban family purchases relative to a previous period.

omy, it is normal for the prices of some things to rise and others to fall because of changing demand and supply. But when the prices of nearly everything rise, inflation occurs. This increases the cost of living. Each dollar spent buys fewer goods and services.

The **consumer price index (CPI)** is the most commonly used measure of changes in the general price level. This index is a statistic issued monthly by the Bureau of Labor Statistics of the U.S. Department of Labor. It is popularly known as the cost-of-living index, although it actually measures changes in a specific group of prices rather than people's living costs. Costs of living are affected by

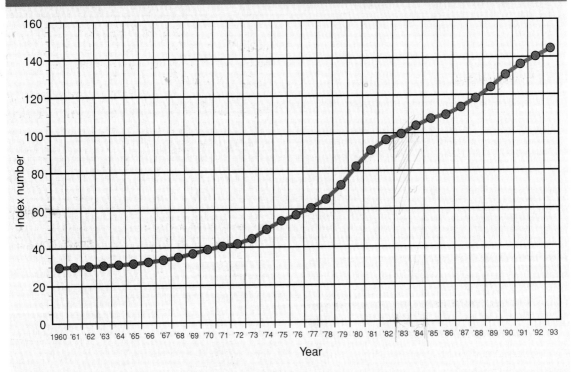

Figure 5.
Consumer Price Index, 1960–1993

Source: U.S. Department of Labor, Bureau of Labor Statistics.

■ Inflation, measured by the Consumer Price Index (CPI), accelerated in the 1970s and moderated somewhat in the recessions of the early 1980s and 1990s, but remains high compared to earlier norms.

Figure 6.

Production Capacity and Inflation

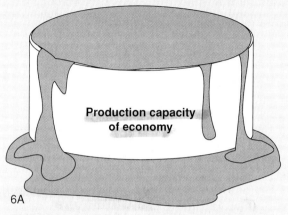
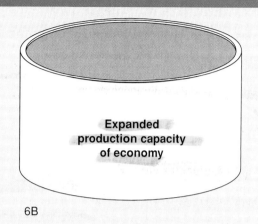

Production capacity of economy

6A

Expanded production capacity of economy

6B

■ When aggregate demand exceeds the full employment level, it causes inflation (6A). However, over a period of time, increased aggregate demand can be satisfied without inflation by increasing the production capacity of the economy (6B).

changes in buying habits as well as by price changes (see Figure 5).

The CPI expresses the price of consumer goods in a given month as a percentage of the price prevailing in some earlier period, known as the **base period**. In computing the index, the total cost of a representative sample of 205 household purchases during the base period is calculated. The cost of that same "market basket" of goods and services is then computed in subsequent months. The base period price level has an index number of 100. If the current cost of the "market basket" is 25% greater than in the base period, the CPI is 125. Figure 5 shows the CPI for the period from 1960 to 1993, with 1982–1984 as the base period.

Demand-Pull Inflation

A basic cause of inflation is excessive demand. In the most extreme cases, when the demand for goods and services exceeds the production capacity of the economy, we have pure **demand-pull inflation**. This is illustrated in Figure 6A, where we again have a tank representing the capacity output of the economy. The amount of purchasing power attempting to buy goods and services is shown in purple.

When demand reaches the top of the tank, the economy is unable to produce additional goods and services in the short run. As a result, the purchasing power overflows the tank and is reflected in the economy as a general rise in prices, or inflation.

When the increase in demand is not too rapid, the economy can adjust. In the long run, producers can expand their capacity to produce more goods and services. If the increase in demand occurs gradually over a period of time, it can be matched by an enlargement of the output capacity of the economy without causing inflation. This is shown in Figure 6B. But when demand increases rapidly at or near full employment, as during a war, the excess purchasing power overflows in the form of inflation, as in Figure 6A.

base period (base year): the reference period for comparison of subsequent changes in an index series; set equal to 100.

demand-pull inflation: a continuing rise in the general price level that occurs when aggregate demand exceeds the full-employment output capacity of the economy.

When inflation gets started, it is likely to be self-reinforcing. If people see that prices are going up, they may attempt to stock up on goods before prices rise even further. This boosts demand and accelerates the inflation. **Speculators** also contribute to inflation. With prices rising rapidly, it is profitable to buy something, hold it for a while, and then sell it. This fuels inflation, not only by adding speculative demand to the market, but also by holding supplies of goods off the market.

Cost-Push Inflation

Inflation can also result from reduced supplies of production inputs as well as from increased total demand. When inflation comes from the supply side, it is called **cost-push inflation**.

A major cause of high inflation in the late 1970s was the increase in energy costs brought on by the OPEC oil cartel. Because energy is an important factor input in the production of so many goods and services, the rise in energy prices increased production costs. Prices rose throughout the economy. The increase in oil prices also raised the demand for oil substitutes, such as coke, a coal residue. Industries that use coke for fuel, the steel industry for instance, found that they had to pay more for it. Because of the increase in this production cost, steel prices went up. This

price rise, in turn, resulted in price increases for all of the goods using steel.

There is often an interaction between demand-pull and cost-push inflation forces, each feeding the other. When the cost of living goes up, labor unions demand higher wages so that their workers can maintain their real incomes and living standards. The wage increases raise production costs, causing producers to increase prices again. Workers try to catch up with the cost of living by higher wage demands, which again increases production costs and the cost of living. Sometimes this wage inflation is built into labor union contracts with a **cost-of-living adjustment (COLA)** clause. The COLA clause calls for automatic wage increases when the consumer price index goes up a specified number of percentage points.

The government has been accused of contributing to cost-push inflation by its environmental controls and other regulations. Government-imposed emission controls and safety requirements for automobiles have increased car prices by several hundred dollars. Smokestack emission controls on industries have increased their production costs, which raises the price of products. Businesses complain that the increase in paperwork required by government reports and regulations has raised their costs of doing business and the prices they must charge.

Monetary Inflation

Demand-pull and cost-push inflation are attributed to changed demand and supply conditions. An alternative view of the cause of inflation is held by the **monetarists**, who believe that changes in the money supply are the most important factor in inflation.

This view is embodied in the **quantity equation**. The quantity equation states that the total value of goods and services purchased during a given period, say a month, is the number of transactions (**T**) times the average level of prices (**P**). This value of total purchases (T × P) must be the same as the quantity of money (**M**) times the average number of times that each dollar of the money supply changes hands,

speculators: people who purchase goods or financial assets in anticipation that prices will rise and they can sell at a profit; speculators can also speculate on a fall in prices.

cost-push inflation: a continuing rise in the general price level that results from increases in production costs.

cost-of-living adjustment (COLA): a frequently used provision of labor contracts that grants wage increases based on changes in the Consumer Price Index; often referred to in negotiations as the "escalator clause."

monetarists: those who believe that changes in the money supply have a determinative effect on economic conditions.

quantity equation (equation of exchange): the quantity of money (**M**) times the velocity of its circulation (**V**) equals the quantity of goods and services transacted (**T**) times their average price (**P**); M × V = T × P.

Case Application

The High Cost of Loving

The increase in the cost of living has been bad enough, but it hasn't been nearly as bad as the increase in the cost of loving. Raymond F. DeVoe Jr., who writes a stock market newsletter, has been calculating a cost of loving (COL) index since 1955. (Please note that the COL index is not the same as COLA, the cost-of-living adjustment.) Since that time, the general price level of consumer goods and services has increased 5.6 times the level in 1955. In other words, if 1955 were the base period, the CPI would have risen from 100 to 560.

To figure the COL, we take a representative sample of goods and services involved in the mating game and compare their prices in 1955 with the prices today. A cost of loving index might be calculated as shown below. The 1994 COL index was 675.

The cost of loving has gone up much more than the CPI. The COL assumes that young men still court young women the same way they did in 1955. Today's courting practices may include fewer candlelight dinners and fewer birthday gifts of expensive perfume. The same type of problem affects the CPI. Changes in lifestyles and consumption habits make comparisons of

the cost of living over a number of years difficult. For this reason, the base period and the contents of the market basket of goods for the CPI are periodically updated.

Economic Reasoning

1. The most inflationary item in the COL was the increase in diamond prices. The price of diamonds increased because people were buying them as a hedge against inflation, and for speculation. Would you call the inflation of diamond prices a demand-pull or a cost-push type of inflation? Why?

2. Which index is a better measure of our purchasing power, the CPI or the COL? Why?

3. Do you think that the high cost of loving has actually affected dating practices? How? Do price changes affect our buying habits in general? What implication does this have for the validity of the CPI?

Table 1   Cost of Loving Index

Item	Number purchased (Q)	Price 1955 (P$_0$)	P$_0$ × Q	Price 1994 (P$_1$)	P$_1$ × Q
Wine for picnic	4	$1.55	$6.20	$7.95	$31.80
First-run movie	14	1.00	14.00	7.00	98.00
Candlelight dinner	6	2.75	16.50	70.00	420.00
Silver bracelet	2	1.29	2.58	14.00	28.00
Dozen roses	2	5.00	10.00	40.00	80.00
Perfume	1	35.00	35.00	95.00	95.00
Diamond ring	1	400.00	400.00	2,500.00	2,500.00
Blood test	1	7.00	7.00	35.00	35.00
Marriage license	1	2.00	2.00	40.00	40.00
			$493.28		$3,377.80

$$\text{COL (1990)} = \frac{P_1 \times Q}{P_0 \times Q} \times 100 = \frac{\$3,377.80}{\$493.28} \times 100 = 675$$

*This index is based on but not identical to the one devised by Raymond F. DeVoe Jr.

called the **velocity of money circulation (V)**. In other words, the quantity equation says that the total spending during a period must be the same as the total value of goods and services transacted. Stated in shorthand equation form, it is $M \times V = T \times P$. If the volume of transactions (T) remains the same, as it would at full employment, and the rate of turnover of money (V) is constant, an increase in the money supply (M) necessarily results in a rise in the price level (P). This relationship between the money supply and the price level is summarized in the quantity equation below.

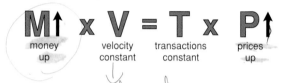

$$M\uparrow \times V = T \times P\uparrow$$

money   velocity   transactions   prices
up   constant   constant   up

rate of turnover of money.

The quantity equation is a truism rather than a statement of economic analysis since the total amount spent must always necessarily be the same as the total amount received. For some time, the quantity equation was out of fashion in economic theory because it was not considered important to solving economic problems. Economists noted that you could have full employment and stable prices with any given money supply, whether it be large or small, because the monetary unit itself is arbitrary. Although the quantity theory of money made a comeback in the 1980s, and the monetarists had a large influence on policy, the lack of correspondence between changes in the money supply and the rate of inflation in recent years has again relegated monetarism to the back seat of economic analysis.

Is There a Trade-off between Unemployment and Inflation?

Unemployment and inflation have plagued economic systems since the beginning of market economies. But in earlier experience, they did not occur together. In this analysis section, we will examine the question of whether we necessarily have less of one when we have more of the other.

Phillips Curve

In 1958 an economist from New Zealand, A. W. "Bill" Phillips, published a paper demonstrating that for a century there had been a trade-off between unemployment and inflation—the more you had of one, the less you had of the other, and vice versa. Historically, economic booms result in full employment, and the high level of aggregate demand causes shortages of goods and services. As a consequence, prices rise.

When the boom collapses, demand falls off, surpluses of goods appear, and workers are laid off. Prices and unemployment generally move in opposite directions. The graphic illustration of this trade-off was named the **Phillips curve** after its detector.

In the last 25 years, however, there has been a controversy over whether the historic relationship between inflation and unemployment still exists. Or did Bill Phillips discover something that expired soon after it was discovered?

The Phillips curve trade-off was alive and healthy in the 1960s, as shown in Figure 7. The unemployment rate is on the horizontal axis, and the inflation rate is on the vertical axis. The line through the inflation-unemployment points for 1960–1968 shows the average change of one variable with a change in the other. It is the Phillips curve.

When the unemployment rate was over 4%, the inflation rate was less than 2%. The higher the unemployment, the lower the infla-

---

velocity of money circulation (V): the average rate at which money changes hands.

Phillips curve: a statistical relationship between increases in the general price level and unemployment.

Figure 7.

Inflation and Unemployment Rates, 1960–1968

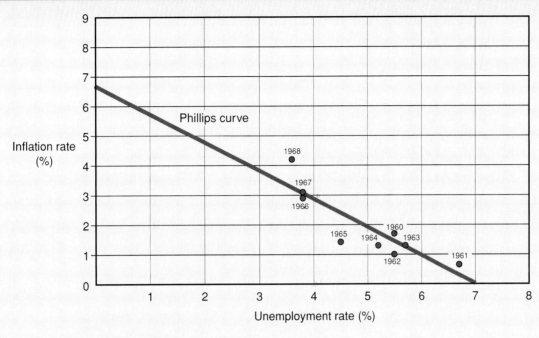

Source: U.S. Department of Labor, Bureau of Labor Statistics.

■ The Phillips curve in the 1960s showed the historic trade-off between inflation and unemployment.

tion. In 1961, when unemployment reached 6.7% of the workforce, the inflation rate was negligible, only 0.7%. On the other hand, when unemployment fell below 4%, the inflation rate rose sharply. In 1968, when unemployment was only 3.6%—full employment—the inflation rate reached 4.2%. This does not seem like a high inflation rate in view of what followed in the 1970s, but at that time it was considered quite high.

Stagflation

In the 1970s the inflation-unemployment relation saw a dramatic change. Instead of having *either* high unemployment or high inflation rates as we had in the 1960s and earlier periods, we had *both* high unemployment and high inflation. When we have a combination of high unemployment and high inflation rates, the situation is called **stagflation**—a combination of stagnation and inflation.

This led some economists to say that there was no longer a Phillips curve trade-off. But the Phillips curve for 1974–1983, the blue line in Figure 8, shows that a trade-off between inflation and unemployment did exist, although at a higher level than in the 1960s. Both variables had shifted upward and the trade-off was not as definitive. Nevertheless, it appears that the Phillips curve still represented the relationship between inflation and unemployment in the short run, even under conditions of stagflation.

Stagflation is very unpleasant, both for the public suffering from it and for the economic policymakers trying to cure it. How did the economy get into that situation in the

> **stagflation:** a term created to describe a situation of simultaneous economic stagnation, high unemployment, and inflation.

Figure 8.

Inflation and Unemployment Rates
1960–1968, 1974–1983, 1984–1993

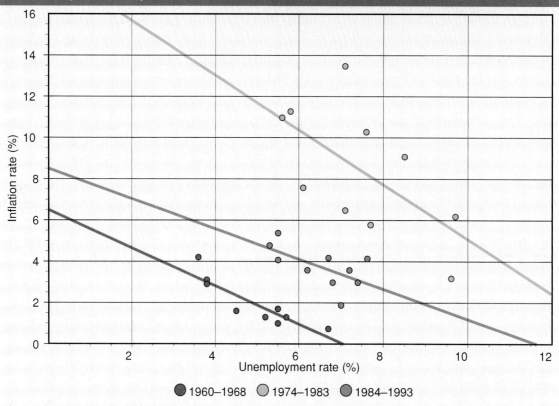

Source: Calculated from data from the U.S. Department of Labor, Bureau of Labor Statistics.

■ The Phillips curve showing the trade-off between inflation and unemployment is not constant over time. It shifts according to economic expectations and other factors. But under any given conditions, the greater the amount of unemployment, the lower inflation is likely to be, and vice versa.

1970s? Traditionally inflation was not supposed to become a problem until the economy was producing at full capacity. The situation represented in Figure 2B on page 282, where there is excess production capacity, provides no reason for prices to go up. Only when aggregate demand exceeded capacity was there expected to be a spillover into inflation, as in Figure 6A on page 287.

Why wasn't this true in the 1970s? Why did the Phillips curve shift upward? To help

us with the answers to these questions, let us look at another set of diagrams that relate **aggregate supply** to demand. Figure 9A shows the same simplified conditions as the output tanks we saw earlier in Figures 2 and 6, but in a different way, by using aggregate demand and supply curves. The aggregate supply curve (AS) is assumed to be perfectly elastic (horizontal) at the existing price level as long as the economy is operating at less than full capacity. When output reaches the full employment level, however, the aggregate supply curve becomes perfectly inelastic (vertical). When aggregate demand is on the elastic part of the supply curve, as it is in demand curves

aggregate supply: the total amount of goods and services available from all industries in the economy.

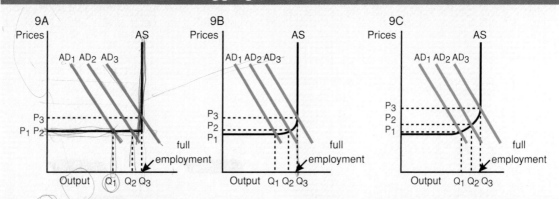

Figure 9.

The Effect of Increases in Aggregate Demand on Prices

- In 9A aggregate supply (AS) is assumed to be perfectly elastic (horizontal) at the existing price level (P_1) when the economy is operating below its full production capacity. However, when output reaches the full employment level (Q_3), the aggregate supply curve (AS) becomes perfectly inelastic (vertical). When aggregate demand is on the elastic part of AS, as with AD_1 and AD_2, demand can increase with no rise in the price level. When demand increases beyond the full employment level, as with AD_3, inflation occurs.

In 9B the situation in which factor prices rise somewhat as production output approaches the full

employment level is illustrated. This is similar to the occurrences of the 1960s. When the economy is operating well below full employment, the price level is nearly constant, as indicated by the point where AD_1 intersects AS. At a higher output level, prices rise slightly, as indicated by the intersection of AS by AD_2. When demand is near full capacity (Q_3), the price level rises sharply, as illustrated by the intersection of AD_3 with AS.

In 9C factor prices rise substantially before output reaches full employment. This illustrates the occurrences of the 1970s.

AD_1 and AD_2, demand can increase with no rise in the price level. However, when demand increases beyond the full employment level, as shown by AD_3, inflation occurs.

The actual supply curve in the 1960s was more like that shown in Figure 9B. When the economy was operating well below full employment, as it was in 1961, the price level was nearly constant. This is indicated by the point where the aggregate demand curve AD_1 intersects the aggregate supply curve in Figure 9B. When the economy was operating at a higher level of output, as in 1965, prices rose as indicated to the point where AD_2 intersects AS. When demand was near full capacity output, as it was from 1966 to 1968, the price level rose sharply. This is represented by the intersection of demand curve AD_3 and AS.

The Phillips curve in Figure 7 and the aggregate supply curve in Figure 9B show the normal relationship between unemployment and inflation prior to the 1970s. How, then, did we get into the stagflation situation? There was ap-

parently a change of the sort shown by the aggregate supply curve in Figure 9C. The price level was no longer stable, even when the economy was operating well below capacity with high unemployment, as with demand AD_1. Higher levels of demand AD_2 and AD_3 created even more extreme inflation.

The aggregate supply curve in Figure 9C indicates what happened in the 1970s to the relationship between employment and output on the one hand and inflation on the other. But it doesn't explain why it happened. The stagflation problem of the 1970s originated in the second half of the 1960s, when the war in Vietnam escalated at the same time that major new domestic social programs got under way. Additional demand resulted from increased government expenditures for these activities. The increased government spending was not offset by higher taxes, thus generating inflationary conditions. A surge in oil prices and resulting energy shortage in the 1970s drove prices higher.

■ The increased military spending during the Vietnam War, which was not offset by higher taxes, was one of many factors that caused both high inflation and high unemployment in the 1970s.

A succession of economic stabilization programs failed to stem the inflation. This failure created expectations in the minds of consumers, workers, and businesspeople that prices would continue to rise. Inflationary expectations probably played a large role in what happened during the decade. When the public loses faith in a stable price level, prices are bid up by people stocking up in anticipation of even higher prices to come. Attempts by labor unions to keep wages in step with, or ahead of, increases in the cost of living and attempts by producers to beat rising production costs result in ever-increasing prices.

It took the shock treatment of a severe recession in the early 1980s to break the inflationary psychology. The Phillips curve shifted back to a lower level (green line, Figure 8), but not as low as during the 1960s. The economy

experienced a period of moderate expansion, another recession, and a recovery, with the inflation-unemployment relationship showing typical Phillips curve behavior at a level in between that of the 1960s and the 1970s.

▦ Natural Rate of Unemployment

The controversy over whether or not the Phillips curve is a valid representation of the relationship between unemployment and inflation has been resolved for the bulk of economists by the recognition of *two* Phillips curves, one short-run and the other long-run. The difference between them results from changing expectations regarding prices and their effect on real wages. When workers have adjusted their expectations to rising inflation, demanding higher wages to maintain their real income level, there will be a higher unemployment rate associated with the higher inflation than there was in the short run before expectations changed.

Economists and policy makers now base their analysis of the relationship between unemployment and inflation on the concept of a **natural rate of unemployment**. The natural rate is that unemployment level that exists in the long run after expectations have adjusted to the level of inflation. A more wordy but more precise term used to define that level of unemployment is the **non-accelerating-inflation rate of unemployment (NAIRU)**. The natural rate of unemployment depends largely on the amount of structural unemployment. But it may also be affected by such things as minimum wage laws, labor mobility, retirement plans, confidence in government policies, foreign competition, and so forth.

There is disagreement over exactly what the NAIRU level of unemployment is in today's labor market. Economist Stuart Weiner has estimated it at 6.25%; the Congressional Budget Office uses the figure of 5.5% in its forecasts; and chief economist Richard Belous of the National Planning Association believes it is closer to 5.5% than to 6%. Whichever figure is correct, there clearly continues to be a trade-off between inflation and unemployment, although at a higher level than in earlier times.

natural rate of unemployment: the equilibrium level of unemployment at full-capacity output consistent with a stable amount of inflation.

non-accelerating-inflation rate of unemployment (NAIRU): a more precise term for the natural rate of unemployment.

The Roller-Coaster Ride

The historical course of economic activity has been similar to a roller-coaster ride, with its climbing, peaking, plunging downward, and bottoming out. Let us take a figurative ride on the business cycle.

We start at the bottom, as one does on roller coasters. The first part of the ride up is not steep. The economy is getting in gear, picking up speed. Factories have a great deal of unused capacity. As demand increases, output can be expanded easily without increasing average production costs. Interest rates are unusually low, making it easy for producers and merchants to obtain capital. This is the recovery phase of the business cycle.

The climb begins to get steeper. More jobs, larger incomes, increased spending, and higher profits create an enthusiastic atmosphere. A confident buying public goes into debt to acquire new cars, appliances, and other consumer durable goods. Would-be entrepreneurs see the profits being made by others and decide to undertake new business ventures. This is the expansion phase of the business cycle. In the rosy glow of prosperity, speculation replaces real investment and price increases accelerate, creating an economic "boom."

After a while the steep climb begins to level off. As labor and other resources become fully employed, production costs rise and cut profit margins. The banking system has become fully loaned up and interest rates increase, making credit hard to obtain. Consumers reach their debt limits and demand

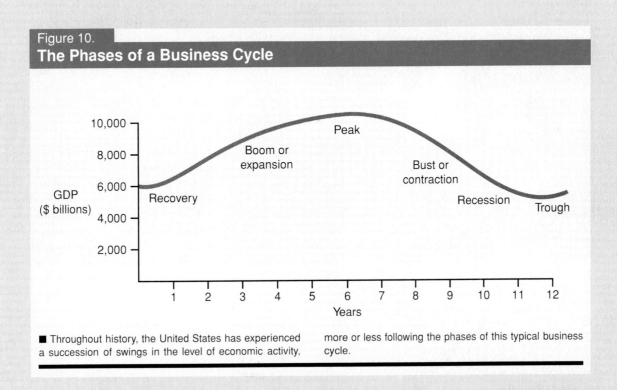

Figure 10.
The Phases of a Business Cycle

■ Throughout history, the United States has experienced a succession of swings in the level of economic activity, more or less following the phases of this typical business cycle.

for durable goods decreases. This is the peak or downturn phase. Some firms fail, affecting the financial situation of their suppliers and creditors, which leads to more failures, resulting in an economic "bust."

As the economy starts its downward plunge, it rapidly gains momentum. Widespread bankruptcies result in a collapse of the credit market. Worker layoffs and falling incomes result in declining sales in all industries. This is the contraction phase of the cycle, which leads to a recession or, if it is severe, a depression.

The ride down seems as if it will never stop, but it does. The economy bottoms out. The rate of business failures slows. Inventories are reduced. Consumer purchases begin to increase. Due to the small amount of lending in the slump, banks have an increased amount of liquidity and interest rates are lowered. The stage is set for the trough or upturn, the last phase of our cyclical roller-coaster ride.

Economic Reasoning

1. At what phase of the business cycle would you expect conditions to be at the upper left end of the Phillips curve? At the lower right end?

2. How does stagflation differ from the traditional business cycle?

3. Which do you think is worse, stagflation or the traditional business cycle? Why?

What Are the Consequences of Unemployment and Inflation?

Having examined the nature and causes of unemployment and inflation and their relationship to each other, we will now take a look at their economic and social consequences.

Income Effects of Unemployment

Unemployed people and their families must continue to pay living costs when their income is cut. Nondiscretionary expenditures such as insurance, housing payments, utility bills, and taxes take a large part of some unemployed people's savings, especially after their eligibility for unemployment compensation is exhausted. The loss of medical insurance coverage resulting from unemployment is a major financial problem for families in case of illness, accident, or pregnancy (see the introductory article for chapter 13, p. 333). The loss of income means a reduction in buying power and living standards for the unemployed and their dependents.

The drop in income of the unemployed also hurts others who are not unemployed. Reduced spending means lower receipts for retail merchants, manufacturers, workers, and others in the chain of production. As we have seen, each person's income generally depends on someone else's spending.

Unemployment reduces the revenues of federal, state, and local governments while at the same time adding to their outlays for unemployment compensation and welfare support. When unemployment increases 1%, the federal treasury alone loses $30 billion in tax revenue and increased welfare and unemployment compensation payments.

Real Output Effects of Unemployment

From the standpoint of the overall economy, a rise in unemployment means a decline in the nation's production. For each 1% of unemployment, the country loses over $100 billion in output. Goods and services not produced because of unemployment are gone forever. This means that the nation as a whole is poorer by $100 billion, not just the unemployed.

The **real output** effects of unemployment continue into the future. Some of the goods not produced during a period of high unemployment are capital goods. The result is reduced growth in the production capacity of the economy that will affect the amount of future output of goods and services. Although the economy resumes growing after a recession, it is on a lower growth path than it would have been. This reduces future production and standards of living.

Social Effects of Unemployment

Unemployment has social as well as economic costs. When people lose their jobs, especially when they cannot find another for an extended period, they tend to become depressed and their health suffers. Suicides increase, families break up, and there is more child abuse. A study by Harvey Brenner of the Johns Hopkins University School of Hygiene and Public Health shows that for every 1% increase in the unemployment rate, there is a 1.9% increase in deaths from stress-related diseases, a 4.1% increase in suicides, a 5.7% increase in homicides, and a 4% increase in commitments to state prisons.

Other studies have found that the mental and physical health of the spouses and children of unemployed workers are also affected. Children in families where one or both parents have lost their jobs are more likely to suffer from malnutrition, child abuse, and behavior problems than children of working parents.

Income Effects of Inflation

In the past 10 years, the purchasing power of the dollar has fallen by over 30%. Taking the

---

real output: the value of output adjusted for changes in prices; the volume of output.

■ Unemployment can lead to many difficulties, even imprisonment for some. These inmates line up outside the barber shop at Sumter County Correctional Institution in Bushnell, Florida.

average of 1982–1984 as the base, when $1.00 would buy a dollar's worth of goods and services, that same dollar in 1993 would buy only $0.69 worth of goods and services. For people whose money income did not keep pace with the rise in prices, these inflated dollars meant a decline in **real income**.

The income effects of inflation are not the same for everyone. Those on a fixed money income are bound to suffer during periods of inflation. One of the great ironies of inflation is that it often penalizes thriftiness. Many people who have worked hard and lived frugally over a working lifetime and who planned to live off their savings in old age have found the purchasing power of their savings has declined substantially as a result of inflation.

real income: money income adjusted for changes in the prices of goods and services.

But not everyone is hurt by inflation. Those whose dollar incomes rise faster than the general price level enjoy a rise in real income. Chief executives of major corporations have been among the big winners in the inflation race, with their income from salaries and bonuses going up much faster than prices. Asset owners also do well in inflationary times. Property owners see the value of their properties rise. Owners of scarce resources and speculators receive windfall profits.

Debtors are another group benefiting substantially from inflation. When the time comes to pay off their loans, they pay them off with dollars that are worth less than the dollars that they borrowed. Because of this, the federal government, with its debt approaching $5 trillion, is the biggest beneficiary of inflation. As people come to anticipate continuing inflation and as these inflationary expectations are reflected in higher interest

Inflation—How High Is Up?

America's experience with inflation in the 1970s was a problem. But here the inflation rate reached "only" 13.3% a year at its height in 1979. In other places inflation has fed on itself to such an extent that it exploded, a condition called hyperinflation. Extreme inflation can paralyze an economy. The bad effects—hoarding, uncertainty, loss of confidence in the value of money, production bottlenecks—may so greatly override the investment-stimulating and output-expanding effects that they virtually halt production.

A classic example of this was the hyperinflation experienced in Germany during the early 1920s. The acceleration in the rate of inflation became so great that firms had to pay workers by the day. If firms refused to pay their workers daily, they would refuse to work at all. Why should they put in a week's work for an agreed-upon wage of 100,000 marks, the workers argued, if prices were rising at such an unpredictable rate that by the end of the week they couldn't be sure 100,000 marks would buy a kilogram of bratwurst and a loaf of bread? The rate of inflation became so extreme by 1923 that prices were literally rising by the hour and workers had to be paid twice a day. As soon as a worker received his morning's pay, he would rush out to the entrance and thrust the large bundle of marks into his wife's hands. She would rush off to spend them within the hour, for in a few hours perhaps that bundle of marks would buy only half as much. With the institution of money shattered, market-directed activity all but collapsed.

That was the most extreme case of inflation in this century, but in recent years there have been other countries that experienced hyperinflation rates. In 1984–1985 Bolivia had hyperinflation that reached an incredible annual rate of 11,750%, and a number of other Latin American and African countries have experienced runaway inflation. They include Brazil (2,750%), Argentina (3,080%), and Peru (7,500%). In these countries, as in Germany in the 1920s, prices of some goods rose daily or even twice a day. This situation greatly complicates life for consumers and producers alike.

■ In post–World War I Germany, hyperinflation made some paper money good only for lighting fires.

Economic Reasoning

1. Which effects of inflation does the case of hyperinflation in Germany during the 1920s illustrate?

2. The German government was unable to sell bonds, so it had to resort to "printing press" money. Why would no one buy German government bonds in the early 1920s?

3. Do you think that hyperinflation could happen in this country? Why do you think it might, or what do you think would prevent it?

rates, for the individual the advantage of incurring new debt disappears.

Real Output Effects of Inflation

The rise of aggregate demand associated with demand-pull inflation tends to increase the real output of the economy up to the full employment level. An increase in demand, given some slack or unused productive capacity, stimulates production. Idle resources are put to work, and idle plant capacity is utilized more fully. These developments may favorably affect business profit expectations and lead to increased investment spending on new plants, equipment, inventories of raw materials, and goods in process.

This is only part of the story, however. As inflation continues and as the system moves closer to full employment, cost-push inflation forces strengthen. Though on the average all prices are rising in a period of inflation, not all individual prices are rising at the same time. Firms that feel reasonably confident that the prices of the things they are selling will rise faster than the prices of what they must buy will have an incentive to expand by investing. Others may find that their costs are rising faster than their selling prices, or they may fear that this will happen. This causes considerable differences in supply responses. The patterns of production change.

Inflation is tricky. It may stimulate production in some areas and simultaneously create bottlenecks, uncertainties, or other difficulties that can hold back production in other areas. Inflation may induce some producers to anticipate future needs for materials, to buy more heavily than they otherwise would, and to hoard the materials.

As inflationary expectations strengthen, interest rates rise well above normal levels, making business investment in plant and equipment too costly. This discourages further expansion of output and thus contributes to higher inflation by creating shortages. On balance, it appears that the higher the inflation rate and the longer the period of time the inflation goes on, the greater will be the negative effects on output.

* What's the difference between recession & depression?

DOTY

Putting It Together

Normal adjustments to changing demand and supply conditions for different products and services in a market economy result in the loss of jobs for some people. Other workers quit their jobs because of dissatisfaction or for other personal reasons. In a healthy economy, these people should be able to find new jobs within a few weeks. While they are seeking employment, they constitute a *frictional unemployment* bloc in the labor force. Unemployment levels of 3–4% were in the past considered normal due to frictional unemployment and those unemployable for one reason or another.

When a whole industry or region has less business because of changing consumer tastes or changing cost conditions, some workers lose their jobs. There may not be enough jobs immediately available in other industries to reemploy them, or they may not have the skills and training necessary to take jobs in other industries. This *structural unemployment* may result in extended periods without work for some people.

The most serious and widespread unemployment, however, is *cyclical unemployment*, which occurs when there is inadequate *aggregate (total) demand* for goods and services. If there is insufficient spending in the economy to purchase all of the goods and services that could be produced, workers will not be able to find jobs. Those workers without jobs are forced to cut back on their consumption, and this results in a further decline in output and a further increase in unemployment.

When unemployment is high for a prolonged period of time, some workers who have been unable to find jobs become discouraged and stop looking. Since they are not actively seeking employment, they are not included in the unemployment statistics. They constitute a segment of *hidden unemployment*. Other workers forced to work only part time are part of this segment as well.

Just as unemployment may be caused by insufficient demand, *inflation* may be the result of too much demand. If demand exceeds

■ A senior at Old Dominion University finds an unusual way of expressing the employment concerns of recent Generation X college graduates.

the capacity of the economy to produce at full employment, prices will rise. Inflationary expectations and speculation tend to accelerate *demand-pull inflation* even more.

Another cause of inflation can be an increase in the costs of production. Shortages of raw materials, higher wages, or government regulations raise prices. The interaction between demand-pull and *cost-push inflation* can result in an inflationary spiral.

According to the *monetarists*, increases in the money supply are inflationary because of the relationship between the quantity of money and the price level. This is expressed by the *quantity equation* $M \times V = T \times P$, where M is the money supply, V is the velocity of circulation of money, T is the number of transactions during the period, and P is the average price level. If output (T) and the rate at which money turns over (V) are constant, there is a direct ratio between changes in the money supply and changes in the price level.

There has historically been a trade-off between the rate of unemployment and the rate of inflation. This relationship is shown by the *Phillips curve*. Phillips curves based on data from earlier periods show that when unemployment was high the inflation rate was low, and vice versa. During the 1970s, however, the economy had simultaneously both high unemployment and high inflation. This situation is referred to as *stagflation*. From 1984 to 1993 stagflation abated, but the trade-off between unemployment and inflation has been at a higher level than in the 1960s and before.

Economists now recognize two Phillips curves, a short-run curve and a long-run curve that exists after workers have adjusted their expectations to take into account inflation. The *natural rate of unemployment* after adjustment of worker expectations, also called the *non-accelerating-inflation rate of unemployment (NAIRU),* depends mainly on the amount of structural unemployment but is influenced by other labor market circumstances.

Unemployment has an effect upon income, real output, and social conditions. The *income effects* result in lower living standards for those who are unemployed, their families, and those who supply them with goods and services. The *real output effects* result in smaller production, investment, and growth for the whole economy. The *social effects* include

health problems, family disintegration, and higher crime levels.

Inflation, too, has income effects and real output effects. The income effects vary for different groups. Some, especially those on fixed incomes, lose, while others, such as debtors, gain. When inflation rates are low, the real output effect of a small rise in prices may be to stimulate production. But when inflation rates are high, speculation takes precedence over production, and rising production costs discourage output. The high interest rates that accompany inflation deter new investment, and productivity and economic growth decline.

Black Thursday and the Great Crash

Crowds gathered on Wall Street on Black Thursday as stock prices declined. The Great Depression was soon to follow.

More on the crash and the Great Depression can be found in *The Great Myths of 1929 and the Lessons to Be Learned* by Harold Bierman (New York: Greenwood Press, 1991); *The Great Depression* by David A. Shannon, ed. (Englewood Cliffs, NJ: Prentice Hall, 1960); *The Great Crash* by John Kenneth Galbraith (Boston: Houghton Mifflin, 1988); *America's Great Depression* by Murray N. Rothbard (Oakland, CA: Liberty Tree Press, 1983); *The Great Slump* by Goronwy Rees (New York: Harper and Row, 1971); and *The World in Depression, 1929–1939* by C. P. Kindleberger (London: Allen Lane, 1973).

Black Thursday, as it is called, was Thursday, October 24, 1929. It was a truly black day for stock market investors, and for the nation as a whole. Stock prices declined rapidly during the morning hours in a panic of selling. The market volume was so large that the stock market ticker did not finish reporting the day's transactions until after midnight.

People's savings were wiped out and many stock speculators were bankrupted within a few hours. Among the many rumors that spread on Wall Street that day was the story that 11 stock speculators had committed suicide. According to a report in the next day's *New York Times,* "A peaceful workman atop a Wall Street building looked down and saw a big crowd watching him, for the rumor had spread that he was going to jump off." Humorist Will Rogers wrote in his newspaper column, "When Wall St. took that tail spin, you had to stand in line to get a window to jump out of." (Actually, the legend of suicide leaps by ruined Wall Street financiers is largely myth. There were only two such suicides from Black Thursday up until the end of the year, while a few other investors took their lives in alternate ways.)

Significant and dramatic as the events on Wall Street were, they were not "the" cause of the Great Depression that followed. The causes were in the fundamental weaknesses in the economy, not just in the excesses of speculation in the stock market. Although the decade of the 1920s was a period of prosperity and growth, not all sectors of the economy participated in the prosperity. The farmers, who constituted a large proportion of the population, were suffering from overproduction and low prices throughout the second half of the decade. The farm population and the low-paid unskilled workers had insufficient purchasing power to absorb all of the goods that were produced by the large investment in production facilities during the boom. Excessive financial speculation was founded on a weak banking structure. There was not yet a Federal Deposit Insurance Corporation, so when defaults by debtors created liquidity problems for some banks and forced them to close, panic withdrawal of deposits from other banks took place, forcing them to close too.

The significance of Black Thursday and the Great Crash was that the events in the stock market revealed the fallacy of faith in endless prosperity. This loss of faith did not happen all at once. For a time there were assurances from many "experts" that the setbacks were only temporary, that the economy was basically sound and would soon turn up again. Instead, it sank further and further into depression until universal pessimism in the 1930s replaced the unbounded optimism of the 1920s.

FOR FURTHER STUDY AND ANALYSIS

Study Questions

1. Mr. Jones was disabled in an accident in 1990 and has not been able to work since. Is he included in the unemployment statistics? Why or why not?

2. If the average propensity to consume (see chapter 5) increased, how might the price level be affected? Under what circumstances would such an increase be inflationary? Under what circumstances would it not necessarily be inflationary?

3. A reduction in space exploration programs has resulted in a loss of jobs in the aerospace industry. This situation is an example of what type of unemployment?

4. Judging from the quantity equation, could the money supply go down and prices go up at the same time? What would have to happen for this to come about?

5. The economy is currently in what phase of business conditions—recovery, boom, peak, bust, contraction, recession, trough, or stagflation? How can you tell?

6. How can the production capacity of the economy expand from the amount shown in Figure 6A to the amount shown in Figure 6B?

7. If an anticipation of price inflation leads business firms to build up inventories of raw materials and semifinished goods, what effect does this have on economic conditions? Why?

8. Assuming an inflation rate of 10% per year for the next 5 years, what would be the effect on the purchasing power of the dollar at the end of that time?

9. If Mrs. Sawyer were living on a fixed pension of $500 a month, how would she fare if inflation occurred at the rate indicated in question 8?

10. Why did homeowners who bought houses in the 1980s benefit from inflation?

Exercises in Analysis

1. Write a short paper on employment conditions in your area.

2. Assume that inflation is taking place and that it appears that it will continue for the foreseeable future. You have a nest egg from an inheritance of $25,000. Write a short paper on what you would do with the money and why.

3. From the following data, calculate the student cost-of-living (SCOL) index for 1995 with 1983 as the base year.

Item	Number Purchased per Semester	1983 Price	1995 Price
Hamburgers	50	$ 1.50	$ 3.00
Jeans	2	25.00	35.00
Books	3	25.00	45.00
Movie tickets	10	5.00	7.00

4. From the statistical tables in the most recent Economic Report of the President (see Further Reading), find the unemployment and inflation rates for the past 4 years. Plot them on a diagram similar to the one in Figure 7 in this chapter.

Further Reading

Case, John. *Understanding Inflation*. New York: William Morrow, 1981. "This book is for people who want to know why prices keep going up. It is not—rest assured—an economics textbook. It contains no equations, one graph, and only a few statistics" (p. 7). Includes an appendix on how the inflation rate is calculated.

Economic Report of the President. Washington, DC: Superintendent of Documents, annual. A report by the president to Congress on the state of the nation's economy. Includes the annual report of the Council of Economic Advisers, which covers a number of macroeconomic subjects such as inflation and unemployment. Also includes an appendix of statistical tables relating to income, employment, and production.

Gowland, David. *Money, Inflation, and Unemployment*. New York: St. Martin's Press, 1992. Covers the role of money in economic stability and the effect of inflation on unemployment.

Layard, Richard, Stephen Nickel, and Richard Jackman. *Unemployment: Macroeconomic Performance and the Labor Market*. New York: Oxford University Press, 1991. A study of the effect of changing aggregate output and inflation on the employment level.

Padoa-Schioppa, Fiorella, ed. *Mismatch and Labor Mobility*. New York: Cambridge University Press, 1991. The proceedings of an international conference on the relationship between labor mobility and unemployment.

Paarlberg, Don. *An Analysis and History of Inflation*. Westport, CT: Praeger, 1993. The causes and course of inflation in earlier periods of economic instability.

Rielhe, Kathlene A. *What Smart People Do When Losing Their Jobs*. New York: John Wiley and Sons, 1991. A practical guide to protecting yourself against the worst consequences of job loss, including the psychological consequences.

Skene, G. Leigh. *Cycles of Inflation and Deflation: Money, Debt, and the 1990s*. Westport, CT: Praeger, 1992. An examination of U.S. business cycles and the monetary policies effected to control price instability.

■ **In order** to deal with economic instability, we must know what to expect in the economy's be- havior. The introductory article discusses the diffi- culties of predicting where the economy is going.

Forecasting or Fortune-Telling?

Citizens of ancient Greece could get a proph- ecy about a military campaign or a long, dan- gerous sea trip by going to the oracle at the temple of Apollo at Delphi. The oracle pre- dicted future events by examining the intes- tines of a goat or by asking for a sign from Apollo. The prophecy was often so vague that no matter what happened the oracle could claim the prophecy had been fulfilled.

The demand for prophecies still flourishes. Businesses and governments go to present- day oracles for help in planning for the future. Increasingly, the oracles to which they go are those of economic model builders such as Chase Econometrics, Wharton Econometric Forecast Associates, Evans Economics, and McGraw-Hill's Data Resources. Complex sys- tems of equations, rather than mystical signs, are the sources of modern prophecy.

A great quantity of statistical data is cranked into their computer models. The data deal with economic variables whose interrela- tionships are shown by sets of mathematical equations. The more complex your economic view, the more equations you must use to fore- cast the results of changes in variables. For example, the Wharton Quarterly Model of the

U.S. economy uses 1,100 equations to forecast hundreds of specific economic changes—in prices, interest rates, automobile sales, retail sales, tax collections, unemployment, and so on.

The track record of the leading forecasting establishments has been far from perfect. In October 1981 Evans Economics predicted that the economy would grow 3.3% in 1982, Whar- ton Associates predicted 2.2% growth, and Chase Econometrics forecast a 2% growth rate. In actuality, the economy shrank by 2.5% in 1982, measured in dollars of constant pur- chasing power. As a group, they greatly un- derestimated the strength and duration of the economic expansion following 1983. And none of them foresaw the high federal government deficits, import surpluses, and high real inter- est rates that marked the 1980s. Even when individual forecasters or forecasting compa- nies have been right in a particular instance, they have not been able to repeat their success consistently.

Why have modern economic oracles not been more successful? One of the problems of the forecasters is caused by the accuracy—or lack of it—of the original data that go into the

forecasting models. The figures published by the agencies responsible for gathering the data are almost never correct when they first appear. Sometimes they are off by a factor of 10. As more accurate data become available, the figures are revised; but it may be 2 years before the final figures are available. Even after revisions, the data may not be reliable.

And why are the economic data so unreliable? Collecting the raw data is not the job of the forecasting businesses. Their function is to determine what the data mean for the industries and firms who are their clients and for the economy as a whole. Only the federal government is in a position to collect and organize economic data on the huge scale needed. But, according to Courtney Slater, former chief economist of the Commerce Department, "Too many statistical series are outmoded, and there are too many data gaps. Information about new industries and rapidly growing economic sectors is often scanty and sometimes misleading." Cuts in the budget for data collection and reporting have made the problem worse.

The unreliability of data is just one problem in economic forecasting. Another problem is understanding what effects a change in one economic variable will have on other variables. Forecasting models are based on past relationships of the variables—for example, the Phillips curve, discussed in the last chapter. But, as we saw, those relationships may change over time, resulting in inaccurate predictions. The pace of such shifts in relationships seems to be accelerating. Management

consultant Peter Drucker describes this as an "age of discontinuity" in which old rules and relationships do not apply anymore.

It is possible to compensate somewhat for unreliable data and inexact models by putting predictions in the form of a range of possibilities rather than as an exact figure. This approach, however, may be too wimpy to impress potential clients and others. According to Herbert Stein, former chairman of the Council of Economic Advisers, "Certitude pays money. It pays in attention, influence. . . . There is no 'don't know' school to which you can belong."

A difficulty that has plagued forecasters from ancient Greece to modern days is the effect of external forces on developments. Wars, disasters, shifts in government policies, all types of unforeseen occurrences can play havoc with even the most astute predictions. For example, oil prices escalated in the 1970s as a result of OPEC manipulations of the petroleum market. That changed the economic picture so much that the forecasters were left with models that were no longer relevant.

Despite their fallibility, the forecasting companies are handsomely rewarded for their services. Not all forecasting involves computers and fat fees, however. The Delphic oracle of old has many contemporary imitators. A Chicago pawnbroker, for instance, indexes economic trends by the percentage of pawnshop items that are redeemed. A psychologist predicts economic ups and downs by the number of patients signing up for expensive therapy. A Los Angeles pet store operator believes that an important economic omen is the number of rhinestone-studded poodle collars the store sells.

The newest twist in forecasting business cycles is the use of lyrics of current popular songs. Harold Zullow, a research fellow in social psychiatry at Columbia University, correctly predicted the recession of 1990–1991 by analyzing the content of the lyrics on Billboard magazine's Hot 100 chart. Studying the hit songs of the past 40 years, Zullow found that when the lyrics of the songs turned from optimistic to pessimistic it signaled that an economic downturn was approaching in 1 to 2 years. What Zullow is unsure of is which is cause and which is effect. Are the song lyrics merely a reflection of underlying currents in society? Or do they reinforce and spread pessimism and bring about the downturn?

How Much Does the Economy Produce?

There are two methods of measuring the total output of the economy. We can measure the sales value of the output of goods and services, or we can measure the incomes received by the workers and the owners of other factors used in production. These two measurements should give us the same figure because the value of what is sold ends up in the pockets of those who produced and distributed it. Income should be the same as the value of the output.

Expenditure Categories
In 1992, the national output of the United States totaled $6,038.5 billion in goods and services. This was the sum of four types of spending: consumer purchases, investment outlays for new capital goods, government spending, and net exports. The total of those expenditures was the **Gross Domestic Product (GDP)**. The 1992 GDP consisted of the outlays shown in Table 1 on page 310. The largest class of spending, shown in the left column of the chart, was **personal consumption expenditures (C)**. They comprised all

> **Gross Domestic Product (GDP):** the sum of the values of all goods and services produced within the country during the year.
>
> **personal consumption expenditures (C):** spending by households on goods and services.

Table 1. The Expenditure Categories Method of Measuring GDP—1992
(Figures in $Billions*)

Households	Investors	Governments	Rest of the world
Consumer durables $497.3	Business structures $172.6	Federal expenditures $448.8	Exports $640.5
+ Nondurable goods $1,300.9	+ Durable equipment $392.9	+ State and local expenditures $683.0	− Imports $670.1
+ Services $2,341.6	+ Residences $223.6		
	+ Additions to inventory $7.3		

Consumption:	$4,139.9
+ Investment:	796.5
+ Government:	1,131.8
+ Net Exports:	(-29.6)
= GDP:	**$6,038.5**

* The subsidiary parts may not add up to the totals because of rounding.

Source: Department of Commerce, Bureau of Economic Analysis.

■ In 1992, by using the expenditure categories method (the total sales value of the domestic output of goods and services), the Gross Domestic Product of the United States was $6,038.5 billion.

household outlays for durable goods, such as automobiles, nondurable goods, such as food and clothing, and services, such as medical care, repairs, and entertainment.

gross private domestic investment (I): private-sector spending on capital equipment, increased stocks of inventories, and new residential housing.

inventories: the value of finished and semifinished goods and raw materials in the hands of producers and distributors.

Gross private domestic investment (I) refers to outlays for capital goods. Such spending enables businesses to maintain and expand their production capacity. The two main types of investment spending are for fixed investment in buildings and for capital equipment, such as machinery. Increases in **inventories** of goods in the hands of producers or on the shelves of dealers are also considered investments. If inventories were to fall during the year it would be disinvestment, a reduction in (I). In addition, in the U.S. system of

■ The labor cost of this worker is added to GDP, but the cost of the materials she is working on, which were purchased from other suppliers, is not added to GDP because that would result in double-counting.

accounts, new residences sold during the year are included in fixed investment.

The **government sector spending (G)** includes both purchases from the private sector (for example, purchase of military equipment) and the costs of government itself (for example, salaries paid to government workers). Government spending is a mixture of consumer-type purchases, such as school lunches, and investment-type purchases, such as hydroelectric dams.

The GDP also includes the net value of U.S. international trade. Since GDP measures only what is produced domestically, we subtract imports (M) from exports (X). The difference is **net exports (X – M)** and is added into the GDP.

Adding these various expenditure categories, the GDP measures the current output of our economy as the grand total of final spending (aggregate demand). It is the sum of spending by the nation's households (C), investors (I), governments (G), and the excess, if any, of the nation's exports over its imports (X – M). Thus, GDP = C + I + G + (X – M).

Before 1992 the measurement used for total output was not Gross Domestic Product but **Gross National Product (GNP).** The difference between the two is that GDP measures income generated by production within our borders. GNP, on the other hand, includes the interest and dividends received by U.S. residents on overseas investments and the retained earnings of foreign branches of U.S. corporations, while excluding such U.S. payments to foreigners. As international investments greatly increased in recent years, the use of GNP as a measure of the actual amount of production activity within this country became less useful, and the decision was made to use GDP instead. Also, GDP is the figure generally used by other countries.

Income Categories

The second method of measuring GDP is to add together all of the incomes earned in production: labor earnings, business profits, interest, and rent payments. This total of income earnings is called **National Income (NI)**. The GDP measurement by income categories is the sum of National Income earned from domestic production plus nonincome costs of production such as depreciation on capital goods, **excise taxes**, and **business transfer payments.** The components of NI and GDP using the income approach for 1992 are shown in Figure 1.

government sector spending (G): spending by the various levels of government on goods and services, including public investment.

net exports (X – M): the value of goods and services exported minus the amount spent on imported goods and services.

Gross National Product (GNP): the sum of the values of all goods and services produced by residents of the country during the year, including earnings on overseas investments and excluding foreign earnings on investments in this country.

National Income (NI): the total of all incomes earned in producing the GNP.

excise taxes: a tax on a particular type of good or service; a sales tax.

business transfer payments: outlay by business for which no good or service is exchanged, such as excise taxes, payouts under deferred compensation arrangements, gifts, and donations.

Figure 1.

The Income Categories Method of Measuring GDP
$ Billions (1992)

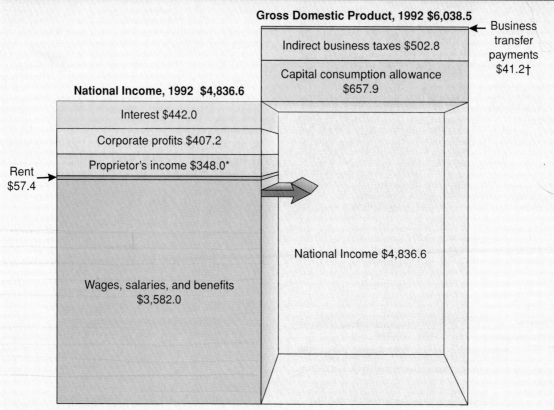

Gross Domestic Product, 1992 $6,038.5

Indirect business taxes $502.8

Capital consumption allowance $657.9

← Business transfer payments $41.2†

National Income, 1992 $4,836.6

Interest $442.0

Corporate profits $407.2

Proprietor's income $348.0*

Rent $57.4

National Income $4,836.6

Wages, salaries, and benefits $3,582.0

* Proprietor's income has been adjusted for capital consumption on private rental property as well as on business property.
† Includes statistical discrepancy.

Source: Department of Commerce, Bureau of Economic Analysis.

■ In 1992, by using the income categories method (the sum of all incomes earned plus capital consumption allowances [depreciation], indirect taxes, and business transfer payments), the Gross Domestic Product of the United States was $6,038.5 billion.

The largest part of National Income consists of the earnings of labor, including professional and managerial salaries. Other income components are proprietors' net income, corporate profits, interest, and rent. The National Income in 1992 totaled $4,836.6 billion. In addition to National Income, GDP also includes cost allocations to cover the depreciation of plant and equipment, listed in Figure 1 as **capital consumption allowances.** It further includes **indirect taxes** such as business excise taxes and other business transfer payments, which are not a part of earnings but do constitute a cost of production. When we add these nonincome costs to National In-

capital consumption allowances: the costs of capital assets consumed in producing GDP.

indirect taxes: taxes collected from businesses that are ultimately paid in full or in part by someone other than the business from which the tax is collected; not income taxes.

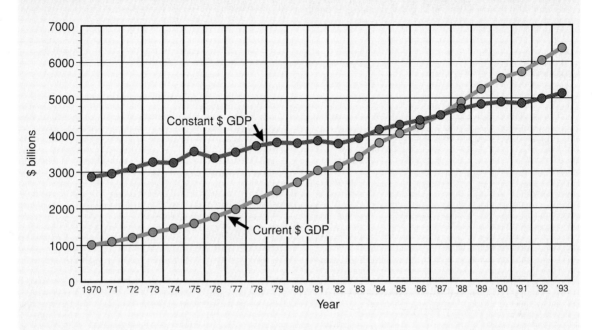

Figure 2.
Current and Constant (1987) Dollar GDP, 1970–1993

Source: Department of Commerce, Bureau of Economic Analysis.

■ Removing the effects of inflation by using 1987 constant dollar measurement gives a real GDP of $5,132.7 billion, as compared to the current 1993 dollar GDP of $6,370.0.

come, we obtain the same GDP figure that we arrived at using the expenditures approach in Table 1, $6,038.5 billion.

Value Added

The GDP is a measure of the total goods and services produced by a nation's economy in a given year. To avoid overstating the real output, the same good must not be counted more than once. For example, if we count the sale of iron ore used in making steel, then count the value of the steel sold, and finally count the selling price of an automobile in which the steel is used, we would be counting the value of the iron ore three times. To avoid double-counting, only the **value added** at each stage of production is counted. The final sale price includes and is equal to all the individual values added at each intermediate stage of production. The worth of production that actually takes place in the industries making goods like automobiles is indicated by the sum of values added. It is not the total prices of intermediate and final sales.

Current and Constant Dollar GDP

In estimating GDP, an item's current worth is the price paid for it. A **current dollar GDP** reflects the current price level of goods and services. Current dollar GDP may increase over time because of inflation.

A real or **constant dollar GDP** is used to remove the effects of inflation in order to

value added: the difference between the value of a firm's sales and its purchases of materials and semi-finished inputs.

current dollar GDP: the value of GNP as measured by figures unadjusted for inflation.

constant dollar GDP (real GDP): the value of GDP adjusted for changes in the price level since a base period.

Harry's Sub Shop

Harry's Sub Shop opened for business in January of 1993 in a good location near a college campus. By pricing his submarine sandwiches at the competitive level of $2.25, Harry soon had all the business he could handle. By year's end, he had sold 34,600 sandwiches and taken in $77,850.

From his revenues, of course, Harry had to pay for the expenses of making and selling the subs. The salami, cheese, pickles, onions, tomatoes, lettuce, rolls, and other ingredients used in the subs had cost $31,240. Out of the difference between the $77,850 taken in and the $31,240 paid for supplies, Harry had to pay an assistant, make the mortgage payments on the building,

Statement of Income (Loss)
Year Ended December 31, 1993

Revenues

Net sales - sandwiches	$77,850.00
34,600 @ $2.25 each	
Cost of Sales	
Supplies (ingredients)	31,240.00
Gross Margin	46,610.00
Other Operating Expenses	24,000.00
Staff (including benefits)	9,500.00
Interest (mortgage)	5,000.00
Depreciation	2,500.00
License fee (annual)	1,500.00
Utilities	4,500.00
Advertising	1,000.00
Net Profit	22,610.00
(before income taxes)	

nues, Harry was left with a net income of $22,610. This wasn't much, but the Sub Shop was only open 25 hours a week, and Harry also ran a catering business on the side.

How much did Harry's Sub Shop add to the 1993 current dollar GDP? One way to look at the answer is to examine how much people spent on Harry's subs. They spent $77,850. The other way to look at it is to add up all of the expenses of producing the subs, including Harry's proprietary income. The $31,240 that Harry paid to his suppliers became wages, rent, interest, profits, and depreciation allowances for all the intermediate firms in the supply chain.

Due to an increase in the cost of ingredients, Harry had to raise the price of his subs to $2.50 in 1994. Because the prices at other eating places in the area also went up, Harry did not lose any sales. He sold the same number of subs in 1994 as he had the year before.

Economic Reasoning

1. What was the value added to national output by Harry's Sub Shop in 1993?

2. What happened to the firm's contribution to the current dollar GDP in 1994 compared to 1993? What happened to its contribution to real or constant dollar GDP in that year compared with the previous year?

3. While Harry was running his two businesses, his wife, Margaret, was taking care of their three children and the house. Since she didn't get paid for this, she was not contributing to GDP. Was she actually making no contribution to the nation's output? What might be the arguments for and against including housework in GDP?

see the real change in output. This measure indicates what the GDP would be if the purchasing power of the dollar had not changed from what it was in the base year (see chapter 11, p. 287). The U.S. **national income accounts** now use 1987 as the base year. Figure 2 shows the real or constant dollar GDP for the years 1970–1993, measured in the value of 1987 dollars (brown line), compared to the GDP measured in current year dollar values for those years (green line). It shows that the real or constant dollar GDP for 1993 was only $5,132.7 billion, as compared to the 1993 current dollar GDP of $6,374.0 billion. The difference reflects price increases since 1987.

What Determines Domestic Output from the Demand-Side Point of View?

There are two principal interpretations of what determines total output. One emphasizes the role of demand in determining how much will be produced; the other emphasizes the role of supply. The demand-side analysis dominated economic thinking and planning from World War II to the 1980s. It stems from the writings of British economist John Maynard Keynes. The model he developed of how the economy works is called **Keynesian economics**.

The Keynesian economic model can be illustrated with the use of the production capacity tank introduced in the previous chapter. As you will recall, the size of the tank represents the maximum capacity of the economy to produce goods and services. Since the total output of goods and services for the year is Gross Domestic Product and the contents of the tank represent that output, we will refer to the tank as the GDP tank. The GDP tank is shown in Figure 3 with the flow of consumer spending.

Consumption Demand

The GDP tank model with consumer spending is related to the circular flow model from chapter 3, shown in Figure 4. The rent, wage, and interest payments from business to households for their productive services that are allocated by the households to consumption purchases are shown in the GDP tank model by the outflow from the bottom of the tank to the consumption sector.

The outflow is marked "C." This is the amount of income generated by production that is allocated to purchase new consumer goods and services. It flows back into the tank where it again becomes income to the producers of those goods and services. The inflow, the amount spent, is also marked "C" because it is equal to the outflow, the amount of their income that households allocate to consumption.

The amount of consumer spending depends basically on people's **disposable income**. Disposable income is income received minus taxes. Most of this disposable income is spent on consumption. In 1992 disposable personal income was $4,500.2 billion. Of this amount, households spent $4,139.9 billion on consumption goods and services. This is the amount shown in the first column of Table 1 (see p. 310) and the amount represented by "C" in the GDP tank model.

The consumption sector is the largest part of aggregate demand, making up over two-thirds of GDP in 1992. But it is not the most important sector as far as economic instability is concerned. The other sectors, although smaller, account for more instability. These

national income accounts: the collective name for various macroeconomic measurements such as GDP and National Income.

Keynesian economics: the body of macroeconomic theories and policies that stem from the model developed by John Maynard Keynes.

disposable income: the amount of after-tax income that households have available for consumption or saving.

Figure 3.

GDP Tank with Consumer Spending

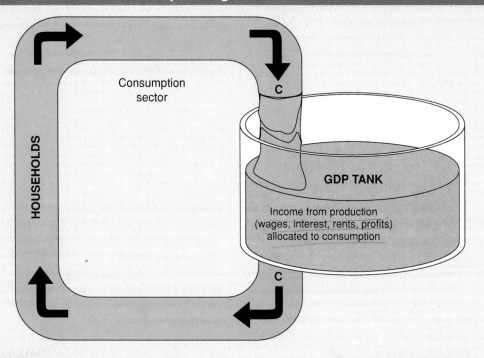

Consumption sector

HOUSEHOLDS

GDP TANK

Income from production
(wages, interest, rents, profits)
allocated to consumption

■ The GDP tank represents the nation's output of goods and services. Consumption demand by households takes the largest part of that output. Purchasing power flows into the top of the tank in the form of consumer spending. It becomes income to the households in payment for their productive services. The income that households allocate to purchase additional consumption goods and services flows out of the bottom of the tank and is returned in the form of new purchasing power.

other sources of demand are investment demand, government demand, and foreign demand. We will add the first two of these demand sectors to the GDP tank model in this chapter and consider the effects of the foreign sector in chapter 16.

Investment Demand

A second determinant of the amount of output is investment demand. Private investment spending, shown in Figure 5 in green, flows into the GDP tank from the pipe marked "I." This is spending by businesses for equipment, factories, office buildings, and inventories. It also includes spending on new residences. As shown in the second column of Table 1, investment demand in 1992 was $796.5 billion.

Investment spending comes principally from savings. The amount of income generated in producing GDP that is allocated to savings is shown flowing out of the GDP tank from the pipe at the bottom marked "S." The savings outflow, however, is not directly connected to the investment inflow. Instead, most savings flow through the banking system or other parts of the financial marketplace. This financial marketplace is represented in Figure 5 by the investment sector holding tank to the right of the GDP tank. Savings flow into the financial markets and are then drawn out to be invested in capital equipment, structures, and inventories. (This does not apply to that part of business investment which is financed out of retained earnings.) In that case the savings flow directly from the company's earnings

■ According to Keynes, these Brunswick County sheriff's deputies do more than "alligator traffic control." Their wages, and other government spending, also add to demand in the economy.

into capital spending without passing through financial markets.)

The amount of savings flowing into the financial markets through pipe "S" is not necessarily the same as the amount of investment spending flowing out of the financial markets through pipe "I." As we saw in chapter 10, the banking system can create money by making loans. In that way investment spending can be greater than intended savings. It would also be possible for the financial markets to absorb more savings than the amount of new investment spending. In that case, the amount of income flowing out of the GDP tank in the form of savings would be larger than the amount of purchasing power flowing into the tank in the form of investment.

Unlike the rate of consumption spending, which normally has a fairly consistent relationship to disposable income and tends to be rather stable, investment spending may be quite unstable. It depends a lot on expectations of future economic conditions, which may be influenced by all kinds of events and are likely to change frequently and violently. Inventory investment is an especially unstable component of investment.

Government Demand

A third source of demand is federal, state, and local government purchases of goods and services. These purchases include armaments, highways, police and fire protection, and schools, among other things. Government spending is added to consumption and investment demand for GDP in Figure 6 on p. 320. It is shown by the red flow from the pipe at the top of the GDP tank marked "G." This amounted to $1,131.8 billion in 1992, as shown in the third column of Table 1.

At the bottom of the tank, income is drawn off by government in the form of taxes through the pipe labeled "T." As with the relation between savings and investment, the amount of income drawn off in taxes is not necessarily the same as the amount of government spending going back into the economy. If the government has a **deficit** in its budget (spending more than it takes in), it is pumping more purchasing power into the economy than it is drawing off in taxes. If, on the other

deficit: a negative balance after expenditures are subtracted from revenues.

Figure 4.
Circular Flow Diagram

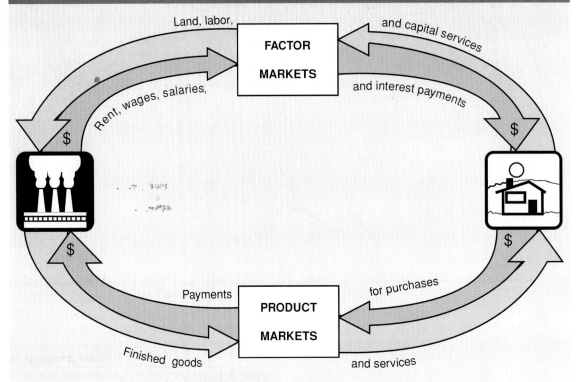

■ The GDP tank diagram with consumer spending (Figure 3) shows the same flow of purchasing power through the economy as this circular flow diagram from chapter 3. Households use the income that they receive from the sale of their labor, land, and capital services in production to purchase the consumption goods and services produced by the firms. The GDP tank diagram, however, is better than the circular flow diagram for showing the effects of the other sectors of the economy, as follows.

hand, the government has a **surplus** (spending less than it takes in), there is an accumulation in the red government sector holding tank. The flow of purchasing power back into the economy is reduced. For the most part, state and local governments must keep their budgets in balance, except for spending on long-term capital projects. It is mainly the federal government deficits or surpluses that affect changes in the income stream.

surplus: a positive balance after expenditures are subtracted from revenues.

Equilibrium Output

Aggregate demand in the domestic sectors of the economy is the total of consumption (C), investment (I), and government (G) spending. The flow of purchasing power from these three sectors determines the quantity of goods and services that can be sold. (The foreign sector is excluded for the present. It will be incorporated in the model in chapter 16.)

The quantity of goods and services demanded in turn determines how much output firms will produce. If the flow of purchasing power from one or more of these sectors is reduced, output and employment will go down. When the expenditure flows are increased, output and employment go up, unless the economy is already at full-capacity production.

Figure 5.

GDP Tank with Investment Spending

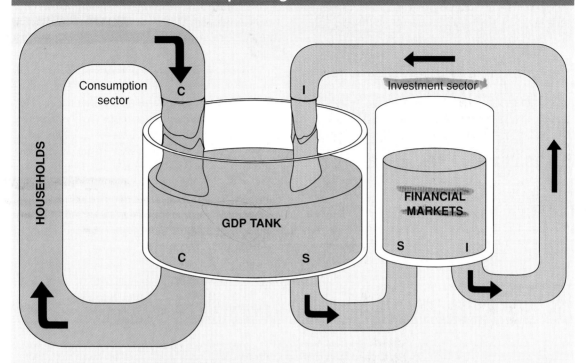

■ Whereas all of the income that households allocate to consumption is spent on consumer goods and services, the income allocated to savings may or may not all be spent on investment goods. Savings go into financial markets; and that amount, or less, or more, may be returned to the economy in the form of investment spending.

In that case, as we saw in Figure 6A in chapter 11, on page 287, the increased demand results in demand-pull inflation rather than increased output.

Production will be at the **equilibrium output level,** whether at full employment or below it, when the additions to purchasing power from domestic consumption (C), investment (I), and government spending (G) are just equal to the leakages from the income tank. These leakages are the income generated in the tank and allocated to consumption (C), intended savings (S), and taxes (T). Since the amount of income allocated to consumption of domestic goods (C) is always the same as the amount of purchasing power returned to the tank in consumer spending (C), only the other two sectors can get out of equilibrium. GDP will be constant when all of the income

that is *drawn out* of GDP in the form of savings (S) and taxes (T) is *returned* to GDP in the form of investment (I) and government (G) spending. When I + G = S + T, output is at an equilibrium level. Output, employment, and income will remain the same as long as there is no change in one of those variables.

If there is a change in one of the demand sectors, there will be a change in the level of GDP. For example, if there is a decrease in investment, purchasing power flowing into the GDP tank from investment and government demand will be less than the outflow into sav-

equilibrium output level: the level of GDP at which aggregate demand (C + I + G + X) is just equal to aggregate supply (C + S + T + M); the level where income leakages (S + T + M) are exactly equal to income additions (I + G + X).

■ Savings that flow out of the GDP and into financial markets are used by businesses to invest in capital equipment, such as these computers.

ings and taxes (I + G < S + T). This causes production to decline, as shown in Figure 7. (This figure is a schematic version of the GDP tank model in Figure 6.) The resulting fall in output and employment reduces people's income.

When their income is reduced, households save less and pay less taxes, as well as reduce their consumption of goods and services. Output, employment, and income will continue to fall until the reduction in investment spending is offset by a comparable decline in savings and taxes, so that inflows again equal outflows (I + G = S + T). A new equilibrium GDP results, with a lower level of output and income accompanied by higher unemployment and unused production capacity. This outcome is shown in Figure 8.

Figure 6.
GDP Tank with Government Spending

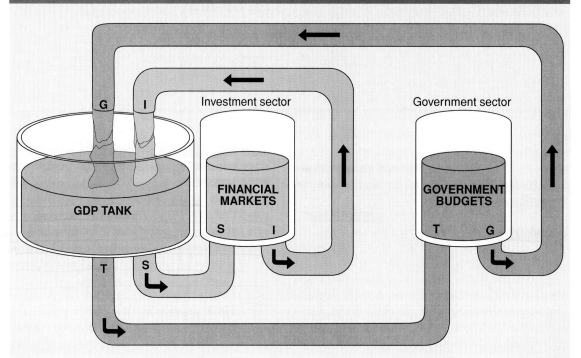

■ Government spending is funded by taxes; but, as with the investment sector, the amount drawn out of the economy in taxes is not necessarily the same as the amount returned to the economy in government spending. Generally, government spending, especially federal government spending, is greater than tax receipts. The government adds more to income than it withdraws, resulting in budget deficits.

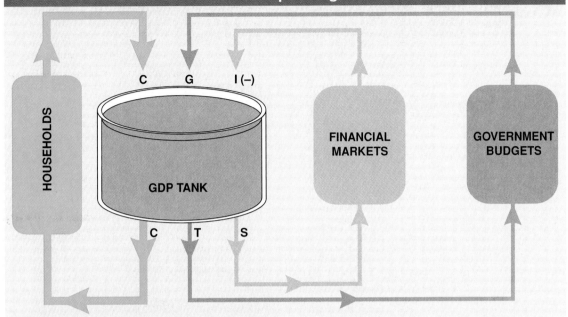

Figure 7.
Effect of a Decrease in Investment Spending

■ If there is a reduction in the amount of investment spending, as indicated by I(–), there will be a decline in aggregate demand. The amount of purchasing power flowing into the economy (C + G + I) will be less than the amount flowing out, (C + T + S). This will lower the level of economic activity, as shown in Figure 8.

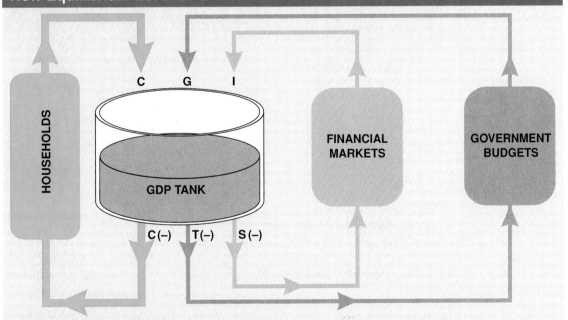

Figure 8.
New Equilibrium Level of GDP

■ The fall in GDP resulting from reduced investment spending will decrease incomes. This will result in reduced consumption, taxes, and savings, as shown by C(–), T(–), and S(–). There will be a new lower equilibrium level GDP when the reduced T + S equals the reduced G + I.

Comparative Case Application

Gaposis

How big is the gap between current output and potential output? That is a question that is getting a lot of attention these days. It is one to which the Federal Reserve, among others, would like an answer. Knowing how big the gap is would make it a lot easier for the Fed to set interest rate policy to avoid inflation. This, in turn, makes it important to a lot of ordinary citizens, such as a couple anxious to buy a new home.

But determining the size of the output gap is filled with uncertainty. As pointed out in the introductory article (p. 307), even an accurate reading on current output is not available, much less an accurate measurement of potential output. Different researchers use different methods to estimate the maximum production that an economy is capable of and come to different conclusions.

One method is to graph output levels over past years and draw a trend line connecting the peaks of production. Extending this trend line to the present gives an estimate of the output that would be produced if the economy were currently at full employment. One problem with this method is that there is on occasion a break in the trend, as there was for the United States in the 1970s, when the estimated growth trend rate fell from 2.7% to 2.1%.

Using this method to estimate the size of the output gap in early 1994, researchers Ger-

ald Holtham and Robert Beange of Lehman Brothers investment bank projected that the United States would reach its output potential during the year unless growth was slowed. At the same time, Japan, Germany, Great Britain, and France were estimated to have output gaps of 5–6%.

Economic Reasoning

1. What part of the GDP tank diagram represents the output gap? If the output gap in the United States goes to zero and demand keeps rising, what would happen on the GDP tank diagram?

2. How does the output gap analysis relate to the natural rate of unemployment or NAIRU, discussed on page 294 of the last chapter? Which is more in danger of inflation, the United States or Japan, Germany, Great Britain, and France? Why?

3. Should the Fed base its interest rate policy decisions on estimates of the output gap, given the uncertain accuracy of those estimates, even if that means stifling the housing market and running the risk of cutting off the recovery? Why or why not?

What Determines Domestic Output from the Supply-Side Point of View?

The demand-side national income model was developed by Keynes in the 1930s and refined after World War II by his intellectual heirs, the neo-Keynesians. It emphasized the importance of aggregate demand in determining the levels of output, employment, and prices. Government macroeconomic policies have been based largely on Keynesian economics. From the 1940s to the 1960s, those policies worked quite well. The economy was more stable than it had been during the 1930s and before.

However, the stagflation of the 1970s raised doubts about Keynesian economic policies. Some economists and politicians advocated a different approach based on **supply-side economics**. This approach was implemented in the economic policies of the 1980s known as "Reaganomics." Supply-side economics is more an approach to policy formulation than it is a model of how the economy operates. In fact, supply-side proponents use the Keynesian model of how the economy works to analyze and explain the effects of their supply-side policies.

Say's Law

Supply-side economics is not entirely new. Its roots go back at least as far as the early nineteenth century, when a French economist by the name of J. B. Say formulated **Say's Law of Markets**. Say's Law states simply that "supply creates its own demand." In a money economy, this means that when an entrepreneur produces something, enough income is created in payments for wages, raw materials, capital, and other costs to purchase what was produced.

The prevailing idea prior to the **Keynesian revolution** in economic thinking was that overproduction or underproduction would not be a problem because demand would always be equal to the amount supplied. If there were a temporary glut, prices would fall and permit the excess goods to be purchased. Full employment would automatically be restored.

The Keynesian model showed that this was not the case. A decrease in investment spending, for example, would mean that some goods that were produced would not be sold, as indicated in Figures 7 and 8 on page 321. There is a good deal of institutional resistance to reducing prices. There is especially resistance by labor unions to a reduction in the price of labor (wages). Demand therefore remains insufficient for full employment. As a result, high unemployment could last for a long time. The experience of the 1930s depression discredited Say's Law and led to the acceptance of Keynes's theories.

Incentives

The emphasis in modern supply-side economics is on the importance of incentives in determining output. Keynesian economics assumes that an increase in aggregate demand automatically results in more goods and services being produced, as long as there is excess capacity in the economy. Supply-side proponents, on the other hand, maintain that increased production will not take place if costs are too high. These high costs include high interest rates and high tax rates.

---

supply-side economics: an approach to macroeconomic problems that focuses on the importance of increasing the supply of goods and services.

Say's Law of Markets: A theory of the French economist J. B. Say, which holds that when goods or services are produced, enough income is generated to purchase what is produced, thereby eliminating the problem of overproduction.

Keynesian revolution: the name given to the transformation in macroeconomic theory and policy that resulted from the ideas of Keynes.

Figure 9.

Supply-Side View of the Effect of a Decrease in Taxes on Aggregate Supply

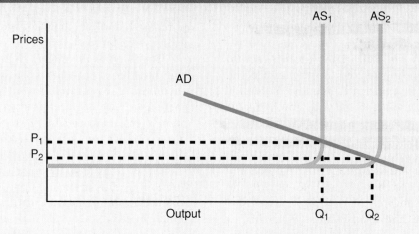

■ Supply-side economics believes a reduction in taxes on businesses will provide an incentive to expand production. This expansion will shift aggregate supply from AS_1 to AS_2 and prices will fall from P_1 to P_2 as output increases from Q_1 to Q_2.

Today's supply-side economists believe that there is a basis of truth in Say's Law. They believe that a reduction of costs, especially taxes, increases the incentive to produce, and that this increased production will create jobs and income. Increasing the net returns to producers by reducing taxes and other costs provides an incentive for them to produce more. They believe that reducing taxes will also cause households to save more, thereby making additional funds available to businesses for investment in new capital equipment. This additional investment will increase aggregate supply, as shown in Figure 9. The expansion of production capacity will shift aggregate supply from AS_1 to AS_2. As a result, there will be a decrease in inflation and unemployment as the general price level falls from P_1 to P_2 and output increases from Q_1 to Q_2.

The advocates of supply-side economics believe that increased monetary incentives can affect the supply of labor as well as the supply of capital. They maintain that reducing marginal tax rates will induce managers and workers to increase their labor input. Worker absenteeism will decline; workers will seek more overtime and second jobs; there will be less voluntary unemployment.

It is true that a reduction in tax rates means an increase in real wages, and the Law of Supply states that an increase in the price of a good or service will increase the amount offered for sale. However, there is some question as to whether this applies to the supply of labor, and under what conditions. If real wages increase, does this cause people to seek more work, or does it cause them to work less and take more leisure time? Studies show that the effect varies among different groups of workers. Many workers prefer more vacation time to higher wages, which suggests that greater real income might actually reduce the amount of labor that they supply.

Government Deficits

Supply-side economics also differs from demand-side economics in another way. It emphasizes the effect of government deficits on the availability and cost of capital to investors in the private sector. When government spends more than it collects in taxes, it fi-

Figure 10.

Effect of Government Borrowing Crowding Out Private Investors

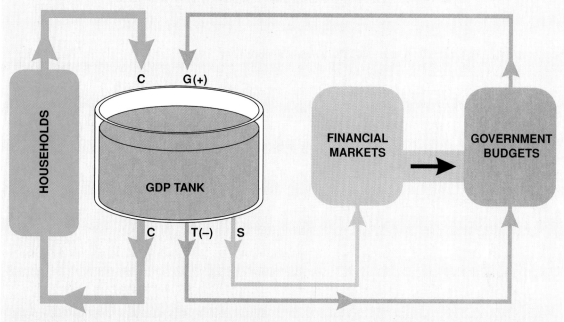

■ When an increase in government spending, G(+), or a decrease in taxes, T(−), is financed by government borrowing, investment sector funds may be diverted from private investment to the government sector. This is the "crowding out" effect shown by connecting flow between the financial markets (green) and government budgets (red). The effect is exaggerated in the diagram by completely eliminating the investment flow.

nances the difference by borrowing money in the financial markets. State and local governments sell **revenue bonds** to finance major projects, and the federal government sells Treasury bills and bonds to finance federal deficits. The sale of these government securities draws large quantities of capital out of the private capital market and raises interest rates. This process is illustrated in Figure 10 above. It is the same as the previous GDP tank models except that government budgets are connected to the financial markets out of which governments siphon off investment capital.

Figure 10 shows current GDP, the purple area in the GDP tank, at less than full employment. Some supply-siders argue that the reason for the unemployment is that the government is **crowding out** private investment,

depriving it of capital. (The crowding-out effect is exaggerated in Figure 10 by showing a complete elimination of private investment flow from the financial sector.)

If the private investors had access to this capital, supply-siders say, they would invest it in new plants and equipment, thereby creating jobs and increasing GDP. But the government returns some of its payments to the economy in the form of income transfers,

revenue bond: a financial obligation issued by a branch of state or local government that has the receipts from a specific revenue source pledged to the obligation's interest and redemption payments.

crowding out: the term given to the effect government has in reducing the amount of financial capital available for private investment.

Spending Like There Is No Tomorrow

■ The economic climate of the 1980s encouraged spending by an elite 20% of the population. Boats like these are one example of this conspicuous consumption.

Americans have not shown much interest in saving in recent years. The private savings rate fell from an average of 7%–8% of disposable income in the 1960s and 1970s to a low of 3.2% in 1987, and in the early 1990s it was less than 5%. This is a much lower savings rate than in other industrialized countries. Why is the savings rate so low?

One of the explanations for a low savings rate is the income security provided by our Social Security system. The Japanese, for instance, must depend much more on lifetime savings to provide for retirement income. Another reason is the ready availability of credit in this country.

The reasons for the especially low savings rate in the last decade, however, may be found in particular economic circumstances of the period. The rise in the values of real estate and of stock portfolios encouraged spending. Owners of those assets could spend more of their income and yet see an increase in the worth of their assets at the same time. This affected the spending habits of the roughly 20% of the population who have substantial assets.

The other 80% of the population did not, in fact, go on a consumption binge. Their real standard of living actually declined during the decade, according to most economists.

The baby boom generation has been saving 2% to 3% less of their income at age 35, the prime saving years, than did their parents at the same age. One view is that they are starting families at a later age than previous generations did, and that their savings rate will increase as they assume family responsibilities.

As for Generation X, the perceived weakness in the financial structure of the Social Security system (see "Social Insecurity," p. 346) may cause them to save more for a secure retirement. Social Security benefits have been cut back to put the system on a sounder footing and are likely to be reduced further.

Economic Reasoning

1. According to Say's Law, what would be the effect of an increase in investment on consumption? Why?

2. Why would supply-side proponents favor a reduction in Social Security benefits?

3. Should the government levy consumption taxes on goods and services to discourage consumption spending and raise revenue for the government, as European governments do? Why or why not?

which are nonproductive and tend only to raise prices and not output. This is the rationale for reducing government spending and balancing the budget.

There has been a controversy among supply-siders between those who believe in the need for tax cuts to provide production incentives and those who fear that the resulting government deficits will crowd out private investment. However, even with the record government deficits, this did not occur. It did not occur in part because the demand by businesses for investment funds was moderate and in part because a large amount of funds was supplied to the U.S. capital market by foreigners, especially the Japanese. But the danger is that if foreign investors pull their money out of the country while the government is running large deficits, it will result in crowding out private investment. This would raise interest rates and choke off economic expansion.

■ Ronald W. Reagan, elected president in 1980, embraced supply-side economics so avidly that the theory became known as Reaganomics. This approach to policy formulation in the 1980s replaced the stagflation of the 1970s, which had raised doubts about Keynesian economic policies.

Putting It Together

The total output of the economy, *Gross Domestic Product (GDP)*, can be measured either by the sales value of the output of goods and services or by the total incomes received in producing these goods and services. In measuring sales, there are four sources of demand for goods and services: *consumption demand, investment demand, government demand,* and *net export demand.* The total expenditures by these four sectors constitute GDP.

In measuring GDP as the total of incomes, we first determine *National Income,* which is the sum of wages, rents, interest, and profits. To arrive at GDP, the amount of capital equipment used up during the year (depreciation) plus *indirect business taxes* and other *business transfer payments* are then added to National Income.

In measuring the value of GDP, we do not include the total sales for each industry. That is because the value of goods produced by fin-

ished goods industries already includes the value of the semifinished goods used to produce the finished products. To avoid double counting, only the *value added* by each industry in the production process is included. In order to compare changes in real output from year to year, the effects of inflation are removed from the figures. This is done by adjusting *current dollar GDP* to eliminate the effect of higher prices. Deflating current dollar GDP by the price index gives us *constant dollar GDP.*

The *Keynesian economic model* is the basis for demand-side economics. The model, including only the domestic sectors for the present, holds that consumption (C), investment (I), and government (G) spending determine an economy's total output. When purchasing power going into the economy from investment and government spending is exactly offset by the allocation (leakages) of income into savings (S) and taxes (T), an economy's output will be at equilibrium level. On the other hand, if the income leakages into S and T are greater than the injections of purchasing power from I and G, then output, employment, and income will fall. Or if spending injections exceed leakages, output will rise, unless the economy is already at full employment.

Keynes's model demonstrated that the economy could be at equilibrium even though it was operating at less than full employment. This contradicted classical theories of economics, including *Say's Law of Markets,* which states that "supply creates its own demand."

Say's Law was an early formulation of *supply-side economics.* Modern supply-side economists claim that Keynesian economic policies are misguided because they ignore the effects of these policies on supply. In order to induce producers to risk their capital, it is necessary to provide adequate profit incentives. Adding to aggregate demand without providing incentives to producers only drives up prices. Supply-siders call for a reduction in tax rates, both on investment income and on labor services, a decrease in government spending by cutting back on government services and transfer payments, and a reduction in cost-increasing government regulations.

■ There are different ways to measure the output of the economy, and different models to explain its operation.

The Keynesian Revolution

John Maynard Keynes (1883–1946)
Keynes was raised in the intellectual environment of Cambridge University where his father, a noted writer on political economy and logic, taught and where his mother was mayor of the city of Cambridge. Upon graduation from the university, he took the examinations for entry into the British Civil Service and received his lowest mark in the economics part of the examinations. His explanation for the low grade was that "the examiners presumably knew less than I did" about economics. His career alternated between government service, teaching, writing, editing, and business, including making a fortune in the commodities market. He was a patron of the arts and married a star ballerina of the Russian Imperial Ballet. In 1942 he was made a peer and became Lord Keynes. He died of a heart attack in 1946.

In addition to *The General Theory*, his other important publications include *The Economic Consequences of the Peace* (1919), in which he predicted the results of the heavy war reparations imposed on Germany that later contributed to the rise of Hitler; *A Treatise on Probability* (1921); and *A Treatise on Money* (1930).

In a 1935 letter to Irish playwright George Bernard Shaw, British economist John Maynard Keynes predicted that the book he was working on would revolutionize the way people thought about economic problems. That book, *The General Theory of Employment, Interest and Money*, was published in 1936. Keynes was prophetic. *The General Theory* did revolutionize economic thinking, and the transformation became known as the "Keynesian revolution," sometimes capitalized as "Keynesian Revolution" to dramatize its significance.

Prior to the publication of *The General Theory*, the working hypothesis of macroeconomics was that the economy had a natural tendency to full employment. Unemployment was assumed to be the result of a *temporary* malfunction. The depth and length of the Great Depression, however, appeared to belie this assumption. In the United States, output fell by almost one-half and prices dropped nearly as much. Unemployment reached as high as one out of every four in the working population. By the time *The General Theory* appeared, the Depression had been going on for over half a decade and it continued, only somewhat abated, until the outbreak of World War II.

The revolutionary model that Keynes presented in *The General Theory* showed how an economy can be stuck at an equilibrium output level far below full employment because of insufficient aggregate demand. The policy implication of the model was that government should take an active role in bringing the economy out of a depression by injecting government spending into the income stream. This increased spending by government at a time of declining tax revenues would, of course, result in large budget deficits. To those who were concerned about the long-run consequences of such policies, Keynes's response was, "In the long run we are all dead."

Keynes wrote in his letter to Shaw that the revolution in economic thinking would not take place overnight. Keynes's theory was elaborated on by a number of other economists, including Joan Robinson (see chapter 6 Perspective). Perhaps the final triumph of the Keynesian revolution was reached when conservative Republican president Richard Nixon said, "I am a Keynesian." Ironically, this triumph of the Keynesian revolution came at a time when the structure of the economy had changed so much that Keynesian economics no longer seemed to provide an adequate solution to our economic problems.

FOR FURTHER STUDY AND ANALYSIS

Study Questions

1. If you tutored a classmate for 10 hours at $8 an hour, what would be the effect on the National Income?

2. In the above case, if you had no expenses, what would be the effect on the nation's output as measured by GDP?

3. Assuming in the above case that you had to spend 50 cents on gas to drive to each 1-hour tutoring session, what would be the value added to GDP by your tutoring?

4. On January 1, 1994, a grocery store had on hand an inventory valued at $240,000. During 1994 the store had bought groceries worth $600,000. Sales for that year came to $800,000. How much did this firm contribute to the investment component of GDP for 1994?

5. If you had a $200,000 "dream house" built, what would be the effect on GDP? What component of aggregate demand would be affected?

6. You are working at a job with a take-home pay of $200 a week. You have been putting $15 into a savings account every week, but you want to build up your savings faster, so you increase it to $25. What effect would this have on GDP?

7. Assuming the economy is at an equilibrium level of output, what are three examples of changes that would cause output to fall?

8. If output were not at the full employment level, what are three examples of changes that would increase GDP?

9. According to Keynesian economics, what would happen to output, employment, and income if government spending were reduced by 50% and taxes by 25%?

10. According to supply-side economics, what would happen to equilibrium GDP if government spending and taxes were both reduced by 50%?

Exercises in Analysis

1. In the *Economic Report of the President* (see Further Reading at the end of chapter 11) or another source, find the changes in current dollar GDP for the most recent year reported compared to the preceding year. Then write a short paper on which components of GDP were principally responsible for the changes.

2. The following are GDP figures for a hypothetical country: Consumption—$2,000; Investment—$300; Government spending—$400; Exports—$150; Savings—$400; Taxes—$400; Imports—$100. From these figures calculate the aggregate demand in the economy. Does the total demand equal the value of current output? If not, what would you expect to happen to output? Why?

3. Write a short paper on what has happened to investment spending, government spending, savings, taxes, output, and employment in the past year. Illustrate with a GDP tank diagram.

4. Write a short paper on whether demand-side economics or supply-side economics is, in your opinion, a better explanation of how the economy behaves and why.

Further Reading

Anderson, Victor. *Alternative Economic Indicators*. New York: Routledge, 1991. Discusses National Income accounting, traditional economic indicators, and social economic indicators. Examines their usefulness for economic policy and development.

Center for Popular Economics. *Economic Report of the People*. Boston: South End Press, 1986. An alternative view of the economy to that in the *Economic Report of the President* (see Further Reading at the end of the last chapter). Discusses supply-side economics in the 1980s.

Evans, Michael K. *The Truth About Supply-Side Economics*. New York: Basic Books, 1981. The myths, the truths, and the policy implications of supply-side economics.

Hailstones, Thomas J. *A Guide to Supply-Side Economics*. New York: Prentice Hall, 1983. Compares the evolution and policies of Keynesian and supply-side economics.

Hall, Peter A. *The Political Power of Economic Ideas: Keynesianism across Nations*. Princeton, NJ: Princeton University Press, 1989. Explores the spread of the Keynesian Revolution from country to country and the effect it had on politics and policies.

Hillard, John, ed. *J. M. Keynes in Retrospect: The Legacy of the Keynesian Revolution*. Aldershot, U.K.: Edward Elgar, 1988. This book is a collection of articles on the Keynesian Revolution in the past and where it stands today.

Kotlikoff, Laurence J. *What Determines Savings?* Cambridge, MA: MIT Press, 1989. There are sections on the motives for savings, the relation of fiscal policy to savings, and how social security and demographics affect savings.

Lambro, Donald. *Land of Opportunity: The Entrepreneurial Spirit in America*. Boston: Little, Brown, 1986. Covers economic forecasting, supply-side economics, and the effects of economic policy in the 1980s.

Rousseas, Stephen. *The Political Economy of Reaganomics*. New York: M. E. Sharp, 1982. An examination of classical supply-side economics, demand-side economics, monetarist supply-side economics, and how "Reaganomics" fit into these schools of thought.

■ **Government spending** and taxing have a large effect on the economy. With the government sector accounting for one-fifth of GDP, there is a great deal of interaction between the public and private sectors. The following article uses a hot policy issue where private and public overlap—the health industry—to introduce the coverage of public finance.

Rx Health Care Reform

The American health care system has been badly in need of a curative. There was no lack of consensus about its problems, but there existed widespread disagreement over the prescription for a cure. President Clinton, among others, thought major surgery was required, while there were those who believed that some minor surgery or a few Band-Aids would take care of the problems.

The worst symptom was the large and growing number of people without health care coverage, amounting to an estimated 39 million by 1994. That was up from 32.6 million in 1988. Those figures refer to the number of people not covered by health insurance at any given time. The total number not covered at some point during the year was more than 51 million.

These increases in the numbers of the uninsured stemmed in large part from layoffs by major firms, which deprived the workers and their families of employer health coverage, and the increased use of part-time and temporary labor with no fringe benefits. In fact, a leading reason for the shift by companies to the use of more contingent workers was to escape the rising costs of health coverage for their labor force.

Costs of health care were rising at double the rate of inflation. Total spending on health rose from 5.9% of GDP in 1965 to 14% in 1992. This was twice the amount spent on education. Unless changes were made in the system, it threatened to take 20% of GDP within another decade. Health care cost the United States much more than it did other countries. In 1991, Great Britain and Japan each spent just 6.6% of their GDP on health care, Germany 8.5%, and France 9.1%. The U.S. health care bill translates into $2,867 for each man, woman, and child. Germany spends about $1,659, France about $1,650, and Canada $1,915. All of these countries have long had universal health care coverage with no one left out. Every large industrialized country enjoyed universal coverage except the United States and South Africa.

The elevated health care costs in this country are to some extent due to the extensive use of high-tech medicine, especially in the final stages of a patient's life. Heart and liver transplants, heart bypass surgery, and other miracles of modern medicine are enormously expensive. A liver transplant and follow-up treatment carry a price tag of $300,000 in the first year. Every year, some 400,000 Americans undergo heart bypass surgery at a total cost of about $12 billion. Angioplasty to unclog blocked arteries is now performed 300,000 times a year at a cost of approximately $10,000 per procedure.

There has been a tendency to employ high-tech medical treatments excessively, even when they could not be shown to improve health outcomes. The use of angioplasty has risen despite a lack of evidence that it prevents heart attacks and in spite of the fact that drug treatment has been shown to yield similar results at a fraction of the cost. A 1988 RAND Corporation survey found that half of the heart bypass operations in a sample of hospitals were at best questionable and at worst useless. But the number of bypass operations continues to rise. Like climbing a mountain, high tech is used because it is there. At half of all deliveries, obstetricians connect the fetus in the womb to an electronic monitor to check on any signs of distress. The rising popularity of this procedure, at a collective cost of $1 billion a year, flies in the face of a number of studies that show no better outcomes than with the use of a stethoscope placed on the mother's abdomen, even in high-risk pregnancies.

The increased use of high-tech procedures has been accompanied by purchase of diagnostic scanners and other costly equipment by hospitals. When every hospital in an area purchases the same equipment in order to stay competitive, it drives up hospital costs and much of the equipment is underutilized.

But the use and overuse of high-tech medicine is only one of the causes of the larger medical costs in this country than in other advanced countries. Another explanation lies in the inflated cost of prescription drugs, among the most expensive in the industrialized world. A General Accounting Office survey done for the U.S. Senate found that for 121 prescription drugs, Canadians paid on the average only 62% as much as U.S. citizens. Residents of the United Kingdom, France, Italy, and Japan pay even less for the same drugs. Only in Germany are the prices of prescription medicines comparable to those in the United States.

Physicians' fees are also substantially higher in this country. According to a 1990 study reported in *The New England Journal of Medicine,* "The quantity of physicians' services is actually lower in the United States than in Canada [but] U.S. fees for procedures are more than three times as high as in Canada." Relative to average incomes in this country, incomes of physicians in the United States are much higher than in other industrialized countries; the mean income of a self-employed American physician is $170,000. But in this regard it should be noted that doctors in other countries do not leave medical school with debts of $50,000 and more, since the cost of their medical education is covered by the government. Important in the greater cost of physician services in this country is the relative proportion of specialists, who are typically more expensive than generalists. Here nearly 80% of the doctors are specialists, while in other Western countries the proportion is half that.

Another costly aspect of American medicine is administrative. The costs of administration in the private sector of the U.S. health care system account for 20% of the total costs. In Canada, where the system is government run (see the Case Application on p. 341), only about 10% of health care costs go for administering the system. Estimates for the bureaucratic costs of health insurance companies, hospitals, and public agencies range as high as $167 billion a year, roughly what Germany and France combined spend on their whole health care systems annually.

Health care costs are also inflated by fraud. Experts in the field estimate that fraud and abuse add between $50 billion and $80 billion to the nation's medical bill each year. This ranges from such lesser abuses as the ordering of unnecessary tests and procedures to pad medical bills to outright scams, such as the $1 billion of false medical lab billings in an elaborate Southern California scheme run by the two Russian immigrant Smushkevich brothers. Government and private health care insurers paid out $50 million in claims before the racket was exposed in 1988.

Failure to cover millions of citizens and the high costs of care are merely the symp-

Figure 1.

Health Care Spending
1991

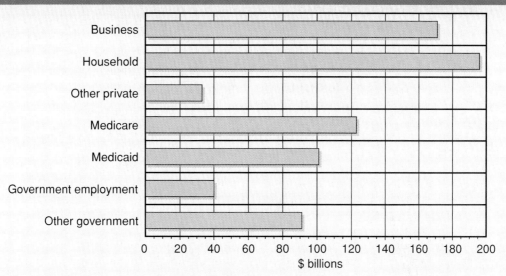

Source: Health Care Financing Administration.

■ Spending on health care in 1991 was about equally divided between private sector spending—by businesses on employee health coverage and by households on insurance and out-of-pocket costs—and government sector spending on Medicare, Medicaid, government employee health coverage, and other programs.

toms of what ails the U.S. health care system. The basic causes are to be found in the structure of the system itself. Unlike most markets in our free-enterprise economy, the market for medical treatment has not been subject to the discipline of price competition for the customers' business. Neither the employer-paid health care plans for workers nor the government Medicare and Medicaid programs for older people, people with disabilities, and the poor provide adequate incentives for patients to economize on their use of medical resources.

Because little or none of the extra cost of more expensive medical treatments comes out of the pockets of the patients, there is no incentive to economize on health care costs. Generally, insured patients do not even know what the costs of the treatments they receive will be. On the supply side of the market, doctors, hospitals, and labs have financial incentives to expand the amount and price of services, while on the demand side there is little motivation for the customer to shop for the less expensive service. The government and the private insurance companies try to hold down costs; but since they depend on the information supplied by the service providers, they are not in a position to be knowledgeable purchasers.

The result of this inefficient market system is that health care costs have escalated to levels that hamper the economy and threaten to drive the federal budget out of control. Health care spending has been growing four times faster than any other component of the federal budget. The percent of total federal revenues going to health care increased from 9% in 1972 to 21% in 1991.

The rapid rise in the private and public costs of health care, along with the inadequacies of the system—lack of universal coverage, exclusion by insurers of people with preexisting conditions, lack of portability of health care coverage for workers changing jobs, insurance that can be canceled in cases of catastrophic illness—led to the demand for reform.

This was by no means the first time comprehensive health care reform was proposed. The first national health care bill was presented to Congress in 1943. Nearly every president since then has pushed for a reform program. Virtually all proposals for changes in the way health care was delivered or paid for were defeated by organized medicine. Those with a vested interest in preserving the status quo have contributed hundreds of millions of dollars to politicians and to media blitzes opposing reform. It took a war chest of only $1 million to defeat the first national health care bill. More recently, Federal Election Commission records show that health care and insurance industry interests funneled $41.4 million just into the House and Senate campaigns of 1992.

■ Chapter Preview

The rapid rise in U.S. health care costs has been one of the factors in increasing federal budget deficits and the national debt. But the American people have come to consider health care, like food and shelter, to be a basic human right. To the extent that the free market does not provide adequate health care at an affordable price, the public looks to government to fill the need. People want the programs that government provides, but they do not want the country to go broke paying for them. In this chapter we will examine the problem of government finance by asking these questions: On what do governments spend money? Where do governments get the money to spend? Who pays for government spending?

■ Learning Objectives

After completing this chapter, you should be able to:

1. Discuss the relative size of government economic activity.

2. List the most important types of federal government spending.

3. List the most important types of state and local government spending.

4. Identify the principal sources of revenue for the federal, state, and local governments, respectively.

5. Explain the criteria for equity in taxation.

6. Describe how "bad" taxes decrease economic efficiency.

7. Define what is meant by the incidence of a tax.

The battle over the current reforms concerned the extent of changes in the system, how big a role the government would play, and how the changes would be paid for. No one can say for sure how the reforms will affect the government budget down the road; but, lacking a cure for the ailing health care system, the road of escalating health care costs was leading not only the government but individuals and businesses as well to the poorhouse.

On What Do Governments Spend Money?

According to public opinion polls, people are not as concerned about the amount of taxes collected as they are about the efficiency with which their tax dollars are spent. This section examines the allocations of spending by the different levels of government.

Size of Government Spending

Just how big is "big government"? About one-third of all money flow in the U.S. economy is channeled through governments. The budgets of all levels of government—federal, state, and local—together equal 34% of the Gross Domestic Product. This is similar to or less than the share of government spending in other advanced economies (37% in the United Kingdom and Germany, 44% in France, 32% in Japan).

That figure, however, overstates the impact of government spending on the economy because a large part of government payments, especially in the federal budget, are not purchases but rather income transfers. In 1993, 70% of all federal expenditures were transfer

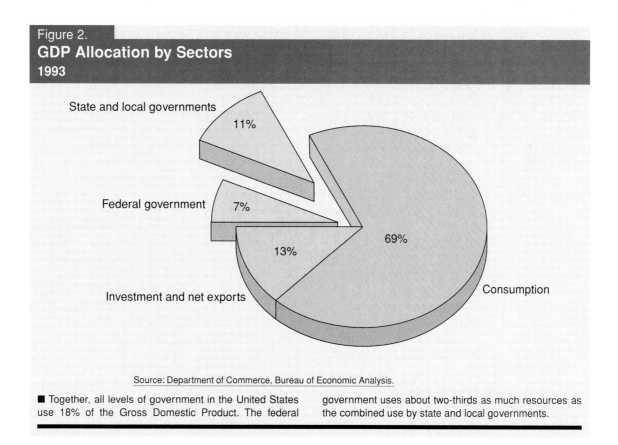

Figure 2.
GDP Allocation by Sectors
1993

State and local governments 11%

Federal government 7%

Investment and net exports 13%

69%

Consumption

Source: Department of Commerce, Bureau of Economic Analysis.

■ Together, all levels of government in the United States use 18% of the Gross Domestic Product. The federal government uses about two-thirds as much resources as the combined use by state and local governments.

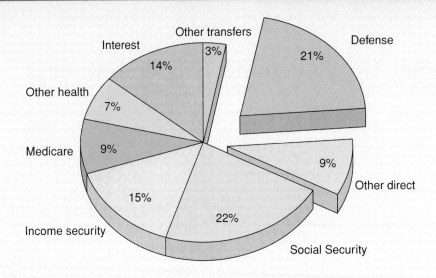

Figure 3.
Federal Government Spending
1993

Other transfers
Interest 14%
Other health 7%
Medicare 9%
Income security 15%
22%
Social Security
3%
Defense 21%
9%
Other direct

Source: U.S. Office of Management and Budget.

■ The largest direct expenditure item in the federal budget is national defense. Altogether, direct spending, represented in this figure by the exploded (set-off) sections, accounts for 30% of the federal budget. The other 70% consists of transfer payments, of which Social Security is the largest. The federal government budget is therefore more important in allocating income than in allocating resources.

payments. If we subtract transfer payments from the total of all government expenditures, then government spending at all levels accounts for less than one-fifth of total spending. The various levels of government purchase 18% of the nation's yearly output of goods and services, of which the federal government accounts for 7% (see Figure 2).

Between 1974 and 1993, total government spending increased by 72% (federal spending by 74%) after adjustment for inflation. Of the increase in federal spending, 45% was accounted for by increased transfer payments to individuals and another 19% by increases in defense spending. The increase in state and local spending was primarily for government services.

Because of the large amount of transfer payments, the federal budget is two-thirds greater than the combined total of both state and local government budgets. But 83% of all

government employees work for state and local governments, whereas only 17% work for the federal government, excluding military personnel. State and local governments employ so many more workers than the federal government because they provide the bulk of public services. Over 13% of all civilian employees in the country work for state and local governments, while the federal government employs less than 3%. The size of the federal workforce has been virtually constant for the last 2 decades and has actually declined by one-fourth as a percentage of the total labor force. Meanwhile, the number of employees in state and local governments has doubled.

Federal Spending

Figure 3 shows the allocation of federal outlays in 1993. The federal budget is divided between purchases of goods and services and transfer payments. The largest single direct

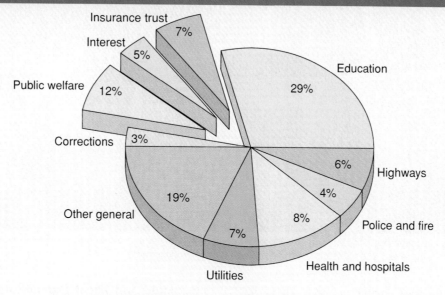

Figure 4.
State and Local Government Spending
1991

Insurance trust 7%

Interest 5%

Public welfare 12%

Corrections 3%

Other general 19%

Utilities 7%

Health and hospitals 8%

Police and fire 4%

Highways 6%

Education 29%

Source: U.S. Bureau of the Census.

■ In contrast to federal spending, which is mainly income transfers, state and local government expeditures are primarily direct spending on goods and services (unexploded sections of Figure 4.) The largest expenditure is for education.

expenditure item in 1993 was for national defense, as it is each year, accounting for over one-fifth of the total budget. All other direct expenditures—for running the executive, legislative, and judicial branches of the government, natural resources and the environment, technology, the space program, transportation, energy, and everything else—accounted for only 9% of the budget. It is this direct spending that makes up the government sector (G) in determining the level of national output (GDP) discussed in the last chapter.

The rest of the budget consists of transfer payments of various sorts. The largest of these in 1993 was Social Security pension and disability benefits. (For a full discussion of Social Security, see the Case Application for the second analysis section of this chapter, p. 346.) Next in size was income security—federal employee pension and disability payments, unemployment compensation, food stamps, and others—with 15% of spending. It was followed

by interest on the national debt, accounting for 14% of the budget. Interest on the debt was only 9% of the budget in 1980; as the debt grows, so does its interest cost. Other major transfers are for Medicare and other health programs. In 1980 Medicare accounted for 5% and other health care spending for 4% of the budget. By 1993 Medicare had grown to 9% and other health programs to 7%. In total, annual health care costs to the federal government increased $182.6 billion between 1980 and 1993.

Since transfer payments account for over two-thirds of the budget, the federal government is more important in allocating income in the economy than it is in allocating resources through its purchases. Furthermore, it is obvious from these figures that reducing "waste and inefficiency in government," insofar as federal government civilian activities are concerned, cannot accomplish a great deal in reducing the deficit. Eliminating all federal

■ Free public education accounts for over one-third of state and local government expenditures. Tax reduction initiatives and higher costs have led to smaller budgets and cutbacks in many classrooms.

government direct spending other than defense would reduce the size of the federal budget by less than 10%. Making government agencies more efficient rather than eliminating them can reduce government spending by only a negligible amount.

Most of the income transfer programs are entitlements, which means that eligible recipients are legally entitled to the payments or services from the government. These entitlements include Social Security benefits, federal employee retirement benefits, Medicaid, Medicare, veterans' benefits, and unemployment assistance. Anyone who is eligible to receive these benefits is, by law, entitled to them, and more and more people have become eligible in recent years. The total number of beneficiaries of these various entitlement programs is now over 70 million, or nearly one of every three persons in the population. These recipients constitute a very large group in support of continuation of these programs. As the age distribution of the population shifts toward older ages, more people become eligible for these programs, and some programs become more expensive because their benefits are indexed to the cost of living. This creates a built-in pressure for continuing increases in transfer payments.

State and Local Expenditures

As shown in Figure 4, state and local governments spend more on education than in any other area. Education absorbs 29% of state and local budgets. In contrast to the federal budget, most state and local expenditures are direct rather than transfer payments.

The interest costs on the debt of state and local governments amount to only 5% of their budgets, much less than for the federal government. This is because state and local governments in general are legally prevented from running deficits in their current spending. Except for capital expenditures such as construction projects that are funded by specific bond issues, state and local government budgets must be in annual balance.

Unable to run current budget deficits to cover shortfalls, burdened with federally mandated programs, limited in revenue collections by taxpayers' revolts and sluggish economies, state and local governments have been caught in a financial squeeze. The result has been dilapidated school buildings, overcrowded classrooms, deteriorating highways, bridges, and public transit, and inadequate water and sewage systems. Two areas of state spending have been increasing: prisons and health care.

Comparative Case Application

Northern Exposure

A number of myths have circulated in the United States about the Canadian health care system, suggested in many cases by those opposed to a single-payer system in the United States. Under a single-payer system, the government (provincial, state, or federal) is responsible for paying for all covered medical treatments. Its opponents have labeled it socialized medicine. But the Canadian system does not fit that description, since the government neither hires the doctors and other health professionals nor owns the hospitals.

One wrongly held view is that patients do not have free choice about the selection of their doctor or hospital under the Canadian system. In fact, under this system, the patient can choose any doctor or hospital and change at will. By contrast, in the United States, the choice of doctor and medical facility has been increasingly constrained by the growth of health maintenance organizations (HMOs) as the primary health care providers for American workers. In an HMO, the patient's choice of doctor and facility is limited to those that belong to that HMO.

Another myth is that Canadians are unhappy with the system. Overall, they are very satisfied with it. Surveys show that the great majority of the population is very pleased with the system, while a minority thinks improvements are needed. By comparison, polls taken in the United States in 1994 found as much as 65% of the population dissatisfied with the American system.

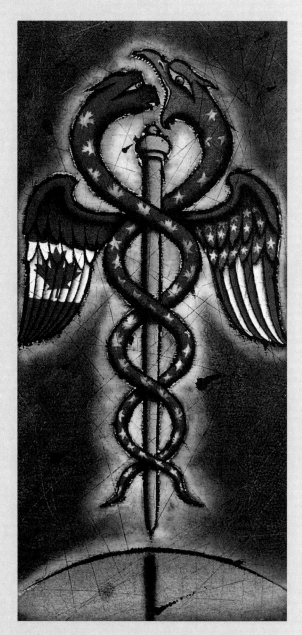

One of the alleged reasons for Canadians' dissatisfaction with their system is supposedly long waits to see a doctor or obtain treatment. For urgent care cases and necessary operations there is no wait. For elective surgery, patients are queued according to the significance of their need.

As for the allegation that most Canadian physicians are unhappy with the system, with great numbers leaving the country to practice elsewhere, that is also untrue. At the time of the first introduction of a government health care system in the 1960s, the medical profession was strongly opposed and attempted to block it. Since then, Canadian doctors have found that, while the system limits the amount they can charge for their services, it also relieves them of such overhead costs as extensive paperwork and the problem of bad debts. At the same time, it does not circumscribe the doctor's freedom in treating patients as much as insurance companies and HMOs do in the United States. Nor has it circumscribed their income. Before the system was introduced, Canadian physicians earned twice the national income average. Now they earn five times as much as the average Canadian.

On the other hand, Canada has not been any more successful than the United States in holding down the rise in health care costs, which have gone up at twice the rate of inflation. But savings on such things as administrative costs (only a quarter of those in the United States) and major medical expenses through better preventive care (prenatal care, for example, holds the infant mortality rate to half that in the United States) result in health care consuming a significantly smaller proportion of the national output in Canada than in the United States. It constitutes about 10% of GDP in Canada compared to 14% here. Both the General Accounting Office and the Congressional Budget Office estimated that a single-payer system could save the nation roughly half a trillion dollars in health care costs within 5 years.

Exposing the myths about the Canadian single-payer health care system is unlikely either to overcome the propaganda campaign against it waged by the U.S. medical and insurance industries, dispel the suspicions Americans have about "big government," or enable the radical change a single-payer system would make in the way health care is organized and paid for in this country. But a better understanding of the system north of the border improves the rationality of the debate over health care reform.

Economic Reasoning

1. Is Canadian government spending on health care a direct expenditure or a transfer payment? How can you tell?

2. What would be the effect on the U.S. federal budget of a single-payer system? Would the proportion of the budget going to health care go up or down or stay about the same? Why?

3. Should the United States adopt a single-payer system similar to Canada's? Why or why not?

Where Do Governments Get the Money to Spend?

In the preceding section, we saw that there are major differences in what the federal government spends money on and what state and local governments spend money on. In this section we will see that there are also major differences in the sources of their funds.

 Federal Government Revenues

The largest source of revenue for the federal government is individual income taxes. As shown in Figure 5, the tax on personal incomes provided 45% of the federal government's revenue in 1993. The personal income tax component of federal receipts has changed little over the past 2 decades.

Next to income taxes, the largest revenue—over one-third—comes from Social Security **payroll taxes**. Social Security taxes have been steadily increasing and making up an ever larger part of federal government income. Over half of the nation's workers, those at the lower end of the income scale, pay more in Social Security contributions than in income taxes.

Corporate income taxes generated 9% of federal revenues in 1993, down from 13% in 1980. Excise taxes—the federal taxes on gasoline, alcohol, cigarettes, and public utility services—customs duties on imports, and miscellaneous receipts such as user fees and earn-

> **payroll tax:** a tax on wages and salaries to finance Social Security and Medicare costs, with equal amounts paid by employee and employer; the 1990 tax rate on each was 7.65%.

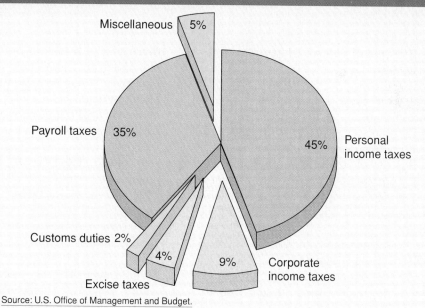

Figure 5.
Federal Government Revenue
1993

- Miscellaneous 5%
- Payroll taxes 35%
- Personal income taxes 45%
- Customs duties 2%
- Excise taxes 4%
- Corporate income taxes 9%

Source: U.S. Office of Management and Budget.

■ The largest source of federal government revenue is personal income taxes. The second largest is payroll taxes from Social Security and federal pension contributions. The largest item in the miscellaneous category is earnings by the Federal Reserve System.

Figure 6.

State and Local Government Revenue
1991

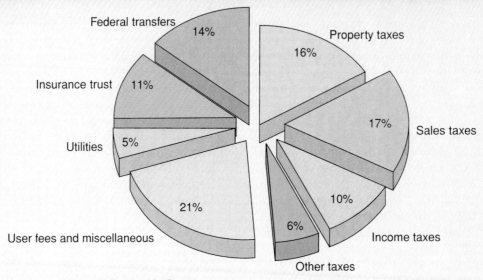

Source: U.S. Bureau of the Census.

■ The largest single source of revenue for the states is sales taxes. The share of revenue from user fees has been increasing, while that of state income taxes has been decreasing. For local governments, the largest revenue source is property taxes. Income transfers from the federal government are important to both state and local governments.

ings by the Federal Reserve System accounted for the balance.

State and Local Government Revenues

As Figure 6 shows, the largest sources of state and local government revenues come from sales taxes, which the states principally depend on, property taxes, which local governments principally depend on, and federal transfers and user fees, which help finance both levels.

The federal income transfers are referred to as **fiscal federalism**, by which a lower branch of government is financed by revenues collected at a higher level of government.

fiscal federalism: tax collection and disbursement of funds by a higher level of government to lower jurisdictions.

Much of the transfers are to cover federally mandated programs, but in recent years the mandated costs have tended to exceed the amounts transferred, leaving the states to make up the difference. States such as Florida and California sued the federal government to recover the costs of educational and health services mandated for illegal immigrants. The amounts of federal transfers to each state in 1992 are shown in Table 1.

State and local governments face increasingly vocal demands from their citizens for improvements in highways, transportation, and other infrastructure; better schools; and pollution control. They are required by mandated federal programs to spend more on Medicaid, social services, and income maintenance. At the same time, federal aid to the states has been declining as a percentage of state revenues. State taxes, meanwhile, have been restricted by the taxpayers' revolt of the 1980s.

Table 1.

Federal Income Transfers to States and the District of Columbia in Order of Amounts per Capita, 1992

State	Federal Aid Total (billions)	Per Capita	State	Federal Aid Total (billions)	Per Capita
District of Columbia	$ 2.0	$3,314	New Jersey	$ 5.2	$ 670
Alaska	$ 0.8	$1,425	South Carolina	$ 2.4	$ 664
Wyoming	$ 0.6	$1,271	Washington	$ 3.4	$ 657
New York	$ 19.3	$1,065	Idaho	$ 0.7	$ 650
Louisiana	$ 4.4	$1,030	Minnesota	$ 2.9	$ 646
Rhode Island	$ 1.0	$ 981	Oklahoma	$ 2.1	$ 643
North Dakota	$ 0.6	$ 948	Ohio	$ 7.1	$ 641
Montana	$ 0.8	$ 929	California	$ 4.3	$ 639
West Virginia	$ 1.7	$ 921	Michigan	$ 6.0	$ 636
Vermont	$ 0.5	$ 882	Wisconsin	$ 3.1	$ 624
New Mexico	$ 1.4	$ 872	Nebraska	$ 1.7	$ 621
Massachusetts	$ 5.2	$ 870	Delaware	$ 0.4	$ 617
Maine	$ 1.0	$ 847	Maryland	$ 2.9	$ 599
South Dakota	$ 0.6	$ 845	Georgia	$ 4.0	$ 597
New Hampshire	$ 0.9	$ 842	Illinois	$ 6.9	$ 596
Mississippi	$ 2.2	$ 839	Iowa	$ 1.7	$ 590
Connecticut	$ 2.6	$ 790	Arizona	$ 2.2	$ 583
Kentucky	$ 3.0	$ 786	North Carolina	$ 4.0	$ 580
Tennessee	$ 3.7	$ 728	Utah	$ 1.0	$ 575
Hawaii	$ 4.8	$ 724	Indiana	$ 3.2	$ 573
Arkansas	$ 1.7	$ 705	Colorado	$ 1.9	$ 549
Pennsylvania	$ 8.3	$ 691	Texas	$ 9.6	$ 546
Oregon	$ 2.2	$ 688	Kansas	$ 2.0	$ 545
National	**$174.4**	**$ 684**	Nevada	$ 0.7	$ 504
Alabama	$ 2.8	$ 676	Florida	$ 6.2	$ 459
Missouri	$ 3.5	$ 674	Virginia	$ 2.8	$ 435

Source: U.S. Bureau of the Census, *Federal Expenditures by State for Fiscal Year 1992.*

■ The federal government provides grants-in-aid and other income transfers to state and local governments under a system of fiscal federalism. Other than the District of Columbia, which is financed by the federal government, the largest federal aid per capita in 1992 went to Alaska—$1,425 per Alaskan. The smallest amount went to Virginia—only $435 for each Virginian.

There are some indications, however, that voters are willing to pay more to get the improved services that they want. In California, where the taxpayer revolt began, and a number of other states, including Florida, Massachusetts, Montana, Nevada, Oklahoma, Texas, and Vermont, either state voters or local governments have passed tax increases to fund specific programs. Voters are apparently willing to accept targeted taxes earmarked for specific purposes that they feel are needed.

Case Application

Social Insecurity

Is the Social Security system going broke? Will there be any money left to pay retirement benefits to the young workers who are contributing to the system now? These are troublesome questions because, since the passage of the Social Security Act in 1935, the Social Security system has become the cornerstone of our society's method of providing economic security to older Americans.

There are actually four separate trust funds under the Social Security program. The principal fund pays *retirement benefits* to those who are past retirement age or to their survivors, and a second fund provides *disability payments* to those who are unable to work any longer for physical or psychological reasons, although they have not reached retirement age. The other two funds are for *hospital* and *supplementary medical* care for older people—the Medicare program.

Unlike private pension plans, the Social Security system does not pay benefits out of returns on investments made with the contributions to the fund. Instead, the current contributions of workers pay the benefits to present retirees. This system worked very well during the time that the labor force was expanding more rapidly than the number of people collecting benefits. But since 1950, the ratio of workers to retirees has been steadily declining. In 1950 there were 16 workers paying Social Security taxes for every person collecting retirement benefits. By 1960 the ratio had been reduced to 5 to 1. Today it is just over 3 to 1. When the baby boom generation, those born between 1946 and 1961, reach retirement age, the ratio is expected to decline to only two workers for each retiree.

The funds—especially the retirement fund—were nearing exhaustion in the early 1980s. To rescue the funds from running out

of money, Congress enacted legislation in 1983 that increased Social Security revenues and reduced benefits. The bill accelerated scheduled increases in payroll taxes, raised the tax rate on the self-employed, and subjected some Social Security retirement benefits to income taxation. On the side of benefits, the most important change was to delay from 65 to 67 the age at which workers could retire with full benefits. That change will not come into effect until the year 2000, when it will be phased in gradually up to the year 2027. Other benefit changes include a reduction in the percentage received by those who retire early, also effective at the turn of the century.

Based on the estimates of the time, those reforms were assumed to take care of the financing of the retirement fund until about the year 2020, when the large number of retiring baby boomers would necessitate additional revenue or cutbacks in benefits. But the estimates were overly optimistic. More realistic data on fertility rates, life expectancies, interest rates, and the performance of the economy show that, with the present financing system, the retirement trust fund will run short sooner than anticipated, perhaps by 2014, when the first wave of baby boomers begins to retire.

To continue benefits at their present levels after that time might require Social Security tax rates of 35% or more. This would probably not be politically acceptable. Even now there is discussion of an emerging intergenerational conflict between younger workers. An average couple retiring now at age 65 can expect cash benefits worth over 3 times the amount they and their employer put in (plus interest). The same couple retiring in 2025 would get only about 1.75 times the original investment. And most young people starting work now can expect to collect less than they pay in over their working lifetimes.

In even more immediate difficulty are the Disability and Medicare funds, which will be exhausted in 1995 and 2001, respectively, unless they're bailed out. Earlier cost-containment measures imposed on hospitals and doctors and higher Medicare patient charges failed to stop the hemorrhaging. This was one of the considerations driving the movement for health care reform.

The idea that the Social Security trust funds are accumulating surpluses now to pay for benefits in the future is something of a fiction. The surpluses are in fact used to help the government to balance the federal budget, because the Social Security accounts are included in the government's overall budget. The government borrows from the trust funds in the same way it borrows from others—by selling them Treasury bonds. By law, the reserves of the funds can be used only to purchase U.S. government securities. The Social Security surpluses thus reduce the government's need to go into the private capital market to finance the deficit. But the government is obligated to repay the funds borrowed, and the total assets of the funds remain intact.

Social Security real benefits are always provided from current real production, whatever the funding system. This has to be the case because every year total consumption must be equal to total production, except for inventory changes and net foreign trade. The present generation cannot produce the goods and services for consumption when it retires. To show how ridiculous the idea is—there could never be enough warehouses built in which to keep the output for later consumption. Therefore, the consumption of retirees will always be provided for by the output of the current labor force. The problem is to make the financing of the transfer as equitable as possible.

Various suggestions have been put forth for solutions to the long-run problems of the Social Security system. One proposal has been to change the method of calculating cost-of-living increases in benefit payments. Since Social Security benefits were indexed to the cost of living in 1975, the real income of retirees has actually increased faster than that of workers. Proposed changes in the method of calculating cost-of-living increases and raising taxes on benefits could result in decreasing real income for retirees.

More radical solutions would involve changing the very basis of financing the Social Security system. One proposal is to change it over into an investment fund like private pension plans rather than a pay-as-you-go system. A modified version of this solution has been put forth that would provide for a sort of "super IRA," allowing workers to contribute to their own tax-sheltered pension plans to supplement Social Security benefits. Another proposal is to eliminate the payroll tax method of financing and pay Social Security benefits out of general tax revenues, just as other transfer payments are made. At the very least, it is argued, the amount of any future deficits in the trust funds should be covered out of general tax revenues rather than further increasing the already substantial payroll tax.

Economic Reasoning

1. How does the financing of Social Security differ from the financing of other government programs?

2. It has been said that Medicare is not properly a part of the Social Security system and should be transferred to the U.S. Department of Health and Human Services. What would be the effects of such a change on the budget?

3. What changes do you think should be made in the Social Security system and why?

Who Pays for Government Spending?

The question of who should pay how much of the cost of government—how the burden should be shared—is a continuing subject of debate. Economics can help enlighten this debate by providing certain criteria that are presented in this analysis section.

Equity

In a democracy, governments can tax the citizens only with their agreement, and people will agree to be taxed only if they perceive the tax system to be fair. One of the conditions of fairness is that people who are equally able to pay should bear the same tax burden. This is **horizontal equity**. An example of failure to fulfill this condition was the so-called "marriage penalty." Because their joint return put them in a higher bracket, a married couple typically paid more taxes on a given income than two people living in one household but who were not married. The income tax rate structure was changed to reduce this marriage penalty, although it still exists. Another question of horizontal equity is the relationship between tax rates on **earned income**, such as wages and salaries, and tax rates on such **nonearned income** as capital gains.

The differential between the tax rates on earned income and on capital gains is smaller than it once was, but there is a move to increase it once again by reducing capital gains taxes to stimulate investment.

Another criterion of a fair tax structure is **vertical equity**, which is based on the concept that those with higher incomes are in a better position to pay taxes with less sacrifice and should therefore pay a larger percentage in taxes. It is felt that the larger the income, the smaller the sacrifice for each dollar paid in taxes. Those below a certain income level, for whom the marginal utility of money is very high because they are living in poverty, pay zero income taxes.

Just what constitutes vertical equity is one of the most heated questions in the subject of taxation. The maximum **marginal tax rate** on high income earners was reduced from 50% to 31% in the 1986 and 1991 tax bills, but the 1993 tax bill again made federal income taxes more progressive by increasing the maximum rate to 39.6%.

A different approach to tax equity is applied in some cases where the proceeds of a tax are directly allocated to a corresponding government service. An example of this is the highway trust fund, which is used to finance the construction and maintenance of our highway system and is financed by gasoline sales taxes and motor vehicle fees. This represents the **benefits principle** of equity in taxation.

Efficiency

Along with their effect on equity, taxes are also judged for their effect on economic efficiency. To be efficient, the tax should neither interfere with the way resources are allocated nor discourage production. An exception to this rule is made in the case of **sin taxes** such as those levied on tobacco and alcohol, in part to reduce their consumption in the public interest.

A higher tax on cigarettes to help pay for health care reform was one part of the program over which there was little disagreement, except from smokers and the tobacco

---

horizontal equity: equality of treatment for all individuals at the same level.

earned income: wages, salaries, and other employee compensation plus earnings from self-employment.

nonearned income: dividends, interest, capital gains, and other nonlabor income.

vertical equity: fair differentiations of treatment of individuals at different levels.

marginal tax rate: the tax rate applied to the last or additional income received.

benefits principle: levy of a tax on an individual to pay the costs of government service in proportion to the individual's benefit from the service.

sin tax: an excise tax levied on commodities that public policy deems undesirable, such as cigarettes and alcohol, in order to limit their consumption.

---

industry. Its appeal stemmed from a combination of advantages: it satisfies the benefits principle in the sense that smokers cause higher health care costs; and as a sin tax it accomplishes the public policy objective of discouraging smoking, especially among the young. There could be a contradiction in the two objectives in that if a tax reduces consumption too much, the revenue it produces declines. But according to estimates of the elasticity of demand for cigarettes (see chapter 5, p. 112), a tax of around $1 per pack maximizes the revenue produced by the tax.

It is, of course, impossible to levy taxes that are completely neutral in their effects on output, but taxes that produce inefficiency should be avoided. A classic example of a "bad" tax was one that was levied in medieval England on the window space of houses. Glass windows were considered a luxury at the time, and those who could afford large houses with lots of windows were assumed to be able to afford the taxes. The result of the tax, however, was that new houses were constructed without windows. This was not a sensible way to build houses. The window tax was inefficient. It was inefficient, not because it didn't produce much tax revenue, although that happened to be the case, but rather because of the adverse effect it had on the allocation of resources. Building houses without windows resulted in lowering the utility from a given amount of output.

All taxes are to some extent inefficient, and there is frequently a conflict between the principles of equity and efficiency in taxation. Finding the right mix of taxes that best satisfies these criteria and also provides the necessary revenue for the functions of government is a perpetual problem.

▨ Incidence

One of the major obstacles to devising an equitable and efficient tax system lies in the difficulty of determining who ultimately pays the tax. The **incidence of a tax** is not necessarily determined by those on whom the tax is levied by the government. Frequently those who pay the tax to the government actually shift it to someone else. Personal income taxes cannot

"STEP UP TO THE CAPTAIN'S OFFICE AND SETTLE!"

■ In the caption under this cartoon of 1895, during President Grover Cleveland's administration, Uncle Sam says: "I'm sorry for you, my unfortunate friends;——I know the Income Tax is 'inquisitorial and oppressive'; but I've *got* to meet the one hundred and sixty million dollars of pension appropriation somehow!"

be shifted, and the incidence of the tax falls on the person who pays it. However, this is not the case with most other taxes. Excise taxes and property taxes on rental and business property, for example, are shifted to consumers. Even employer payroll taxes are shifted—to consumers in the form of higher prices and to workers in the form of lower wages. The federal personal income tax has historically been a **progressive tax** because the tax paid as a percentage of income increases as income rises.

> **incidence of a tax:** the amount of a tax that ultimately falls on households, irrespective of who initially pays the tax.
>
> **progressive tax:** a tax rate that increases as the income on which the tax is based grows larger.

Reflections in the Tax Mirror: Which Is Fairest of Them All?

Taxes are not pretty. In fact, though always unpopular, taxes in recent years have become downright ugly in the eyes of taxpayers. Yet the government services and benefits they pay for are in increasing demand.

The problem faced by legislators and executives at all levels of government is how to extract the necessary revenue from the citizenry with the least amount of pain and squealing. A multiplicity of taxes, surcharges, user fees, and license fees have recently been imposed on such things as credit reports and debt collections (Pennsylvania), dog and cat kenneling (Minnesota), ski equipment rentals (Lakewood, Colorado), and a $30 fee imposed on ex-convicts in Michigan's Washtenaw County for each monthly visit to their probation officer.

Although such revenue sources raise less public opposition than general tax increases, the collection costs are often so great as to offset a large part of the revenue. Substantial revenue sources are needed to pay for government services and benefits, but which type of tax is least undesirable? The federal income tax is under attack, especially by supply-side adherents (see p. 324), as a disincentive to work and investment. State sales taxes are criticized for their regressive effect on low-income earners. Local property taxes are both regressive and obstacles to home ownership.

The alternative revenue source most often proposed is the value-added tax (VAT). The United States is the only major industrialized nation that does not have some type of VAT. Its revenue-generating power is enormous. The Congressional Budget Office has esti-mated that a VAT of 5% would bring in more than $100 billion annually.

The VAT is related to the concept of value added discussed in relation to calculating GDP (p. 313). At each stage of producing a good, the producer adds an amount of value to the raw materials or semifinished goods pur-chased from suppliers. With VAT, the producer is required to send the designated percentage of that value added to the government and include it in the cost passed on to the next production or distribution stage. When the fin-ished product is sold to the customer, the price includes the total of the value-added taxes paid at each stage of production and distribution.

Generally, in countries that use a VAT, the amount of the tax paid on an item is not in-dicated on the sales tag, only a statement that the price includes the VAT. The public, there-fore, does not have a constant tax irritant to react to. There is likely to be less squealing than with the normal sales tax added to the price of a purchase at the time of sale.

Economic Reasoning

1. What is the incidence of the value-added tax?

2. Is a VAT regressive, proportional, or progressive? Why?

3. Should the VAT be adopted in the United States? Why or why not?

Most taxes other than income taxes are **regressive taxes** as a result of shifting the incidence of the tax to consumers. This is due to the fact that the lower a person's income, the larger a percentage of that income is spent on the goods and services whose prices include the taxes. As a result, low-income consumers pay a larger percentage of their income on sales taxes, gasoline taxes, utility taxes, and so forth. Even though they may not own property, property taxes take a higher percentage of their income as property owners shift the tax to renters in the form of higher rents.

A **proportional tax** would take the same percentage of income from taxpayers at all income levels. When the federal income tax was more progressive, the total of all types of taxes in the country—federal, state, and local—was considered roughly proportional.

Putting It Together

Total government spending—federal, state, and local—amounts to about one-third of GDP. A large part of this represents *transfer payments* of income to individuals rather than government purchases or salaries for government employees. If these transfer payments are subtracted, government spending at all levels accounts for less than one-fifth of the nation's economic activity.

The largest item of direct spending in the federal budget is national defense, which accounts for over one-fifth of the total budget. All other direct expenditures account for 9% of the budget. All of the rest of federal government spending consists of transfer payments, the largest of which is Social Security. Next largest in size are income security and interest on the national debt. For state and local governments, the major expense is education. Most state and local government spending is for direct purchases rather than transfer payments.

The largest revenue source for the federal government is *personal income taxes.* After that comes Social Security *payroll taxes.* State and local governments obtain their revenues from *sales taxes,* the largest revenue producer for the states, *property taxes,* the largest for

local governments, user fees, and grants from the federal government under a system of *fiscal federalism.*

To make the tax system work, the public must perceive it as being fair. One criterion for fairness is that people in similar economic

regressive tax: a levy that takes a higher proportion from low incomes in taxes than it takes from high incomes.

proportional tax: a levy that takes the same proportion in taxes from low and high incomes.

situations should pay similar amounts in taxes. This is referred to as *horizontal equity.* Another criterion is that people with higher incomes should pay proportionally more taxes than people with lower incomes. This is referred to as *vertical equity.* A third criterion, applied to certain government programs, is that those who benefit from a government service should pay directly for that service. This is the *benefits principle* of equity.

Taxes should be levied in a way that least affects the allocation of resources and least discourages economic activity. If a tax results in some goods not being produced that otherwise would be produced, it is a "bad" tax. Public policy makes an exception in the case of *sin taxes,* such as alcohol and tobacco excise taxes, which are levied in part to reduce the consumption of items that society wishes to discourage.

Taxes frequently are not borne by the person who initially pays the tax. Taxes other than income taxes are shifted to consumers in the form of higher prices or to workers in the form of lower wages. How the tax burden is allocated is the *incidence of the tax.* Taxes that take a larger percentage of higher incomes than lower incomes are *progressive.* Those that take the same percentage from all income levels are *proportional,* and those that take a larger percentage from low incomes are *regressive.*

The Growth of Big Government

More information on the growth of government spending can be found in *Deficit Financing: Public Budgeting in Its Institutional and Historical Context* (1992) by Donald F. Kettl; *The Inevitability of Government Growth* (1990) by Harold B. Vetter and John F. Walker; and *Growth of Government in the West* (1978) by G. Warren Nutler.

At the end of the 1920s total expenditures for all levels of government amounted to less than 10% of GDP (Gross Domestic Product). For the past 27 years they have been 30% to 35%. How did government grow so much in the second half of this century? Where is the growth of government taking us?

These are just some of the questions raised by the debate over "big government."

The size of government relative to GNP (Gross National Product) doubled in the early 1930s, due primarily to the decline in GNP during the Great Depression rather than to an increase in government spending. The ratio of government expenditures to total output doubled again during World War II but dropped back to less than 20% after the war. It rose above 25% during the Korean War and the "cold war" years of the early 1950s. It remained around 27–28% until 1968, when a combination of the Vietnam War expansion and increased domestic social spending on the "War on Poverty" raised government outlays above 30% of GNP. Since then government spending has hovered around one-third of total spending in the economy.

These figures on total government spending, however, do not reveal the important changes that have been occurring in the types of government spending. One significant change has been in the proportions of total government spending accounted for by the three levels of government. In the 1920s local government spending accounted for about half of the total. It fell to below 10% in the 1940s and today is over 22%. State government spending is almost the same amount. Meanwhile, the federal government's share reached a peak during World War II and has gradually declined since. Although federal outlays are greater than the combined spending of state and local governments, part of that federal government spending goes for funding state and local government programs under fiscal federalism.

The picture is also affected by changes in the makeup of federal spending. In the 1920s only about 10% of federal expenditures were transfer payments. This has increased over the years until today transfer payments account for over half of the federal budget. As a result, state and local government spending plays a larger part in economic allocations than does federal spending. In terms of economic activity and the number of employees, the growth of "big government" is now personified not so much by the federal government as by the growth in state and local spending.

FOR FURTHER STUDY AND ANALYSIS

Study Questions

1. What types of government spending are included in GDP? What types are most readily subject to cost cutting?

2. How many people in your family and how many friends or acquaintances of yours are receiving transfer payments? What type of transfer payments are they receiving?

3. Have there been any recent reductions in government services in your area? What were they? In which level of government did they occur?

4. If a candidate for national office promised, if elected, to double the efficiency of federal government operations and thereby reduce taxes by half, why might you question that promise? What promises might that candidate make about tax reduction that you would find feasible?

5. Approximately how much have you paid in excise taxes (taxes other than those on income) in the past 3 days? On what items?

6. What revenues do state (provincial) and local governments receive, other than taxes? What is the impact on various income groups of these revenue sources?

7. What is the current outlook for the Social Security system? Do you believe that you will benefit from it in the future?

8. Why is it assumed that wealthier people have a smaller marginal utility for money than people with lower incomes?

9. What are three things, other than cigarettes and liquor, whose production is affected by a tax? What is the effect of the tax? What is the incidence of the tax?

10. How did the most recent tax legislation affect the equity of the tax burden?

Exercises in Analysis

1. Write a report on changes in the federal, state (or province), and local funding of your school over the last 5 years. Have the funds increased at a greater rate, the same, or a lesser rate than the inflation rate? What adjustments have been made in school expenditures as a consequence?

2. Write a report on the sources of funding for your state or provincial budget.

3. From a taxpayer's guide, list five personal income tax deductions and five business tax deductions. Why do you think these deductions are allowed?

4. Write a short paper on what you believe are the problems of the Social Security system and the best solution of those problems.

Further Reading

Bennett, Arnold, and Orvil Adams, eds. *Looking North for Health: What We Can Learn from Canada's Health Care System.* San Francisco: Jossey-Bass, 1993. Topics include health care in the Canadian community, a comparison of the two systems, patient and taxpayer polling results, and the political aspects of planning and implementing the Canadian system.

Coddington, Dean C. *The Crisis in Health Care: Costs, Choices, and Strategies.* San Francisco: Jossey-Bass, 1990. Examines what has happened to health care costs in the United States and the results of U.S. medical policy.

Danziger, Shelden, and Peter Gottschalk, eds. *Uneven Tides: Rising Inequality in the 1990s.* New York: Russell Sage Foundation, 1993. Covers the trend in inequality, the rising importance of skill in the labor market, the effect of de-unionization on earnings inequality, and the effect of federal taxes and cash transfers on income distribution.

Fullerton, Don, and Diane Lim Rogers. *Who Bears the Lifetime Tax Burden?* Washington, DC: Brookings Institution, 1993. A study of the incidence of taxes and how different taxes are shifted.

Konner, Melvin. *Medicine at the Crossroads: The Crisis in Health Care.* New York: Pantheon Books, 1993. A critical view of U.S. medical care policy and the associated costs.

Marmor, Theodore R., Jerry L. Mashaw, and Phillip L. Harvey. *America's Misunderstood Welfare State: Persistent Myths, Enduring Realities.* New York: Basic Books, 1990. Evaluates U.S. social policy, its public welfare system, Social Security, and Medicare.

Myles, John, and Jill Quadagno, eds. *States, Labor Markets, and the Future of Old Age Policy.* Philadelphia: Temple University Press, 1991. An examination of how older people are treated under government policy, continued employment of seniors, early retirement, and Social Security.

Patrick, Donald L., and Pennifer Erickson. *Health Status and Health Policy: Quality of Life in Health Care Evaluation and Resource Allocation.* New York: Oxford University Press, 1992. Evaluates medical care in the United States from the standpoint of its overall effect on patients and the costs associated with current policies.

Peterson, Peter G., and Neil Howe. *On Borrowed Time: How the Growth in Entitlement Spending Threatens America's Future.* San Francisco: ICS Press, 1988. An alarmist view of where Social Security, federal pensions, and inflation of health care costs are leading the country.

Weiss, Lawrence David. *No Benefit: Crisis in America's Health Insurance Industry.* Boulder, CO: Westview Press, 1992. Reviews the historical development and current profile of the commercial health insurance industry, including price fixing and conspiracy in the industry, employer cost-cutting strategies, and how the uninsured were created.

Chapter 14. Policies for Economic Stability and Growth

■ **The government** budget has a big impact on the economy, for good or evil. Fear is widespread that the federal debt is dangerously evil. This introductory article looks at the basis of that fear.

The Debt Bogeyman

Is it Jason? Is it Freddy? Or is it just a pretend spook in a white sheet? In the minds of some, the national debt is a dangerous threat. To others, it is a minor nuisance. How seriously should we be concerned about the size of the national debt?

In the dozen years between the time Ronald Reagan took office in 1981 and Bill Clinton's inauguration in 1993, the national debt ballooned from $994 billion to $4.4 trillion. Relative to total output, a more significant way to consider it than the raw figures, the debt went from 33% of GDP to 69% in those years, more than doubling as a real economic burden.

Those are frightening numbers, all right. But before panic sets in, we might get a perspective by looking at earlier debt-to-GDP ratios (see Figure 1). In 1946, at the end of World War II, the debt was 127% of GDP. Ten years later it was still high at 71%, just about the same as in 1993. In these postwar years the economy did not collapse as a result of the high debt. This was, in fact, a period of rising prosperity. Excluding 1946–1947, when the economy was converting from wartime to peacetime production and growth was nega-

tive, the average real growth rate in total output for 1948–1955 was 4.3%. The only comparable period of sustained growth that high for that length of time since then was 1962–1970, when real growth averaged 4.7%.

Judging by the historical data, the absolute size of the debt-to-GDP ratio does not seem to be a problem. But whether the ratio is rising or falling may be. In both of the periods of greatest sustained growth described above, the ratio was falling. In the period 1981–1993, during which the debt escalated, on the other hand, real growth averaged only 2.4%. In the best consecutive 8 years of that time, it averaged 3.4%, about a percentage point lower than in the earlier periods. To put the effect of a difference of 1% in GDP growth rate in perspective, we can say that over a period of 5 years it is equivalent to the whole of the federal deficit.

There are many factors affecting the economy besides the national debt, and high or low growth rates of GDP are not necessarily dependent on the size of the debt or whether it is increasing or decreasing. But a majority of the American public, many politicians, and some economists think it is critically impor-

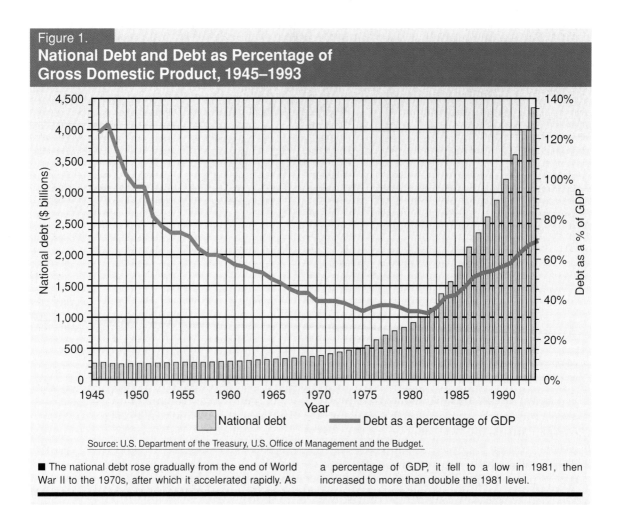

Figure 1.
National Debt and Debt as Percentage of Gross Domestic Product, 1945–1993

Source: U.S. Department of the Treasury, U.S. Office of Management and the Budget.

National debt

Debt as a percentage of GDP

■ The national debt rose gradually from the end of World War II to the 1970s, after which it accelerated rapidly. As a percentage of GDP, it fell to a low in 1981, then increased to more than double the 1981 level.

tant. Egged on by H. Ross Perot, who compared the federal deficits to a "crazy aunt" we keep locked in the basement, opinion polls put the deficit and the size of the debt among the public's greatest worries, along with jobs and crime.

One unwarranted fear about the national debt is that it will bankrupt the country. For one thing, the federal debt cannot bankrupt the country in any literal sense. As we saw in chapter 10, the government can create as much money as it needs. For another, we owe 86% of the federal debt to ourselves. The Treasury securities that constitute the debt are held by American citizens, banks, the Fed, and other domestic institutions. You cannot go bankrupt owing money to yourself. The remaining 14% of the debt is held by foreign individuals, banks, governments, and other foreign institutions. The interest payments on

the foreign-held part of the debt tend to lower the value of the dollar in relation to other currencies; but, as we shall see in chapter 16, that is not necessarily a bad thing.

More fundamentally, bankruptcy means that one's debts exceed the value of one's assets. Large as the national debt is, it is a small fraction of the value of the assets of the country. National bankruptcy is one phrase used too loosely in discussions of the debt. Another is that the debt represents a forward shifting of costs from the present generation to future generations.

The allegation that a large national debt is a burden shifted onto the shoulders of future generations is also not true in a literal way. Interest on the debt and repayments of the principal paid *by* future generations are paid *to* future generations. As noted in the dis-

■ The monetary policy of the United States is under the control of the Federal Reserve Board, which uses its power of regulating required and excess reserves to manage the supply of money. Shown above is the Federal Reserve Bank of Minneapolis, Minnesota, part of the Federal Reserve System.

cussion of Social Security in the previous chapter (p. 347), each generation consumes what it produces, except for net foreign trade. (The effect on future generations of a current foreign trade deficit is considered in chapter 16, p. 430.) With that exception, each generation's consumption levels and living standards are determined by its own output, not by the deficits of earlier generations.

The problems posed by the national debt are not simplistic "bankruptcy" or "shifting the debt burden" problems, but that is the way the public perceives them. Legislators responded to the public's concern in 1994 by attempting to pass, for the fourth time in a dozen years, a balanced budget amendment to the U.S. Constitution. The amendment would require that the federal budget be balanced every year. A 1994 CNN–USA Today poll showed 66% of Americans in support of such a measure.

There is certainly good reason to halt the escalation of the debt that occurred from 1981–1993. If the debt/GDP ratio continued to climb at that rate, it would have a number of unfortunate consequences: it would be inflationary by expanding the money supply; it would increase the share of the federal budget going to pay interest on debt; and it would raise interest rates, discouraging investment and growth. One of the reasons cited for the low GDP growth rates from 1981–1993 was the crowding-out effect of government borrowing to cover the deficit (see chapter 12, p. 325). But perhaps the worst consequence of the swollen debt is its crippling effect on stabilization policy.

All of these are strong arguments for reining in the federal government deficits. But whether a balanced budget amendment is the right answer to the problem is questionable. Even if you believe that Congress and the administration are fiscal alcoholics, unable to resist intoxicating deficits, to shackle them with a balanced budget amendment is probably not the right cure. For one thing, Congress and the president have keys to the shackles. Con-

gress's key is a sufficiently large majority—60% in the 1994 bill—to override the budget constraint. The president's key is to declare a national emergency. Another available escape is for Congress simply to declare more types of spending off-budget, as it did the savings and loan bailout money.

Thus, a balanced budget amendment could, on the one hand, be easily evaded in some circumstances while, on the other, imposing too rigid a constraint in different circumstances. A requirement that the budget must be balanced every year would tie one of the hands of stabilization policy. A better approach to the problem would be for Congress and the administration to enter a voluntary program of deficit abstinence.

■ **Chapter Preview**

According to the Employment Act of 1946 and the Full Employment and Balanced Growth Act of 1978, the federal government has a responsibility to maintain full employment, reasonably stable prices, and economic growth. Continuously large budget deficits and rising national debt make the meeting of those responsibilities more difficult. This chapter will examine the specific tools that the government has at its disposal for influencing economic activity by asking the following questions: What can the government do about unemployment and inflation? How can fiscal policy help stabilize the economy? How can monetary policy help stabilize the economy? How can economic growth be increased?

■ **Learning Objectives**

After completing this chapter, you should be able to:

1. Discuss the problem of the large national debt.

2. Identify the government's two major instruments of stabilization policy.

3. Differentiate between annually balanced budgets, cyclically balanced budgets, and functional finance.

4. Explain how discretionary fiscal policy works from the Keynesian and supply-side viewpoints.

5. Describe the multiplier effect.

6. Define and give examples of automatic stabilizers.

7. Explain how monetary policy is implemented.

8. Explain the investment/GDP ratio and the capital/output ratio and describe their importance.

9. Describe the effects on economic growth of the labor-force participation rate and investment in human capital.

What Can the Government Do about Unemployment and Inflation?

The government's two principal instruments for managing the economy are fiscal policy and monetary policy. Fiscal policy involves taxing and spending by the government, while monetary policy involves control of the money supply and interest rates.

Fiscal Policy

In earlier periods, the national debt increased greatly during major wars and as a result of major depressions. The growth of the debt between 1981 and 1993 was unprecedented, not only in size but because we neither fought a major war, excluding the "cold war," nor spent our way out of a major depression. We did, however, reduce taxes in 1981 to counter a recession. The type of tax cut enacted in the 1981 tax bill represented a new direction in the government's **fiscal policy**. Previous major tax cuts to combat recession had been aimed at stimulating demand by increasing disposable income. A tax reduction leaves people with more purchasing power and thus increases aggregate demand. The 1981 tax bill, on the other hand, was intended to increase output by making production and investment profitable for any level of demand and by stimulating savings to finance the investment. It was a supply-side tax bill, designed to leave more money in the hands of those with a higher propensity to save rather than those with a higher propensity to consume.

The difference between Keynesian and supply-side fiscal policy also showed up in the treatment of government expenditures. Supply-side economics called for a reduction in government spending in order to reduce the government's competition with the private sector of the economy for labor, capital, and other resources. Reducing the growth of government spending during a time of high unemployment was the exact opposite of the Keynesian policies that the United States had pursued since World War II. According to demand-side economics, a recession should be offset by increasing government spending.

The policy of combining increased spending with reduced taxes to combat a recession results in government budget deficits. Before the experiences of the 1930s and before the writings of Keynes, it was traditionally held that the government should have an **annually balanced budget**. If the federal government took $25 out of the spending stream in taxes in a given fiscal year, it should put $25 into the spending stream through its purchases of goods and services. However, such a budgetary policy can be destabilizing. As an economy moves into a recession, tax receipts fall as production, employment, and income decline. If an annually balanced budget policy is followed, the government must then cut spending, or raise taxes, or do both. Such policies would make a recession worse by reducing aggregate demand.

On the other side of the business cycle, during a period of economic expansion, tax receipts automatically rise as sales, price, and income increases generate more taxes. To balance the budget, a tax cut or a spending increase would be necessary. Either action would tend to be inflationary by increasing aggregate demand.

Instead of an annually balanced budget, a **cyclically balanced budget** would allow active fiscal policy to stabilize the economy. Short-run deficits and surpluses would be used to stabilize recessions and booms, but the

> **fiscal policy:** the use of federal government spending, taxing, and debt management to influence general economic activity.
>
> **annually balanced budget:** a budgetary principle calling for the revenue and expenditures of a government to be equal during the course of a year.
>
> **cyclically balanced budget:** a budgetary principle calling for the balancing of the budget over the course of a complete business cycle rather than in a particular fiscal or calendar year; over the course of the cycle, tax receipts and expenditures would balance.

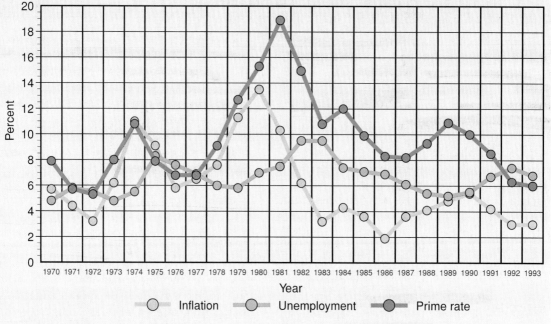

Figure 2.
Economic Instability, 1970–1993

Year

⬭ Inflation   ⬤ Unemployment   ⬤ Prime rate

Sources: Inflation and unemployment rates: U.S. Department of Labor, Bureau of Labor Statistics.
Prime interest rates: Federal Reserve System.

■ The magnitude of economic fluctuations in the 1980s, as shown by the swings in inflation, unemployment, and interest rates, was greater than at any time in the last 40 years. Achieving economic stability is more difficult as a result of external shocks, unanticipated reactions of the public to policy measures, and the constraints on policy imposed by a large national debt.

deficits would offset the surpluses and the budget would balance over the course of the business cycle. There are problems, however, with this approach. Financially, recessions and booms may not cancel each other out, and the budget may not balance over the long run. Also, it is politically far more popular to reduce taxes and increase spending than to increase taxes or cut spending. Fiscal policy under these conditions might thus have an inflation bias.

A third budget philosophy, **functional finance**, sees noninflationary full employment as the most important economic goal; balanc-

functional finance: the use of fiscal policy to stabilize the economy without regard to the policy's effect on a balanced government budget.

ing the budget becomes a secondary objective. Under this philosophy, taxes and spending should be administered at whatever level is necessary to promote full employment without increasing prices. This policy might leave the budget permanently out of balance.

A fourth alternative has been proposed recently as a guide to budget management. It recognizes that there are two basic types of government spending—spending on current services and spending for capital investment. The rationale for the proposal is that spending for current consumption should be covered by revenues, but that capital spending on infrastructure can be financed by deficit spending since it increases future production. (See discussion of infrastructure investment later in this chapter, p. 376.) This budget approach

Who's at the Wheel?

The economy has been on a wild ride in the last 2 decades. It has had three recessions, including the worst recession since the Great Depression of the 1930s. It has experienced the second longest economic expansion since World War II. It has had record-breaking inflation, record-breaking interest rates, and record-breaking government deficits and national debt. Most of these developments came as a surprise.

As the introductory article for chapter 12 showed (p. 307), predicting where the economy is going has always been more or less a guessing game. But these days the pace of change seems to have speeded up, while our ability to anticipate and correct for changes in direction has diminished. It is as if we were at the wheel of a speeding car with the gas pedal pressed to the floor and the windshield painted black.

Just who *is* at the wheel in control of the economy? The Full Employment Act, passed in 1946 and amended in 1978, assigns to the federal government a legal responsibility to ensure maximum employment, production, and purchasing power. In order to accomplish this, the Council of Economic Advisers is designated to advise the president on economic policy and to submit a yearly report to Congress on the state of the economy. The Federal Reserve Board has the responsibility for pursuing a monetary policy that is stabilizing. But the best-laid plans of those responsible for maintaining full employment and stable prices are subject to two types of forces that may defeat them: unforeseen, uncontrollable external events and the behavior of you, me, and the rest of the public.

While external events—wars, fluctuating petroleum prices, economic instability abroad—complicate the job of stabilizing the U.S. economy, an even bigger problem for policymakers is the unpredictable behavior of the public. If we decide to spend less, we can cause a recession or make an existing one worse. If we spend more, we may contribute to inflation.

Attempts to make us behave in a particular way have been less than successful. In the 1980s income tax rates were cut and Individual Retirement Accounts (IRAs) were established, allowing people to shelter part of their income from taxes. These measures were expected to motivate the public to save more. The United States has a savings rate far below that of other industrialized countries. We generally save only 5–6% of our income, compared to 18% in Japan and 12% in Germany. But instead of the savings rate increasing in this country as the policymakers expected, the rate fell below 3%.

Individuals watch government policy for clues as to what actions they should take to protect and promote their personal economic well-being. For example, if the Federal Reserve increases the money supply to encourage more production and investment, people take this as an indicator that inflation is coming. The result of these "rational expectations" is a rise in long-term interest rates to compensate for the anticipated inflation, thereby discouraging new investment and checkmating the Fed's move.

Economic Reasoning

1. When income tax rates were cut in the 1980s in the hopes that the public would increase their savings, was this an example of fiscal policy or monetary policy?

2. Why do people take an increase in the money supply as an indication that inflation is coming?

3. Should the government get around the problem of public behavior that negates stabilization policies by, for example, forcing people to save more or imposing a ceiling on interest rates? Why or why not?

has been called the **golden rule**. Increased future GDP will generate tax revenues to pay the interest and principal costs on the resulting debt.

Monetary Policy

Neither the president nor Congress has control over **monetary policy**; rather it is under the control of the Federal Reserve Board. The money supply is managed indirectly by the Fed, through its direction of financial institutions' required and excess reserves. By employing the control techniques described in chapter 10, the Fed can vary the volume of excess reserves. This action affects the ability of lending institutions to grant loans and thereby their ability to increase the money supply.

In a recession, the level of aggregate demand is below that necessary for full employment. In that situation, the Fed, through its monetary policy actions, brings about an increase in the volume of bank reserves. Bankers are then able to grant more loans. The loans stimulate higher total spending in the economy, and income and employment rise. Conversely, to combat inflation, the Fed uses its controls to decrease the volume of bank reserves. Bankers grant fewer loans, and there is less total spending in the economy.

How Does Fiscal Policy Help Stabilize the Economy?

The principal reason for government taxing and spending is not to stabilize the economy, but rather to provide the services that citizens require from government. However, the fiscal activities of government can be managed to counteract cyclical fluctuations.

Discretionary Fiscal Policy

Decisions about increasing or decreasing taxes and decreasing or increasing government spending are referred to as **discretionary fiscal policy**. Keynesian and supply-side economists differ on how discretionary fiscal policy should be implemented.

golden rule: a budget approach that calls for current services to be covered by revenues while paying for capital expenditures with deficit financing.

monetary policy: actions of the Federal Reserve Board to produce changes in the money supply, the availability of loanable funds, or the level of interest rates in an attempt to influence general economic activity.

discretionary fiscal policy: fiscal policy measures activated by overt decisions.

Keynesians focus on the use of fiscal policy to compensate for inadequate or excessive demand in the private sector. How Keynesian fiscal policy is used to combat unemployment can be traced in the GDP tank diagram in Figure 3.

If the amount of purchasing power flowing into the economy from consumption (C), government (G), and investment (I) demand is not sufficient to provide full employment, as indicated by the level in the tank, the government can increase demand by larger expenditures, causing more purchasing power to flow from government (G+), and/or by reducing taxes (T–), taking less from the income stream. If the tax cuts are directed primarily at the lower-income groups, which have the highest propensity to consume, nearly all of the tax savings will be allocated to increased consumption (C+), which stimulates production and employment.

Supply-side fiscal policy also calls for a reduction in taxes when aggregate demand is too low. But government spending is reduced rather than increased in order not to put the government in competition with the private

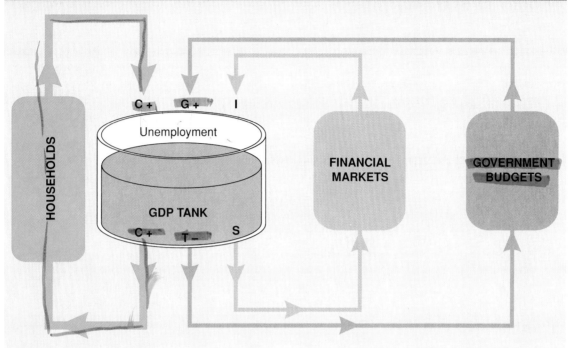

Figure 3.
Keynesian Unemployment Policy

C +   G +   I

Unemployment

HOUSEHOLDS

GDP TANK

C +   T –   S

FINANCIAL MARKETS

GOVERNMENT BUDGETS

■ Keynesian fiscal policy to increase GDP and reduce unemployment is to lower taxes (T–) and increase spending (G+) in the government sector (red). This results in an increase in purchasing power and demand

(C+) in the consumption sector (blue). The increased demand raises the GDP level (purple) and reduces unemployment.

sector for productive resources and financial capital. The purpose of reducing the leakage into taxes (T–) in the supply-side approach is not to increase consumption (C), but rather to increase savings (S+) and investment (I+), as shown in Figure 4. Therefore, the tax cuts are directed toward businesses and toward individuals in high tax brackets, who save more, rather than toward consumers.

The use of discretionary fiscal policy to combat recession at a time when the government is already running large deficits is difficult. With deficits at record levels and a large national debt, increasing the deficit and debt further to combat the recession is not an attractive policy option. It could lead to a loss of confidence in the financial security of the U.S. government on the part of the American public, business, and foreign investors. Interest rates would have to

be raised to sell the government securities necessary to finance the deficit. Higher interest rates are the opposite of the monetary policy needed to overcome recession. This problem is one of the most troublesome aspects of the expanded debt.

The Multiplier Effect

Fiscal policy can be used not only to combat unemployment caused by insufficient aggregate demand, but also to combat inflation caused by too much demand. In either case, fiscal policy is more effective as a result of the **multiplier effect**. The multiplier effect refers

multiplier effect: the process by which an initial increase in income results in a total income increase that is a multiple of the initial increase.

Figure 4.

Supply-Side Unemployment Policy

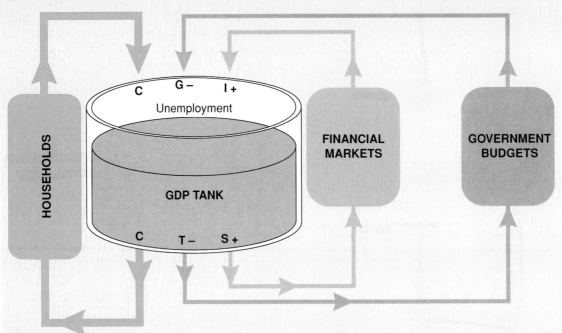

■ Supply-side fiscal policy to reduce unemployment is to lower taxes (T–) and spending (G–) in the government sector (red) in order to increase savings (S+) and investment (I+) in the investment sector (green). The reduction in taxes provides incentives and financial capital for in-creased investment. The added investment increases the level of GDP and reduces unemployment. At the same time, lower government spending reduces competition in the factor markets for real and financial resources, help-ing to hold down prices and interest rates.

to the magnified impact on national income of an initial increase or decrease in spending. It is similar in principle to the money multiplier in chapter 10 (p. 267).

Suppose, for example, an outsider comes into your community and spends $100 on a single purchase. Someone's income would increase by $100 with that expenditure. The income receiver would probably not hold onto the $100 very long but would spend most of it, say four-fifths ($80), on increased consumption of goods and services. The rest would go to taxes and into savings. Those who receive

the $80 that was spent would now spend four-fifths of that amount, or $64. The process, as shown in Table 1, would continue until the original influx of $100 had generated additional income to the community of another $400 for a total of $500.

The multiplier effect is based on the assumption that people, on the average, spend a certain fraction of any increase in income after taxes and put the rest into savings. The smaller the amount that leaks into savings in each round of spending, the larger will be the **multiplier**. In the above example, the multiplier was 5 since an initial increase in spending of $100 ultimately resulted in a total increase in spending of $500. The size of the multiplier is easy to calculate if you know the percentage of new income that goes into taxes and savings. The multiplier is found by divid-

multiplier: the ratio of the ultimate increase in income, caused by an initial increase in spending, to that initial increase.

Table 1.

Table 1. The Multiplier Effect
Initial Spending
Increase $100

Person 1	C $ 80.00	S + T $ 20.00
Person 2	C $ 64.00	S + T $ 16.00
Person 3	C $ 51.20	S + T $ 12.80
All others	C $204.80	S + T $ 51.20
Total (Including initial $100)	C $500.00	S + T $100.00

An initial increase in spending of $100 (when leakage to savings and taxes is 20%) will multiply through the community until it has generated an additional $400 in consumption spending (C) for a total of $500. Total leakages to savings and taxes (S + T) will be $100.

■ Carmen Motta, a single mother, photographed in one of the two small rooms she shares with her four children in a New York City welfare hotel, receives welfare payments and food stamps every month. These automatic stabilizers help cushion economic shock in a depressed economy.

ing the savings rate plus the tax rate, expressed in decimal form, into 1. If savings plus taxes are 20% of new income, you divide 1 by .20, which gives a multiplier of 5.

$$\text{Multiplier} = \frac{1}{\text{Savings rate + tax rate}} = \frac{1}{.20} = 5$$

The multiplier process takes time to work. It is usually a matter of a few months before the major part of the effect is completed.

Automatic Stabilizers

In order to put discretionary fiscal policy to work, the government must do something—must take some action. But there is another type of stabilization that takes effect as a result of automatic changes in government spending and revenue collections. These **automatic stabilizers** help increase incomes in a depressed economy and decrease incomes in an inflationary economy.

Automatic stabilizers consist of taxes, which automatically rise and fall with changes in income, or some form of payments designed to redistribute income. Most types of welfare and other government transfer payments, such as Aid to Families with Dependent Children and unemployment compensation, are based on the income of the recipient. When a person's income falls to a designated level, government expenditures provide income supplements. These supplements add to the spending stream, pushing aggregate demand up. By themselves, automatic stabilizers are not strong enough to reverse a trend, but they do cushion the economic shock until discretionary fiscal policy can be implemented.

automatic stabilizers: changes in government payments and tax receipts that automatically result from fluctuations in national income and act to aid in offsetting those fluctuations.

Comparative Case Application

Look Who's Virtuous Now

Not long ago, Uncle Sam was looked down on as the industrialized world's biggest spendthrift. In 1991, the combined deficits of all levels of government, including the Social Security trust funds, were 4.5% of GDP. The other major countries had smaller relative budget deficits or, like Japan, surpluses.

By 1994, however, the growth in U.S. GDP combined with a reduction in the deficit resulted in a reduction of the deficit percentage of GDP to 2.7%. Meanwhile, recessions in Europe, Canada, and Japan hurt their GDP and tax receipts while at the same time increasing government outlays on unemployment and other income security programs and on economic stimulus measures.

As a result, budget deficits were projected at 3% of GDP in Japan and higher in Canada and Europe. Deficits for Great Britain and France were projected at 6% of GDP or higher and Italy above 8%.

But there is a difference in the nature of the deficit numbers for the United States and the other countries. The United States enjoyed a cyclical low in its deficit/GDP ratio because of the expanding economy. The other countries, however, were at or near their recession troughs, having begun the downswing subsequent to the United States, and consequently had cyclically high deficits.

When all of the countries return to full employment, the remaining deficits will be structural. A structural deficit is the amount of the deficit under normal economic condi-

Table 4.   Tax Revenues as a Percentage of Gross Domestic Product 1980–1990

(Covers national and local taxes and Social Security contributions)

Country	1980	1985	1990
United States	29.5	29.2	29.9
Canada	31.6	33.1	37.1
United Kingdom	35.3	37.9	36.7
Germany*	38.2	38.1	37.7
France	41.7	44.5	43.7
Italy	30.2	34.4	39.1
Japan	25.4	27.6	31.3

* Former West Germany (prior to unification).

tions, when there is neither recession nor excess demand. It is the deficit resulting from a country's tax and budgeting system. Since the United States has the lowest taxes relative to GDP of any of the leading producers (Table 4) and spends more on national defense, it tends to have higher structural deficits than the other countries.

Although the United States appeared to be more virtuous than the other major industrial countries with respect to the deficit/GDP ratio in 1994, it is unlikely to maintain that reputation. As long as the United States opts to have more government benefits and national defense than it is willing to pay for, it will have a high structural deficit.

Economic Reasoning

1. Are the government outlays on unemployment benefits and other income security spending a part of discretionary fiscal policy or automatic stabilizers?

2. With higher tax rates than the United States, do the other countries shown in Table 4 have a larger or smaller multiplier than the United States? How can you tell?

3. Do you think the United States should reduce its structural deficit? How?

How Can Monetary Policy Help Stabilize the Economy?

The three measures available to the Federal Reserve for affecting bank reserves—changing legal reserve requirements, discounting, and open market operations—were discussed in chapter 10 on pages 263–268. Now we will look at the way these monetary controls are used in stabilization policy and examine what the targets of monetary policy are.

Monetary Policy Tools

Open market operations are the Fed's most flexible tool of monetary control and the most utilized. If the Fed undertakes to curb inflation, it offers U.S. government securities, which it has in its possession as a result of earlier purchases, for sale at an attractive price. Financial institutions, other businesses, or individuals buy these securities. Regardless of who purchases them, reserves are transferred from commercial banks' reserve accounts to the Fed to pay for the securities. This reduces the ability of the banks to expand their lending activity and may even force them to contract credit. The resulting limitation on the money supply raises interest rates, thus reducing aggregate demand, especially for capital goods, new housing, and consumer credit purchases of durable goods such as new cars.

If the problem is too little aggregate demand rather than too much, the Fed purchases government securities from banks, other businesses, or individuals. This action by the Fed pumps more reserves into the banking system and has an expansionary effect on the economy.

As an alternative to or in addition to selling securities to combat inflation, the Fed can also raise the discount rate it charges on loans to financial institutions. A rise in the discount rate is contractionary because it limits the money supply and raises other interest rates, while a reduction in the discount rate is expansionary.

The most forceful monetary tool the Fed has is its power to change the required reserve ratio. Because this is also the least flexible tool, it is infrequently used. Raising the reserve ratio from, say, 10% to 12% of banks' deposit liabilities would wipe out a large por-

---

Table 2. **How the Federal Reserve Attempts to Combat Inflation**

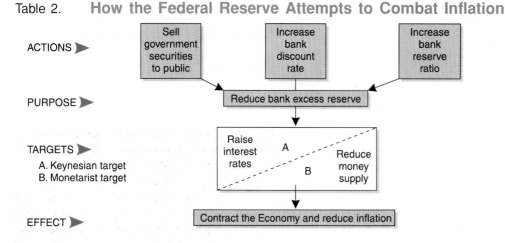

ACTIONS ▶

PURPOSE ▶

TARGETS ▶
  A. Keynesian target
  B. Monetarist target

EFFECT ▶

In times of high unemployment the Federal Reserve might try to expand the economy by taking these actions in the opposite manner.

Figure 5.

Demand Deposit Turnover Rate, 1975–1991

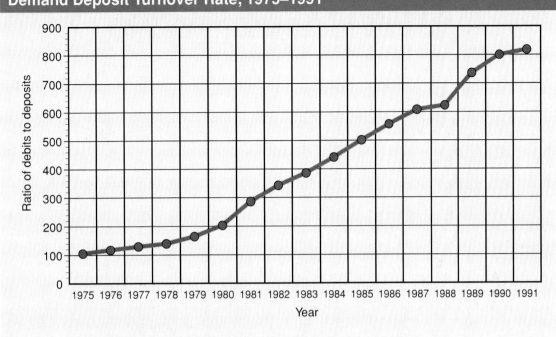

Source: Board of Governors of the Federal Reserve System, *Federal Reserve Bulletin.*

■ The bank deposit turnover rate, one measure of the velocity of circulation of money, indicates the number of times a deposit dollar is used during a period. It is not constant, as assumed by the quantity theory of money (quantity equation).

tion of their excess reserves and force them to contract credit. That would have a deflationary effect on economic activity. Lowering the legal reserve requirement, on the other hand, would make it possible for banks to extend more credit on easier terms. This might have an expansionary effect on economic activity, depending on economic conditions. If the economic outlook is very poor, businesses still might not borrow and invest—even at low interest rates. Consequently, although monetary policy can contract excessive aggregate demand in a boom period, it may be powerless to stimulate demand to bring about a recovery at the bottom of the cycle.

Monetary policy, as well as fiscal policy, is constrained by the existing budget deficits and large national debt. For example, tightening the money supply and raising interest rates to curb inflation would have consequences for the federal budget. An increase in interest rates raises the cost of carrying the debt. This would increase government outlays at a time when spending should be reduced.

Controlling Interest Rates

The traditional target of Federal Reserve monetary policy has been the control of interest rates. Specifically, the Fed attempts to control the Federal Funds rate, the interest rate banks charge each other on short-term lending of excess reserves. By controlling the Federal Funds rate, the Fed can influence the various other interest rates that are charged on loans. By causing interest rates to rise, the Fed would have a deflationary effect on economic activity and prices, and by causing

Target Practice at the Fed

For the Federal Reserve, controlling the money supply today is like playing an electronic game in which you have a number of targets moving in different directions and only one shot. Managing the money supply is more complicated and more difficult than it used to be. Prior to 1979, the Fed aimed directly at controlling interest rates to stabilize the economy. In that year it switched to a policy of controlling the money supply, specifically the amount of M1, rather than controlling interest rates. This change reflected the influence of the monetarist economists (see p. 288) on policy.

However, because of the growth of new types of money accounts—the NOW and ATS accounts and money market funds that lie somewhere in between the traditional demand deposit and savings accounts—the M1 money supply became less relevant. The Fed then shifted its target to the broader measure M2, which includes those near monies.

The Fed still felt that it had a responsibility for maintaining stability in the financial markets. To do this, the Fed attempted to control sharp swings in interest rates. However, since the money supply affects interest rates and vice versa, when the Fed chooses to shoot at one target, it's bound to miss the other. If it hits the lower money supply target, it is bound to miss the stable interest rate target when the lower money supply causes a rise in interest rates.

Faced with an apparent breakdown in the relationship between M2 and inflation and growth, the Federal Reserve chairman announced in 1993 that the Fed was no longer going to target control of the broad M2 money supply to achieve its objectives. According to the chairman's announcement, the Fed would pay more attention to real short-term interest rates. But it is difficult to determine what the real interest rate equilibrium is.

Whether the reason is because it has not been able to decide which target it is shooting at or because it is simply unable to hit the target, the Fed has been criticized in the past for its failure to prevent cyclical swings of inflation and recession. There have been proposals to make the Federal Reserve more directly accountable to the president and/or Congress. Instead of having the Board of Governors appointed for periods of 14 years as at present, one of the more extreme proposals would require all of the governors to submit their resignations to the president if the Fed missed its target by more than one percentage point during the year. The resignations would be submitted along with an explanation of what went wrong. The president would then have the choice of accepting the explanation and sharing the blame or accepting the resignations.

Economic Reasoning

1. What initial target is the Fed aiming at when it attempts to affect the Federal Funds rate?

2. One of the explanations given for the Fed's inability to hit its money supply target is the time lag involved in the response of the economy to changes in Fed policies. Why don't the tools of monetary policy immediately affect the money supply?

3. Do you think that the Federal Reserve ought to be made more directly responsible to the president and Congress? What would be the advantages and disadvantages of this?

interest rates to fall, it would have an expansionary effect.

A great deal of criticism has been directed at the Fed for mistakes in the timing of its actions. In the past, it often seemed to wait too long before putting on the brakes in a boom period, allowing the inflation rate to become exceedingly high before raising interest rates sufficiently to cool the economy. When it finally did act, the results of this action too often appeared after the turning point in the economy and resulted in emphasizing the severity of the downturn. Similarly, in upswings the Fed delayed too long raising interest rates, resulting in inflation. These mistakes in timing were due partly to time lags in receiving and evaluating data on what was actually happening in the economy.

As the economy recovered from the 1991 recession, the Fed appeared determined not to repeat previous mistakes of delay in implementing monetary stabilization measures. It initiated interest rate increases prior to any evidence of inflating prices. In doing so it was criticized in some quarters for raising rates prematurely and thereby weakening the recovery. The Fed aimed at a slow expansion that would, it hoped, continue over a long period of time.

Control of the Money Supply

Rather than controlling interest rates directly, the Fed may aim at keeping the money supply growth at a predetermined level as it did in the 1980s. According to the quantity theory of money, $M \times V = T \times P$, if the money supply (M) goes up at the same rate as the increase in transactions (T), the price level (P) will remain constant and we will not have inflation—that is, if the velocity of circulation of money (V) does not change (see chapter 11, p. 288).

Actually, the velocity has been on a long-term rising trend since the Great Depression. This in itself would not be a problem since it could be taken into account in setting the growth rate of M. But problems arise when V jumps around unpredictably and when it moves in a destabilizing direction. Studies indicate that when we have inflation and high interest rates, V accelerates. This offsets the stabilizing effects of limiting M and thus makes it difficult for a monetarist approach to stability to achieve satisfactory results.

A strict monetarist approach, as advocated by its foremost proponent, Milton Friedman (see Perspective, p. 383), would have a "monetary rule" setting annual increases in the money supply equal to the average long-run increase in real GDP.

How Can Economic Growth Be Increased?

The danger posed by a large national debt is not that it will bankrupt the country or shift the real cost of interest payments and repayment of principle from the present generation to future generations. The actual danger is that it will hamper economic growth, leaving future generations poorer than they would be otherwise.

Importance of Economic Growth

Our standard of living is determined largely by the rate of economic growth. At the 3% real growth rate that characterized the U.S. economy in the last 2 decades, our standard of living doubles in 24 years, with a constant population. If the growth rate were as fast as the 4.58% achieved by the Japanese economy, where the population size actually *is* static, the standard of living would double in just two-thirds the time—less than 16 years.

Figure 6 shows the inflation-adjusted GDP growth of the United States for 1940 to 1995, with growth for 1994–1995 projected at 3% per year. As can be seen from the graph, the economy grew at a higher rate in the 1960s and 1970s than it has since then. Those decades were a period when the national debt was relatively low and the debt/GDP ratio falling. The size of the national debt is just one of the many factors that go into determining

Figure 6.

Real Gross Domestic Product, 1940–1995
(1987 dollars)

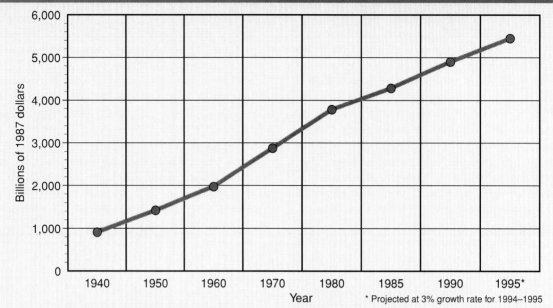

Source: U.S. Department of Commerce, Bureau of Economic Analysis (except 1995 projection).

* Projected at 3% growth rate for 1994–1995

■ The growth of GDP is the main determinant of our standard of living. In the decades of the 1960s and the 1970s, when the national debt was relatively low and the debt/GDP ratio was falling, the U.S. economy grew at significantly higher rates than it has since.

the growth rate of the economy, but it may be an important one.

A higher growth rate makes it easier to solve many economic problems, from balancing the budget to stabilizing the economy to overcoming poverty.

Increasing Capital Investment

The proportion of a nation's output that goes into private capital formation in the form of fixed equipment and business structures is another important determinant of growth. The measure of that proportion is the **investment/GDP ratio**, the fraction of each year's GDP that is allocated to investment goods.

investment/GDP ratio: the proportion of GDP that is allocated to private investment.

Figure 7 shows the U.S. investment/GDP ratio for the years 1960–1993, expressed as a percentage. Prior to 1976, we were putting about 9–11% of our output into fixed, nonresidential investment (which excludes investment in inventories and housing). This was less than the investment/GDP ratios in the countries of Western Europe, especially in what was West Germany, where it was almost 50% greater than here, and Japan, where it was twice as great. As a result those countries grew more rapidly than the United States.

United States investment rates increased from 1976 to 1981, then declined. From 1977 to 1988 the investment/GDP ratio was above 11%, higher than in the previous period. The rate of growth of output, however, did not increase along with the higher investment ratio. On the basis of historical experience, it is not surprising that we did not immediately see a

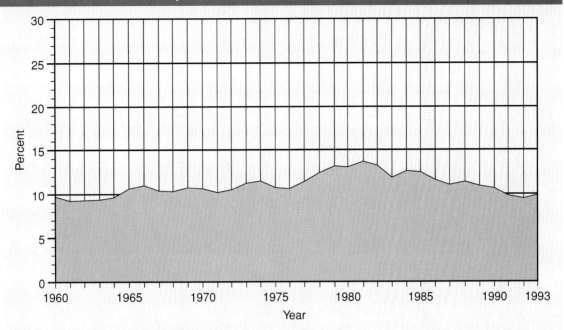

Figure 7.
Investment/GDP Ratio*, 1960–1993

Y-axis: Percent (0 to 30); X-axis: Year (1960 to 1993)

* Fixed nonresidential investment as a percentage of GDP.

Source: Calculated from data from the U.S. Department of Commerce, Bureau of Economic Analysis.

■ Investment in business equipment and structures as a percentage of total output was unusually high in the 1980s, but it did not show up in higher growth rates. The reasons may be a lag in increased productivity due to time for assimilating the new technology, or decreasing capital efficiency, or inadequate investment in human capital.

productivity payoff from the new investment. There is a lag of some years between the introduction of new technology and the resulting growth that it generates. For example, productivity failed to grow much for 20 years after the introduction of the assembly line in 1901.

It has taken companies time to assimilate the new technologies and make the best use of them. Some firms that have automated their operations have realized significant productivity gains, while others have not. For some reason, office automation has led to less of a reduction in white-collar staffing than factory automation has led to displacement of blue-collar labor. As a result, productivity gains have been much larger in manufacturing than in services.

The effects of increasing the investment/GDP ratio are shown in Figures 8 and 9. In Figure 8 there is an initial reduction in consumption spending (C−) to finance increased savings-investment (S+ and I+). This results in increasing the production capacity of the economy, shown in Figure 9 by an expanded GDP tank. More production means more consumption (C+) and higher levels of savings and tax receipts (S+ and T+), which make possible more investment and government services (I+ and G+).

The real cost of economic growth is the current consumption that must be given up in order to save for investment in new capital formation. One of the controversial questions in public policy is, "Whose consumption is going to be reduced in order to free the resources

Figure 8.
Increasing Investment/GDP Ratio

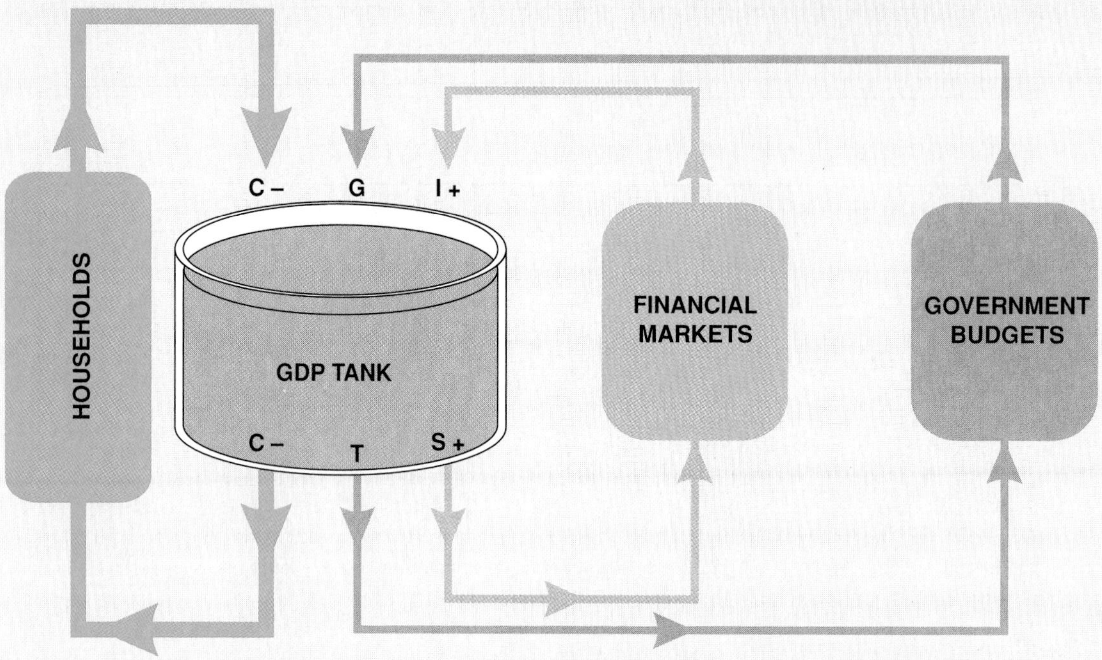

HOUSEHOLDS

C –   G   I +

GDP TANK

C –   T   S +

FINANCIAL MARKETS

GOVERNMENT BUDGETS

■ The investment/GDP ratio can be increased by shifting spending from the consumption (blue) sector to the investment (green) sector to finance the production of more investment goods (I+).

for increased investment?" Government policies can make the solution to this problem easier by reducing the unemployment level, increasing the total of resources engaged in production.

Another way in which stabilization policies and growth policies are interconnected is through interest rates. For example, anything that causes higher interest rates, such as the large national debt, discourages investment in increased production capacity. As another example, the peace dividend discussed in the chapter 2 introductory article "Swords into Plowshares" will benefit economic growth in two ways. It will lower the deficit and thus reduce upward pressure on interest rates. At the same time it will free up resources from military production, especially scarce scientific and technical labor, encouraging investment in civilian production facilities that are more productive of real growth.

Reducing government spending on infrastructure—highways, bridges, harbors, transportation, water supplies, sewage treatment—would, on the other hand, result in discouraging private investment by making it less productive. Better highways speed delivery for businesses; deep-water harbors facilitate foreign trade; adequate water and sewage facilities encourage new plant construction. This type of government investment in improved infrastructure provides a long-run stimulus to private investment as well as a short-run stimulus to employment in construction. The disadvantages are that, all other things being equal, it increases the deficit and national debt and competes with the private sector for resources.

Among the proposals for promoting more real investment are measures to encourage a change in business focus from a fixation on short-term profits to a longer-term outlook.

Figure 9.

Results of Increasing Investment/GDP Ratio

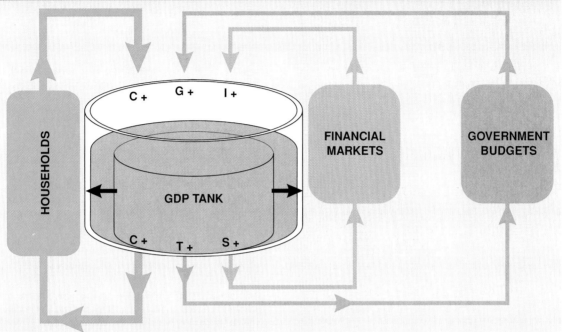

■ As a result of increasing the investment/GDP ratio, the production capacity of the economy increases, as shown by the expansion of the GDP tank. This increases income, with a multiplied expansion of consumption spending (C+). More income also means more allocation to savings (S+) and taxes (T+). This provides the funds to finance further increases in investment (I+) and increased government services (G+)

Presently, company executives with **stock options** are motivated to concentrate on short-term profits to produce rapid increases in the prices of their firms' securities. This motivation might be changed by providing tax incentives to reward performance over a long period of time.

Diverting resources to the production of investment goods may initially reduce consumption levels, but it increases the total production capacity of the economy. In the long run, more production means more real income. There will be multiplied effects on consumption spending, increased savings, and an increase in tax receipts for the government.

Increasing Capital Efficiency

The quantity of capital investment is not the only thing that affects growth. The quality of investment may be even more important. If new investment consists simply of more of the same type of capital equipment without a change in technology, the growth of output will not be as large as if the new investment goods are more technologically advanced. In fact, increased capital efficiency from new technology has contributed more to growth than the actual amount of capital.

The new technologies made possible by the microprocessor are an important means of increasing productivity, the amount of output per hour of labor. The promise of such programs as DFMA, FMS, and CIM, discussed in chapter 7 (p. 171), is to give us more output for our investment dollar by increased capital efficiency. The efficiency of capital is measured

stock option: the right to purchase a specific amount of a corporation's stock at a fixed price. Often part of the compensation package for a company's top executives.

■ Above, a worker at the National Institute of Standards and Technology monitors the performance of a robot. The Institute, part of the U.S. Commerce Department, provides training to workers in small firms to help improve their productivity.

Country	Female (ages 25–54)		Male (ages 25–54)	
	1980	1991	1980	1991
United States	63.8	74.0	93.4	92.3
Canada	60.1	75.8	94.8	92.5
United Kingdom	63.4	72.9	95.4	93.4
France	63.0	73.7	96.4	95.3
Italy	39.9*	49.9	93.1*	90.7
Sweden	82.9	90.5	95.4	94.6
Japan	56.7	65.0	97.0	97.2

* Ages 25–59

Source: Organization for Economic Cooperation and Development, *Labour Force Statistics.*

■ The participation of women in the labor force has greatly increased in the United States in the last decade, contributing to the growth of the economy. Among Western industrialized countries, their participation rate is second only to that in Sweden.

by the **capital/output ratio**. The capital/output ratio is the relationship of investment in capital equipment to the resulting increase in production output. The ratio varies from industry to industry, but an investment of $4 in new equipment may increase output by $1 a year. If the efficiency of FMS were to reduce the capital/output ratio in an industry from 4:1 to 3:1, economic growth stemming from new investment in the industry would increase by one-third.

The government is engaged in an effort to help companies improve productivity from the new technologies. The Commerce Depart-

ment's National Institute of Standards and Technology (NIST) provides instruction to workers in small firms to train them in computer-aided manufacturing, which involves programming machines to be controlled electronically rather than by hand, and using blueprints. This change can cut production times for many jobs by as much as 50%. NIST has established regional centers in Ohio, South Carolina, and New York. These centers are the technological equivalent of the agriculture extension agents that helped make American agriculture the world's most productive.

Increasing Labor Force Participation Rate

An increase in the percentage of the population that is in the labor force can increase output even without an increase in productivity. A sizable part of U.S. economic growth that has taken place in recent years has been the result of increased **labor force participation rate**.

capital/output ratio: the ratio of the cost of new investment goods to the value of the annual output produced by those investment goods.

labor force participation rate: the percentage of the working-age population, or of a subgroup of the population, that is in the labor force.

This is partly due to the baby boom generation entering the labor force and partly because a much larger percentage of married women hold jobs than was the case in earlier years. This is especially true for younger couples between the ages of 25 and 35. In 1973 in such families 47% of the wives worked; now over two-thirds do. The labor force participation rate of women in the United States is higher than in all other Western bloc countries with the exception of Canada and Sweden.

The study by Edward F. Denison on U.S. economic growth from 1929 to 1982 (chapter 7, p. 170) shows that the increase in labor input was the largest single factor contributing to growth. Its contribution to growth has increased steadily since 1964. But with a baby bust generation following on the heels of the baby boom generation, a decrease in labor force participation rates by males, and indications that increases in women's participation in the labor force will not continue at the same level, economic growth in coming years will have to depend on factors other than increases in the labor force participation rate.

Increasing Investment in Human Capital

Investment in new types of capital equipment can substantially increase intensive growth only if there is skilled labor available to implement the new technology. Investment in human capital involves investment in the public school system, university education, occupational skills training programs, and on-the-job training. The role that business firms can play in improving the quality of human capital was discussed in chapter 7, but basic education skills have been primarily the responsibility of government.

As noted previously, a competent labor force with the necessary skills and training is required to operate the emerging high-tech economy. The most basic competency requirement is literacy, and the rate of illiteracy in the United States is shocking. One in five adults lacks the minimum reading and writing skills even to meet the demands of daily living. Another 20–30% of the population are

■ A competent labor force with the necessary skills and training is required to function in the emerging high-tech economy. On-the-job training is one way that businesses can make the investment in human capital keep pace with the investment in capital equipment.

only marginally capable of being productive workers. Some 13% of high school students graduate with the reading and writing skills of sixth graders, and another 1 million students drop out of school each year without graduating. Many of the students who graduate from high school and go on to college are so unprepared that an estimated two-thirds of the colleges and universities find it necessary to provide remedial reading and writing courses for them. The Japanese population, by comparison, has a literacy rate of 95%.

This decline in the educational quality of the workforce is one explanation for the stagnation of labor productivity that the country has experienced since 1973. Up to then productivity had been growing at the rate of 2% a year from as far back as 1900. Since 1973, however, the productivity growth rate has been only a little more than half that, 1.2% per year. This has affected our ability to compete in the world and our standard of living.

If the United States is to take advantage of the second Industrial Revolution, it must invest not only in high-tech hardware but also in high-tech human capital.

Investing in the Future

Policies to promote economic growth call for a longer time horizon than stabilization policies. Some growth measures may have a relatively quick payoff. For instance, increased investment in production plant and equipment can expand output in a matter of months. However, if the investment does not raise productivity as well as production, the output may not be competitive.

Advances in technology that do raise productivity take time to yield results. Studies of the learning curve (chapter 7, p. 169) show that the harvest period for technological innovations in U.S. firms is longer than in some other countries. Particularly in the service industries, the increase in computer technology put in place in the 1980s showed little productivity improvement by 1990.

The growth instrument with the longest period for results is investment in human capital. But the fact that it has a long payoff interval does not mean that it should not be given high priority in national policy. Technological advances will not produce results without a workforce that has the skills to make use of sophisticated equipment. Automated equipment that is designed for very simple work tasks, referred to as "idiot-proof" machines, does not provide the high-productivity growth that raises living standards.

A 1990 study by the Commission on the Skills of the American Workforce compared the education-training systems in the United States, West Germany, Japan, Sweden, Denmark, Ireland, and Singapore. It found that all of the other countries except Ireland provide far better schooling and job training than the United States for those youth not going on to college.

It also found that the other countries have much more effective national systems for facilitating high school graduates' movement into industry. It characterizes the system in the United States, or virtual absence of any system, as "the worst of any industrialized country."

The commission study recommended a drastic overhaul in the way that the nation educates and trains that portion of its citizens who will not graduate from a 4-year college, some 70%. One proposal of the study was for a national fund to upgrade worker skills. The fund would be financed by a 1% tax on business payrolls. Employers could avoid the tax by spending an equivalent amount on their own company training programs.

Economic Reasoning

1. Of the factors that affect economic growth, which one produces results in the shortest period of time and which one takes the longest to increase the growth rate?

2. Why is the growth measure that takes effect most quickly not necessarily the one that public policy should concentrate on?

3. Should the recommendation of the Commission on the Skills of the American Workforce that employers be required to spend an amount equal to 1% of their payroll on in-house or national training programs be adopted into law? Why or why not?

Putting It Together

Since the 1930s, the federal government has used *fiscal policy* and *monetary policy* as the principal means to stabilize prices and maintain full employment. In implementing fiscal policy, the government adapts its spending and taxing activities in order to increase aggregate demand when there is unemployment and to decrease aggregate demand when there is inflation. Prior to the 1930s, government policy was an *annually balanced budget*. The Great Depression and the spread of the ideas of John Maynard Keynes led the government to adopt new policies that purposely created deficits in the budget to compensate for inadequate demand in the private sector and to provide for full employment.

It would be well for the government to have budget surpluses at times to counteract inflation. Over the whole business cycle, if the surpluses offset the deficits, we would have a *cyclically balanced budget*. Some economists argue that balancing the budget either annually or cyclically is not important. What is important is to do what is required for stabilization at any given time. This is *functional finance*.

The Keynesian method of solving unemployment by use of *discretionary fiscal policy* is to increase government spending on goods and services in order to expand aggregate demand, raise production, and thus stimulate employment. By increasing transfer payments, for example with cash subsidies to lower-income families, the government provides larger purchasing power to the private sector, which also increases aggregate demand. On the taxation side, the Keynesians would cut taxes to boost consumption spending, thus increasing production and stimulating employment.

The amount of increased government spending and/or decreased taxes necessary to bring about full employment depends on the *multiplier*. Any increase in sales provides purchasing power to those producing the goods and services, most of which they in turn use to purchase additional goods and services. The total increase in spending is a multiple of the original increase in sales. The smaller the propensity to save, the larger is the *multiplier effect*.

Supply-side economic policy also involves the use of tax cuts, but with a different purpose. The objective of supply-side tax cuts is to make production and investment more profitable and thereby provide incentives to businesses, workers, and other factor inputs to make more of these inputs available for production. The resulting increase in economic activity would create more jobs, and the rising output of goods and services would reduce or eliminate price increases by reducing scarcity.

In addition to the discretionary fiscal policy tools used by the federal government,

■ The Federal Reserve System regulates the United States' monetary policy. The president and Congress control fiscal policy. Together, these institutions work to stabilize the economy and increase economic growth.

there are *automatic stabilizers* built into the economy. These are tax provisions and government expenditures, such as unemployment insurance payments, that help counteract cyclical fluctuations.

The principal tools of Federal Reserve monetary policy are open market operations, changes in the discount rate, and changes in the required reserve ratio. Prior to the 1980s, Fed policy was targeted on the control of interest rates. Since then, the target has been the control of the money supply itself.

The monetarist approach assumes that if the money supply is allowed to rise only at the rate of the average long-run increase in real output, the price level will be stabilized. Monetarist theory is based on a constant velocity of circulation of money, which may not be the case.

Economic growth is promoted by having a higher proportion of total output flow into new investment—raising the *investment/GDP ratio*. Another determinant of growth is the ratio between the amount of new capital spending in an industry and the increase in output resulting from that investment—the *capital/output ratio*. If the capital/output ratio is low, there is a larger increase in output for a given amount of capital spending, and the profit incentives for investment are greater.

Raising the *labor force participation rate,* while it may in the short run reduce labor productivity, increases total and per-capita output and is a significant growth factor. In the United States in the last 2 decades, increased participation by women in the labor force has

■ Occupational training is an important factor in the upgrading of human capital that leads to economic growth. Here, in the Step Up project in Chicago, federal housing rehabilitation money is used to train poor residents in construction jobs.

contributed to intensive growth and raised per capita income. Growth also results from upgrading human capital through additional education and occupational training.

Monetarism—Does Money Matter?

Milton Friedman (born 1912)
Friedman was born in Brooklyn, New York, and attended the University of Chicago and Rutgers University. He received a Ph.D. from Columbia University in 1946. During his schooling Friedman worked on the research staff of the National Bureau for Economic Research and in the tax research division of the U.S. Treasury Department. He taught for 1 year at the University of Minnesota before returning to the University of Chicago, where he spent the rest of his teaching career, becoming the Paul Snowden Russell Distinguished Service Professor of Economics. In 1977 he became a senior Research Fellow at the Hoover Institution at Stanford University. Friedman served as the president of the American Economics Association in 1967 and was awarded the Nobel Prize in economics in 1976. He has repeatedly proven to be a formidable opponent in his numerous public debates with liberal economists because of the great amount of data he has developed from his prodigious research. He is not only the leading spokesman for monetarism but also for the conservative economic viewpoint associated with the Chicago School. Among his publications are *Essays in Positive Economics* (1953), *Inflation: Cause and Consequences* (1963), *A Theoretical Framework for Monetary Analysis* (1972), *There's No Such Thing as a Free Lunch* (1975), and *Price Theory* (1976).

In the early years of the Keynesian revolution, during the 1940s and early 1950s, the role of money in determining the level of economic activity was generally dismissed as having no relevance to economic stabilization policy. Keynes's discussion of the role of prices in *The General Theory* was interpreted by many of his followers to mean that wage rates were rigid, except at full employment when increasing demand would cause inflation of wages and other prices. Some latter-day Keynesian followers (neo-Keynesians) have noted that the assumption about fixed wages and prices was only a simplifying assumption that Keynes dropped in later chapters when he discussed the effects of price changes. Still others say that what he meant was that wages *should* be rigid to prevent even greater economic instability.

In any event, the role of prices and money was largely ignored in discussions of macroeconomic theory and economic stabilization policy. Everywhere, that is, except at the University of Chicago, where the quantity theory of money ($M \times V = T \times P$) was kept alive and nurtured by a group of economists that came to be known as "The Chicago School." The foremost member of the Chicago School of economists was Milton Friedman.

In his monumental study (with Anna Schwartz), *A Monetary History of the United States, 1867–1960,* Friedman demonstrated a close correlation between changes in the money supply on the one hand and inflation and the level of economic activity on the other. In his view, it was fiscal policy that was irrelevant. Promoted by Friedman and other Chicago School economists and reinforced by the persistent inflation of the 1970s, monetarism had a strong influence on both theory and policy in the early 1980s.

The rise of monetarism to the forefront of macroeconomics did not last long, however. In the area of theory, monetarism proved unable to explain what was happening any better than, or as well as, Keynesian economics. On the basis of monetarist analysis, Friedman predicted a recession in early 1984, followed by renewed inflation. Neither of these things happened, either then or for some years after.

On the policy side, the implementation of monetarist policies by the Fed did put a halt to inflation in 1981–1982 by contracting the money supply and bringing about the most severe recession since the depression of the 1930s, but that was no great trick. The real trick is to restrain inflation and at the same time provide full employment and a healthy growth rate. Monetarist policies were not any more successful in accomplishing this than previous approaches.

FOR FURTHER STUDY AND ANALYSIS

Study Questions

1. If there had been such a thing at the time, would fiscal stabilization policy have been very effective in the early years of this century when the federal government was quite small? Why or why not?

2. Why would annually balanced budgets make discretionary fiscal policy impossible?

3. What determines how much output will flow out of the economic "pump" after a given amount of priming?

4. Why are the automatic stabilizers built into our economy in themselves insufficient to maintain full employment?

5. What explains the difference in the effectiveness of monetary policy at opposite ends of the business cycle?

6. What might cause an increase in the velocity of circulation of money?

7. The investment/GDP ratio is based only on private investment. What are some examples of government spending that might increase economic growth?

8. Why does the capital/output ratio vary among different industries within a country? Which U.S. industries would you expect to have a high capital/output ratio? Which ones would you expect to have a low capital/output ratio?

9. Why has the U.S. labor force participation rate increased? What could be done to in-crease it further? What events might cause it to decrease?

10. What are some examples of technological improvements that do not require investment in new capital equipment? Why are these more beneficial for accelerating growth than those that do require new capital equipment?

Exercises in Analysis

1. Using the most recent Economic Report of the President or other sources, write a short paper on the government's recent fiscal and monetary policies.

2. From news accounts of current government stabilization measures, write a short paper on whether those measures represent Keynesian (demand-side) economic policies, supply-side economic policies, or monetarist economic policies.

3. Assume you are an economist on the staff of the Federal Reserve Board and the series of leading economic indicators suggests that the economy is headed into a severe recession. Write a report to the board recommending what actions it should take.

4. Write a report on investments in human capital in your area.

Further Reading

Biven, W. Carl. *Who Killed John Maynard Keynes?* Homewood, IL: Dow Jones–Irwin, 1989. Reviews basic Keynesian propositions and shows how they were replaced by monetarism, rational expectations, and Reaganomics. Concludes that the alternative formulations have not proved satisfactory and suggests a return to reworked Keynesian ideas.

Buiter, William H. *Principles of Budgetary and Financial Policy.* Cambridge, MA: MIT Press, 1990. Covers the question of the crowding out of private investment by government borrowing.

Burdekin, Richard C., and Farrakh K. Langdana. *Budget Deficits and Economic Performance.* New York: Routledge, 1992. An intercountry comparison of deficit financing, especially in the European Union.

Calleo, David P. *The Bankrupting of America: How the Federal Budget Is Impoverishing the Nation.* New York: William Morrow, 1992. An extremist outlook on the consequences of U.S. fiscal policy.

Friedman, Benjamin. *Day of Reckoning.* New York: Random House, 1988. "This book is about debt: debt and the material and moral impoverishment that inevitably follow, no less for a nation than for an individual or family, from continually borrowing for no purpose other than to live beyond one's means" (p. vii).

Friedman, Milton. *Monetarist Economics.* Cambridge, MA: Basil Blackwell, 1991. The leading proponent of monetarist economics explains the takes on monetary policy by the Chicago School of economics. See Perspective on page 383.

Kotlikoff, Laurence. *Generational Accounting: Knowing Who Pays, and When, for What We Spend.* New York: Free Press, 1992. Explains how tax burdens affect different generations and the real impact of budget deficits and debt interest payments.

Lindsey, Lawrence. *The Growth Experiment: How the New Tax Policy Is Transforming the U.S. Economy.* New York: Basic Books, 1990. This is a justification for supply-side tax policy. It maintains that the tax cuts of the 1980s were not the cause of the federal deficits, although conceding that they contributed to making the deficits greater than they would otherwise have been.

Lynch, Thomas D., ed. *Federal Budget and Financial Management Reform.* New York: Quorum Books, 1991. Includes an evaluation of proposals for reforming the Congressional budget process and an examination of the possibilities of privatization in federal budget reform.

Minarik, Joseph. *Making America's Budget Policy: From the 1980s to the 1990s.* Armonk, NY: M. E. Sharp, 1990. A review of taxes, federal budgets, and budget deficits during the Reagan years.

Ortner, Robert. *Voodoo Deficits.* Homewood, IL: Dow Jones–Irwin, 1990. Supply-side economic policy and how budget deficits are not what they seem. The role of international competition and the U.S. balance of trade is examined.

The economy of the United States is closely integrated into the world economy. Our economic policies have a major impact on other countries and vice versa.

Chapter 15. International Trade

Trading with other nations enables us to increase our living standards, but some people are hurt in the process. Restricting the amount of foreign trade is a subject of continuing controversy.

Chapter 16 International Finance and the National Economy

International payments are made and exchange rates of currencies are determined in the foreign exchange market. There is a close interconnection between the international payments balance and domestic equilibrium.

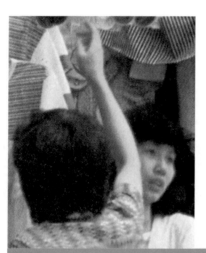

Chapter 17. Alternative Economic Systems

There have been extreme changes in the formerly communist systems in recent years. Other economic systems are also changing, although not as drastically. Economic systems are more similar than before, but there are still significant differences in the way they operate and how well they perform.

Chapter 18. World Economic Development

Two-thirds of the people in the world live in countries with low living standards and numerous obstacles to development. The prospects for overcoming poverty in less developed countries depend to a large extent on how the world meets the population, debt, and environmental threats.

■ **The motivations** for international trade are basically no different from those for trade within a country, but nations have imposed special regulations and restrictions on foreign trade. In order to reduce the trade-limiting effects of those constraints, nations negotiate agreements to reduce the restrictions. These agreements generate a great deal of controversy, as in the two recent instances discussed in the introductory article.

Do You Hear a Giant Sucking Sound Yet?

The debate in Washington over the North American Free Trade Agreement (NAFTA), establishing a free trade area among the United States, Canada, and Mexico, rose to an unusually frenzied pitch. Among the heated charges was businessman/politician H. Ross Perot's prediction that if trade barriers between the United States and Mexico were eliminated, there would be heard a "giant sucking sound" as American jobs were siphoned off to low-pay Mexico.

The opposition to NAFTA came from a strange coalition of organizations and individuals that are generally not on the same side of public policy questions. Besides Perot, the strongest opponents were the labor unions. Labor leaders exerted a great deal of pressure on their traditional allies in the Democratic Party. They threatened to cut off campaign contributions and to actively work to defeat in the next election any Democrat who voted for the NAFTA pact.

Environmental organizations were split over the issue, some opposing NAFTA and others supporting it. Ralph Nader, who came to national prominence as a consumer advocate, mounted a vigorous campaign in opposition to NAFTA. This seemed a strange position for a consumer advocate to take, since, whatever its effect on jobs, free trade is generally conceded to benefit consumers through lower prices. When questioned about his position, Nader held Japan up as a model of the benefits of protectionism, ignoring the heavy cost to Japanese consumers from their government's protection of sheltered industries.

But the main battle for the hearts and minds of voters over NAFTA centered in its effect on jobs. Perot claimed that as many as 5.9 million jobs would be lost to Mexico, asserting that even jobs in such high-technology industries as guided missiles and space vehicles were "at risk." A less exaggerated estimate came from Washington's Economic Policy Institute, projecting the possibility of a 490,000 job loss. On the other side, the International Economics Institute estimated a net gain of 171,000 American jobs.

The heat of the argument over NAFTA's effect on jobs was misplaced. Whether the effect turned out to be plus or minus, it would not be very significant relative to total domestic employment fluctuations. If the job change turned out to be some 200,000, whether in the

positive or negative direction, it would be no more than the monthly seasonal adjustment in employment figures.

Looked at in larger perspective, the NAFTA battle was really over what future direction the U.S. economy should take. Should the nation attempt to protect and retain relatively low-skill manufacturing jobs in the face of increasing competition from less developed countries in traditional industries? Or should it let those jobs go and shift its capital and labor resources into high-tech and service industries?

The opposition of the labor unions to the type of change represented by NAFTA is understandable. Their base of strength is in the manufacturing industries threatened by such a change. That base has already been seriously eroded. They are fighting a rear-guard action to slow down further erosion. On a personal level, many of their members are too old or too ill-equipped educationally to retrain for more skilled jobs. If they lose their present jobs, they are unlikely ever to have another job that pays as well.

Despite the formidable opposition to NAFTA, it passed Congress by a narrow margin and was signed into law. The heat of political passion over NAFTA anticipated Congressional consideration of an even more significant trade treaty among the 124 countries of the General Agreement on Tariffs and Trade (GATT). The agreement ended the eighth round of negotiations since GATT was first established in 1947. The negotiations among the three countries over the terms of NAFTA were a breeze compared to the quarrelsome, drawn-out negotiations over this latest version of GATT. The discussions began in September of 1986 at Punta del Este in Uruguay, giving the name "Uruguay Round" to the meetings, which continued off and on for 7 years in different locations over various continents.

The main sticking points were agricultural protection, a particularly French obstacle; protection against the piracy of intellectual property such as patents, copyrights, and trademarks, important to U.S. negotiators; and freedom from restrictions on foreign competition in the service sector, especially banking and financial services. Hard-fought compromises and an implicit agreement to continue the disagreement on some issues, such as opening markets to financial services, finally resulted in conclusion of the Uruguay Round in December 1993. A year later in December 1994, Congress approved the now GATT.

The agreement slashes tariffs on industrial goods by an average of about one-third, requires cuts in subsidies by European countries to their farmers, restricts piracy of intellectual property such as music, films, and software, and extends free trade rules to many services that were not covered in past agreements.

It also sets up a new organization to continue the process of trade liberalization—the World Trade Organization (WTO). Establishment of the WTO finally completes the objectives of the Bretton Woods System, devised by the World War II Allies in 1944 at Bretton

Woods, New Hampshire, to form a group of international organizations for facilitating economic relations in the postwar world. A charter for a proposed International Trade Organization (ITO) was drawn up at a conference in Havana, Cuba, in 1948. But the ITO was the one Bretton Woods organization that failed to materialize, largely because of protectionist forces in the U.S. Congress. Fifty years later we now have the WTO, which may possibly avert a repetition of the marathon 7-year Uruguay Round negotiations.

Why Do We Trade with Other Countries?

Trade between countries results from specialization of production. In chapter 3, absolute and comparative advantage were introduced to explain specialization in the use of resources. These concepts are especially applicable to international trade. It might be useful for you to review the explanation on pages 62–63 before taking up the discussion that follows.

Absolute Advantage

The South American country of Ecuador has excellent climate and terrain for growing coffee, cocoa, and bananas. It has an absolute advantage over the United States in the production of these goods. The United States, on the other hand, has an absolute advantage over Ecuador in many manufactured goods such as computers, airplanes, and electric razors. Ecuador does not have the capital equipment, technology, or trained personnel to produce these things economically. Thus there is trade between the two countries, based on their respective absolute advantages, that benefits each country.

Comparative Advantage

During the GATT negotiations, there was pressure on U.S. trade representatives from the textile industry to restrict imports. Textile imports from Singapore, China, the Philippines, and other countries have eliminated a large part of the market for U.S. textiles. The United States is an efficient producer of textiles, but labor and capital in this country are more efficient in the production of other goods.

Figure 1.

World Trade in Goods, 1992

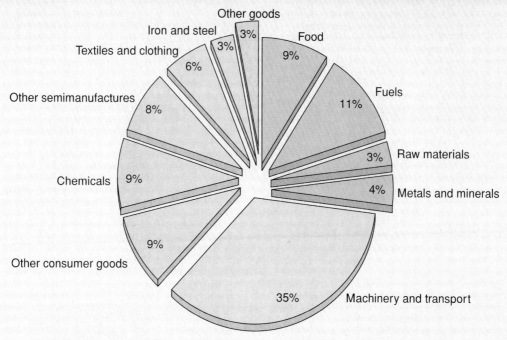

Source: General Agreement on Tariffs and Trade.

■ Trade among countries is based on absolute and comparative advantage. Trade in primary products (shown in green) is more likely to be based on absolute advantage, while trade in manufactured goods (shown in blue) is more likely to be based on comparative advantage.

As an example, let us assume that the United States has an absolute advantage over the Philippines in the production of both electric drills and raincoats. However, the efficiency advantage of the United States is greater in producing drills than producing raincoats. The United States has a comparative advantage in drills with respect to the Philippines. The advantage of a cheaper labor supply in the Philippines is not sufficient to offset the technological superiority of the United States in manufacturing drills.

The Philippines may not be able to produce raincoats as efficiently as they could be produced in the United States either, but the production of raincoats is adaptable to different levels of technology. With lower wage rates, Philippine manufacturers can use a more labor-intensive method of producing raincoats and can sell them more cheaply in the United States

than can American producers. Therefore, the Philippines exports raincoats to the United States on the basis of its comparative advantage in producing them.

Even though the United States is absolutely more efficient in raincoat production than the Philippines, the opportunity costs of producing raincoats there are lower than in the United States. Let us assume that when the Philippines produces one raincoat, it must give up the production of one drill. We'll assume that production of one raincoat in the United States, however, means that two drills will not be produced here. Thus, the opportunity cost, or real cost, of producing a raincoat in the United States is two drills, compared to an opportunity cost of only one drill in the Philippines. In effect, we must give up only one-half of a raincoat when a drill is produced in the United States, compared to the sacrifice

■ Countries, like individuals, find it profitable to produce those goods that they are best suited to produce. One country may be very efficient in the production of both electric drills and raincoats, but another country will have a comparative advantage in the production of raincoats if its opportunity costs for that production are low.

of a whole raincoat when a drill is produced in the Philippines.

Specialization

As was found in the case of individuals in chapter 3, countries find it profitable to produce those goods that they are best suited to produce. Countries like the Philippines, with a relative abundance of labor but not capital, tend to specialize in industries that are **labor-intensive,** such as textiles and clothing. Other countries with large amounts of capital per worker, such as the United States, tend

to specialize in high-technology industries. By doing what they do best, nations can maximize the value of their output and thus maximize their standard of living. As a result, specialization of production requires that each nation must engage in trade to sell its surplus production and acquire what it does not produce.

Increasing Costs

Sometimes specialization is complete. Between Ecuador and the United States, there is complete specialization in the cocoa and aircraft industries. Ecuador does not manufacture any airplanes and the United States does not grow cocoa commercially. For most products, however, specialization is only partial. The United States imports most of the raincoats that are sold in this country, but it still produces a quantity of raincoats. The Philippines imports most of the electrical equipment that it needs, including drills, but it does produce some electrical equipment itself. Instead of complete specialization, we more often have **limited specialization**.

The reason for this limited specialization is the existence of **increasing costs**. The Philippines can produce some electrical equipment that is competitive with that produced by the United States. However, because of its limited supplies of skilled labor and capital equipment, it cannot increase the output of its electrical equipment industry sufficiently to satisfy all of its domestic needs without running into higher production costs. The concept of increasing costs was illustrated in Figure 3 of chapter 2 (p. 42) in connection with the trade-off between the production of civilian goods and the production of armaments.

labor-intensive: refers to production processes that employ a large amount of labor relative to the amount of capital equipment.

limited specialization: specialization in producing goods or services according to comparative advantage when the specialization is not complete due to increasing costs (decreasing returns).

increasing costs: a rise in average production costs as the quantity of output of the good increases.

Comparative Case Application

The Odd Trio

As a prelude to NAFTA, the United States and Canada entered into a free trade agreement in 1989. That agreement generated a great deal of controversy in Canada, with Canadians charging that a great many Canadian jobs had been lost to the United States.

Between 1989 and 1992, U.S. merchandise exports to Canada increased from $78.8 billion to $90.6 billion, a healthy 15% gain in just 3 years. But imports from Canada rose almost as much, from $88 billion to $98.5 billion, a 12% increase. Furthermore, Canada continued to have a favorable trade balance with the United States of $7.9 billion. The principal cause of job losses in Canada in the early 1990s was the onset of recession, not the reduction of trade barriers.

Canada is the most important trading partner of the United States, taking 20% of our total merchandise exports. Mexico is our third most important trading partner, after Japan, taking 9% of total exports.

But there the similarity ends. In contrast with the deficit trade balance with Canada, the United States has a surplus trade balance of $5.4 billion with Mexico. And the types of goods traded with Mexico are much different from the goods traded with Canada. The United States imports five times as much fruit and vegetables from Mexico as from Canada and three times as much apparel and clothing accessories. On the other hand, the United States purchases a great deal of pulp and paper from Canada and virtually none from Mexico. It also purchases eight times as much specialized industrial machinery from Canada as from Mexico.

Canada and the United States have similar economic system structures. They both have highly industrialized economies with a great deal of capital investment per worker. Both are well endowed with natural resources, although primary production is relatively more important in Canada. Mexico is much less industrialized. The United States and Canada employ approximately the same amount of energy per capita, while Mexico uses less than one-fifth as much per capita because of its lower level of industrialization.

Can such a mismatched trio succeed as partners? Will the gains in trade between the two like partners be greater than or less than the trade gains between the dissimilar partners? Which partner or partners will benefit most from NAFTA? Or will the benefits be shared equally? All of the partners should benefit from increased trade, but only time will tell who receives the most benefits.

Economic Reasoning

1. Which of the merchandise trades cited in the case application are likely based on absolute advantage and which on comparative advantage?

2. Which of the goods are subject to increasing costs? Why?

3. Do you think the United States will gain more benefits from trade with Canada or from trade with Mexico as a result of NAFTA? Why?

Who Benefits and Who Is Hurt by Foreign Trade?

Specialization, according to absolute or comparative advantage, results in a net gain to both of the trading partners in foreign trade. However, not everyone in a country benefits equally from foreign trade. Some individuals or firms in a country may even suffer economic losses as a result.

Consumer Benefits

Without foreign trade, there are some things that we would be unable to enjoy. Chocolate lovers would probably not appreciate cocoa grown in hothouses in this country as a substitute for the beans grown in Ecuador. Even if they were willing to drink it, they wouldn't be able to afford much domestically grown cocoa because it would be very expensive.

However, most imports, unlike cocoa, are items that we can and do produce domestically. Those items that are produced by domestic firms and are also imported are called **import-competing**. Consumers benefit from

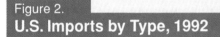

import-competing industry: a domestic industry that produces the same or a close substitute good that competes in the domestic market with imports.

Figure 2.
U.S. Imports by Type, 1992

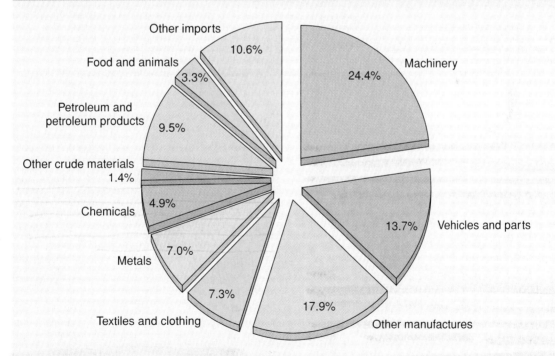

Other imports 10.6%

Food and animals 3.3%

Petroleum and petroleum products 9.5%

Other crude materials 1.4%

Chemicals 4.9%

Metals 7.0%

Textiles and clothing 7.3%

Other manufactures 17.9%

Vehicles and parts 13.7%

Machinery 24.4%

Source: U.S. Bureau of the Census, *U.S. Merchandise Trade.*

■ The largest category of U.S. imports is machinery. This includes such things as electrical equipment, power-generating machinery, telecommunications apparatus, and specialized industrial machinery.

Figure 3.
U.S. Exports by Type, 1992

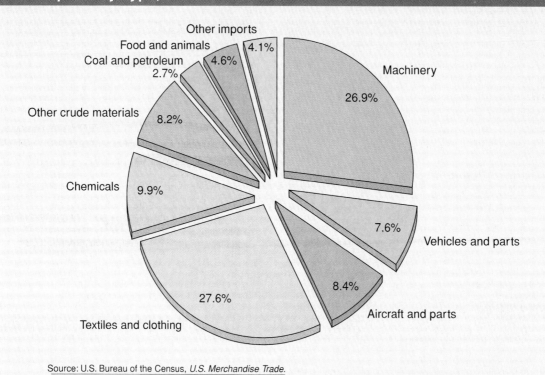

Other imports
Food and animals
Coal and petroleum
2.7%
4.6%
4.1%
Machinery
26.9%
Other crude materials
8.2%
Chemicals 9.9%
7.6%
Vehicles and parts
27.6%
8.4%
Textiles and clothing
Aircraft and parts

Source: U.S. Bureau of the Census, *U.S. Merchandise Trade*.

■ The largest type of U.S. exports, as with imports, is machinery. The world economic system is highly inte- grated, with most trade taking place among industrialized countries that have similar economies.

the availability of imported goods because they have more selection, foreign products are very often less expensive or of better quality, and the import competition helps keep down the price of domestically produced goods.

The different types of imports into the United States during 1992 are shown in Figure 2 on the previous page, which gives the percentage of total imports for each major type of commodity imported. The largest category of imports was machinery. The most significant items in this category were electrical equipment, telecommunications apparatus, power generating, and specialized industrial machinery. The United States is also an exporter of these types of products. This illustrates how integrated the world economy has become. By far the largest part of U.S. trade is with other industri-

alized countries that have similar production systems. Worldwide, three-quarters of exports go from developed countries to other developed countries. Comparative advantage now rests largely on very specific products within broad categories. For example, 70% of worldwide exports of friction bearings go to countries that also export bearings.

Altogether, the United States purchased $535.5 billion worth of goods from abroad in 1992. In addition, U.S. tourists and business travelers spent $55.3 billion abroad and the military spent $13.4 billion. Payments for other foreign services amounted to $54.7 billion. One out of every 10 dollars that we spent in 1992 was spent on imports of goods and services. This is not a particularly large import ratio compared to that of most other countries. For example, Germany and Great

Table 1. United States Export, Import-Competing, and Domestic Industries

Export Industries	Import-Competing Industries	Domestic Industries
Computers	Textiles and clothing	Construction
Aircraft	Steel and other metals	Health services
Chemicals	Autos and parts	K–12 education
Instruments	Furniture	Personal services
Lumber and paper products	Consumer electronics	Wholesale
Financial services	Cement	Domestic transport
Films and other media	Shoes and luggage	Printing and publishing
Higher education	Toys and jewelry	Rubber and plastic products

Sources: U.S. Bureau of the Census, *U.S. Merchandise Trade: Exports, General Imports, and Imports for Consumption;* U.S. Department of Commerce, Bureau of Economic Analysis, *Survey of Current Business.*

■ The export sector creates jobs and raises wages for workers in the exporting industries. Workers in the import-competing industries suffer job losses and lower wages. Jobs in the domestic sector industries are not affected by trade, but the workers in those industries, along with workers in the other sectors, benefit from greater availability, lower prices, and improved quality of goods and services in the import-competing sector.

Britain spend one out of every five dollars on imports. For the United States, however, this amount of import spending is much higher than it has been historically.

Producer and Worker Benefits

Many industries and workers also benefit in various ways from foreign trade. Some American industries depend on raw materials that can only be acquired abroad. Other firms purchase semifinished components for their products from foreign sources, including both independent producers and subsidiaries of American firms abroad.

Perhaps the most important benefit of foreign trade to producers and workers, however, is providing markets for our export industries. The United States exported $439.3 billion worth of civilian goods in 1992. The major merchandise export industries are shown in Figure 3. Machinery, including computers and power generators, accounted for more than a quarter of all merchandise exports.

Merchandise exports generated 9.1% of our national income in 1992. In addition to merchandise exports, the country transferred $10.9 billion worth of military goods under military agency sales contracts in 1992. Foreigners also spent $71.6 billion on U.S. travel and transportation and $96 billion on other services.

Our exports create jobs and increase the income of all the suppliers of the export industries as well as provide profits to the owners. The U.S. industries that benefit from sizable exports are shown in the first column of Table 1.

Import-Competing Firms' and Workers' Losses

The heavy pressure exerted by some industries on Congress for protection from imports is a good indication of which groups are hurt by foreign trade. Pressure from the automobile industry and the United Auto Workers union resulted in restrictions on automobile imports. The textile, steel, furniture, and other import-competing industries plead for more protection. The closing of plants and loss of jobs in these industries have caused hardships.

Steel Industry Does an About-Face

For years, the U.S. steel industry led the fight *for* free trade. Today, it is fighting *against* free trade.

The emergence of a mature, efficient steel industry in Germany, Japan, South Korea, and elsewhere has tipped the scales. Not only have U.S. steel firms been priced out of many foreign markets, they are in a struggle with foreign competitors for the profitable North American steel market.

The steel industry is suffering from lagging productivity and the higher costs associated with environmental protection regulations. As a result of rising production costs, the price of a ton of domestic steel is so high that American steel users are finding it more cost effective to import larger and larger quantities from foreign suppliers. In order to reduce the price differentials of domestic steel compared to foreign steel, U.S. steel firms have pleaded for relief from environmental controls as well as new restrictions on the importation of foreign steel.

Both labor and management in the steel industry are now far more sensitive to the implications of their low productivity. Steel output in the United States declined from a peak of 116.6 million tons in 1978 to 88.3 million tons in 1991. Between 1970 and 1991, the U.S. share of world steel ingot and castings production fell from 20% to 11%. But some small steel plants, using advanced smelting technology—the so-called minimills—have been able to undersell imported steel and are increasing their sales.

The steel industry claims that the problem is not so much high production costs in the United States as it is unfair competition from foreign producers, subsidized by their governments. The Commerce Department declared that steel imported from nine countries was, in fact, subsidized and being sold in the United States at unfairly low prices. As a result, the government imposed an additional tax on foreign steel

■ The U.S. steel industry, suffering from lagging productivity and the high costs of government regulation, is fighting for protection from foreign competition.

that ran as high as $250 a ton on some imports. Higher steel prices as a result cost U.S. consumers at least $5 billion annually.

Economic Reasoning

1. Who will gain and who will lose as a result of the higher taxes on steel imports?

2. Why was the steel industry at one time in favor of free trade?

3. Do you think that the steel industry should get more protection from imports? Why or why not?

■ Appealing to pride in domestic manufacture has become an important sales strategy for firms in import-competing industries.

Free trade can be costly to workers and owners in import-competing industries. But these costs are no different from the costs resulting from domestic competition. For example, the once-thriving U.S. railroad industry was devastated by competition from the automobile and trucking industries. The market mechanism allocates resources to their most efficient employment in accordance with costs and consumer demand.

Mobility of Capital and Labor

If sales of the textile industry are reduced because of imports, while sales of aircraft are increased because of export demand, capital and labor should move from the textile industry to the aircraft industry. The difficulty is that these factors of production are not perfect substitutes for one another, and the transfer of some factors from one employment activity to another can cause hardships. Workers in southern textile mills may not want or be able to move to western aircraft factories or have the necessary skills. Fixed capital has even less mobility: textile industry machinery, for example, cannot be used to produce airplanes.

Domestic Consumers of Export Industries

International trade equalizes the prices of products. Before trade, the price of electric drills was relatively low in the United States and relatively high in the Philippines. With trade, the price of drills tends to rise in the United States and fall in the Philippines as some of the U.S. output is exported. Eventually, this adjustment process leads to equal prices in both countries, except for transportation costs and import taxes. The American consumer of drills finally pays a higher price for domestically produced drills.

How Do We Restrict Foreign Trade?

International trade would be larger than it is if it were not for the restrictions countries put on it. These restrictions take various forms.

Tariffs

Tariffs are a tax on imports either on the value of the imports or per unit of quantity imported. Tariffs could be used for revenue purposes, but in recent times their principal purpose has been to shelter domestic firms from foreign competition. U.S. tariffs have historically been imposed on selective goods and have been relatively high. High tariffs result in a small quantity of imports and as a consequence do not generate much tax revenue.

Empowered by the Reciprocal Trade Agreement Act of 1934 and its extensions, U.S. presidents have steadily reduced tariffs through **bilateral trade negotiations** (see Figure 4). These negotiated reductions depended upon the willingness of other countries to lower tariffs imposed on U.S. exports. Because bilateral negotiations can create confus-

> **free trade:** international trade that is unrestricted by government protectionist measures.
>
> **tariff:** a tax placed on an imported good; also, the whole schedule of a country's import duties.
>
> **bilateral trade negotiations:** trade negotiations between two countries only.

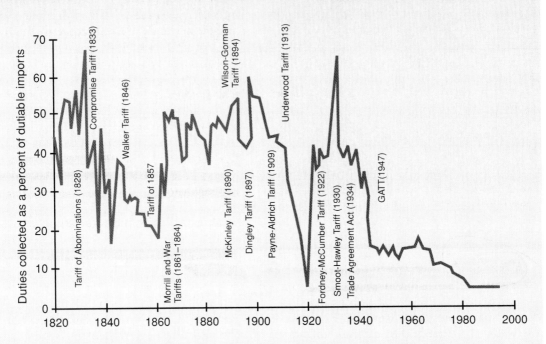

Figure 4.
U. S. Tariff History

■ Since the early 1800s average tariff rates have fluctuated widely. Since the early 1930s, however, the trend has been downward.

ing multiple tariff rates for different nations, **most-favored-nation clauses** in trade agreements extend the benefits of tariff reductions negotiated with one country to all other countries that accord the United States similar treatment. The United States has been reluctant to extend the benefits of the most-favored-nation treatment to some countries, notably the Soviet Union while it existed. Trade negotiations with these countries continue on a purely bilateral basis.

The original 1947 General Agreement on Tariffs and Trade provided for nondiscrimination among the cooperating nations. It set a pattern for **multilateral trade negotiations** as a substitute for bilateral trade negotiations. When all of the participating countries negotiate simultaneously, the possibilities for making deals for tariff reductions are greatly expanded. Through a succession of GATT agreements, tariffs have been markedly reduced. Although some significant exceptions exist, trade between the United States and the rest of the world is much freer today than it has ever been before.

Quotas

Restrictions on the quantity of a good that may be imported or exported during a given time period are called **quotas**. They are established either in physical terms—a set number of tons of a commodity, for example—or in value terms—a set number of dollars' worth of a commodity. Quotas may be directed toward one or a number of specific countries, or they can be established without regard to the country of origin. The quota may be stated in absolute terms; that is, a fixed quantity or value of a commodity may be allowed to enter a country. Alternatively, the quota may be stated as a tariff quota, which allows a given quantity or value of commodity to enter a country duty free or at a low tariff, with larger quantities or values entering at a higher rate of duty.

Quotas have been largely responsible for limiting Japanese auto penetration in European markets. France has restricted Japanese cars to 3% of total sales, and tough quotas in Italy and Spain have held Japan's share of their markets to less than 1%. The main difference in the effect of a tariff and a quota—at least an absolute quota—is that the tariff still allows the price system in the importing country to allocate goods and resources. Quotas, on the other hand, set an absolute limit and, no matter how high the domestic price is above the price abroad, no more can be imported. The Uruguay Round of GATT succeeded in further reducing the use of quotas as a protectionist device.

Nontariff Barriers

Besides tariffs and quotas, there are a number of other ways of restricting imports. These are termed **nontariff barriers**. If industries lobbying for protection are unable to get high tariffs or import quotas imposed, they still have other weapons. For example, a requirement may be imposed that all goods that have foreign components must have labels affixed. This labeling can serve to encourage nationalistic sentiments. In addition, labeling adds to the costs of the foreign producer.

An informal type of barrier to foreign imports is to make the clearing of foreign goods through customs difficult and time consuming, and therefore expensive. Imported goods can be made subject to a series of tests and inspections for reasons of safety, health, and general public welfare. These nontariff barri-

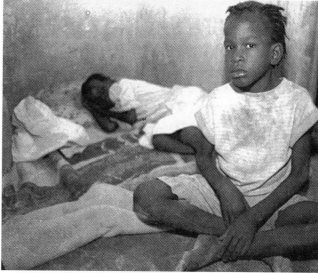

■ The oil embargo and other sanctions in Haiti, whose purpose was to bring about restoration of democratic government, also resulted in the deaths of as many as 1,000 children each month.

ers, when applied and enforced, can be very effective in discouraging imports.

Export Embargoes

Export embargoes are prohibitions on the export of commodities, capital, or technology. They are sometimes imposed for political reasons, such as the 1980 embargo on exports of U.S. grain to the Soviet Union because of the Soviet invasion of Afghanistan, the 1990 embargo on Iraq arising from Iraq's invasion of Kuwait, and the embargo on Haiti to force a restoration of democratic government.

Export embargoes might instead be used to prevent other countries from having access to valuable new technologies. They could also be imposed to block the outflow of important raw materials and thus keep down their prices to domestic producers.

nontariff barriers: restrictions on imports resulting from requirements for special marking, test, or standards enforced on imported goods or the time delays in clearing them for importation.

export embargo: a prohibition of the export of a commodity, capital, or technology.

Protection Japanese-Style

American producers regularly complain that the Japanese market is particularly tough to crack. Public officials in the United States insist that the enormous trade deficit with Japan—$51 billion in 1992—must be reduced.

The Japanese, for their part, claim that they have greatly reduced their tariffs in recent years; the average tariff level of Japan is in fact below that of the United States. If Japanese tariffs are not especially high, why is it so difficult for U.S. businesses to penetrate the Japanese market?

One area in which Japan does have stiff import restrictions is on agricultural products. Quotas on imports of meat and fruit create large price differences between the Japanese market and the American market—$20 a pound for steak and $35 for melons in Tokyo, for example.

However, the main obstacles to selling more American products in Japan are not formal trade barriers. One of them is Japanese government red tape. For instance, documentation and testing of American cars sold in Japan add as much as $500 to the price of each car. Testing for the safety of U.S. health care products is required in Japan, even if similar tests have already been performed for the same products marketed in the United States.

Another problem for foreigners in penetrating the Japanese market is the existence of giant integrated Japanese firms that produce goods all the way from the raw material stage to the finished product. Foreign suppliers of intermediate products have no chance of selling them to the vertically integrated Japanese firms. Even the smaller Japanese producers are frozen out of their own domestic markets in this way. As a result, some of them are now entering into joint production and marketing arrangements with American and

■ When the trade-barrier dilemma between the United States and Japan is settled, these young Japanese, the shinjinrui (under-30 generation), who are interested in trendy fashions, could become an important market target for the American fashion industry.

other foreign firms—taking advantage of trade liberalization pressures on the Japanese government—in order to gain an entry into their *own country's* markets!

But perhaps the greatest barrier American business has to overcome is cultural. The formalities and informalities of Japanese business conduct are significantly different from those in the West. Personal relationships are more important in Japanese business dealings. Socializing over a cup of tea is an essential ingredient in business negotiations. The Japanese characterize such business dealings as "wet," in contrast to the "dry," more businesslike and less personal, practices in the United States and other Western countries.

It takes considerable time for U.S. firms to develop a market in Japan. American business has been criticized for having a too-short profit horizon. Any proposed business activity that doesn't promise to show profits within a few months is rejected. The small number of American businesspeople who take the time to learn the Japanese language attests to a lack of commitment to nurturing the Japanese market. By comparison, a Japanese business representative may spend 10–15 years in the United States making contacts and learning the language. Some American firms that have put forth the effort have had success with sales in Japan; included among these firms are IBM, Schick, Coca-Cola, and McDonald's.

Economic Reasoning

1. What type of nontariff barriers, other than quotas, restrict imports into Japan? Can you think of any similar barriers that restrict imports into the United States?

2. Would U.S. farmers and ranchers be able to export more to Japan if the Japanese applied tariffs rather than quotas to imports of agricultural products? What are the assumptions underlying your answer?

3. Americans' lack of ability in speaking foreign languages is said to hamper the country in business dealings, international understanding, and cultural growth. Do you think that more study of foreign languages should be required of American students? What would be the trade-off of increased language requirements in our schools?

Should Foreign Trade Be Restricted?

As can be seen in Figure 4 on page 400, the level of protectionist sentiment in this country has fluctuated widely, though over the years **protectionism** has generally been high. Since the GATT agreement in 1947, trade barriers have been greatly reduced. But the fierce opposition to NAFTA showed that protectionism is still alive and well in the United States. Why does the protectionist movement keep reappearing? This analysis section examines some of the arguments over free trade versus protectionism.

Traditional Protectionist Arguments

The most common justification given for protectionism is that it is supposed to increase domestic employment by protecting the U.S. worker from the unfair competition of cheap foreign labor. But trade is based on comparative, not absolute, advantage. Low foreign wages do not necessarily create comparative advantage for those countries. The wage issue, in essence, ignores the productivity of workers. Wages of American workers are high because of their high productivity. The low wages of foreign workers are due to their low productivity. When their productivity increases, so do their wages. Imports, as a result of specialization according to comparative advantage, increase the real wages of American workers.

Furthermore, competition from foreign producers increases productivity in an industry. A 1993 study by William Lewis of McKinsey & Company and others examined productivity in nine manufacturing industries in Japan, Germany, and the United States.

> **protectionism:** measures taken by the government in order to limit or exclude imports that compete with domestic production.
>
> **infant industry argument:** the contention that it is economically justified to provide trade protection to a new industry in a country to enable it to grow to a size that would result in production costs that are competitive with those of foreign producers.
>
> **terms of trade:** the ratio of average export prices to average import prices.

They examined the reasons for productivity differences in each of the industries among the three countries. They concluded that it was not differences in capital equipment, labor education, or managerial techniques that accounted most for differing productivity, but the degree of foreign and domestic competition in the industry. In Japan, the auto, auto parts, consumer electronics, metal working, and steel industries—all of which are subjected to vigorous foreign and domestic competition—have high productivity rates. In the processed foods, soap and detergent, and beer industries, on the other hand—which are sheltered in Japan—the U.S. firms have productivity rates as much as 70% higher than the Japanese firms.

A second argument for protectionism is that imports represent a leakage of spending from the economic system and that a reduction in spending for imports would increase domestic aggregate demand. This argument is true as far as it goes, but one country's imports are another's exports. The imposition of tariffs generally causes retaliation, reducing employment in U.S. export industries as much or more than the increased employment in import-competing industries.

One situation in which protection can be justified for a period of time is where a *new industry* could be efficient and competitive if it had a chance to mature and achieve economies of scale. This argument holds that newly established industries need to be protected until they reach levels of production that allow them to be competitive in the world market. The costs of temporary trade restrictions might be worth paying in order to gain a long-run benefit. This **infant industry argument** may have limited validity for underdeveloped countries, but it generally has little applicability in the United States or other mature economies.

Terms of Trade

The average price of exports relative to the price of imports is called the **terms of trade**. It shows how many units of imports can be purchased with a given amount of exports.

Countries may desire to improve the terms of trade in order to increase their purchasing power in the international marketplace. They want the value of the goods they export to increase relative to the value of the goods they import. They would then be able to buy more imports for the same quantity of exports, thus raising their standard of living.

The terms of trade can be altered either by a reduced price for imports or an increased price of exports. For example, the prices paid to foreign exporters may be forced down by imposing tariffs or quotas. The higher retail prices resulting from import restrictions cause the quantity demanded in the importing country to fall. In response to the lower demand, foreign producers will reduce their export prices, resulting in an increase in the terms of trade for the country imposing the tariff or quota. However, when one country attempts to turn the terms of trade in its favor in this fashion, it invites retaliation from others.

Neomercantilist Arguments

The **mercantilists** around the time of Queen Elizabeth I believed that the strength of a nation lay in how much gold and other precious metals it held. They believed a country must export more than it imported. For if there is an excess of exports over imports, goods and services will flow out of the country; and in payment, gold will flow into the country. An exception to their export drive was the export of machinery. England prohibited the export of textile machinery, or even the plans for constructing it, because that would have enabled France and other rivals to compete with English textiles.

The **neomercantilists** of today are reviving the ideas of the seventeenth-century mercantilists. They argue that, whereas in the past comparative advantage came in large part from the basic resources of a country, comparative advantage for a modern industrialized economy is primarily a function of technology. Thus, a country will retain a comparative advantage only as long as it retains a technological lead over other countries. When technology is being rapidly exported, as it is now, a domestic industry has less time to capitalize on any com-

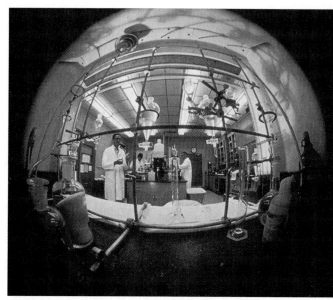

■ Neomercantilists contend that exporting high technology can cause a country to lose its competitive advantage.

parative advantage that it might have due to superior technology. If the industry loses this comparative advantage, it is faced with resource dislocation and the accompanying structural unemployment.

No one can deny that technology is more mobile today than it has ever been. A country can lose its comparative advantage if it does not remain technologically superior. A major strength of the U.S. economy has been its ability to generate technology. Many claim that to be its fundamental comparative advantage. The question is should it—or can it—prevent the export of its technology to Japan and other countries? Or, failing that, should it restrict

mercantilists: those who advocated mercantilism, a doctrine that dominated policies in many countries from the sixteenth to the eighteenth centuries. It held that exports should be maximized and imports minimized to generate an inflow of gold, and that exports of machinery and technology should be prohibited to prevent competition from foreign producers.

neomercantilists: contemporary advocates of mercantilist trade policies to restrict imports, maximize exports of consumer products, and restrict exports of capital equipment and technology to prevent competition from foreign producers.

the importation of the products of that technology?

Protectionist arguments fail to take into account the basic rationale for trade—to raise standards of living by maximizing the efficiency of resource allocation through comparative advantage. Furthermore, the matter of technology transfer is becoming a two-way street as Japan and Western Europe devote more resources to research and development.

However, since the nation as a whole benefits from the advantages of foreign competition and new technology, it must be prepared to compensate those who are injured in the process. In the United States, **trade adjustment assistance** is given by the government to industries injured by foreign competition to help capital and labor shift to new products.

Restrictions to Solve Foreign Payments Problems

If a country's imports exceed its exports, it will have a deficit in its foreign payments. The method of correcting the deficit under free trade and free currency conditions would be to let the value of the country's currency fall relative to other countries until its exports became inexpensive enough to compete in world markets. The protectionist method would be to restrict imports and perhaps also restrict investments in foreign countries. This solution to the problem of a foreign deficit could work only if other countries did not retaliate.

■ Unemployed men stand in a breadline at the New York Municipal Lodging House during the Depression in 1930. The effects of the Depression were made worse by the strongly protectionist Smoot-Hawley Tariff of 1930, the subject of the Perspective on page 410.

trade adjustment assistance: supplementary unemployment payments to workers who have lost their jobs because of import competition, and assistance to firms in shifting to other types of production.

Bastiat's Petition

The controversy between protectionists and free traders has remained very much alive, as the current pressure for increased protection from foreign competition shows. The most extreme protectionist position was neatly satirized in the nineteenth century by French economist Frederic Bastiat (1801–1850) in his famous "Petition of the Manufacturers of Candles, Waxlights, Lamps, Candlesticks, Strut Lamps, Snuffers, Extinguishers, and the Producers of Oil, Tallow, Resin, Alcohol, and Generally Everything Connected with Lighting," which was addressed to the French parliament.

Gentlemen:

We are suffering from the intolerable competition of a foreign rival, placed, it would seem, in a condition so far superior to our own for the production of light, that he absolutely *inundates* our *national market* with it at a price fabulously reduced.... This rival ... is no other than the sun.

What we pray for is ... a law ordering the shutting up of all windows, skylights ... in a word of all openings, holes, chinks, and fissures.... If you shut up as much as possible all access to natural light and create a demand for artificial light, which of our French manufacturers will not benefit by it?

Make your choice, but be logical; for as long as you exclude, as you do, iron, corn, foreign fabrics, *in proportion* as their prices approximate to zero, what inconsistency it would be to admit the light of the sun, the price of which is already at zero during the entire day!

Economic Reasoning

1. What type of protectionist argument was Bastiat satirizing?

2. If the French parliament had adopted Bastiat's petition, what effect would this have had on the manufacturers of candles, wax lights, lamps, and candlesticks? What would have been the effect on the French economy?

3. Do you think that the U.S. industries that are suffering from import competition should be accorded protection? Why or why not? Is there a difference between the argument for restricting the imports of textiles, steel, or Japanese automobiles and Bastiat's petition to restrict the competition from the sun?

Putting It Together

Specialization according to absolute or comparative advantage means that resources are employed efficiently and total world output increases. Specialization may be complete, especially in smaller countries with a limited variety of resources. But most often specialization is *limited*. Countries both produce and import a specific item. The reason they do not produce enough for their needs, even though they are capable of producing the item, is because of *increasing costs*. Increasing the output of the industry would raise costs due to a limited supply of factor inputs. It is resource availability that determines the nature and extent of specialization.

Consumers are the greatest beneficiaries of foreign trade. Because goods are made where they can be produced most inexpensively, consumers' real purchasing power is maximized. Production firms that use imported raw material and components are also beneficiaries of trade. Export industries and their workers also benefit. Losses are sustained by firms that must compete with imports. These losses are more lasting and severe when the mobility of capital and labor between

different industries is limited. Domestic consumers of the products of export industries will also suffer to the extent that the export demand raises the prices of the products.

Tariffs and *quotas* are methods of restricting imports. *Nontariff barriers,* such as regulations on labeling, packaging, and testing, also restrict imports. On rare occasions, exports may be taxed or prohibited when the authorities believe that it is in the best interest of the country to do so.

In order to reduce trade barriers, nations negotiate mutual concessions in *bilateral* or *multilateral trade negotiations.* When a nation grants a tariff reduction or other trade concession on imports of a good from one country through these negotiations, it automatically extends the concession to all other countries to whom it extends *most-favored-nation* treatment.

Among the older *protectionist* arguments are the "cheap foreign labor" argument, which maintains that the wages of American workers are held down by competition from low-wage workers abroad, notwithstanding that the foreign wages are low because the foreign labor is not very productive. Other current justifications for protection, such as to stimulate domestic employment or improve the terms of trade, usually ignore the likelihood of retaliation.

Neomercantilist arguments for restricting exports of American capital and technology contradict the principle of comparative advantage. Another reason given for imposing import restrictions is to attempt to eliminate a deficit in the nation's foreign payments. Under free trade and free currency conditions, however, this should not be necessary because the deficit should be corrected by a fall in the value of the country's currency, which would stimulate exports and curb imports.

The only protectionist argument that has received limited approval by most economists is the *infant industry* argument. This argument holds that a country that has the resource endowment for a particular industry to be efficient can justifiably protect that industry from foreign competition during the industry's early growth period. The assumption is that import restrictions will be removed when the industry matures. This argument may have validity for underdeveloped nations but generally has little application to developed economies.

■ Retail stores throughout the United States, such as this Connecticut shop, feature a wide range of products that have been handmade or manufactured in countries where labor costs are low.

◢PERSPECTIVE◣

Smoot-Hawley Revisited

For additional information on Smoot-Hawley and U.S. tariff history, see John M. Dobson, *Two Centuries of Tariffs* (Washington, D.C.: United States Trade Commission, 1976); David A. Lake, *Power, Protection, and Free Trade* (Ithaca, NY: Cornell University Press, 1988); Stefanie Ann Lenway, *The Politics of U.S. International Trade* (Boston: Pitman, 1985); and F. W. Taussig, *The Tariff History of the United States* (New York: Augustus M. Kelley, 1967).

In 1930 a thousand members of the American Economics Association begged Congress to defeat the Smoot-Hawley Tariff Bill. However, their petitions fell on deaf ears. Unemployment was rising, and Congress reasoned that if workers were displaced because of cheap foreign imports, then why not curtail the imports and protect the United States worker? It proceeded to enact the most restrictive set of import duties ever adopted in the United States.

Passage of this legislation turned some economists' worst fears into reality. It set in motion massive, worldwide trade restrictions. The powerful and not-so-powerful nations of the world responded to the Smoot-Hawley Tariff of 1930 out of self-protection and self-interest. They did not have enough dollars or gold to continue to pay for U.S. goods if the United States bought less from them. And they reasoned that if it was advantageous for the United States to protect its industries from foreign competition, then it was equally advantageous for them to protect their industries from American competition. The result was a marked reduction in world trade—a reduction that left the export industries of most countries in shambles. Incomes fell. Unemployment grew. The intensity of the Great Depression increased.

The loss of export markets was especially hard on farmers. The farm economy had been in a depression since the mid-1920s, years before the crash hit industry and commerce. Exports were an outlet for excess American farm production prior to Smoot-Hawley.

The irony of Smoot-Hawley was that all during the preceding decade the United States had an excess of exports over imports. In 1928 the export surplus was over $1 billion, more than $9 billion in today's dollars. During the years leading up to Smoot-Hawley, the United States on balance gained, not lost, jobs from foreign trade.

Raising the barriers against the import of goods from abroad made it impossible for other countries to pay their accumulated debts to American banks and other lenders. The consequent defaults added more pressure on the crumbling U.S. financial structure.

Once the international trading system was virtually destroyed by the protectionist policies of the early 1930s, it was slow to recover. The lessons learned as a result of Smoot-Hawley and its aftermath conditioned the international approach to trade following World War II. Led by the United States, the western countries adopted GATT and other agreements intended to liberalize trade and avoid in the future the havoc that followed Smoot-Hawley.

FOR FURTHER STUDY AND ANALYSIS

Study Questions

1. If the United States has an absolute advantage in the production of rubber boots, does it necessarily follow that it will also have a comparative advantage in producing rubber boots? Explain.

2. Why could a country have a comparative advantage in the production of a certain quantity of a good but a comparative disadvantage in producing larger quantities of that same good?

3. If all countries followed their comparative advantage and world output increased, who would get this increased output?

4. Does your state or province have any export industries? What are they? Does it have any import-competing industries? Which ones?

5. Since some people benefit from an increase in foreign trade while others lose, although the total benefits exceed the total losses, how could the benefits be redistributed so that everybody gains?

6. Were tariff duties as a percent of dutiable imports ever as low before as they are now? When?

7. Why do quotas result in less efficient resource use than do tariffs?

8. How could the United States take better advantage of its technological innovation?

9. Why are small countries not as likely to encounter retaliation when they increase trade restrictions as large countries are?

10. A U.S. congressman favoring trade restrictions on textile imports released figures showing that foreign-made apparel cost 97% of the average retail price for U.S.–made goods. Does this indicate that consumers would not be much affected by restrictions on imports of apparel? Explain.

Exercises in Analysis

1. Locate five imported items in stores in your area. List the items, where they were produced, what materials were used in their manufacture, and whether competing products manufactured in the United States were also available. For those items in which foreign-made and U.S. goods competed, compare the prices. If the prices differed, explain why. If the prices were identical or nearly the same, explain why.

2. Write a short paper on the impact of foreign trade on your area. Include such information as: what local businesses export all or part of their production; what local businesses are in direct competition with imported products; what local businesses use imported raw materials; and whether any local businesses provide tourist services to foreigners.

3. In the *Readers' Guide to Periodical Literature* in the library, or another source, find a recent article on U.S. trade policy. Write a short paper summarizing the article and explaining what effects the trade policies discussed are likely to have on the economy.

4. Write a brief paper arguing for or against increased protection for U.S. industries.

Further Reading

Adams, John. *International Economics: A Self-Teaching Introduction to the Basic Concepts.* 3rd ed. New York: St. Martin's Press, 1989. A programmed instruction primer on classical and modern trade theory and international finance.

Anderson, Terry L., ed. *NAFTA and the Environment.* San Francisco: Pacific Research Institute for Public Policy, 1993. Attempts to evaluate the environmental impacts stemming from the agreement and its effect on trade and resources.

Batra, Ravi. *The Myth of Free Trade: A Plan for America's Economic Revival.* New York: C. Scribner's Sons, 1993. Batra takes a contrarian view of the effects of free trade on the U.S. economy. "Few realize that the cause of America's unprecedented economic debacle is the policy of free trade" in his opinion. He advocates an increase in average tariffs from 5% to 40%.

Bhagwati, Jagdish N. *Political Economy and International Economics.* Cambridge, MA: MIT Press, 1991. Written by perhaps the most prolific economist writing in the field of international economics, this book covers the theory and policy of free trade versus protectionism.

Friman, H. Richard. *Patchwork Protectionism: Textile Trade Policy in the United States, Japan, and West Germany.* Ithaca, New York: Cornell University Press, 1990. A case study of the use of government trade policies in three countries to shelter and promote a particular industry.

Jackson, Tim. *Japan, America, and the New European Market.* Boston: Houghton Mifflin, 1993. Focuses on the success of Japanese industrial/trade policy. Contrasts the pitfalls of European industrial policy.

Khosrow, Fatemi, ed. *North American Free Trade Agreement: Opportunities and Challenges.* New York: St. Martin's Press, 1993. Evaluates the prospective consequences of NAFTA, depending on how commercial policies are implemented.

Lawrence, Robert Z., and Charles L. Schultze, eds. *An American Trade Strategy: Options for the 1990s.* Washington, DC: Brookings Institution, 1990. The arguments for free trade versus protectionism in contemporary U.S. trade policy are examined in this scholarly work.

Leuenberger, Theodor, and Martin E. Weinstein, eds. *Europe, Japan, and America in the 1990s: Cooperation and Competition.* New York: Springer-Verlag, 1992. A look at economic relations among the three centers of world economic power, viewed from a number of different perspectives.

Lincoln, Edward J. *Japan's Unequal Trade.* Washington, DC: Brookings Institution, 1990. How Japan maintains a favorable trade balance with the United States through a variety of nontariff barriers to trade.

Low, Patrick. *Trading Free: The GATT and U.S. Trade Policy.* New York: Twentieth Century Fund Press, 1993. An examination of the trade policy disputes in the Uruguay Round and the goals of U.S. commercial policy.

Saborio, Sylvia, ed. *The Premise and the Promise: Free Trade in the Americas*. New Brunswick, NJ: Transaction Publishers, 1992. How the liberalizing of trade measures in an American trading bloc will affect the economies of Latin America and United States.

Thurow, Lester C. *Head to Head: The Coming Economic Battle among Japan, Europe, and America*. New York: William Morrow, 1992. One of the best-known contemporary economists examines the changing nature of international economic relations and how the nation should respond.

U.S. National Commission for Employment Policy. *The Employment Effects of the North American Free Trade Agreement: Recommendations and Background Studies*. Washington, DC: National Commission for Employment Policy, 1992. Studies concerning the impacts on jobs of North American economic integration.

Yoffie, David B., ed. *Beyond Free Trade: Firms, Governments, and Global Competition*. Boston, MA: Harvard Business School Press, 1993. This study finds that patterns of international trade result from five factors: traditional production advantages in an industry, the international structure of the industry, specific characteristics of multinational firms, government policy, and the inertia of history.

16. International Finance and the National Economy

■ **International transactions** impact the domestic economy in a variety of ways. The effects can be positive or negative—or both, depending on your viewpoint. The following introductory article takes a satirical look at the contradictions posed by international transactions, with the help of Lewis Carroll's familiar characters.

Alice in the Wonderland of International Finance

According to the *Economist,* a British journal of political economy, there are only some 600 people in the world who really understand how the international monetary system works. The editors of the *Economist* believe that it is unfortunate that the rest of us don't take more interest in the subject because it "affects everybody's everyday lives. What happens to exchange rates, trade, interest rates, and debt translates into jobs, the safety of a nest egg, the cost of a foreign holiday. For millions, it can mean the difference between tolerable and intolerable poverty" (*Economist,* October 5, 1985, p. 5).

What the magazine does not reveal is that, in addition to the 600 academic economists, government officials, and commercial moneymen, there is another "expert" on the workings of the international monetary system—a little girl by the name of Alice who learned the secrets of international finance while on a visit to Wonderland, one of the few places where it is understood.

The subject first came to Alice's attention when the Queen of Hearts announced that her land would make war on the Land of the Rising Sun. The reason for the war, it seemed, was that the Land of the Rising Sun was sending them too many things.

"Are these things it is sending you things that you don't want?" asked Alice.

"Don't ask impudent questions, little girl," said the Queen.

The helpful White Rabbit pulled on Alice's sleeve and whispered in her ear, "Oh, no, we like the things they send us very much. They are better than the things we have here, but they are sending too many things and won't take enough from us in return."

Alice thought this a peculiar reason for starting a war, but before she could ask any more questions, the Dormouse came running up, all out of breath, exclaiming, "The dollar is sinking. The dollar is sinking."

Upon hearing this news, some of those in attendance cheered and others moaned. The March Hare scampered off to see his broker.

"Why is the dollar sinking?" inquired Alice.

"Don't ask stupid questions," said the Queen. "The dollar is sinking because of the floating exchange rate system."

"Oh, dear," said Alice, "I hope no one is hurt when the dollar sinks."

"Lots of people will be hurt," replied the King, gleefully. "The importers will get killed. So much the worse for them. Consumers will have to pay more for all of those things from the Land of the Rising Sun and won't be able to afford them. So much the worse for them. Producers will have to pay more for imported raw materials and will have to raise their selling prices. So much the worse for them."

"But that is terrible," Alice said. "What caused the dollar to sink? Can't we rescue it?"

"Get that ninny of a girl out of my sight," screamed the Queen, "or I'll have her head."

The White Rabbit took Alice aside where he could explain to her the facts of international exchange rate policy. "We purposely caused the dollar to sink so that we would have to pay more for the things we get from the Land of the Rising Sun and other lands," he said. "The other lands will, of course, pay less for what we send them. They weren't very happy about it, but we threatened them with a trade war if they didn't go along. So the finance ministers of the other six lands in the Group of Seven agreed to cooperate with us in sinking the dollar."

"How do you sink the dollar?" asked Alice.

"The Queen was right. You are a ninny," said the Rabbit. "You sink the dollar by floating more of them. The more dollars you float, the lower the dollar sinks."

"This all gets curiouser and curiouser," thought Alice. "Everything in the World of International Finance seems to be upside-down."

Just then she heard a commotion and went to see what the cause of it was. There was the Queen, purple with rage, shouting "Cut off their heads! Cut off their heads!"

"Oh, my, whose head does she want to cut off now?" asked Alice.

"She has proof that the foreign exporters of hats are being subsidized by their governments to sell us hats below their costs of production," responded the Gryphon. "It has made the Queen furious and the Mad Hatter even madder."

"But if they are selling us hats below the costs of producing them, aren't they giving us something for nothing?" puzzled Alice. "Shouldn't we thank them instead of cutting off their heads?"

"You might at first think so," replied the Gryphon, "but if we took their low-priced hats, what would the Mad Hatter do?"

"Couldn't he make something else that no one wants to give us?" asked Alice.

The Gryphon, normally quite polite, looked at her with visible disdain. "But then he wouldn't be the Mad Hatter anymore, would he?

"Oh, my," sighed Alice. "I don't think that I will ever understand international finance. The more you have to pay for something, the better. If people outside your land want to give you something, they should have their heads cut off. If they send you too much of what you want, you declare war on them. If your currency floats too high, you try to sink it. It seems to me that

■ **Chapter Preview**

■ **Chapter Preview**

The Cheshire cat was smiling at the contradictions in our attitudes and policies with regard to international trade and finance. These contradictions are partly inherent in the problems posed by the foreign sector of the economy. But they are also in part the result of a lack of understanding of how the international financial system works and how it impacts the national economy. This chapter will attempt to make it more understandable by covering the following questions: How do we pay for imports? What happens when exports and imports do not balance? What is the relationship between international finance and the national economy?

■ **Learning Objectives**

After completing this chapter, you should be able to:

1. Explain how payments are made for imports.

2. Distinguish between fixed and freely fluctuating exchange rates and explain how the rate of exchange is determined under each system.

3. Differentiate between currency depreciation, currency appreciation, devaluation, and revaluation.

4. Define balance of payments and list the different accounts in the balance of payments.

5. Distinguish between a favorable and an unfavorable balance of trade.

6. Explain basic deficit and the role of the residual accounts in the balance of payments.

7. Explain national economic equilibrium and illustrate with a schematic GDP tank diagram.

8. Show how an import surplus allows the economy to consume more than it produces.

9. Describe the role of foreign investment in compensating for insufficient domestic savings and taxes.

in the World of International Finance nothing is the way it's supposed to be."

At this, she heard a chuckle. Turning in the direction from which it came, Alice saw the Cheshire cat grinning at her from the bough of a tree. "When you understand that, you understand everything there is to know about international finance." said the cat. Having pronounced that bit of wisdom, the cat grinned even wider and gradually began to disappear, from its tail forward, until all that was left behind was its smile.

How Do We Pay for Imports?

One answer to the question, "How do we pay for imports?" is that we pay for imports with exports. But, although bartering is more common in international trade than in domestic trade, most imports are paid for with a medium of exchange. The problem is that a different medium of exchange and a different unit of measurement are used in each country: dollars in the United States, pounds in the United Kingdom, marks in Germany, and yen in Japan. How can importers pay in their currency and exporters receive payment at the same time in theirs?

▓ **Foreign Exchange Market**

The conversion of U.S. dollars into foreign currency occurs in the **foreign exchange market**. Here the price of any one money in terms of another is set either by market forces of demand and supply, or by government price-

---

foreign exchange market: a set of institutions, including large banks in the world's financial centers, private brokers, and government central banks and other agencies, that deal in the exchange of one country's money for another's.

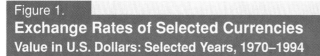

Figure 1.

Exchange Rates of Selected Currencies
Value in U.S. Dollars: Selected Years, 1970–1994

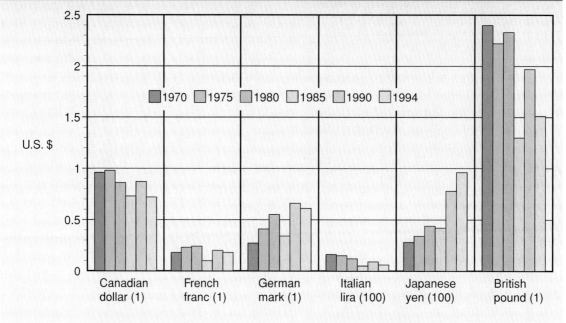

Source: Board of Governors of the Federal Reserve System, *Federal Reserve Bulletin*.

■ Since the system of fixed exchange rates was abandoned in the early 1970s, currency exchange rates have fluctuated widely. The exchange rates are dependent on foreign trade and investments.

fixing, or by a combination of both. Once the price has been set, a foreign currency can be bought very easily through a bank.

Local banks obtain foreign money from centrally located **correspondent banks** that deal in the foreign exchange market. These are generally the larger banks in principal trading centers such as New York, London, Frankfurt, and Tokyo. Such banks supply their customers and other banks with foreign money from balances they hold abroad. For example, the Chase Manhattan Bank may have an account with the Midlands Bank in London. If an American cloth importer needs British pounds to pay for a shipment of En-

correspondent bank: a bank in another city or country that a bank has an arrangement with to provide deposit transfer or other services.

glish woolens, the Chase Manhattan Bank will sell the importer some pounds in its London account. The American importer can use these pounds to pay the British exporter. The account balance held in Britain by the Chase bank was created by payments made by Britons for U.S. goods or in settlement of accounts owed to American citizens from other transactions.

Exchange Rates

The foreign exchange rate expresses the price of one money in terms of another. Like any price, an exchange rate may vary in the free play of market forces. For example, the British pound was priced at $2.40 in 1970. It declined to $1.30 in 1985, and in 1994 it was worth approximately $1.50.

Exchange rates were not always allowed to fluctuate in that fashion. From the end of World War II to the early 1970s, the major

TUESDAY, AUGUST 9, 1994

Currency	Foreign Currency in Dollars Tue.	Mon.	Dollars in Foreign Currency Tue.	Mon.
f-Argent (Peso)	1.0100	1.0100	.9901	.9901
Australia (Dollar)	.7440	.7412	1.3441	1.3492
Austria (Schilling)	.0899	.0897	11.127	11.145
c-Belgium (Franc)	.0306	.0307	32.63	32.60
Brazil(Real)	1.1111	1.0989	.9000	.9100
Britain (Pound)	1.5375	1.5380	.6504	.6502
30-day fwd	1.5367	1.5372	.6507	.6505
60-day fwd	1.5359	1.5362	.6511	.6510
90-day fwd	1.5350	1.5352	.6515	.6514
Canada (Dollar)	.7283	.7262	1.3730	1.3770
30-day fwd	.7278	.7256	1.3740	1.3781
60-day fwd	.7274	.7251	1.3748	1.3791
90-day fwd	.7270	.7247	1.3755	1.3799
y-Chile (Peso)	.002437	.002417	410.35	413.72
China (Yuan)	.1162	.1164	8.6023	8.5899
Colombia (Peso)	.001231	.001226	812.57	815.62
c-CzechRep(Koruna)	.0353	.0352	28.30	28.44
Denmark (Krone)	.1602	.1606	6.2420	6.2270
ECU	1.20710	1.21070	.8284	.8260
z-Ecudr (Sucre)	.000453	.000456	2207.02	2192.02
d-Egypt (Pound)	.2961	.2961	3.3775	3.3775
Finland (Mark)	.1925	.1919	5.1935	5.2120
France (Franc)	.1846	.1843	5.4170	5.4255
Germany (Mark)	.6323	.6309	1.5815	1.5850
30-day fwd	.6321	.6307	1.5821	1.5856
60-day fwd	.6320	.6306	1.5822	1.5857
90-day fwd	.6321	.6306	1.5821	1.5857
Greece (Drachma)	.004188	.004184	238.80	239.00
Hong Kong (Dollar)	.1294	.1294	7.7252	7.7250
Hungary (Forint)	.0091	.0091	109.52	109.90
y-India (Rupee)	.0319	.0319	31.350	31.350
Indnsia (Rupiah)	.000463	.000462	2161.04	2165.02
Ireland (Punt)	1.5208	1.5215	.6575	.6572
Israel (Shekel)	.3298	.3298	3.0320	3.0320
Italy (Lira)	.000631	.000631	1586.00	1586.00
Japan (Yen)	.009875	.009830	101.27	101.73
30-day fwd	.009896	.009851	101.05	101.51
60-day fwd	.009916	.009871	100.85	101.31
90-day fwd	.009941	.009893	100.59	101.08
Jordan (Dinar)	1.4704	1.4725	.68009	.67912

Currency	Foreign Currency in Dollars Tue.	Mon.	Dollars in Foreign Currency Tue.	Mon.
Lebanon (Pound)	.000597	.000596	1675.00	1676.50
Malaysia (Ringgit)	.3880	.3873	2.5770	2.5820
z-Mexico (Peso)	.295421	.295334	3.3850	3.3860
N. Zealand (Dollar)	.6001	.6041	1.6664	1.6554
Nethrinds(Guilder)	.5618	.5620	1.7800	1.7795
Norway (Krone)	.1444	.1445	6.9270	6.9210
Pakistan (Rupee)	.0326	.0328	30.53	30.53
y-Peru (New Sol)	.4651	.4695	2.150	2.130
z-Phlpins (Peso)	.0384	.0383	26.03	26.10
Poland (Zloty)	.000044	.000044	22906	22906
Portugal (Escudo)	.006223	.006223	160.69	160.70
a-Russia (Ruble)	.000479	.000485	2087.00	2060.00
Saudi Arab (Riyal)	.2667	.2666	3.7500	3.7503
Singapore (Dollar)	.6645	.6644	1.5050	1.5052
So. Africa (Rand)	.0316	.0316	31.69	31.69
f-So. Africa(Rand)	.2773	.2770	3.6065	3.6100
f-So.Africa(Rand)	.2183	.2186	4.5800	4.5750
So. Korea (Won)	.001242	.001244	805.10	803.90
Spain (Peseta)	.007692	.007678	130.00	130.25
Sweden (Krona)	.1285	.1291	7.7810	7.7475
Switzerlnd (Franc)	.7485	.7485	1.3360	1.3360
30-day fwd	.7483	.7483	1.3364	1.3364
60-day fwd	.7481	.7480	1.3368	1.3369
90-day fwd	.7476	.7475	1.3376	1.3378
Taiwan (NT $)	.0378	.0378	26.46	26.48
Thailand (Baht)	.03994	.04005	25.04	24.97
Turkey (Lira)	.000032	.000032	31308.66	31251.72
U.A.E. (Dirham)	.2723	.2723	3.6727	3.6727
f-Uruguay (Peso)	.198020	.200000	5.05	5.00
z-Venzuel (Bolivar)	.0053	.0053	190.0000	187.0000

ECU: European Currency Unit, a basket of European currencies.
The Federal Reserve Board's index of the value of the dollar against
10 other currencies weighted on the basis of trade was 89.94
Tuesday, off 0.10 points or 0.11 percent from Monday's 90.04. A
year ago the index was 94.47
  a-fixing, Moscow Interbank Currency Exchange
  c-commercial rate, d-free market rate, f-financial rate, y-official
  rate, z-floating rate.
  Prices as of 3:00 p.m. Eastern Time from Telerate Systems and
other sources.

■ The exchange rates of currencies on the international market change daily in response to the forces of demand and supply. This newspaper clipping shows one day's values of various currencies in relation to the U.S. dollar.

Western countries maintained a system of **fixed exchange rates**. For the system to work, each country had to accept or supply money at the fixed rate. If a nation ran short of a particular foreign money, it could resort to short-term loans from the **International Monetary Fund (IMF)** to maintain the fixed price. But because of chronic imbalances in the demand and supply of various countries' currencies (especially the U.S. dollar), the system of fixed rates was abandoned.

The opposite of a fixed-rate system is one of **freely fluctuating exchange rates** that vary daily in response to demand and supply. With such rates, increased demand for a foreign money results in a rise in its price in terms of domestic currency. Conversely, increased supplies of a particular national currency depress its price. Such price changes increase the uncertainty and risk of international transactions.

If the supply of a country's currency in the foreign exchange market is greater than the demand for that currency, the currency will depreciate. Depreciation means that a unit of the country's currency will buy less of other currencies than it did previously. One common reason for **currency depreciation** is domestic inflation. If the general level of prices is going up faster in one country than in others, that country will find it difficult to export goods, while at the same time it will be importing more from overseas. This results in a surplus of the country's currency on the foreign exchange market, which lowers its exchange rate value. The opposite of depreciation is **currency appreciation**, an increase in the foreign value of currency.

Under a fixed exchange rate system, with exchange rates set by the government, a lowering of the exchange rate by government regulation is a **devaluation**. If the government raises the exchange rate of its currency under a fixed exchange rate system, that is termed **revaluation**.

Even under a freely fluctuating exchange rate system, government central banks may attempt to control exchange rate movements

(Continued on page 422) ⟹

---

fixed exchange rates: exchange rates between currencies that are legally set by the respective countries.

International Monetary Fund (IMF): an organization established in 1946 to assist in operation of the world monetary system by regulating the exchange practices of countries and providing liquidity to member countries that have payment problems.

freely fluctuating exchange rates: an exchange-rate system by which the relative values of different currencies are determined by demand and supply rather than by government fiat.

currency depreciation: a decline in the value of a country's currency relative to other currencies as a result of an increase in its supply relative to the demand for it.

currency appreciation: an increase in the value of a country's currency relative to other currencies as a result of a decrease in its supply relative to the demand for it.

devaluation: a decrease in the value of a country's currency relative to other currencies due to an official government reduction in the exchange rate under a fixed-rate system.

revaluation: an increase in the value of a country's currency relative to other currencies due to an official government increase in the exchange rate under a fixed-rate system.

The Hunt for the Elusive Ecu

Have you ever seen an ecu? Before you answer, you should be warned that this is a trick question—no one has ever seen an ecu. But that does not mean they do not exist; they most assuredly do.

The ecu is the European Currency Unit. It was established in 1981 as the official unit of account (unit of measurement) for the members of the European Community (EC). It was originally intended only to serve administrative purposes in defining the relationships among the various EC currencies. But the ecu has proved so useful in financial markets that the value of business dealings transacted in ecus has now reached the hundreds of billions. This includes mortgages, life insurance policies, traveler's checks, certificates of deposit, corporate and government bonds, and even

Table 1.	Value of the European Currency Unit June 10, 1994		
Currency	ECU Ratio	$ Exchange Rate	ECU $ Value
British pound	0.08784	1.509	0.1326
Danish krone	0.1976	0.154	0.0304
French franc	1.332	0.176	0.2344
Greek drachma	1.440	0.00399	0.0057
Irish pound	0.00852	1.468	0.0125
Italian lira	151.8	0.00062	0.0941
Dutch guilder	0.2198	0.535	0.1176
Deutsche mark	0.6242	0.600	0.3745
Belgian franc	3.301	0.029	0.0957
Luxembourg franc	0.130	0.029	0.0038
Spanish peseta	6.885	0.0073	0.0503
Portuguese escudo	1.393	0.0058	0.0081
	Value of the ecu in U.S. dollars		$1.1597

Visa and MasterCard payments, all denominated in ecus. The menu of Luxembourg's elegant La Gaichel restaurant goes so far as to list the prices of its dishes in ecus rather than Luxembourg francs.

The worth of an ecu is determined by a basket of the EC currencies, each one contributing a fraction of the ecu's value. The amount of each currency that goes into determining the value of the ecu is shown in Table 1.

Column 2 shows the ratio of the column 1 currency that is used in making up the ecu. To get the ecu value in any particular currency, say, the U.S. dollar, the ratio of each currency in the basket is multiplied times its current dollar exchange rate, and the results are added. Column 3 shows the U.S. dollar exchange rate for the EC currencies on June 10, 1994. The ecu ratio in column 2 times the exchange rate in column 3 is shown in column 4. The sum of the ratios times the individual exchange rates gives the ecu/dollar exchange rate. On June 10, 1994, the ecu was worth approximately $1.16.

The values of the individual EC currencies are maintained at a rate fixed to the ecu, with a possible fluctuation of plus or minus 15%. If any currency deviates from its fixed ecu value by more than that, the EC central banks must intervene to bring the currency's value back to the par value determined by the ecu basket formula. This helps to eliminate the uncertainty of exchange rate instability for EC businesses and investors.

The ecu has been useful as a unit of measurement for trade and investments among the EC countries. But with the signing of the 1993 Maastricht treaty by the members of the EC—now called the European Union (EU) in some quarters—they have agreed to have a common European currency, a true unit of exchange, by 1997 at the earliest or 1999 at the latest. If their plan is not sabotaged by recession, inflation, or divergent domestic monetary policies in the member countries, you may actually see an ecu before the end of the century.

Economic Reasoning

1. Why is the ecu ratio so much larger for the Italian lira than it is for the French franc? (Hint: compare their exchange rates.)

2. What could cause the peseta to depreciate more than 15%? What could the central banks do to bring it back to its ecu par value as determined by the ecu formula?

3. If a North American Economic Community evolves from NAFTA, should the dollar be replaced by a nacu (North American Currency Unit)? Why or why not?

■ The stamp shown here presents a glimpse of the probable future of economic cooperation in Europe. When Italy issued this 500-lira stamp to commemorate the elections for the 12-member European Parliament in 1989, it printed the stamp's equivalent value in ecus. Europe does not yet have a single currency, and thus ecus are still a technical measure rather than a spendable currency. Still, the European Union is working toward monetary union, and the ecu may well soon supplement, or even supplant, the British pound, German mark, French franc, and other national currencies.

■ The imports that this ship brings to the United States are represented by the flow marked M on the GDP tank diagram (Figure 3) on page 427. To continue the metaphor used in the text, by floating more dollars a country can increase its exports.

▥▶ *(Continued from page 419)*

within limits or otherwise manipulate the rate. For example, if a country's currency is exchanging at such a high rate that it hurts exports, as was the case with the U.S. dollar in the mid-1980s, the central bank may lower the rate by selling its own currency on the foreign exchange market. As the White Rabbit explained to Alice in the chapter introduction, the added supply floated on the market results in lowering the currency's exchange rate.

What Happens When Exports and Imports Do Not Balance?

Under a system of freely fluctuating exchange rates, the exchange rate for a currency is determined by the demand for and supply of that currency in the foreign exchange market. If a country's international transactions are out of balance, the exchange rate for the country's currency will be unstable.

balance of payments: an annual summary of all economic transactions between a country and the rest of the world during the year.

Balance of Payments

The accounting record of all international transactions between the residents of one country and the residents of the rest of the world is the country's **balance of payments**. When a country imports something, the cost shows up in its balance of payments. Similarly, when a country exports something, the receipts from the sale are recorded in the balance of payments (see Table 2).

The balance of payments is divided into different types of transactions. The imports

Table 2. Simplified Hypothetical Balance of Payments for Country A for a Given Year (Billions of Dollars)

Credit Items		Debit Items	
(Foreign earnings by Country A)		(Liabilities of Country A to Foreigners)	
Current Account		Current Account	
Exports of merchandise	$224	Imports of merchandise	$249
Tourist expenditures in Country A	22	Country A tourist expenditures abroad	30
Earnings from investments abroad	75	Earnings by foreign investments in Country A	33
Military and economic aid from abroad	0	Military and economic aid to other countries	17
Capital Account		Capital Account	
New Foreign investments in Country A	20	New investments by Country A abroad	45
Basic Balance Total	$341	Basic Balance Total	$374

Basic deficit ($374 − $341) = $33

Residual Account			
New bank deposits by foreigners in Country A	$30		
Gold exports	1		
International Monetary Fund loan	2		
Balance Items Total	$33		
Balance of Payments Total	$374	Balance of Payments Total	$374

and exports of goods and services are recorded in the **current account** section of the balance of payments. Take, for example, the importation of French cheese. This is a merchandise import in the current account section. The difference between merchandise imports and merchandise exports is the **balance of trade**. If merchandise exports during the year are greater than merchandise imports, the balance of trade is said to be **favorable**. If imports are greater than exports, the balance of trade is said to be **unfavorable.**

But the current account includes more than just merchandise trade. It also includes services. One major type of service "import" is foreign travel. If the French cheese had been consumed by an American tourist in a Paris café, the effect on the U.S. balance of payments would have been the same as if it had been imported. The consumption of the cheese gave rise to a foreign claim on American dol-

lars, which in this case would presumably have to be paid before the tourist left the café.

Military assistance, foreign aid, government remittances, and private gifts are special types of current transactions for which there may be no actual material import. The "import" may be national security or goodwill. But note the basic rule: if it results in a money outflow, it is an import-type transaction. Profits, dividends, and

current account: those transactions in the balance of payments consisting of merchandise and service imports and exports and unilateral transfers (gifts).

balance of trade: the net deficit or surplus in a country's merchandise trade; the difference between merchandise imports and exports.

favorable balance of trade: the surplus in a country's merchandise trade when exports during the year are greater than imports.

unfavorable balance of trade: the deficit in a country's merchandise trade when imports during the year are greater than exports.

interest earned by Americans on foreign assets are export-type transactions. What is exported is the use of American capital.

International Capital Flows

At the time when capital is transferred abroad, it appears in the balance of payments in the **long-term** or **short-term capital** accounts. The long-term capital account summarizes the flow of public and private investment into and out of the country. This includes only those new investments undertaken during the year. If an American firm builds a plant abroad or if an individual buys stock in a foreign company, these are import-type transactions.

The short-term capital account consists of liquid funds transferred from one country to another, such as transfers of bank deposits. The greater part of this type of transfer consists of money payments for merchandise, service, and investment transactions. The purchase of English woolens in the example on page 418 constituted an import entry in the U.S. current account. Then when the U.S. importer paid the British exporter by transferring funds to the exporter from an account at the Midlands Bank in London, an export-type entry in the U.S. short-term capital account occurred. The two entries offset each other in the balance of payments.

In the sense that for every transaction there is an import or export on one side of the balance of payments and an offsetting transfer of the payment on the other side, the balance of payments always balances. What, then, is meant by a deficit or a surplus in the balance of payments? The current account transac-

■ Whether a U.S. citizen eats this French cheese as a tourist in a Paris café or buys it in the imported-cheese section of an American supermarket, the effect on the U.S. balance of payments will be the same. Consumption of the cheese gives rise to a foreign claim on American dollars.

tions, the long-term capital account transactions, and certain short-term capital account transactions, such as foreigners investing in U.S. money market funds, are considered spontaneous transactions motivated by market conditions. If a country's total import-type payments are greater than its total export-type receipts for these transactions, the difference is the country's **basic deficit**. It is this deficit that we read about in the newspapers.

The balance of payments system has two means to offset a basic deficit and bring the accounts into balance. Either foreigners can, in effect, extend credit to the deficit country by holding larger amounts of the country's currency, which are in the nature of IOUs, or the deficit can be covered by an export of gold. Short-term capital and gold movements constitute the **residual accounts** that bring the balance of payments into balance. If the deficit country does not have gold to export and foreigners are not willing to accept more of its money, it can turn to the International Monetary Fund for a loan to temporarily solve its balance of payments problem while it attempts to eliminate its basic deficit.

Under a freely fluctuating exchange rate system, the existence of a basic deficit results in a depreciation of the country's currency. An excess of imports over exports results in more of the country's currency going into the foreign exchange market than is demanded. As a result of the excess supply, the exchange rate falls. The lower exchange rate helps to eliminate the basic deficit by increasing exports and decreasing imports.

long-term capital: direct investment in plant and equipment or portfolio investments in stocks and bonds.

short-term capital: transfers of demand deposits or liquid investments such as money market funds, CDs, or Treasury bills.

basic deficit: the excess of import-type transactions over export-type transactions in a country's current, long-term capital and noninduced, short-term capital movements in the balance of payments.

residual accounts: the short-term capital transfers and monetary gold transactions that compensate for the imbalance in a country's basic balance in its international payments.

The World's Biggest Debtor

The United States was once creditor to the world. It provided more investment capital to other countries than any nation. Now it is the world's biggest debtor. No other country, not even the big debtor countries in Latin America and Eastern Europe, has a bigger net foreign deficit.

It was only in 1989 that the United States became a net debtor for the first time since 1914. During all the intervening years, as befits a prosperous, capital-rich nation, the country had lent abroad much more than it borrowed. Countries in need of more investment capital than they could muster from their domestic sources borrowed from the United States in various ways. There was private capital flow to other countries in the form of direct investment by U.S. companies in foreign subsidiaries. There was additional private lending by means of purchases of foreign stocks and bonds, as well as commercial bank loans to foreign firms or governments. Besides these private capital flows, the U.S. government lent to less developed countries both directly and through international lending agencies.

In 1982, however, the positive net foreign asset position of the United States began to decline as a result of rising foreign investment in this country relative to U.S. investment abroad. Up to 1989 the total amount of foreign assets held by U.S. residents, valued at market value, was greater than the total claims by foreigners against the assets of this country. Since then the United States has had an increasing net foreign debt (see Figure 2). The reasons were the large balance-of-trade deficits run up by the United States and the attractiveness of U.S. securities to foreign investors.

These two causes were related. The low savings rate in the United States resulted in a high propensity to consume, including the consumption of imported goods. This resulted in growing trade deficits. The low savings rate and large government budget deficits also meant high interest rates, which made U.S. securities attractive to foreign investors. The United States has long been a desirable place for foreigners to invest their funds because of its political stability.

In a sense, then, the increasing foreign debt of the United States was due in part to the strength of its economy rather than its weakness—foreigners wanted to invest here because returns were greater and more secure. For the United States, the inflow of foreign capital was very useful in helping to finance its record federal budget deficits, compensating for the low savings rate of the U.S. population. Foreigners increased their holdings of U.S. Treasury securities from $296.3 billion in 1987 to $560.6 billion in 1992, helping to finance our growing federal budget deficits in those years.

Nevertheless, it created an uneasy situation because foreign funds can be withdrawn very rapidly if the outlook changes. If there were a flight of capital from the country, the international value of the dollar would come tumbling down, and a shortage of domestic capital would make it difficult for the government and businesses to raise money, driving interest rates higher. The danger of that happening became more apparent when a crisis in the Middle East caused foreign capital to flow out of the country rather than flowing in, as was customary in previous world crises. With its large government and foreign deficits and the deteriorating value of the dollar, the

Figure 2.

U.S. International Investment Position, 1984–1992

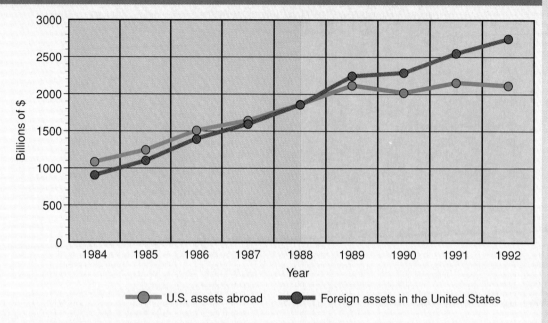

Source: U.S. Department of Commerce, Bureau of Economic Analysis.

■ Between 1914 and 1988 the United States was a net creditor with respect of the rest of the world (green shaded area). Since then, its net obligation to foreign investors has grown rapidly (red shaded area).

United States no longer appeared to be the safe haven for world capital that it had been in the past.

Economic Reasoning

1. How do foreign investments in the United States affect the U.S. balance of payments? If Table 2 (see p. 423) was the balance-of-payments statement for the United States, in what account would the sales of Treasury securities to foreign buyers appear?

2. How will the earnings of foreigners on their U.S. investments affect the exchange rate of the dollar in the future? Why?

3. Is it a good thing to have foreigners finance part of our federal budget deficits? Why or why not?

What Is the Relationship between International Finance and the National Economy?

In chapter 12 we examined the conditions of national economic equilibrium when we considered the domestic sectors of the economy. In this analysis section, we will see how the foreign sector affects macroeconomic equilibrium.

The Foreign Sector in the National Economy

In discussing gross domestic product (chapter 12, p. 309), we noted that aggregate demand was the sum of consumer demand (C), investment demand (I), government demand (G),

and net foreign demand (X − M). The first three sectors were included in the GDP tank model in chapter 12 showing domestic equilibrium. Figure 3 adds the foreign sector (pictured in brown) to the three domestic sectors of the economy in the GDP tank diagram.

The amount of income that consumers and businesses allocate to imports, indicated by M, flows out of the tank into the foreign sector. The expenditures by foreigners on U.S. exports flow from the foreign sector into the GDP tank as demand for goods and services,

---

Figure 3.
GDP Tank National Income Model Including the Foreign Sector

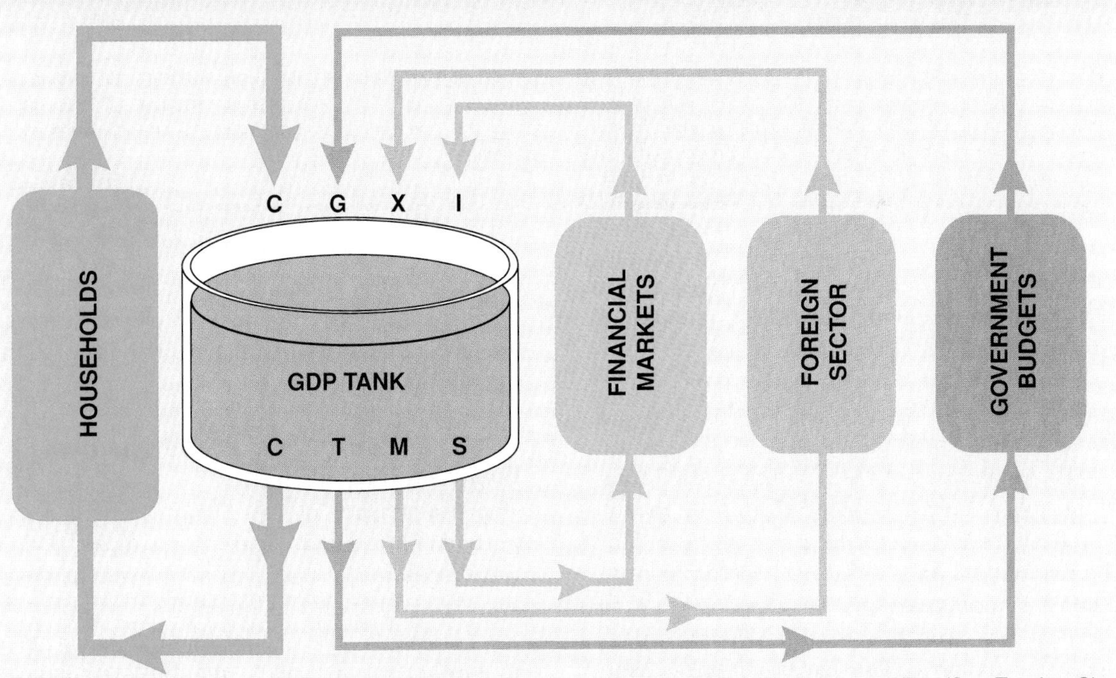

■ Economic equilibrium requires that the allocations of GDP income to savings (S), taxes (T), and imports (M) be equal to the purchasing power flowing back into the economy from investment (I), government spending (G), and exports (X). In the United States in recent years, the amount of savings and taxes has been less than investment and government spending (S + T < I + G). The difference has been compensated by an excess of imports over exports (M > X), so that savings, taxes, and imports together equal the total of investment, government spending, and exports (S + T + M = I + G + X).

Figure 4.

Foreign Sector Financing of U.S. Domestic Deficits

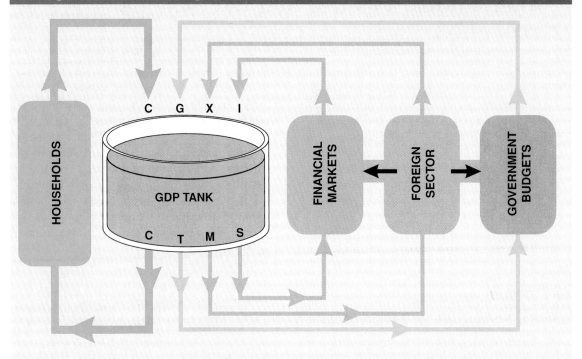

■ There is more income going to the foreign sector from imports (M) than is being returned to the economy in export demand (X). The excess dollars in the foreign sector (brown) are invested in U.S. private financial markets (green) and U.S. Treasury securities (red). The import surplus has permitted the economy to consume (including I and G) more than it produces. It also has been the source of foreign capital to finance domestic deficits.

shown by X. As was the case with the investment and government sectors, the amount of purchasing power flowing out of the economy for imports is not necessarily the same as the amount of purchasing power flowing into the economy for export purchases.

If the balance of trade is unfavorable, as it has been for the United States in recent years, there are more dollars flowing out of the economy into the foreign sector in payment for imports than there are flowing into the economy from the foreign sector in payment for exports. The excess dollars accumulated by foreigners could be held as deposit balances in U.S. banks. Or they could be used to buy monetary gold. But most of the excess dollars from the foreign sector have been used for capital investment in the United States. They have been used

to buy securities, both government and private, and to purchase or create real assets such as office buildings, chemical plants, and automobile factories.

▓▓▓ The Foreign Sector and National Economic Equilibrium

The economy is in equilibrium when aggregate demand equals aggregate supply (review the discussion of equilibrium output in chapter 12, pp. 318–321). Considering only the domestic sectors, the U.S. economy has not been in equilibrium for some time. Saving has been less than investment and taxes have been less than government spending. As a result, the amount of funds flowing into the investment and government sectors has been less than the amounts flowing from those sectors into the demand for goods and services.

■ Outflow from the foreign sector into U.S. financial markets consists of investments in corporate stocks and bonds, as well as direct investments in new plants and equipment and the acquisition of existing companies.

The difference between the amounts allocated to savings and taxes and the total of investment and government spending (S + T < I + G) has been made up by an excess of imports over exports (M > X). In other words, the U.S. import surplus has compensated for the deficiency in our savings and taxes. This results in savings, taxes, and imports equaling investment, government spending, and exports (S + T + M = I + G + X). Since aggregate demand (I + G + X) equals aggregate supply (S + T + M), the national economy is in equilibrium.

The United States has been living beyond its means, consuming and investing more than it has been producing. But the foreign sector has balanced the domestic sectors. Foreigners made it possible for aggregate demand to exceed aggregate supply in the domestic sectors by sending us more goods and services

than we send them and lending the accumulated dollars back to us to finance our deficits.

This process is shown in Figure 4. A portion of the funds flowing out of the economy in payments for imports (the M outflow from the bottom of the tank) are channeled from the foreign sector into U.S. financial markets (the green sector) and into financing government deficits (red). The flow to the private sector consists of both portfolio investments in corporate stocks and bonds and direct investments in new plant and equipment, as well as the acquisition of existing companies and other real assets. The flow into the government sector consists principally of the purchase of U.S. Treasury securities.

These investments compensated for the imbalance in aggregate demand and supply in the domestic sectors of the economy. The import surpluses gave rise to dollar balances in

Table 3.   Foreign Direct Investments in the United States, 1991

Country	Total Investments ($ millions)
United Kingdom	106,064
Japan	86,658
Netherlands	63,848
Canada	30,002
Germany	28,171
Switzerland	17,594
Other Europe	42,450
Other Areas	32,790

Source: U.S. Bureau of Economic Analysis, *Survey of Current Business.*

■ Foreign investments in the United States have played an important role in compensating for domestic spending in excess of savings and taxes.

the hands of foreigners. When those dollars were invested, they paid for our excess domestic spending. The American banking system can create money to finance investments and fund government deficits, as we discovered in chapter 10 (p. 263). But the banking system cannot provide the economy with additional resources and products that allow us to consume (including I and G) more than we produce. Only the foreign sector can do that.

Although the Queen of Hearts in the introductory story wanted to make war on the Land of the Rising Sun for not buying as much from us as it sold to us, the fact is that it was only by means of our import surplus that we managed to have the level of consumption, investment, and government spending that we have had in recent years. Of course, we will have to pay the piper for our excess consumption dance in the form of future interest and dividends on the foreign debt. Unless we continue increasing our foreign debt indefinitely, which the rest of the world will not permit, this will mean consuming less than we produce in the future.

Case Application

Selling America

Rockefeller Center in New York bears the name of one of the most powerful financial dynasties in American history. But there is now a different name on the ownership papers— Mitsubishi Estate Company. Mitsubishi owns the controlling interest in Rockefeller Center. Mamma Leone's restaurant, a well-known New York tourist spot, now belongs to Kyotaru Company, a Japanese restaurant firm.

These, along with such purchases as Columbia Pictures, San Francisco's Mark Hopkins Hotel, and exclusive Beverly Hills real estate, are all Japanese acquisitions. Less newsworthy but more important are sizable foreign investments in such basic industries as chemicals; glass, stone, and clay; primary metals; printing and publishing; and electrical machinery. Foreign ownership of these industries ranges from $28 billion in the machinery industry to $49 billion in the chemical industry.

Of particular concern is the amount of foreign capital invested in U.S. high-tech industries. Hitachi purchased 80% of National Advanced Systems, a manufacturer of mainframe computers, for $309 million, and TDK took over all of disk drive chip producer Silicon Systems for $200 million.

With the recession in Japan in the early 1990s and the collapse of land and other asset values there, Japanese investors were forced to contract their overseas acquisitions and even to liquidate some earlier purchases. But so long as private and government spending in the United States exceeds the amount of savings, resulting in negative trade balances, we can expect the excess dollars in the foreign exchange market to be used by overseas investors to acquire U.S. assets.

Although the focus of attention has been on Japanese acquisition of American compa-

■ Rockefeller Center, in which Mitsubishi has a controlling interest, is a towering symbol of foreign investment in United States businesses, real estate, and basic industries—the result of negative trade balances. Excess dollars in the foreign exchange market will be used in this way as long as private and government spending in the United States exceed savings and taxes.

nies and property, Japan is only in second place as a foreign owner of U.S. assets. Its investments trail far behind those of the United Kingdom (see Table 3).

The rising foreign ownership of U.S. assets has alarmed many Americans. Do foreigners have too much power over our economy? Can they use their ownership of American business to injure the country? Are we losing control of our destiny?

For the most part, these fears are groundless. The government can always intervene if there is any hostile intent. The real problem, according to economist Martin Feldstein, president of the National Bureau of Economic Research, is the effect of the low U.S. savings rate. "A trade deficit," says Feldstein, "is not an indication that a nation has low productivity or low-quality products. It is an indication that the domestic investment rate is high relative to the rate of saving. The basic accounting identity is that the trade deficit equals the excess of investment over saving. . . . We inevitably have a trade deficit if we as a nation spend more on investment than we save to finance investment."

The trade deficit finances the investment by foreigners in U.S. companies, property, and financial assets such as Treasury securities. Investments in a country by foreigners are not necessarily a bad thing. They are, in fact, necessary so long as total domestic consumption exceeds production. But a net inflow of capital is more appropriate for less developed countries (as we shall see in chapter 18) than it is for a mature industrial country such as the United States.

The meaning for the United States is that our excess consumption now might be expected to result in lower levels of consumption in the future than would otherwise be possible. But the foreign capital inflow compensates for our low savings rate by enabling the United States to invest more than our level of savings permits. The current investment financed by capital inflow means more production and consumption in the future. Part of that production, however, will be transferred to foreign investors in the form of interest and dividend payments. If the investments were financed domestically, there would be no such transfers. This is the exception to the statement in chapter 14 that "each generation's consumption levels and living standards are determined by its own output, not by the deficits of earlier generations" (p. 359).

Economic Reasoning

1. Referring to Figure 4, where did the funds come from for the Mitsubishi purchase of Rockefeller Center and the Kyotaru purchase of Mamma Leone's?

2. Does Figure 4 illustrate Martin Feldstein's statement? How?

3. Should the United States restrict foreigners from acquiring assets in this country such as businesses, real estate, and financial securities? Why or why not?

Putting It Together

■ The Cheshire Cat was smiling at the contradictions in our attitudes and policies with regard to international trade and finance. These contradictions partly are inherent in the problems posed by the foreign sector of the economy. But they are also in part the result of a lack of understanding of how the international financial system works and how it impacts the national economy.

Payments for international transactions are made through the *foreign exchange market,* which consists mainly of major banks in the financial capitals of the world, plus some other foreign exchange dealers and brokers. *Correspondent banks,* which possess deposit accounts in banks overseas, facilitate the purchase of foreign exchange.

Under the *freely fluctuating exchange rate system* currently in existence, the exchange rate for a country's currency is determined by the demand for and supply of the country's currency in the foreign exchange market. An increase in the supply of a country's currency on the exchange market will cause the currency to depreciate in value. An increase in the value of a country's currency is called *appreciation;* a decrease is called *depreciation.* Under a system of *fixed exchange rates,* governments set the rates of exchange for their currencies. If the government lowers the international value of its currency, it is *devaluation;* raising the value is *revaluation.*

The summation of foreign transactions of a country is its *balance of payments.* The net of merchandise imports and exports is the *balance of trade.* If exports are larger than imports, the balance of trade is said to be *favorable;* if imports are larger, it is *unfavorable.*

In addition to merchandise exports and imports, the balance of payments includes service exports and imports in the *current account,* foreign investments in the *long-term capital* account, and short-term capital movements and monetary gold in the *residual accounts.* When receipts from abroad in the current and long-term capital accounts are less than foreign spending, there is a *basic deficit.* This basic deficit is covered by a short-term capital inflow or gold exports so that the balance of payments balances.

Export demand added to consumption, investment, and government demand makes up aggregate demand for the nation's output. If imports exceed exports, the excess dollars in the foreign sector are used to finance foreign investments in the United States.

The economy is in equilibrium when aggregate demand equals aggregate supply. Since demand in U.S. domestic sectors has been greater than supply, the foreign sector made up the difference. Imports have been greater than exports, offsetting the deficiency in savings and taxes and making $S + T + M$ equal to $I + G + X$. The foreign sector has provided the additional resources and products that have allowed the United States to consume more than it produced. The excess dollars in the foreign sector have been channeled into investments and the purchase of U.S. Treasury securities.

Bring Back Gold?

For additional information on the gold standard, see *The International Gold Standard Re-interpreted* (1940) by W. A. Brown Jr.; *The Downfall of the Gold Standard* (1936) by C. G. Cassel; *Gold or Credit* (1965) by Francis Cassel; *The Gold Standard in Theory and Practice* (1947) by R. G. Hautrey; *Gold and the Gold Standard* (1944) by E. W. Kemmerer; *Gold and the Dollar Crisis* (1961) by Robert Triffin; *The Rise and Fall of the Gold Standard* (1934) by C. M. Webb; and *A Tool of Power: The Political History of Money* (1977) by W. Wiseley.

The extreme fluctuations of currency values under the system of freely fluctuating exchange rates (see Figure 1, p. 418) have given rise to calls for a return to the gold standard. Under the gold standard, which was in effect from the 1830s to the 1930s and in a modified form in the United States up to 1971, the value of a currency was defined by how much gold it was worth. The U.S. government specified the value of the dollar at $35 per ounce of gold. It maintained this value of the dollar by offering to both buy and sell gold at that price, thereby ensuring that the value of the dollar would be stable with respect to gold and other gold standard currencies.

Those advocating a return to the gold standard believe that it would stabilize exchange rates and prevent a return of inflation by imposing a monetary discipline on our government that the current paper money standard does not. If a country were to permit inflation, its imports would exceed its exports and the surplus of its currency on the foreign exchange market would be used by foreigners to buy its gold. The resulting drain on its gold reserves would force the government to reduce the domestic money supply and stop the inflation.

The problem with the gold standard when it was in effect was that it made the domestic economy a slave to what happened abroad. If, for example, other countries were in a recession, exports to those countries would fall. This resulted in an outflow of gold to cover the difference between export earnings and import spending. Following the "rules of the game" for the gold standard, the government would permit the outflow of gold to deflate the domestic economy. In this way, recessions would be "imported." That is basically why the worldwide depression in the 1930s put an end to the international gold standard. Governments refused to follow the rules because doing so would increase unemployment.

After the Depression, the United States continued to value its currency in gold but restricted its sales of gold only to official transactions, not to private gold dealers. Other countries valued their currencies either in terms of the dollar or the British pound. In 1971, with the foreign trade deficit threatening to deplete its gold supply, the United States first devalued the dollar and later abandoned any ties to gold, setting the U.S. dollar free to fluctuate according to demand and supply in the foreign exchange market.

For those who today advocate a return to the gold standard, it should be noted that during the time that the gold standard was in effect there were periods that were highly inflationary as well as periods of severe depression.

FOR FURTHER STUDY AND ANALYSIS

Study Questions

1. Assuming that the price of the Swiss franc is 80 cents (U.S.), if there is a large increase in the demand for Swiss watches in this country, what would you expect to happen to the franc-dollar exchange rate under a system of freely fluctuating exchange rates?

2. How does inflation affect the international value of a country's currency? Does it cause the currency to appreciate or depreciate?

3. Why does a rise in U.S. interest rates affect the foreign exchange rate of the dollar? Would it cause the dollar to appreciate or depreciate?

4. In what sense is an export surplus favorable to the exporting country? In what way might an export surplus not be favorable?

5. If a Japanese investor redeems (cashes in) a U.S. Treasury bond, is that an export-type transaction in the U.S. balance of payments or an import-type transaction? How can you tell?

6. Can a country have a surplus in its balance of trade and at the same time have a basic deficit in its balance of payments? How?

7. What determines the amount of income that consumers allocate to imports? What determines the level of exports?

8. If foreigners reduced their investments in the United States, how would this be shown in the GDP tank diagram? What effect would it have on exports and/or imports? Why?

9. Why do dollars earned by foreign exporters always return to (or never leave) the United States?

10. Under the gold standard, if the U.S. dollar was valued at $35 per ounce of gold and the French franc was 700 francs per ounce of gold, what was the exchange rate between the dollar and the franc?

Exercises in Analysis

1. Call or visit a local bank and ask if they sell bank drafts drawn in French francs. Ask what exchange rate they give. Compare the exchange rate quoted by the bank with the exchange rate listed for French francs in the *Wall Street Journal* or the business section of your newspaper. Put the information you gathered in a report along with your explanation of the difference, if any, in the exchange rate quoted by your bank and the exchange rate listed in the paper.

2. Do a report on what has happened to the foreign exchange rate of the dollar since 1994. If the exchange rate has gone up or down since then, explain why.

3. From the most recent *Economic Report of the President* or other sources, find the U.S. balance of payments for the last year reported. Write a brief analysis of the balance of trade position and the balance of payments position of the United States.

4. Make a report on the current equilibrium position of the U.S. economy. Show what has happened to the investment, government, and foreign sectors. Illustrate with a schematic GDP tank diagram.

Further Reading

Bergsten, C. Fred. *America in the World Economy: A Strategy for the 1990s.* Washington, DC: Institute for International Economics, 1988. Discusses how the current account deficit can be eliminated, domestic politics in trade policy, foreign direct investment in the United States, and international monetary reform, among other topics.

Frieden, Jeffry A. *Banking on the World: The Politics of American International Finance.* New York: Harper & Row, 1987. "International finance is the pivot around which the world economy twists and turns, and it affects politics and economics in every nation" (p. 1). Discusses the effects of foreign borrowing, the future of international finance, and the effect on American politics of international finance.

Genberg, Hans, and Alexander K. Swoboda, eds. *World Financial Markets after 1992.* New York: Kegan Paul International, 1993. A study of how the international financial system affects economies, with a particular focus on the European Economic Community.

Hormats, Robert D. *American Albatross: The Foreign Debt Dilemma.* New York: Priority Press Publications, 1988. Examines the economic conditions that have given rise to the growth of U.S. external debt since 1981. Evaluates economic policies that have caused a large increase in the foreign debt.

Kindleberger, Charles P. *The International Economic Order.* Cambridge, MA: MIT Press, 1988. Part I of the book comprises essays on the international capital and foreign exchange markets. The author discusses distress in international financial markets and whether there is going to be a global depression. Contained in Part II are essays on the European Community, economic development, and international public goods.

McKenzie, Richard B., and Dwight R. Lee. *Quicksilver Capital: How the Rapid Movement of Wealth Has Changed the World.* New York: Free Press, 1991. Discusses the effects of international capital movements and their impact on economic relations among countries.

Panic, M. *European Monetary Union: Lessons from the Classical Gold Standard.* New York: St. Martin's Press, 1992. The gold standard, although it has not been around for decades, still maintains a place in the discussions of international monetary policy in Europe. The French, in particular, are still preoccupied with gold standard considerations.

Riboud, Jacques. *A Stable External Currency for Europe.* New York: St. Martin's Press, 1991. Covers the monetary policy of the EC countries and the role of the European currency unit.

Rosow, Jerome M., ed. *The Global Marketplace.* New York: Facts on File, 1988. A collection of essays by chief executives of corporations engaged in international trade and finance.

Smith, Dale L., and James Lee Ray, eds. *The 1992 Project and the Future of Integration in Europe.* Armonk, NY: M. E. Sharp, 1993. Examines the benefits deriving from European integration and monetary policy coordination and the effect of monetary integration on business. Covers the arguments for free trade with the rest of the world versus "fortress Europe."

Solomon, Anthony M. *The Dollar, Debt, and the Trade Deficit*. New York: New York University Press, 1987. A collection of Solomon's lectures on the U.S. balance of trade, the foreign debt, and the U.S. foreign exchange problem.

Swann, Dennis, ed. *The Single European Market and Beyond: A Study of the Wider Impli-* *cations of the Single European Act*. New York: Routledge, 1992. Analyses the effects of establishing the European Monetary Union and its demands on intra-European monetary policies.

Tolchin, Martin, and Susan Tolchin. *Buying into America: How Foreign Money Is Changing the Face of Our Nation*. New York: Times Books, 1988. Examines the effects, both positive and negative, of foreign investment in the United States. Specific cases are studied to show the changes resulting from foreign investment.

Chapter 17. Alternative Economic Systems

■ **The previous chapters** have concentrated on how market economies function, in particular that of the United States. This chapter deals with economic systems that are structured differently. The range of alternative economic systems has shrunk in recent years. But there are nevertheless distinct characteristics today in the structure and functioning of various systems. This introductory article provides a background to the chapter discussion of contemporary economic systems.

The Death of the Isms

The traditional alternatives to capitalism—communism, socialism, welfare statism—are fading into history. The breakup of the Soviet Union effectively ended communism as a major alternative to the capitalist system. It must be noted that, given the overwhelming economic and social problems in Russia and other former Soviet Union states—unemployment, crime, declining standards of living—many of their citizens are calling for a return of the relative stability and order provided under communism. But it is not expected that the market genie can be put back in the bottle. Privatization, political freedom, and disillusionment with the results of the old system make the return of communism unlikely. The system that evolves in the former communist bloc, however, is not likely to be a carbon copy of American capitalism.

The system that existed in the Soviet Union was not true communism. The government owned the means of production—the factories, farms (with some exceptions), and stores—and production decisions were made at the top. Under a true communist system, workers would own and run the businesses directly. Such a system was in place in only one country, Yugoslavia. In the Soviet Union and the other so-called communist countries, the economic system was more accurately described as state socialism.

In the Soviet system, 5-year plans were drawn up that were intended to allocate all resources according to the production priorities determined by the central planning authorities. The highest-priority sectors were military production and investment in heavy industry. Until the last decade of the communist regime, production of consumer goods was given low priority. This resulted in shortages and long lines of shoppers attempting to purchase the limited supplies available.

Public dissatisfaction with the system led to an attempt to reform it with *perestroika* (restructuring) under Mikhail Gorbachev, who became head of state in the Soviet Union in 1985. Gorbachev believed that introducing production incentives and eliminating bureaucratic inefficiency from the system could save it.

Perestroika was, in fact, an attempt to transform the state socialism of the Soviet Union into a form of market socialism. Under market socialism, the means of production would be largely owned and operated by the

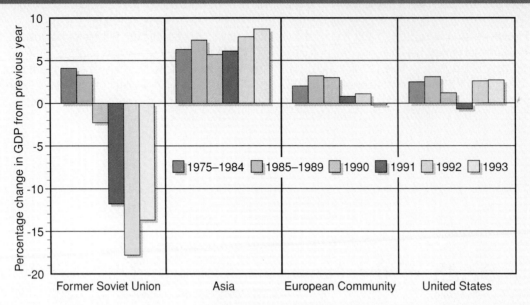

Figure 1.

Growth Rates in Three Groups of Countries and the United States
Selected Years, 1975–1993

Legend: ■ 1975–1984 ■ 1985–1989 ■ 1990 ■ 1991 ■ 1992 ■ 1993

Categories: Former Soviet Union, Asia, European Community, United States

Y-axis: Percentage change in GDP from previous year

Source: U.S. Department of Commerce; International Monetary Fund.

■ The countries of the former Soviet Union have experienced negative growth rates since its dissolution. The highest rates have been achieved in Asia, especially among the industrializing countries of East Asia that have authoritarian governments.

government; but production decisions and production methods would be determined by market demand and supply rather than by a central planning body.

Gorbachev and perestroika did not succeed, and in 1991 the Soviet Union dissolved into separate states. Russia, by far the largest state with three-quarters of the land and half of the total population, was headed by economic reformer Boris Yeltsin. Yeltsin, in consultation with Harvard economist Jeffrey Sachs, attempted to transform the Russian economy into a market system by "shock therapy." The near-term result was that unemployment ensued as state enterprises laid off workers, shortages became worse, and inflation ran rampant.

Sachs maintained that shock therapy was the only choice and that a gradual transition from a command economy to a market system would result in chaos as plant managers were subjected neither to the discipline of central authority nor the discipline of the marketplace. He pointed to the radical reform in Poland, for which he was also an adviser and which appeared successful, as evidence that shock therapy could work.

However, the economic pain inflicted on the Russian people by inflation and job losses gave unreconstructed communist bureaucrats and other reactionaries in the Russian parliament an opportunity to block further radical reforms of the system and get rid of leading reformers in the government—and Sachs along with them. Nevertheless, privatization continued apace (chapter 3, p. 68), and even the reactionaries did not propose a return to the old communist system.

Some countries, such as China, Vietnam, and Cuba, continued to maintain official allegiance to communism. But their economic systems are so changed in the direction of market

capitalism that the father of communism, Karl Marx (see Perspective, p. 462), would certainly disown them from the grave.

The countries of Western Europe are changing as well. The high costs of their cradle-to-grave welfare systems cannot be sustained in the face of increasing international competition in a highly integrated world economy. To remain competitive with North America, Japan, and the industrializing countries of East Asia, they must lower labor costs. This has meant a reduction in the generosity of their unemployment, retirement, and labor fringe benefits.

At the same time, the United States—considered the most capitalistic major nation—is far from a pure market economy. Spending by the various levels of government amounts to 34% of GDP; and, after eliminating transfer payments from government spending, U.S. government units account for 18% of the resource usage in the economy. These figures show that the United States is not pure capitalism but a mixture.

■ Chapter Preview

With the death of the isms, economic systems have lost their sharp distinctions. But within the mixed economies of today's world, there are differences in the structure and in the performance of various systems. We shall examine these differences within the framework of the goals of an economic system presented in chapter 2: How is the goal of efficiency satisfied in different economic systems? How is the goal of stability satisfied in different economic systems? How is the goal of growth satisfied in different economic systems? How are socioeconomic goals satisfied in different economic systems?

■ Learning Objectives

After completing this chapter, you should be able to:

1. Explain how resource allocation has changed in the transition from central planning to market-directed economies.

2. Describe the implementation of privatizing government enterprises in different systems.

3. Compare labor productivity in Russia to labor productivity in China.

4. Explain total factor productivity.

5. Contrast monetary stability in different economic systems.

6. Describe unemployment problems in different systems.

7. Explain the factors contributing to economic growth in different systems.

8. Describe the socioeconomic problems found in different systems.

The fact is that all economies are mixed economies to one degree or another. But the particular mixture can be very important. The importance can be seen in the widely different economic growth rates achieved under different systems. The growth of GDP in 1993 ranged from a minus 12% in Russia (a fall of 12% in total output from the year before) to a plus 13% in China.

One ism that has not died is authoritarianism. Some of the world's fastest-growing economies are those in East Asia with authoritarian governments. They include (with their 1993 growth rates): Singapore (11%), Taiwan (6%), South Korea (7%), Malaysia (8%), and Thailand (7%). While not centrally planned, as the Soviet system was, the governments in these countries intervene in the economy to direct industry and trade. They do not adhere to the principle of Adam Smith's "invisible hand" of the market to guide the economy (chapter 4 Perspective, p. 101). The success of these countries challenges the laissez-faire idea that economic systems should be left to the unfettered direction of the marketplace.

How Is the Goal of Efficiency Satisfied in Different Economic Systems?

In theory, **central planning** should have been an efficient system for organizing an economy. It was supposed to ensure that resources would be allocated to meet production needs in the order of their priority without the wastes of marketplace miscalculations and the booms and busts of **capitalism**. In practice, it turned out to be quite inefficient. This section examines the efficiency of economic systems after the death of the isms.

Resource Allocation

Under the system of **communism** as practiced in the Soviet Union and other communist countries, which was in fact **state socialism**, resources were allocated by a central planning bureau according to priorities established by the political authorities. Because communist accounting practices made no distinction between those goods that were sold and those that went into accumulated stock of goods on hand, the volume of production was all that mattered. Resource allocation was very inefficient because goods continued to be produced that could not be sold, while other goods were in short supply.

Market forces are doing today what central planners refused to do; to the extent that the market is allowed to operate, it is concentrating resources in the production sectors that are in demand and in which the economy has a comparative advantage. For Russia, this means producing refrigerators, not cameras, which can be acquired more cheaply, and of better quality, from Asian producers. For China, it means producing clothing for export in return for high-tech machinery imports. For Poland, it means the production of heating systems, not VCRs.

But the rationalization of resource allocation is hindered by the problem of what to do with the millions of employees in the state enterprises that cannot compete in the market. These firms constitute a giant program of

> **central planning:** a method of resource allocation in which the top leadership makes the major decisions on production, distribution, and coordination.
>
> **capitalism:** an economic system based on the right of private ownership of most of the means of production, such as businesses, farms, mines, and natural resources, as well as private property, such as homes and automobiles.
>
> **communism:** according to Karl Marx, the last stage of economic development after the state has withered away and work and consumption are engaged in communally; in common usage, frequently used to designate state socialist economies.
>
> **state (authoritarian) socialism:** a command economy in which virtually all of the means of production are in the hands of the state and decision making is centralized.

make-work. They are too big to let fail and too sick and unprofitable to sell. Unemployment is already large, and shutting down more of the state enterprises would increase it to unmanageable levels. This threat has led to a reactionary trend in Russia, Poland, and other Eastern European countries. If the reactionary politicians in Russia succeed in halting reforms and rolling them back—for example, by resuming large-scale defense production or increasing government subsidies to the least efficient state plants—the prospects for achieving an efficient system are poor.

There has also been a scaling down in China of plans to shut down 140,000 state-owned factories. Altogether they ran up a $3.7 billion loss in 1993, which drove up the government deficit and contributed to inflation. Because of the traditional "iron rice bowl" policy in China—which guarantees workers housing, health care, and other benefits—the government does not allow plants to lay off workers even when there is no work for them.

Aside from the problem of displaced labor, most of the reform governments in the former centrally planned countries do not want to go all of the way down the capitalist road. They wish to maintain basic industries as government enterprises. Their model is not pure capitalism, but **market socialism**. China, for example, has stated that its objective is to create a "socialist market economy." The Polish government intends to hold onto industries considered "strategic," such as power and telecommunications firms. Other former communist countries have given similar indications.

Privatization

The principal method of moving from a centrally planned to a market economy has been through **privatization** of the state enterprises. In Russia, this was accomplished through a program by which vouchers, which could be exchanged for shares of stock in privatized firms, were issued to each person (chapter 3, p. 69). One of the objectives of the voucher program was to give the workers a stake in the success of the companies they worked for, providing an incentive for more efficient production. As it turned out, the work-

■ In Russia, a voucher program was initiated to help move the country from a centrally planned to a market economy through privatization of state enterprises. Every citizen was issued vouchers that could be exchanged for shares of stock in privatized firms.

ers initially had little faith in the success of the privatized firms and many sold their vouchers at discounted prices. Privatization in Poland was accompanied by scandals concerning the distribution of shares of privatized companies, which enriched some insiders at the expense of the public. These scandals resulted in the firing of the official involved and the resignation of the finance minister.

Despite these problems, privatization is achieving its objectives. Retail and nearly all other service industries have been put in the private sector in the Eastern European countries. As a result, shortages and long waits for service in the service sector are a thing of the

market socialism: an economic system in which the means of production are publicly or collectively owned, and the allocation of resources is market-directed by the pricing system.

privatization: the process of selling government enterprises to private buyers and/or turning government services over to private sector operation.

■ France joined Great Britain and Italy in their programs of privatization of state industries by selling shares of the Banque National de Paris, and other companies, to private investors in 1992–1993.

past. In manufacturing, the majority of firms have been privatized. By mid-1994 Russia had transferred 70% of its state-owned enterprises to private hands. This has increased supplies in some areas, but speculation has created shortages in others.

The countries of Western Europe have also undertaken to privatize their government enterprises. These enterprises came into existence to satisfy certain social objectives, but unfavorable experiences with government ownership of utilities and other basic industries have led the countries to embark on a program of privatization. Their aim is to increase efficiency in those industries. Following Britain's lead under Margaret Thatcher in the 1980s, France and Italy have undertaken to sell off large state industries by offering shares to private investors. In 1993–1994, France sold the Banque National de Paris, the giant chemical firm Rhône-Poulenc, the nation's biggest oil company, Elf Aquitaine, and even the country's largest car maker, Renault.

Italy's privatization sales included three banks, an electric power company, and a larger insurer.

The goals of privatization in Western Europe are to get politics out of the operations of the industries, to raise badly needed cash for recession-strapped governments, and to force more efficiency in the firms by subjecting them to the discipline of the market.

In the United States, privatization has been taking place at the local rather than the national level, although there is occasional discussion of privatizing the U.S. postal system. In an attempt to save money, state and local governments have been turning more of their functions over to private for-profit companies. States and localities contract with private firms to provide the services that have traditionally been provided by government employees. Private contracting of public services has long been used for some services such as garbage collection and road repair. But as budget pressures have forced city, county, and state governments to seek cost reductions, some are hiring private firms to take over a variety of government services. In many instances, privatization has been successful; in others it has not.

Production Efficiency

One of the objectives of privatization, in addition to obtaining a more efficient allocation of resources, is increasing production efficiency, especially labor productivity. Privatization results in incentives to minimize costs of production. Under state ownership, firms could count on the government to bail them out if they did not cover their expenses. With the arbitrary price system used in central planning, there was no accurate way to determine whether a firm was unprofitable. After Russian state enterprises were subjected to market pricing, it turned out that some actually *subtracted* value from the raw materials used. Russia's steel industry, which produced twice as much steel as the United States, was so inefficient that the value of its output was less than the real cost of the energy and raw materials that it consumed. The same was true of the machine-tool industry.

Whether or not the privatization of state enterprises in Russia will improve efficiency in the short run is questionable. In most of the plants, management and organizational behavior remained the same after privatization as before. Workers and managers of the plants held most of the shares in the privatized firms. There was a pact between them that if management promised not to let go any workers, the workers would use their shares to support management in office. Then there is the problem in Russia of the loss of a work ethic after 70 years of communism, the development of what the labor newspaper *Trud* has called "a psychology of permanent dependence."

Passive labor attitudes like those found in Russia have not emerged in China, however, despite efforts during "the Great Proletarian Cultural Revolution" of the mid-1960s to stamp out personal incentives. Unit labor costs in China have been falling at the rate of 12% a year, even while real wages have been rising.

One of the reasons for high productivity rates in China and other East Asian countries is their investment in human capital. They have emphasized the importance of public education, especially at the lower grade levels. And they are providing the same education to girls as to boys. Thus, although women are not in the labor force in large numbers, they give their children a great deal of home education both before and after the children start school. This helps to explain the high test scores attained by East Asian children in internationally standardized tests. It also explains why the children grow into productive workers.

Total Factor Productivity

In order to be productive, labor must be combined with physical capital in the most effective way. Part of the recent success of the East Asian economies is their high savings/investment rates. In 1965 they were saving on average 20% of GDP. By the early 1990s, East Asian countries as a whole were saving and investing 35% of their GDP, three times the rate in the United States.

But the absolute amount of investment in human and physical capital does not entirely account for the level of productivity achieved. The way in which labor and capital equipment are combined affects the efficiency and growth of the economic system. One measure of the efficiency of the labor/capital combine is **total factor productivity (TFP)**. TFP accounts for the increase in output that is not otherwise accounted for by increases in the labor force and capital investment. Some of the explanation for a high TFP can be attributed to the more effective utilization of labor discussed in chapter 7 (pp. 169–174). The openness of an economic system to new production ideas and the willingness to put them into practice can increase TFP. The high TFP resulting from Japan's willingness to adopt new ways of organizing production helps to explain its "economic miracle."

total factor productivity (TFP): the increase in output in excess of the amounts attributed to additional labor and physical capital inputs; results from combining labor and capital in a production process that has increased efficiency.

Yankee Capitalists Tackle the Wild East

The leading nineteenth-century newspaper publisher, Horace Greeley, advised ambitious Yankees seeking their fortune to "Go west, young man, go west." Today, some enterprising young Americans are heading to economically wild Eastern Europe to start up businesses. Prague, the capital of the Czech Republic, has attracted a number of young would-be entrepreneurs. More mature Yankee capitalists, including such well-known consumer institutions as Pizza Hut, Coca-Cola, and McDonald's, have made large investments in Russia.

But the major impact on former Soviet bloc economies is likely to come from less well-known Yankee capitalists, who are bringing their hard currency and production know-how to a region that is badly in need of both. They are attracted by the inducements of Russia's low wages for an educated workforce, wealth of natural resources, and large market population with great pent-up consumption desires. These are the positive enticements to foreign capital. On the negative side are the poor work habits of the labor force—conditioned by decades of an implicit communist labor-management pact summarized in the statement "We pretend to work and they pretend to pay us"—as well as the inadequate business and property laws, the corruption by officials and criminal activities in general, and the difficulty of taking profits out of the country in hard currency.

Because of these negatives, the type of American and other foreign companies in the vanguard of investment in Russia, beyond the fast food/soft drink firms establishing a foothold for the future, have been the natural resource extraction industries. Exploitation of cheap natural resources in a place with low-cost labor has always been an attraction to foreign capital.

Oil producers are especially eager to develop what they hope will be a bonanza of black gold in the region. One of the early arrivals, in 1991 prior to the dissolution of the Soviet Union, was the White Nights joint venture between Texas-based Anglo-Swisse and Connecticut-based Phibro Energy, in partnership with a Soviet oil producer. The objective of the joint venture was to apply American capital and technology to oil exploration in Siberia.

The operation soon ran into a number of setbacks. The bank in which White Nights' deposits were held became insolvent and in December 1991 closed its doors, losing the firm $2 million. In June 1992, the Russian government decreed that firms earning hard currency from their exports must exchange half their earnings for rubles.

The sophisticated drilling equipment that White Nights shipped 3,000 miles to western Siberia proved too expensive to operate in the harsh Siberian conditions, where temperatures drop to 45 degrees below zero Fahrenheit. The operation switched to the use of modified Russian rigs, which could do the job at one-fifth the cost.

Other problems were less easy to overcome. The relatively luxurious living accommodations provided for the American managers and workers aroused resentment from the local workers. The joint venture was attacked in the press for mistreating its Russian employees and "plundering Russia's underground riches."

The partners nevertheless persisted and even planned to set up two more ventures in Russia. If potential earnings are sufficiently large, the profit motive overcomes a great deal of adversity.

Economic Reasoning

1. Did the use of sophisticated drilling equipment by the White Nights operation increase production efficiency? Why or why not?

2. How can foreign capital investment improve the efficiency of resource allocation in the former Soviet states?

3. Do foreign capital investments in Russian natural resource industries constitute a "plundering of Russia's underground riches"? Why or why not?

How Is the Goal of Stability Satisfied in Different Economic Systems?

Closely associated with a system's efficiency is its stability. An economic system cannot operate efficiently under conditions of high inflation or with high unemployment.

Inflation

Theoretically, countries with central planning can keep prices almost perfectly stable because most prices are established by state agencies. Before the Soviet government became concerned about shortages of consumer goods, prices were quite stable. The official Soviet price index changed by less than 1% in 15 years. But when the government tried to alleviate the persistent shortages of goods and housing, prices increased drastically.

After the dissolution of the Soviet Union, inflation in Russia reached an annual rate of 245% in January 1992. The acting prime minister, Yegor Gaidar, convinced the Russian central bank to hold down money and credit growth in order to bring down the inflation rate. As a result of this monetary tightening, inflation was reduced to 9% by August. But as credit dried up, state enterprises were unable to meet their financial obligations. Pressure from the managers of the enterprises and from the parliament led Yeltsin to replace the head of the central bank. The new head reversed the tight money policy, flooding the economy with credit and taking it to the brink of hyperinflation. (For a discussion of hyperinflation, see chapter 11, p. 299.) At the end of the year, Gaidar himself was replaced by a prime minister more acceptable to the reactionaries in parliament.

The International Monetary Fund was concerned that any credits provided to Russia would be wasted under such inflationary conditions. Unless the inflation was brought under control, international credits would not be able to stabilize the value of the ruble. Therefore, the IMF made the granting of further credits, which were required for Russia to import needed goods in the face of the sharp de-

■ This employee of a Russian bank is changing the rates quoted for foreign currency as the ruble dropped to new lows. After the dissolution of the Soviet Union, inflation reached an annual rate of 245% by January 1992, and it continues to soar.

preciation of the ruble, contingent upon the return of price stability. By early 1994, inflation was again reduced to below 10%.

Other former communist countries also experienced high rates of inflation when they went to a market system and freed prices. There was a great deal of pent-up demand that the production system could not meet. Inflation in Poland reached a peak rate of 640% in 1989 but was slowed to 38% for 1993.

China managed to avoid the extreme inflation levels of the Eastern European countries. But in the first part of 1994, the overheated Chinese economy had an inflation level over 24%. China's monetary system has not evolved sufficiently to provide mechanisms for controlling inflation. The only means for the government to cap the rise in prices is to set price ceilings on those goods over which it has market control, such as grain, or to slow the growth of the economy by throttling industry expansion.

In order to reduce the pace of price increases, the Chinese government introduced an austerity program. This caused a collapse of speculation in property and moderated the surge in industrial production but did not significantly abate the inflation rate.

The United States and Western European countries have much more sophisticated instruments for controlling the money supply (chapter 10, p. 263, and chapter 14, p. 372). But their abilities to stabilize their economies are limited by conflicting goals. The monetary arrangements of the European Union almost foundered at the Union's 1993 inception when different countries attempted to pursue incompatible monetary policies. Germany was in the process of absorbing the former East Germany into the combined state, and government budgetary outlays associated with the process threatened inflation. To prevent inflation, the German central bank raised interest rates. This came at a time when Europe was sunk in the worst recession since the 1930s.

In order to combat the recession, France, Britain, and other members of the EU desired to lower interest rates. They were restricted in their ability to do so by the threat of capital flight. If they introduced low interest rates while Germany maintained high interest rates, capital would flow out of those countries to the German capital market. Speculation that this would happen drove their exchange rates to depreciate below the 2.5% range permitted under EU monetary agreements. Although the range was subsequently increased to 15% to accommodate this disturbance, the experience cast doubt on whether the goal of a common currency could be achieved. The lesson was that even sophisticated monetary controls cannot rescue systems from instability if there are conflicting goals.

Unemployment

Although inflation was brought somewhat under control in Eastern Europe, unemployment continued to rise. Official Russian figures on the number of unemployed understate the true unemployment rate by millions. The official statistics report only those who register at unemployment offices. Most unemployed workers do not register because they gain nothing by doing so. Furthermore, unemployment carries a stigma in Russia where, prior to 1991, it was considered a crime. No one knows the true number of unemployed. Besides those who have no jobs, there are additional millions of hidden unemployed in the state enterprises who are formally employed but have no work to do. Russia's total output fell more between 1990 and 1993 than did America's during the Great Depression of the 1930s.

Unemployment also hit other Eastern European countries when they opened their economies to market competition. Poland's textile and electronics industries could not compete with imports, resulting in mass layoffs. Its defense industry lost its main customer, the Soviet Union, with the dissolution of the communist Warsaw Pact. By the end of 1993, the unemployment level reached 16%. Burgeoning new service businesses such as restaurants and Western-style supermarkets helped take up the slack, but further layoffs in the remaining state enterprises threatened to drive unemployment to even higher levels, levels that the public would not accept. In the second quarter of 1994, 40% of the labor force still worked in state-owned firms in Poland. Concern over unemployment and the loss of the economic security that existed under communism led to growing public dissatisfaction with the economic reforms. Changing social relations, occasioned by the rise of a new class of successful businesspeople and high-income professionals, caused resentment on the part of those groups left behind—the uneducated, the elderly, and the rural population. This dissatisfaction resulted in the election in September 1993 of a conservative/reactionary government that included many former communist officials.

Similar dissatisfaction in Hungary led, in May 1994, to similar political results. Unemployment had gone from near zero to 12% and was accompanied by soaring inflation, this in a nation that was the most liberal and market oriented among the old Soviet bloc countries.

The least dissatisfied populace was that of the Czech Republic. The Czech government undertook an initial dose of shock therapy—freeing prices and devaluing the currency—but followed this by protecting Czech enterprises from the consequences of free-market competition. Hidden unemployment rose to over 20% of the labor force; but firms were kept solvent by being allowed to take on high debt levels, not by government subsidies. Privatization in the service sector and an export boom cushioned the transition. However, closure of the 20% to 30% of industrial firms that were unprofitable still had to be faced at some point.

Unemployment is not a problem in the booming economies of China and the **authoritarian nations** of East Asia. Singapore, Taiwan, and South Korea are the leading examples of the area's government-directed market economies, along with Malaysia and Thailand. Even international financial agencies committed to free-market policies have been forced by the success of these countries to recognize the possible benefits of "market-friendly state intervention." Government intervention may take the form of directing credit to chosen industries, protecting infant industries with protective tariffs, and subsidizing technology, as evidenced by the success of the South Korean consumer electronics industry. The governments are also able to keep special-interest lobbies at bay and prevent the corruption that hinders development and leads to instability in many African and Latin American countries.

The countries of Western Europe experienced unemployment levels in the early 1990s that were inconceivable in earlier years. Western European countries, which had once been accustomed to unemployment rates of 2%, found themselves saddled with double-digit unemployment rates. The high costs this imposed on their generous unemployment benefits and other elements of the social safety net forced a painful reconsideration of their social policies (discussed in the last section of this chapter).

Even Germany, which suffered from the opposite problem of labor shortages during most of the postwar period, experienced rising unemployment. After the absorption into the German economy of East Germany, with its open unemployment rate of 18% and hidden unemployment of an estimated 30%, unemployment became worse.

Germany was unaccustomed to this instability. The structure of economic institutions in Germany is designed to maintain stability. Its core is *Mitbestimmung,* or codetermination, which gives workers extensive consultative powers. By law, workers have half of the seats on the supervisory board of a firm and all of the places on a workers' council, which must be consulted on most decisions. Such laws govern all aspects of the German economy and take precedence over the dictates of the market. The purpose of this body of laws is to achieve economic outcomes in which everybody's rights and interests are protected. This system resulted in a high degree of stability of employment until it was faced with the necessity to ingest a problem-ridden East German economy.

authoritarian nations: one-party states that have no effective political opposition; may be benign governments with the best interests of the whole people as their goal, or may be self-serving of the interests of the ruling group.

The Loose Cannon

The second largest nation to emerge from the dissolution of the Soviet Union, next in size to Russia, is Ukraine. At the time of independence in August 1991, Ukraine appeared to be in a strong position to take advantage of its industrial base (steel production, television manufacture), its raw materials (iron ore, sugar), its population of 52 million, and its proximity to Western European markets—it is located on the far western border of the former Soviet Union—to compete in the new economic situation.

At first, Ukraine seemed on the road to fulfilling the promise of rapid transition to a market economy. Prices were liberated, a program of privatization initiated, and a commitment made to land reform and a balanced budget. But the promising start soon turned into a disaster. The Ukrainian prime minister for most of 1992 lavished unbudgeted credits on industry, generating inflation and disguised unemployment. By the beginning of 1993, inflation was running at a rate of 30% *per month*.

It was estimated that the cost of food increased 4,300 times between the date of independence and March 1993. Ukrainians were reduced to poverty subsistence level, resorting to homegrown food and barter to survive. The state controls over prices and trade that had been lifted after independence were reinstated, but the economic situation continued to deteriorate.

Rather than reducing the government's role in the economy, Ukrainian government spending went from 48% of GDP in the last year before independence to 70% in the year after independence. The government budget for 1993 called for spending equal to 73% of GDP, but the likelihood was that it would rise to as much as 90%.

The Ukrainian government has only one way of financing its deficits—printing money. The consequence has been hyperinflation.

Beginning in January 1994, the National Bank attempted for a second time to control inflation by imposing a tight monetary policy. But without decontrolling prices, which the government refused to do, a tight monetary policy results in the inability of firms to make payments to their suppliers and workers, bringing economic activity to a halt.

Economic Reasoning

1. How stable was the Ukrainian economy in the 2 years after its liberation from the Soviet Union? What were the indications?

2. Why did Ukrainian government spending result in hyperinflation? (For help in answering this question, you might want to review the discussion of monetary inflation in chapter 11, p. 288.)

3. Should the Ukrainian government decontrol prices despite the enormous rise in the cost of living that has already taken place? Why or why not?

How Is the Goal of Growth Satisfied in Different Economic Systems?

Economic systems are frequently judged by the rate of economic growth they achieve. A high growth rate raises living standards and makes economic problems easier to manage. Growth is affected by efficiency and stability, but it is a dynamic process that is determined by more than static factors. In this section we will examine how different systems perform with respect to growth.

Capital Investment

A key determinant in the rate of economic growth is the amount of current output that goes into the creation of capital rather than into consumption. Under central planning in the communist countries this was easy to control. The Soviet record in annual growth in real GDP was exceptional during the decades of its industrial development. The long-run average growth rate for the Soviet Union, starting in 1928 with the first 5-year plan and lasting to the 1960s, excluding the war years, has not been matched by any other country over such a period of time, either in aggregate or per capita terms. A large part of the explanation for that exceptional growth performance was the high savings rate achieved by depriving the consumption and housing sectors of resources in order to maximize industrial and military growth.

The period of exceptional growth in the Soviet Union came to a halt in the 1970s. Growth factors such as the increasing industrial labor force and the high investment/GDP ratio that had powered the earlier growth period were played out. They were not replaced by such other growth factors as improved technology (except in the high-priority military and space industries), or increased labor productivity. When development of heavy industry held priority, increases in total output came quickly. When more resources were allocated to consumer goods and services, productivity gains did not come as easily.

Today, the question in Russia and the other former Soviet republics is not how high is the growth rate, but how to stop the downward slide in output. It is hoped that market incentives and foreign investment capital, attracted by the cheapness of labor and other resources, will stimulate growth. But as of 1994, the inefficiency of the old system, the decline in output from state enterprises, and other negative factors have outweighed the positive stimulants.

Some of the formerly subjugated Eastern European countries are doing better since the dissolution of the Soviet Union than Russia and the other Soviet republics. Poland's economy grew by 4% in 1993, and those of Hungary and the Czech Republic were expected to resume economic growth in 1994. The economy of Estonia, one of the three Baltic states along with Latvia and Lithuania, was projected by the International Monetary Fund to grow 6% in 1994. All of these countries are capable of sustaining real growth rates of 6% a year for a period of time under favorable circumstances. Unlike Russia, they have a past history, preceding World War II, of market economies, free labor organizations, and an entrepreneurial class.

As noted in the introductory article for this chapter, the outstanding success stories of economic growth come out of East Asia. China and the so-called "Four Tigers"—Singapore, Hong Kong, Taiwan, South Korea—along with Thailand, Malaysia, and Indonesia have growth rates that surpass those of any other region. In the nineteenth century, it required around 50 years for Great Britain and America to double per capita real income. The Asian tigers and China are achieving this in a single decade. In addition to high savings/investment rates, their exceptionally rapid growth is due to the catch-up phenomenon described later.

China's growth rate has slowed since the 13% rates of 1992 and 1993. Such rates were

Figure 2.

Share of Investments in Gross Domestic Product, 1992

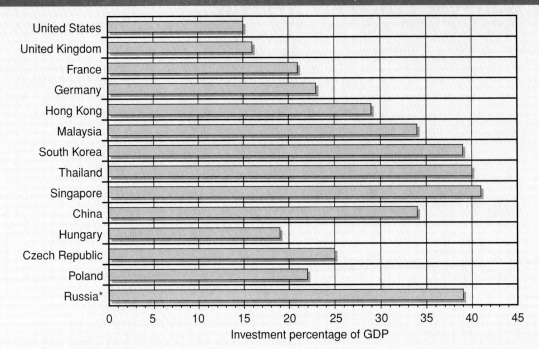

* The investment percentage shown for Russia may not be comparable to figures for other countries due to different data reporting methods. Data estimates for the economies of the former Soviet Union are under review by the World Bank.

Source: World Bank, *World Bank Atlas 1994.*

■ In the fast-growing countries of East Asia, investment is a high percentage of GDP.

not sustainable without incurring unacceptably high inflation rates. Therefore, the government took measures to cool off the overheated economy by restricting credit for industry expansion. But the expansionary forces have proved difficult to retard.

Meanwhile, Western European countries are suffering from lagging growth. The anticipation of closer economic integration of their economies in the European Union caused a spurt of investment in the 1980s, but this petered out in the early 1990s as recession set in. It has been suggested that the EU should repay its—philosophical, not actual—debt to the U.S.–funded Marshall Plan, which helped to rebuild the Western European countries after World War II, by providing similar aid to rebuild the economies of Eastern Europe. If the EU did so, providing unilateral aid as well

as investment capital to the Eastern European countries, it would be a stimulant to growth in the EU countries.

Labor

Economic growth in different systems is affected by their investment in human capital as well as investment in capital equipment. Growth can also be increased, at least on a one-time basis, by an increase in the labor force participation rate. The labor force participation rate, which was probably higher in the Soviet Union than in any other industrial nation, played a major role in accounting for the high Soviet growth rate. The Soviets were very successful in moving people from the countryside to the city and into the active labor force. Furthermore, the economic role of women in the Soviet economy was greater

■ Women filled important roles in every sector of the Soviet economy and they continue to do so in Russia today. Here, economist Irina Tolkacheva works with an employee in the bank transfers department of the Tver Universal Bank.

than anywhere in the West. Women were important in every sector of the Soviet economy, providing manual labor in construction, operating transportation equipment, and serving in professions such as medicine.

Up to now, the labor participation rate of women in East Asian societies has been low. But as their economies modernize, it can be expected to increase. That may enable those countries to continue growing at a higher-than-normal rate for a period of time after other growth factors, such as the exceptionally high savings rates, have run their course. As for their investment in human capital, an emphasis on public investment in education was cited above as one of the reasons for the economic successes in East Asia. In fact, economic growth in China before 1979 came entirely from greater investment in capital and education, not at all from improved efficiency.

Public investment in education can be complemented by the investment of companies in training their workers. German firms have extensive worker training programs, which are credited in part for the quality of German products. German companies are more inclined to invest in this training than are American firms because of the greater stability of the German labor force. One of the results of *Mitbestimmung* is that there is a more loyal relationship between German companies and their employees that results in less labor turnover, justifying company investment in worker training.

Catch-up

Industrializing countries can obtain a big boost to their growth by adopting advanced technology and production methods already in use in the industrialized countries. This process is termed **catch-up**. Catch-up has been important in growth spurts of different countries historically. For example, rapid growth in the United States in the nineteenth century was due in large part to adopting production technologies from England.

In order for catch-up to work effectively, a country must be open to other economies. Foreign trade is the conduit by which technology spreads. It not only provides access to new technologies, but it furnishes incentives to adopt them.

The factor that most clearly distinguishes the economies of those East Asian countries that are succeeding from those that are stagnant or declining—North Korea, Vietnam, Myanmar, the Philippines—is that the latter group is closed off from the international economy. All of the East Asian countries are to some degree authoritarian, but the successful ones combine "soft authoritarianism" with economic engagement in the international economy. The unsuccessful ones close off their societies—and economies—to protect them from foreign influences.

The nations of Eastern Europe, while industrial countries, were cut off from the technologies of the West during their period under communism. In the 1990s, the more progressive of the Eastern European economies—Poland, Hungary, the Czech Republic, and possibly others such as the Baltic countries—should experience high growth benefits from catch-up. Their economies are already being integrated into those of Western Europe through trade; and they wish to join the European Community as soon as possible, although that is not likely before the end of the century.

catch-up: the growth process by which an industrializing country adopts advanced technology and production methods already in use by industrialized countries.

Comparative

Case Application

The Titan Ages

Between the 1950s and the 1990s, Japan, despite its relatively small geographic size and limited natural resources, became a giant among the world's economies. Its real rate of economic growth rose from 6% in the late 1950s to 9% in the mid-1960s and to 12% in the early 1970s. It captured an increasing share of world markets, taking one industry market after another away from U.S. producers. Japan's success served as a model for the smaller nations of East Asia, which are now in the process of replicating it.

The structure of the Japanese economy that helped in achieving these successes had some unique features. One of the important features was the *keiretsu,* giant integrated companies whose various divisions supported each other. There was close cooperation between the banks that financed the companies, the producing firms, and the merchandising concerns that distributed the goods.

Another institution, especially important to Japan's export drive, was the Ministry of International Trade and Industry (MITI). MITI devised the industrial policy to be followed by Japanese producers, targeting a succession of export markets, that managed to capture a large share of world trade and build Japan into the world's second largest economy after the United States.

The Japanese growth rate, however, has been slowing down since 1973. Its economic growth, like its population, is aging. The benefits of catch-up began to fade in the 1970s, and a decline in the rate of growth of the labor force set in. The long-term real growth rate projected for the Japanese economy has been reduced from the 6% that was anticipated in 1978 to a recent official projection of 3.5%.

But even this lowered growth expectation is substantially higher than the growth rates of the United States and other advanced industrial economies. The titan of Asia is slowing with age, but it is still capable of great economic feats.

Economic Reasoning

1. Which factors contributing to economic growth in Japan have changed since the 1970s?

2. How might an increase in the consumption sector as a portion of total Japanese output affect the economic growth rate? Why?

3. Should the United States have an industrial policy that would determine investment and export objectives for different industries? Why or why not?

How Are Socioeconomic Goals Satisfied in Different Economic Systems?

Since the ultimate purpose of economic activity is to raise living standards and improve the life of the people, socioeconomic goals are as important in evaluating a country's performance as the more strictly economic goals.

Protecting the Environment

The area occupied by the former Soviet Union has been labeled "a toxic wasteland." The environment was sacrificed in the attempt to meet the goals of the 5-year plans. According to Murray Feshbach and Alfred Friendly Jr. in their book *Ecocide in the U.S.S.R.,* "When historians finally conduct an autopsy on Soviet communism, they may reach the verdict of death by ecocide." The environmental pollution remaining as a legacy of the Soviet system includes poisoned air, food, and water.

Under the Soviets, in 1 year the Ukrainian Republic alone emitted 22 billion pounds of toxic substances. This was eight times the rate of air pollution in the United States. On one occasion, air in the industrial center of Nizhniy Tagil in the Russian Republic became so polluted that car drivers had to drive with headlights on in the middle of the day. People became dizzy and fell ill. The air breathed by tens of millions of Russians today is polluted by at least five times the "safe" levels of various harmful chemicals.

Compounding the damage done by industrial pollutants spewed in the air, a denuding of vast forest land in Siberia has eliminated one of the world's primary natural air cleaners. The 5 million acres of Siberian forest cut down each year constitutes as serious a threat to world climatology as the destruction of the Brazilian rain forests.

Ecological damage was equally bad under central planning in the smaller Eastern European countries. Decades of pushing industrial output without any environmental controls have been costly in human health. To satisfy the demands of heavy industry for plentiful power, governments subsidized electric power production and ignored conservation. As a result, Poland, for example, emits six times as much air pollutants for each unit of output

■ Russian workers scoop up oil and mud at a recent Arctic oil spill in Siberia. Oil pipeline leaks have ruined enormous areas of land. Environmental pollution, which has also poisoned air, food, and water, is a legacy of the Soviet system.

produced as the countries of Western Europe. Air pollution from Eastern European countries is killing the forests of Western Europe, and toxic wastes are poisoning the Baltic Sea.

Lake Baikal, one of the largest and deepest freshwater lakes in the world, is home to an exceptional variety of living organisms, some of which can be found nowhere else in the world. But the lake has suffered serious damage from logging operations, pulp and paper mills, and nearby construction. Another great body of water, the once enormous Aral Sea, has been dried up by water diversion, resulting in global effects. Rivers that fed the inland sea were diverted for irrigation projects leaving the body to evaporate. The consequence has been a great plain of salt and dust, raising temperatures in the region as much as three degrees and increasing particulate matter in the Earth's atmosphere by more than 5%.

Large tracts of land have been despoiled by spills from oil pipeline leaks. To save on costs of constructing the pipelines, cutoff valves were installed only every 30 miles rather than at safer 3-mile intervals. According to one report, an amount of oil equivalent to four *Exxon Valdez* tanker discharges in Alaska is spilled on the ground every day in Russia. One spill in Siberia has created a pool of oil that is 4 miles wide, 7 miles long, and 6 feet deep.

But perhaps the most serious environmental threat the world inherited from the Soviet Union is nuclear radiation. The Soviets recklessly exploded nuclear devices for such mundane purposes as moving earth for dam-building projects, thereby spreading unknown amounts of radioactive contamination. They also dumped nuclear reactors and other radioactive waste into the sea. There is a continuing threat from accident-prone nuclear power installations. The accident at Chernobyl in 1986 (chapter 2, p. 47) and its radiation consequences are well documented. Less well known are the four other serious nuclear accidents that have occurred and hundreds of less serious accidents. A few of the inherently unsafe nuclear reactors built during the communist era have been shut down, but hundreds of reactors are still operating, and they are aging and becoming more dangerous due to inadequate maintenance. In 1992, over 200 nuclear accidents or safety mishaps were reported in Russia.

Pollution, worsening sanitary conditions, and a collapse of the health care system have brought about *falling* life expectancy in Russia in recent years, an unusual occurrence anywhere. Half of the drinking water is contaminated by chemical and organic toxins, and 10% of the food is contaminated. The life expectancy of adult men in Russia has fallen to 60 years, lower than that in such countries as Indonesia and the Philippines and parts of Africa. The fact that the longevity decline is highest in Russia's male population suggests that vodka overindulgence may also play a role.

As we know, even advanced market economies have no built-in protection against environmental pollution. The United States and the other Western industrial countries have contributed more to air and water pollution than the rest of the world combined. Any system, whether it be centrally or market controlled, must first recognize the problem, rather than denying it, and then adopt measures to reduce pollution. If the will is there to do so, it may be easier to stop pollution in authoritarian societies than in *laissez-faire* ones. Singapore, a "soft authoritarian" state, is notable for the cleanliness of its environment along with its high rate of economic growth.

Economic Security

Living standards in the Soviet Union were low for an industrialized country, but people were assured of a job and a pension that at least provided subsistence. Today that economic security no longer exists. As a result of inflation, those living on fixed job or pension incomes frequently cannot afford even the necessities. The average monthly old-age pension in 1994 amounted to the dollar equivalent of $31.40. At the same time, a gallon of milk cost $1.80, a pound of butter $1.35, and the cheapest winter coat $47.00. Rent is very low, but added to it is the average monthly electricity cost of $4.70. Thus pensioners and workers with fixed incomes have difficulty covering basic food costs, much less being able to afford the luxury products that are now coming into the country from the West.

The **welfare states** of Western Europe find themselves in an opposite situation from the former communist countries—their unemployment, pension, and other benefits are turning out to be too generous. The social safety nets that those countries put in place during the heady years of high growth and rising living standards are proving too costly in this time of slower growth and increased international competition. They are causing budget deficits for government and high labor costs for business.

In Germany, one-third of the GDP now goes for spending on social programs. Germany was the country where social security originated. Today, the social insurance contributions, shared 50-50 by workers and their employers, amount to almost 40% of gross pay. The financial burden of the pension system will become increasingly difficult as the German population ages, with the number of Germans over 65 rising 50% by the year 2015. The government is trying to find ways to reduce the future pension liabilities, which amount to 1.6 times current GDP. It is also seeking to reduce unemployment compensation from 58% of previous earnings to 55% and set a cut-off time for benefits.

Other European countries have already moved to reduce the generosity of welfare state benefits. In the Netherlands, students were eligible for unemployment benefits as soon as they graduated, but no longer. Dutch workers were eligible for benefit payments amounting to 70% of their last gross wage if they suffered from either physical or psychological disabilities. One out of every seven people in the working population was on disability allowance, one-third of the recipients claiming that they were suffering from "stress." In 1993 eligibility for the disability program was tightened, and regular reassessment of each case imposed.

However, there is no intent in the European countries to dismantle their social safety nets entirely. Even the modest reductions have been met with fierce opposition. What is

■ Gangsterism is the new "ism" in Russia. Here, armed guards keep watch at an American business in Moscow. The alternative, paying protection money to extortion gangs, is the choice of an estimated 80% of the private businesses in the country.

in process is reducing the welfare state "generous grandfather" to a more modest "helpful uncle" role.

Economic Equity

In Russia, communism has been replaced by gangsterism. It is estimated that 80% of the private businesses in Russia pay protection money to extortion gangs. Those businesspeople that refuse are dealt with ruthlessly. In 1993, there were 30 murders of bankers and 94 murders of people classified as entrepreneurs in Russia. It is alleged that there are 5,000 organized gangs that control the economy.

welfare state (democratic socialism): an economic system that combines state ownership of some basic industries with a market system, extensive social services, income redistribution, and democratic political institutions.

■ In China the income of farmers, like these vegetable growers outside Beijing, averages less than half of the wages of city workers.

Aside from such blatant criminal activity, and perhaps more significant, if less visible, is the graft and corruption in the normal course of doing business. There are old-comrade networks of bureaucrats that have set up private companies to trade in land, natural resources, and foreign currencies. They use illegal exports of oil and other resources to transfer billions to their accounts in Western banks. State enterprises that were privatized but remained under the control of their former managers have been stripped of their assets.

Many ordinary Russians feel that they are at the mercy of the new *biznismeni,* a word often used to mean crooks and swindlers. Even if the wealth that people see flaunted by the privileged—expensive foreign cars and luxury imported items that would cost the average Russian a year's salary—were honestly obtained, the traditional Russian character resents inequality in itself. This, along with the unemployment and other hardships that have accompanied reform, helps to explain the political successes of the reactionaries in the Russian parliament.

When China dropped communist orthodoxy and embarked on a program of modernization of its economy in 1978, it adopted the slogan "To get rich is glorious." And many Chinese *are* getting rich, but millions more are left out of the modernizing sector of the economy in which incomes are rising. China, nomi-

nally a communist state with equality as a maxim, has greater inequality of income than capitalistic Taiwan and South Korea. More than a million Chinese have become "dollar millionaires." An estimated 5% of the population is affluent by Chinese standards.

The general public sees graft and corruption as the cause of the inequality. Payoffs and connections are found at every level. Even government party officials are constantly being found embezzling money. The perception of widespread corruption is causing popular opposition to liberalization of the economy. But the principal source of income inequality is the gap between urban and rural incomes. Farmers average less than half of a city worker's wages. The growing wealth in China needs to spread from the big cities and special economic zones on the coast to the interior and the lagging sectors. Ending liberalization would slow this spread.

The economic system in the United States has its own socioeconomic failings to answer for. Among these are the large numbers of homeless people, the failure to provide all citizens with health care, a murder rate and an incarceration rate that are far in excess of any other industrialized nation, and a school system that is failing both children and society. No "perfect" economic system exists, but an examination of other systems—their successes and their failings—will help us to shape ours.

The Lands of the Midnight Sun—Fading Beacons

The Nordic countries—Norway, Sweden, Finland, and Denmark—have been viewed as shining beacons of enlightened societies. They have enjoyed high living standards, equality of income distribution with virtually no poverty, low crime rates, and cradle-to-grave security.

Sweden led the way for European social welfare states when it elected the Social Democratic Party to power in 1932. Its system offered a third way between capitalism and communism, providing the best of both worlds. It incorporated the efficiency of a market system and the civil liberties and individual rights of a democracy while at the same time furnishing high-quality medical services for all, subsidized modern housing, income security for the aged, and excellent public services in transportation, communication, and child care. Unemployment was kept low by joint action of the government and trade unions to direct unemployed workers into retraining programs, resulting in government jobs if no private jobs were to be had.

The other Nordic countries had similar welfare state systems. But all of this had to be paid for by very high tax rates. Marginal income tax rates ranged as high as 80% on the largest incomes. The costs of the welfare programs grew to the point that taxpayers could not—or would not—continue to support the system.

The breaking point came with the recession of the early 1990s. As long as unemployment remained low, it was possible to pay benefits up to 90% of previous earnings. But when unemployment rates climbed toward 20% of the workforce, as it did for example in Finland, the system could no longer be supported.

The four Nordic countries are adjusting differently to the financial strains. Sweden and Finland have sharply cut back on social spending. The Norwegian government, blessed by large income from the country's North Sea oil production, has only modestly trimmed its benefits. The crisis affected Denmark least because it was the first of the four nations to join the European Community. As a result, it had already been in the process of shrinking government outlays, even before the recession hit, in order to satisfy currency stabilization requirements of the EC.

How far the Nordic countries will have to go in reducing their welfare state benefits remains to be seen. They would like to retain as much as possible the systems that provided them with their high living standards in the past.

Economic Reasoning

1. In what ways have the Nordic countries satisfied the goal of economic security?

2. How did they achieve a large degree of economic equity?

3. Is the welfare state system better or worse than laissez-faire capitalism? Why?

Putting It Together

Although theoretically efficient, *central planning* turned out to be quite inefficient in practice. The system was intended to avoid the market wastes of *capitalism,* but as practiced in the countries with *communism* as their nominal system, which was in fact *state socialism,* resources were allocated quite inefficiently by their central planning bureaus. Because communist accounting methods made no distinction between production and sales, goods continued to be produced that could not be sold, while other goods were scarce. The shift from central planning to a market system in those countries has moved to rationalize the allocation of resources, but the existing state enterprises are not competitive.

China and other communist countries that are reforming their systems do not intend to become pure market economies. They are moving toward a system of *market socialism,* or what the Chinese describe as a "socialist market economy."

The move from centrally planned systems to market-directed systems is being accomplished through *privatization.* In Russia, this took the form of issuing vouchers to its citizens, which could be exchanged for shares of stock in privatized state enterprises.

Privatization of government enterprises is also occurring in the mixed economies of the West. Western European countries are privatizing state businesses in order to remove them from political intervention and make them more efficient. In the United States, state and local governments are privatizing government services to reduce the costs of government.

In addition to being inefficient in allocation, state socialism in the Soviet Union was also inefficient in production. Privatization is intended to increase productivity, especially labor productivity, by providing incentives.

China and other nations in East Asia are achieving rapid gains in labor productivity by investing in human capital. They emphasize and put resources into education. They are also obtaining increased productivity from combining capital and labor in effective ways.

As a result, they have high *total factor productivity (TFP).*

Another measure of the performance of an economic system is its stability. Central planning in the Soviet Union was able to maintain relatively stable prices and employment, though at the cost of persistent shortages. Moving to a market system has resulted in high inflation rates and a large amount of actual and disguised unemployment.

The overheated Chinese economy experienced high rates of inflation, which could only be checked by the imposition of an austerity program. The tools of monetary management in China are too rudimentary to support a sophisticated monetary policy.

Even the Western countries, with their much more developed monetary management tools, find difficulty in achieving low inflation and low unemployment as a result of conflicting objectives within and between countries.

Economic growth was exceptionally high in the Soviet Union during its period of industrialization from the 1920s to the 1960s. The high growth was accomplished by allocating resources to heavy industry and the military at the expense of the production of consumer goods and housing. It was also boosted by a large increase in the labor force participation rate, bringing women into the labor force in all types of occupations.

The highest rates of economic growth today are found in China and a number of the smaller states of East Asia. They have very high savings/investment rates, an emphasis on education at the lower grade levels, and more or less authoritarian governments that actively intervene in economic matters.

Another reason for the high growth rates in East Asian countries is the *catch-up* phenomenon. Industrializing countries are able to increase efficiency and growth by adopting advanced technology and production methods from the already industrialized countries. For catch-up to be effective, a country must have an economy open to trade and investment with the rest of the world. Those East Asian countries that have not enjoyed economic growth are the ones with closed economies.

As for socioeconomic goals, the Soviet Union had a very poor record in protecting the environment. Its air, water, and soil pollution, in particular radioactive poisoning of the environment, has left a destructive legacy for the former Soviet nations and the rest of the world as well.

Western market economies have contributed much more than their share to world environmental pollution. "Soft authoritarian" societies, such as Singapore, may find it easier to halt pollution.

The citizens of the Soviet Union enjoyed a good measure of economic security, albeit at a low standard of living for most. During the reform movement, with its accompanying unemployment and rising costs of living for those on fixed incomes, that economic security has been lost.

The *welfare states* of Western Europe are reducing the generosity of their social welfare programs because the costs have become higher than they can bear. The expense of unemployment, pension, and other benefits has created large government deficits and raised labor costs to levels that make competition with foreign products difficult.

Russia and other former Soviet states are beset by extortion and other gangster activities and by corruption and pilfering in state and privatized businesses. China is also experiencing a high degree of corruption, which magnifies the income discrepancies between the urban and rural populations.

The system in the United States also suffers from economic and socioeconomic failings. Comparing economic systems increases our ability to understand and deal with those problems.

Marx on Capitalism

Karl Marx (1818–1883)
Marx was born in Germany, the son of a lawyer. Entering Bonn University at the age of 17, he intended to be a lawyer, too. However, after being arrested for public intoxication, he was transferred by his father to Berlin University, which was a more academic institution. There he became a brilliant student and developed a passionate interest in philosophy. After receiving a doctorate from the University of Jena in 1841, he turned to journalism. In 1843 he married the daughter of an aristocratic family from his hometown and moved to Paris. It was there that his interest in communism began. There also he began a collaboration with Frederick Engels that would continue for a lifetime. Together they wrote the *Manifesto of the Communist Party* in 1848. They went to Cologne, Germany, to edit a liberal paper backing the German revolution. The revolution failed and Marx, having been banished from Germany and then expelled from Paris, moved to London. He spent the remainder of his life in London, most of it without funds and in poor health, studying, writing, and organizing the Communist International. The first volume of his major work, *Capital (Das Kapital),* was published in 1867. The second and third volumes were compiled and published by Engels from Marx's unfinished manuscripts after his death in 1883.

In 1867 Karl Marx predicted the demise of capitalism. He did not say just when capitalism would expire, but he did explain why and how. Capitalism had to be replaced, according to Marx, because the evolution of society's institutions is a natural and inevitable process of history. This evolution takes place as a result of class struggles—the struggle between lower socioeconomic classes and higher socioeconomic classes over the fruits of production.

According to Marx, all history can be explained by the conflict between opposing forces, thesis and antithesis. Out of this conflict change emerges through synthesis. Marx contended that the direction of social change is determined by such concrete factors as machinery. This philosophy of the inevitability of change resulting from the struggle of opposites and determined by concrete realities rather than ideas is called dialectical materialism. It is the basic philosophy of communism.

The evolution of society into capitalism resulted from the arrival of machines and the factory system. It created two contending forces—the capitalist class or bourgeoisie, which owns the means of production, and the wage workers or proletariat class, which has to sell its labor to live.

Marx seized on the labor theory of value of the classical economists to explain why labor is the source of all surplus value (profit), which is appropriated by capitalists and invested in more machinery. The increasing accumulation of capital equipment, according to Marx, results in increasing output with a smaller labor force. As a result, the workers do not have enough purchasing power to remove from the market all of the output of goods produced by the increasing stock of capital. The consequence, he thought, would be cyclical depressions of increasing severity, leading to revolution.

Marx expected the new synthesis to be socialism. He predicted that there would be two phases of the transition from capitalism to the new synthesis. In the first phase, there would be a "dictatorship of the proletariat" in which the workers would take power. This government by the working class would subsequently give way to a communal society in which the slogan, "From each according to his ability, to each according to his needs," could at last be realized.

The collapse of communist, actually state socialist, systems in the USSR and elsewhere has dimmed the reputation of Marx as a prophet, but his place in history as a social critic and a major influence on events in the twentieth century is secure.

FOR FURTHER STUDY AND ANALYSIS

Study Questions

1. Why is a market system thought to be more efficient in allocating resources than a centrally planned system?

2. Why was it difficult for the centrally planned economies to engage profitably in foreign trade based on comparative advantage?

3. What differences can you find in the satisfaction of economic goals in Russia compared to China?

4. How is privatization intended to improve the efficiency of resource allocation?

5. Why does a market system result in more innovation than a centrally planned system?

6. What is the relationship between total factor productivity and catch-up?

7. Why did inflation in Russia cause depreciation of the ruble? (For help, refer back to the discussion of exchange rates in the previous chapter.)

8. What conflicts do you find in satisfying the different economic objectives in the countries discussed?

9. How does investment in human capital complement investment in capital equipment?

10. What indications do you find of convergence in the different types of economic systems in recent years?

Exercises in Analysis

1. Make two lists, a list of the similarities among different economic systems and a list of the differences.

2. From investment publications, an investment broker, or other source, find what American companies have investments in the countries of the former Soviet Union. List the companies, what they produce, the amounts of their investments, and other relevant information.

3. Select two countries that are undergoing economic transitions to a changed system. Write a paper comparing the relative success of their reforms.

4. Write a short paper on why you believe that the system of communism (state socialism) was abandoned by the communist nations.

Further Reading

Adam, Jan. *Planning and Market in Soviet and East European Thought, 1960s–1992*. New York: St. Martin's Press, 1993. Examines the working of central planning and the changing mix of planning and market in the evolving mixed economies.

Baldassari, Mario, and Robert Mundell, eds. *Building the New Europe. Vol. 2, Eastern Europe's Transition to a Market Economy*. New York: St. Martin's Press, 1993. Contains contributions from academic scholars from East and West Europe and other specialists on the policies and experiences of the changing economic systems of Eastern European countries.

Clarke, Simon, ed. *The State Debate*. New York: St. Martin's Press, 1991. Compares capitalist and communist systems and their performance since 1945.

Corbo, Vittorio, Fabrizio Coricelli, and Jan Bossak, eds. *Reforming Central and Eastern European Economies*. Washington, DC: World Book Publications, 1991. The study covers both macro- and microeconomic aspects of the transition from centrally planned systems to market systems. Compares three alternative programs for privatization.

Graubard, Stephen R., ed. *Exit from Communism*. New Brunswick, NJ: Transaction Publishers, 1993. Examines the postcommunist systems in Eastern Europe. Covers the roles of nationalism and socialism in the evolving systems.

Grundmann, Reiner. *Marxism and Ecology*. New York: Oxford University Press, 1991. Studies the place of ecology in Marxian economic doctrines, the nature of communist government environmental policies, and their ecological effects.

Le Grand, Julian, and Saul Estrin. *Market Socialism*. Oxford: Clarendon Press, 1989. Contains articles on how markets can be used to achieve socialist ends.

Lichtenstein, Peter M. *China at the Brink: The Political Economy of Reform and Retrenchment in the Post-Mao Era*. New York: Praeger, 1991. A study of Chinese economic policy since 1976.

Nellis, John. *Improving the Performance of Soviet Enterprises*. Washington, DC: World Bank Publications, 1991. Increased autonomy of state enterprise managers has allowed new forms of production to emerge. The study compares the productivity of state enterprises under the former Soviet Union with that of these new enterprises.

Ralston, Richard E., ed. *Communism: Its Rise and Fall in the 20th Century*. Boston: Christian Science Publications Society, 1991. A historical study of communism in Europe. Deals primarily with the political and governmental aspects of communism.

Sakakibara, Eisuke. *Beyond Capitalism: The Japanese Model of Market Economics*. Lanham, MD: University Press of America, 1993. Economic conditions in Japan and Japanese economic policy. Examines the unique workings of capitalism in the mixed economy of Japan.

Wedel, Janine R., ed. *The Unplanned Society: Poland during and after Communism*. New York: Columbia University Press, 1992. Social conditions in Poland at the time communism was introduced and changes under the communist system. The informal economic system after the fall of communism.

Wright, Anthony. *Socialisms: Theories and Practices*. Oxford: Oxford University Press, 1986. Covers the evolution of socialism, its arguments, doctrines, and methods.

Chapter 18. World Economic Development

■ **The nonindustrialized** countries of Africa, Asia, and Latin America are groping for the best economic system to attain economic development. China has chosen one type of system, discussed in the last chapter. India has chosen a different path. The other nonindustrialized countries, and the rest of the world, are watching the outcome in these two most populous nations.

Number Two Has to Try Harder

In a case application in the previous chapter, Japan was described as an economic giant. There are two other countries in Asia that constitute physical giants—China and India. If their economies catch up with their physical size, they may surpass Japan, the United States, and everyone else in the next century. Taken together, their populations compose 38% of the world's population, their land area 10%.

China is the larger of the two giants, both physically and economically. It has a population larger by one-third than that of India and nearly three times the land area. China's GDP is approximately twice that of India. But India, in part because of the challenge posed by its mighty neighbor, has recently awakened from its bureaucratic slumber.

Prior to 1991, the Indian government maintained tight controls over the economy and the activities of the country's businesspeople. Officials issued licenses to companies that gave them exclusive rights to manufacture certain products. Foreign competitors of Indian firms were kept out by high tariffs and other trade restrictions. Even among domestic producers, competition in the marketplace was discouraged. With few exceptions, Indian companies were prohibited from putting new products on the market, diversifying into new areas, or investing overseas.

Taking as a model the central planning of the Soviet Union, the Indian government regulated output, prices, and distribution. Key prices were centrally administered; critical materials, credit, and foreign exchange were rationed; taxes were complex and tax rates high; labor laws were very restrictive. The Indian economy was so inefficient that its total factor productivity growth from 1960 to 1985 averaged a minus 0.4% per year. The value of the increase in output was less than the value of the increased amount of resources used to produce it.

Attempts by Indian prime ministers in the 1980s to liberalize the economy were largely thwarted by government bureaucrats and special interests in the private sector who benefited from the status quo. It took an economic crisis in 1991 to force change. When the Soviet Union, India's second largest export market and the source of cheap oil, dissolved, and Iraq's occupation of Kuwait cut off remittances from Indians working in the Gulf states, India's foreign exchange reserves fell so low that it could not afford even essential fuel imports.

■ This billboard for Coca Cola, positioned at a busy Delhi intersection, reflects the attitude of American businesspeople, who are glad to take advantage of India's liberalized rules for foreign investment.

This crisis combined with the specter of an energized Chinese economy, growing at three times the rate of the Indian economy, to force a new start at liberalization. Now an Indian company can invest in whatever product or area it chooses with no government permission required. There has been a shift away from heavy industry into investment in consumer products and high-tech products. The growth industries include telecommunications, aircraft, nuclear reactors, pharmaceuticals, and computer software.

The Indian economy has also been opened to foreign investment, though with limitations. A list of 34 high-priority industries has been drawn up in which foreign investment up to 51% of equity in the company receives automatic government approval. Among the American companies taking advantage of the liberalized rules to make large investments in India have been General Electric, General Motors, Coca-Cola, Pepsi, and Philip Morris. There was twice

the amount of American investment going into India in 1994 as into China.

Tariff rates on Indian imports, which reached 300% in 1991, were reduced to an average of 65% by 1994 and were projected to fall to 25% by 1998. Exports from India have been growing at the rate of 20% a year. It is the world's second largest exporter of computer software, after the United States. Overall, the United States is India's largest export customer, taking one-fifth of its total exports.

The Indian economy has some institutional advantages over that of China, especially for attracting foreign capital. One of these is its well-developed legal system and courts, which enforce the laws fairly. This is a legacy of two centuries of British occupation in India. Another advantage is India's somewhat modern financial system and monetary control institutions. China, on the other hand, lacks an independent legal system, laws to protect private property rights, or bankruptcy

laws. Its central bank does not have the ability to control the monetary system; nor does the country have a developed commercial banking system and financial market. The stability provided by India's legal and financial institutions makes it less risky for foreign capital, lured to India by its increasingly open domestic market and large pool of skilled labor.

But India still faces obstacles to economic development that, unless they are resolved, will keep it second to China as mainland Asia's leading power. Although a good deal of economic liberalization has taken place at the national level, the individual Indian states wield a great deal of power over economic activities in their territories; and they remain largely committed to bureaucratic control. The encouragement of foreign investment by the national government is not matched by state governments. The agriculture, irrigation, power, road transport, health, and education sectors, accounting for more than half of the nation's GDP, are under control of the states. Government enterprises, such as electric power and the system of transportation canals, are heavily subsidized. Private companies find

■ Chapter Preview

As part of the "developed" world, it is difficult for us to appreciate fully the vast gap between our way of life and the way of life that exists in the less developed two-thirds of the world. Even in countries such as India and China that have embarked on modernization of their economies, the average worker earns a bare subsistence wage. This chapter will address the problem of economic development by examining three basic questions: How do standards of living compare? What makes countries poor? What are the prospects for world economic development?

■ Learning Objectives

After completing this chapter, you should be able to:

1. Discuss the ways of comparing living standards among countries.

2. Name the regions where poverty is most prevalent and list four low-income countries in those regions.

3. Explain the problems that cause countries to be poor.

4. Explain the significance of the population growth rate in economic development.

5. Describe the role of foreign indebtedness with respect to the LDCs.

6. Discuss the relationship between economic development and environmental pollution.

themselves in the position that, even if they are losing money, they still need government permission to shut down.

However, just as the national government was forced to change its policies by the realities of the economic situation, the state governments are now feeling the pressure of events. Their finances are being squeezed by the necessity to pay for the coal needed by their power plants. The financial drain of large subsidies to inefficient public enterprises is making it difficult for them to pay even the salaries of their civil servants. The effect of these pressures is overcoming bureaucratic resistance to change.

The Indian economy is the most tradition-bound of all the world's major countries. It still has labor laws and practices that hearken back to eighteenth-century mercantilism—for example, heavy taxes on machine-made matches to promote jobs in the production of hand-made matches. If India is to emerge from the economic shadow of China, it must free itself from the bonds of tradition.

The smaller LDCs are watching the development race between democratic India and autocratic China to see which system succeeds best. Currently, India is in second place. But this might be a race in which the tortoise beats the hare. An autocratic system can institute changes in a shorter period of time than a democratic system, especially one as bureaucratic as that of India. But it may be that India's legal, judicial, financial, and democratic institutions serve it better in the long run than China's autocratic system.

How Do Standards of Living Compare?

Most of the world's peoples do not live in the types of countries whose economies have been discussed in the preceding chapters. Two-thirds of the world's population live in nonindustrialized countries. These countries are referred to by various designations, the most common and inclusive being **less developed countries (LDCs)**. However, there are wide differences among the various LDCs in their living standards, potential for development, rate of development, and problems to be overcome in achieving development. In this analysis section, we will examine living standards in the LDCs.

> **less developed countries (LDC):** nonindustrialized countries generally characterized by a poverty income level, a labor force primarily employed in agriculture, extensive underemployment, and illiteracy, and located in Africa, Asia, or Latin America.
>
> **per capita income:** total National Income (or GNP) divided by the population size.
>
> **World Bank (International Bank for Reconstruction and Development—IBRD):** a specialized agency of the United Nations that began operations in 1945 first to help countries rebuild facilities destroyed in World War II and subsequently to help finance development of the LDCs.

▤ Poverty

Most of the world's population is found in countries with a **per capita income** of only a few hundred dollars a year. These countries are located in Asia, Africa, and Latin America. They are largely agricultural—as much as 80% of the population engaged in agriculture—with only small and inefficient manufacturing sectors. This subjects their income earnings to the wide price fluctuations characteristic of commodity markets.

The **World Bank** classifies countries as low-income, middle-income, upper-middle-income, and high-income economies. India and China still rank as low-income economies, with 1992 per capita GNP of only $310 for India and $470 for China.

The low-income countries are mainly in South Asia and sub-Saharan Africa (African countries that lie south of the Sahara desert). They have an average per capita output of only $390 a year. But the average covers countries with populations living under quite different conditions and with quite different prospects. India has always had a small number of super-rich families—land owners, favored businesspeople with monopoly pow-

Figure 1.

GNP Per Capita, 1992
By Income Class of Economy

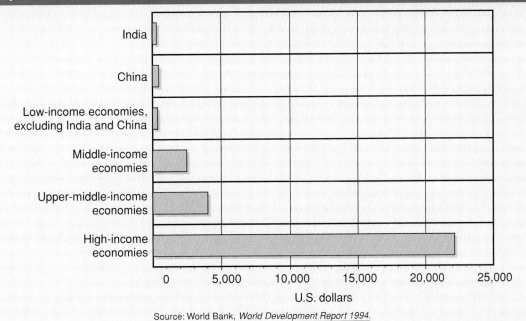

Source: World Bank, *World Development Report 1994*.

■ India's output per person is somewhat below the average for all low-income economies, other than India and China. China's per capita output is higher than the average for other low-income countries. The industrialized high-income countries have per capita outputs many times those of the LDCs and the industrializing countries.

ers. China, even after the Cultural Revolution, which attempted to stamp out the elite class, had its own wealthy class—corrupt politicians, generals, overseas Chinese businesspeople.

But the economic growth in Asia during the 1980s produced a large new class of rich, by poor country standards, with incomes above $30,000 measured in U.S. dollars. It is estimated that there are over 8 million of these high-income families in Asia, not counting Japan, and the number is growing rapidly. There is a second group of middle-income households with incomes above $18,000 and a third much larger group of families that are on the verge of middle-income status, who participate in the consumer economy. Assuming four persons per household in these groups, projections are that, by the year 2000, Asia will have 1 billion consumers with middle-class tastes. It is these figures that have

attracted the attention of foreign producers and investors.

The prospects for sub-Saharan Africa are much more bleak. In many countries of the region, the GNP per capita is falling. During the period from 1980 to 1992, per capita GNP fell by an average annual rate of 3.6% in Mozambique, 4.3% in Niger, and 2.4% in Madagascar. The Ivory Coast, previously classified as a lower-middle-income country, has inexorably been sliding into the low-income class with per capita GNP falling an average of 4.7% a year. For the region as a whole, GNP per capita fell 0.8% a year from 1980 to 1991.

Other regions besides sub-Saharan Africa have been experiencing negative per capita growth rates. North Africa and the Middle East have experienced the largest decline, and per capita growth in Latin America and the Caribbean has also been negative. But the situation in these areas is not as desperate

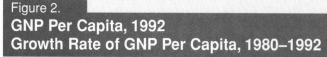

Figure 2.
GNP Per Capita, 1992
Growth Rate of GNP Per Capita, 1980–1992

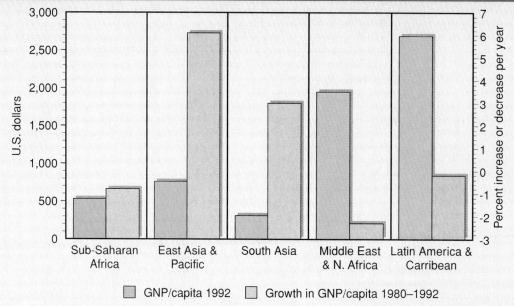

GNP/capita 1992   Growth in GNP/capita 1980–1992

Source: World Bank, *World Development Report 1994*.

■ The East Asia and Pacific region and the South Asia region, along with sub-Saharan Africa, have the lowest output per person among the LDC areas (left scale). The Asian regions, however, have been experiencing high growth rates since 1980, especially East Asia with an average growth in per capita GNP of over 6% during the period (right scale). The LDC regions outside Asia, on the other hand, have experienced negative growth rates during this period.

because they are middle income, and the economic and political situation in many of the troubled countries is improving. The situation in sub-Saharan Africa, however, is going from bad to worse. The one hopeful development has been the political resolution of the South African racial problem, where an economic renaissance could lead the whole southern African region into an economic expansion.

▨ Income Distribution

Per capita GNP does not accurately show the actual extent of poverty in less developed countries. Many LDCs have highly skewed income distributions, with a large percentage of total income going to a small percentage of the population. In Tanzania the highest 10% of income receivers get 47% of the total income, while the poorest 20% must exist on

only 2.4% and the lower 60% share less than 19%. In the Western Hemisphere, Honduras has a similarly skewed distribution, with 48% of income going to the wealthiest 10% of the population and less than 3% to the lowest 20% on the income scale.

The income distribution in India and China is not so extremely skewed as in the above examples. In India the highest 10% of income receivers gets 27% of the income and in China 25% The bottom 20% receives 8.8% of income in India and 6.4% in China. These income distribution patterns compare favorably with income inequality in the United States (see Table 2 in chapter 9, p. 232). But they are not typical of the inequality of income distribution in most LDCs.

The type of unequal income distribution that results from inherited wealth, particu-

Table 1.   Basic Social Indicators

Country	Adult Illiteracy (%) 1990	Life Expectancy at Birth (years) 1992	Infant Mortality (per 1,000 live births) 1992	Population per Physician 1990
Low-income	40	62	73	11,190
China	27	69	31	n.a.
India	52	61	79	2,460
Indonesia	23	60	66	7,030
Pakistan	65	59	95	2,940
Bangladesh	65	55	91	n.a.
Middle-income	n.a.	68	43	2,020
Russia	n.a.	69*	20	210
Philippines	10	65	40	8,120
Iran	46	65	65	3,140
Turkey	19	67	54	1,260
Thailand	7	69	26	4,360
Upper-middle-income	15	69	40	1,140
Brazil	19	66	57	n.a.
Mexico	13	70	35	n.a.
South Korea	4	71	13	1,070
South Africa	n.a.	63	53	1,750
Argentina	5	71	29	n.a.
High-income	n.a.	77	7	420
United States	less than 5%	77	9	420
Japan	less than 5%	79	5	610
Germany	less than 5%	76	6	370
United Kingdom	less than 5%	76	7	n.a.
Italy	less than 5%	77	8	210

*According to the World Bank, estimates for Russia "are subject to more than the usual range of uncertainty." This life expectancy figure is higher than independent estimates.

Source: World Bank, *World Development Report 1994.*

larly land ownership, which is typical of LDC agrarian societies, differs from the inequality in income distribution that results from development activities. The former perpetuates poverty, while the latter results in increasing demand for labor, thereby raising incomes down the line. This is the current development in China and, to a lesser extent, in India.

▩ Social Indicators

Per capita output and per capita income are the most direct measures of poverty. However, they do not give a complete picture of the comparison of living standards in differ-

ent countries. Table 1 shows some basic **social indicators** for each income class of countries and data for the largest five countries in each group. The table lists their adult illiteracy rate, life expectancy at birth, infant mortality rate, and the number of people per physician.

Although China is among the low-income countries, a newborn Chinese baby has a life expectancy of 69 years. That is higher than

(Continued on page 476) ⇒

social indicators: noneconomic statistics that reflect a country's standard of living.

A Tale of Two Countries

Kenya and Tanzania are two sub-Saharan African countries that have much in common. They share a common border in east Africa. It was near this border, in the Olduvai Gorge of Tanzania, that British paleontologist Louis B. Leakey discovered the remains of our earliest ancestors, who lived there about 1.75 million years ago. You might say that this part of the world got a head start in economic development. However, today it is among the world's poorest areas.

In addition to their common border and ancestry, Kenya and Tanzania have other similarities. They are similar in population size—26 million in 1992—and high population growth rates—3.6% for Kenya and 3.0% for Tanzania. They were both administered as colonies by Great Britain until they gained their independence in the early 1960s. Each of them has a one-party political system, disrupted by strife among the various tribal factions.

Kenya has 40 separate ethnic groups, the largest of which is the Kikuyu, who dominate the political scene. Jomo Samiburati ("Call me Sammy") is a Kikuyu. He was named after the father of Kenya's independence movement and its first president, Jomo Kenyatta. Sammy is not interested in politics, however. He is interested in making money. He is a driver and guide for tourist groups on safari to Kenya's game preserves. In addition to his native Bantu dialect, he speaks Swahili, the official language of Kenya, fluent English, and some French, German, and Italian. He learned the foreign languages from movies and tourists; he never went further than the primary grades in school. His income is far above the average for Kenya, but he will not say just how much. However, his expenses are also far above average. Nairobi, the capital of Kenya, is a very expensive city to live in compared to his native village. He is the father of six children under the age of 10, four of whom are in school. He also has two nephews living with him whose schooling he is paying for; they are sons of a brother still living in their home village, where secondary school is not available. Most weeks that Sammy is on safari, he drives for 6 days; he gets home to see his wife and children and recuperate for only one day before going out again. It is a tough life, but he is ambitious for himself and his children.

Across the border in Tanzania, 200 miles to the southwest, lives Mkwamasi, a Maasai tribesman. Mkwamasi follows the traditional Maasai occupation of herding cattle. Over 7 feet tall, he makes an imposing figure striding across the plain in bright orange-red flowing dress, carrying a spear for protection from the lions and other wild animals. He grazes his cattle over the vast Serengeti Plain, sometimes following the seasonal grass up into Kenya. The land the Maasai tribe have traditionally inhabited is now divided between Kenya and Tanzania. If Sammy were to cross the Tanzanian border without a passport, he would be arrested. But Mkwamasi has no passport, nor for that matter any document of any sort—no driver's license, no Social Security card, no birth certificate. He has virtually no money income. The cattle herd provides the principal subsistence for him and his village. He drinks their milk, frequently mixed with their blood, and eats their meat. Some Maasai are now turning to farming, but not his village. The village is much different from the native village of Samiburati in Kenya with its houses and

Table 2.   Basic Indicators for Kenya and Tanzania

Country	GNP per Capita		Inflation Rate (%) Avg. 1980–92	Agriculture as % of GDP 1992	Life Expectancy at Birth 1992	Infant Mortality (per 1,000 live births) 1992
	Dollars 1992	Growth (%) Avg. 1980–92				
Kenya	310	0.2	9.3	27	59	66
Tanzania	110	0.0	25.3	61	51	92

Source: World Bank, *World Development Report 1994.*

streets. The Maasai village is a circle of 15 low thatched-roof huts made of sticks and mud, surrounded by a fence of bushes and woven branches. The huts have dirt floors, crawling with insects, and are pitch black inside except for the glow of charcoal embers in the cooking fire and a small ventilation hole in one wall. The entrance is a baffled maze to keep out the weather and unwelcome intruders, animal or human. In the center of the village is a stick enclosure for animals. But mainly the central area is full of children, none of whom attend school, and their mothers. Five of the children, ranging in age from 6 months to 11 years old, are those of Mkwamasi. Two older sons are with him herding the cattle. The lifestyles of Samiburati and Mkwamasi are not typical of Kenya and Tanzania respectively, but they do symbolize the differences between the two countries and, in fact, the contrasts between traditional and developing societies in Africa and elsewhere. Despite their similar backgrounds, the economies of Kenya and Tanzania perform quite differently. Economic and social indicators for the two countries are given in Table 2.

Both countries are classified as low-income countries, but the per capita GNP of Kenya is nearly three times that of Tanzania. Tanzania is still primarily agricultural, with 61% of GDP consisting of agricultural output. The structure of the Kenyan economy is more diverse, with only 27% in agriculture. The social indicators of life expectancy and infant mortality are more favorable for Kenya.

But in one important respect, their economic performance—or perhaps one should say nonperformance—is similar. Like most African countries, output growth in both economies has been stagnant in recent years, with zero growth in Tanzania and only 0.2% growth in Kenya.

Economic Reasoning

1. Are Kenya and Tanzania above or below the average of sub-Saharan African countries in their GNP per capita? Is the growth rate of their GNP per capita greater or less than that of sub-Saharan African countries in general?

2. What differences between the economies of the two countries are shown in Table 2 that might explain the better performance of the Kenyan economy in the 1980s? Why?

3. Do you think that the Kenya and Tanzania economies would perform better under multiparty political systems than with only one legal party in each country? Why or why not?

■ Ninety-three percent of China's primary-age children are enrolled in school, like this kindergarten student at a factory school in Beijing.

➠ *(Continued from page 473)*

most of the world outside of the high-income industrialized countries (see Table 1). Also, the infant mortality rate in China is a fraction of that in other low-income countries. China is similarly in a much more favorable position relative to most low-income countries with respect to literacy. As shown in Table 1, only 27% of the adult Chinese population is illiterate, compared to 52% in India and an average of 40% in all low-income countries.

Another social indicator of the standard of living in a country is the nutrition level, especially important during the early years of childhood. The prevalence of malnutrition among children under five averaged 63% in India from 1987 to 1992. During that same period, malnutrition in China affected "only" 31% of the children. There is not enough information available to give the malnutrition average for all low-income countries; but among those for which estimates are available, India is exceeded only by Bangladesh in the level of malnutrition among children. This is an especially important social indicator because of its effect on child development, ability to learn in school, and future productivity as an adult.

What Makes Countries Poor?

Why are more than 3 billion people subsisting on an average income of less than $400 a year? Why, after 45 years of World Bank and country-to-country development assistance, is nearly 60% of the world population still living in LDCs? These questions do not have clear answers. The path to economic development is difficult and complicated. But there are certain basic development lessons that are clear—certain problems that must be overcome in order for countries to achieve self-sustaining growth.

> **vicious circle of poverty:** the pattern of economic stagnation resulting from a lack of surplus of production to invest in capital goods to increase productivity.
>
> **economic surplus:** a margin of output over and above consumption needs that can be allocated to investment for intensive growth.

▒ Lack of Capital, Technology, and Human Capital

In order to grow and develop, a low-income country must surmount a number of severe problems. Perhaps the most difficult of these is breaking the **vicious circle of poverty**. Per capita output in LDCs is close to the subsistence level. There is no **economic surplus** to allocate to capital accumulation or technological progress. As a result, productivity remains low and the subsistence standard of living is perpetuated.

One indication of the rate of capital accumulation is the percentage of total output allocated to investment goods. In India gross domestic investment equaled 23% of GDP in 1992. This is close to the average for low income countries, excluding China. (Current data on the investment/GDP ratio is not available for China, but it is undoubtedly higher than the average for other low-income countries.)

Figure 3.
The Growth-Consumption Choice

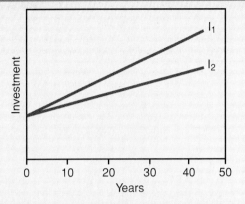

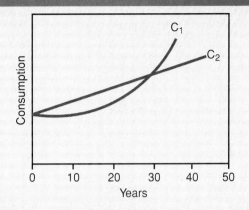

■ By sacrificing present consumption (C₁), an economy will be able to invest more (I₁) and be able to grow more rapidly than at consumption level (C₂) and investment level (I₂). This long-term strategy eventually creates more consumption.

Unlike many other LDCs, however, India finances nearly all of its investment out of domestic savings. In 1992 gross savings amounted to 22% of GDP, leaving a gap of only 1% of investment to be financed out of resource transfers from abroad. Most other low-income countries had much larger gaps between investment and savings that had to be filled by foreign borrowing. This leads to debt problems that can hinder development down the road, as discussed in the last section of this chapter.

Another measure of a country's progress in economic development is the rate of growth in investment. For the period 1980–1992, India averaged a healthy growth rate of 5.3% in gross domestic investment. Many African countries, on the other hand, experienced negative growth rates of gross domestic investment during that time.

In order to encourage a high rate of private investment, it is necessary for a nation to have in place an adequate infrastructure of transportation and communication facilities, electric power, safe water supplies, and educational facilities. Table 3 shows the infrastructure available in India and the four other largest of the low-income countries.

For an LDC, India is well equipped with infrastructure. In transportation it has by far

the greatest length of railway trackage relative to GDP and is second only to Zimbabwe in paved road density relative to population. (These figures are not available for China.)

The LDCs are looking to the new technologies of satellite and fiber-optics transmission to leapfrog into the telecommunications age. China is embarking on a massive program for installing telecommunications equipment. It plans to pour some $100 billion into telecom equipment by the year 2000, adding 80 million phone lines. By the end of 1995 it expects to have in place high-capacity optical fiber links to each of its 26 provincial capitals, except Lhasa in Tibet, and also to Hong Kong, Singapore, Taiwan, and Thailand.

India is in a good position to take advantage of technology because of its high number of college-educated workers, another legacy of the British colonial period, which emphasized education. More engineers graduate each year in India than in China and South Korea combined. As a result, India should be able to fully exploit the benefits of catch-up. With the reduction in bureaucratic restrictions on business and investments that is taking place and with the incentive of opening its markets to world competition, the country can be expected to make rapid gains in production technology.

Table 3.   **Infrastructure in the Five Largest**
Low-Income Countries

Country	Households with Electricity (% of total) 1984	Telephone Mainlines (per 1,000 persons) 1990	Paved Roads (km. per mill. persons) 1988	Population with Access to Safe Water (%) 1990	Rail Traffic (km. per mill. $ GDP) 1990
China	n.a.	n.a.	n.a.	72	n.a.
India	54	6	893	73	593
Indonesia	14	6	160	51	n.a.
Pakistan	31	8	229	55	168
Bangladesh	n.a.	2	59	78	41

Source: World Bank, *World Development Report 1994.*

Among the five largest low-income countries for which data is available, India is better equipped in transportation and household electric power infrastructure than the others.

The university system provides not only a source of white-collar and professional workers, but also a large supply of teachers. It is therefore ironic that India should have such a high illiteracy rate, twice that of China. One reason for the low literacy rate in India is the use of child labor in rural parts of the country. The income of these children is needed by their families on the edge of poverty. For example, some 80,000 children work in the hand-made match factories, handling toxic chemicals and working up to 60 hours a week. More than 80% of them are girls. Four-fifths of the girls work full-time and receive no schooling. Among the boys working in the match factories, however, most work only part-time while also attending school. The reason for this is that when a girl gets married in India her work benefits the family she marries into; her birth family gets no economic return on any investment they put into educating her.

While India has an extensive system of higher education, it provides a much smaller percentage of its children with primary and secondary education than does China. One of the major obstacles to economic development in most LDCs is the lack of literate, skilled labor. In China, virtually all children receive a primary school education, and over half are enrolled in secondary schools. It has almost as many children enrolled in school as the total population of the United States. The investment by China in its human capital by providing universal education will have large returns in productivity and economic development.

The percentage of children educated in India is substantially lower. Less than a third of Indian girls are enrolled in secondary school. The failure to provide a basic education to all children is a handicap to economic development in India and most other LDCs.

▇ Overpopulation
Educated and trained human capital is an asset to economic growth. Increased numbers of mouths to feed are not. A nation's standard of living is determined by the amount of food, housing, and other goods and services available to each person. The number of people and the rate of population increase are important factors in this measure. For many developing nations, overpopulation can be a major obstacle to improving living standards.

An aggressive government birth control program in India, which at one time even resorted to forced sterilization, has reduced the population growth rate to 2.1%, a relatively small population growth rate compared to the average of 2.6% for other low-income countries except China. Nevertheless, the population of

■ A couple and their son take a ride in Sichuan Province in China. Since 1979 the Chinese government has promoted policies to encourage one-child families.

India is projected to reach 1 billion by the year 2000 and to surpass the population size of China before stabilizing.

China's population is already over 1 billion—one-fifth of the world's population living on 7% of the world's land area. In the early years after the revolution, the leaders of communist China regarded a huge population as a resource that could be used to develop the economy rapidly. They subsequently recognized the cost of a high population growth rate. Between 1953 and 1978, a sizable 58% of the increase in output was allocated for the additions to the population, leaving only 42% for investment and improved living standards. In 1979 a one-child-per-family policy was initiated. There is an effective program for population control that combines education in family planning and birth control clinics with government propaganda and community pressure for smaller families. There are rewards for those who adhere to family planning regulations and penalties for those who do not. If a newly married couple agrees to have only one child, they receive a lump sum reward of rice and money, the child gets a full adult grain ration and a double fruit and vegetable ration, and the child is allotted a private plot of 75 square meters instead of the usual 50. If the child dies, the couple is allowed to have another. However, if they break their promise and have two children, they must repay all of the rewards they received.

Through such aggressive population control methods, the rate of population increase has been dramatically reduced. But because of the large numbers of young people approaching the age of establishing families, the size of China's population will continue to increase for some time to come despite the lower birthrate. It is expected to reach 1.68 billion before it stabilizes. India's hypothetical population stability size is projected at 1.89 billion.

Other developing countries have made headway in bringing population growth under control, but about one-fourth of the world, mainly the poorest countries, still have explosive population growth. The average fertility rate for sub-Saharan African countries is 6.1 children per woman. The problem of providing the necessities of life for ever-increasing numbers of population is one of the most serious facing all developing countries.

▬ Exploitation

Another barrier that underdeveloped countries must overcome is **exploitation**, external and internal. Many of the LDCs were pre-

> **exploitation:** obtaining labor services, raw materials, or finished goods for a price that is less than their true value.

Figure 4.
Population Growth Rates, 1970–1992, and Projected Growth Rates, 1992–2000

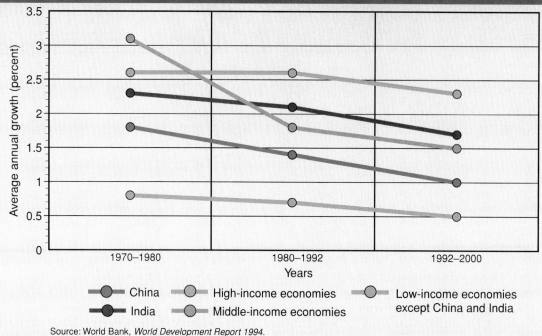

China   **High-income economies**   **Low-income economies except China and India**

India   **Middle-income economies**

Source: World Bank, *World Development Report 1994*.

■ Rising income for an economy is accompanied by a fall in the growth rate of the population. China is an unusual case because it has low population growth rate even though it is still a low-income economy.

---

viously colonies of other countries. The intended purpose of the colonies was to provide the mother country with a supply of raw materials and to buy its processed goods. Other nations, such as China, although not formally colonies, were frequently used by more powerful states for their own purposes.

The African countries as they exist today are artificial creations of the occupying colonial countries of Europe. Between 1870 and 1914, France, Britain, and Germany colonized 8,600,000 square miles of African territory with a population of 72 million. Those countries, along with Belgium, Portugal, Italy, and Spain, subjugated virtually the whole of the African continent.

They carved out African countries for administrative purposes, whose borders bore no relation to tribal boundaries or the natural flow of commerce. When the countries were liberated from colonial rule after World War II, they were left with local armies employing modern weapons but without the political infrastructure needed for stability. The result has been incessant tribal warfare and political strife.

Another obstacle to development is the internal exploitation of one class by another. LDCs are predominantly agricultural, with ownership of the land usually concentrated in the hands of a wealthy elite class, which also controls the government. The landless peasants are kept at a subsistence level. In pre-revolutionary China, less than 10% of the population owned 70–80% of the land, with landowners extracting from peasants rent and crop shares, levying taxes and taking graft from their taxes, and charging them exorbitant interest rates on their debts. The landowners could even seize the children of a poor family in payment of the family's debt.

This type of exploitation of the masses was overthrown by the 1949 revolution. Land reform, income redistribution programs, rural development, and education programs all have contributed to improving the conditions of the peasants. Famine, a regular recurrence in China throughout history, has been eliminated. But the 1989 Tiananmen Square crushing of the liberalization movement demonstrated that the pattern of authoritarian control of the Chinese people continues still.

Economic Policies

Misguided government policies frequently contribute to the difficulties of LDCs. India's restrictive bureaucratic regulations on trade and investment effectively blocked economic development. Recent financial reforms have eliminated many of the restrictions on banks and other financial institutions. Other reforms have removed obstacles to foreign trade and investment in India. Since 1991, peak tariff rates in India have been reduced by more than half, but the liberalization process has a long way to go.

In China government policies have slowed the inflow of foreign capital as well. There is often a disparity between government policy and investor aims. According to a report on the attempt of an American automobile firm to produce in China, "The Western executives placed the highest possible value on economic efficiency, even if it led to differentials in income or unemployment; by contrast, they found that Chinese state enterprises were more willing to tolerate inefficiency for the sake of equality of income, full employment, and social order" (*Beijing Jeep*, p. 307; see Further Reading at the end of this chapter).

There have been a number of government strategies pursued by other LDCs that have undermined their economic development in the long run. One common strategy, particularly among African countries, has been the exploitation of agriculture to provide cheap food for the growing urban populations. Holding down agricultural prices is popular with the politically powerful urban areas but has often resulted in a decrease in agricultural output so that countries that historically were self-sufficient have had to begin importing food. The food imports absorb scarce foreign exchange needed to pay for machinery imports to modernize production.

Another policy frequently adopted by LDCs, including many in Latin America, has been a concentration on developing import-substitution industries. Protectionist measures are enacted to keep out imported manufactured goods, leaving the market to high-cost domestic producers. This policy is popular both with the producers and with labor unions. However, it results in inflation and inefficient production.

Many LDCs spend an excessive amount on the military. Military expenditures in the LDCs have increased from $24 billion in 1960 to over $200 billion today. In Angola, Chad, Pakistan, Oman, Nicaragua, Syria, Uganda, and Zaire, for example, spending on arms is at least double the amount spent on health and education. In Iraq and Somalia, the amount spent on the military is five times greater than the amount spent on health and education.

Successful government development strategies in LDCs are not policies that are politically popular in the short run. Successful development strategies call for government budget restraint—avoiding grandiose projects and large military spending in favor of strengthening the country's basic infrastructure, encouraging competition in industry, and maintaining a stable environment for investment.

The Economically Dark Continent

Africa is the world's poorest continent and the only one where the people are poorer now than they were in 1980. Prospects for the future do not look good. The African countries, except for South Africa, cannot look forward to regaining their 1970s standard of living during the next half century.

How did they get into such a situation? It resulted from the legacy of colonialism, misguided and greedy political leadership, and explosive population growth. After independence, most African governments instituted highly regulated economic systems, similar to the bureaucratic regulations described in the introductory article on India. One big difference with India, however, is that India has legal and judicial institutions that control corruption in the bureaucracy. African countries have no such protection, and governmental graft is unbridled. In Nigeria, some $3 billion, amounting to 10% of GDP, was siphoned out of government accounts through government graft.

In west Africa, a more urgent problem than corrupt politicians has arisen—criminal anarchy. Crime is so rampant in west Africa that U.S. and European airlines have suspended landing at airports there. In Sierra Leone, the government army itself is part of the problem, threatening vehicle drivers and passengers at highway checkpoints.

Disease is another factor in Africa's impoverishment. Of the approximately 12 million people worldwide whose blood is HIV positive, 8 million are in Africa. It is malaria, however, that is the greatest medical drag on the African economies. Unlike AIDS, it is easy to catch through nonsexual contact; and most people in sub-Saharan Africa have recurring bouts of the disease throughout their entire lives, sapping their energies.

But the main reason why Africa is doomed to decades of poverty is overpopulation. At 3% a year, Africa's population growth rate is half again larger than that of any other continent. Meanwhile, food production is going up by only 1% to 2% a year, as has for some 30 years. Only one in five children born in Africa today receives nutrition adequate to lead a healthy and productive life.

Africa, a basket case of LDCs, needs a great deal of help from abroad, both public and private. But the rich countries of the Northern Hemisphere and the international lending agencies are reluctant to pour money down a sinkhole of corruption and exploding population. And foreign investors, attracted by the cheap labor in Africa, are put off by bribes demanded for every permit, the difficulty of enforcing contracts, and a totally inadequate infrastructure.

Economic Reasoning

1. What are some of the causes of poverty in Africa?

2. How does the vicious circle of poverty help to explain Africa's economic decline?

3. Can Africa's difficulties be blamed on exploitation by the colonial powers that dominated it until after World War II? Why or why not?

What Are the Prospects for World Economic Development?

In order to accomplish economic development, LDCs have to overcome the problems hindering their economic growth and mobilize their resources effectively. Some of the factors limiting economic development, however, are worldwide in scope and require international cooperation.

The Population Bomb

World population, which stands at over 5.5 billion, is climbing at the rate of 1.7% per year. Total population is projected to increase by 50% by the year 2025. It is possible for food production to match the population increase, but the assumption that it will is problematic. There is the problem of the high costs of en-

ergy required to increase productivity per acre. Up to now, the world's total food production capacity has been more than sufficient to feed all of the world's people. The problems that have arisen have been the result of poor distribution of the food supplies relative to population needs and inadequate transportation and distribution mechanisms.

Since 1965, the population growth in the industrial nations has fallen from a rate of 1.2% per year to 0.6% per year. The populations of less developed countries, however, are still expanding at a much faster pace—2% annually, 2.6% excluding China and India. About 95% of the world's population growth is taking place in the LDCs. Even if birthrates are re-

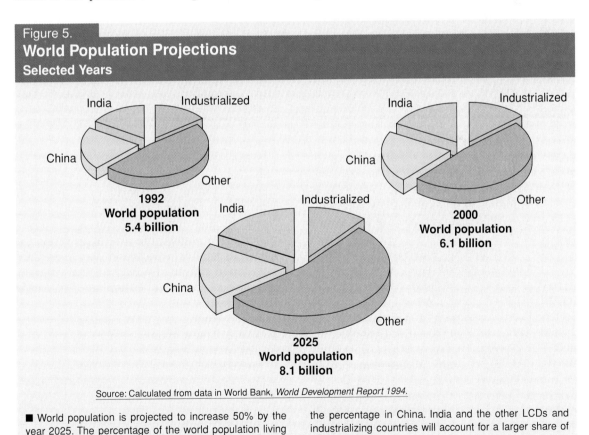

Figure 5.
World Population Projections
Selected Years

1992
World population
5.4 billion

2000
World population
6.1 billion

2025
World population
8.1 billion

Source: Calculated from data in World Bank, *World Development Report 1994*.

■ World population is projected to increase 50% by the year 2025. The percentage of the world population living in the presently industrialized countries will fall, as will the percentage in China. India and the other LCDs and industrializing countries will account for a larger share of world population.

Figure 6.

Projected World Population Growth by Geographic Area, 1992–2025

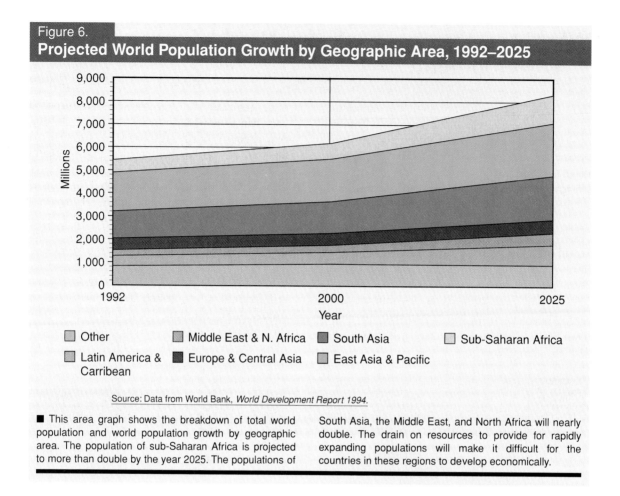

Source: Data from World Bank, *World Development Report 1994*.

■ This area graph shows the breakdown of total world population and world population growth by geographic area. The population of sub-Saharan Africa is projected to more than double by the year 2025. The populations of South Asia, the Middle East, and North Africa will nearly double. The drain on resources to provide for rapidly expanding populations will make it difficult for the countries in these regions to develop economically.

duced, the LDC populations will continue to grow rapidly for some time to come because of their large numbers of young people. The LDCs are adding 80 times as many young people to the world's population as are the developed countries.

The countries of sub-Saharan Africa have population growth rates averaging 3% per year, half again as large as the average for all LDCs. A growth rate of 3% may not appear to be very large; but at a steady 3% growth rate, the population will double in just over 23 years. In many LDCs, especially those in Africa, virtually all economic gains from development efforts are canceled out by population growth. In the poorest countries, malnutrition results in illness, blindness, and death of large numbers of children. Starvation is a costly and cruel form of population control.

The world population boom will strain not only food resources but international relations. According to reports by Georgetown University's Center for Strategic and International Studies, overpopulation is already a major factor underlying and aggravating political turmoil in Africa and the Near East. Population growth also increases the pressure on nonfood resources, on energy, and on the environment.

But resource use does not depend just on numbers. Those mainly responsible for using up the world's resources are the populations of the industrialized countries. It has been estimated that the average resident in a developed country uses up 50 times more of the world's natural and environmental resources than does the average LDC resident. In the industrialized West, the average annual per capita energy consumption is 120 times as much as in the poorest LDCs. If, as the developing countries industrialize, they use as great amounts of energy and raw materials as the industrialized countries already do, the world's resource base will be insufficient to sustain the growth.

The Debt Bomb

Of more immediate concern to many LDCs than the overpopulation problem is their debt crisis. The two problems are not unrelated. In order to provide for the food and other needs of their growing populations and at the same time invest to expand and modernize their production capacity, developing countries have borrowed to the hilt from foreign banks and international lending institutions. India's external debt in 1992 amounted to $77 billion, China's to $69 billion. Indonesia's external debt was even greater at $84 billion. Among the industrializing countries of the upper-middle-income group, Brazil had an external debt of $121 billion, Mexico $113 billion, and Argentina $68 billion.

Most of the debt in the upper-middle-income economies was incurred when their income from commodity exports was high and growing. They—and their lenders—expected that they would have no trouble paying the interest and paying off the loans out of earnings from their raw materials, which were in short supply. With the collapse of many primary products markets in the 1980s, the borrowing countries were unable to meet their interest payments. This created a financial crisis that threatened the international financial structure. Rescheduling of the loan payments and forgiveness by Western bank lenders of some of the interest due averted a massive default by LDC borrowers, but they are still burdened by the large debts. They are forced by the World Bank and other international lenders to pursue politically unpopular austerity measures. These include curbing government spending and the inflation rate, freeing up markets, and disposing of money-losing nationalized industries.

The conditions imposed on the debtor countries have meant cutbacks in social programs, higher unemployment, and shortages

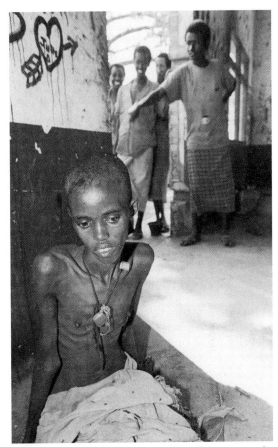

■ Too weak to walk, a teenage Somalian woman sits outside an orphanage awaiting food handouts. Political turmoil in 1991–1992 resulted in widespread famine and a substantial drop in economic output.

of imported goods. These austerity measures have caused social unrest that threatens to topple the governments in some countries. Their leaders are walking a tightrope between defaulting on the loans—thereby alienating the creditors and cutting off future financial assistance, foreign investment, and even essential imports—and economically squeezing their populations to the point of revolution. Some 40 impoverished countries in sub-Saharan Africa collectively pay about $1 billion a month in interest on their external debt. According to the president of Nigeria, "Indebtedness is the single major obstacle to development of the continent. The debt is crippling. We cannot continue this way." The fuse continues to burn on the LDC debt bomb.

The Environmental Bomb

Less developed countries attempting to industrialize rapidly—China, India, Brazil, Mexico—are running into severe environmental problems. Their skies are choked with soot and fumes, their waterways are poisoned with chemical wastes, and their lands are denuded of trees. The increase in mineral fuel prices (oil, kerosene, coal) in the 1970s forced millions of people in the underdeveloped nations to resort to using wood as their principal fuel for cooking and heating. The result was a massive denuding of the land of trees. This, in turn, caused erosion of the topsoil, reducing agricultural output.

The external costs of industrialization in the LDCs are enormous. Few efforts have been made to internalize those external costs because of the economic burden of doing so (see chapter 8, p. 206). With insufficient capital for normal investment purposes, the LDCs have been unwilling to divert resources into environmental protection. Furthermore, they lack the technology needed to cure such environmental problems as smokestack emissions.

The growing concern over ozone depletion and global warming in the industrialized countries leaves the developing world indifferent. After all, they argue, the high-income nations became wealthy exploiting the environment. Is it fair now to ask the LDCs to sacrifice their own growth to satisfy world environmental concerns? In view of the consequences of global warming for everyone on spaceship Earth, it may be in the interest of the wealthy countries to subsidize such measures as the preservation of tropical rain forests in the LDCs.

Utopia or Apocalypse

What does the future hold in store for the LDCs? The futurologists are busy writing scenarios and most of them are rather grim. They

■ Preserving the rain forests is in the economic interest of all people; but the fact that these forests are located primarily in less developed or developing countries makes the question of how this can be accomplished a controversial one.

have presented a superinflation scenario, a worldwide depression scenario, a World War III scenario, and a wars of redistribution scenario. The pessimists far outnumber the optimists because there is so little evidence that anything significant is being done to change the present course.

The optimists, however, claim that we have the technological and organizational tools to overcome the problems. They point out that there have been many earlier predictions of impending doom, but although there have been periodic catastrophes such as famine and depression, the world's economy and standards of living have continued to improve. Many economists are optimists because they believe in a system that is self-adjusting and self-correcting. They believe in the "invisible hand" (Adam Smith's term) directing the adjustments necessary to solve the problems.

South of the Border

One instructive case in economic development is close at hand, just south of the border—Mexico. It is a case that is of great importance to the United States. If Mexico should fail to achieve development and rising living standards, the consequences for the United States would be at best increased illegal immigration or at worst a Mexican revolution and the emergence of a hostile, terroristic nation on our border.

Mexico is faced with the whole range of problems discussed previously—rapid population growth, a huge foreign debt, and severe environmental pollution. Air pollution in Mexico City is the worst of any city in the world. Mexico is 11th in the world in population. Its population growth rate has fallen by one-third since the 1970s but is still twice as high as that of the United States and nearly three times the average of high-income economies. Every newborn baby stretches the nation's resources that much further. The baby must be fed, clothed, and educated. Eventually, that baby will join the long line of those already waiting to be employed.

It is this last problem that most worries the economic planners in Mexico. Until mid-1982, when it was hit by a currency crisis resulting from its foreign indebtedness, the Mexican economy was growing at the healthy rate of 8% a year. Since then its GDP has grown at only an average of 1.5% a year. The economy needs to grow by at least 5% a year in real terms just to create the jobs needed by the added numbers entering the labor force. It has been unable to create the 1 million new jobs needed each year. As a result, hundreds of thousands annually join the ranks of the unemployed. Independent estimates of Mexican unemployment put the figure at 25% to 30%, including those scraping a living in the informal economy, far higher than official government unemployment figures.

For those without work, life is hard. Public welfare programs are nearly nonexistent. Many of the poor crowd into the cities and some must beg for their livelihood. Others head for the U.S. border in an attempt to escape the poverty of their homeland. It is hoped that the North American Free Trade Agreement will increase employment opportunities in Mexico, and, in consequence, reduce the number of illegal immigrants entering the United States.

The collapse of world oil prices in the 1980s put Mexico into a financial crisis. During the years of rising oil prices, it had borrowed heavily from foreign banks and the World Bank to finance its expansion, counting on oil revenues to pay the interest on the loans and repay the debt. When its petroleum income shrank drastically, it was no longer able to meet its obligations. In 1988 the IMF advanced Mexico $3.64 billion, including more than $1 billion for interest and principal payments on old debt.

For its part, Mexico cut its budget deficit by 20%, sold off two-thirds of the 1,200 businesses it owned to private investors, and pressured labor and business to restrain wage and price increases in order to reduce the inflation rate. The consequences of its economic difficulties and the austerity program included a 20% fall in the standard of living for the average Mexican family and a deterioration of public services. The telephone system, for example, was devastated by lack of maintenance and investment. To make a call, it required up to 10 tries to get a line that worked.

■ Air pollution in Mexico City (above) is the worst of any city in the world.

As part of the reform program, Mexico turned away from its traditional protectionist trade policies by eliminating some tariffs, reducing other obstacles to trade, and inviting in foreign investment without the previous restrictions such as requiring Mexican partners. As a result, it has had an inflow of about $25 billion in foreign capital.

To meet the stiffer competition in the marketplace that will result from NAFTA, Mexican companies are restructuring to increase productivity. Manufacturing productivity increased 19% between 1990 and 1992. One of the results, however, is that companies have had to scrap plants and machinery sooner than they would otherwise. As a result, total capital stock has barely increased despite a growth in investment from 20% of GDP in 1988 to 24% in 1992.

At the time of the restructuring of Mexico's foreign debt in 1988, it owed $102 billion.

In 1992 the external debt was up to $113 billion and its current account deficit amounted to $22.8 billion. The foreign debt is again putting a cloud over Mexico's growth prospects.

Economic Reasoning

1. Which of the development problems discussed in this section of the chapter are faced by Mexico?

2. How could Mexico's large population of young people be turned into a human capital asset rather than a liability?

3. Should U.S. banks that have lent money to Mexico "forgive" a portion of the debt on condition that Mexico does not default on the major part? Should they lend Mexico additional funds? Why or why not?

Putting It Together

Two-thirds of the world's people live in poverty in the *less developed countries (LDCs)* of Asia, Africa, and Latin America. These countries are largely agricultural with small, inefficient manufacturing sectors and *per capita incomes* of only a few hundred dollars a year.

Income distribution in the LDCs is generally skewed so that a small percentage of income receivers have most of the income. Various *social indicators* such as illiteracy, life expectancy at birth, and infant mortality, along with the economic indicators, reveal a country's standard of living.

The poverty in developing countries stems from a number of factors. The *vicious circle of poverty* perpetuates low productivity because a lack of capital and the resulting low incomes do not provide an economic surplus with which to create capital. The lack of capital, modern technology, and productive human capital result in low GDP per capita.

Rapid population growth compounds the problem of insufficient capital by consuming virtually all production. This prevents the accumulation of a sufficient quantity of capital upon which growth and development can build.

Colonialism left a legacy of economic and social effects in these developing countries. Though some things left by colonial powers are beneficial, colonialism has had many negative effects. The world economic system prior to World War II was based on taking raw materials from the colonies to use in the industries of Western countries. This did not give Third World countries a chance to develop industries on their own. Today, domestic exploitation of one class by another retards development.

Misguided government policies have also interfered with growth. Many LDCs have embarked on ambitious industrialization programs, neglecting agriculture. The results of these programs too often were high-cost, poor-quality manufactured goods, food shortages, and serious balance-of-payments problems. Protectionist trade policies have frequently resulted in high-cost production and inflation with falling real income.

There is a race between world population growth—the population bomb—and increased food production. The long-run specter of food shortages, resource depletion, and environmental pollution is a threat not only to LDCs, but to the industrialized countries as well. The world's resources may be insufficient to satisfy demand if the developing countries begin to use them up at the same per capita rate as the industrialized countries do now.

A pressing problem for many LDCs is meeting the payments on their large external debt—the debt bomb. If they default they will lose international credit and foreign investment, and perhaps have their imports cut off. But if the governments tighten their domestic economic belts in order to avoid defaulting, their citizens may revolt.

The Malthusian Dilemma

Thomas Robert Malthus (1766–1834)
Robert Malthus was born in Surrey, England. He studied for the ministry at Cambridge, from which was derived the deprecatory reference to him by some of his later critics as "Parson Malthus." He was appointed professor of modern history and political economy at the Haileybury College of the East India Company, where he remained until his death. He was a friend and frequent correspondent of David Ricardo, who occasionally passed on to him tips on good investments in the commodities markets. Malthus did not act on the advice given by his successful friend and lived a life of genteel penury. In addition to six editions of the *Essay on Population,* Malthus wrote a text on the *Principles of Political Economy* (1820) and a number of pamphlets on such topics as prices, money, gold, rent, and foreign trade policy.

In his *Essay on Population* (1798), Thomas Robert Malthus predicted that the growth of population was bound to outrun the world's food supply. According to his calculations, population grew at a geometric ratio (1, 2, 4, 8, 16, etc.), while food production at most grew at an arithmetic ratio (1, 2, 3, 4, 5, etc.).

As a result, population would always push against the limit of food supplies and would be held in check by famine, as well as war and disease. Under these circumstances, there could be no improvement in living standards.

In the second edition of the *Essay on Population,* Malthus suggested that there might be a way to avoid mass starvation. He recognized that "moral restraint" might serve as a preventive check on population growth. He defined moral restraint as postponing marriage and also strict sexual continence prior to marriage. He was not, however, very hopeful that sufficient moral restraint would be practiced by the British working class to alleviate the population problem.

It was Malthus's very gloomy prediction of worldwide mass starvation that gave economics the designation of "the dismal science." So far, Malthus's expectations have not been fulfilled. On the whole, the world's population is better fed now than it has ever been in history. Malthus did not foresee the vast new areas that would be brought under cultivation in the New World and elsewhere, nor could he foresee the dramatic improvements in transportation that would make the New World's produce available throughout the world. Even less could he foresee the improvements in agricultural productivity that were to result from the agricultural revolution of the late nineteenth and early twentieth centuries and the green revolution that has resulted in more productive seed hybrids and improved irrigation and fertilization in the last 3 decades.

However, there are many today who believe that Malthus was basically right and only his timing was mistaken. These "neo-Malthusians" maintain that at the present rates of reproduction in many countries throughout the world, the population is bound to outrun the food-producing capacity of the earth, perhaps early in the next century. Even today the balance between food and population is precarious, with no reserves of staples in storage that could sustain the world over a series of shortfall production years resulting from drought or other production interruptions in major growing areas.

FOR FURTHER STUDY AND ANALYSIS

Study Questions

1. How do India and China compare in progressing toward the goal of economic development?

2. How can the LDCs increase the amount of capital available for investment in development projects to increase their rate of economic growth?

3. Why are educational and health programs important to economic growth?

4. What would it mean for a country if its population growth rate was higher than the growth rate of the GDP?

5. How does the existence of large amounts of unemployment and underemployment in LDCs affect their decisions about development strategies? What economic sectors might be stressed, and what kind of technology might be used in those circumstances?

6. Why does a poor country typically have a much higher birthrate than a developed country? What causes the birthrate to fall as income levels rise?

7. How does income distribution in the LDCs compare with the income distribution figures given for the United States in chapter 9 (p. 232)?

8. What policies should the governments of LDCs pursue in order to bring about economic development?

9. Why do LDCs accumulate so much international debt?

10. Why does environmental pollution get worse as a country begins to develop?

Exercises in Analysis

1. Compare the East Asia and Pacific region with the Latin America and Caribbean region with respect to GNP per capita and growth in GNP per capita. Write a short paper on the differences and what might account for them.

2. Select an LDC that interests you, other than the ones discussed in this chapter, and write a paper on its economy and prospects for development.

3. Write a paper on world population growth, the problems it poses, the possible solutions to those problems, and the prospects for the future.

4. Write an essay on one or all of the international problems hindering economic development, and the international cooperation to overcome them.

Further Reading

Barkin, David. *Distorted Development: Mexico in the World Economy.* Boulder, CO: Westview Press, 1990. An analysis of economic conditions and development policies in Mexico. Covers the role of the agricultural sector and the impact of Mexico's large foreign debt.

Cooper, Frederick, ed. *Confronting Historical Paradigms: Peasants, Labor, and the Capitalist World System in Africa and Latin America.* Madison, WI: University of Wisconsin Press, 1993. An examination of the economic and social conditions in the LDCs of Africa and Latin America. Evaluates the effect of capitalism on the agrarian societies of these countries.

Feinberg, Richard E., et al. *Economic Reform in Three Giants: U.S. Foreign Policy and the USSR, China, and India.* New Brunswick, NJ: Transaction Books, 1990. Covers economic reforms in three of the world's largest countries and discusses the international political ramifications.

Ghosh, Arun, *Planning in India: The Challenge for the Nineties.* New Delhi: Sage Publications, 1992. Examines the program of decentralization in government control over the Indian economy.

Gooptu, Sudarshan. *Debt Reduction and Development: The Case of Mexico.* New York: Praeger, 1993. Explains the means by which Mexico has handled its large foreign debt through a program of austerity and governmental fiscal restraint.

Grossman, Gene M. *Pollution and Growth: What Do We Know?* London: Center for Economic Policy Research, 1993. Reviews recent empirical studies on the relationship between pollution and per capita income in both developed and developing countries. Findings show that, although some local pollution problems, such as urban water and air pollution, exhibit an inverted U-shaped curve with respect to rising income—increasing to a certain income level and then falling—more large-scale environmental problems such as acid rain and carbon dioxide in the atmosphere steadily get worse.

Harrison, Paul. *The Third Revolution: Environment, Population and a Sustainable World.* New York: I. B. Tauris, 1992. Focuses on the relationship between population and the environment. The previous two revolutions implied by the title were the agricultural revolution and the industrial revolution. Both "were the response to pressures of population growth on the environment." The current revolution, according to Harrison, is brought on by waste.

International Investment Corporation Economics Department. *Internal and External Investments in Developing Countries: Financing Corporate Growth in the Developing World.* Washington, DC: World Bank Publications, 1991. Discusses corporate capital structures in industrial and developing countries, identifying similarities and differences. Compares the capital structures in fast-growing countries to those in slower-growing countries.

Leonard, H. Jeffrey, ed. *Divesting Nature's Capital: The Political Economy of Environ-*

mental Abuse in the Third World. New York: Holmes & Meier, 1985. Articles on the role of natural resources and the environment in economic development and the policies that have resulted in environmental degradation.

Leonard, H. Jeffrey. *Pollution and the Struggle for the World Product: Multinational Corporations, Environment, and International Comparative Advantage. Cambridge: Cambridge* University Press, 1988. A more technical treatment than the preceding book, it examines the relationship between industrial strategy and environmental pollution in both advanced and industrializing economies.

Lombardi, Richard W. *Debt Trap: Rethinking the Logic of Development.* New York: Praeger, 1985. The impact of multinational banking in the Third World and the debt crisis.

Mann, Jim. *Beijing Jeep: The Short, Unhappy Romance of American Business in China.* New York: Simon & Schuster, 1989. A newspaper reporter's account of trials and tribulations accompanying the attempts of American Motors and, after its takeover of American Motors, Chrysler to produce Cherokee Jeeps in China prior to the Tiananmen Square massacre.

Overholt, William. *The Rise of China.* New York: W. W. Norton, 1993. The author presents a very optimistic view of the economic prospects of China, predicting that it will be the next economic superpower. He sees difficulties to be faced in the conflicts between rich and poor regions and possible succession struggles, but he believes that pragmatism will overcome these difficulties.

Rosen, George. *Contrasting Styles of Industrial Reform: China and India in the 1980s.* Chicago: University of Chicago Press, 1992. A comparison of economic policies in India and China and the results of their differing paths to economic development.

Tidrick, Gene, and Chen Jiyuan, eds. *China's Industrial Reform.* New York: Oxford University Press, 1987. Contains articles on factor allocation and enterprise incentives; planning, supply, and marketing; and enterprise organization in China.

Todaro, Michael, *Economic Development in the Third World,* 4th edition. New York: Longman, 1989. Describes the characteristics of LDCs, the problems and policies of development, and foreign aid and investment.

Torres, J. F. *New Directions in Third World Countries: The Failure of U.S. Foreign Policy.* New York: Ashgate Publishing, 1993. This book focuses particularly on Latin American economic development. It criticizes the United States for supporting the military status quo in Latin American countries and argues instead for a "bottoms-up" development program in which the poor are directly involved in planning and implementation.

White, James C., ed. *Global Climate Change: Linking Energy, Environment, Economy, and Equity.* New York: Plenum Press, 1992. The author writes that "the nations of the world are not facing up to the global environmental needs. We are failing to recognize the potential severity of approaching problems and are not investing enough in prevention and amelioration to stem the deterioration of our environment."

Glossary

This glossary has been prepared to provide you with a convenient and ready reference as you encounter terms in *The Study of Ecoomics* that you wish to review. It includes the definition of each of the economic concepts contained in the in-text glossary.

Altogether there are a total of 373 items contained here. The number in *italics* following the **boldface** entry is the page number on which the item is first discussed in the text. For other references to each term in the text you should consult the index, which begins on page 513.

A.

absolute advantage *62;* when each of two producers can produce a different good or service more efficiently than can the other producer, each of the producers has an absolute advantage in the good or service that he produces most efficiently.

affirmative action program *238;* a program devised by employers to increase their hiring of women and minorities; frequently mandated by government regulations.

aggregate concentration *177;* a measure of the proportion of the total sales of all industries accounted for by the largest firms in the country. There is no common standard for measuring the aggregate concentration ratio.

aggregate demand *281;* the total effective demand for the nation's output of goods and services.

aggregate supply *292;* the total amount of goods and services available from all industries in the economy.

Aid to Families with Dependent Children (AFDC) *239;* a federally subsidized public assistance program to provide income maintenance and social services to needy families with dependent children.

annually balanced budget *361;* a budgetary principle calling for the revenue and expenditures of a government to be equal during the course of a year.

antitrust legislation *192;* laws that prohibit or limit monopolies or monopolistic practices.

authoritarian nations *449;* one-party states that have no effective political opposition; may be benign governments with the best interests of the whole people as their goal, or may be self-serving of the interests of the ruling group.

automatic stabilizers *367;* changes in government payments and tax receipts that automatically result from fluctuations in national income and act to aid in offsetting those fluctuations.

automatic transfer services (ATS) *258;* a type of account that provides for the depository institution to automatically transfer funds from the depositor's savings account to her or his checking account when it has been drawn down.

automation *171;* production techniques that adjust automatically to the needs of the processing operation by the use of control devices.

average costs *138;* total costs divided by the number of units produced.

average propensity to consume *114;* the percentage of after-tax income which, on the average, consumers spend on goods and services.

average propensity to save *114;* the percentage of after-tax income which, on the average, consumers save.

B.

balance of payments *422;* an annual summary of all economic transactions between a country and the rest of the world during the year.

balance of trade *423;* the net deficit or surplus in a country's merchandise trade; the difference between merchandise imports and exports.

barrier to entry *178;* an obstacle to the entry of new firms into an industry.

barter *258;* direct exchange of goods and services without the use of money.

base period (base year) *287;* the reference period for comparison of subsequent changes in an index series; set equal to 100.

basic deficit *424;* the excess of import-type transactions over export-type transactions in a country's current, long-term capital and noninduced, short-term capital movements in the balance of payments.

benefits principle *348;* levy of a tax on an individual to pay the costs of government service in proportion to the individual's benefit from the service.

bilateral trade negotiations *399;* trade negotiations between two countries only.

bond *263;* a long-term, interest-bearing certificate issued by a business firm or government that promises to pay the bondholder a specified sum of money on a specified date.

boycott *165;* refusal by consumers to buy the products or services of a firm.

break-even point *143;* the output level of a firm at which total revenue equals total costs (TR = TC).

business process reengineering (BPR) *174;* a reorganization of a company to make use of just-in-time methods, DFMA and DMS, and multidisciplinary teams of workers aimed at production in least time with no defects.

business transfer payments *311;* outlay by business for which no good or service is exchanged, such as excise taxes, payouts under deferred compensation arrangements, gifts, and donations.

C.

capital *9;* the means of production, including factories, office buildings, machinery, tools, and equipment; alternatively, it can mean financial capital, the money to acquire the foregoing and employ land and labor resources.

capital consumption allowances *312;* the costs of capital assets consumed in producing GDP.

capital equipment *167;* the machinery and tools used to produce goods and services.

capital gain *236;* net income realized from an increase in the market value of a real or financial asset when it is sold.

capitalism *442;* an economic system based on the right of private ownership of most of the means of production, such as businesses, farms, mines, and natural resources, as well as private property, such as homes and automobiles.

capital/output ratio *378;* the ratio of the cost of new investment goods to the value of the annual output produced by those investment goods.

cartel *147;* an industry in which the firms have an agreement to set prices and/or divide the market among members of the cartel.

catch-up *453;* the growth process by which an industrializing country adopts advanced technology and production methods already in use by industrialized countries.

central bank *263;* a government institution that controls the issuance of currency, provides banking services to the government and to the other banks, and implements the nation's monetary policy; in the United States the Federal Reserve is the central bank.

central planning *442;* a method of resource allocation in which the top leadership makes the major decisions on production, distribution, and coordination.

centrally directed (command) economy *65;* an economic system in which the basic questions of what, how, and for whom to produce are resolved primarily by governmental authority.

certificate of deposit (CD) *258;* a deposit of a specified sum of money for a specified period of time that cannot be redeemed prior to the date specified.

chart *20;* a graphical representation of statistical data or other information.

check *255;* a written order to a depository institution to pay a person or institution named on it a specified sum of money.

circular flow diagram *75;* a schematic drawing showing the economic relationships between the major sectors of an economic system.

collective bargaining *221;* a process by which decisions regarding the wages, hours, and conditions of employment are determined by the interaction of workers acting through their unions and employers.

collective good (public good) *198;* an economic good (includes services) that is supplied by the government either with no direct payment by the recipient or at a price less than the cost of providing it.

command-and-control regulations *206;* a system of administrative or statutory rules that requires the use of specific control devices to reduce pollution.

commodity *260;* an economic good.

communism *442;* according to Karl Marx, the last stage of economic development after the state has withered away and work and consumption are engaged in communally; in common usage, frequently used to designate state socialist economies.

community demand schedule *86;* the sum of all the individual demand schedules in a particular market showing the total quantities demanded by the buyers in the market at each of the various possible prices.

comparative advantage *63;* when one producer has an efficiency advantage over another producer in two separate products, but has a greater advantage in one product than in the other, the efficient producer has a comparative advantage in the product in which he has the greater relative efficiency; and the inefficient producer, on the other hand, has a comparative advantage in the product in which his efficiency disadvantage is not as large.

complement *91;* a product that is employed jointly in conjunction with another product.

computer-integrated manufacturing (CIM) *172;* a system of integrating all the operations of different departments in a plant by means of a central computer and a network of workstation computers.

concentration ratio *177;* the percentage of total sales of an industry accounted for by the largest four firms. An alternative measure is the percentage of sales accounted for by the largest eight firms.

constant dollar GDP (real GDP) *313;* the value of GDP adjusted for changes in the price level since a base period.

consumer equilibrium *119;* the condition in which consumers allocate their income in such a way that the last dollar spent on each good or service and the last dollar saved provide equal amounts of utility.

consumer price index (CPI) *286;* a statistical measure of changes in the prices of a representative sample of urban family purchases relative to a previous period.

consumer sovereignty *114;* the condition in a market economy by which consumer decisions about which goods and services to purchase determine resource allocation.

consumer tastes and preferences *91;* individual liking or partiality for specific goods or services.

cooperatives *130;* producer and worker cooperatives are associations in which the members join in production and marketing and share the profits. Consumer cooperatives are associations of consumers engaged in retail trade, sharing the profits as a dividend among the members.

corporation *130;* a business enterprise that is chartered by a state government or, occasionally, by the federal government to do business as a legal entity.

correspondent bank *418;* a bank in another city or country that a bank has an arrangement with to provide deposit transfer or other services.

cost-of-living adjustment (COLA) *288;* a frequently used provision of labor contracts that grants wage increases based on changes in the Consumer Price Index; often referred to in negotiations as the "escalator clause."

cost-push inflation *288;* a continuing rise in the general price level that results from increases in production costs.

cross-training *170;* giving workers training in performing more than one task.

crowding out *325;* the term given to the effect government has in reducing the amount of financial capital available for private investment.

currency *253;* that part of the money supply consisting of coins and paper bills.

currency appreciation *419;* an increase in the value of a country's currency relative to other currencies as a result of a decrease in its supply relative to the demand for it.

currency depreciation *419;* a decline in the value of a country's currency relative to other currencies as a result of an increase in its supply relative to the demand for it.

current account *423;* those transactions in the balance of payments consisting of merchandise and service imports and exports and unilateral transfers (gifts).

current dollar GDP *313;* the value of GNP as measured by figures unadjusted for inflation.

cyclical unemployment *281;* the lack of work that occurs because the total effective demand for goods and services is insufficient to employ all workers in the labor force.

cyclically balanced budget *361;* a budgetary principle calling for the balancing of the budget over the course of a complete business cycle rather than in a particular fiscal or calendar year; over the course of the cycle, tax receipts and expenditures would balance.

D.

deficit *317;* a negative balance after expenditures are subtracted from revenues.

demand *85;* the relationship between the quantities of a good or service that consumers desire to purchase at any particular time and the various prices that can exist for the good or service.

demand curve *85;* a graphic representation of the relationship between price and quantity demanded.

demand deposits (checking accounts) *255;* liabilities of depository institutions to their customers that are payable on demand.

demand schedule *85;* a table recording the number of units of a good or service demanded at various possible prices.

demand-pull inflation *287;* a continuing rise in the general price level that occurs when aggregate demand exceeds the full-employment output capacity of the economy.

deposit liabilities *266;* the amount that a depository institution is obligated to pay out to its depositors.

depository institutions *265;* financial institutions that maintain deposit account obligations to their customers; includes commercial banks, savings banks, savings and loan associations, and credit unions.

depreciation *137;* the costs of buildings, machinery, tools, and equipment that are allocated to output during a given production period.

depression *282;* a severe and prolonged period of decline in the level of business activity.

deregulation *194;* the process of eliminating government regulations and reducing the scope and power of regulatory bodies.

derived demand *218;* the demand for a factor of production, not because it directly provides utility, but because it is needed to produce finished products that do provide utility.

design for manufacturability and assembly (DFMA) *172;* a system of designing products in which the design engineers consult with manufacturing personnel during the designing process to avoid designs that will be difficult or costly to manufacture.

devaluation *419;* a decrease in the value of a country's currency relative to other currencies due to an official government reduction in the exchange rate under a fixed-rate system.

diagram *23;* a graph that shows the relationship between two or more variables that may or may not have values that can actually be measured; a graphical model.

differentiated competition *148;* an industry in which there are a large number of firms producing similar but not identical products; sometimes called monopolistic competition.

differentiated products *148;* similar but not identical products produced by different firms.

diminishing marginal utility *116;* the common condition in which the marginal utility obtained from consuming an additional unit of a good or service is smaller than the marginal utility obtained from consuming the preceding unit of the good or service.

diminishing returns *142;* the common condition in which additional inputs produce successively smaller increments of output.

direct relationship *23;* a relationship between two variables in which their values increase and decrease together.

discount rate *265;* the interest rate charged by the Federal Reserve on loans to depository institutions.

discounting *267;* assigning a present value to future returns; making a loan with the interest subtracted in advance from the principal.

discretionary fiscal policy *364;* fiscal policy measures activated by overt decisions.

disposable income *315;* the amount of after-tax income that households have available for consumption or saving.

E.

earned income *348;* wages, salaries, and other employee compensation plus earnings from self-employment.

earned income tax credit (EITC) *239;* a federal tax credit for poor families with earnings that offsets their tax liabilities and, for the poorest, provides a tax subsidy.

economic concept *17;* a word or phrase that conveys an economic idea.

economic good *12;* any good or service that sells for a price; that is, a good that is not free.

economic growth *50;* an increase in the production capacity of the economy.

economic model *17;* a simplified representation of the cause-and-effect relationships in a particular situation. Models may be in verbal, graphic, or equation form.

economic profits *139;* earnings on invested capital that are in excess of the normal rate of return.

economic reasoning *12;* the application of theoretical and factual tools of economic analysis to explaining economic developments or solving economic problems.

economic surplus *476;* a margin of output over and above consumption needs that can be allocated to investment for intensive growth.

economies of scale *178;* decreasing costs per unit as plant size increases.

eco-tax *206;* a fee levied by the government on each unit of environmental pollutant emitted.

effective demand *91;* the desire and the ability to purchase a certain number of units of a good or service at a given price.

efficiency *48;* maximizing the amount of output obtained from a given amount of resources or minimizing the amount of resources used for a given amount of output.

elastic *110;* a demand condition in which the relative size of the change in quantity demanded is greater than the size of the price change.

elasticity ratio *112;* a measurement of the degree of the response of a change in quantity to a change in price.

employee involvement (EI) *172;* various programs for incorporating hourly-wage workers in decision making; may involve decisions on production methods, work scheduling, and purchase of capital equipment.

entitlement program *238;* government benefits that qualified recipients are entitled to by law, such as Social Security old-age benefits.

entrepreneur *10;* a business innovator who sees the opportunity to make a profit from a new product, new process, or unexploited raw material and then brings together the land, labor, and capital to exploit the opportunity, risking failure.

equilibrium output level *319;* the level of GDP at which aggregate demand (C + I + G + X) is just equal to aggregate supply (C + S + T + M); the level where income leakages (S + T + M) are exactly equal to income additions (I + G + X).

equilibrium price *89;* the price at which the quantity of a good or service offered by suppliers is exactly equal to the quantity that is demanded by purchasers in a particular period of time.

equity *114;* the owner's share of the value of property or other assets, net of mortgages or other liabilities.

excess reserves *266;* reserves of depository institutions over and above the legally required minimum on deposit with the Federal Reserve.

excise taxes *311;* a tax on a particular type of good or service; a sales tax.

exploitation *479;* obtaining labor services, raw materials, or finished goods for a price that is less than their true value.

export embargo *401;* a prohibition of the export of a commodity, capital, or technology.

external costs *205;* costs of the production process that are not carried by the producer unit or by the purchaser of the product and are therefore not taken into consideration in production and consumption decisions.

external economies *199;* benefits that accrue to parties other than the producer and purchaser of the good or service; benefits for which payment is not collected.

externalities *200;* external economies or external diseconomies (external costs).

F.

factor incomes *72;* the return to factors of production as a reward for productive activity.

factor market *70;* a market in which resources and semifinished products are exchanged.

factor share *228;* the part of national income received by a particular factor of production.

factors of production *9;* another name for the production resources of land (natural resources), labor, and capital (machinery and buildings).

favorable balance of trade *423;* the surplus in a country's merchandise trade when exports during the year are greater than imports.

Fed *263;* Federal Reserve System.

Fed Board of Governors *264;* the governing body of the Federal Reserve System, consisting of seven members appointed by the president for 14-year terms.

Federal Funds market *268;* the market among depository institutions for temporary transfer of excess reserves from one institution to another.

Federal Funds rate *268;* the interest rate paid on Federal Funds borrowed.

Federal Open Market Committee *268;* a committee consisting of the Federal Reserve Board and the presidents of five regional Federal Reserve banks that decides on the purchase or sale of government securities by the Federal Reserve to implement monetary policy.

Federal Reserve System (Fed) *253;* the central bank of the United States; a system established by the Federal Reserve Act of 1913 to issue paper currency, supervise the nation's banking system, and implement monetary policy.

financial capital *10;* the money to acquire the factors of production.

fiscal federalism *344;* tax collection and disbursement of funds by a higher level of government to lower jurisdictions.

fiscal policy *361;* the use of federal government spending, taxing, and debt management to influence general economic activity.

fixed costs *137;* production costs that do not change with changes in the quantity of output.

fixed exchange rates *419;* exchange rates between currencies that are legally set by the respective countries.

flexible manufacturing systems (FMS) *172;* the use of computer-controlled capital equipment that can be readily shifted from the production of one part to a different part.

food stamps *238;* certificates that can be used in place of money to purchase food items.

"for whom" question *45;* the question concerning the decisions made by an economy about income distribution—who gets how much of the goods and services produced.

foreign exchange market *417;* a set of institutions, including large banks in the world's financial centers, private brokers, and government central banks and other agencies, that deal in the exchange of one country's money for another's.

free good *12;* a production or consumption good that does not have a direct cost.

free trade *399;* international trade that is unrestricted by government protectionist measures.

freely fluctuating exchange rates *419;* an exchange-rate system by which the relative values of different currencies are determined by demand and supply rather than by government fiat.

frictional unemployment *279;* the lack of work that occurs from time lost changing jobs.

full employment *50;* employment of nearly everyone who desires to work. In practice, an unemployment level of not more than 4–5% is considered full employment.

full employment aggregate demand *281;* the level of total effective demand that is just sufficient to employ all workers in the labor force.

functional finance *362;* the use of fiscal policy to stabilize the economy without regard to the policy's effect on a balanced government budget.

functional income distribution *227;* the shares of total income distributed according to the type of factor service for which they are paid, that is, rent as a payment for land, wages for labor, and interest for capital.

G.

golden rule *364;* a budget approach that calls for current services to be covered by revenues while paying for capital expenditures with deficit financing.

government sector spending (G) *311;* spending by the various levels of government on goods and services, including public investment.

Gross Domestic Product (GDP) *309;* the sum of the values of all goods and services produced within the country during the year.

Gross National Product (GNP) *311;* the sum of the values of all goods and services produced by residents of the country during the year, including earnings on overseas investments and excluding foreign earnings on investments in this country.

gross private domestic investment (I) *310;* private-sector spending on capital equipment, increased stocks of inventories, and new residential housing.

H.

hidden unemployment *282;* that part of the unemployed population not reflected in official unemployment figures.

homogeneous products *148;* identical products produced by different firms.

horizontal equity *348;* equality of treatment for all individuals at the same level.

household *72;* an economic unit consisting of an individual or a family.

"how" question *44;* the question concerning the decisions made by an economy about the technology used to produce goods and services.

human capital *169;* labor that is literate, skilled, trained, healthy, and economically motivated.

hypothesis *11;* a tentative explanation of an event; used as a basis for further research.

I.

implicit interest *231;* income that derives from the use of capital but is not paid as interest but rather as a part of accounting profits.

implicit wages *227;* income that is the result of labor input but is not received in the form of wages or salaries, but in some other form such as net proprietor's income (profits).

import-competing industry *395;* a domestic industry that produces the same or a close substitute good that competes in the domestic market with imports.

incentive *71;* a motivation to undertake an action or to refrain from undertaking an action; in a market economy profits are the incentive to produce.

incidence of a tax *349;* the amount of a tax that ultimately falls on households, irrespective of who initially pays the tax.

income effect *83;* the effect of a change in the price of a good or service on the amount purchased that results from a change in purchasing power of the consumer's income due to the price change.

increasing costs *393;* a rise in average production costs as the quantity of output of the good increases.

indirect taxes *312;* taxes collected from businesses that are ultimately paid in full or in part by someone other than the business from which the tax is collected; not income taxes.

industry consortium *193;* a combination of firms in an industry to carry out a common purpose.

inelastic *110;* a demand condition in which the relative size of the change in the quantity demanded is less than the size of the price change.

infant industry argument *404;* the contention that it is economically justified to provide trade protection to a new industry in a country to enable it to grow to a size that would result in production costs that are competitive with those of foreign producers.

inflation *49;* a continuously rising general price level, resulting in a reduction in the purchasing power of money.

infrastructure *45;* an economy's stock of capital—much of it publicly owned—that provides basic services to producers and consumers. Includes such facilities as highways, electric power, water supplies, educational institutions, and health services.

institutions *15;* decision-making units, established practices, or laws.

interdependence *63;* the relationship between individuals and institutions in a country or between countries that arises because of specialization of production.

interest *72;* a factor payment for the use of capital.

internalize external costs *206;* the process of transforming external costs into internal costs so that the producer and consumer of a good pay the full cost of its production.

International Monetary Fund (IMF) *419;* an organization established in 1946 to assist in operation of the world monetary system by regulating the exchange practices of countries and providing liquidity to member countries that have payment problems.

inventories *310;* the value of finished and semifinished goods and raw materials in the hands of producers and distributors.

inverse relationship *23;* a relationship between two variables in which the value of one decreases as the value of the other increases.

investment/GDP ratio *374;* the proportion of GDP that is allocated to private investment.

J.

job action *222;* a concerted action by employees to disrupt production or distribution in order to put pressure on employers to grant concessions. Job actions may consist of lesser actions such as work slowdowns or work-to-rule (performing the minimum tasks stipulated in the job description) as an alternative to a strike.

junk bonds *168;* bonds that are issued paying higher than normal interest rates because they have a greater risk of default.

just-in-time *171;* a system that provides for raw materials and subassemblies to be delivered by suppliers to the location where they will be processed at the time they are needed rather than being stored in inventories.

K.

Keynesian economics *315;* the body of macro-economic theories and policies that stem from the model developed by John Maynard Keynes.

Keynesian revolution *323;* the name given to the transformation in macroeconomic theory and policy that resulted from the ideas of Keynes.

kickback *178;* the return of a portion of a payment or commission in accordance with a secret agreement.

L.

L *258;* a measure of the money supply that includes M3 plus commercial paper, savings bonds, and government securities with maturities of 18 months or less.

labor *9;* all human resources, including manual, clerical, technical, professional, and managerial labor.

labor force participation rate *378;* the percentage of the working-age population, or of a subgroup of the population, that is in the labor force.

labor-intensive *393;* refers to production processes that employ a large amount of labor relative to the amount of capital equipment.

land *9;* all natural resources, including fields, forests, mineral deposits, the sea, and other gifts of nature.

law of demand *83;* the quantity demanded of a good or service varies inversely with its price; the lower the price the larger the quantity demanded, and the higher the price the smaller the quantity demanded.

law of supply *88;* the quantity supplied of a good or service varies directly with its price; the lower the price the smaller the quantity supplied, and the higher the price the larger the quantity supplied.

learning curve *169;* a diagram showing how labor productivity or labor costs change as the total number of units produced by a new plant or with new technology increases over time.

legal reserve requirement (required reserves) *265;* the minimum amount of reserves that a depository institution must have on deposit with the Federal Reserve bank, stated as a percentage of its deposit liabilities.

less developed countries (LDC) *470;* nonindustrialized countries generally characterized by a poverty income level, a labor force primarily employed in agriculture, extensive underemployment, and illiteracy, and located in Africa, Asia, or Latin America.

limited liability *131;* a legal provision that protects individual stockholders of a corporation from being sued by creditors of the corporation to collect unpaid debts of the firm.

limited specialization *393;* specialization in producing goods or services according to comparative advantage when the specialization is not complete due to increasing costs (decreasing returns).

liquidity *258;* the degree of ease with which an asset can be converted into cash without appreciable loss in value.

long run *95;* a period of time sufficiently long that the amount of all factor inputs can be varied.

long-term capital *424;* direct investment in plant and equipment or portfolio investments in stocks and bonds.

Lorenz curve *232;* a diagram showing the distribution of income among groups of people; an indicator of the degree of inequality of income distribution.

luxury *109;* a good or service which increases satisfaction but is not considered essential to well-being.

M.

M1 *255;* a measure of the money supply that includes currency in circulation, demand deposit accounts, negotiable order of withdrawal (NOW) accounts, automatic transfer savings (ATS) accounts, traveler's checks, and checkable money market accounts.

M2 *258;* a measure of the money supply that includes M1 plus savings deposits, small time deposits (CDs), and certain money market mutual funds.

M3 *258;* a measure of the money supply that includes M2 plus large time deposits (CDs).

macroeconomics *xviii;* the area of economic studies that deals with the overall functioning of an economy, total production output, employment, and price level.

marginal cost *146;* the addition to total cost from the production of an additional unit of output.

marginal revenue *146;* the addition to total revenue from the sale of an additional unit of output.

marginal tax rate *348;* the tax rate applied to the last or additional income received.

marginal utility *116;* the amount of satisfaction a consumer derives from consuming one additional unit (or the last unit consumed) of a particular good or service.

market concentration *177;* a measure of the number of firms in an industry.

market economy *65;* an economic system in which the basic questions of what, how, and for whom to produce are resolved primarily by buyers and sellers interacting in markets.

market socialism *443;* an economic system in which the means of production are publicly or collectively owned, and the allocation of resources is market-directed by the pricing system.

marketplace (market) *65;* a network of dealings between buyers and sellers of a resource or product (good or service); the dealings may take place at a particular location, or they may take place by communication at a distance with no face-to-face contact between buyers and sellers.

maximum profit level *143;* the output level of a firm at which the revenue from one additional unit of production (marginal revenue) is equal to the cost of producing that unit (marginal cost).

Medicaid *239;* a federally subsidized, state-administered program to pay for medical and hospital costs of low-income families.

medium of exchange *258;* a commodity accepted by common consent in payment for goods and services and as settlement of debts and contracts.

mercantilists *405;* those who advocated mercantilism, a doctrine that dominated policies in many countries from the sixteenth to the eighteenth centuries. It held that exports should be maximized and imports minimized to generate an inflow of gold, and that exports of machinery and technology should be prohibited to prevent competition from foreign producers.

merger *178;* a contractual joining of the assets of one formerly independent company with those of another; may be a horizontal merger of companies producing the same product, a vertical merger of companies producing different stages of a product in the same industry, or a conglomerate merger of companies producing in different industries.

merit goods *199;* goods (including services) that have a social value over and above their utility for the individual consumer.

microeconomics *xviii;* the area of economic studies that deals with individual units in an economy, households, business firms, labor unions, and workers.

minimum wage laws *221;* federal or state laws that prohibit employers from paying less than a specified hourly wage to their employees.

misallocation of resources *178;* not producing the mix of products and services that would maximize consumer satisfaction.

mixed economy *67;* an economic system in which the basic questions of what, how, and for whom to produce are resolved by a mixture of market forces with governmental direction and/or custom and tradition.

monetarists *288;* those who believe that changes in the money supply have a determinative effect on economic conditions.

monetary policy *364;* actions of the Federal Reserve Board to produce changes in the money supply, the availability of loanable funds, or the level of interest rates in an attempt to influence general economic activity.

money market mutual fund *258;* an investment fund that pools the assets of investors and puts the cash into debt securities that mature in less than 1 year: short-term bank CDs, commercial paper of corporations, and 6-month Treasury bills.

money multiplier *267;* the ratio of the maximum increase in the money supply to an increase in bank reserves. Determined by the required reserve ratio.

monopolistic pricing *178;* setting a price above the level necessary to bring a product to market by restricting the supply of the product.

most-favored-nation clause *400;* a provision in trade agreements that extends lower tariff concessions granted to one country to all other countries that are accorded most-favored-nation treatment.

multilateral trade negotiations *400;* simultaneous trade negotiations among a number of countries.

multiplier *366;* the ratio of the ultimate increase in income, caused by an initial increase in spending, to that initial increase.

multiplier effect *365;* the process by which an initial increase in income results in a total income increase that is a multiple of the initial increase.

N.

National Income (NI) *311;* the total of all incomes earned in producing the GNP.

national income accounts *315;* the collective name for various macroeconomic measurements such as GDP and National Income.

natural monopoly *193;* an industry in which the economies of scale are so extensive that a single firm can supply the whole market more efficiently than two or more firms could; natural monopolies are generally public utilities.

natural rate of unemployment *294;* the equilibrium level of unemployment at full-capacity output consistent with a stable amount of inflation.

near money (monies) *255;* assets with a specified monetary value that are readily redeemable as money; savings accounts, certificates of deposit, and shares in money market mutual funds.

necessity *109;* a good or service which is considered essential to a person's well-being.

negotiable order of withdrawal (NOW) accounts *255;* savings and loan bank customer accounts on which checks can be drawn.

neomercantilists *405;* contemporary advocates of mercantilist trade policies to restrict imports, maximize exports of consumer products, and restrict exports of capital equipment and technology to prevent competition from foreign producers.

net exports (X – M) *311;* the value of goods and services exported minus the amount spent on imported goods and services.

net value *220;* the market value of a worker's output after subtracting the other production costs, such as raw materials.

non-accelerating-inflation rate of unemployment (NAIRU) *294;* a more precise term for the natural rate of unemployment.

nonearned income *348;* dividends, interest, capital gains, and other nonlabor income.

nontariff barriers *401;* restrictions on imports resulting from requirements for special marking, test, or standards enforced on imported goods or the time delays in clearing them for importation.

normal rate of return *139;* the rate of earnings on invested capital that is normal for a given degree of risk.

O.

oligopoly *147;* a shared monopoly in which there is no explicit agreement among the firms.

open market operations *265;* the purchase or sale of government securities by the Federal Reserve to implement monetary policy.

opportunity cost *40;* real economic cost of a good or service produced measured by the value of the sacrificed alternative.

other checkable deposits *255;* accounts, other than demand deposit accounts in commercial banks, on which checks can be drawn, principally negotiable order of withdrawal (NOW) accounts in savings and loan banks.

P.

partnership *130;* a nonincorporated business enterprise with two or more owners.

payroll tax *343;* a tax on wages and salaries to finance Social Security and Medicare costs, with equal amounts paid by employee and employer; the 1990 tax rate on each was 7.65%.

per capita income *470;* total National Income (or GNP) divided by the population size.

perfectly elastic *111;* a demand condition in which the quantity demanded varies from zero to infinity when there is a change in the price.

perfectly inelastic *111;* a demand condition in which there is no change in the quantity demanded when price changes.

personal consumption expenditures (C) *309;* spending by households on goods and services.

personal income distribution *231;* the pattern of income distribution according to the relative size of people's income.

Phillips curve *290;* a statistical relationship between increases in the general price level and unemployment.

poverty line *236;* the family income level below which people are officially classified as poor.

predatory business practice *178;* any action on the part of a firm carried out solely to interfere with a competitor.

price discrimination *178;* selling a product to two different buyers at different prices where all other conditions are the same.

price elasticity of demand *110;* the relative size of the change in the quantity demanded of a good or service as a result of a small change in its price.

price leadership *148;* a common practice in shared monopoly industries by which one of the firms in the industry, normally one of the largest, changes its prices, and the other firms follow its lead.

price stability *49;* a constant average level of prices for all goods and services.

privatization *443;* the process of selling government enterprises to private buyers and/or turning government services over to private sector operation.

process innovation *171;* introducing improved methods of organizing production.

product differentiation *179;* a device used by business firms to distinguish their product from the products of other firms in the same industry.

product market *70;* a market in which finished goods and services are exchanged.

production inputs (inputs) *72;* the factors of production used in producing a good or service.

production possibility frontier (PPF) *41;* the line on a graph showing the different maximum output combinations of goods or services that can be obtained from a fixed amount of resources.

productivity *162;* a ratio of the amount of output per unit of input; denotes the efficiency with which resources (people, tools, knowledge, and energy) are used to produce goods and services; usually measured as output per hour of labor.

profits *139;* the net returns after subtracting total costs from total revenue. If costs are greater than revenue, profits are negative.

progressive tax *349;* a tax rate that increases as the income on which the tax is based grows larger.

promissory note (IOU) *261;* a written obligation to pay a specified amount at a specified time.

proportional tax *351;* a levy that takes the same proportion in taxes from low and high incomes.

proprietorship *130;* a business enterprise with a single private owner.

protectionism *404;* measures taken by the government in order to limit or exclude imports that compete with domestic production.

public utility *144;* an industry that produces an essential public service such as electricity, gas, water, and telephone service; normally, a single firm is granted a local monopoly to provide the service.

public utility commission *193;* a regulatory body whose members are appointed by government to set rates and services provided by public utility firms.

pure competition *141;* a condition prevailing in an industry in which there are such a large number of firms producing a standardized product that no single firm can noticeably affect the market price by changing its output; also an industry in which firms can easily enter or leave.

pure monopoly *144;* an industry in which there is only one firm.

Q.

quantity demanded *83;* the amount of a good or service that consumers would purchase at a particular price.

quantity equation (equation of exchange) *288;* the quantity of money **(M)** times the velocity of its circulation **(V)** equals the quantity of goods and services transacted **(T)** times their average price **(P)**; $M \times V = T \times P$.

quota *400;* a limit on the quantity or value of a good that can be imported in a given time period.

R.

rate discrimination (price discrimination)
192; charging different customers different
rates for services of equal production cost.

real capital *133;* the buildings, machinery,
tools, and equipment used in production.

real income *298;* money income adjusted for
changes in the prices of goods and services.

real interest rate *119;* the quoted interest
rate calculated on an annual basis and adjusted for changes in the purchasing power
of money during the duration of the loan.

real investment *167;* the purchase of business structures and capital equipment; investment measured in dollars of constant value to
adjust for inflation.

real output *297;* the value of output adjusted
for changes in prices; the volume of output.

recession *281;* a decline for at least 2 successive quarters in the nation's total output of
goods and services.

regressive tax *351;* a levy that takes a
higher proportion from low incomes in taxes
than it takes from high incomes.

rent *72;* a factor payment for the use of land.

required reserves *265;* see legal reserve requirement.

reserve requirement ratio *266;* the percentage of a depository institution's deposit obligations to its depositors that must be
maintained in reserves.

residual accounts *424;* the short-term capital
transfers and monetary gold transactions that
compensate for the imbalance in a country's
basic balance in its international payments.

resources *9;* the inputs that are used in production. Includes natural resources (minerals,
timber, rivers), labor (blue collar, white collar),
and capital (machinery, buildings).

revaluation *419;* an increase in the value of
a country's currency relative to other currencies due to an official government increase in
the exchange rate under a fixed-rate system.

revenue *139;* the receipts from sales of
goods and services.

revenue bond *325;* a financial obligation issued by a branch of state or local government that has the receipts from a specific
revenue source pledged to the obligation's interest and redemption payments.

S.

savings deposits *255;* liabilities of depository
institutions to their customers that are not
transferable by check and for which the institution may require advance notice before withdrawal.

Say's Law of Markets *323;* A theory of the
French economist J. B. Say, which holds that
when goods or services are produced,
enough income is generated to purchase
what is produced, thereby eliminating the
problem of overproduction.

scarcity *9;* the limited resources for production relative to the demand for goods and
services.

scientific method *11;* a procedure used by
scientists to develop explanations for events
and test the validity of those explanations.

shared monopoly *147;* an industry in which
there are only a few firms; more specifically,
an industry in which four or fewer firms account for more than 50% of industry sales.

shift in demand *96;* a change in the quantity
of a good or service that would be purchased
at each possible price.

shift in supply *96;* a change in the quantity
of a good or service that would be offered for
sale at each possible price.

short run *93;* a period of time so short that the amount of some factor inputs cannot be varied.

short-term capital *424;* transfers of demand deposits or liquid investments such as money market funds, CDs, or Treasury bills.

sin tax *348;* an excise tax levied on commodities that public policy deems undesirable, such as cigarettes and alcohol, in order to limit their consumption.

social indicators *473;* noneconomic statistics that reflect a country's standard of living.

socioeconomic goal *52;* the type of social goal that has important economic dimensions.

specialization *61;* concentrating the activity of a unit of a production resource—especially labor—on a single task or production operation. Also applies to the specialization of nations in producing those goods and services that their resources are best suited to produce.

speculators *288;* people who purchase goods or financial assets in anticipation that prices will rise and they can sell at a profit; speculators can also speculate on a fall in prices.

stagflation *291;* a term created to describe a situation of simultaneous economic stagnation, high unemployment, and inflation.

state (authoritarian) socialism *442;* a command economy in which virtually all of the means of production are in the hands of the state and decision making is centralized.

statistics *15;* the data on economic variables; also the techniques of analyzing, interpreting, and presenting data.

stock option *377;* the right to purchase a specific amount of a corporation's stock at a fixed price. Often part of the compensation package for a company's top executives.

store of value *260;* a means of conserving purchasing power for a future time.

strike *222;* a collective refusal by employees to work.

structural unemployment *280;* the lack of work that occurs because of changes in the basic characteristics of a market, such as a new substitute product, a change in consumer tastes, or new technology in production.

substitute *91;* a product that is interchangeable in use with another product.

substitution effect *84;* the effect of a change in the price of a good or service on the amount purchased that results from the consumer substituting a relatively less expensive alternative.

supply *87;* the relationship between the quantities of a good or service that sellers wish to market at any particular time and the various prices that can exist for the good or service.

supply curve *88;* a graphic representation of the relationship between price and quantity supplied.

supply schedule *87;* a table recording the number of units of a good or service supplied at various possible prices.

supply-side economics *323;* an approach to macroeconomic problems that focuses on the importance of increasing the supply of goods and services.

surplus *318;* a positive balance after expenditures are subtracted from revenues.

T.

tariff *399;* a tax placed on an imported good; also, the whole schedule of a country's import duties.

technology *10;* the body of skills and knowledge that comprises the processes used in production.

terms of trade *404;* the ratio of average export prices to average import prices.

time series *21;* the changes in the values of a variable over time; a chart in which time—generally years—is one of the variables.

total costs *138;* the sum of fixed costs and variable costs.

total factor productivity (TFP) *445;* the increase in output in excess of the amounts attributed to additional labor and physical capital inputs; results from combining labor and capital in a production process that has increased efficiency.

total revenue *139;* the sum of receipts from all of the units sold; price × quantity.

total utility *116;* the amount of satisfaction a consumer derives from all of the units of a particular good or service consumed in a given time period.

trade adjustment assistance *406;* supplementary unemployment payments to workers who have lost their jobs because of import competition, and assistance to firms in shifting to other types of production.

trade-off *40;* the choice between alternative uses for a given quantity of a resource.

traditional economy *66;* an economic system in which the basic questions of what, how, and for whom to produce are resolved primarily by custom and tradition.

transfer payments *238;* expenditures for which no goods or services are exchanged. Welfare, Social Security, and unemployment compensation are government transfer payments.

Treasury bill *263;* a short-term, marketable federal government security with a maturity of 1 year or less.

trust *191;* a combination of producers in the same industry under joint direction for the purpose of exerting monopoly power.

U.

underemployed *283;* workers who cannot obtain full-time employment or who are working at jobs for which they are overqualified.

unfavorable balance of trade *423;* the deficit in a country's merchandise trade when imports during the year are greater than exports.

unit of measurement (standard of value or unit of account) *258;* a common denominator of value in which prices are stated and accounts recorded.

unitary elasticity *112;* a demand condition in which the relative change in the quantity demanded is the same as the size of the price change.

utility *116;* the amount of satisfaction a consumer derives from consumption of a good or service.

V.

value added *313;* the difference between the value of a firm's sales and its purchases of materials and semifinished inputs.

variable *17;* a quantity—such as number of workers, amount of carbon dioxide, or interest rate—whose value changes in relationship to changes in the values of other associated items.

variable costs *138;* production costs that change with changes in the quantity of output.

velocity of money circulation (V) *290;* the average rate at which money changes hands.

vertical equity *348;* fair differentiations of treatment of individuals at different levels.

vertically integrated *179;* separate divisions of one company producing the different stages of a product and marketing their output to one another.

vicious circle of poverty *476;* the pattern of economic stagnation resulting from a lack of surplus of production to invest in capital goods to increase productivity.

W.

wage or salary *72;* a factor payment for labor service.

welfare state (democratic socialism) *457;* an economic system that combines state ownership of some basic industries with a market system, extensive social services, income redistribution, and democratic political institutions.

"what" question *44;* the question concerning the decisions made by an economy about how much of the different alternative goods and services will be produced with the available resources.

workfare *239;* originally a program that required nonexempt welfare recipients to work at public service jobs for a given number of hours a month; now may also include job training and wage subsidies.

World Bank (International Bank for Reconstruction and Development—IBRD) *470;* a specialized agency of the United Nations that began operations in 1945 first to help countries rebuild facilities destroyed in World War II and subsequently to help finance development of the LDCs.

Index

This index has been prepard to help you easily find important information contained in *The Study of Economics*. It includes names, literary references, and subject entries.

The index is alphabetically arranged by *principal entry*. Each principal entry is immediately followed by the page or page numbers of the text on which it appears or by a *subentry* or series of *subentries* with page references to enable you to find the discussion of a particular aspect of the principal entry. **Bold face** page numbers are references to in-text glossary items. These items can also be found in the general glossary beginning on page 495.

G.

U.

Ukraine, 450, 455
Ultraviolet (UV) rays, 6
Underemployed, **283**
Unemployment, 49, 50; aggregate demand and, 281–282; causes of, 279–283; compensation in U.S. vs. Europe, 284–285; cyclical, 281; defense budget and, 38; in different economic systems, 448–449, 459; frictional, 279–280; as global issue, 284–285; hidden, 282–283, 448, 449; income effects of, 297; inflation and, 290–294; natural rate of, 294; real output effects of, 297; social effects of, 297; structural, 280–281; underemployment and, 283
Unemployment compensation, 367; in Europe vs. United States, 284–285
Unfavorable balance of trade, **423**
Unions. *See* Labor unions
Unit of measurement (standard of value or unit of account), **258**
Unitary elasticity, **112**
United Kingdom. *See* Great Britain
United States: comparative advantage and, 391–393; currency value and, 254; debt in, 357–360; foreign direct investment in, 430, 431–432; health care reform in, 333–337; industrial performance in, vs. Japan, 159–181; investment/GDP ratio in, 374; NAFTA and, 389–390, 394; privatization in, 444; trade deficit of, 425–426, 428, 429–430, 431–432, 434; unemployment compensation in, vs. Europe, 284–285

Universal health care coverage, lack of, in U.S., 333, 334–336, 341, 342
Upper-middle-income economies, 470, 473
USAir, 197
Utility, **116**–117
Utility companies, 73, 74

V.

Value added, **313**
Value judgments, in economics, 15
Value-added tax (VAT), 352
Variable, **17,** 25
Variable costs, **138**
Variables in graphs, 21, 25
"Veblen effect," 123
Veblen, Thorstein, 123
Velocity of money circulation (V), 288, **290**
Verleger, Philip, 99
Vertical equity, **348**
Vertically integrated, **179**
Veterinarian, cattle health and the, 62
Vicious circle of poverty, **476,** 489
Videotape recording machines (VTRs), 160
Vietnam, 440–441
von Hayek, Friedrich August, 211

W.

Wage or salary, **72,** 76
Wages: available capital and, 220–221; derived demand and, 218; implicit, 227–228; labor supply and, 218–220; labor unions and, 221–224. *See also* Income
Wagner Act, 221–222
Wal-Mart, 278

Waste Makers, The (Packard), 55
Watt, James, 77
Wealth of Nations, The (Smith), 101
Weather, global warming and, 6
Weight loss businesses, 43
Welfare state (democratic socialism), 441, **457,** 459
Western Electric, 189, 194
Western Europe, economic systems of, 441, 444, 448, 449, 452, 457. *See also* Europe
Whale oil, as lubricant, 94
Whale products, ban on, 94
Wharton Quarterly Model of the U.S. economy, 307
"What" question, **44,** 48, 54
White Nights, 446
White-collar workers, 9
Wildcat banking, 251
"Willingness to pay" approach, to placing monetary value on human life, 207–208
Window tax, in medieval England, 349
Winston, Clifford, 195
Women, in labor force, 452–453
"Work cells," 173
Work ethic, in Russia, 445
Worker protection, 204–205
Workfare, **239**
Workforce. *See* Labor
WordPerfect, 150–151
World Bank, **470,** 485
World Trade Organization (WTO), 390–391

Y.

Yeltsin, Boris, 440, 447

Z.

Zullow, Harold, 309

Chase Manhattan Archives; 53 Matsushita; 54 Rafal Olbinski; 55 John Kenneth Galbraith

Chapter 3 58 Library of Congress; 60 National Cattlemen's Association; Mike Eagle; 62 courtesy New York Convention and Visitors' Bureau; 65 courtesy Union Electric; 66 Kit Porter; 67 TVA Washington Office and Tom Sweeten; 68 Reuters/Bettmann; 71 Pamela Carley; 73 Bettmann; 74 Solar Products Manufacturing Corp.; 76 Library of Congress; 77 The Bettmann Archive, Inc.

Chapter 4 80 Pamela Carley; 82 USDA, Mike Eagle; 89 Pamela Carley; 91 Pamela Carley; 92 Hind; 93 courtesy Morrison Knudsen Corporation; 94 Line drawing by Lucretia Breazeale Hamilton/University of Arizona Press; 96 Pamela Carley; 99 Geo; 100 Pamela Carley; 101 The Bettmann Archive, Inc.

Chapter 5 106 courtesy World Health Organization; 108 Mike Eagle; 110 courtesy Philips; 113 Pamela Carley; 114 courtesy Chase Manhattan Archives; 116 AP/Wide World; 118 Cheryl Greenleaf; 120 Pamela Carley; 122 World Health Organization; 123 The Bettmann Archive, Inc.

Chapter 6 126 AP/Wide World; 129 Mike Eagle; 132 courtesy Ben & Jerry's; 133 courtesy Chrysler Corporation; 136 NYT Pictures; 138 USDA; 141 courtesy Ford New Holland; 144 courtesy Ford New Holland; 149 Pamela Carley; 152 Equitable Agri-Business; 154 The Bettmann Archive, Inc.

Chapter 7 158 Houston Industries, Inc.; 161 Mike Eagle; 164 Eastman Chemical Company; 165 courtesy StarKist Seafood Company; 170 courtesy TRW; 173 Pratt & Whitney; 175 courtesy IBM; 176 courtesy IBM; 179 Pamela Carley; 180 Reuters/Bettmann; 182 Houston Industries, Inc.; 184 NYT Pictures

Chapter 8 188 Picture Cube; 190 Mike Eagle; 192 The Bettmann Archive, Inc.; 194 courtesy General Electric; 195 © Kevin Horan/Picture Group; 198 courtesy Federal Aviation Association; 199 AP/Wide World; 200 The National Gallery of Art; 202 courtesy General Motors; 205 Steve Delaney/EPA; 208 Charles Vitelli; 209 Pamela Carley; 210 Steve Delaney/EPA; 211 UPI/Bettmann

Chapter 9 214 SuperStock; 216 Susan Harris/NYT Pictures; 217 Mike Eagle; 221 Library of Congress; 225 AP/Wide World; 231 Reuters/Bettmann; 234 Sara Krulwich/NYT Pictures; 237 Michelle V. Agins/ NYT Pictures; 238 Pamela Carley; 239 courtesy 415 Society; 242 SuperStock; 244 The Bettmann Archive, Inc.

Chapter 10 250 courtesy Krause Publications; 252 Mike Eagle; 255 Pamela Carley; 256 UPI/ Bettmann; 259 courtesy American Red Cross; 260 North American Atlas, London, 1977, Historic Picture

Services, Inc.; 261 courtesy Krause Publications; 262 Pamela Carley; 263 UN photo by Nagata; 271 Timothy Wright/NYT Pictures; 272 courtesy Krause Publications; 273 Library of Congress

Chapter 11 276 Robert Neubecker; 278 Mike Eagle; 281 Reuters/Bettmann; 294 UPI/Bettmann; 296 courtesy Busch Gardens; 298 UPI/Bettmann; 299 UPI/Bettmann; 300 Doty; 301 Bob Firek/Old Dominion University, Office of Public Information; 302 Robert Neubecker; 303 UPI/Bettmann

Chapter 12 306 Mike Eagle; 308 Mike Eagle; 311 courtesy Pratt & Whitney; 317 AP/Wide World; 320 courtesy TRW; 326 Pamela Carley; 327 White House photo; 328 Mike Eagle; 329 UPI/Bettmann

Chapter 13 332 Margot Thompson/Three in a Box; 336 Mike Eagle; 340 courtesy Apple Computer; 341 Pol Turgeon; 349 The Bettmann Archive, Inc.; 350 courtesy The White House; 351 Margot Thompson/Three in a Box; 353 K. Jewell/Congressional News Photos

Chapter 14 356 courtesy Busch Gardens; 359 Federal Reserve Bank; 360 Mike Eagle; 367 NYT Pictures; 378 National Institute of Standards and Technology; 379 Pratt & Whitney; 381 Federal Reserve Bank; 382 Todd Buchanan/NYT Pictures; 383 UPI/Bettmann

Chapter 15 388 Painting by David Cutler, courtesy of Yellow Freight System; 390 Mike Eagle; 393 Pamela Carley; 398 American Iron and Steel Institute; 399 Crafted with Pride in America; 401 Alyx Kellington/NYT Pictures; 402 Reuters/Bettmann; 405 EPA/Documerica; 406 EPA/Documerica; 407 UPI/Bettmann; 408 Painting by David Cutler, courtesy of Yellow Freight System; 409 courtesy Dorothy Fink; 410 Library of Congress

Chapter 16 414 Mike Eagle; 416 Mike Eagle; 422 courtesy the Port Authority of New York and New Jersey; 424 Pamela Carley; 429 John Beckmann; 430 Mike Eagle; 431 Woodfin Camp; 433 Mike Eagle; 434 courtesy Chase Manhattan Archives

Chapter 17 438 Reuters/Bettmann; 441 Mike Eagle; 443 Itar-Tass/Sovfoto; 444 courtesy Banque National de Paris; 447 Reuters/Bettmann; 453 Itar-Tass/ Sovfoto; 455 Alexander Zemlianichenko; 457 Otto Pohl/NYT; 468 US–China Review; 460 Reuters/Bettmann; 462 Library of Congress

Chapter 18 466 Reuters/Bettmann; 468 Reuters/Bettmann; 469 Mike Eagle; 476 UN photo by John Isaac; 479 UN photo; 485 Reuters/Bettmann; 486 Pamela Carley; 488 AP/Wide World; 489 Jeff Hacker; 490 The Bettmann Archive, Inc.

Publisher   Irving E. Rockwood

Editor   John S. L. Holland

Copy Editors   Josh Safran and Dorothy Fink

Production Manager   Brenda S. Filley

Designers   Richard Stalzer and Charles Vitelli

Typesetting Supervisor   Libra Ann Cusack

Typesetter   Juliana Arbo

Proofreader   Diane Barker

Graphics   Shawn Callahan

Art Editor   Elizabeth L. Hansen

Manufactured in compliance with NASTA specifications.

The body of the text was set in Century Schoolbook.

Charts and graphs were rendered by the DPG.
Cartoons were drawn by Mike Eagle.

The text was printed in web offset lithography and
bound by William C. Brown Communications, Inc.,
Dubuque, IA.

Manufactured in the United States of America.
Cover design by Richard Stalzer.